Lecture Notes in Computer Scienc

Commenced Publication in 1973
Founding and Former Series Editors:
Gerhard Goos, Juris Hartmanis, and Jan van Leeuwen

Editorial Board

David Hutchison
Lancaster University, UK

Takeo Kanade
Carnegie Mellon University, Pittsburgh, PA, USA

Josef Kittler
University of Surrey, Guildford, UK

Jon M. Kleinberg
Cornell University, Ithaca, NY, USA

Alfred Kobsa
University of California, Irvine, CA, USA

Friedemann Mattern
ETH Zurich, Switzerland

John C. Mitchell
Stanford University, CA, USA

Moni Naor
Weizmann Institute of Science, Rehovot, Israel

Oscar Nierstrasz
University of Bern, Switzerland

C. Pandu Rangan
Indian Institute of Technology, Madras, India

Bernhard Steffen
TU Dortmund University, Germany

Madhu Sudan
Microsoft Research, Cambridge, MA, USA

Demetri Terzopoulos
University of California, Los Angeles, CA, USA

Doug Tygar
University of California, Berkeley, CA, USA

Gerhard Weikum
Max Planck Institute for Informatics, Saarbruecken, Germany

Alfredo Petrosino   Lucia Maddalena
Pietro Pala et al. (Eds.)

New Trends in Image Analysis and Processing – ICIAP 2013

ICIAP 2013 International Workshops
Naples, Italy, September 9-13, 2013
Proceedings

 Springer

Volume Editors

see next page

Cover illustration: "ICIAP 2013" by Laura Zoé (2013)

ISSN 0302-9743   e-ISSN 1611-3349
ISBN 978-3-642-41189-2   e-ISBN 978-3-642-41190-8
DOI 10.1007/978-3-642-41190-8
Springer Heidelberg New York Dordrecht London

Library of Congress Control Number: 2013948504

CR Subject Classification (1998): I.5, I.2.9-10, I.4, K.4, J.3, I.7, H.5, H.3, F.2

LNCS Sublibrary: SL 6 – Image Processing, Computer Vision, Pattern Recognition, and Graphics

Typesetting: Camera-ready by author, data conversion by Scientific Publishing Services, Chennai, India

Printed on acid-free paper

Springer is part of Springer Science+Business Media (www.springer.com)

Volume Editors

Alfredo Petrosino
Department of Science and Technology
University of Naples Parthenope, Italy
alfredo.petrosino@uniparthenope.it

Lucia Maddalena
Institute for High Performance
Computing and Networking
National Research Council, Italy
lucia.maddalena@cnr.it

Pietro Pala
Department of Information
Engineering
University of Florence, Italy
pietro.pala@unifi.it

Virginio Cantoni
Department of Industrial
and Information Engineering
University of Pavia, Italy
virginio.cantoni@unipv.it

Michele Ceccarelli
Department of Biological
and Environmental Science
University of Sannio, Italy
ceccarelli@unisannio.it

Robert F. Murphy
Department of Biological Sciences
Carnegie Mellon University, USA
murphy@cmu.edu

Alberto Del Bimbo
Department of Information
Engineering
University of Florence, Italy
delbimbo@dsi.unifi.it

Maja Pantic
Department of Computing
Imperial College London, UK
m.pantic@imperial.ac.uk

Costantino Grana
Department of Engineering
University of Modena and
Reggio Emilia, Italy
costantino.grana@unimore.it

Johan Oomen
Netherlands Institute for Sound and Vision
The Netherlands
joomen@beeldengeluid.nl

Giuseppe Serra
Department of Engineering
University of Modena and
Reggio Emilia, Italy
giuseppe.serra@unimore.it

Marco Leo
Institute of Optics
National Research Council, Italy
marco.leo@cnr.it

Danilo P. Mandic
Department of Electrical and
Electronic Engineering
Imperial College of London
d.mandic@imperial.ac.uk

Giuseppe Pirlo
Department of Computer Science
University of Bari, Italy
giuseppe.pirlo@uniba.it

Michael Fairhurst
School of Engineering and Digital Arts
The University of Kent, UK
M.C.Fairhurst@kent.ac.uk

Donato Impedovo
Dyrecta Lab, Italy
impedovo@gmail.com

Preface

This volume contains the papers accepted for presentation at the workshops hosted by the 17th International Conference on Image Analysis and Processing (ICIAP 2013), held in Naples, Italy, September 9–13, 2013, in the magnificent Castel dell'Ovo, (www.iciap2013-naples.org), organized by the CVPR Lab of the University of Naples Parthenope (cvprlab.uniparthneope.it).

The International Conference on Image Analysis and Processing (ICIAP) is an established biennial scientific meeting promoted by the Italian Group of Researchers in Pattern Recognition (GIRPR), which is the Italian IAPR Member Society, and covers topics related to theoretical and experimental areas of image analysis and pattern recognition with emphasis on different applications. ICIAP 2013 was endorsed by the International Association for Pattern Recognition (IAPR), the IEEE Computer Society's Technical Committee on Pattern Analysis and Machine Intelligence (TCPAMI), and the IEEE Computational Intelligence Society (CIS).

ICIAP 2013 hosted a range of workshops focusing on topics of interest to the pattern recognition, image analysis, and computer vision communities, exploring emergent research directions or spotlight cross-disciplinary links with related fields and/or application areas. Five individual workshops were selected to complement ICIAP 2013 in Naples, three one-day and two half-day workshops. The topics addressed constituted a good mix between novel current trends in computer vision and the fundamentals of image analysis and pattern recongniton.

- *ACVR 2013*, the First International Workshop on Assistive Computer Vision and Robotics.
- *EAHSP 2013*, the International Workshop on Emerging Aspects on Handwritten Signature Processing.
- *MM4CH 2013*, the 2nd International Workshop on Multimedia for Cultural Heritage.
- *PR PS BB 2013*, the 2nd International Workshop on Pattern Recognition in Proteomics, Structural Biology, and Bioinformatics.
- *SBA 2013*, the International Workshop on Social Behaviour Analysis.

The *ACVR 2013* workshop was aimed to give an overview of the state of the art of perception and interaction methodologies involved in this area with special attention to aspects related to computer vision and robotics. Assistive technologies provide a set of advanced tools that can improve the quality of life not only for disabled people, patients, and elderly, but also for healthy people struggling with everyday actions. After a period of slow but steady progress, this scientific area seems to be mature for new research and application breakthroughs. The rapid progress in the development of integrated micro-mechatronic tools has boosted this process. However, many problems remain open especially as regards environment perception and interaction of these technological tools with people. The ACVR 2013 workshop was organized by Marco Leo from the Institute of Optics and the Institute of Intelligent Systems for Automation of the National Research Council (Italy) and by Danilo Mandic from the Department of Electrical and Electronic Engineering of the Imperial College of London (UK). Based on rigorous peer reviews by the Program Committee members and the reviewers, six papers were selected for presentation in an half-day workshop. All the papers thoroughly cover a broad range of topics related to the research areas of assistive technologies, addressing major advances in knowledge and effective use of computer vision and robotics in a variety of applications. ACVR 2013 also included an outstanding presentation given by Andrea Cavallaro of the Queen Mary University of London (UK) about new techniques for localizing people and understanding their interactions, which is a desirable yet demanding task for assistive computer vision applications.

The *EAHSP 2013* workshop, organized by Michael Fairhurst of The University of Kent (UK), Donato Impedovo of Dyrecta Lab (Italy), and Giuseppe Pirlo of the University of Bari (Italy), focused on the frontiers of research and applications in the field of static and dynamic signature analysis and processing. Indeed, in the era of Internet, there is a growing interest for personal verification, and a handwritten signature is one of the most useful biometric traits, since the verification of a person's identity by signature analysis does not involve an invasive measurement procedure. Furthermore, handwritten signatures are a well-established means of personal identification, and their use is widespread and well-recognized by administrative and financial institutions.

Handwritten signature analysis and processing is a multi-disciplinary field involving aspects of disciplines ranging from human anatomy to engineering, from neuroscience to computer and system sciences. Also from the application point of view, signature analysis and processing is useful in many fields, from security to physical areas, from security for internet-based systems to forensic and medical applications. The ten papers accepted for presentation to EAHSP 2013 define a useful scenario of the field from both the scientific and applicative point of view.

The *MM4CH 2013* workshop, organized by Costantino Grana and Giuseppe Serra of the University of Modena e Reggio Emilia (Italy) and Johan Oomen from the Netherlands Institute for Sound and Vision (The Netherlands), had the aim of creating a profitable informal working day to discuss together hot topics in multimedia applied to cultural heritage. Multimedia technologies have recently created the conditions for a true revolution in the cultural heritage area, with reference to the study, valorization, and fruition of artistic works. The use of these technologies allows us to create new digital cultural experiences by means of personalized and engaging interaction. New multimedia technologies could be used to design new approaches to the comprehension and fruition of the artistic heritage, for example through smart, context-aware artifacts and enhanced interfaces with the support of features like story-telling, gaming, and learning. To these aims, open and flexible platforms are needed, to allow building services that support use of cultural resources for research and education. A likely expectation is the involvement of a wider range of users of cultural resources in diverse contexts and considerably altered ways to experience and share cultural knowledge between participants. The scientific community has shown great interest in this timely topic. Indeed, 27 papers were received and, after the review process, 17 were accepted (acceptance rate 62%). Papers were contributed from 14 different countries (Austria, China, the Czech Republic, France, Greece, India, Italy, Morocco, The Netherlands, Norway, Poland, Switzerland, the UK, and the USA) demonstrating the universal importance of cultural heritage.

The *PR PS BB 2013* workshop covers topics related to pattern recognition in proteomics, structural biology, and bioinformatics. The amount and complexity of bioinformatics data, such as DNA and protein sequences, genetic information, biomedical text, and molecular data, exploded in the past decade. The importance of studying such amounts of data, for the analysis of structural building blocks, their comparison, and their classification is instrumental to practical problems of the maximum impact, such as the design of a small molecule to bind a known protein or the scan of drugs libraries to detect a suitable inhibitor for a target molecule. Advanced pattern recognition methods can also play a significant role in high-throughput functional genomics and system biology, where the classification of complex large-scale expression profiles, and their link with motif discovery and inference of gene regulatory networks, is a major research challenge in the field of computational biology. However, current pattern recognition techniques to tackle these huge data are still not sufficient. The development of approaches for the improvement of current performance was the scope of the PR PS BB 2013 workshop, organized by Virginio Cantoni of the University of Pavia (Italy), Michele Ceccarelli of the University of Sannio (Italy), and Robert Murphy, Carnegie Mellon University (USA). Featuring 13 accepted papers, the workshop was intended, through its informal nature, as the foremost platform for exchanging ideas and giving to top researchers, practitioners, and students from around the world, of the computing and biological communities, excellent opportunities to meet, interact, and find synergies.

The *SBA 2013* workshop, organized by Alberto Del Bimbo and Pietro Pala of the University of Florence (Italy) and Maja Pantic of the Imperial College London (UK), aimed to bring together researchers to advocate and promote research into human behavior and social interactions analysis, to disseminate their most recent research results, to discuss rigorously and systematically potential solutions and challenges, and to promote new collaborations among researchers. In the new digital age, progress and development in science and technology have a great impact on our daily activities and lifestyle. Models and tools for the automatic analysis of human behavior and social interactions are increasing their relevance in a broad range of application domains, including entertainment, security, surveillance, human–computer interfaces, and psychology among other fields. The availability of new devices capable of multimodal data acquisition paves the way to new solutions to the analysis and recognition of human activities in social contexts, hand and body gestures, facial expressions, interactions with objects, and expressive speech. All submitted papers were reviewed by at least three PC members or external reviewers who volunteered to contribute their time and expertise to the review process. The 14 accepted papers, coming from 7 different countries worldwide, were organized into 3 sessions: 3D Behaviour Analysis; Social and Multimodal Analysis; and Applications, Benchmarking, Verification. The technical program featured one invited talk, by Alessandro Vinciarelli from the University of Glasgow, and oral presentation of all the accepted regular papers.

Many people helped make the ICIAP 2013 workshops a success. I would like to thank all the ICIAP 2013 workshop organizers and their organizations for soliciting and reviewing submissions, which guaranteed the high quality of the technical program, all the members of the Program Committees, who dedicated their time and energy to reviewing the papers, and the authors for having submitted their own valuable work. Special thanks should be tributed to all those involved in the preparation of the event, especially Lucia Maddalena for her unfaltering dedication to the coordination of the event.

All these people made it possible to build such a rich supplementary program beside the main ICIAP 2013 scientific program, which justified, for the first time for ICIAP, the publication of ICIAP 2013 workshops proceedings in a separate volume.

September 2013   Alfredo Petrosino

ACVR 2013 Organization

General Chairs

Marco Leo (Italy)   Danilo P. Mandic (UK)

Steering Committee

Cosimo Distante (Italy)   Annalisa Milella (Italy)
David Looney (UK)

Program Committee

Salvatore M. Anzalone (France)   Liliana Lo Presti (USA)
Donato Di Paola (Italy)   Pier Luigi Mazzeo (Italy)
Cem Direkoglu (Ireland)   Markos Mentzelopoulos (UK)
Arcangelo Distante (Italy)   Mikel Rodriguez (France)
Flavio Esposito (USA)   Davide Scaramuzza (Switzerland)
Giovanni Indiveri (Italy)   Paolo Spagnolo (Italy)
Henry Kautz (USA)

Endorsing Institutions

International Association for Pattern Recognition (IAPR)
IEEE Computer Society's Technical Committee on Pattern Analysis and
Machine Intelligence (IEEE-TCPAMI)
IEEE Computational Intelligence Society (IEEE-CIS)
Italian Group of Researchers in Pattern Recognition (GIRPR)
National Group for Scientific Computing (GNCS)

Institutional Patronage

Università di Napoli Parthenope, Italy
Campania Regional Board, Italy
National Research Council of Italy (CNR), Italy

Sponsoring Institutions

Italian Ministry of Education, University and Research (MIUR), Italy
Italian Ministry of Economic Development (MiSE), Italy
Comune di Napoli, Italy
Google Inc., USA
Ansaldo STS, Italy
Italian Aerospace Research Center (CIRA), Italy
Selex ES, Italy
ST-Microelectronics, Italy
Unlimited Software srl, Italy

Acknowledgments

We acknowledge the support of the Project PT2LOG, National Operational
Program for "Research and Competitiveness" 2007-2013, made available by the
Italian Ministry of Education, University and Research (MIUR) and the Ministry
of Economic Development (MiSE).

ICIAP 2013 Organization

Organizing Institution

CVPR Lab of the University of Naples Parthenope, Italy
http://cvprlab.uniparthenope.it

General Chair

Alfredo Petrosino   University of Naples Parthenope, Italy

Area Chairs

Pattern Recognition and Machine Learning:

Marco Gori	University of Siena, Italy
Kai Yu	Baidu Inc., Germany

Human Recognition Systems:

Paola Campadelli	University of Milan, Italy
Caroline Pantofaru	Google, USA

BioMedical Imaging Applications:

Joan Martì	Universitat de Girona, Spain
Francesco Tortorella	University of Cassino, Italy

Multimedia Interaction and Processing:

Rita Cucchiara	University of Modena and Reggio Emilia, Italy
Fatih Porikli	MERL, USA

3D Computer Vision:

Shaogang Gong	Queen Mary University of London, UK
Vittorio Murino	University of Verona and IIT, Italy

Understanding Objects and Space:

Silvio Savarese	University of Michigan, USA
Jiambo Shi	University of Pennsylvania, USA

Steering Committee

Virginio Cantoni	University of Pavia, Italy
Luigi Cordella	University of Naples Federico II, Italy
Alberto Del Bimbo	University of Florence, Italy
Marco Ferretti	University of Pavia, Italy

Fabio Roli   University of Cagliari, Italy
Gabriella Sanniti di Baja   ICIB-CNR, Italy

Local Committee Chairs

Alessio Ferone   University of Naples Parthenope, Italy
Maria Frucci   ICIB-CNR, Italy

Workshop Chairs

Lucia Maddalena   ICAR-CNR, Italy
Pietro Pala   University of Florence, Italy

Tutorial Chairs

Francesco Isgrò   University of Naples Federico II, Italy
Giosuè Lo Bosco   University of Palermo, Italy

Industrial Liason Chairs

Michele Nappi   University of Salerno, Italy
Francesco Camastra   University of Naples Parthenope, Italy

International Program Committee

Jake Aggarwal, USA   Kalman Palagyi, Hungary
Marco Andreetto, USA   Witold Pedrycz, Canada
Edoardo Ardizzone, Italy   Marcello Pelillo, Italy
Isabelle Bloch, France   Fatih Porikli, USA
Gunilla Borgefors, Sweden   Carlo Sansone, Italy
Alfred Bruckstein, Israel   Raimondo Schettini, Italy
Rama Chellappa, USA   Mubarak Shah, USA
Leila De Floriani, Italy   Josè Ruiz Shulcloper, Cuba
Aytul Ercil, Turkey   Stefano Soatto, USA
Gianluca Foresti, Italy   Arnold Smeulders, The Netherlands
Ashish Ghosh, India   Steven Tanimoto, USA
Edwin Hancock, UK   Massimo Tistarelli, Italy
Xiaoyi Jiang, Germany   John Tsotsos, Canada
Etienne Kerre, Belgium   Shimon Ullman, Israel
Walter Kropatsch, Austria   Mario Vento, Italy
Yanxi Liu, USA   Alessandro Verri, Italy
Gerard Medioni, USA   Hezy Yeshurun, Israel
Alain Merigot, France   Ramin Zabih, USA
Ram Nevatia, USA   Bertrand Zavidovique, France
Sankar Kumar Pal, India   Jacek Zurada, USA

EAHSP 2013 Organization

General Chairs

Giuseppe Pirlo (Italy)   Michael Fairhurst (UK)
Donato Impedovo (Italy)

Program Committee

Marjory Abreu (Brazil)   Angelo Marcelli (Italy)
Michael Blumenstein (Australia)   Javier Ortega-Garcia (Spain)
Alexander Filatov (USA)   Umapada Pal (India)
Sonia Garcia Salicetti (France)   Rejean Plamondon (Canada)
Laurent Huette (France)   Robert Sabourin (Canada)
Marcus Liwicki (Germany)   Nicole Vincent (France)
Muhammad Imran Malik (Germany)   Elias Zois (Greece)

Additional Reviewers

Donato Barbuzzi (Italy)   Francesco Maurizio Mangini (Italy)

MM4CH 2013 Organization

General Chairs

Costantino Grana (Italy)   Giuseppe Serra (Italy)
Johan Oomen (The Netherlands)

Program Committee

Maristella Agosti (Italy)   Martin Kampel (Austria)
Olga Regina Pereira Bellon (Brazil)   Eamonn Keogh (USA)
Lamberto Ballan (Italy)   Martha Larson (The Netherlands)
Tsuhan Chen (USA)   Josep Lladós (Spain)
Rita Cucchiara (Italy)   Luca Mainetti (Italy)
Alberto Del Bimbo (Italy)   Jan Nouza (Czech Republic)
Matteo Dellepiane (Italy)   Nicola Orio (Italy)
Kate Fernie (UK)   Edgar Roman-Rangel (Switzerland)
Antonio Gentile (Italy)   Enrique Vidal (Spain)

Sponsors

Gruppo Italiano Ricercatori in Pattern Recognition
Università degli Studi di Modena e Reggio Emilia
Franco Cosimo Panini Editore
Laboratorio Imagelab

PR PS BB 2013 Organization

General Chairs

Virginio Cantoni (Italy)
Michele Ceccarelli (Italy)

Robert Murphy (USA)

Program Committee

Pierre Baldi (USA)
Paola Bertolazzi (Italy)
Mario Cannataro (Italy)
Virginio Cantoni (Italy)
Alessandra Carbone (France)
Jens Michael Cartsensen (Denmark)
Rita Casadio (Italy)
Michele Ceccarelli (Italy)
Angelo Facchiano (Italy)
Concettina Guerra (USA)
Alamgir Hossain (UK)

Tom Lenaerts (Belgium)
Le Ly (Vietnam)
Giuseppe Maino (Italy)
Elena Marchiori (The Netherlands)
Giancarlo Mauri (Italy)
Giovanni Paolella (Italy)
Alfredo Petrosino (Italy)
Michael Schroeder (Germany)
Ekaterina Shelest (Germany)
Roberto Tagliaferri (Italy)
Alfredo Vellido (Spain)

Additional Reviewers

Luigi Cerulo (Italy)
Fulvio D'Angelo (Italy)

Pietro Zoppoli (USA)

Workshop Organization and Scientific Secretary

Alessandra Setti (Italy)

SBA 2013 Organization

General Chairs

Alberto Del Bimbo (Italy)   Pietro Pala (Italy)
Maja Pantic (UK)

Program Committee

Andrew Bagdanov (Spain)   David Marshall (UK)
Stefano Berretti (Italy)   Mohammad Soleymani (UK)
Michael Bronstein (Switzerland)   Michela Spagnuolo (Italy)
Petros Daras (Greece)   Anuj Srivastava (USA)
Hatice Gunes (UK)   Michel Valstar (UK)
Irene Kotsia (UK)   Hazem Wannous (France)
Tung-Ying Lee (Taiwan)   Stefanos Zafeiriou (UK)
Giuseppe Lisanti (Italy)

Sponsors

STC Social Networking

Table of Contents

MM4CH 2013 - 2nd International Workshop on Multimedia for Cultural Heritage

PR PS BB 2013 - 2nd International Workshop on Pattern Recognition in Proteomics, Structural Biology and Bioinformatics

SBA 2013 - International Workshop on Social Behaviour Analysis

A Robust Hand Pose Estimation Algorithm for Hand Rehabilitation

Francesca Cordella[1], Francesco Di Corato[2],
Loredana Zollo[3], and Bruno Siciliano[1]

[1] PRISMA Lab, Department of Electrical Engineering and Information Technology,
Università di Napoli Federico II, via Claudio 21, 80125 Napoli, Italy
{francesca.cordella,bruno.siciliano}@unina.it
[2] Research Center "E. Piaggio", Università di Pisa, largo Lucio Lazzarino, 1, 56100
Pisa, Italy
francesco.dicorato@for.unipi.it
[3] Laboratory of Biomedical Robotics and Biomicrosystems, Università Campus
Bio-Medico, via Alvaro del Portillo 21, 00128 Roma, Italy
l.zollo@unicampus.it

Abstract. During a rehabilitation session, patient activity should be continuously monitored in order to correct wrong movements and to follow patient improvements. Therefore, the application of human motion tracking techniques to rehabilitation is finding more and more consensus. The aim of this paper is to propose a novel, low-cost method for hand pose estimation by using a monocular motion sensing device and a robust marker-based pose estimation approach based on the Unscented Kalman Filter. The hand kinematics is used to enclose geometrical constraints in the estimation process. The approach is applied for evaluating some significant kinematic parameters necessary for understanding human hand motor improvements during rehabilitation. In particular, the parameters evaluated for the hand fingers are joint positions, angles, Range Of Motion and trajectory. Moreover, the position, orientation and velocity of the wrist are estimated.

Keywords: hand pose estimation, rehabilitation, Unscented Kalman Filter.

1 Introduction

Cerebrovascular diseases, such as stroke, are the third leading cause of death in industrialized countries and the leading cause of permanent disability [1]. This leads to a remarkable demand of healthcare services with consequently increasing public expenses. The aim of neurorehabilitation is to help patient relearn sensori-motor capabilities by exploiting the plasticity of the neuromuscular system: motor patterns are relearned through repeated execution of predefined movements [2]. Patient monitoring is needed to evaluate the quality of the performed movements, modify the therapy if needed, apply corrective actions and assess patient performance. Systems for human movement tracking applied to

A. Petrosino, L. Maddalena, P. Pala (Eds.): ICIAP 2013 Workshops, LNCS 8158, pp. 1–10, 2013.
© Springer-Verlag Berlin Heidelberg 2013

rehabilitation [3] are usually divided into two categories: non-visual tracking systems and visual tracking systems. In this paper the attention is focused on systems belonging to the latter class, which are in turn classified as marker-based and marker-less systems. Marker-based motion analysis systems use optoelectronic cameras and reflective markers: although these systems provide an accurate estimation of joints [4], they are expensive and cumbersome. Further, they require a completely structured environment to perform calibration and acquisition. Marker-less systems rely on Computer Vision algorithms that are sensitive to environmental conditions, but usually use one or two cameras making the system cheap and space-saving.

Vision-based techniques for estimating the hand pose are usually grouped into two categories [5]: Model-based and single frame pose estimation. Model-based visual pose estimation consists of finding the best matching between a group of features characterizing the input image and a group of model features. In order to reduce the computational cost of searching, a prediction step is considered. Multiple hypothesis around the prediction are considered to avoid local minima and discontinuities [6] in the matching. In particular, Bayesian filtering techniques using Monte Carlo methods, such as particle filters [7], [8], [9] are applied. Single frame pose estimation does not make assumptions on time coherence, making the problem very hard to solve. Global search over a database of templates [10] and motion constraints [11], [12] are viable solution.

The hand pose estimation approach presented in this paper tries to merge computer-vision and marker-based techniques proposing a cheap system (that facilitates a fundamental step for hand pose estimation: the triangulation process of the visual features) using a monocular camera, with reduced computational cost, easy to implement and robust. It performs the visual analysis of human hand motion and records hand joint kinematics during movements in a robust and repeatable way making the system adapt for home based rehabilitation.

The paper is structured as follows: in Section 2 the hand kinematic model is introduced; in Section 3 the hand pose estimation algorithm is explained; results about the hand pose estimation are presented in Section 4. Finally, conclusions and future work are proposed in Section 5.

1.1 Notation

The exposition relies on a notation very common in the Computer Vision and Robotics community: the generic pose (rotation R_{ij} and translation T_{ij}) of the frame $\mathcal{I}$ with respect to the frame $\mathcal{J}$ is denoted with the group transformation $g_{ij} = \{R_{ij}, T_{ij}\} \in SE(3)$, which maps a vector expressed in the frame $\mathcal{I}$, into a vector expressed in the frame $\mathcal{J}$. $SE(3)$ is the special Euclidean group for the rigid transformations. The notation is simplified for the pose of the wrist frame with respect to a proper fixed reference frame (e.g. the camera frame, $g_{wc} = \{R_{wc}, T_{wc}\}$), for which the subscripts are dropped, for cleaner notation, and it is denoted simply as $g = \{R, T\}$. The inverse transformation is indicated with the notation $g_{ij}^{-1} \triangleq \{R_{ij}^T, -R_{ij}^T T_{ij}\} \in SE(3)$. The *action* of the group transformation g_{jk} on g_{ij}, usually denoted with the symbol $\circ$, to indicate function composition, is indicated with a simple product, i.e. $g_{ik} = g_{jk}g_{ij}$, being by definition: $g_{ik} \triangleq \{R_{jk}R_{ij}, R_{jk}T_{ij} + T_{jk}\}$. The same notation is used for the action of the transformation $g_{jk} \in SE(3)$ on a vector $P_j \in \mathbb{R}^3$, which is indicated as $P_k = g_{jk}P_j$, that is: $P_k \triangleq R_{jk}P_j + T_{jk}$.

2   Hand Kinematic Model

Long fingers are considered as kinematic chains composed of 3 links with 4 Degrees of Freedom (DoFs): 2 DoFs for the MetaCarpo-Phalangeal (MCP) joint and 1 DoF each for the Proximal Inter-Phalangeal (PIP) and Distal Inter-Phalangeal (DIP) joints respectively. It has been assumed a coupling between PIP and DIP joints ($\theta_{DIP} = \frac{2}{3}\theta_{PIP}$) [13]. The thumb is modeled as proposed in [14] with 5 DOFs. The fingers are considered as 5 kinematic chains having the origin in common (i.e. the wrist). Fig. 1 shows the joint reference frames (left) and the Denavit-Hartenberg parameters for the index finger and for the thumb (right). The remaining long-fingers (middle, ring and little) are assumed kinematically equivalent to the index.

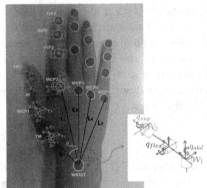

Joint #	a_i	α_i	d_i	θ_i
1	0	$-90°$	0	θ_{abd}^{MCP2}
2	L_P^{index}	$0°$	0	θ_{flex}^{MCP2}
3	L_M^{index}	$0°$	0	θ^{PIP2}
4	L_D^{index}	0	0	θ^{DIP2}

Joint #	a_i	α_i	d_i	θ_i
1	0	$-90°$	0	θ_{abd}^{TM}
2	L_P^{thumb}	$90°$	0	θ_{flex}^{TM}
3	0	$-90°$	0	θ_{abd}^{MCP1}
4	L_M^{thumb}	$0°$	0	θ_{flex}^{MCP1}
5	L_D^{thumb}	$0°$	0	θ^{IP}

Fig. 1. (left) Protocol used for marker positioning and joint reference frames in the hand starting position. The system reference frame, positioned (in red) on the hand wrist, has the X-axis along the line connecting the marker $WRIST$ with the marker $MCP3$, the Z-axis perpendicular to the palm plane and the Y-axis defined with the right hand rule. (right) DH parameters of the index finger (top) and of the thumb (bottom).

The wrist is modeled as a system with 6 DoFs, consisting of 3 components of translation and 3 angles of rotation (Adduction/Abduction, Flexion/Extension, Pronation/Supination). It is easy to show that these angles correspond to the Euler angles in configuration ZYX. Finally, the palm is assumed to be composed of rigid segments linked to the wrist and its anatomy is assumed known. For the purposes of this work, the arm is supposed not to change its orientation during

motion, thus it can be assumed that changes in hand orientation are due to actu-
ation of the wrist joints only. The DH parameters are evaluated in such a way as to
obtain a generic algorithm valid for different hand sizes. Therefore, the algorithm
envisages an initial calibration phase, where marker centers are detected manually in the first image acquired by the camera and the link lengths are measured,
by means of the depth information provided by the vision system. It is assumed
that the camera focal axis is perpendicular to the plane where the hand lies.

3 Hand Pose Estimation

3.1 Detection and Tracking

In order to estimate the hand pose, 21 markers, made of blue paper, are placed
on the subject hand, as shown in Fig. 1 and a fast detector based on color histogram and a connected component labeling algorithm has been implemented.
The Asus Xtion Prolive motion sensing device working at $30\,fps$ and consisting
of an InfraRed (IR) laser emitter, an IR camera for measuring depth information and a RGB camera, with a resolution of 640×480, has been used. The
same marker detection algorithm has already been adopted by the authors in a
previous work, hence a more detailed explanation can be found in [15]. In the
same work, the authors claimed that using simple detection algorithms like the
one used may render the task of associating visual measurements to physical
markers or deciding whether a given measurement is an outlier or a valid marker
projection difficult. For this reason, since a model of the hand is available, the
marker tracking problem has been reformulated into a stochastic optimization
problem. This renders the proposed algorithm robust with respect to outliers
and markers entering and exiting from the field of view.

3.2 Filtering Motion and Pose

The pose parameters – position, $T(t)$ and orientation, $R(t)$ – of the wrist with
respect to its initial pose (corresponding to the first image), together with the
kinematics of the 17 finger joints can be modeled according to the following
discrete-time kinematic model:

$$\begin{cases} T(t+1) = T(t) + v(t)\,dt \\ v(t+1) = v(t) + \eta_v(t)\,dt \\ R(t+1) = R(t)\,e^{(\Omega(t)dt)} \\ \theta_i(t+1) = \theta_i(t) + \eta_{\theta_i}(t)\,dt, \ i = 1,\dots,17 \end{cases} \tag{1}$$

where $\Omega(t) = \eta_\omega(t)\wedge$, being $\wedge$ the skew-symmetric operator, $\eta_v(t)$, $\eta_\omega(t)$ and
$\eta_{\theta_i}(t)$ are zero-mean white noises with constant variance, modeling the hand
motions as random walks, and dt is the base sample time, chosen coincident
with the sampling rate of the camera. The rotation matrix $R(t)$ is parametrized
via Euler angles and encodes the current value of wrist joint angles. The output
model is represented by the projection of the visible markers on the image space

$$y_i(t) = \pi\left(g_{w_0 c}\,g(t)\,T_{m_i w}(\Theta)\right) + \nu_i(t), \ i \in \mathcal{V}(t) \subseteq \{1, 2, \dots, 21\} \tag{2}$$

where $\pi\left(\right):\mathbb{R}^3\to\mathbb{R}P^2$ denotes the projective operator, according to the pinhole model, $g\left(t\right)=\{R\left(t\right),T\left(t\right)\}\in SE\left(3\right)$ and $T_{m_iw}\left(\Theta\right)$ is the $3D$ position of the i-th marker with respect to the wrist reference frame. This position is a function of the hand kinematic parameters Θ, i.e. the joint angles θ_i and the DH parameters, and can be obtained via direct kinematic. The group transformation $g_{w_0c}\in SE\left(3\right)$ is the pose (translation and rotation) between the camera frame and the frame $\mathcal{W}_0$ corresponding to the wrist initial pose, which is assumed known, and $\nu_i\left(t\right)$ is a zero-mean white noise with variance R_i, assumed constant among features. A possible algorithm for the iterative estimation of the relative transformation g_{w_0c} can be found in [16]. The set $\mathcal{V}\left(t\right)$ denotes the group of visible markers at the current time (omitting the clutters). It incorporates the time index since the markers may move out of the field of view or be occluded.

According to the kinematic model (1) and the output model (2) a nonlinear estimation scheme has been designed. The aim of the filter is to estimate the state $x\left(t\right)$ of the system, consisting of: i) the motion variables, $T\left(t\right),v\left(t\right)$ and the Euler angles parametrization of the rotation matrix $R\left(t\right)$, and ii) the joint angles $\theta_i\left(t\right)$ of the fingers. In this paper, given the non linearity of the model with respect to the state and the orientation noise terms, the Augmented Unscented Kalman Filter algorithm presented in [17] has been used. The peculiarity of the adopted estimation scheme, compared with the classical UKF approach [18], is the possibility to easily deal with non-affine noise terms in the state/measurement model. For the remaining part, the technique is a classical UKF as in [18].

3.3   Robust Tracking and Estimation

The challenge in the proposed approach is twofold: above all, using simple detection algorithms like the one described in Sect. 3.1 may render the task of associating a-priori a projection to a physical marker difficult; moreover, the algorithm is desired to be robust with respect to the presence of outliers, occlusions and markers entering and exiting from the field of view.

In [15], the tracking problem has been solved by using Sequential Monte Carlo methods, via adaptation of existing techniques in the framework of multiple target tracking. In that case, the model of the hand has not been available and the markers have been assumed to be independent targets moving on the image plane. On the contrary, the present work takes advantage of the knowledge of the hand model, which allows to constrain the motion of the markers onto the image plane. Thus, the tracking problem is formulated as a stochastic optimization problem embedded into the pose estimation algorithm. The general approach has been presented in [16]. For this aim, the outputs given by the blob detection algorithm, for the image at the time t, are considered a random sequence of M_t measurements $\mathbf{y}_t=\{y_1\left(t\right),y_2\left(t\right),...,y_{M_t}\left(t\right)\}$ of blob candidates. In general, the condition $M_t\neq 21$ holds, which means that the sequence $\mathbf{y}_t$ does contain projections of visible markers and clutters. The association between measurements and markers/clutters is considered unknown. It is assumed that the sequence $\mathbf{y}_t$ is conditionally independent from every other sequence in the past and that the association of each $y_i(t) \in \mathbf{y}_t$ is conditionally independent from the past history of associations. The filtering problem is thus solved by using a probabilistic technique. To this end, consider a latent variable $a_i(t)$, modeling the measurement-to-marker association:

$$a_i(t) = \begin{cases} 0, & \text{if } y_i(t) \text{ is a clutter} \\ j, & \text{if } y_i(t) \text{ is the projection of marker } j \end{cases} \qquad (3)$$

Introducing the latent variable is the same as considering the non linear model (2), in compact form $y(t) = h(x(t))$, as a conditional measurement model over the variable $a_i(t)$. In fact, it is possible to condition the output function over a certain value of the latent variable: i.e. $y_i(t) = h\left(x(t) \middle| a_i(t) = j \neq 0\right)$, with the meaning of selecting the rows corresponding to the projection of the marker j from the function $h(x(t))$. If $a_i(t) = 0$, the output model reduces to $y_i = \nu_o$, $\nu_o \sim \mathcal{N}(\bar{\nu}_o, \Sigma_o)$. It is desired to find the most probable value of the variable $a_i(t)$, $\forall i = 1, \ldots, M_t$, that is for every measurement collected at the current time step. The association problem can be recast as maximizing the belief that the current measurement $y_i(t) \in \mathbf{y}_t$ is either the projection of a visible marker or a clutter. Formalizing, the aim is to find the maximum of the posterior distribution:

$$p\left(a_i(t) \middle| y_i(t), \mathbf{y}_{0:t-1}\right) \propto p\left(y_i(t) \middle| a_i(t), \mathbf{y}_{0:t-1}\right) p\left(a_i(t)\right) \qquad (4)$$

given the current measurement $y_i(t)$ and the whole history of the measurements up to the previous step. The previous equation has been obtained via application of Bayes' rule. The *prior* $p(a_i(t))$ is determined by the a priori knowledge of clutter and marker association event probabilities [15,16], while the density $p\left(y_i \middle| a_i, \mathbf{y}_{0:t-1}\right)$ is the likelihood that the current measurement is associated to a given marker or to a clutter. This distribution can be obtained via marginalization of a proper joint density:

$$p\left(y_i \middle| a_i, \mathbf{y}_{0:t-1}\right) = \int p\left(y_i \middle| x, a_i, \mathbf{y}_{t-1}\right) p\left(x \middle| a_i, \mathbf{y}_{t-1}\right) dx \qquad (5)$$

$$= \int p\left(y_i \middle| x, a_i, \mathbf{y}_{t-1}\right) p\left(x \middle| \mathbf{y}_{t-1}\right) dx \qquad (6)$$

where the last equality is obvious since the prediction of the motion parameters of the wrist does not depend on the value of the association for the current measurements set. Fixing a certain guess for the association, $a_i(t) = j$, $j \neq 0$, the density $p\left(y_i \middle| a_i, \mathbf{y}_{0:t-1}\right)$ is the Kalman Filter likelihood of the measurement $y_i(t)$, given the prediction of the marker j, i.e. given the conditioning of the measurement model over *that* value of the latent variable. Thus, given the predicted state-related Sigma-Points [17], $\mathbf{X}_{n,t/t-1}^x$, $n = 1, \ldots, L$, computed by employing the nonlinear state model, their transformation through the conditioned measurement function can be obtained, as in the classical UKF:

$$\mathbf{Y}_{n,t/t-1}^j = h\left(\mathbf{X}_{n,t/t-1}^x \middle| a_i = j\right) \qquad (7)$$

The superscript j on the transformed Sigma-Points of the output, indicates that $Y_{n,t/t-1}^j$ refers to the predicted projection of the marker j, for which the association is being tested. The mean and covariance of the measurement vector are calculated as:

$$\widehat{y_j^-} = \sum_{n=0}^{L} W_m^n \mathbf{Y}_{n,t/t-1}^j \tag{8}$$

$$P_{yy,j}^- = \sum_{n=0}^{L} W_c^n \left(\mathbf{Y}_{n,t/t-1}^j - \widehat{y_j^-} \right) \left(\mathbf{Y}_{n,t/t-1}^j - \widehat{y_j^-} \right)^T + R_i \tag{9}$$

where W_c^n and W_m^n are the weights associated to the Sigma-Points [17], $\widehat{y_j^-}$ is the predicted projection of the marker j and $P_{yy,j}^-$ its covariance, while R_i is the covariance matrix of the measurements, assumed known. Thus, the probability of the association $a_i = j$ (eq. (6)) can be computed as:

$$p\left(a_i = j \middle| y_i, \mathbf{y}_{0:t-1}\right) \propto \mathcal{N}\left(y_i - \widehat{y_j^-}, P_{yy,j}^-\right) p\left(a_i = j\right) \tag{10}$$

being $\mathcal{N}()$ the multivariate normal distribution of proper mean value and covariance. It is worth to mention that, when testing the association to a clutter, $a_i = 0$, Equation (10) is written as $p\left(a_i = 0 \middle| y_i, \mathbf{y}_{0:t-1}\right) \propto (1/RES) \, p\left(a_i = 0\right)$, where RES is the image resolution, meaning that a clutter can happen everywhere in the image. The set of possible associations is discrete, thus the (discrete) value of the association posterior distribution can be computed by inspecting all the possible values of the associations [16]. Selecting the maximum probability among the ones in equation (10) gives the most probable value of the variable $a_i(t)$, corresponding to the measurement $y_i(t)$. The association problem is solved by repeating the above procedure for all the measurements in the set $\mathbf{y}_t$. Degenerate cases, like multiple associations of different measurements to the same marker and so on, have been considered also, in this work, which solution is detailed in [16]. After the association problem is solved, the correction step can take place, employing the visible markers and the associated image projections, as in the classical UKF.

4   Experimental Validation of Hand Pose Estimation Algorithm

Monitoring human hand joint motion during a rehabilitation session allows extracting quantitative indicators about patient performance. In particular, measure of ROM, A/A and F/E angles of the fingers, wrist orientation and velocity, finger trajectories provide an indication of the ability of a person to perform a movement [19] [20]. The proposed algorithm has been experimentally tested for tracking the whole hand and extracting the above mentioned kinematic parameters during F/E and A/A movements of the fingers and of the wrist and during reach and grasp action. These are standard movements used for understanding the behaviour of each hand joint during a common rehabilitation session. The paper wants to provide a proof-of-concept of the pose estimation approach for evaluating those parameters; hence, the study is still preliminary and is based on

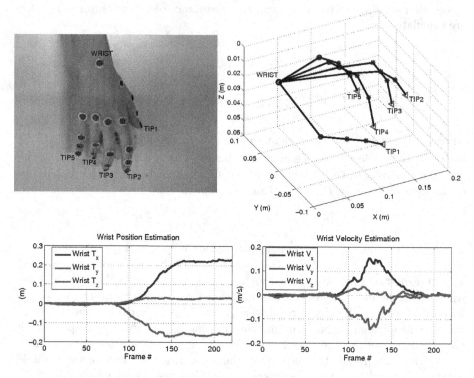

Fig. 2. Pose estimation result (top-right) corresponding to the grasping action of the observed hand (top-left). Position and velocity over time of the wrist during the reaching and grasping phases (bottom). Note that the detector failed with the markers on the thumb due to partial occlusion and shadows, however the pose estimation is still coherent.

the experimental tests on one subject. The participant (a healthy woman of 34 years old) was seated in front of a table with the right hand placed on it. In the starting configuration of the hand, the four fingers are fully extended, the thumb is adducted and the wrist is in a neutral position. The subject was asked to perform reach and grasp actions and finger movements for evaluating joint RoMs paying special attention not to rotate the arm. Fig. 2 shows the final instant of the grasping experiment and the related pose estimation of the hand. Moreover, the acquired data have also been used for analyzing the wrist behaviour in the reaching phase. In particular, Fig. 2, bottom, shows the wrist trajectory and velocity during the reach and grasp action. Fig. 3 shows finger A/A angles and wrist joint angles behaviour. The plotted results are reasonable, in fact it is possible to note that the measured A/A RoMs respect the values of published data on human beings [21]. The previously listed indicators are also extracted but are not reported for the sake of brevity. In conclusion, the approach could be easily used for patient performance evaluation during a rehabilitation session.

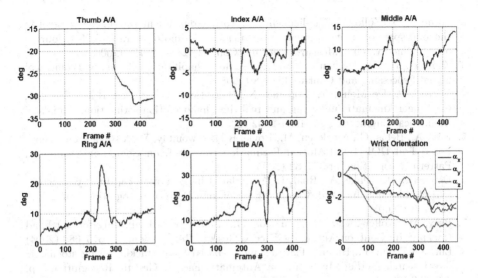

Fig. 3. Fingers A/A motion and wrist angle components during the range of motion experiment

5   Conclusion

In this paper, a novel and low-cost method for hand pose estimation has been proposed. The hand tracking problem has been formulated as a non-linear estimation problem solved by using UKF and considering the interdependence of the markers by introducing the hand kinematic model. Information about the joint orientation, position, trajectory and velocity have been extracted in order to demonstrate that the proposed pose estimation algorithm can be adopted for finding kinematics parameters about the whole hand. The approach can have useful applications in rehabilitation providing quantitative information about the performed task, such as the measurement of joint motion. Further improvements will be devoted to verify the accuracy of the approach by means of a comparison with a ground truth obtained with an optoelectronic system and to test the approach on real patients.

Acknowledgements. This work was supported in part by the National PRIN Project ROCOCÒ – COoperative and COllaborative RObotics (CUP E61J11000300001) and partly by the National PRIN Project HandBot (CUP: B81J12002680008).

References

1. Pellegrino, G., Tomasevic, L., Tombini, M., Assenza, G., Gallotta, E., Sterzi, S., Giacobbe, V., Zollo, L., Guglielmelli, E., Cavallo, G., Vernieri, F., Tecchio, F.: Interhemispheric coupling changes associate with motor improvements after robotic stroke rehabilitation. Restorative Neurology and Neuroscience (2012)

2. Formica, D., Zollo, L., Guglielmelli, E.: Torque-dependent compliance control in the joint space of an operational robotic machine for motor therapy. ASME Journal of Dynamic Systems, Measurement, and Control 128, 152–158 (2006)
3. Zhou, H., Hu, H.: Human motion tracking for rehabilitation–A survey. Biomedical Signal Processing and Control 3, 1–18 (2008)
4. Cerveri, P., De Momi, E., Lopomo, N., Baud-Bovy, G., Barros, R.M., Ferrigno, G.: Finger kinematic modeling and real-time hand motion estimation. Annals of Biomedical Engineering 35, 1989–2002 (2007)
5. Erol, A., Bebis, G., Nicolescu, M., Boyle, R.D., Twombly, X.: A Review on Vision-Based Full DOF Hand Motion Estimation. In: Conf. on Computer Vision and Pattern Recognition, pp. 75–82 (2005)
6. Deutscher, J., Blake, A., Reid, I.: Articulated body motion capture by annealed particle filtering. In: Conf. Computer Vision and Pattern Recognition, vol. 2, pp. 126–133 (2000)
7. Bray, M., Koller-Meier, E., Van Gool, L.: Smart particle filtering for 3D hand tracking. In: Conf. on Automatic Face & Gesture Recognition, pp. 675–680 (2004)
8. Lin, J.Y., Wu, Y., Huang, T.S.: 3D model-based hand tracking using stochastic direct search method. In: Conf. on Automatic Face & Gesture Recognition, pp. 693–698 (2004)
9. Chang, W.Y., Chen, C.S., Hung, Y.P.: Appearance-guided particle filtering for articulated hand tracking. In: Conf. on Computer Vision and Pattern Recognition, vol. 1, pp. 235–242 (2005)
10. Stenger, B., Thayananthan, A., Torr, P.H.S., Cipolla, R.: Hand pose estimation using hierarchical detection. In: Sebe, N., Lew, M., Huang, T.S. (eds.) ECCV/HCI 2004. LNCS, vol. 3058, pp. 105–116. Springer, Heidelberg (2004)
11. Chua, C.S., Guan, H.Y., Ho, Y.K.: Model-based finger posture estimation. In: Asian Conference on Computer Vision (2000)
12. Lee, J., Kunii, T.: Constraint-based hand animation. In: Models and Techniques in Computer Animation, 110–127 (1993)
13. Lin, J., Wu, Y., Huang, T.S.: Modeling the Constraints of Human Hand Motion. In: Proceeding Workshop on Human Motion, pp. 121–126 (2000)
14. Parasuraman, S., Zhen, C.C.S.: Development of Robot Assisted Hand Stroke Rehabilitation System. In: Conf. on Computer and Automation Engineering, pp. 70–74 (2009)
15. Cordella, F., Di Corato, F., Zollo, L., Siciliano, B., van der Smagt, P.: Patient performance evaluation using Kinect and Monte Carlo-Based finger tracking. In: Conf. on Biomedical Robotics and Biomechatronics, pp. 1967–1972 (2012)
16. Di Corato, F.: A Unified Framework for Constrained Visual-Inertial Navigation with Guaranteed Convergence. PhD Dissertation, University of Pisa (May 2013)
17. Kandepu, R., Foss, B., Imsland, L.: Applying the unscented Kalman filter for nonlinear state estimation. Journal of Process Control 18(7-8), 753–768 (2008)
18. Wan, E.A., Van der Merwe, R.: The unscented Kalman filter for nonlinear estimation. In: Symposium on Adaptive Systems for Signal Processing, Communications, and Control, pp. 153–158 (2000)
19. Zollo, L., Rossini, L., Bravi, M., Magrone, G., Sterzi, S., Guglielmelli, E.: Quantitative evaluation of upper-limb motor control in robot-aided rehabilitation. Medical and Biological Engineering and Computing 9(49), 1131–1144 (2011)
20. Formica, D., Krebs, H.I., Charles, S.K., Zollo, L., Guglielmelli, E., Hogan, N.: Passive wrist joint stiffness estimation. Journal of Neurophysiology (2012)
21. Berger, R.A., Weiss, A.P.C.: Hand surgery (2004)

Natural User Interfaces in Volume Visualisation Using Microsoft Kinect

Anastassia Angelopoulou[1], José García-Rodríguez[2], Alexandra Psarrou[1], Markos Mentzelopoulos[1], Bharat Reddy[1], Sergio Orts-Escolano[2], Jose Antonio Serra[2], and Andrew Lewis[3]

[1] Dept. of Computer Science and Software Engineering,
University of Westminster, UK
{agelopa,psarroa,mentzem,bharat.reddy}@wmin.ac.uk
[2] Dept. of Computing Technology, University of Alicante, Spain
{jgarcia,sorts,jserra}@dtic.ua.es
[3] Dept. of Engineering and Information Technology, University of Griffith, Australia
a.lewis@griffith.edu.au

Abstract. This paper presents the integration of human-machine interaction technologies within a virtual reality environment to allow for real-time manipulation of $3D$ objects using different gestures. We demonstrate our approach by developing a fully operational, natural user interface (NUI) system, which provides a front-end framework for back-end applications that use more traditional forms of input, such as wear cable sensors attached to the users. The implementation is a user-friendly system that has immense potential in a number of fields, especially in the medical sciences where it would be possible to increase the productivity of surgeons by providing them with easy access to relevant MRI scans.

Keywords: Growing Neural Gas, 3D Sensors, Natural User Interfaces, Volume Visualisation.

1 Introduction

Volume visualization is an important form of scientific visualisation, allowing investigation of, for example, medical scanned data such as CT and MRI data, seismic survey data, and computational fluid dynamic (CFD) data [3,10]. To better understand volumetric datasets, people use computer hardware and software to manipulate the data and generate 2D projections for viewing. Much research on volume visualisation has been focused on volume rendering (how to render larger sets of data faster with a higher level of realism) or transfer function generation (how to highlight the regions of interest). To help improve the efficiency and efficacy of volume visualisation, one can integrate virtual reality environments (VEs) and human computer interaction (HCI) technologies in volume visualisation applications. However, these volume visualisation systems require accurate tracking of posture and movement which is provided by wear cable sensors attached to the users. Over the last decades there has been an

A. Petrosino, L. Maddalena, P. Pala (Eds.): ICIAP 2013 Workshops, LNCS 8158, pp. 11–19, 2013.

increasing interest in using neural networks and computer vision techniques to allow users to directly explore and manipulate objects in a more natural and intuitive environment without the use of electromagnetic tracking systems. With the recent rise of motion sensing cameras, most notably Microsofts Kinect, gesture recognition has added an extra dimension to human-machine interaction [9].

This paper presents a virtual reality visualisation system (VirtVis) that has been designed and developed to use various virtual tools that allow users to directly explore and manipulate the volume data in $3D$ space. Many innovations have been integrated into this system, including an optimisation of the hand using the GNG network, an intuitive HCI paradigm tailored for volume visualisation in VEs, and geometric tools that can assist users to fully reveal the internal structure of volumetric datasets. Usability experiments have demonstrated that volume visualisation tasks can be performed significant better in virtual reality viewing conditions, and that using these geometric tools can significantly improve the efficiency and efficacy of the volume visualisation process. The HCI interaction used in VirtVis is based on natural and intuitive hand gestures. To manipulate a virtual object, the user physically reaches to grasp and move it as though it was real.

The remainder of the paper is organised as follows. Section 2 gives a theoretical background over sensor-free systems and our choice of selection. Section 3 discusses the implementation of the proposed system, before we conclude in Section 4.

2   Sensor-Free Systems

Human gestures form an integral part in our verbal and non-verbal communication. We use them to reinforce meaning not always conveyed through speech, to describe the shape of objects, to play games, to communicate in noisy environments, and to convey meaning to elderly people and people with special needs. We can use gestures as expressive body motions or to translate non-verbal languages that consist of a set of well defined gestures and hand postures with complete lexical and grammatical specifications as in the case of sign languages.

Hand gestures, which are effectively a $2D$ projection of a $3D$ object, can become very complex for any recognition system. Systems that follow a model-based method [1,13], require an accurate $3D$ model that captures efficiently the hand's high Degrees of Freedom (DOF) articulation and elasticity. The main drawback of this method is that it requires massive calculations which makes it unrealistic for real-time implementation. Since this method is too complicated to implement, the most widespread alternative is the feature-based method [7] where features such as the geometric properties of the hand can be analysed using either Neural Networks (NN) [14,16] or stochastic models such as Hidden Markov Models (HMMs) [4,15].

We decided to use the former for the representation of human gestures since our model should perform at high computational efficiency making it ideal for real time environments, have low quantisation error, and allow for efficient transformation of the objects. More specifically, we have used the GNG model since is superior in terms of computational efficiency, is robust against noise, and can handle complex distributions [2,12,13]. As for a sensor-free hardware platform which will allow the user to move freely and naturally in any environment we decided to use Microsoft Kinect since it combines an RGB camera, infrared depth sensor and multiarray microphone with a proprietary layer of software that allows human body and voice recognition.

2.1   Growing Neural Gas (GNG)

GNG [6] is an unsupervised incremental self-organising network independent of the topology of the input distribution or space. It uses a growth mechanism inherited from the Growth Cell Structure [5] together with the Competitive Hebbian Learning (CHL) rule [8] to construct a network of the input date set. In some cases the probability distribution of the input data set is discrete and is given by the characteristic function $\xi_w : \mathbb{R}^q \to \{0,1\}$ with ξ_w defined by

$$\xi_w = \begin{cases} 1 \text{ if } \xi \in W \\ 0 \text{ if } \xi \in W^c \end{cases} \tag{1}$$

In the network ξ_w represents the random input signal generated from the set $W \subseteq \mathbb{R}^q$ and W^c is the complement of $W \in \mathbb{R}^q$. The growing process starts with two nodes, and new nodes are incrementally inserted until a predefined conditioned is satisfied, such as the maximum number of nodes or available time. During the learning process local error measures are gathered to determine where to insert new nodes. New nodes are inserted near the node with the highest accumulated error and new connections between the winner node and its topological neighbours are created.

The GNG algorithm consists of the following:

- A set A of cluster centres known as nodes. Each node $c \in N$ has its associated reference vector $\{x_c\}_{c=1}^N \in \mathbb{R}^q$. The reference vectors indicate the nodes' position or *receptive field centre* in the input distribution. The nodes move towards the input distribution by adapting their position to the input's geometry using a winner take all mapping.
- Local accumulated error measurements and insertion of nodes. Each node $c \in N$ with its associated reference vector $\{x_c\}_{c=1}^N \in \mathbb{R}^q$ has an error variable E_{x_c} which is updated at every iteration according to:

$$\Delta E_{x_\nu} = \|\xi_w - x_\nu\|^2 \tag{2}$$

The local accumulated error is a statistical measure and is used for the insertion and the distribution of new nodes. Nodes with larger errors will cover greater area of the input probability distribution, since their distance from the generated signal is updated by the squared distance. Knowing where the error is large, if the number of the associated reference vectors belonging to the input space is an integer multiple of a parameter λ, a new node x_r is inserted halfway between the node with the largest local accumulated error x_q and its neighbour x_f.

$$x_r = \frac{x_q + x_f}{2} \tag{3}$$

All connections are updated and local errors are decreased by:

$$\Delta E_{x_q} = -\alpha E_{x_q} \tag{4}$$

$$\Delta E_{x_f} = -\alpha E_{x_f} \tag{5}$$

A global decrease according to:

$$\Delta E_{x_c} = -\beta E_{x_c} \tag{6}$$

is performed to all local errors by a constant β. This is important since new errors will gain greater influence in the network resulting in a better representation of the topology.

- A set C of edges (connections) between pair of nodes. These connections are not weighted and its purpose is to define the topological structure. The edges are determined using the competitive hebbian learning method. The updating rule of the algorithm is expressed as:

$$\Delta x_\nu = \epsilon_x(\xi_w - x_\nu) \tag{7}$$

$$\Delta x_c = \epsilon_n(\xi_w - x_c), \forall c \in N \tag{8}$$

where ϵ_x and ϵ_n represent the constant learning rates for the winner node x_ν and its topological neighbours x_c. An *edge aging scheme* is used to remove connections that are invalid due to the activation of the node during the adaptation process.

2.2   3D Hand Representation with GNG

Figure 1 shows the ability of GNG to preserve the input data topology. Identifying the points of the input data that belong to the objects allows the network to adapt its structure to this input subspace, obtaining an induced Delaunay triangulation of the object. GNG has been adapted using the Point Cloud Library (PCL)[1] for the 3D surface representation. The main difference with the original GNG algorithm is the omission of insertion/deletion actions after the first frame. Since no neurons are added the system keeps the correspondence during the whole sequence, solving intrinsically the problem of correspondence. This adaptive method is also able to face real-time constraints, because the number λ of times that the internal loop is performed can be chosen according to the time available between two successive frames that depend on the acquisition rate. The mean time to obtain a GNG on a frame is about 10ms., using the adaptive method. Thus, GNG provides a reduction of the input data, while preserving its structure.

---

[1] The Point Cloud Library (or PCL) is a large scale, open project [11] for 2D/3D image and point cloud processing.

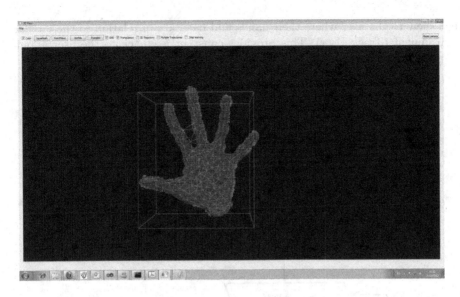

Fig. 1. 3D Hand representation with GNG

2.3   Microsoft Kinect

The Microsoft Kinect, is an accessory for Microsofts popular Xbox 360 gaming console that removes or reduces the need for a controller by enabling motion tracking in the Xbox 360, and allowing users to use their hands and bodies to play games that can receive this information. All the experimental phase is based on the use of real-world sequences obtained by the Kinect sensor. Such sensors belong to the so-called RGB-D cameras since they provide RGB format images with depth information per pixel. Specifically, Microsoft's Kinect sensor is able to get screenshots of 640x480 pixels and its corresponding depth information, based on an infrared projector combined with a CMOS sensor with a resolution of 320x240 pixels, and can reach rates of up to 30 frames per second. A first processing of sensor data enables obtaining the component in the z axis of coordinates of the points in the three dimensional space.

For the segmentation of the hands from the background, a hybrid technique based on depth information and skin colour has been used. A modification of the Point Cloud Library (PCL) for the 3D surface representation of the objects was used to support the 3D mesh reconstruction of the points based on the GNG algorithm discussed in Section 2. In the past, point clouds have mainly been created using 3D scanners. However, with the advent of technology such as Kinect it is now possible to acquire a point cloud for an object by using the depth sensor functionality. The construction of the VirtVis system is given in Figure 2. The main functionalities of the system as can be seen in the flowchart (User Modifies Object) are a menu system displayed on the screen, where the user can select an option by putting their hand mark over the option and holding for a few seconds (e.g. reset, change object, fly-through), and three indicators that show to the user where their hands and head are in relation to the virtual environment (Track User). This provides constant feedback to the user about the positioning of their hands.

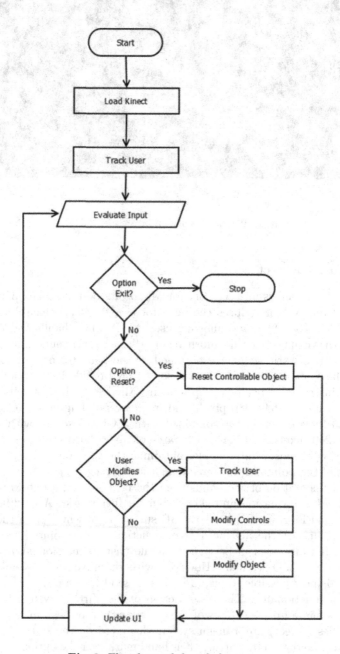

Fig. 2. Flowchart of the whole system

3 Experiments

Several experiments have been performed for the validation of our system. To carry out all the experiments we used the Kinect SDK which provides a Runtime class in C# that, once initialised, acts as an interface between the Kinect and our system. The Runtime is initialised with the first active Kinect system that the program finds, and is initialised with a number of Runtime options that allow skeletal tracking, video display, and multi-player interfaces. Skeleton Tracking is done via the Kinect Skeleton Engine, which provides, through the SkeletonFrameReady event, positions for up to two skeletons, and various joints on this skeleton. These joints positions are given according to the Kinects field of view, and are converted from our system to screen sized dimensions to accurately represent control of objects on screen.

The depth frame is constantly displayed in the top left hand corner of the screen to provide a reference to the user of what the Kinect is picking up so they can better position themselves for a good user interaction experience. Figure 3 shows the VirtVis main window. The system is based around the users head position, represented as an area that begins at 20% of the distance from the Kinect to the user, and ends at 80% of the distance. If one or both of the users hands are in this box, they are defined as active, and will do different things based on which hands are active. For example, when both hands are active, the user has activated the objects scaling functionality. Object scaling is calculated by taking the vector distance between the left and right hands, as well as the vector distance between the left and right shoulders. Shoulder joints are calculated to make the scaling functionality more intuitive by ensuring that if the hands are inside the shoulders, the object is smaller and when outside the object is bigger.

A modified version of PCL is used to save a reconstructed surface representation of the hand performing a gesture. Once the user has been tracked a timer is started. The user is notified that they have three seconds to get their right hand into position for the point cloud to be taken. After these three seconds the

Fig. 3. An example of a cube object being transformed using different gestures. Two levels of fly-through functionality have been implemented similar to what is used in the volume visualisation systems.

functionality within PCL takes the point cloud of the right hand and reconstructs the surface using the GNG algorithm discussed in section 2.

Usability testing has been conducted with the User Acceptance Testing (UAT). UAT is common in agile methodology where tests are written as short one-stop requirements where testers are asked to indicate whether a requirement was met, partially met, or not met at all. Figure 4 shows the results of the user experience testing. There was found to be some ambivalence amongst users about whether

Input	Tester1	Tester2	Tester3	Tester4	Tester5	Met	Partially Met	Not Met	Score (%)
Natural User Interface									
I am able to control the object with my hands									
I am able to move an object on screen from one position to another	Met	Met	Met	Met	Met	5	0	0	100
I am able to increase and decrease the size of an object on screen	Met	Met	Met	Met	Met	5	0	0	100
I am able to rotate an object on screen	Met	Met	Met	Met	Met	5	0	0	100
Keyboard Interface									
I am able to reset the environment I am working in	Partially Met	Met	Met	Partially Met	Met	3	2	0	80
I am able to access a menu that contains relevant options	Met	Met	Met	Met	Met	5	0	0	100
I am able to change the 3D object I am working with	Not Met	Not Met	Not Met	Not Met	Not Met	0	0	5	0
User Experience									
I am able to view the object I can control, and am able to see them transformed in real-time	Met	Met	Met	Met	Met	5	0	0	100
I am able to view where my hands are in relation to the virtual environment	Met	Met	Met	Met	Met	5	0	0	100
I am able to use a visual menu that extends the functionality of the environment									
Reset	Met	Met	Met	Met	Met	5	0	0	100
Change Object	Not Met	Not Met	Not Met	Not Met	Not Met	0	0	5	0
Fly-Through	Met	Met	Met	Met	Met	5	0	0	100
Met	8	9	9	8	9				
Partially Met	1	0	0	1	0			Average Test Score (%)	
Not Met	2	2	2	2	2				
Score (%)	77.27273	81.81818	81.81818	77.27273	81.81818			80	

Fig. 4. User Acceptance Testing results

the reset requirement was met. Using the UAT scoring matrix, the requirement has been assigned a test score of 80%. Two out of five testers indicated that this functionality was partially met; indicating to the interviewer that they felt the reset functionality should reset the entire window as opposed to just the object. However, this is not necessary as the main environment is the controllable object and a window reset can be done by restarting the application.

4   Conclusions and Future Work

In this paper we have presented an architecture to represent gestures based on neural networks and 3D sensors. The system operates a fully functional natural user interface (NUI) with 3D reconstruction of hands, an intuitive HCI paradigm, and tools for fly-through interactivity as is used in volume visualisation applications. As for future work, we will improve the system performance at all stages to achieve a natural interface that allows us to interact with any object manipulation system.

References

1. Albrecht, I., Haber, J., Seidel, H.: Construction and animation of anatomically based human hand models. In: Proc. of the 2003 ACM SIGGRAPH/Eurographics Symposium on Computer Animation, pp. 98–109 (2003)
2. Angelopoulou, A., Psarrou, A., García Rodríguez, J.: A Growing Neural Gas Algorithm with Applications in Hand Modelling and Tracking. In: Cabestany, J., Rojas, I., Joya, G. (eds.) IWANN 2011, Part II. LNCS, vol. 6692, pp. 236–243. Springer, Heidelberg (2011)
3. Calhoun, P.S., Kuszyk, B., Heath, D., Carley, J., Fishman, E.: Three-dimensional volume rendering of spiral CT data: Theory and method. RadioGraphics 19(3), 745–764 (1999)
4. Eddy, S.: Hidden Markov Models. Current Opinion in Structural Biology 6(3), 361–365 (1996)
5. Fritzke, B.: Growing Cell Structures - A self-organising network for unsupervised and supervised learning. The Journal of Neural Networks 7(9), 1441–1460 (1994)
6. Fritzke, B.: A growing Neural Gas Network Learns Topologies. In: Advances in Neural Information Processing Systems 7 (NIPS 1994), pp. 625–632 (1995)
7. Koike, H., Sato, Y., Kobayashi, Y.: Integrating Paper and Digital Information on Enhanced Desk: A Method for Real Time Finger Tracking on an Augmented Desk System. ACM Transactions on Computer-Human Interaction 8(4), 307–322 (2001)
8. Martinez, T., Schulten, K.: Topology Representing Networks. The Journal of Neural Networks 7(3), 507–522 (1994)
9. Ravikiran, J., Mahesh, K., Mahishi, S.: R., D., Sudheender, S., Pujari, N.: Finger detection for sign language recognition. In: International MultiConference of Engineers & Computer Scientists, p. 489 (2009)
10. Rosenblum, L.J.: Scientific Visualization: Advances and challenges, vol. 4 (1994)
11. Rusu, R., Cousins, S.: 3D is here: Point Cloud Library, PCL (2011)
12. Stergiopoulou, E., Papamarkos, N.: Hand gesture recognition using a neural network shape fitting technique. Engineering Applications of Artificial Intelligence 22(8), 1141–1158 (2009)
13. Sui, C.: Appearance-based hand gesture identification. Master of Engineering, University of New South Wales (2011)
14. Vamplew, P., Adams, A.: Recognition of Sign Language Gestures using Neural Networks. Australian Journal of Intelligent Information Processing Systems 5(2), 94–102 (1998)
15. Wong, S., Ranganath, S.: Automatic Sign Language Analysis: A Survey and the Future beyond Lexical Meaning. IEEE Transactions on Pattern Analysis and Machine Intelligence, 873–891 (2005)
16. Yang, J., Bang, W., Choi, E., Cho, S., Oh, J., Cho, J., Kim, S., Ki, E., Kim, D.: A 3D Hand-drawn Gesture Input Device Using Fuzzy ARTMAP-based Recognizer. Journal of Systemics, Cybernetics and Informatics 4(3), 1–7 (2009)

A Fast and Precise HOG-Adaboost Based Visual Support System Capable to Recognize Pedestrian and Estimate Their Distance

Kishino Takahisa, Zhe Sun, and Ruggero Micheletto

Yokohama City University, Graduate School of Nanobioscience,
22-2 Seto Kanazawa-ku, 236-0027 Yokohama, Japan
{n115208c,n125213e,ruggero}@yokohama-cu.ac.jp
http://ruggero.sci.yokohama-cu.ac.jp/

Abstract. In this paper,we present a visual support system the visually impaired. Our detection algorithm is based on the well known Histograms of Oriented Gradients (HOG) method, due to its high detection rate and versatility[5]. However, the accuracy of object recognition rate is reduced because of high false detection rate. In order to solve that, multiple parts model and triple phase detection have been implemented. These additional filtering stages were conducted by separate action on different area of the sample, considering deformations and translations. We demonstrated that this approach has raised the accuracy and speed of calculation. Through an evaluation experiment based on a large dataset, we found that false detection has been improved by 18.9% in respect to standard HOG detectors. Experimental tests have also shown the system ability to estimate the distance of the pedestrian by the use of a simple perspective model. The system has been tested on several photographic datasets and have shown excellent performances also in ambiguous cases.

Keywords: Pedestrian detection, HOG methods, distance evaluation, single-camera, Adaboost.

1 Introduction

In this study, we present steps toward the realization of an automatic pedestrian detection system for the visually impaired. Today, the visually impaired has many obstacles to walk outside and despite the advancement of technology in many fields, we often see blind people accompanied by friends or by a dog. Widespread devices to help these persons are not common yet. However, we think that audio support devices that are based on a GPS route navigation systems[8] are promising and may be successful. And they also present dangers because of possible collision by other pedestrian.

Many of the pedestrian detecting systems typically apply standard computer vision techniques[11], such as background subtraction or background modelling[10]. Since the camera is given to the visually impaired, the images are shot directly from the user viewpoint. As an alternative for background subtraction, it is possible to

A. Petrosino, L. Maddalena, P. Pala (Eds.): ICIAP 2013 Workshops, LNCS 8158, pp. 20–29, 2013.

use the approach of detecting multiple and deformable parts. This approach will be used in this study and its results shown. We will demonstrate that it is possible to reduce the effect of a variable and dynamic background and obtain high quality detection and robust results.

Our system consists of an algorithm that acts in two phases: pedestrian detection and estimation of distance. In the detection phase, it scans the image for the pedestrian shape standing in front of the camera. We improved a standard HOG method introducing a multiple part model to it.

1.1 Comparison of HOG, SIFT and PCA-SIFT

We realized that HOG method is more suitable than other methods because of its geometrical and optical transfer invariance, and because it shows low computational complexity and high velocity [9].

Table 1. A rough comparison between HOG, SIFT and PCA-SIFT methods for pedestrian recognition

	Speed	Scale	Rotation
HOG	best	best	common
SIFT	common	good	good
PCA-SIFT	good	common	best

2 System Model

This section describes the pedestrian detection system and the distance estimation process.

2.1 Histograms of Oriented Gradients

The underlying building blocks of our method are the Histograms of Oriented Gradients (HOG)[4]. HOG representation captures the gradient structure that is characteristic of the human shape. A magnitude m and orientation θ of gradients at each pixel are given by the equation:

$$m(x, y) = \sqrt{f_x(x, y)^2 + f_y(x, y)^2} \qquad (1)$$

$$\theta(x, y) = \tan^{-1} \frac{f_x(x, y)}{f_y(x, y)} \qquad (2)$$

where $f_x(x, y) = L(x + 1, y) - L(x - 1, y)$, $f_y(x, y) = L(x, y + 1) - L(x, y - 1)$ and $L(x, y)$ is proportional to the brightness of a pixel. θ is discretized into one of nine orientation bins. Each pixel is assigned the orientation of its gradient, with a strength that depends on m. The image is divided into $n * n$

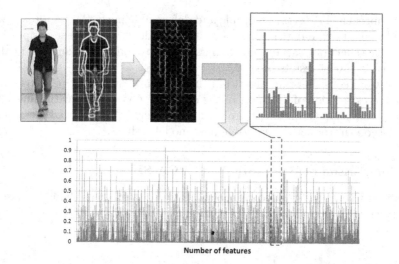

Fig. 1. An example of the HOG process. The HOG analysis acts on *cells* that contain the images edges of the image captured by the camera. The edges are evaluated for orientation θ and an *orientation magnitude* m value is calculated for each cell and normalized . The magnitudes m are normalized by *blocks* (see text for details). These normalized magnitudes are stored as an one-dimensional histogram and represent the main feature of the image that will be compared with a database of positive or negative samples for the human recognition process.

not overlapping pixel regions that are called *cells* and each group of cells is integrated into a *block*. The blocks can overlap with each other. These gradient features are represented as one-dimensional histogram, as shown in Figure 1.

2.2   Multiple Parts Model

The pedestrian have diverse postures (e.g. looking down, checking the phone). From the point of view of the camera held by the subject, the relative changes in the parts (e.g. head, arm) position are especially important. So our system is required to deal with various poses without making mistakes. One of the methods to detect diverse human poses, consists of divide the target object into several parts [6] and consider the whole as the composition of them. Thus our method treats the person model as a cluster consisting of three parts, that define the complete body, the head and the legs, see Figure. 2. The model of the pedestrian is composed by a base filter and two secondary models (P_1, P_2). The base filter F_0 covers the entire human and defines the rough pedestrian location. The secondary models represent the head and feet parts. In general each secondary model is given by the relation:

$$P_i = (F_i, v_i, s_i)$$

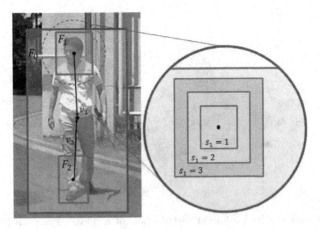

Fig. 2. A sketch representing how the multiple part analysis is done. We apply the HOG algorithm firstly on the whole screen and by the use of a mean-shift clustering procedure the position of the person body is located. To realize a more robust analysis we apply the HOG algorithm again twice in order to locate the head and the feet parts of the image. This further analysis is made using the three different sizes s_i as mentioned in the text to reduce error.

Here i is the part number, F_i is the part filter for the specific ith element, v_i is a two dimensional vector locating the center of a box enclosing the part and finally s_i gives the size of the box. There are three sizes for each box to reduce error.

We have considered that using higher resolution is essential to reduce false detections. Therefore each part filter f_i has a higher HOG resolution than its base. The position of each filter can move at each scene, remaining confined within its base filter range. The filter can act externally to the base filter provided it is overlapping with it at least 50% of its area. In this way the variability is enough to recognize the region of the body in diverse position without incurring in errors.

2.3   Classifier Construction

To optimize performances we used a cascade AdaBoost classifier[13,14] trained by the main HOG features[12]. When the processing is complete, the final classifier $H(x)$ is a linear combination of several weak classifiers $h_t(x)$. The number of weak classifiers is T and it is equal in number as the learning samples.

$$H(x) = \sum_{t=1}^{T} \alpha_t h_t(x)$$

where x is the input feature data, t is number of learning round. α_t is the weight of the tth learning data, this it is given by the equation:

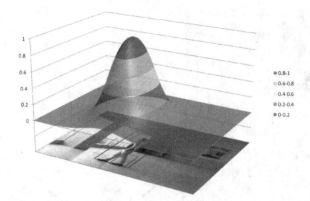

Fig. 3. An example of the likelihood distribution of a image. For each image frame captured by the camera, a likelihood map is generated in real time. This map is obtained from output values of the classifiers that scans the image in an iterative process. When a region of the image is found to have similar features to the human profile accordingly to a database of learning data, that area is assigned a higher likelihood.

$$\alpha_t = \frac{1}{2}\ln\frac{1-e_t}{e_t}$$

where e_t is the weight summation of each learning sample at tth learning round.

In other words, the output value of the final classifier represents the level of resemblance to human profile of a particular area on the image. When the classifier is applied to the image area where a human is present, it outputs a high value. By iteration of raster scans, a map that associates the human likelihood to the image is generated. As shown in Figure 3, our classifier likelihood is mainly distributed over the human profile in the example.

The features of HOG are compared with positive samples (human images) and negative ones (background object and other non-human images). The features that exhibit greater differences between positive and negative samples are considered for an efficient classifier, about 200 classifiers were selected in this study.

We also compared the AdaBoost classifier algorithm with the SVM classifier and we realized that a weak classifier AdaBoost with high-speed detection is more suitable for pedestrian recognition[7].

2.4   Distance Range Estimation

To notify the user of collision risks, our system estimate the distance to pedestrian that are located ahead the camera[3]. As the image is shot from a single camera the distance should be estimated by perspective projection. There are two clues to estimate distance by perspective: the size of pedestrian in the image and its position. Since the size of pedestrian depends on the person body height, our system derives the approximate range using the position of the pedestrian. We assume a planar road surface and that a camera optical axis is parallel to the road surface, even though the system is robust enough to accept small perturbations around these conditions (see Figure.4 with a diagram of the imaging geometry).

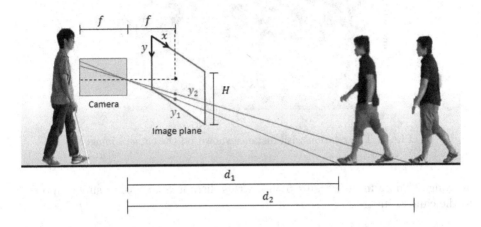

Fig. 4. Ideal image geometry in the perspective model for distance estimation. See text for details.

The camera is held by the user at height h. The distance to the pedestrian from the camera is d. The point on the road at the distance d is projected onto the image plane at the position y. This is the image coordinates given by the equation:

$$y = \frac{fh}{d} + \frac{H}{2}$$

where f is the camera focal length expressed in pixel and H is the full screen size.

When a first pedestrian is at a distance d_1 and a distant pedestrian is at d_2, the points of contact are projected onto the image at y_1 and y_2. As shown in the example of Figure. 4, y_1 results to be smaller than y_2. To calculate the distance to a pedestrian the system detects the person foot and its range is estimated from the following formula:

$$d = \frac{1}{fh}(y - \frac{H}{2})$$

In the current algorithm the camera is set at $h = 1.4$m and as an indication to notify of the collision risk, pedestrian are grouped by their distance into three range levels: near-range (4m or less), medium-range (between 4m and 8m), and

Fig. 5. The relation with distance shown on the camera image

far-range (8m or more). Figure.5 shows this distant relationship superimposed to the camera image.

3   Experiment and Results

3.1   Experiment

To evaluate detection accuracy, we prepared a dataset.Using this dataset we compare two methods of detection, conventional HOG and our multi parts detector. Table 2 shows the accuracy result.

Even if the conventional HOG detector has a better detection rate than our method, the difference in accuracy is just 3.2%. On the contrary, compared to the conventional HOG method, our method have a 18.92% better false detection performance. Since our method have a flexible positioning of each part the decrease in detection rate is low. Instead the false detection result, the conventional HOG method is more likely to falsely detect objects with a complex texture. Overall, our method makes a slight sacrifice in detection rate, to obtain an improved lower false detection rate.

3.2   Pedestrian Detection

The process of detecting the pedestrian from an image consists of a detection window that scans the image over and over. The scale and position of this window are changed in scale and position in an optimized way. In this way it is possible to detect humans whose size is diverse. These images are taken in multiple locations, with a resolution of 640*480 pixels.

Table 2. Accuracy rate for HOG and our multiple model method. The "miss" parameter shows the percentage of missed target, while "false" include the missed targets and the detection of false targets.

	precision	miss	false
HOG	91.90	9.10	25.21
Multiple Model	88.70	11.30	6.29

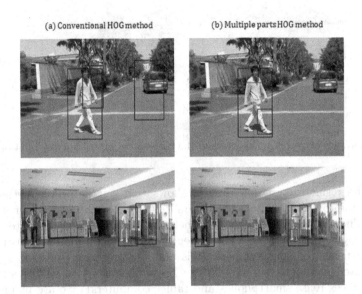

Fig. 6. Examples of detection images over complex and moving backgrounds. On the left are shown the results with a conventional HOG approach: moving car and other objects are falsely detected. On the right our multiple part HOG approach solves this problem when tested on the same video frames.

In Figure.6 we show a comparative result of pedestrian detection examples. The conventional method shows false detections due to complex background. Because our method operates with three phase detection, it works better and is more robust than the conventional HOG method. Our method is able to detect pedestrian accurately in these non-ideal environments. Figure. 7 shows the result of estimating the distance of each person. We see that the position of each pedestrian can be estimated with good approximation. Based on this result, our system can compute the collision risk and notify the user of approaching pedestrian.

4   Conclusions and Perspective

In this study, we proposed a pedestrian detection system which can estimate the distance to targets with a single camera by the use of a multiple-parts HOG

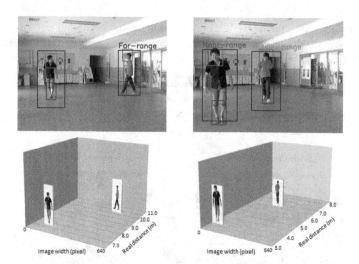

Fig. 7. Examples of detection images and the corresponding distance estimation range

model. The result of test experiments shows that our detection method has a 18.92% improvement in false detection rate against the conventional HOG method. The system was also able to detect pedestrian in complicated backgrounds moving environments. The system was able to estimate the distance of pedestrian using the single camera. It is possible to derive collision risk from the estimated distance. Our system can be implemented on simple and convenient devices (e.g., smartphones and tablet computers). We are planning to improve the system developed up to now to work as a support application in real environments. Especially there we want to focus on two parameters, real time processing and pedestrian tracking. Our system takes more CPU time than the simple HOG method. We have to optimize processing time and simultaneously realize the tracking of the pedestrian to support the user to decide the direction of avoidance. We plan to use time-series filtering, Kalman filter [2] or Particle filter [1]. By applying a time-series filter algorithm, faster process time is expected because of the determinate scan area. The new filtering will also enable to improve the accuracy because of the tracking information relative to the target person.

References

1. Brasnett, P., Mihaylova, L., Bull, D., Canagarajah, N.: Sequential monte carlo tracking by fusing multiple cues in video sequences. Image vision Computing 25(8), 1217–1227 (2007)
2. Cuevas, E., Zaldiver, D., Rojas, R.: Kalman filter for vision tracking. Fachbereich Mathematik und Informatic. Technical Report B, Freie Universitat Berlin (2005)
3. Hoiem, D., Efros, A.A., Hebert, M.: Putting objects in perspective. Pattern Analysis and Machine Intelligence 2 (2006)

4. Dalal, N., Triggs, B.: Histograms of oriented gradients for human detection. In: CVPR, pp. 886–893 (2005)
5. Suard, F., Rakotomamonjy, A., Bensrhair, A., Broggi, A.: Pedestrian detection using infrared images and histograms of oriented gradients. In: Proc. IEEE Conf. Intell. Vehicles, pp. 206–212 (2006)
6. Felzenszwalb, P., Girschick, R., McAllester, D.: Cascade object detection with deformable part models. In: CVPR, pp. 1–8 (2010)
7. Han, F., Shan, Y., Cekander, R., Sawhney, H.S., Kumar, R.: A two-stage approach to people and vehicle detection with hog-based svm. In: Performance Metrics for Intelligent Systems Workshop in conjunction with the IEEE Safety, Security, and Rescue Robotics Conference, pp. 134–136 (2006)
8. Helal, A., Moore, S., Ramachandran, B.: Drishti: An integrated navigation system for the visually impaired and disabled. In: Fifth International Symposium on Wearable Computers (ISWC 2001), pp. 149–156 (2001)
9. Juan, L., Gwun, O.: A comparison of sift, pca-sift and surf. International Journal of Image Processing 3, 143–152 (2009)
10. Montabone, S., Soto, A.: Human detection using a mobile platform and novel features derived from a visual saliency mechanism. Image and Vision Computing 28(3), 391–402 (2010)
11. Felzenszwalb, P.F., Girshick, R.B., McAllester, D., Ramanan, D.: Object detection with discriminatively trained part based models. Pattern Analysis and Machine Intelligence, 1627–1645 (2010)
12. Zhu, Q., Avidan, S., Yeh, M.C., Cheng, K.T.: Fast human detection using a cascade of histograms of oriented gradients. Mitsubishi Electric Research Laboratories, pp. 1491–1498 (2006)
13. Yan, X., Luo, Y.: Recognizing human actions using a new descriptor based on spatial-temporal interest points and weighted-output classifier. Neurocomputing 87, 51–61 (2012)
14. Zhang, T., Liu, S., Xu, C., Lu, H.: Boosted multi-class semi-supervised learning for human action recognition. Pattern Recognition 44(10-11, SI), 2334–2342 (2011)

Mobile Visual Assistive Apps:
Benchmarks of Vision Algorithm Performance

Jose Rivera-Rubio, Saad Idrees, Ioannis Alexiou,
Lucas Hadjilucas, and Anil A. Bharath

BICV Group, Department of Bioengineering, Imperial College,
Exhibition Road, London SW7 2AZ, U.K.
{jose.rivera,saad.idrees12,i.alexiou09,1h205,a.bharath}@imperial.ac.uk
http://www.bg.ic.ac.uk/research/a.bharath/

Abstract. Although the use of computer vision to analyse images from smartphones is in its infancy, the opportunity to exploit these devices for various assistive applications is beginning to emerge. In this paper, we consider two potential applications of computer vision in the assistive context for blind and partially sighted users. These two applications are intended to help provide answers to the questions of "Where am I?" and "What am I holding?".

First, we suggest how to go about providing estimates of the indoor location of a user through queries submitted by a smartphone camera against a database of *visual paths* – descriptions of the visual appearance of common journeys that might be taken. Our proposal is that such journeys could be harvested from, for example, sighted volunteers. Initial tests using bootstrap statistics do indeed suggest that there is sufficient information within such visual path data to provide indications of: a) along which of several routes a user might be navigating; b) where along a particular path they might be.

We will also discuss a pilot benchmarking database and test set for answering the second question of "What am I holding?". We evaluated the role of video sequences, rather than individual images, in such a query context, and suggest how the extra information provided by temporal structure could significantly improve the reliability of search results, an important consideration for assistive applications.

Keywords: Image-based localisation, path-planning, mobile assistive devices, object categorisation, mobile computer vision.

1   Introduction

Low vision brings many challenges to an individual, including reduced independence and social exclusion. The World Health Organisation estimates (2012) that more than 285 million people worldwide suffer from low vision or blindness. Due to changing demographics and greater incidence of disease – e.g. diabetes – blindness and failing sight are increasing in prevalence. The cost to society includes direct health care expenditure, care-giver time and lost productivity.

A. Petrosino, L. Maddalena, P. Pala (Eds.): ICIAP 2013 Workshops, LNCS 8158, pp. 30–40, 2013.
© Springer-Verlag Berlin Heidelberg 2013

Enabling people with visual impairment to increase participation will help address social exclusion and improve self-esteem and psychological well-being. There is the potential of near-commodity smartphones, backed by appropriate computer vision algorithms and supporting processes, to address this need.

1.1   A Solution in Waiting?

The growth in availability of camera-equipped smartphones, networks, methods of social networking and crowdsourcing of data offers new solutions to develop assistive systems that could be scaled in performance and capability[5,11]. The services/capabilities that could be offered include:

Navigation: GPS does not offer sufficient precision or reliability for indoor manoeuvring. A combination of visual cues, translated into speech or tactile information, is desirable.

Shopping: Other challenges include shopping and product recognition, both in shops and at home. The technology for visual object recognition from mobile devices has arrived for sighted users: the challenges to deployment for visually-impaired users includes a) the existence of accessible label databases, that are free from commercial bias; b) changing retrieval algorithms and systems to place more emphasis on strong match confidence; c) techniques for conveying information readily to blind and partially-sighted users.

Personal Safety: As a partially sighted user, one is faced with a number of hurdles when undertaking journeys away from a familiar environment, and lack of confidence about the "unseen" can be a significant contributing factor to reduced mobility. Where does the pavement end? Where is the entrance to the bus, and are there stairs? Are there obstructions at head-height?

In summary, the overarching need is to increase the possibility for independent living; in a hugely visually-oriented built environment, sighted users rely on visual cues, signage, and recognition of structures such as doorways. Can these cues be reliably translated into semantically appropriate information using computer vision? Therefore we focus on the feasibility of answering two questions with existing technology from visual cues: "Where am I?" and "What am I holding?".

2   Where Am I?

Techniques for WiFi localisation are entering mainstream use through, at one level, estimates obtained from the physical locations of WiFi access points, simple measures of signal strength or approaches such as "Walkie-Markie" [8], which use multiple signatures to infer location. These technologies hold great potential. However, accurate localisation still relies strongly on reasonable accurate motion models, and the collection of other cues, such as accelerometry or gyroscopes [10].

Indeed, no matter how good other sources of information are, few can replace the contextual information of visual inference. During navigation, using natural vision, sighted individuals are able to *from one consistent information source*:

a) recognise their location relative to previous journeys; b) locate entrances and exits; c) detect obstructions; d) recognise people; e) assess human intent; f) identify objects or activities of personal interest.

Invoking computer vision to *simultaneously* solve all of these tasks is a current challenge. Our purpose is to assess the feasibility and accuracy of existing computer vision techniques to meet some of these needs. The primary question we address in this section relates to the first topic in the list above: can we use computer vision to recognise location against previous journeys.

2.1   Related Approaches

Several methods of indoor localisation using smartphone-relevant technology have been described, including RSSI, dead-reckoning, and combinations for techniques that harvest environmental cues [10], [8].

Related approaches to this problem involve the use of techniques such as SLAM [1] and PTAM [3]. These methods are near state-of-the-art for monocular robot navigation, allowing geometry of a space to be mapped out dynamically at the same time that self-localisation is achieved. Indeed, Pradeep and colleagues successfully applied this to a demonstration for indoor navigation in an assistive device [6].

2.2   Visual Paths

Methods such as SLAM and PTAM attempt to simultaneously map world geometry and localise a camera within that geometry. Our question is slightly different: we seek to identify where we might be relative to previous journeys taken along the same route, either by ourselves or other people. Thus, we introduce the idea of the *visual path*, a stream of descriptions captured from visual information as we traverse from location A to location B, or from location C to D. Such streams could be captured from the cameras of other users moving in the same physical space.

We can split the path localisation problem into two distinct tasks. The first is to determine which of P possible paths one is navigating along, and the second is to determine where along a particular visual path one is located. In the context of computer vision, a key question concerns the *distinctiveness* of information along paths, either as indicators of a particular journey or as indicators of location along a known journey. Note that we do not explicitly attempt to localise with respect to a map – our suggestion is to localise with respect to a journey. In the context of many users, this would appear to be a sensible way to harvest information about locations that might be frequently reconfigured in a manner that would reduce dependence on an explicit mapping processes.

Though SLAM and PTAM are strong candidates for assistive techniques, there is also the need to combine mapping with object detection. Putting these systems in the category of mapping and localisation, we explore the possibility that rather than mapping out a space, a user might be more interested in merely following a path that has been traversed by others. It is in this long-term, collaborative context that the visual path concept would sit: we wish to allow users to compare their journeys against those of others through these visual paths.

In tracing along different paths, we might ask how distinctive the visual content is along one path relative to the appearance along another. We used a standard keypoint and descriptor type approaches to describe visual paths captured by users as they walked along indoor environments.

We first studied the distribution of a similarity metric, γ, based on a modification of Lowe's ratio test for discriminating descriptors [4]. The modification takes the form of an L_∞-type normalisation on the distribution of squared Euclidean distances between distinctive descriptors that are close matches between database images along a set of P possible paths C_p, $p = 1, 2, \ldots, P$.

2.3   Visual Path Descriptions

First, consider a number $M_p^{(i)}$ of descriptor vectors, $\mathbf{v}_m^{(i)}, m = 1, 2, \ldots, M^{(i)}$ produced from an image, $\mathbf{I}_p^{(i)}$, with each vector being of dimension $L \times 1$. These descriptors are stacked into the rows of an $M^{(i)} \times L$ descriptor matrix, $\mathbf{V}_p^{(i)}$ associated with image $\mathbf{I}_p^{(i)}$. A *set* of images, $\{\mathbf{I}_p^{(i)}\}_{i=1,2,\ldots N_p}$ is now collected for path C_p, and for each of these, a descriptor matrix is produced. A visual path C_p is then encoded by the set of matrices of descriptors, denoted $\mathcal{M}_p = \{\mathbf{V}_p^{(i)}\}_{i=1,2,\ldots,N_p}$ generated from the set of images taken along that path.

Query images, $\mathbf{J}^{(j)}$, $j = 1, 2, \ldots, N_q$ are now acquired, separately. A particular query image is also mapped to matrix of descriptors $\mathbf{Q}^{(j)}$. We wish to know which of the P paths the query image $\mathbf{J}^{(j)}$ has been taken on; this is answered by comparing the query descriptor matrix against the set of path descriptors for all paths, $\{\mathcal{M}_p\}_{p=1,2,\ldots,P}$.

2.4   Pairwise Descriptor Comparisons

Let us first consider the comparison of individual query descriptors, $\mathbf{v}_n^{(j)}, n = 1, 2, \ldots, N^{(j)}$ arising from a single query image. The Euclidean distance metric in L-dimensional space is widely used in assessing descriptor distances in computer vision. Let $\mathbf{D}^{(i|n)}$ be the $M^{(i)} \times L$ matrix defined by

$$\mathbf{D}_p^{(i|n)} = \mathbb{1}_{M^{(i)} \times 1} \otimes \mathbf{v}_n^{(j)} - \mathbf{V}_p^{(i)} \tag{1}$$

where $\mathbb{1}$ is a vector of ones, and $\otimes$ denotes the Kronecker product. Then the elements along the diagonal of

$$\mathbf{D}_p^{(i|n)} [\mathbf{D}_p^{(i|n)}]^T \tag{2}$$

are collated into a vector, $\mathbf{d}_p^{(i|n)} \in [0, \mathbb{R}^+]^{M^{(i)}}$ of squared Euclidean distances between the nth descriptor from a query image and each of the $M^{(i)}$ descriptors derived from the ith image along the path C_p.

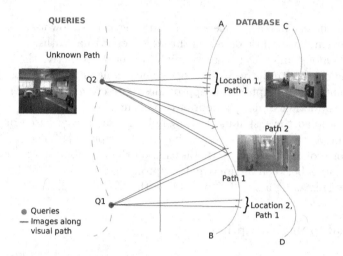

Fig. 1. Diagram illustrating the nature of visual paths and queries. There are different paths recorded in the databases. The statistical tests reported in this paper compare the within-path queries and between-path queries, as well as within-path, between-location scores based on image comparisons.

2.5   Query Descriptor Rejection

Many descriptors in the query image will not be sufficiently distinct to be useful in matching. The distribution of distances contained in vector $\mathbf{d}_p^{(i|n)}$ is used in a first stage filtering for distinctiveness by order-statistic filtering. A query descriptor $\mathbf{v}_n^{(j)}$ is considered suitable for use in assessing similarity between a pair of images only if $d_{[1]}^{(i|n)} < \alpha \cdot d_{[2]}^{(i|n)}$ where $d_{[1]}^{(i|n)}, d_{[2]}^{(i|n)}, \ldots$ denotes the sorted elements of the vector $\mathbf{d}_p^{(i|n)}$ in increasing order (the path subscript p is temporarily suppressed to include the order-statistic of elements). $0 < \alpha < 1$ is set to around 0.7, and any *query* descriptors that do not satisfy this condition are discarded. All image query vectors are subjected to the same test. Those that pass the test allow an "average" distance based on best matching descriptors to be used to determine how close a single query image is to a single database image. That is, for a single image query we calculate

$$\mu_p^{(i,j)} = \frac{1}{|\mathcal{D}|} \sum_{n \in \mathcal{D}} d_{[1]}^{(i|n)} \tag{3}$$

where $\mathcal{D}$ is the set of query descriptors that pass the distinctiveness test, as described here. Again, note that path subscript p has been omitted from the right-hand side of this expression to represent the sorted distances.

2.6   The γ Score

We calculated $\mu_p^{(i,j)}$ across all query images $\mathbf{J}^{(j)}$, $j = 1, 2, \ldots, N_q$ and all path images $\{\{I_p^{(i)}\}_{i=1,2,\ldots,N_p}\}_{p=1,2,\ldots P}$. A γ score is then defined to produce a score,

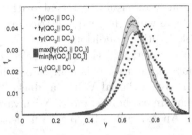 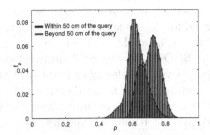

(a) Distributions for the γ metric.   (b) Distributions for the ρ metric.

Fig. 2. Tests of visual distinctiveness along paths. (a) path level queries, capturing the behaviour of the γ metric for inter- and intra-path distributions and (b) locations within a path, illustrating the distribution trends of the ρ-metric, all within a single 80m path, but at different distances either within or outside 50cm from known query submissions.

$\gamma^{(i,j)}$, as a measure of similarity between image pairs (i,j) relative to path p such that $0 < \gamma \leq 1$.

$$\gamma^{(i,j)} = \frac{||\mu_p^{(i,j)}||_\infty - \mu_p^{(i,j)}}{||\mu_p^{(i,j)}||_\infty} \tag{4}$$

The γ measure is applied between pairs of query and database images, and one may identify two types of categories that these query comparisons fall into. In the first case, the images come from the same path (although query and visual path database are, of course, distinct). In the other case, queries come from different paths. The results are shown in Fig. 2(a).

A second type of score, ρ, was created with a slightly different normalisation criterion based on observing the maximum within-path distance distributions, i.e. for a given path index, p. The behaviour of this score was studied using query images as taken with ground-truth locations, measured with a surveyor's wheel; again, probability density estimates of scores are estimated from hundreds of thousands of descriptor comparisons.

3   What Am I Holding?

An increasing use for smartphones involves using *visual search* in which a photograph taken with the phone is used as a query into a catalogue of database items. Common items include paperbacks (books), compact-disc packaging and, increasingly, art. A closely related approach is the use of barcodes on items to look up both price information and more detailed product information.

For the visually impaired, barcodes may be difficult to locate, and one would wish to allow recognition on objects and products from different points of view.

The quality of a query image might also be below that of a sighted user. For this reason, it is appropriate to assess the ability of visual search algorithms, designed for large-scale categorisation, to perform when the image queries are of low quality, as might occur in poor or variable lighting conditions.

The SHORT database [7] provides such a dataset; and though it lacks the category-level complexity of real-world product databases, it is compliant with other datasets used in computer vision, such as the Pascal VOC database [2]. SHORT includes data acquired from 20 different smartphone cameras, with varying degrees of resolution and image quality. An example of typical queries is shown in Fig. 3 below.

Fig. 3. The SHORT database contains thousands of query images that form a representative set of examples of smartphone queries containing everyday household or packaged food products

The dataset contains a mixture of stills and video clips, including more than 55,000 video frames and more than 1,900 still images. Image sizes range from under 100,000 pixels to over 6 megapixels.

3.1   Evaluation of Sequential Video Frames

In this section we analyse how we can use sequential frames from a video of an object in order to improve classification accuracy. First, multiple sequential images from a video were queried, and each image was matched to one of the thirty categories of the SHORT-30 database using the descriptor matching as described in Sections 2.4 and 2.5. A histogram of the matches was computed for several videos of the same object, as shown in Fig. 4(a). Even though the total number of incorrect matches increases as we query more video frames, they are distributed across a range of object categories in the database. As shown, the correct object often has a higher number of hits than the incorrect ones. Therefore we propose to use the "individual voting" as a metric to classify an object based on querying sequential images from a video of a hand-held object. Further analysis was undertaken in order to determine the number of video frames that are required for the total number of correct matches to exceed the number of individual total incorrect matches. Preliminary results, Figure 4(b), shows that the number of total incorrect matches to individual objects rises slowly while the number of total matches to the correct object increases rapidly. The above analyses were undertaken for several videos and object categories under the SHORT-30 dataset. Classification accuracy using different numbers of query frames and the above metric is presented in Section 4.2.

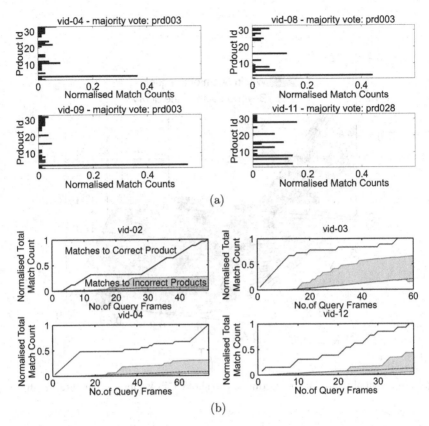

Fig. 4. Evaluation of sequential video frames. (a) Distribution of matches across different categories of SHORT-30 dataset for four videos of the same query object. (b) Fraction of correctly matched queries to incorrect matches for videoframe sequences. Note that there is a distribution of incorrect matches across multiple categories as the number of sequential query frames increases.

4 Experimental Results

4.1 Navigation

We acquired a number of visual paths with a mobile phone (Nexus 4). These simply take the form of video acquisitions, captured with the phone pointing in the direction of motion, and recording at 30fps at 1920×1080 resolution. The images were then downsampled to a resolution of 192×108 pixels. The number of images captured along the paths raises the complexity of the image matching problem task: there are typically 2000 images per path.

For the analysis of the distribution of the metrics γ and ρ, as shown in Fig. 2, we have used VLFEAT's [9] implementation of SIFT [4] descriptors.

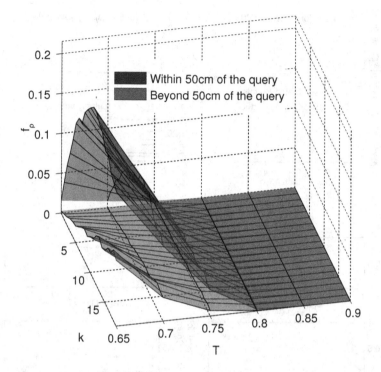

Fig. 5. Fraction of values of ρ exceeding a threshold T in k consecutive database frames

The use of bootstrap statistics was appropriate for this study because, for example, in the navigational context, it allows sampling distributions of distances across the whole image database of around 400,000 possible pairings of visual path images.

In the case of the ρ metric, these bootstrapped measurements have revealed the existence of visual distinctiveness between positions that are "close" or "far" along a path from a given query. In Fig. 2(b) we have double-filtered the distribution of the ρ values with a one-point moving average. This clearly shows that values of ρ closer to one are useful for discriminating positions belonging to a specific visual path. These results have motivated the search for a threshold on the values of ρ and the use of consecutive database frames to maximise discriminability, as illustrated in Fig. 5.

4.2 Classification Accuracy Based on Sequential Video Frames

Classification accuracy using the individual voting metric (Section 3.1) was computed for six categories of SHORT-30 dataset (Table 1). A video $\mathbf{Q}$, comprising of query frames $Q_i, i = 1, 2, ..., N$, is classified as the k-th category, C_k, to which the majority of query frames, Q_i, were matched to. The accuracy was calculated for classifying twelve videos of each object based on different limits for the number of queries allowed, N.

Table 1 shows that the classification accuracy increases as we increase the limit of query frames, except for occasional dips which occur due to instability as a person rotates the object in their hand. In comparison to the classification accuracy of individual queries, classification based on sequential video frame queries gives a much higher accuracy.

Table 1. Classification accuracy of different objects for different number of sequential query frames. Accuracy is defined as the number of videos correctly classified divided by the total number of videos queried.

ID	Single frame Acc (%)	10 frames		30 frames		50 frames		70 frames		90 frames	
		Acc	Std	Acc	Std	Acc	Std	Acc	Std	Acc	Std
prd001	37.89	85.71	34.99	85.71	34.99	85.71	34.99	92.86	25.75	92.86	25.75
prd002	55.56	75.00	43.30	75.00	43.30	66.67	47.14	75.00	43.30	91.67	27.64
prd003	40.87	73.33	44.22	73.33	44.22	80.00	40.00	80.00	40.00	80.00	40.00
prd005	43.14	62.50	48.41	62.50	48.41	62.50	48.41	87.50	33.07	87.50	33.07
prd006	80.61	92.31	26.65	100.00	0.00	100.00	0.00	100.00	0.00	100.00	0.00
prd007	46.15	78.57	41.03	78.57	41.03	92.86	25.75	92.86	25.75	92.86	25.75

5   Discussion and Conclusions

There are several conclusions to the pilot work that we have reported here. First, in the navigation context, there is an opportunity to use information from visual paths to provide an indication of which path a user might be on relative to previous journeys. Although this study is at quite an early stage, it does indeed indicate that distinctive information can be harvested from visual paths with great ease. For example, the resolutions of the images used in Section 2 contained only 1% of the pixels in the captured images! Yet, decisions on γ do seem to allow reasonably accurate estimates of where one is likely to be along a path, subject to appropriate verification being performed, perhaps using higher resolution images. With extra processing to perform geometric verification of match locations along the path, the idea of mapping images to a location looks quite feasible.

In the navigational context, the possibility of obscured views has not been considered, either during path collection or query collection. However, the density of our queries is also low relative to the number of queries we would normally take. For example, at a normal walking rate, one could easily collect more than 10 frames within 1 metre. Such an image sampling rate would give more opportunity to capture unobscured visual patches along a path. The caveat is that one would have to include modules for recognising obstructions or moving objects, such as people, within the frame, and remove query descriptors at spatial scales that would include such regions. Since one of the key roles for incorporating computer vision into navigational aids would be to detect path obstructions and hazards, this does not seem to be out of the realms of possible system-level scenarios.

In the context of hand-held objects from the SHORT-30 database, a real application would be expected to have thousands of products. Our current size is more appropriate to home use by a single user. The retrieval mechanisms described here are not scalable: we did not use visual words in this study, although our tests are indicative of what one might apply in a post bag of visual words (BOVW) verification of rankings based on descriptor distances.

Perhaps the most surprising factor of both of the feasibility studies reported here – hand-held object recognition and the visual paths, is that the features used for both cases rely on the same set of tools: image descriptors that can be computed very quickly. This is the subject for ongoing research in this area.

References

1. Durrant-Whyte, H., Bailey, T.: Robotics and Automation Magazine 13(99), 80 (2006)
2. Everingham, M., Gool, L., Williams, C.K.I., Winn, J., Zisserman, A.: The Pascal Visual Object Classes (VOC) Challenge. International Journal of Computer Vision 88(2), 303–338 (2009)
3. Klein, G., Murray, D.: Parallel Tracking and Mapping on a camera phone (2009)
4. Lowe, D.: Distinctive image features from scale-invariant keypoints. International Journal of Computer Vision (2004)
5. Manduchi, R., Coughlan, J. (Computer) Vision without Sight. Communications of the ACM 55(1), 96–104 (2012)
6. Pradeep, V., Medioni, G., Weiland, J.: Robot Vision for the Visually Impaired. In: IEEE International Conference on Computer Vision and Pattern Recognition (CVPR), CVAVI 2010, pp. 15–22 (2010)
7. Rivera-Rubio, J., Idrees, S., Alexiou, I., Bharath, A.A.: The SHORT-30 database. Object recognition in an increasingly mobile world. In: British Machine Vision Association Meetings: Vision in an Increasingly Mobile World, London (2013)
8. Shen, G., Chen, Z., Zhang, P., Moscibroda, T., Zhang, Y.: Walkie-Markie: Indoor Pathway Mapping Made Easy, pp. 85–98, research.microsoft.com
9. Vedaldi, A., Fulkerson, B.: VLFeat: An Open and Portable Library of Computer Vision Algorithms (2008), http://www.vlfeat.org/
10. Wang, H., Sen, S., Elgohary, A., Farid, M., Youssef, M.: Unsupervised Indoor Localization. In: MobiSys. ACM (2012)
11. Worsfold, J., Chandler, E.: Wayfinding project. Tech. rep., Royal National Institute of Blind People, London (2010)

Tracking Posture and Head Movements of Impaired People During Interactions with Robots

Salvatore Maria Anzalone and Mohamed Chetouani

Institute of Intelligent Systems and Robotics,
University Pierre and Marie Curie, 75005 Paris, France
mohamed.chetouani@upmc.fr

Abstract. Social robots are starting to be used in assistive scenarios as natural tool to help impaired people in their daily life activities and in rehabilitation activities. A central problem of such kind of systems is the tracking of humans activity in a reliable way. The system presented in this paper tries to address this problem through the use of an RGB-D sensor. State of art algorithms are used to detect and track the body posture and the heads pose of each human partner.

Keywords: People tracking, posture estimation, head orientation, human-robot interaction.

1 Introduction

Social robotics focuses on developing robots able to collaborate with humans as their reliable partners [4] [3]. Particular scenario for such kind of robots is their use as assistive technology. While traditional assistive technologies became more and more robust and reliable [9], researchers started to develop new assistive systems using robots able to help impaired people in a more natural and effective waye [15]. Such kind of applications are very different and each of them uses a particular kind of robot. As instance, due to the rapid ongoing aging of the population, lot of researchers focused on the use of robots to assist elderly people: in this case intelligent environments, domotic tools and robots have been used in conjunction to help elderlies in their daily life activities [5] [1]. Other researches focused on the use of robots in rehabilitation activities. Interesting example of such kind of applications are several studies in which robots have been integrated in therapies with humans, such as improving the attention deficits of autistic children [11]. It is important to point out that researchers focused not only on humanoid robot but also on animal shaped robot or on wheeled robot, accordingly to the constraints of the particular application conceived.

In all these works on assistive robotics, more than in other standard social robotics applications, a key point is the fine perception of the humans. Body behaviours are instinctively used by humans as a natural communication way with the others [6]: a social robot able to interact in a strict and collaborative

A. Petrosino, L. Maddalena, P. Pala (Eds.): ICIAP 2013 Workshops, LNCS 8158, pp. 41–49, 2013.

way with humans, as instance as caregiver of impaired people, should be able not only to recognize the human speech but also to recognize and interpret the body language [2]. Moreover, people behaviours and body movements can contain information that can be useful to the doctors to correctly diagnose and characterize the impairment [12].

The system presented in this paper is a human body tracking system that can be used in conjunction with a robot to organize interactive session of behavioural data acquiring from impaired people. In particular, this system has been conceived as assessment tool of autistic children behaviours during therapeutic sessions involving the use of the robot.

The system proposed uses an RGB-D sensor to detect and to track body features of each human involved in the interactions with a robot caregiver. The state of art about the human behaviour analysis suggests that the body posture, the head movements and the eye gazing are extremely important information on the description of the human behaviours. According to this, the system focuses on the postures, defined as the the tracks of all the joints of the human body, and on the head gesture, that can be seen as a good approximation of the human gaze. Due to technological constraint of such RGB-D sensors used, the eye gazing can not be taken in account: despite its importance, the low resolution of the sensor make the system unable to collect such important information.

Several experiments have been performed to evaluate the performances of the presented system. Results shown in this paper have been collected through the analysis of the behaviour of healthy people, both adult and children.

2   System Overview

The presented system allow robots to gather information about posture and head movements of human partners during direct interactions. In particular, each human that interacts with the robot is modeled through a 3d description that takes in charge the body posture, in terms of the angles of each limb of the body, and the head posture, in term of its pitch and yaw. This data is collected by the use of a RGB-D sensor that is conveniently placed in the environment according to its geometry, in order to retrieve a good perspective of the environment.

The system has been implemented through several software modules able to communicate via messages streams or via remote procedure calls, by the use of the ROS platform, Robot Operating System, that offers such kind of capabilities.

As shown in figure 1, data coming from the RGB-D sensor is used by the "Skeleton Tracker" module to detect the presence of humans in the environment. In this case the module is able to localize and track in three dimensions the articulations of each person. These identified positions are used to select inside the RGB images the areas in which the corresponding heads of each person should appear. A "Face Tracking" module is then able to detect the faces from these selections, to estimate their pose in terms of pitch and yaw. Two face trackers based on Active Appearance Models [7] have been used: one based on the Constrained Local Models algorithm [8]; another one based on the Generalized Adaptive View algorithm [10].

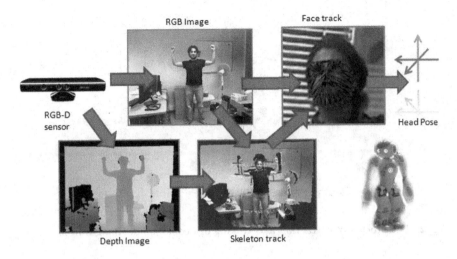

Fig. 1. The gaze recognition pipeline: skeleton traking; head detection; gaze estimation

Data collected by this system can be used in real time to obtain a feedback about the human activity: the robot can use the collected information to act in a coherent way. Moreover, the same data can be treated offline in order to extract information that can be relevant for the doctors in the assessment of the impairment.

3 People Detection

Human activity is detected by the use of the 3d information perceived by the RGB-D data through the use of a multiple skeleton tracking system provided by OpenNi [13]. In particular, each person will be tracked in the space in terms of their joints information. This data will permit the retrieving of posture, limb and arm movements and gestures information.

Depth information acquired by the sensor is elaborated to distinguish the body of each person from the environment. This is achieved through a background subtraction technique applied to the depth image.

The depth image left is then segmented and classified according a per-point approach, labeling each depth point of the body as a particular body part. As shown in figure 2, a total of 31 body patches distributed among the body has been considered. The body patch labeling uses depth invariants and 3D translation invariants features that try to describe to which part of the body each depth pixel belongs to. The classification process is based on a randomized decision forest of such features that results in a dense probabilistic skeleton with body parts labeled accordingly. The training process of such classifier employed a database of 500k labeled frames captured through motion capture in hundred of different scenarios, such as dancing, kicking, running. Each estimated patch

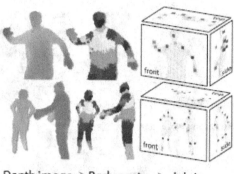

Depth image → Body parts → Joints

Fig. 2. The process of extraction and traking of people joints (Images from [13])

is finally employed, according to its density, to extract the position of each joint of the body, correspondent to each patch.

4   Head Tracking

Once located an estimation of the 3d position of the head of each human in the environment, the system reproject it to the RGB image, in order to select on it a a section in which the head of each subject should appear. A face tracker algorithm is then applied to the crops in order to estimate a model in terms of pitch and yaw of each head found.

Two algorithms have been used: the Constrained Local Models algorithm and the Generalized Adaptive View-based Appearance Model. Both of them can be used with three dimensional, depth map based data, but, due to the huge noise of the sensor used, the simple use of RGB images has been chosen.

The CLM algorithm follows the Active Appearance Model approach: both try to model faces via a statistical description based on a set of landmarks. Shapes of faces are deformed iteratively according to the landmarks positions, to find a best fit with the actual face image. In particular, the standard AAM algorithm tries to compute a model of faces according to their shape and their appearance. The shape model is calculated from a set of keypoints spread over a face, as its contour, the border of the lips, the nose and the eyes. In particular, a data set of labeled faces has been chosen as training set of the algorithm. The shape model is obtained from the mean and the variance of the PCA transformation of the facial key points of all the faces in the training set. It will be described as the mean shape parametrized by the variance. The appearance model will be built by normalizing the grayscale image of the face, wrapping it over its mean shape. Also in this case, the model will be obtained from the PCA transformation of the wrapped faces in the training set, described by its mean and parametrized according to the variance. The shape model and the appearance model will be fused to obtain a full face model using another PCA transformation: this will result in a parametrized model able to take in account both shape and appearance of the faces. During its normal usage, the AAM algorithm will calculate the error between the current model and the its actual appearance. The error will control the change of the model parameters iteratively, to better approximate the actual appearance, minimizing it. In particular, the error will encode how the parameters of the model should be changed: this relation is learnt in the training step and is used iteratively, providing also high speed performances to the whole system.

The CLM algorithm can be seen as a slightly variation of the AAM algorithm: also in this case the face model is composed by a conjunction of space model and appearance model. However, in this case the appearance model is built employing local features: a patch of pixels around each keypoint is considered, instead of using the whole wrapped face as in the AAM algorithm. Moreover, also the model fitting is different: to adapt the parameters to the actual face the Nelder-Meade simplex algorithm is employed.

The GAVAM algorithm tracker follows a different path: it tries to integrate several state of art approaches in order to obtain a reliable head pose estimation. In particular, a static pose estimator has been fused with a derivative tracker and with a keypoint-based pose estimator. The static pose estimator is able to recognize faces in a single frame, but neglects all the useful temporal information. This issue is coped by a derivative approach: the head position and orientation is tracked through the frames sequence. However, this last system gives high precision in short time scales, but its accuracy becomes very weak over the time. Then, this is integrated with a local keypoint approach that uses templates, in a similar way of AAM and CLM, to track the head over the time.

5   Experimental Results

The system has been evaluated in direct interaction scenarios, involving a Nao robot. A population of both adult and children has been chosen to estimate the performances of the system.

Fig. 3. Data capture session: motion capture makers are placed on the helmet and on the arm

A motion capture system have been used to capture the pose of the head of three adult subjects. Markers have been placed over the ears, on the left and on the right, and above the forehead. Such information has been used as ground truth of the system.

As shown in figure 3, each human partner was asked to stand in front of the robot, at 1.5mt from the RGB-D sensor, and to imitate the robot movements, that turned his head on the left and on the right, for three times.

Table 1. Head's pose estimation performances using Gavam and CLM approaches

Head Pose	Gavam	CLM
Pitch	61%	49%
Yaw	79%	93%
Overall	70%	71%

Data obtained by presented system has been evaluated, correlating it with the ground truth perceived by the motion capture: the whole performances of the two algorithms are similar, but, as shown in table 1, a fine analysis of the the pitch recognition and the yaw recognition results shows that the best performances are obtained by the usage of both algorithm together: the Gavam approach to recognize the heads pitch, while the CLM approach to recognize the heads yaw.

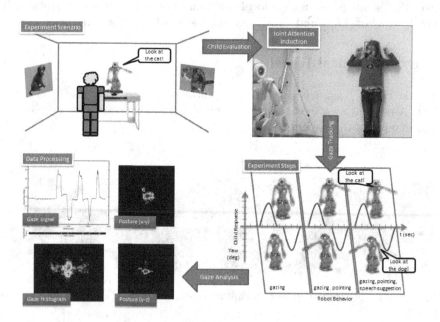

Fig. 4. A children during the joint attention induction experiment

Other experiments have been conducted with 15 healthy children in an age between 6 and 10 years old. The goal has been to collect data of their behaviour in a simple joint attention experiment [14] [16]. As show in figure 4, the robot Nao tries to induce in them joint attention by looking towards two animal figures placed on the two opposite sides of the room, alternatively. The induction is repeated three times: the first time the robot just looks towards each figure; the second time it tries to add more informative content by looking and pointing each figure; the third time it will add to these behaviours a vocalization of the object, look at the cat, look at the dog.

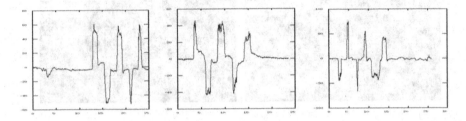

Fig. 5. The head's yaw variation among the time (deg/sec) during the joint attention experiment of three different healthy children

Head pose and body posture information of each child can be recorded and analyzed off-line. In particular, the head pose estimation has been collected using the Gavam approach to retrieve the heads pitch and using the CLM approach to retrieve the heads yaw, according to the results here discussed. Figures 5 show the heads yaw of three typical healthy children: each of them respond to the joint attention induction pushed by the Nao robot, moving the head towards the left and the right sides.

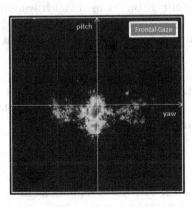

Fig. 6. The average histogram of the head movements (yaw-pitch) of healthy children

A different way to gather important information about the head pose behavior of the children is by considering the histogram of their head movements, on the yaw-pitch plane. The histogram in figure 6 shows how the attention of the child is captured on the left, on the right and on the center, characterized to the three spots corresponding to the two focus of attention, the figures of animals on the two sides, and to the robot, placed just above the RGB-D sensor, in front of the child.

The same histogram can be assessed for the children pose: in particular, figure 7 shows the histogram of the displacements from the average positions of the body.

Fig. 7. The average histogram of the position (top-view and front-view) of healthy children

6 Conclusions and Future Works

In this paper a system able to recognize and track human body activities has been presented. The system is conceived for human robot interaction contexts, in particular where the robot is employed as an assistive tool for impaired people. Using a RGB-D sensor, the system is able to capture human postures and head poses. The information collected can used as real-time input of a robotic system, as well as, to help doctors in the correct assessment of an impairment.

Several experiments have been conducted to evaluate the performances of the system in real contexts. Results shown the potentialities and the lacks of this approach. Results also encourage on the use of such system as an assessment tool of able to retrieve social engagement cues. In particular, the system will be used to help therapists on stimulating autistic children in joint attention activities.

Acknowledgements. Authors would like to thank to Dr. A. Carbone and T. Luiz for their kind collaboration. The current study was supported by a grant from the European Commission (FP7: Michelangelo under grant agreement n. 288241), and the fund Entreprendre pour aider.

References

1. Anzalone, S.M., Ghidoni, S., Menegatti, E., Pagello, E.: A multimodal distributed intelligent environment for a safer home. In: Intelligent Autonomous Systems 12, pp. 775–785. Springer Berlin Heidelberg (2013)

2. Asada, M., Hosoda, K., Kuniyoshi, Y., Ishiguro, H., Inui, T., Yoshikawa, Y., Ogino, M., Yoshida, C.: Cognitive developmental robotics: a survey. Autonomous Mental Development, IEEE Transactions on 1(1), 12–34 (2009)
3. Breazeal, C.: Toward sociable robots. Robotics and Autonomous Systems 42(3-4) (2003)
4. Breazeal, C.: Designing sociable robots. The MIT Press (2004)
5. Cesta, A., Cortellessa, G., Giuliani, M.V., Pecora, F., Scopelliti, M., Tiberio, L.: Psychological implications of domestic assistive technology for the elderly. Psych-Nology Journal 5(3), 229–252 (2007)
6. Cochet, H., Vauclair, J.: Pointing gesture in young children. Gesture and Multimodal Development p. 7 (2012)
7. Cootes, T.F., Edwards, G.J., Taylor, C.J.: Active appearance models. Pattern Analysis and Machine Intelligence, IEEE Transactions on 23(6), 681–685 (2001)
8. Cristinacce, D., Cootes, T.: Feature detection and tracking with constrained local models. In: Proc. British Machine Vision Conference. vol. 3, pp. 929–938 (2006)
9. Maor, D., Currie, J., Drewry, R.: The effectiveness of assistive technologies for children with special needs: a review of research-based studies. European Journal of Special Needs Education 26(3), 283–298 (2011)
10. Morency, L.P., Whitehill, J., Movellan, J.: Generalized adaptive view-based appearance model: Integrated framework for monocular head pose estimation. In: Automatic Face & Gesture Recognition, 2008. FG'08. 8th IEEE International Conference on. pp. 1–8. IEEE (2008)
11. Pioggia, G., Igliozzi, R., Ferro, M., Ahluwalia, A., Muratori, F., De Rossi, D.: An android for enhancing social skills and emotion recognition in people with autism. Neural Systems and Rehabilitation Engineering, IEEE Transactions on 13(4), 507–515 (2005)
12. Scassellati, B., Admoni, H., Mataric, M.: Robots for use in autism research. Annual Review of Biomedical Engineering 14, 275–294 (2012)
13. Shotton, J., Fitzgibbon, A., Cook, M., Sharp, T., Finocchio, M., Moore, R., Kipman, A., Blake, A.: Real-time human pose recognition in parts from single depth images. In: Proceedings of the 2011 IEEE Conference on Computer Vision and Pattern Recognition. pp. 1297–1304. CVPR '11, IEEE Computer Society, Washington, DC, USA (2011)
14. Sumioka, H., Hosoda, K., Yoshikawa, Y., Asada, M.: Acquisition of joint attention through natural interaction utilizing motion cues. Advanced Robotics 21(9), 983–999 (2007)
15. Tapus, A., Mataric, M.J., Scassellati, B.: Socially assistive robotics. IEEE Robotics and Automation Magazine 14(1), 35 (2007)
16. Yoshikawa, Y., Nakano, T., Asada, M., Ishiguro, H.: Multimodal joint attention through cross facilitative learning based on μx principle. In: Development and Learning, 2008. ICDL 2008. 7th IEEE International Conference on. pp. 226–231. IEEE (2008)

Scene Perception and Recognition
for Human-Robot Co-operation

Nikhil Somani[1], Emmanuel Dean-León[2], Caixia Cai[1], and Alois Knoll[1,*]

[1] Technische Universität München, Fakultät für Informatik,
Boltzmannstrae 3, 85748 Garching bei München, Germany
{somani,caica,knoll}@in.tum.de
[2] Cyber-Physical Systems, Fortiss - An-Institut der Technischen Universität München
Guerickestr. 25 80805 München, Germany
dean@fortiss.org

Abstract. In this paper, an intuitive interface for collaborative tasks involving a human and a standard industrial robot is presented. The target for this interface is a worker who is experienced in manufacturing processes but has no experience in conventional industrial robot programming. Physical Human-Robot Interaction (pHRI) and interactive GUI control using hand gestures offered by this interface allows this novice user to instruct industrial robots with ease. This interface combines state of the art perception capabilities with first order logic reasoning to generate semantic description of the process plan. This semantic representation creates the possibility of including human and robot tasks in the same plan and also reduces the complexity of problem analysis by allowing process planning at semantic level, thereby isolating the problem description and analysis from the execution and scenario-specific parameters.

Keywords: Perception, HRI, Reasoning.

1 Introduction

Industrial robotics, which was hitherto mostly used in structured environments, is currently witnessing a phase where a lot of effort is directed towards applications of standard industrial robots in small and medium sized industries with short production lines, where the scenarios are rather unstructured and rapidly changing. One important challenge for conventional industrial robot systems in these situations is the necessity to re-program the robot whenever the scenario or manufacturing process changes, which requires an expert robot programmer. Standard industrial robot systems also face limitations in their ability to adapt

* The research leading to these results has received funding from the European Union Seventh Framework Programme (FP7/2007-2013) under grant agreement n 287787 in the project SMErobotics, the European Robotics Initiative for Strengthening the Competitiveness of SMEs in Manufacturing by integrating aspects of cognitive systems.

A. Petrosino, L. Maddalena, P. Pala (Eds.): ICIAP 2013 Workshops, LNCS 8158, pp. 50–59, 2013.

to these environments, and with the complexity of some tasks which seem relatively easier to humans. A partial solution could be to extend the capabilities of the current industrial robots by providing intelligence to these robot systems through perception [14] and reasoning [13] capabilities. This extension of capabilities does not solve the problem completely because these industries typically contain a mixture of tasks, some of which are highly suitable for robots while some others are difficult to model or inefficient for robots and are better suited for humans. This problem stimulates the need for co-operative activities where humans and robots act as co-workers, using the concept of symbiotic Human Robot Interaction (sHRI). This work presents an interface for collaborative human-robot tasks in such industrial environments.

For a robot to be able to work cooperatively with a human, both parties need to be able to comprehend each other's activities and communicate with each other in an intuitive and natural way. In the social robotics and personal robotics communities, meaningful information from human activities is extracted in an abstract or semantic form to achieve this purpose. In an activity containing roles for both human and robot, the level of detail at which the human instructions are specified is important. In several works involving HRI [7,15], human instructions are preferred at an abstract or semantic level. In this case, the scene perception and recognition module is an important component in these intelligent robotic systems. On one hand, the information provided by the perception module is used by reasoning engines to generate an abstraction of the world and learn tasks at this abstract level by human demonstration. On the other hand, the perception module provides scenario specific information which is used by the low-level execution and control modules for plan execution.

The perception problem in this context involves detecting and recognizing various objects and actors in the scene. The objects in the scene consist of workpieces relevant to the task and obstacles, while actors involved are humans, and the robot itself. The most important part of the perception module presented in this work is an object detection, recognition and pose estimation module, which uses 3D point cloud data obtained from low-cost depth sensors and can handle noisy data, partial views and occlusions. The popular approaches for this task can be broadly classified as: local color keypoint [12], local shape keypoint [16], global descriptors [10], geometric [6], primitive shape graph [11]. Global descriptors such as VFH [10] require a tedious training phase where all required object views need to be generated using a pan-tilt unit. Besides, its performance decreases in case of occlusions and partial views. The advantage of these methods, however, lies in their computational speed. Some other methods such as [11], [9] provide robustness to occlusions, partial views and noisy data but are relatively slow and not suitable for real-time applications. In this paper, an extension to the ORR [9] method has been proposed, which enhances its robustness to noisy sensor data and also increases its speed.

To distinguish objects having identical geometry but different color, the Point Cloud is first segmented using color information and then used for object detection. There are several popular approaches for Point Cloud segmentation such as

Conditional Euclidean Clustering [5], Region Growing [4], and graph-cuts based segmentation methods [2]. In this paper, a combination of multi-label graph-cuts based optimization [2] and Conditional Euclidean Clustering [5] is used for color-based segmentation of point clouds.

The major contribution of this article is the integration of the presented perception [14] and reasoning modules [13] in an HRI application. An intuitive interface for instructing industrial robots in unstructured environments typically found in SME's is developed, where scene understanding is a key aspect for HRI and co-operative Human-Robot tasks.

2   Shape Based Object Recognition

The approach presented here is an extension of the ORR method [9], called Primitive Shape Object Recognition Ransac (PSORR) [14]. This approach has two phases : (1) an offline phase where the model point clouds are processed and stored, (2) an online phase where the scene cloud is processed and matched with the models for recognition and pose estimation.

2.1   Primitive Shape Decomposition

This step is very important for the algorithm because the hypothesis generation and pose estimation steps are based on this decomposition. The hypothesis verification step, which is a major bottleneck in most algorithms such as ORR, can also be significantly simplified and sped-up using this decomposition.

Fig. 1. Primitive Shape Decomposition example : (a) original Point Cloud (b) result of Primitive Shape Decomposition

An example of such a decomposition is shown in Fig. 1, where the original scene cloud is shown in Fig. 1 (a) and its decomposition into primitive shapes is shown in Fig. 1 (b).

Hypothesis for primitive shapes are generated by randomly sampling points in the point cloud. Once the hypotheses have been generated, each point in the cloud is checked to determine whether it satisfies the hypotheses.

Each primitive shape has a *fitness_score* associated with it, which indicates how well the primitive matches the point clouds, see Eq. 1.

$$fitness\_score = (inliers/total\_points) + K * descriptor\_length \qquad (1)$$

where, the first fraction represents the inlier ratio, i.e., the ratio of points which satisfy the primitive shape (*inliers*) to the total number of points in the input cloud (*total_points*), *descriptor_length* represents the complexity of the primitive shape (e.g. the number of values required to represent the shape). The constant K determines the relative weighting of the two factors.

The merging strategy, based on minimum descriptor length (MDL) [8], is a greedy approach where pairs of primitive shapes are selected and merged if the combined primitive shape has a better fitness score than the individual primitive shapes. This continues till there are no more primitive shapes which can be merged.

Planes and cylinders are chosen as primitive shapes for this implementation since they are easy to model and efficient to detect compared to complicated primitives such as ellipsoid or torus. The algorithm, however, is designed to work for any kind of primitive for which a fitness score can be defined according to Eq. 1.

2.2 Hypothesis Generation

An Oriented Point Pair (OPP) (u, v) contains two points along with their normal directions: $u = (p_u, n_u)$ and $v = (p_v, n_v)$. A feature vector $f(u, v)$ is computed from this point pair, see Eq. 2.

$$f(u, v) = (\|p_u - p_v\|, \angle(n_u, n_v), \angle(n_u, p_v - p_u), \angle(n_v, p_u - p_v))^T, \quad (2)$$

The central idea in the ORR method is to obtain OPP's from both the scene and model point clouds and match them using their feature vectors. For efficient matching of OPP's, a Hash Table is generated containing the feature vectors from the model point cloud. The keys for this table are the three angles in Eq. 2. Each Hash Cell contains a list of models ($M_i \in M$) and the associated feature vectors. Every feature vector f has a homogeneous transformation matrix F associated with it, see Eq. 3.

$$F_{uv} = \begin{pmatrix} \frac{p_{uv} \times n_{uv}}{\|p_{uv} \times n_{uv}\|} & \frac{p_{uv}}{\|p_{uv}\|} & \frac{p_{uv} \times n_{uv} \times p_{uv}}{\|p_{uv} \times n_{uv} \times p_{uv}\|} & \frac{p_u + p_v}{2} \\ 0 & 0 & 0 & 1 \end{pmatrix}, \quad (3)$$

where $p_{uv} = p_v - p_u$ and $n_{uv} = n_u + n_v$. Hence, for each match f_{wx} in the hash table corresponding to f_{uv} in the scene, a transformation estimate (T_i) can be obtained, which forms a hypothesis $h_i = \{T_i, M_i\} \in H$ for the model (M_i) in the scene, $T = F_{wx} F_{uv}^{-1}$. The raw point clouds are generally noisy, especially the normal directions. The original ORR method is sensitive to noise in the normal directions and hence, randomly selecting points to generate the feature vectors requires more hypothesis until a good OPP is found. In the PSORR method, every plane in the scene point cloud's primitive shape decomposition is considered as an oriented point (u) with the centroid of the plane as the point (p_u) and the normal direction as the orientation (n_u). The normal directions for these oriented points are very stable because they are computed considering hundreds of points lying on the plane. Therefore, we can use these centroids instead of the whole cloud to compute and match features, which leads to a significantly less number of hypotheses.

If full views of the objects are available in the scene cloud, the Hash Table for the model cloud can also be computed in a similar fashion considering only the centroids of the primitive shapes. However, in case of partial views or occlusions, the centroid for the scene cloud primitives might not match the model centroids. To handle this, the point pairs for the model cloud are generated by randomly sampling points from every pair of distinct primitive shapes.

2.3   Efficient Hypothesis Verification

Since the model and scene clouds are decomposed into primitive shapes and represented as Primitive Shape Graphs (PSG), hypothesis verification using point cloud matching is equivalent to matching all the primitive shapes in their PSG's. Matching these primitive shapes can be approximated by finding the intersection of their Minimum Volume Bounding Boxes (MVBB's) [1].

The i-th MVBB comprises 8 vertices $v^i_{1,..,8}$, which are connected by 12 edges $l^i_{1,..,12}$ and forms 6 faces $f^i_{1,..,6}$. To find the intersecting volume between MVBB's i and j, the points p^i at which the lines which form the edges of MVBB i intersect the faces of MVBB j are computed. Similarly, p^j are computed. Vertices v^i of the first MVBB which lie inside the MVBB j and vertices v^j of the second which lie inside the MVBB i are also computed. The intersection volume is then the volume of the convex hull formed by the set of points $\left(p^i \cup p^j \cup v^i \cup v^j\right)$.

The fitness score for this match is the ratio of the total intersection volume to the sum volumes of the primitive shapes in the model point cloud. This score is an approximation of the actual match but the speed-ups achieved by this approximation are more significant compared to the error due to approximation.

2.4   Results

Fig. 2 (c) shows an example of the results obtained using the PSORR algorithm, where a partial view of the object is present in the scene cloud, which is much sparser than the model cloud. The algorithm is able to recognize all the object and estimate their poses accurately. The average number of hypotheses required by the PSORR algorithm are nearly 50 times less than the ORR algorithm. Also, the hypothesis verification step is nearly 100 times faster than conventional approaches where point clouds are matched using octrees. Including the additional cost of primitive shape decomposition, the PSORR algorithm is still 5 times faster than the ORR algorithm for the industrial workpieces used in our experiments.

The algorithm has been designed to work with point cloud data and can handle occlusions and partial views. Hence, this data may be from a single frame, combined from several frames over a time interval or fused from several depth sensors in the scene.

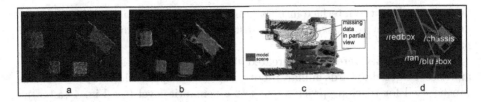

Fig. 2. Example of object recognition using a combination color and shape information: (a) Color Based segmentation (b) Detected Object Clusters (c) PSORR result for partial view of sparse scene cloud (d) Final result of Object Recognition using shape and color information

3 Combining Shape and Color Information

Shape information is often not sufficient for object recognition tasks. For example, some workpieces may have the same shape but different color. A combination of multi-label graph-cuts based optimization [2] and Conditional Euclidean Clustering [5] is used for color-based segmentation of point clouds, followed by cluster recognition and pose estimation using the PSORR method described in Sect. 2.2.

The color based segmentation problem is posed as a multi-label graph-cuts optimization problem. A graph $G = \{V, E\}$ is constructed such that each point in the point cloud is a vertex $v_i \in V$. An edge E_{ij} connects neighboring vertices v_i and v_j. Labels $l_i \in L$ are defined such that each label represents a color. Each l_i is defined by a Gaussian $N(\mu_i, \Sigma_i)$ in the HSV space. Each of these vertices needs to be assigned a label which indicates the color of the object to which the point belongs. The energy term associated with this graph is defined by $D = D_p + D_s + D_l$.

D_p is the data term. It represents the likelihood that the node v_i belongs to the label L_j. D_s is the smoothness term, which represents the energy due to spatially incoherent labels. It can be considered as an interaction term between neighboring nodes, where neighbors prefer to have same labels. D_l is the label swap term. It is an indication of the likelihood of swapping labels for a given vertex. These terms are generally set offline using color models. In this context, the labels which are likely to get mixed up easily (e.g. white and metal) are assigned a higher probability whereas labels which are unlikely to get mixed up (e.g. red and blue) are assigned lower probability.

Fig. 2 shows an example of the results obtained using this approach.

4 Intuitive Interface for Human-Robot Collaboration

The scene perception and recognition algorithm, along with the reasoning module [13] are used to create an interface for human-robot interaction. The perception and reasoning modules help in creating an abstract semantic representation of the world containing objects, actors and tasks. This representation is a key factor in making the interface intuitive for the user since the user can now communicate with the robot system at an abstract level without the need of numeric parameters.

A mixed reality interface is created using scene perception and reasoning modules, targeted towards human-robot co-operation applications. This interface can be used for teaching process plans at a semantic level (see Fig. 4 (a,b,c)), and execute them in different scenarios without requiring any modifications (see Fig. 4 (d,e,f)). This interface can also be used for executing process plans with both human and robot tasks, see Fig. 4 (g,h,i). Fig. 3 shows an example with the different phases of this interface, where it can be noted that the generated process plan contains semantic names of the objects and not the numeric level data in the form of poses taught to the robot.

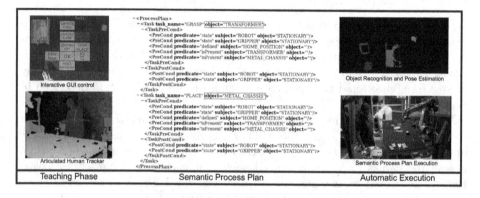

Fig. 3. Overview of Intuitive Interface for Human-Robot Collaboration

4.1 Teaching Process Plans

An articulated Human Tracker is used to recognize the hand positions and use it to control the projected GUI, see Fig. 4 (a). This module enables the user to physically interact with the robot, grab it and move it to the correct position for grasping and placing objects, see Fig. 4 (b-c). The perception module (Sect. 3) detects the objects present in the scene and a reasoning engine associates objects with the taught poses to automatically generate a semantic script of this process plan in STRIPS [3] format, see Fig. 3. The robot system learns process plans and their associated paramters at a semantic level throught this interface. The perception and reasoning module make this learnt process plan independent of the scenario and robot specific details.

4.2 Automatic Plan Execution

The user can place the objects to be assembled anywhere in the working area to begin the plan execution. The system first checks if all pre-conditions for the task

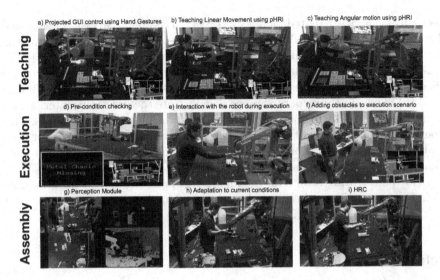

Fig. 4. a,b,c) Teaching Application, d,e,f) Execution and Plan generation of taught Task. g,h,i) HRC in an assembly process.

are satisfied and informs the user in case something is missing, see Fig. 4 (d). The human can physically interact with the robot during the execution and move it by grabbing its end-effector, see Fig. 4 (e). The user can also add obstacles in the path of the robot, which are detected using the perception module and avoided during plan execution, see Fig. 4 (f). All these interactions and changes in the scenario don't require modifications in the process plan script because object positions and obstacles are scenario-specific entities and, like the physical interaction, are handled at the low-level execution. This is the main advantage of decoupling the Problem Space from the Solution Space. The process plan is generated using only information from the Problem Space. The associated execution parameters are loaded on demand. The Perception Module provides the updated information of the current objects in the scene. Therefore, these execution-specific parameters are continuously updated.

4.3   Assembly Task with Human-Robot Co-operation

In this demonstration, we highlight another important advantage achieved using a semantic description of the process plans - possibility of symbiotic human-robot collaboration, which is one of the primary goals of this research. Once the robot is taught the *Pick_And_Place* process plan, it can be instructed to perform this plan on different objects. The application in mind is the assembly of a power converter box. This operation consists of a number of steps, actors and objects which are identified by the perception/reasoning module, Fig. 4 (g), some of which are complex high precision assembly tasks suitable for the human, while some involve lifting heavy objects which are more suitable for the robot. In the situation where precision assembly is required for a heavy object, a co-operative task is performed where the robot grasps the object and the human guides it by physically grasping the robot end-effector and moving it to the desired place position, Fig. 4 (i). The *Low-Level Execution Engine* switches between motion modalities and control schemes according the current conditions (external perturbations) of the scene, Fig. 4 (h). Thus, in this experiment, we demonstrate the use of this interface for human tasks, robot tasks and co-operative tasks which require both actors. This experiment also highlights that it is relatively easy to understand, edit or even create such a plan from scratch since it is at a semantic level and is abstracted from scenario or execution specific details.

A video illustrating results for the algorithms presented in this paper and its use in the applications mentioned above can be found at: http://youtu.be/Jgn9NqGKgnI.

References

1. Barequet, G., Har-Peled, S.: Efficiently approximating the minimum-volume bounding box of a point set in three dimensions. J. Algorithms 38, 91–109 (2001)
2. Delong, A., Osokin, A., Isack, H.N., Boykov, Y.: Fast approximate energy minimization with label costs. Int. J. Comput. Vision 96(1), 1–27 (2012), http://dx.doi.org/10.1007/s11263-011-0437-z
3. Fikes, R.E., Nilsson, N.J.: Strips: A new approach to the application of theorem proving to problem solving. Tech. Rep. 43R, AI Center, SRI International (May 1971)
4. Gonzalez, R.C., Woods, R.: Digital Image Processing, 2nd edn. Prentice Hall, New Jersey (2002)
5. Hastie, T., Tibshirani, R., Friedman, J.: 14.3.12 Hierarchical clustering The Elements of Statistical Learning, 2nd edn. Springer, New York (2009) ISBN 0-387-84857-6
6. Hu, G.: 3-D object matching in the hough space. In: Intelligent Systems for the 21st Century Systems, Man and Cybernetics, vol. 3, pp. 2718–2723 (1995)
7. Kirsch, A., Kruse, T., Sisbot, E.A., Alami, R., Lawitzky, M., Brscic, D., Hirche, S., Basili, P., Glasauer, S.: Plan-based control of joint human-robot activities. Künstliche Intelligenz 24, 223–231 (2010)
8. Leonardis, A., Gupta, A., Bajcsy, R.: Segmentation of range images as the search for geometric parametric models. Int. J. Comput. Vision 14(3), 253–277 (1995), http://dx.doi.org/10.1007/BF01679685
9. Papazov, C., Haddadin, S., Parusel, S., Krieger, K., Burschka, D.: Rigid 3D geometry matching for grasping of known objects in cluttered scenes. International Journal of Robotic Research 31, 538–553 (2012)
10. Rusu, R.B., Bradski, G., Thibaux, R., Hsu, J.: Fast 3D recognition and pose using the viewpoint feature histogram. In: 2010 IEEE/RSJ Intelligent Robots and Systems (IROS), pp. 2155–2162 (2010)
11. Schnabel, R., Wessel, R., Wahl, R., Klein, R.: Shape recognition in 3D point-clouds. In: Skala, V. (ed.) The 16th International Conference in Central Europe on Computer Graphics, Visualization and Computer Vision 2008. UNION Agency-Science Press (February 2008)

12. Sipiran, I., Bustos, B.: Harris 3D: A robust extension of the harris operator for interest point detection on 3D meshes. Vis. Comput. 27(11), 963–976 (2011), http://dx.doi.org/10.1007/s00371-011-0610-y

13. Somani, N., Dean, E., Cai, C., Knoll, A.: Perception and reasoning for scene understanding in human-robot interaction scenarios. In: Proceedings of the 2nd Workshop on Recognition and Action for Scene Understanding at the 15th International Conference on Computer Analysis of Images and Patterns (2013)

14. Somani, N., Dean, E., Cai, C., Knoll, A.: Scene perception and recognition in industrial environments for human-robot interaction. In: Proceedings of the 9th International Symposium on Visual Computing (2013)

15. Zhang, T., Hasanuzzaman, M., Ampornaramveth, V., Kiatisevi, P., Ueno, H.: Human-robot interaction control for industrial robot arm through software platform for agents and knowledge management. In: 2004 IEEE Systems, Man and Cybernetics, vol. 3, pp. 2865–2870 (October 2004)

16. Zhong, Y.: Intrinsic shape signatures: A shape descriptor for 3D object recognition. In: 2009 IEEE Computer Vision Workshops (ICCV Workshops), pp. 689–696 (2009)

Two Bioinspired Methods
for Dynamic Signatures Analysis

Jânio Canuto[1], Bernadette Dorizzi[1], and Jugurta Montalvão[2]

[1] Institut Mines-Telecom, Telecom SudParis, CNRS UMR5157 SAMOVAR,
Évry, France
{janio.canuto,bernadette.dorizzi}@telecom-sudparis.eu
[2] Federal University of Sergipe (UFS), Electrical Engineering Department (DEL)
São Cristóvão, Sergipe, Brazil
jmontalvao@ufs.br

Abstract. This work focuses on the problem of dynamic signature segmentation and representation. A brief review of segmentation techniques for online signatures and movement modelling is provided. Two dynamic signature segmentation/representation methods are proposed. These methods are based on psychophysical evidences that led to the well-known Minimum Jerk Model. These methods are alternatives to the existing techniques and are very simple to implement. Experimental evidence indicates that the Minimum Jerk is in fact a good choice for signature representation amongst the family of quadratic derivative cost functions defined in Section 2.

Keywords: Dynamic Signatures, Segmentation, Minimum Jerk.

1 Introduction

Handwritten signatures result from voluntary but typically complex gestures of the human hand. As result of their particularities, in most cultures, these graphically recorded gestures have been used for centuries to authenticate documents. Some less straightforward uses of handwritten signatures analysis may include mental illness detection or daily stress measurement.

Beyond potential applications, modelling gestures behind signatures and development of proper ways for identification of basic components (i.e., segments) is a challenging enough matter for scientific research. Segmentation is a crucial step that strongly influences the performance of signature verification systems and, therefore, a special attention has been drawn into this task over the last few decades [1].

This work aims at providing two new signature segmentation methods, based on psychophysiological evidences that led to the development of the well-known Minimum Jerk principle for movement planning. We focus on dynamic signatures, which are represented as a time series of pen-tip position coordinates acquired at a fixed sample rate through the use of specific recording devices, such as tablets, digitizers or smartphones.

A. Petrosino, L. Maddalena, P. Pala (Eds.): ICIAP 2013 Workshops, LNCS 8158, pp. 60–68, 2013.

The work is structured as follows: in Section 2 we perform a review of previous works on signature segmentation and movement modelling, with an emphasis on the Minimum Jerk model. In Section 3 we present the proposed algorithms along with some experimental results. Finally, in Section 4, conclusions are drawn.

2   Previous Works

2.1   Signature Segmentation

Global features (e.g. length, maxima, minima, and mean velocity) are commonly used in signature verification systems but are not very discriminative. Such features can be made local if applied to *elements* of a segmented signature. Using localized features is sometimes referred to as a stroke-based approach. Although this decomposition has shown to provide good results, it leads to the non-trivial segmentation task [2].

Indeed, signature segmentation is a very complex task due to the high variability between different signatures provided by the same writer. These variations include stretching, compression, omission and addition of parts of the drawing. Segmentation techniques might derive from specific characteristics of handwriting movements or provide segmentations that are well suited for particular verification methods. In [1] we can find a brief review of such methods that are divided in four categories according to which principle they are based on: pen-up/pen-down signals, velocity analysis, perceptual relevant points and dynamic time warping.

For dynamic signatures, a common and very simple segmentation technique uses pressure information for determining writing units, which are determined as the written part between a pen-down and a pen-up movement.

Segmentation techniques based on velocity analysis use different approaches, ranging from simple detection of null [3] velocity to curvilinear velocity signals. The stroke identification step on the Sigma-Lognormal model [4] can also be placed on such category.

A different class of segmentation methods are those based on the detection of perceptually important points. The importance of a point is determined by the rate of change of the writing angle around it. We can also include in this category techniques based on the detection of geometric extremes [5].

In order to allow the segmentation of many signatures into the same number of segments, dynamic time warping (DTW) has been widely used.

Combinations of different techniques can also be found in the literature, in [6] a combination of pressure (first category), velocity (second category) and angle change (third category) is used for segmentation. Further references for dynamic signature segmentations methods can be found in [1].

2.2   Movement Modelling

The study of how the central nervous system (CNS) generates and controls the movement has yielded many computational models, some relying on biological neural network behaviours, artificial neural networks, equilibrium point hypothesis, coupled oscillators and minimization principles [4].

From a movement planning perspective, the general problem might be posed as follows: It is assumed that human movements are optimally planned according to a latent optimality criterion. Therefore, we need to find what is the optimality criterion used by the CNS. From this formulation, the optimal control theory seems to be the most complete and adequate way for finding an answer [7].

All minimization principles for movement modelling are part of the optimal control approach. Many optimization criteria have been proposed in the literature and can roughly be divided in four categories: kinematic criteria (e.g. minimum jerk), dynamic criteria (e.g. minimum torque-change), muscular and neural criteria (e.g. minimum effort) and energetic criteria (e.g. minimum total work). A detailed review of such criteria can be found in [7] and references therein. Amongst these criteria, Minimum Jerk (MJ) and Minimum Torque-Change (MTC) are the most used in the literature.

Some of these models have already been used for handwriting representation, but only the sigma-lognormal model, which is based on the kinematics theory of rapid human movement, has been used for signature modelling [4]. We, on the other hand, use in our proposed methods the Minimum Jerk principle [8] which to the authors' knowledge has not yet been applied to signature analysis.

Therefore, we now present a more detailed description of the Minimum Jerk model.

The Minimum Jerk Model. This model belongs to the category of the quadratic derivative kinematic criteria, which have a general cost function defined as:

$$C = \frac{1}{2} \int_0^T \left(\frac{d^n x(t)}{dt^n}\right)^2 + \left(\frac{d^n y(t)}{dt^n}\right)^2 dt \tag{1}$$

where T is the movement duration, $x(t)$ and $y(t)$ are the horizontal and vertical position time series respectively. This class of optimum criteria has as general solution polynomials of order $2n - 1$. The *jerk* is defined as the third derivative of the movement, therefore $n = 3$ and the general solution is a fifth-order polynomial. Other well-known kinematic criteria such as acceleration, snap and crackle can be obtained by setting n equal to 2, 4 and 5 respectively.

In [8] this family of optimum criteria has been studied up to $n = 10$, and the authors concluded that the Minimum Jerk is the most suitable for human movement modelling. They were able to properly reproduce the two-thirds power law using the minimum jerk. Using the peak to average velocity ratio as a single scalar projection of velocity profiles, they also found that the MJ is the best suited criterion. Indeed, previous experimental evidences showed that this ratio is about 1.8 (with 10% standard deviation) for reaching movements and the MJ yields a ratio of 1.875 for this class of movements.

Some works point that the Minimum Jerk model is unable to produce asymmetric velocity profiles [7, 9], however this is only true if velocity and acceleration at both the beginning and the end of the movement are null, which is not a requirement of the model itself. Furthermore, in [7] it is noted that MJ predictions are not in agreement with experimental data when the movement occurs on the vertical plane or when the target is not a single point but an infinite set of point (a straight line, for instance); however MJ predictions work properly on the horizontal plane for point-to-point movements. These conditions can both be assumed for a signing movement.

3   Proposed Method

All experiments described in this section have been performed over the MCYT-100 Database [10], which consists of 25 genuine and 25 forged signatures from 100 different writers. These signatures have been acquired with a Wacom® Tablet at a fixed sample rate of 100Hz. In our experiments, since we are focused on segmentation and representation, and not on verification, only the genuine subset has been used.

Our first segmentation method is based on the peak to mean velocity ratio observed on the psychophysical experiments realized during the developments of the MJ principle. We sequentially search for signature segments that comply with the expected 1.8 ratio.

In other words, we segment the signature as a series of point-to-point reaching movements. This method can be categorized amongst the velocity analysis segment techniques. For a given signature, the algorithm can be described as follows:

```
1. Compute the velocity magnitude, V
2. Set START = 1, END = START+1, S(1) = 1 and C = 2
3. Get the velocity, VS, between START and END
4. Compute the ratio, R, between maximum VS and mean VS
5. If R >= 1.8
   5.1. Set S(C) = END
   5.2. Set START = END+1, END = START+1 and C = C+1
6. If R < 1.8 set END = END+1
8. If END <= length of V go to step 3.
9. Return S
```

This extremely simple procedure provides a stable segmentation amongst different signatures of the same writer, with an average coefficient of variation of 13% for all writers. In Figure 1 are shown some examples of segmentation for five different signatures of two writers on the MCYT-100 Database.

It is interesting noting that using this method we are able to remove small artefacts that are often present at the beginning and end of the acquired signatures. The obtained segmentations roughly correspond to changes in the dynamic behaviour (e.g. loops, waves and straight lines).

Visual inspection of the obtained segmentation seems to yield "natural" segments. This technique has the advantages of not being tied to any verification technique, and can be used for any signature analysis task. Furthermore, the 1.8 threshold used for segmentation is based on sound psychophysical experiments that have been reproduced many times over the last 30 years.

This segmentation does not provide a model for the resulting elements, as those in the Sigma-Lognormal model. One could use the result of the MJ principle (i.e. a fifth order polynomial) in order to model each of the resulting segments, however not all of the elements can be properly modelled by such simple functions, resulting in a very poor reconstruction quality, especially on signatures containing many consecutive loops.

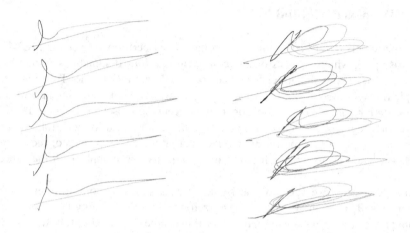

Fig. 1. Segmentation of five different signatures of two writers using the velocity ratio criterion

The reconstruction quality is measured through the Velocity SNR, as in [4], defined as:

$$SNR_v = 10 \log \left(\frac{\int_0^T [v_x^2(t) + v_y^2] dt}{\int_0^T \left[\left(v_x(t) - v_{xx}(t) \right)^2 + \left(v_y(t) - v_{yy}(t) \right)^2 \right] dt} \right) \tag{2}$$

where $v_x(t)$ and $v_y(t)$ are respectively the horizontal and vertical velocities on the original signature, and $v_{xx}(t)$ and $v_{yy}(t)$ are the horizontal and vertical velocities of the reconstructed signature, respectively. For the abovementioned representation an average SNR_V of 10.7 dB is obtained for the MCYT-100 database.

We now propose a second method, based on the MJ Model itself, that result in a piecewise polynomial representation of the signature. This approach models each "writing element" as a fifth order polynomial. The procedure consists in sequentially finding the longer segments that can be adequately represented (according to a given reconstruction quality threshold) by a fifth order polynomial [11].

Notice that the 1.8 peak to mean velocity ratio is *only* observed on reaching movements, in which starting and ending velocity and acceleration are considered to be null (thus, resulting in a symmetric velocity profile), different boundary conditions on the MJ Model lead to different velocity ratios and velocity profiles. Therefore, fitting the fifth-order polynomial to the signature data allows for a better representation of the velocity profiles and can provide not only segmentation but an adequate representation for each segment. The algorithm for this method can be described as follows:

```
1. Normalize the trajectory through a min-max procedure
2. Set L = 1
3. Set R = L + 5
4. Fit a 5th order polynomial to the points in the inter-
   val [X(L):X(R)]
5. Calculate the Velocity SNR for the interval
6. If SNR >= Threshold
   6.1. Set R = R+1 and go to step 4.
7. If SNR < Threshold
   7.1. Set L = R-1 and go to step 3.
8. If R > length of X, stop.
9. Return the list of L values.
```

This procedure is still very simple but much more computationally intensive than the previous one because of the fitting procedure. We chose not to use the Jerk value itself because the numerical estimation of third order derivatives from time-sampled data leads to large numerical errors. We now have a piecewise polynomial representation of signing movements that can be properly predicted by the MJ model.

One of the advantages of such procedure is that the representation quality can be chosen by the user to fit his/her needs. In Figure 2 we present the segmentation obtained for the same signatures shown in Figure 1 with a SNR_v of 15dB.

Fig. 2. Segmentation of five different signatures of two writers using the MJ criterion at 15dB SNR

Even though for the signatures on the right column in Figure 2 we observe more segments than using the first method, on average, for the whole database this procedure produce fewer segments than the previous one. Furthermore, the number of segments obtained for each writer is more stable than before, with a coefficient of variation of 7.3%, that is even lower than the variability for the lengths of the signatures which is of 8%.

Now the obtained signature elements are basically arcs and single loops, most of them containing at least one inflection point. Along with the automatic segmentation we have an alternative representation for the signature as a sequence of fifth order polynomials. Considering the trade-off between compression rate and reconstruction quality, we did experiments similar to those in [8] with different cost functions belonging to the family defined by Equation (1), with n ranging from one to five. Once again the Minimum Jerk ($n = 3$) seems to be the best option, acting as a limit to the compression-quality trade-off. For a SNR of 15dB all of the higher order ($n \geq 3$) solutions attain the same compression rate of 73.3%. In Figure 3 we show the compression-quality trade-off curves for each different cost function.

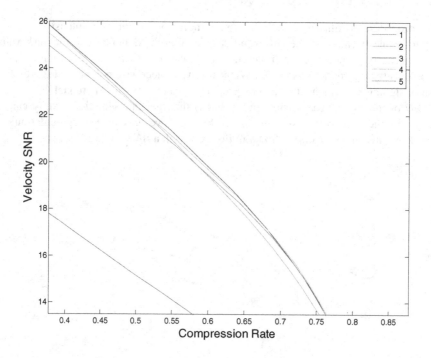

Fig. 3. Representation quality and compression rate tradeoff for minimum velocity ($n = 1$), acceleration ($n = 2$), jerk ($n = 3$), snap ($n = 4$) and crackle ($n = 5$)

4   Conclusions and Future Work

Two methods for automatic signature segmentation and one for signature representation have been presented. These methods are based on the Minimum Jerk Principle and to the authors knowledge it is the first use of such principle for online signatures.

Both methods are very easy to implement and can be used as alternatives to existing methods.

As pointed out before, it is hard to determine if our approach is better than existing methods because such evaluation strongly depends on what the segmentation/representation is going to be used to. An advantage of the proposed model is the possibility of choosing the desired representation error.

The proposed method can be understood as an alternative use of the Minimum Jerk criterion as a basis function for a piecewise representation. In such way the commonly used velocity and acceleration constraints are not needed as well as any manually inserted via-points.

We believe that the ratio between the number of segments obtained by such method and the original length of the signature may be used as a *"complexity"* measure in a similar fashion to the Normalized Lempel-Ziv Complexity [12], we have an on-going work on the demonstration of this link between detected segments and Lempel-Ziv Complexity.

The next step in our work consists in integrating the proposed methods in a recognition system in order to obtain a higher level assessment of its impact. We intend to analyze two main aspects: the reduction of the computational cost due to the use of a more compact representation and the effect of such model in the system performance.

Furthermore, since the Minimum Jerk Model is derived from the analysis of healthy individuals' movements, this *complexity* measure may be used in the early diagnosis of motor diseases such as Parkinson's and Dyskinesia.

References

1. Impedovo, D., Pirlo, G.: Automatic Signature Verification: The State of the Art. IEEE Trans. Syst., Man, and Cybern. – Part C: App. and Rev. 38(5), 609–635 (2008)
2. Yue, K.W., Wijesoma, W.S.: Improved Segmentation and Segment Association for Online Signature Verification. In: Proc. IEEE Int. Conf. Syst., Man, Cybern., vol. 4, pp. 2752–2756 (2000)
3. Dolfing, J.G.A., Aarts, E.H.L., van Oosterhout, J.J.G.M.: On-line Signature Verification with Hidden Markov Models. In: Proc. 4th Int. Conf. Pat. Rec., vol. 2, pp. 1309–1312 (1998)
4. Plamondon, R., O'Reilly, C., Galbally, J., Almaksour, A., Anquetil, E.: Recent developments in the study of rapid human movements with the kinematic theory: Applications to handwriting and signature synthesis. Pat. Rec. Letters (June 15, 2012) (in press)
5. Lee, J., Yoon, H.-S., Soh, J., Chun, B.T., Chung, Y.K.: Using geometric extrema for segment-to-segment characteristics comparison in online signature verification. Pat. Rec. 37, 93–103 (2004)
6. Qu, T., Saddik, A.E., Adler, A.: A stroke based algorithm for dynamic signature verification. In: Proc. Can. Conf. Ele. Comp. Eng. (CCECE), pp. 461–464 (2004)
7. Berret, B.: Integration de la force gravitaire dans la planification motrice et le controle des mouvements du bras et du corps. PhD Thesis, Pozzo, T., Gauthier, J.-P. (advisors), Bougogne Univesity (2008)

8. Richardson, M.J.E., Flash, T.: Comparing Smooth Arm Movements with the Two-Thirds Power Law and the Related Segmented-Control Hypothesis. J. Neuroscience 22(18), 8201–8211 (2002)
9. Dijoua, M., Plamondon, R.: The Limit Profile of a Rapid Movement Velocity. Human Movement Science 29(1), 48–61 (2010)
10. Ortega-Garcia, J., Fierrez-Aguilar, J., Simon, D., Gonzalez, J., Faundez-Zanuv, M., Espinosa, V., Satue, A., Hermanez, I., Igarza, J.J., Vivaracho, C., Escudero, D., Moro, Q.I.: MCYT baseline corpus: a bimodal biometric database. IEEE Proc. Vis., Im., Sig. Proc. 150(6), 395–401 (2003)
11. Canuto, J., Dorizzi, B., Montalvão, J.: Dynamic Signatures Representation Using the Minimum Jerk Principle. In: Proc. 4th IEEE Biosig. Biorob. Conf. (ISSNIP), pp. 1–6 (2013)
12. Ziv, J.: Coding Theorems for Individual Sequences. IEEE Trans. Inf. Theory IT-24(4), 405–412 (1978)

Online Signature Verification:
Improving Performance through
Pre-classification Based on Global Features

Marianela Parodi and Juan Carlos Gómez

Lab. for System Dynamics and Signal Processing, FCEIA,
Universidad Nacional de Rosario, and CIFASIS, Argentina
{parodi,gomez}@cifasis-conicet.gov.ar

Abstract. In this paper, a pre-classification stage based on global features is incorporated to an online signature verification system for the purposes of improving its performance. The pre-classifier makes use of the discriminative power of some global features to discard (by declaring them as forgeries) those signatures for which the associated global feature is far away from its respective mean. For the remaining signatures, features based on a wavelet approximation of the time functions associated with the signing process, are extracted, and a Random Forest based classification is performed. The experimental results show that the proposed pre-classification approach, when based on the apppropriate global feature, is capable of getting error rate improvements with respect to the case where no pre-classification is performed. The approach also has the advantages of simplifying and speeding up the verification process.

Keywords: Online Signature Verification, Global Features, Pre-classification.

1 Introduction

Signature verification is the most popular method for identity verification since people are familiar with the use of signatures in their everyday life [1]. Two categories of signature verification systems can be distinguished taking into account the acquisition device, namely, offline (only the signature image is available) and online systems (dynamic information about the signing process is available).

In online systems, the signature is parameterized by several discrete time functions, such as, pen coordinates, pen pressure and, when available, pen altitude and azimuth angles. Researchers have long argued about the effectiveness of these different time functions for verification purposes [2], [3]. To choose the features that could be extracted from them is also an important design step. The different features can be classified into local, calculated for each point in the time sequence, and global, calculated from the whole signature. Many researchers accept that approaches based on local features achieve better performance than those based on global features, but still there are others who favor the use of global features [4], [5]. In fact, it is interesting to use global features since they

A. Petrosino, L. Maddalena, P. Pala (Eds.): ICIAP 2013 Workshops, LNCS 8158, pp. 69–76, 2013.

have the advantage of being simple features, usually more intuitive than local ones, and can be easily computed and compared. Furthermore, it would be reasonable to expect that local and global features could provide complementary information [5]. To combine both types of features in such a way that their main characteristics could be exploited, is an interesting and still open challenge. In [6], an online signature verification system is designed as a multilevel system which uses three different signature representations, one based on global features and the other two based on local features. In addition, several fusion strategies have been proposed in the literature. In [5], fusion strategies based on the max and sum rules are compared. Some approaches using a pre-classification stage based on global features for the purposes of early detecting bad forgeries, have been proposed in the mid 1990's in [6] and [7]. Global features, such as signature total time duration and pen down duration, have been used in those papers.

In this paper, global based features are used for pre-classification purposes. The idea is to pre-classify signatures, declaring as forgeries those that are far away from their mean, in terms of the global based feature being considered. It is expected that this could help to quickly recognize and classify gross forgeries, speeding up and simplifying the verification process. The remaining signatures continue with the subsequent classification stage which consists in extracting new features (time function based ones modeled by the coefficients in their wavelet approximations) in order to achieve a more detailed representation, and classifying them on the basis of a Random Forest (RF) classifier. For the verification experiments, two different signature styles are considered, namely, Western and Chinese, of one of the most recent publicly available Signature Databases.

2   Pre-classification Approach

In this paper, features based on global parameters as well as features based on time functions (modeled by their wavelet based approximations), are used. Since these different types of features could provide complementary information, the idea is to exploit their intrinsic characteristics. When using global based features, it would be expectable to get a rough and quick representation of the signature. This could be useful to have an idea of some distinctive characteristics and detect some anomalies of the signature. On the other hand, if a more precise representation is needed, the time function based features could provide more detailed information, at the cost of a more time consuming feature extraction.

Global based features are then used for pre-classification purposes. It is reasonable to expect that some global based features, such as signature total time duration, pen down duration and average pressure, for the genuine samples would be far away from the corresponding ones for the forged samples. This is illustrated in Fig. 1 (left), where the distributions of the global based feature "signature total time duration" for the genuine (left) and forged (right) signatures of an author in the database, are depicted.

The idea is then to classify as a forgery those signatures for which the global features differ significantly from the corresponding genuine feature mean.

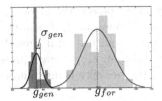

Decision rule
If $\|g_{test} - \bar{g}_{train}\| > \alpha\sigma_{train}$ *then* signature=forgery   *else* continue classification

Fig. 1. Distribution of the global feature "signature total time duration" for the genuine and forged signatures of an author in the database (left). Pre-classification decision rule (right).

In particular, the decision rule shown in Fig. 1 (right) is considered, being g_{test} the global based feature corresponding to the test signature, $\bar{g}_{train}$ and σ_{train} the global based feature mean and standard deviation values over the genuine training set, respectively, and α a coefficient defining the threshold.

Coefficient α is computed, for each global based feature, in three different ways for comparison purposes, namely, as: i. the maximum, or ii. the mean, or iii. the minimum, over all the authors in the Training Set of the database, of the maximum, over all the signatures of each author, of the absolute difference between the global feature value of the test signature and the global based feature mean of the genuine training set, normalized by the standard deviation of the set. That is (for case i.):

$$\alpha = \max_{A} \max_{A_i} \left\{ \frac{|g_{test} - \bar{g}_{train}|}{\sigma_{train}} \right\} \tag{1}$$

where A is the set of all the authors in the Training Set and A_i denotes the i-th author in the same set.

A different approach is considered in [7], where only the signature total time duration is used for pre-classification purposes. In that paper, the threshold is computed as a fraction of the $\bar{g}_{train}$, and it is heuristically set to 0.2.

3   Feature Extraction

Typically, the measured data consists of three discrete time functions: pen coordinates x and y, and pen pressure p. In addition, several extended functions can be computed from them [4], [8]. Previous to the feature extraction, the original x and y pen coordinates are normalized regarding scale and translation.

3.1   Global Based Features

Several global based features can be extracted from the measured and extended time functions. In [4], a feature selection is performed on a set of 46 global features which seem to be the most commonly used in the literature. In [5], subsets of global features are selected from an initial set of 100 features. In the present paper, the global based features are selected to be discriminative enough in order for the proposed pre-classification to be succesful. In order to analyze and compare their individual discriminative power, the following global based features, corresponding to the better ranked ones by the feature selection performed in [4] and [5], are used in this paper: signature total time duration T, pen down duration T_{pd}, positive x velocity duration T_{v_x}, average pressure $\bar{P}$, maximum pressure P_M and the time at which the pressure is maximum T_{P_M}.

3.2   Time Function Based Features

Several extended time functions can be computed from the measured ones. In this paper, the path velocity magnitude v_T, the path-tangent angle θ, the total acceleration a_T and the log curvature radius ρ are computed as in [8]. The set of time function based features is then composed by x, y, p, v_T, θ, a_T and ρ, and their first and second order time derivatives.

A wavelet approximation of the time functions is proposed to model them. The Discrete Wavelet Transform (DWT) decomposes the signal at different resolution levels, splitting it in low (*approximation*) and high (*details*) frequency components. The idea here is to use the DWT approximation coefficients to represent the time functions. Resampling of the time functions, previous to the DWT decomposition, is needed in order to have a fixed-length feature vector. To use a fixed-length feature vector represents an advantage since it makes the comparison between two signatures easier. In [3] and [9], fixed-length representations are proposed based on the Fast Fourier Transform (FFT) and Legendre Polynomials series expansions, respectively. The approximation accuracy is determined by the chosen resolution level, which also determines the length of the resulting feature vector. Since this length has to be kept reasonably small, there will be a trade-off between accuracy and feature vector length. The design parameter is then the length of the feature vector, which determines the resolution level to be used. The widely used db4 wavelets [10] is employed for the representation of the time functions.

4   Experiments

The SigComp2011 Dataset [11] is used for the verification experiments. It has two separate datasets, containing Western (Dutch) and Chinese signatures, respectively. Each dataset, is divided into a Training and a Testing Set. Skilled forgeries (in which forgers are allowed to practice the reference signature for as long as they deem it necessary) are available. The signatures were acquired using a ballpoint pen on paper over a WACOM Tablet, which is the natural writing process. The measured data are the pen coordinates x and y, and pressure p.

In order to compare the discriminative power of the different global based features, experiments using each one of them for pre-classification purposes were carried out. In addition, the three different ways of computing the coefficient α, defining the threshold $\alpha\sigma_{train}$, are also tested.

For each dataset (Dutch and Chinese), the optimization of the meta-parameters of the system is performed over the corresponding Training Set while the corresponding Testing Set is used for independent testing purposes. The meta-parameters of the system are: α for the pre-classification stage, the normalized length of the resampled time functions, the resolution level for the wavelet approximations, and the number of trees and randomly selected splitting variables for the RF classifier. To obtain statistically significant results, a 5-fold cross-validation (5-fold CV) is performed over the Testing Set to estimate the verification errors. For each instance of the 5-fold CV, a signature of a particular writer from one of the testing sets in the 5-fold CV is fed to the system. After its pre-processing, one of the global based features (g_{test}) presented in Subsection 3.1 is extracted from it. Then, the pre-classification is performed as follows: the g_{test} value of the input signature is compared with the $\bar{g}_{train}$ (mean value of the same feature) computed over the current writer's genuine signatures available in the corresponding training set of the 5-fold CV. If the difference between these values is larger than the corresponding threshold for that global based feature, the signature is declared to be a forgery. If this is not the case, the signature is subjected to the subsequent classification stage, as follows: the DWT approximation coefficients are computed for the different time funtions presented in Subsection 3.2. Then, a RF [12] classifier is trained by the genuine class consisting of the current writer's genuine signatures available in the corresponding training set of the 5-fold CV, and a forged class which consists of the genuine signatures of all the remaining writers in the dataset available in the same training set. The result of the verification process is then either the result of the pre-classification (the input signature is considered a forgery), or the result of the RF classifier. If the result is given by the pre-classification, the verification process is speeded up.

To evaluate the performance, the EER (Equal Error Rate) is calculated, using the Bosaris toolkit, from the Detection Error TradeOff (DET) Curve as the point in the curve where the FRR (False Rejection Rate) equals the FAR (False Acceptance Rate). The cost of the log-likelihood ratios $\hat{C}_{llr}$ and its minimal possible value $\hat{C}_{llr}^{min}$ [13] are computed using the toolkit as well [14]. A smaller value of $\hat{C}_{llr}^{min}$ indicates a better performance of the system.

5 Results and Discussion

The experiments were performed using 500 trees and $\sqrt{P}$ randomly selected splitting variables (P = feature vector dimension), for the RF classifier. The time functions were resampled to a normalized length of 256. The wavelet resolution level was set to 3, in order to obtain a feature vector of a reasonable length.

The verification results, with pre-classification, for the six global based features considered, and the three different values of α, are shown in Table 1, for the Dutch (left) and Chinese (right) data, respectively. The best results are indicated in **boldfaced** style. In order to analyze the advantages of using the proposed pre-classification scheme, the results obtained without pre-classification are also included in the last row section of Table 1. For the purposes of comparison, the results in [9], based on Legendre polynomials representations (without pre-classification), are also included in that section.

Table 1. Verification results for the Dutch (left) and Chinese (right) Datasets

		Dutch Dataset						Chinese Dataset					
		T	T_{pd}	T_{vx}	$\hat{P}$	P_M	T_{P_M}	T	T_{pd}	T_{vx}	$\hat{P}$	P_M	T_{P_M}
α_{max}	EER	5.35	6.22	4.95	4.93	6.58	7.08	5.65	7.64	7.01	7.05	7,84	7.91
	$\hat{C}_{llr}$	0.2374	0.2389	0.2283	0.2123	0.2544	0.2704	0.2244	0.3017	0.2644	0.2631	0.2918	0.2849
	$\hat{C}_{llr}^{min}$	**0.2015**	0.2053	**0.167**	**0.1683**	0.2146	0.2408	**0.193**	0.2532	**0.2188**	**0.2155**	**0.2437**	0.2512
α_{mean}	EER	5.98	6.61	6.64	6.01	8.17	8.91	4.93	7.63	6.88	6.92	8.42	8.85
	$\hat{C}_{llr}$	0.2562	0.2728	0.265	0.2558	0.3019	0.3039	0.2008	0.293	0.2745	0.2719	0.3215	0.3331
	$\hat{C}_{llr}^{min}$	0.2263	0.2418	0.2413	0.2272	0.2763	0.2848	**0.1781**	0.2505	**0.228**	**0.2311**	0.2834	0.2861
α_{min}	EER	14.94	15.91	13.24	10.63	10.63	10.2	11.4	14.8	10.47	10.22	12.67	12.16
	$\hat{C}_{llr}$	0.388	0.4407	0.3839	0.3484	0.3484	0.3382	0.3336	0.4532	0.3383	0.3331	0.427	0.3849
	$\hat{C}_{llr}^{min}$	0.3827	0.4247	0.3656	0.335	0.335	0.3235	0.3183	0.4148	0.3113	0.314	0.3873	0.3589

	Without pre-class	Results in [9]	Without pre-class	Results in [9]
EER	6.78	5.91	7.9	10.03
$\hat{C}_{llr}$	0.2491	0.237	0.3126	0.36
$\hat{C}_{llr}^{min}$	0.2055	0.195	0.2476	0,2969

The actual values of α belong to the intervals: $[3,4]$, $[2,3]$ and $[1,2]$, for the max, the mean and the min criteria, respectively. When choosing α_{max}, the threshold is conservative, while when α_{min} is chosen, the threshold allows for more signatures to be pre-classified at the cost of larger errors (in the sense of classifying genuine signatures as forgeries). Then, selecting the mean criterion for computing α is a trade-off between these extreme values. This is confirmed by the results in Table 1, where the results using α_{max} are, in most of the cases, better than the results using α_{mean}, while using α_{min} leads to the worst results. In Fig. 2, the percentage of signatures that are pre-classified out of the total amount of signatures, for each of the three α criteria, are shown for the Dutch (right) and Chinese (left) data, respectively.

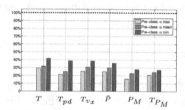 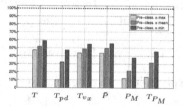

Fig. 2. Percentage of signatures pre-classified as forgeries, using the three different α values to compute the threshold

From Table 1, it can be seen that the proposed pre-classification does improve the error rates with respect to the case of not using it, and the ones in [9] (where no pre-classification takes place). This is not the case for every value of α, since when using α_{min} the results are not good due to the fact that several genuine signatures may be wrongly classified as forgeries. For the Dutch data, the error rates improve only when using the most conservative threshold (defined by α_{max}). Then, if the trade-off (mean) value of α would to be used, there would be no error improvements. This shows that many genuine signatures are beyond $2\sigma_{gen}$. This is probably due to the fact that the feature genuine distribution is not a Gaussian. For the Chinese data, the error rates are still improved when using the trade-off α. Moreover, the best error rate is achieved in this case. Then, for this data, the threshold can be chosen to be a more robust one.

The pre-classifications based on P_M, T_{P_M} and T_{pd} did not get any error rate improvements. In the cases of P_M and T_{P_M}, this seems to be reasonable. The time at which the pressure is maximum T_{P_M} is probably an unstable feature, since people is not likely to be consistent in the time where the pen pressure reaches a peak. The value of P_M, is likely to be dependant on the writing surface, the pen, etc., making it hard to make pre-classification decisions based only on this feature. On the other hand, in the case of T_{pd}, the result was unexpected, since it is believed that forgers are not able to accurately reproduce the pen down time of the genuine writers. The global based features used for pre-classification, leading to error rate improvements, were: T, T_{v_x} and $\bar{P}$. In the case of T, the results do nothing but confirm the well known fact that this feature is a good discriminator [7]. The average pressure $\bar{P}$, is likely to be more consistent than the other pressure based features analyzed here, since people may not make considerable changes in the average pressure when signing. Finally, T_{v_x} proved to have a high discriminative power. Since T_{v_x} indicates the time in which the writer is writing forward, its discriminative power is probably due to the fact that forgers may go back several times during the writing process.

The best error rates were achieved by a pre-classification based on α_{max} and T_{v_x}, and on α_{mean} and T, for the Dutch and Chinese data, respectively. For the Chinese data, the result is not surprising since T is a highly discriminative feature. For the Dutch data, the result could be explained based on the fact that, in most of the cases, horizontal traces are more significant than vertical ones. Then, differences in the time in which the writer is writing forward would indicate that a forged signing process is taking place.

In addition to the error rate improvements, the pre-classification helps to simplify and speed up the verification process. From Fig. 2, it can be seen that, still in the most conservative cases (using α_{max}, where the amount of pre-classified signatures is minimum), an important part of the whole set of signatures is discarded (more than 40% and 25%, for the best cases of the Chinese and Dutch data, respectively), making the system to further process less signatures.

6   Conclusions

A pre-classification approach on the basis of global based features, was proposed to be included in an online signature verification system. The proposed pre-classification approach proved to be capable of exploiting the discriminative power of the global based features to improve the overall performance with respect to the case where no pre-classification is carried out. In addition, the incorporation of the pre-classification stage proved to have the advantages of simplifying and speeding up the signature verification process.

Finally, the proposed pre-classification approach has the advantage of being very simple, since it is based only on one global based feature, but proved to be powerful, allowing improvements regarding the verification errors, the process speed and the simplicity of the whole signature verification system.

References

1. Impedovo, D., Pirlo, G.: Automatic signature verification: The state of the art. IEEE Trans. on Syst., Man, and Cybern. - Part C: Appl. and Reviews 38(5), 609–635 (2008)
2. Maramatsu, D., Matsumoto, T.: Effectiveness of pen pressure, azimuth, and altitude features for online signature verification. In: Proc. of Int. Conf. on Biomet., pp. 503–512 (2007)
3. Yanikoglu, B., Kholmatov, A.: Online signature verification using fourier descriptors. EURASIP J. on Advances in Signal Process., 230–275 (2009)
4. Richiardi, J., Ketabdar, H., Drygajlo, A.: Local and global feature selection for online signature verification. In: Proc. of 8th Int. Conf. on Doc. Anal. and Recognit., Seoul, Korea (2005)
5. Fierrez-Aguilar, J., Nanni, L., Lopez-Peñalba, J., Ortega-Garcia, J., Maltoni, D.: An on-line signature verification system based on fusion of local and global information. In: Proc. IAPR Int. Conf. on Audio- and Video-Based Biomet. Person Authentic., New York, NY, USA, pp. 523–532 (2005)
6. Plamondon, R.: The design of an on-line signature verification system: from theory to practice. Int. J. on Pattern Recognit. and Artif. Intell. 8(3), 795–811 (1994)
7. Lee, L.L., Berger, T., Aviczer, E.: Reliable on-line human signature verification systems. IEEE Trans. on Pattern Anal. and Machine Intell. 18(6), 643–647 (1996)
8. Fierrez-Aguilar, J., Ortega-Garcia, J., Ramos-Castro, D., Gonzalez-Rodriguez, J.: HMM-based on-line signature verification: Feature extraction and signature modelling. Pattern Recognit. Lett. 28, 2325–2334 (2007)
9. Parodi, M., Gómez, J.C., Liwicki, M.: Online signature verification based on legendre series representation. Robustness assessment of different feature combinations. In: Proc. of 13th Int. Conf. on Frontiers in Handwriting Recognit, Bari, Italy, pp. 377–382 (September 2012)
10. Daubechies, I.: Ten Lectures on Wavelets. SIAM, Pennsylvania (1992)
11. Liwicki, M., Malik, M.I., den Heuvel, C.E., Chen, X., Berger, C., Stoel, R., Blumenstein, M., Found, B.: Signature verification competition for online and offline skilled forgeries (SigComp2011). In: Proceedings of 11th Int. Conf. on Doc. Anal. and Recognit., Beijing, China (September 2011)
12. Breiman, L.: Random forests. Technical report, Stat. Dep., Univ. of California, Berkeley (2001)
13. Gonzalez-Rodriguez, J., Fierrez-Aguilar, J., Ramos-Castro, D., Ortega-Garcia, J.: Bayesian analysis of fingerprint, face and signature evidences with automatic biometric systems. Forensic Sci. Int. 155, 126–140 (2005)
14. Brümmer, N., du Preez, J.: Application-independent evaluation of speaker detection. Comput. Speech & Language 20, 230–275 (2006)

Event Based Offline Signature Modeling Using Grid Source Probabilistic Coding

Konstantina Barkoula[1], Elias Zois[2], Evangelos Zervas[2], and George Economou[1]

[1] Physics Dept., University of Patras, Patras, Greece
kbarkoula@gmail.com, economou@upatras.gr
[2] Electronics Dept., Technological Educational Institution of Athens, Athens, Greece
{ezois,ezervas}@teiath.gr

Abstract. A new offline handwritten signature modeling is introduced that confluences disciplines from grid feature extraction and information theory. The proposed scheme advances further a previously reported feature extraction technique which exploits pixel transitions along the signature trace over predetermined two pixel paths. In this new work the feature components, partitioned in groups, are considered as events of a grid based discrete space probabilistic source. Based on the 16-ary F_{CB2} feature, a set of 87 orthogonal event schemes, organized in tetrads, is identified. Next an entropy rule is drawn in order to declare the most appropriate tetrad scheme for representing a writer's signature. When skilled forgery is encountered verification results derived on both the GPDS300 dataset and a proprietary one, indicate enhanced EER rates compared to other approaches, including the previous reference of F_{CB2} as well.

Keywords: Signature Verification, Grid Features, Information Theory, Events.

1 Introduction

It is now entrenched throughout a vast collection of research papers and extensive surveys that the signature remains a popular way for humans to declare their identity in many application areas [1]. Automated Signature Verification Systems (ASVS) are broadly divided into two major categories depending on the method that the signature is acquired. Both online and offline ASVS must cope with the fact that the process of creating handwritten signatures, even when they originate from a well trained genuine writer, may carry natural variations, defined in the literature as inter-writer variability It is widely accepted that the online ASVS are generally more efficient when compared to offline ASVS. A commonly used figure of merit which many researchers employ in order to characterize the efficiency of their ASVS is the equal error rate (EER) which is calculated from the ROC or DET plots of both types of error rates.

Offline ASVS objective is to efficiently map an image into a mathematical space which will represent the image by means of its corresponding features and

A. Petrosino, L. Maddalena, P. Pala (Eds.): ICIAP 2013 Workshops, LNCS 8158, pp. 77–85, 2013.

computational intelligence techniques [2]-[3]. Feature extraction is one of the most challenging tasks when ASVS are designed. There are many philosophies including global based methods which address the image as a whole and extract features from it [2], and local based methods which include geometrically and graph based approaches [4]-[5].

Another philosophy with potential increasing interest exploits the signature using a coarse or fine detail grid which is imposed upon the image. Then the features are calculated as a function of the granularity of the image grid. The reader may find relative references from the work of Baltzakis and Papamarkos [6], Vargas et al. [7], Kumar et al. [8], Impedovo et al. [9], Shekar and Bharathi [10], Swanepoel and Coetzer [11], Kalera et al. [12], Gilperez et al. [13], Parodi et al. [14] along with many others. In a recent work provided by Tselios et al. [15] a novel method was presented which models the signatures by considering the histogram of specific pixel transitions along predefined paths within pre-confined Chebyshev distances of two (F_{CB2} feature). The feature extraction ideas have been evolved by modeling the feature components in a probabilistic context which allows us to represent the feature generation procedure as a discrete space random source. The F_{CB2} symbols (messages) that the random source outputs when a signature pixel is accounted are considered to be members of a predetermined alphabet. They are handled according to the description of the event concept and they are complemented along with their corresponding probabilistic moments. Thus, the 16 possible combinations of F_{CB2} transition paths are organized in groups with the use of an F_T-event collection where subscript T denotes the size of each feature group [16]. The result is an evolved feature description which is expected to enhance the representation of handwriting. An example is provided by selecting the 87 orthogonal permissible groups of four F_4 collection tetrads, hereafter called 'schemes', where in group formation orthogonality and non-redundancy constraints are taken into account. During the training phase the most appropriate event scheme is selected in order to represent each genuine writer by an ad-hoc minimum entropy selection algorithm. Verification results have been drawn with the use of two databases, the GPDS300 and a proprietary one by means of the EER figure of merit.

The remaining of the work is divided as follows: Section 2 provide the preprocessing stage and the feature extraction method. Section 3 describes the verification protocol and section 4 provides the preliminary results along with the conclusions.

2   Feature Extraction Method

2.1   Preprocessing Steps

The preprocessing of scanned signature images consists of signature black and white conversion, skeletonization, cropping and segmentation. Initially, greyscale images are converted to black and white using Otsu's thresholding method [17]. Then, the morphological operation of signature's skeleton extraction is applied on the black and white signature image to eliminate the effects of the pens' ink variety, while preserving strokes' connectivity [2]. The most informative window (MIW) of the bounding rectangle is found in a similar way as in [15] and the part of signature's image outside this rectangle is cropped out. The outcome of the preprocessing steps outcome is depicted in Fig. 1.

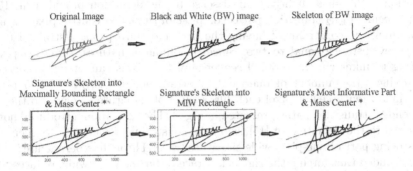

Fig. 1. Signature's Scanned Image Preprocessing Steps

Feature vectors can be extracted from the whole MIW of the signature, from segments of signature's MIW or from their combinations. Signature's MIW segmentation is an extension of the idea of equimass sampling grids [18]-[19]. The equimass sampling grids approach divides the number of black pixels of an image, denoted as mass, by the number of grid divisions in $x-$ or $y-$ direction. Then grid lines are placed in each direction such that each grid strip approximately contains an equal amount of black pixels. Equimass sampling grid segmentation provides strips of the signature with uniform size of signature pixels instead of the trivial distance grid segmentation which provides segments of equal area. The segmentation technique is further enhanced by relaxing the 'grid'-constraint of signature's MIW. This is achieved by keeping the approximately equal mass per segment constraint. Therefore, grid lines are placed in either $x-$ or $y-$ direction such that each grid strip contains the same number of black pixels, equal to mass divided by the number of strips. Each strip is segmented independently of each other, such that (approximately) equimass criterion holds among each segment of the strip. In this way, the resulting segmentation is not a grid segmentation, but an almost equimass rectangular image segmentation. The result is depicted in Fig. 2.

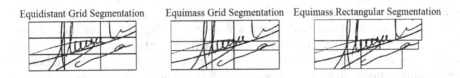

Fig. 2. MIW Signature Segmentation Techniques

2.2 Grid Based Feature Extraction

The proposed representation of the MIW of an offline signature in the feature space pursues modeling the distribution of the co-occurrences of black pixel transition paths of the signature strokes. The set of black pixel transition paths that are used as a basis for signature strokes modeling is the set of F_{CB2} pixel transition paths, in a slightly relaxed sense to the definition provided in [15]. To be specific, F_{CB2} transition paths comprise of three consecutive pixels while maintaining the constraint of having the first and third pixels restrained to a Chebyshev distance equal to two. Since, in offline signatures, signature-pixel ordering is unknown, the ordered sequence of the pixels cannot be estimated. This reduces the number of queried F_{CB2} transition paths, in a 5×5 pixel grid window, with center pixel each black pixel of signature's image, to the 16 independent transition paths presented in Fig. 3. The relaxation introduced now, compared to the definition of [15], is on the constraint of the three consecutive pixels being part of one-pixel wide signature trace. Through experimentation it was concluded that forcing the signature trace to be one-pixel wide, reduces the ability of F_{CB2} co-occurrence modeling. Thus, one-pixel wide constraints have been eliminated. This relaxation has no impact on the 16 basic F_{CB2} elements of the basis used for signature modeling.

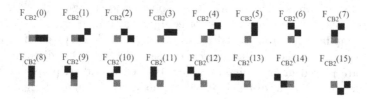

Fig. 3. The basis of the 16 F_{CB2} transition paths (center pixel of the 5×5 grid in red)

2.3 Event Based Modeling

Let (Ω, B, P) denote the probability space on which all our possible outcomes are defined. By definition, Ω is the sample space which consists of all 16 F_{CB2} components (symbols) produced by a discrete memory-less source whereas B is a sigma field (the event space) that contains all possible occurrences of symbols' combinations from the F_{CB2} alphabet. That is, B is the largest possible σ-field [20] which is the collection of all subsets of Ω and is called the power set. Discrete symbols of the sequence are produced at the center pixel of the 5×5 moving grid as it slides over the signature trajectory. In addition, the usual independent variable of time that normally applies a specific ordering to the data is not existent here, as it is of interest only the occurrence of symbols and not their ordered sequence. It is advantageous in our case to explicitly treat the notion of the signature pixels indexes (i, j) as a transformation of sequences produced by the source. As a consequence, the feature extraction grid can be identified as a discrete space - discrete alphabet source.

To overcome the problem of 2^{16} space management we group Ω into T subsets and we define the sub-s-fields B_t as the power sets for each Ω. In this work we choose to group the 16-$F_{CB2}(i)$ components into ensembles of four tetrads (call it hereafter F_4-collection) thus resulting to $4 \times 2^4 = 64$ possible event combinations. According to the exposed material, a discrete source, designated as S_n, can be defined by its emitted symbols and consequent events which are now members of one F_4 collection. The entropy of source S_n is defined as in [1], where $p_{S_n}(\alpha)$ is the distribution of the source events α. This novel modeling of the feature generation process is an evolution of the previous method as it was described in [15]. It attempts to model the distribution of the signature pixel transitions as an information source, while the F_4 collection has been utilized in order to extract events of features along with their corresponding probabilities.

$$H_{F_T} = H(S_n) = - \sum_{\alpha \in S_n} p_{S_n}(\alpha) \ln(p_{S_n}(\alpha)) \tag{1}$$

From the complete set of all the possible ensembles of the F_4 collection only 87 orthogonal cases (hereafter denoted as schemes) shall be enabled along with their corresponding probabilities. The term orthogonal denotes that each component in a subspace of a F_4 tetrad event set cannot be derived as a union of the same subspace F_4 event combination. This constraint provides each signature with 87 different F_4 orthogonal tetrads event sets, found through exhaustive search. In the verification stage that follows, a selection algorithm must be applied in order to choose the most appropriate scheme for each writer. The set Ω, along with one of the feasible orthogonal F_4 partitions ($T = 4$) and its accompanied power set is depicted in Fig. 4.

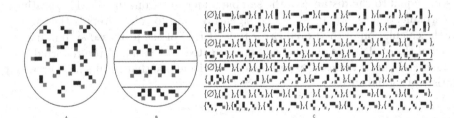

Fig. 4. (A) Sample space, (B) One orthogonal F_4 collection (c) Power set for each tetrad

3   Verification Procedure

3.1   Verification Protocol

During the training phase for each writer and all of his signatures samples and segments an appropriate common scheme should be selected. We call hereafter the set of the appropriate schemes per segment for feature extraction as the representative schemes set (RSS). The selection of the RSS of an orthogonal F_4 collection of F_{CB2} for signature modeling in the current approach is based on the criterion of the most uniform event distribution. The intuition behind this criterion is that the more uniformly the F_{CB2} components along with their set of events are met, the more relevant is the selected scheme to the signature's trace underlying mapping of motor movement. The uniformity of the distribution of symbols within a group g of F_{CB2} components is evaluated using the entropy of the probability mass function P of the sixteen possible combinations of each F_4 collection within each g group. For each one of the four power sets of a F_4 collection an entropy value is calculated namely $H_{41},, H_{42}, H_{43}$ and H_{44}. The sum of them identifies the representative entropy for the scheme applied on the examined signature trace. The RSS is determined from the reference set as defined in section 2.3. For a segment the RSS is the one that provides the minimum sum of entropies along the relevant segment of nref number the signatures of the reference set:

$$H_{F_4} = \sum_{g=1}^{4} H_{4g}, \quad H_S = \sum_{nref} H_{F_4}, \quad RSS = \operatorname{argmin}\{H_S\}, s = 1 : 87 \qquad (2)$$

For each signer, nref number of genuine and an equal number of simulated-forgery signature samples are randomly chosen for training the classifier. The genuine samples are used initially to determine the RSS. Then, the feature vectors of all signatures of the reference set are extracted using the RSS and feed a hard-margin SVM classifier using radial basis kernel. The remaining genuine and simulated forgery signatures' feature vectors using the determined RSS feed the SVM classifier directly for testing, similar to SVM FLV scheme used in [15]. In our implementation, the SVM classifier apart from the class decision, calculates a score equal to the distance of the sample under test from the SVM separating hyperplane. This score for all tested signatures and for all writers is then used for the calculation of the Equal Error Rate (EER) of the proposed system using a global threshold. The experiments are repeated 20 times and the reported results are the mean values of experiment's repetitions, so that results have greater statistical significance.

3.2   Databases

The efficiency of the proposed method has been investigated with two databases of 8-bit grey scale signatures: a Greek signers' (CORPUS1) [15] and GPDS-300 (CORPUS2) [7]. CORPUS1 is comprised from 105 genuine and 21 simulated forgery signature samples for each of the 69 signers of the database. CORPUS2 has 24 genuine signatures and 30 simulated forgeries for each of the 300 signers of the database and is publicly available. During the experiments two schemes of randomly selected training and testing samples were used for comparison with the outcomes of contemporary research in the field. In the first scheme, 12 genuine and 12 simulated-forgery reference samples per writer are used, while in the second scheme 5 genuine and 5 simulated forgery reference samples are used.

The remaining samples are used for testing. The feature vector is a combination of feature extraction from the whole signature's MIW and from the four segments of the 2×2 equimass rectangular segmentation of the MIW relevant to 'S2' scheme used in [15] for comparison.

4   Verification Results and Comparisons

According to the discussion presented above, FAR, FRR and the relevant EER rates, are evaluated for (a) CORPUS 1 withnref = 5 and nref = 12 and (b) CORPUS 2 with nref = 5 and nref = 12. The corresponding results are presented in Table 1 by means of the minimum mean FAR, FRR and EER values for the repetitions of the experimental sets of the current work. The results are promising compared to recently reported ones. In the case of CORPUS 1 the derived results are compared with the results relevant to those reported in [15] for feature level simulated forgery verification tests using 'S2' scheme using (a) nref = 5 and (b) the mean value of nref = 10 and nref = 15 tests for comparison with our test using nref = 12 and presented in Table 2. Concerning CORPUS 2, the results of recently reported research work using nref = 5 and nref = 12, along with the results of the current approach are presented in Table 3.

Table 1. Experimental Results: Mean FAR, FRR and EER values for the defined experimental sets for minimum observed EER values

Experimental Set	FAR (%)	FRR (%)	EER (%)
Corpus 1, nref = 5	2.59	4.23	3.42
Corpus 2, nref = 5	11.29	5.48	8.37
Corpus 1, nref = 12	1.77	2.01	1.83
Corpus 2, nref = 12	6.52	3.23	4.88

Table 2. CORPUS 1: Comparison results of EER (%) values with relevant framework in [15]

[15] for nref = 5	9.16	Current work for nref = 5	3.42
[15] mean EER for nref = 10 and nref = 15	4.65	Current work for nref = 12	1.83

Table 3. CORPUS 2: Comparison results of EER (%) values with recent research approaches

[15] for nref = 5	12.32	Current work for nref = 5	8.37
[7] GPDS-100 for nref = 5	12.02		
[14] nref = 13 (only genuine train samples)	4.21	Current work for nref = 12	4.88
[7] for nref = 12	6.2		
[15] mean EER (nref = 10) & (nref = 15)	8.26		
[8] for nref = 12	13.76		
[21] for nref = 12	15.11		
[22] nref = 12 (only genuine train samples)	15.4		

5   Conclusions

In this work a handwritten signature model based on the powerset of an event topology is evaluated for offline signature verification. Early results on two signature databases suggest that the proposed feature extraction method is promising; It is the authors intention to follow the dissimilarity framework in order to verify the effectiveness of the proposed approach.

References

1. Impedovo, D., Pirlo, G.: Automatic signature verification: The state of the art. IEEE Transactions on Systems Man and Cybernetics 38, 609–635 (2008)
2. Gonzalez, R.C., Woods, R.E.: Digital Image processing. Addison-Wesley (1992)
3. Duda, R.O., Hart, P.E., Stork, D.G.: Pattern classification. John Wiley & Sons (2000)
4. Ferrer, M., Alsono, J., Travieso, C.: Off-line geometric parameters for automatic signature verification using fixed point arithmetic. IEEE Transactions on Pattern Analysis and Machine Intelligence 27, 993–997 (2005)
5. Chen, S., Srihari, S.: A new off-line signature verification method based on graph matching. In: Int. Conf. on Pattern Recognition, pp. 869–872. IEEE (2006)
6. Baltzakis, H., Papamarkos, N.: A new signature verification technique based on a two-stage neural network classifier. Engineering Applications of Artificial Intelligence 14, 95–103 (2001)
7. Vargas, J.F., Ferrer, M.A., Travieso, C.M., Alonso, J.B.: Off-line signature verification based on grey level information using texture features. Pattern Recognition 44, 375–385 (2011)
8. Kumar, R., Sharma, J.D., Chanda, B.: Writer independent off-line signature verification using surroundedness feature. Pattern Recognition Letters 33, 301–308 (2012)
9. Impedovo, D., Pirlo, G., Sarcinella, L., Stasolla, E., Trullo, C.A.: Analysis of Stability in Static Signatures using Cosine Similarity. In: Int. Conf. on Frontiers in Handwriting Recognition (ICFHR 2012), pp. 231–235. IEEE Press (2012)
10. Shekar, B.H., Bharathi, R.K.: LOG-Grid based off-line signature verification. In: Mohan, S., Kumar, S.S. (eds.) Fourth International Conference on Signal and Image Processing 2012. LNEE, vol. 222, pp. 321–330. Springer India (2013)
11. Swanepoel, J.P., Coester, J.: Off-line signature verification using flexible grid features and classifiers fusion. In: Int. Conf. on Frontiers in Handwriting Recognition (ICFHR 2012), pp. 297–302. IEEE Press (2012)
12. Kalera, M.K., Shrihari, S., Xu, A.: Offine line signature verification using distance statistics. Int. J. of Pattern Recognition and Artificial Intelligence, 1339–1360 (2005)
13. Gilperez, A., Alonso-Fernandez, F., Pecharroman, S., Fierrez-Aguilar, J., Ortega-Garcia, J.: Off-line signature verification using contour features. In: Int. Conf. on Frontiers in Handwriting Recognition, ICFHR 2008 (2008)
14. Parodi, M., Gomez, J.C., Belaid, A.: A circular grid-based rotation invariant feature extraction approach for off-line signature verification. In: 11th Int. Conf. on Document Analysis and Recognition, pp. 1289–1293. IEEE Press (2011)
15. Tselios, K., Zois, E.N., Siores, E., Nassiopoulos, A., Economou, G.: Grid-based feature distributions for off-line signature verification. IET Biometrics, 1–10 (2012)

16. Gray, R.M.: Entropy and information theory. Springer, New York (2013)
17. Otsu, N.: A threshold selection method from gray-level histogram. IEEE Transactions on Systems, Man and Cybernetics 6, 62–66 (1979)
18. Favata, J., Srikantan, G.: A multiple feature/resolution approach to handprinted digit and character recognition. Int. J. Imaging Syst. Technol. 7, 304–311 (1996)
19. Impedovo, D., Pirlo, G., Sarcinella, L., Stasolla, E., Trullo, C.A.: Analysis of Stability in Static Signatures using Cosine Similarity. In: Int. Conf. on Frontiers in Handwriting Recognition (ICFHR 2012), pp. 231–235. IEEE Press (2012)
20. Hazewinkel, M.: Encyclopedia of Mathematics. Springer (2001)
21. Nguyen, V., Kawazoe, Y., Wakabayashi, T., Pal, U., Blumenstein, M.: Performance Analysis of the Gradient Feature and the Modified Direction Feature for Off-line Signature Verification. In: Int. Conf. on Frontiers in Handwriting Recognition, pp. 303–307 (2010)
22. Yilmaz, M.B., Yanikoglu, B., Tirkaz, C., Kholmatov, A.: Offline signature verification using classifier combination of HOG and LBP features. In: Proc. Int. J. Conf. Biometrics, pp. 1–7 (2011)

Learning Strategies for Knowledge-Base Updating in Online Signature Verification Systems

Giuseppe Pirlo[1], Donato Impedovo[2], and Donato Barbuzzi[1]

[1] Department of Computer Science, University of Bari, Bari, Italy
{giuseppe.pirlo,donato.barbuzzi}@uniba.it
[2] Department of Electrical and Electronic Engineering, Polytechnic of Bari, Bari, Italy
impedovo@deemail.poliba.it

Abstract. Updating of reference information is a crucial task for automatic signature verification. In fact, signature characteristics vary in time and whatever approach is considered the effectiveness of a signature verification system strongly depends on the extent to which reference information is able to model the changeable characteristics of users' signatures. This paper addresses the problem of knowledge-base updating in multi-expert signature verification systems and introduces a new strategy which exploits the collective behavior of classifiers to select the most profitable samples for knowledge-base updating. The experimental tests, carried out using the SUSig database, demonstrate the effectiveness of the new strategy.

Keywords: Signature Verification, Feedback-based Strategy, Multi Expert System.

1   Introduction

Biometrics is an emerging field of research and technology that involves the recognition of individuals through their physical or behavioural traits. Examples of physical attributes are fingerprints, facial features, the iris, DNA, etc. Some behavioural characteristics are the signature, the voice and keystroke dynamics, among others [1, 2, 3].

A biometric system can either verify or identify. In verification mode, it authenticates the person's identity on the basis of his/her claimed identity. Instead, in identification mode, it establishes the person's identity (among those enrolled in a database) without the subjects having to claim their identity [4, 5].

Signature verification occupies a very special place in biometrics. A signature is a biometric trait generated by a complex process originating in the signer's brain as a motor control "program", implemented through the neuromuscular system and left on the writing surface by a handwriting device [6, 7]. The three main phases of automatic signature verification are: data acquisition and preprocessing, feature extraction and classification [3]. During enrolment phase, the input signatures are processed and their personal features are extracted and stored into knowledge base. During the classification phase, personal features extracted from an inputted signature are compared

A. Petrosino, L. Maddalena, P. Pala (Eds.): ICIAP 2013 Workshops, LNCS 8158, pp. 86–94, 2013.

against the information in the knowledge base, in order to judge the authenticity of the inputted signature [8].

Recently, it has been observed that the verification accuracy can be also improved combining multiple experts. The idea is not to rely on a single decision making scheme but to use several designs (experts) for decision making [9, 10]. In fact, the collective behavior of a set of classifiers can convey more information that those of each classifier of the set, and this information can be exploited for classification aims [11, 12]. When multiple experts are considered, the collective behavior of the set of individual experts can be exploited to dynamically update the knowledge-base of the system, according to suitable feed-back based strategies. In fact, a handwritten signatures is the result of a complex process depending on the psychophysical state of the signer and the conditions under which the signature apposition process occurs. Therefore, although complex theories have been proposed to model the psychophysical mechanisms underlying handwriting [6, 7], ink-depository processes [13] and regional distribution of information [14, 15, 16], signature verification still remains an open challenge since a signature is judge to be genuine or a forgery only on the basis of a few reference specimens.

This paper proposes, as Figure 1 shows, the selection of the valuable samples useful to update the knowledge-base of all experts of the set, correctly recognized by the multi-expert system.

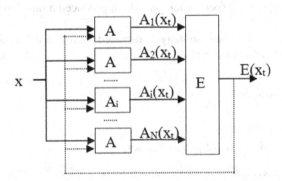

Fig. 1. Feedback in the Multi-Expert Parallel System

Tests have been performed on the task of automatic signature verification, on the SUSig database by considering different types of features. Two different combination techniques (Majority Vote, Weighted Majority vote) have been used at abstract level. The results demonstrate that the proposed strategy is effective in terms of reduction of the false rejection rate (FRR) of genuine signatures and of the false acceptance rate (FAR) of forgery signatures.

The paper is organized as follows: Section 2 presents the background of retraining rules and the different feedback-based strategies. Operating conditions and results are, respectively, in Section 3 and 4. Section 5 reports a discussion and the conclusion of the work.

2   Background of Retraining Rules

2.1   Related Work

In literature, several methods have been proposed for solving the retraining classifier issue, when new labeled data became available. So, the simplest way to update the knowledge base of classifier is probably to use the entire new dataset to retrain the system given the initial training condition or, depending by the classifier, the sets of new and old data. On the other hand, many interesting algorithms can be adopted in order to select (or focus the attention on) specific samples. In particular, the algorithm AdaBoost [17, 18] is able to improve performance of a classifier on a given data set by focusing the learner attention on difficult instances. Even if this approach is very powerful, it works well in the case of weak classifiers, moreover not all the learning algorithms accept weights for the incoming samples. Another interesting approach is the bagging one: a number of weak classifiers trained on different subset (random instance) of the entire dataset are combined by means of the simple majority voting [19]. Bagging and AdaBoost algorithms are adapted when considering a single classifier but applied to a ME system, them performance are boosted. Finally, it has been observed that the collective behavior of classifiers can be considered to select the most profitable samples in order to update the knowledge base of classifiers.

In the past, samples to be used for retraining were selected by considering those, misclassified by a specific expert of the set, which produced a misclassification at the ME level [20, 21, 22].

In the next paragraph a new strategy is depicted taking into account of a multi-expert system that works in supervised learning.

2.2   Selecting Instances

Let be:

- C_j, for j=1,2,...,M, the set of pattern classes;

- $P = \{x_k \mid k = 1,2,..., K\}$, a set of pattern to be feed to the Multi Expert (ME) system. P is considered to be partitioned into S subsets $P_1, P_2, ..., P_s, ..., P_S$, being $P_s=\{x_k \in P \mid k \in [N_s \cdot (s-1)+1, N_s \cdot s]\}$ and $N_s=K/S$ (N_s integer), that are fed to the multi-expert system. In particular, P_1 is used for learning only, whereas $P_2, P_3,...,P_s,...,P_S$ are used both for classification and learning (when necessary);

- $y_s \in \Omega$, the label for the x_s pattern, $\Omega = \{C_1, C_2,...,C_M\}$;

- A_i the *i-th* classifier for $i = 1,2,..., N$;

- $F_i(k) = (F_{i,1}(k), F_{i,2}(k),..., F_{i,r}(k),..., F_{i,R}(k))$ the feature vector used by A_i for representing the pattern $x_k \in P$ (for the sake of simplicity it is here assumed that each classifier uses R real values as features);

- $KB_i(k)$, the knowledge base of A_i after the processing of P_k. In particular $KB_i(k) = \left(KB_i^1(k), KB_i^2(k), \ldots, KB_i^M(k)\right)$;
- E the multi expert system which combines H_i hypothesis in order to obtain the final one.

In first stage ($s=1$), the classifier A_i is trained using the patterns $x_k \in P^*_i = P_1$. Therefore, the knowledge base $KB_i(s)$ of A_i is initially defined as:

$$KB_i(s) = (KB^1_i(s), KB^2_i(s), \ldots, KB^j_i(s), \ldots, KB^M_i(s)) \qquad (1a)$$

where, for $j=1,2,\ldots,M$:

$$KB^j_i(s) = (F^j_{i,1}(s), F^j_{i,2}(s), \ldots, F^j_{i,r}(s), \ldots, F^j_{i,R}(s)) \qquad (1b)$$

being $F^j_{i,r}(s)$ the set of the *r-th* feature of the *i-th* classifier for the patterns of the class C_j that belongs to P^*_i.

Successively, the subsets $P_2, P_3, \ldots, P_s, \ldots, P_S$ is provided to the multi-classifier system both for classification and for learning. The "leave-one-out" method is used to test the multi-expert system. When considering new labeled data (samples of $P_2, P_3, \ldots, P_s, \ldots, P_S$), a naïve and not naïve strategy can be used.

The naïve strategy uses all the available new patterns to update the knowledge base of each individual classifier:

- $\forall x_t \in P_s : update\_KB_i$ \qquad (2)

The second approach is derived from AdaBoost and bagging. A_i is updated by considering all its samples correctly recognized by ME system:

- $\forall x_t \in P_s \ni' \left(E(x_t) = y_t\right) : update\_KB_i$ \qquad (3)

In order to inspect and take advantage of the common behavior of the ensemble of classifiers, the following simple strategy is evaluated and compared to the previous.

3   Operating Conditions

3.1   Classifier and Combination Techniques

The classifier used for the experimentation is a Naïve Bayes Classifier. This fits, in the training phase, a multivariate normal density to each class C_j by considering a diagonal covariance matrix. Given an input to be classified, the Maximum a Posteriori (MAP) decision rule is adopted to select the most probable hypothesis among the different classes.

Also many approaches have been considered so far for classifiers combination. These approaches differ in terms of type of output they combine, system topology and degree of a-priori knowledge they use [9, 10]. The combination technique plays a crucial role in the selection of new patterns to be feed to the classifier in the proposed approach. In this work the following decision combination techniques have been considered and compared: Majority Vote (MV) and Weighted Majority Vote (WMV). MV just considers labels provided by the individual classifiers, it is generally adopted if no knowledge is available about performance of classifiers so that they are equal-considered. The second approach can be adopted by considering weights related to the performance of individual classifiers on a specific dataset. Given the case depicted in this work, it seems to be more realistic, in fact the behavior of classifiers can be evaluated, for instance, on the new available dataset. In particular, let ε_i be the error rate of the i-th classifier evaluated on the last available training set, the weight assigned to

$$A_i \text{ is, } w_i = \log(1/\beta_i) \text{ being } \beta_i = \varepsilon_i/(1-\varepsilon_i) \tag{4}$$

3.2 SUSig Handwritten Signature Database

The SUSig database consists of online signatures donated by 100 people (29 women and 71 men) [23]. The database was collected in two separate sessions that were approximately one week apart. Each person supplied 10 samples of his/her regular signature in each session, for a total of 20 genuine signatures, without any constraints on how to sign. Each person was then asked to forge a randomly selected user's signature. So, 10 forged signatures were produced.

Therefore, in our case a multi-expert system for on-line signature verification has been considered P={xj | j=1,2,...,30} (classes "0" and "1") has been used. Figure 2 presents some samples of handwritten signatures [23].

Fig. 2. Sample genuine signature from SUSig

The DB has been initially partitioned into 2 subsets:

- $P_1=\{x_1,\ldots,x_8,x_{11},\ldots,x_{18},x_{21},\ldots,x_{28}\}$,
- $P_2=\{x_9,x_{10},x_{19},x_{20},x_{29},x_{30}\}$.

In particular, P_1 represents the set usually adopted for training and test considering the "leave-one-out" method on SUSig DB [21]. P_2 is the feedback dataset. Each signature is partitioned into 5 stroke, successively, for each stroke, the following set of features have been considered:

- F_1: features set 1: mean and variance of the distances between two consecutive points;
- F_2: features set 2: mean and variance of pressure between two consecutive points;
- F_3: features set 3: mean and variance of the velocity and acceleration between two consecutive points.

4   Results

This section presents the results in terms of false rejection rate (FRR) of genuine signatures and the false acceptance rate (FAR) of forgery signatures. We combined, adopting a multi-expert system, the three set of features (F1, F2 and F3) and a classifier NB. The label "X-feed" refers to the use of the X modality for the feedback training process: "All" is the feedback of the entire set. "MV" and "WMV" are feedback at ME level adopting, respectively, the majority vote and the weighted majority vote schema.

Tables 1 show results related to the use of NB classifier and majority vote as combination technique. P1 is used for training and test in "leave-one-out" approach and P2 is used for feedback learning. The first column (No-feed) reports results related to the use of P1 for training and test, without applying any feedback (0 Selected Samples), while the approach All-feed uses all samples belonging to the new set in order to update the knowledge base of each single classifier (All Selected Samples). For MV-feed an improvement both of the FAR is 1.36% and of the FRR is 0.59% respect to the use of the entire new dataset.

Table 1. NB, MV Combination Technique, Feedback – P_2

	No-feed	MV-feed	All-feed
FAR	5.39	**3.69**	5.05
FRR	6.25	**5.58**	6.17

In particular, figure 3 shows that MV-feed outperforms each other feedback-based strategy.

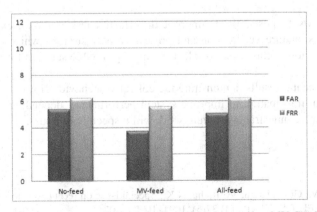

Fig. 3. Comparison between different feedback-based strategies: MV Combination

Finally, Tables 2 show results related to the use of NB classifier and weighted majority vote as combination technique. P1 is used for training and test in "leave-one-out" approach and P2 is used for feedback learning. In this case, for WMV-feed an improvement both of the FAR is 0.68% and of the FRR is 1.32% compared to the use of the All-feed strategy where entire new dataset is used for the feedback. More specifically, figure 4 shows that the results provided by the WMV-feed approach are superior to those obtained by All-feed.

Table 2. NB, WMV Combination Technique, Feedback – P$_2$

	No-feed	WMV-feed	All-feed
FAR	5.19	**2.95**	3.63
FRR	9.57	**5.81**	7.13

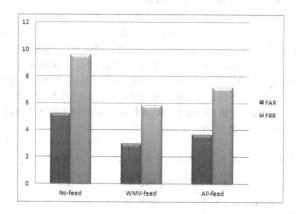

Fig. 4. Comparison between different feedback-based strategies. WMV Combination.

5   Discussion and Conclusion

This paper shows the possibility to improve the effectiveness of a multi-expert system for automatic signature verification and presents a new strategy which exploits the collective behavior of classifiers to select the most profitable samples for knowledge-base updating.

The experimental results demonstrate the collective behavior of a set of classifiers provides useful information to improve system performance, depending on the feature type and matching strategy. Future work will inspect these issues.

References

1. Boyer, K.W., Govindaraju, V., Ratha, N.K.: Special issue on recent advances in biometric systems. IEEE T-SMC – Part B 37(5), 1091–1095 (2007)

2. Prabhakar, S., Kittler, J., Maltoni, D., O'Gorman, L., Tan, T.: Special issue on biometrics: Progress and directions. IEEE T-PAMI 29(4), 513–516 (2007)
3. Impedovo, D., Pirlo, G.: Automatic Signature Verification – State of the Art. IEEE Transactions on Systems, Man and Cybernetics – Part C: Applications and Review 38(5), 609–635 (2008)
4. Jain, A.K., Hong, L., Pankanti, S.: Biometric identification. Commun. ACM 43(2), 91–98 (2000)
5. Jain, A.K., Flynn, P., Ross, A.: Handbook of Biometrics. Springer, NewYork (2007)
6. Plamondon, R.: A kinematic theory of rapid human movements: Part I: Movement representation and generation. Biol. Cybern. 72(4), 295–307 (1995)
7. Plamondon, R.: A kinematic theory of rapid human movements: Part III: Kinetic outcomes. Biol. Cybern. (1997)
8. Impedovo, D., Pirlo, G., Plamondon, R.: Handwritten Signature Verification: New Advancements and Open Issues. In: Proc. XIII International Conference on Frontiers in Handwriting Recognition (ICFHR 2012), Monopoli, Bari, Italy, pp. 18–20, 365–370 (2012)
9. Kittler, J., Hatef, M., Duin, R.P.W., Matias, J.: On combining classifiers. IEEE Trans. on PAMI 20(3), 226–239 (1998)
10. Di Lecce, V., Dimauro, G., Guerriero, A., Impedovo, S., Pirlo, G., Salzo, A.: A Multiexpert System for Dynamic Signature Verification. In: Kittler, J., Roli, F. (eds.) MCS 2000. LNCS, vol. 1857, pp. 320–329. Springer, Heidelberg (2000)
11. Barbuzzi, D., Impedovo, D., Pirlo, G.: Supervised Learning Strategies in Multi-Classifier Systems. In: Proc. 11th International Conference on Information Science, Signal Processing and their Applications (ISSPA 2012), Montreal, Canada, July 3-5, pp. 1215–1220 (2012)
12. Pirlo, G., Trullo, C.A., Impedovo, D.: A Feedback-based multi-classifier system. In: Proceedings of the 10th International Conference on Document Analysis and Recognition (ICDAR-10), Barcelona, Spain, July 26-29, pp. 713–717. IEEE Computer Society Press (2009)
13. Franke, K., Rose, S.: Ink-deposition analysis using temporal data. In: Proc. 10th Int. Workshop Front. Handwriting Recognition (IWFHR), La Baule, France, pp. 447–453 (2006)
14. Pirlo, G., Impedovo, D.: Fuzzy-Zoning-Based Classification for Handwritten Characters. IEEE Trans. on Fuzzy Systems 19(4), 780–785 (2011)
15. Impedovo, S., Ferrante, A., Modugno, R., Pirlo, G.: Feature Membership Functions in Voronoi-based Zoning. In: Serra, R., Cucchiara, R. (eds.) AI*IA 2009. LNCS, vol. 5883, pp. 202–211. Springer, Heidelberg (2009)
16. Impedovo, S., Modugno, R., Ferrante, A., Pirlo, G.: Zoning Methods for Hand-written Character Recognition: An Overview. In: Proceedings of the 12th International Conference on Frontiers in Handwriting Recognition (ICFHR-12), Kolkata, India, November 16-18, pp. 329–334. IEEE Computer Society Press (2010)
17. Schapire, R.E.: The strength of weak learnability. Machine Learning 5(2), 197–227 (1990)
18. Polikar, R.: Bootstrap-Inspired Techniques in Computational Intelligence. IEEE Signal Processing Magazine 24(4), 59–72 (2007)
19. Freud, Y., Schapire, R.E.: Decision-theoretic generalization of on-line learning and an application to boosting. J. of Comp. and System Sciences 55(1), 119–139 (1997)
20. Impedovo, D., Pirlo, G.: Updating Knowledge in Feedback-based Multi-Classifier Systems. In: Proc. of ICDAR, pp. 227–231 (2011)

21. Barbuzzi, D., Impedovo, D., Pirlo, G.: Feedback-Based Strategies In Multi-Expert Systems. In: Sesto Convegno del Gruppo Italiano Ricercatori in Pattern Recognition (2012)
22. Barbuzzi, D., Impedovo, D., Pirlo, G.: Benchmarking of Update Learning Strategies on Digit Classifier Systems. In: Proceedings of the 13th International Conference on Frontiers in Handwriting Recognition, pp. 35–40 (2012)
23. Kholmatov, A., Yanikoglu, B.: SUSIG: an on-line signature database, associated protocols and benchmark results. Pattern Analysis and Applications, 1–10 (2008)

A Dissimilarity-Based Approach
for Biometric Fuzzy Vaults–Application
to Handwritten Signature Images

George S. Eskander, Robert Sabourin, and Eric Granger

Laboratoire d'imagerie, de vision et d'intelligence artificielle
Ecole de technologie supérieure, Université du Québec, Montréal, Canada
geskander@livia.etsmtl.ca, {robert.sabourin,eric.granger}@etsmtl.ca

Abstract. Bio-Cryptographic systems enforce authenticity of cryptographic applications like data encryption and digital signatures. Instead of
simple user passwords, biometrics, such as, fingerprint and handwritten signatures, are employed to access the cryptographic secret keys.
The Fuzzy Vault scheme (FV) is massively employed to produce bio-
cryptogra-phic systems, as it absorbs variability in biometric signals.
However, the FV design problem is not well formulated in the literature,
and different approaches are applied for the different biometric traits.
In this paper, a generic FV design approach, that could be applied to
different biometrics, is introduced. The FV decoding functionality is formulated as a simple classifier that operates in a dissimilarity representation space. A boosting feature selection (BFS) method is employed for
optimizing this classifier. Application of the proposed approach to offline
signature biometrics confirms its viability. Experimental results on the
Brazilian signature database (that includes various forgeries) have shown
FV recognition accuracy of 90% and system entropy of about 69-bits.

Keywords: Fuzzy Vault, Bio-Cryptography, Offline Signatures,
Dissimilarity Representation.

1 Introduction

Cryptographic systems deal with the security of stored or transmitted information. For instance, data encryption methods provide a way for confidentiality,
as only authorized persons, who possess the decryption key, can decrypt and
understand the encrypted information. Also, the digital signature technology
guarantee data integrity. A person digitally signs and transmits the information, by means of his signing key. A receiving party can verify that the received
information are not changed during transmission.

The drawback of cryptography lies in its dependency on secret cryptographic
keys, that if compromised, security of the whole system is compromised. Although the cryptographic keys are too long to be guessed by impostors, they are
also too long to be memorized by the legitimate users. This problem is alleviated
through storing the key in a secure place, e.g., a smart card, and a user retrieves

A. Petrosino, L. Maddalena, P. Pala (Eds.): ICIAP 2013 Workshops, LNCS 8158, pp. 95–102, 2013.
© Springer-Verlag Berlin Heidelberg 2013

his key by providing a simple password. Such token/password solution forms a weak point in a security system, as whatever strong is the cryptographic key, overall system security is determined by the password length. Moreover, these authentication measures are not strongly associated with the user identity, so they cannot really distinguish between attackers and legitimate users. Any person who steals the password and the card can retrieve the cryptographic key and access the system.

Biometrics, which are human traits like fingerprint, iris, face, handwritten signatures, etc., are employed to alleviate the cryptographic key management problem. This new technology is known as bio-cryptography or crypto-biometrics, where cryptographic keys are secured by means of biometrics instead of the traditional passwords [1]. As biometrics are strongly associated with user identity, and it is less likely that they are stolen or forgotten, so they guarantee authenticity of the cryptographic systems users. However, design of the bio-cryptographic systems is challenging due to the fuzzy nature of the biometric traits. The intra-personal variability and inter-personal similarity of biometric signals lead to false rejection of authorized users and acceptance of unauthorized users, respectively.

The Fuzzy Vault Scheme (FV) [2] is employed to produce bio-cryptographic systems based on different biometric traits. This scheme locks the cryptographic key by means of locking features extracted from a biometric template. To unlock the FV, and retrieve the key, a genuine biometric sample is used to extract some unlocking features. The key can be unlocked only if the locking and unlocking features overlap substantially. As identical matching between the biometric template and the query sample is not required, so the FV absorbs some of the biometric variability.

In literature, different design approaches are proposed to design FV systems based on different biometric traits, and no generic approach is introduced. In this paper, a generic FV design approach is introduced. The functionality of the FV system is formulated as a simple classifier that operates in a dissimilarity space [3], where distances between a query sample and a FV constitute the classification space. Optimizing the parameters and input features of this classifier lead to accurate FV decoding. As a proof of concept, the proposed formulation is applied to the offline signature biometrics, and have shown promising results. The boosting feature selection method (BFS) [4] is employed here to optimize the FV model, while different optimization techniques may be applicable.

The rest of this paper is organized as follows. The next section presents a background on the FV scheme as applied to biometrics. The proposed dissimilarity-based formulation of the FV design problem is illustrated in section 3. Application of the proposed method to the offline signature biometrics, and the experimental results are presented and discussed in section 4.

2   Biometric Fuzzy Vaults

A FV scheme locks a cryptographic key K by means of a biometric template T. To unlock K, a biometric query sample Q is provided by the user. Figure 1

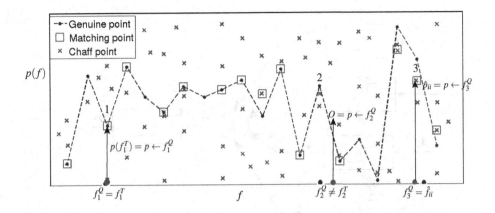

Fig. 1. Illustration of the FV locking/unlocking process

illustrates this locking/unlocking process. For key locking, K is split into $k+1$ strings and constitutes a coefficient vector $C = \{c_0, c_1, c_2, ..., c_k\}$. A polynomial p of degree k is encoded using C, where $p(x) = c_k x^k + c_{k-1} x^{k-1} + ... + c_1 x + c_0$. Then, a locking set $F^T = \{f_i^T\}_{i=1}^t$ is extracted from T. The polynomial is evaluated for all points in F^T and constitutes the set $p(F^T) = \{p(f_i^T)\}_{i=1}^t$. The points $(F^T, p(F^T))$ constitutes the genuine vault points.

It is known that, for a polynomial of degree k, only $k+1$ points on its curve are needed to reconstruct the polynomial equation. So, the genuine vault points can be used to reconstruct the polynomial p, and thereby the cryptographic key K. Hence, any person who accesses the genuine points can retrieve the key. Accordingly, to conceal these data from attackers, a set of z chaff (noise) points ($\hat{F} = \{\hat{f}_{ii}\}_{ii=1}^z$, $\hat{P} = \{\hat{p}_{ii}\}_{ii=1}^z$) are generated. Then, the chaff and genuine points are mixed to constitute the fuzzy vault V_T of length r points. Security of the vault relies on the amount of concealing chaffs. In case that an impostor accesses the vault data, he has to search for at least $k+1$ genuine points, out of $r = t + z$ points of the FV. This search task becomes infeasible with high number of chaff points z.

The proper way to unlock K from the vault V_T, by legitimate users, is to apply a biometric query sample Q. An unlocking set $F^Q = \{f_j^Q\}_{j=1}^t$ is extracted from Q. Then, the chaff points are filtered by matching items of F^Q against all items in V_T. In the ideal case, each feature encoded in F^Q locates the corresponding genuine feature encoded in F^T (e.g., point 1 in Figure 1). On the other hand, due to the fuzzy nature of biometrics, some elements of F^Q differ from their corresponding elements in F^T, and two types of errors might occur, namely erasures and noise. For the erasures case, f_i^Q does not match with any vault point, so it does not add any element to the matching set (e.g., point 2 in Figure 1). For the noise case, a feature f_i^Q might equate a chaff $\hat{f}_{ii}$, so that it adds a noise point $(\hat{f}_{ii}, \hat{p}_{ii})$ to the matching set (e.g., point 3 in Figure 1).

Finally, the resulting matching set is fed to a polynomial reconstruction algorithm, to reconstruct the encoded polynomial p. This process succeeds only if

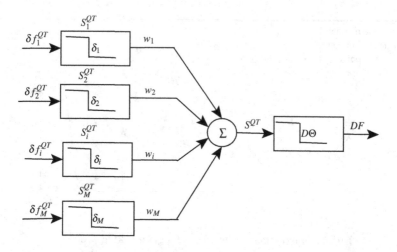

Fig. 2. Proposed formulation of the FV design problem

the matching set contains at least $k+1$ genuine points. However, even if enough genuine points exists, it is not possible to differentiate between the genuine and noise points. To overcome this, FV decoders employ error correction codes, like Reed-Solomon (R-S). The genuine set $(F^T, p(F^T))$ is considered as a code word of length t, that encodes a secret message of length $k+1$, where there are $t-k-1$ redundancy elements. During the decoding process, some noise is added to this code producing a corrupted version of it. The error correction codes can correct some of these errors and recover the secret message.

In literature, the FV design problem is addressed with different approaches. Generally, authors proposed methodologies to absorb the dissimilarities between template and query biometric signals, so that they are within the error correction capacity of the decoder. For instance, fingerprint-based FVs are proposed by Nandakumar et al., where query samples are aligned with the templates [5]. The FV design problem needs to be well formulated, so that a generic approach could be applied to the different biometrics.

3   Dissimilarity-Based Formulation of the FV System

The proposed approach relies on the concept of dissimilarity representation [3]. Instead of representing an object by a set of absolute measurements (features), distances between the objects are considered as features. This concept applies to the FV scheme. A query sample is classified as genuine or forgery, depending on its distance to the FV template.

Figure 2 illustrates the proposed formulation of the FV design problem. Assume $F = \{f_i\}_{i=1}^M$ is a vector of features extracted from a biometric signal. The FV decoder does not concern with the absolute feature values, but rather the difference between the locking and unlocking features. Accordingly, the feature representation is translated to a dissimilarity feature representation $\Delta F = \{\delta f_i^{QT}\}_{i=1}^M$,

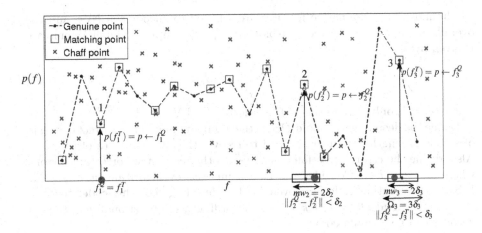

Fig. 3. Illustration of proposed dissimilarity-based FV locking/unlocking process

where $\delta f_i^{QT} = \| f_i^Q - f_i^T \|$ is the distance between the query and template signals, as measured by the feature f_i. In this new space, it is easier to locate a subset of features with similar values for intra-user samples, and that have dissimilar values when extracted from inter-personal samples. For traditional FV decoders, an unlocking feature locates a locking FV point, only if they are identical. Due to the variability of biometrics, it rarely happens that two feature instances are identical. To alleviate this, we modify the FV decoding functionality, so it consideres similar measurements as being identical. In order to define what the term "similar" means, we define $\Delta = \{\delta_i\}_{i=1}^M$, where δ_i is a threshold for a dissimilarity feature δf_i and $\delta f_i^{QT} < \delta_i$ only if Q is a genuine sample.

The vector Δ is used during the FV unlocking process, for matching unlocking features with the FV points adaptively, based on the expected feature variability. An unlocking element f_i^Q is considered matching a FV element f_i^T if they lie in a matching window $m_i = 2 \times \delta_i$. Figure 3 illustrates the viability of the adaptive matching a method. On contrary to the strict matching shown in Figure 1, point 2 could be filtered from the chaff points as $\delta f_2^{QT} < \delta_2$. Also, the dissimilarity thresholds vector Δ, is used during the FV locking phase, for adaptive chaff generation. The chaff points are generated so that they have equal separation space Ω. This separation space is computed for each feature f_i, so that $\Omega_i = 3 \times \delta_i$. By this method, it is less likely that an unlocking element f_i^Q equates a chaff element f_{ii}. For instance, point 3 in Figure 3 is filtered, and f_3^Q did not collide with the chaff f_{ii}, as the chaff are generated outside the matching window w_3.

Accordingly, similarity of the samples Q and T, as measured by a feature f_i is given by:

$$S_i^{QT} = \begin{cases} 1 & if \ (\delta f_i^Q < \delta_i) \\ 0 & otherwise \end{cases} \quad (1)$$

The most t discriminative features are selected to encode the FVs, and the overall similarity score between the biometric query samples and its FV template is given by:

$$S^{QT} = \sum_{i=1}^{M}(w_i \times S_i). \tag{2}$$

where $w_i = 1$, only if the feature f_i is selected for FV encoding.

Define the decoding threshold $D\Theta$ as the minimum number of correct elements of a code of length t, that are needed to recover the encoded word of length k. Also, define the error correction capacity ε as the maximum correctable errors, where $\varepsilon = t - D\Theta$. Consider the Berlekamp-Massey algorithm, as a specific R-S error correction code employed for FV decoding. For this code, the $\varepsilon = (t - k - 1)/2$, and $D\Theta = (t + k + 1)/2$. Accordingly, the functionality of the FV decoder can be formulated as:

$$DF = sign(S^{QT} - D\Theta). \tag{3}$$

where DF is positive if the FV is decoded successfully, and it is negative otherwise. It is obvious that, good design of a FV decoder implies that DF is positive only for genuine query samples. This functionality relies on the elements that produce the similarity score S^{QT} and on the parameters that control the decoding threshold $D\Theta$. These elements and parameters have to be optimized for accurate FV decoding accuracy.

4   Application to the Offline Signature Biometrics

The proposed FV design approach is applied to the offline handwritten signatures, where digitized signature images are used to lock/unlock the FVs. In the preliminary version of this work [6], only the feature selection task is employed. In this paper, the feature dissimilarity is modeled and used to implement the proposed adaptive chaff generation and matching methods.

Although the proposed model of the FV system can be optimized by employing different supervised learning or optimization methods, we employed a Boosting feature selection (BFS) algorithm [3] for feature selection and feature dissimilarity modeling. BFS facilitates selection of a single feature at every boosting iteration, while learning its decision threshold. In case that BFS is employed in a dissimilarity representation space, the algorithm learns the dissimilarity threshold δ_i for every feature feature f_i. To this end, the enrolling signature images are first represented as vectors in a high dimensional feature space. This representation is projected on a dissimilarity representation space, where pairwise feature distances are computed. Boosting feature selection is employed in this space, producing a compact space with the intra-personal distances are minimized and the inter-personal distances are maximized. The feature dissimilarity thresholds are modeled in this space. This method is originally introduced by Rivard et al., to develop writer-independent offline signature verification systems [7]. Recently, we adapted these systems for specific users by tuning their

Table 1. Performance of the proposed FV implementation

Measure %	Previous work[6] (Only ESC)	Proposed Method (ESC+DPDF)	
		Strict matching	Adaptive matching
FRR	25	28	11.53
FAR_{random}	3	2	2.05
FAR_{simple}	7	3	2.39
$FAR_{simulated}$	36	22	24.38
AER	17.75	13.75	10.08

Table 2. Impact of Chaff Quantity on the FV Performance

Chaff separation (Ω)	Without chaff	Fixed separation				Adaptive separation	
		0.2	0.10	0.05	0.025	2δ	3δ
No. of FV points (r)	20	200	400	800	1600	1768	1528
No. of chaff points (z)	0	180	380	780	1580	1748	1508
Security	0-bits	45-bits	52-bits	60-bits	68-bits	69-bits	68-bits
FRR	5.25	11.53	28.94	55.53	75.81	7.03	6.13
FAR_{random}	2.74	2.05	1.06	0.58	0.31	2.40	2.31
FAR_{simple}	3.49	2.39	1.58	0.88	0.49	2.89	3.26
$FAR_{simulated}$	33.14	24.38	15.63	8.15	3.42	29.77	31.06
AER_{all}	11.15	10.08	11.80	16.28	20.00	10.52	10.69

universal representations for specific users [8]. In this paper, training of such user-specific verification systems is employed in the dissimilarity representation space, as a wrapper to select discriminative FV locking features, and to learn the dissimilarity thresholds. This process is out of the scope of this paper, and more details are found in [9].

In the preliminary version of this work [6], we employed Extended-Shadow-Code (ESC) features. Here, we investigate a multi-type feature extraction approach, where Directional Probability Density Function (DPDF) is also employed. The Brazilian database is used for proof-of-concept simulations. The FV system is tested for 60 users, with 40 query samples per user (10 genuine signatures, 10 random, 10 simple, and 10 simulated forgeries). The Average Error Rate (AER) is employed for performance evaluation, where $AER = (FRR + FAR_{random} + FAR_{simple} + FAR_{simulated})/4$. For more details about feature extractions, experimental DB and testing protocol, see [7].

Table 1 reports the performance of the signature-based FVs. In [6], only ESC features are employed. While when the DPDF features are added, the performance is enhanced as AER is reduced from 17.75% to 13.75%. Applying the adaptive matching method, enhanced the performance as AER is reduced from 13.75% to 10.08%.

Table 2 shows the impact of adaptive chaff generation method. It is clear that the FRR is low when no chaff points are generated, while this implementation is not secure. The traditional chaff generation method, is to generate chaff points with fixed separation space between them. In such case, there is a trade-off between security and robustness. For instance, with small separation, e.g., 0.025, there are 40 FV points generated with the same index (1 genuine + 39 chaff points). In this case, a high number of chaffs (1580) is generated, while system entropy is 68-bits and $FRR = 75\%$. On the other hand, by applying the adaptive chaff generation method, high number of chaffs could be generated (1508), with minimal impact on the system robustness ($FRR = 6\%$).

5   Conclusions and Future Work

In this paper, the FV design problem is formulated based on the dissimilarity representation concept. The proposed formulation facilitates selection of FV encoding features, from large number of feature extractions. Features are translated to a dissimilarity representation space, so their dissimilarities can be modeled. Features with discriminative dissimilarities are selected for FV encoding, and their modeled dissimilarities controls the chaff generation and matching processes. The method is applied to the offline signature biometrics, where boosting feature selection algorithm is employed for training. The proposed method, however, is general and future work will address different biometrics, feature selection and optimization techniques. Also, all of the model parameters maybe optimized for higher FV decoding performance.

Acknowledgments. This work was supported by the Natural Sciences and Engineering Research Council of Canada and BancTec Inc.

References

1. Uludag, U., Pankanti, S., Prabhakar, S., Jain, A.K.: Biometric Cryptosystems: Issues and Challenges. Proceedings of the IEEE 92(6), 948–960 (2004)
2. Juels, A., Sudan, M.: A Fuzzy Vault scheme. In: Proc. IEEE Int. Symp. Inf. Theory, Switzerland, p. 408 (2002)
3. Pekalska, E., Duin, R.P.W.: Dissimilarity representations allow for building good classifiers. PR Letters 23(8), 161–166 (2002)
4. Tieu, K., Viola, P.: Boosting image retrieval. International Journal of Computer Vision 56(1), 17–36 (2004)
5. Nandakumar, K., Jain, A.K., Pankanti, S.: Fingerprint based Fuzzy Vault: Implementation and Performance. IEEE TIFS 2(4), 744–757 (2007)
6. Eskander, G.S., Sabourin, R., Granger, E.: Signature based Fuzzy Vaults with boosted feature selection. In: SSCI-CIBIM 2011, Paris, pp. 131–138 (2011)
7. Rivard, D., Granger, E., Sabourin, R.: Multi-Feature extraction and selection in writer-independent offline signature verification. IJDAR 16(1), 83–103 (2013)
8. Eskander, G.S., Sabourin, R., Granger, E.: Adaptation of writer-independent systems for offline signature verification. In: ICFHR 2012, Bari, Italy, pp. 432–437 (2012)
9. Eskander, G.S., Sabourin, R., Granger, E.: On the Dissimilarity Representation and Prototype Selection for Signature-Based Bio-Cryptographic Systems. In: SIMBAD 2013, York, UK, July 3-5 (accepted for publication, 2013)

Local Features
for Forensic Signature Verification

Muhammad Imran Malik[1], Marcus Liwicki[1,2], and Andreas Dengel[1]

[1] German Research Center for Artificial Intelligence
(DFKI GmbH) Kaiserslautern, Germany
`firstname.lastname@dfki.de`
[2] University of Fribourg, Switzerland
`marcus.liwicki@unifr.ch`

Abstract. In this paper we present a novel comparison among three
local features based offline systems for forensic signature verification.
Forensic signature verification involves various signing behaviors, e.g.,
disguised signatures, which are generally not considered by Pattern
Recognition (PR) researchers. The first system is based on nine local
features with Gaussian Mixture Models (GMMs) classification. The second system utilizes a combination of scale-invariant Speeded Up Robust
Features (SURF) and Fast Retina Keypoints (FREAK). The third system is based on a combination of Features from Accelerated Segment
Test (FAST) and FREAK. All of these systems are evaluated on the
dataset of the 4NSigComp2010 signature verification competition which
is the first publicly available dataset containing disguised signatures. Results indicate that our local features based systems outperform all the
participants of the said competition both in terms of time and equal
error rate.

Keywords: Signature verification, disguised signatures, forensic handwriting examination, local features, GMM, SURF, FAST, FREAK.

1 Introduction

Signature verification is in focus of research since decades. Traditionally, automatic signature verification is divided into two broad categories, online and
offline, depending on the mode of the handwritten input. If both the spatial as
well as temporal information regarding signatures are available to the systems,
verification is performed on online data. In the case where temporal information
is not available and the systems must utilize the spatial information gleaned
through scanned or camera captured documents, verification is performed on
offline data [1–3].

In many recent works signature verification has been considered as a two-
class pattern classification problem [3]. Here an automated system has to decide
whether or not a given signature belongs to a referenced authentic author. If
the system could not find enough evidence of a forgery from the questioned

A. Petrosino, L. Maddalena, P. Pala (Eds.): ICIAP 2013 Workshops, LNCS 8158, pp. 103–111, 2013.

signature feature vector, it simply considers the signature as genuine belonging to the referenced authentic author, otherwise it declares the signature as forged.

Apart from the above mentioned two class classification paradigm, another important genre of signatures especially for Forensic Handwriting Examiners (FHEs) is the disguised signatures. A disguised signature is written originally by an authentic author but with the purpose of later denial. Here an authentic author disguises his/her signatures to make them look like a forgery. The purpose of disguising signatures can be hundreds, e.g., a person trying to withdraw money from his/her own bank account via offline signatures on the bank check and trying to deny the check signatures after some time, or even making a false copy of his/her will etc., but they appear often in forensic casework. The category of disguised signatures has been addressed during the ICFHR 4NsigComp 2010 [4]. This was the first attempt to include disguised signatures into a signature verification competition. The systems had to decide whether the author wrote a signature in a natural way, with an intension of a disguise, or whether it has been forged by another writer.

In this paper we investigate three local features based methods on the publicly available 4NSigComp2010 signature verification competition data set. The first system is based on nine local features with Gaussian Mixture Models (GMMs) classification. The second system utilizes a combination of scale-invariant Speeded Up Robust Features (SURF) and Fast Retina Keypoints (FREAK). The third system is based on a combination of Features from Accelerated Segment Test (FAST) and FREAK.

The rest of this paper is organized as follows. Section 2 covers some of the important related work. Section 3 explains the three offline signature verification systems considered in this study. Section 4 explains the dataset used in this study, reports on the experimental results and provides a comparative analysis of the results. Section 5 concludes the paper and gives some ideas for future work.

2   Related Work

Signature verification has remained an active field since the last few decades. The state-of-the-art of signature verification from late 1980's to 2000 are presented in [1], and [2]. Later methods have been summarized in [3]. Throughout these years, various classification methods based on global and/or local features have been presented. A majority of these methods have been tested for detection of genuine and forged signatures but disguised signatures are generally neglected apart from some initial research, like [1], and in some comparative studies of local and global feature based methods, like [5].

Note that, unlike disguised signatures, disguised handwriting in general is previously considered in some PR-research like [6]. However, [6] only focuses the classification of disguise versus genuine handwriting which does not completely suffice the needs of FHEs.

Some local features based methods such as Scale Invariant Feature Transform (SIFT) are used for writer retrieval and identification, as in [7], but identification and retrieval differ from signature verification in their essence, also disguised signatures are not explicitly focused as yet which is a novel aspect of our study. Similarly some improvements in the basic SIFT descriptors have been suggested in recent past for character recognition, such as in [8], and [9]. The SURF Keypoint detector, which we have used to initially identify the signatures' local regions of interest in one of our experiments, in conjunction with SURF keypoint descriptor has been previously used heavily for object and character recognition, such as in [10–12]. Similarly, the FAST keypoint detector, which we have also used to initially identify the signatures' local regions of interest in one of our systems, has been previously used mainly for problems like multiple object tracking [13], object recognition for smart phone platforms [14], and recognition of degraded handwritten characters [15].

The novelty of our work, however, is the way local features are averaged and applied for signature verification to cater the complete verification paradigm including disguised signatures as well as the comparison we have performed among the three approaches with respect to time and memory.

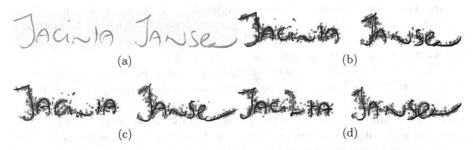

(a)   (b)

(c)   (d)

Fig. 1. Some example signatures. (a): A genuine reference signature, (b): Keypoints extracted from the genuine reference signature, (c): Keypoints extracted from a questioned forged signature, (d): Keypoints extracted from a questioned disguised signature (red=matching, blue=non-matching with the questioned signatures keypoints).

3 Local Features Based Systems

In this section we provide a short description of the three local features based offline signature verification systems considered in this study. Note that for the system 1 (i.e., SURF-FREAK) and system 2 (i.e., FAST-FREAK) we followed the same methodology of local interest point/areas detection and description. The difference between the two systems, however, is that in the first system we used the Speeded Up Robust Features (SURF) for detecting the signatures' local areas of interest and in the second system we used the Features from Accelerated Segment Test (FAST) for local interest areas detection. Later, in both the systems, we used the Fast Retina Keypoints (FREAK) descriptors of these local areas of interest in order to perform classification. In the following Section 3.1 we will describe the methodology we followed for the first two systems. Later in

Section 3.2 we will describe the third local features based system we applied in this study.

3.1   Methodology: System 1 and System 2

The proposed approach for signature verification is based on part-based/local features. To perform part-based analysis, it is first required to extract keypoints/ areas of interest from the signature images. The regions around these keypoints are then described using different descriptors. Hence, in the proposed approach in System 2, FAST [16] keypoint detector is used to detect keypoints in signature images. FAST keypoint detector is computationally efficient in comparison to well known keypoint detection methods, e.g., SIFT [17], Harris [18], and SURF [12] (we also compare results when we used SURF keypoint detector for finding the potential local areas of interest, in System 1). In addition, FAST gives a strong response on edges, which makes it suitable for the task of signature verification. Once the keypoints are detected, descriptor for each of the keypoints is computed using recently proposed part based descriptor, FREAK [19]. FREAK is a binary keypoint descriptor inspired by the retina in human visual system. These features are efficiently computed by sampling area around the keypoint on retinal pattern and encoding it as a binary string by comparing image intensities over this pattern. FREAK features are computationally very efficient in comparison to the well known part-based descriptors, i.e., SIFT [17] and SURF [12]. As the descriptors extracted using FREAK are binary, therefore Hamming distance is used for comparison of descriptors of query and reference signatures. The use of Hamming distance in-turn makes it computationally more efficient as it can be computed using a simple XOR operation on bit level. To categorize a signature as genuine, forged, or disguised, first it is binarized using the well known global binarization method OTSU [20]. We preferred using OTSU since we had fairly high resolution signature images and OTSU is also computationally efficient. After binarization, we applied the SURF/FAST keypoint detector on all the reference signatures, separately, to get the local areas of interest from these signatures. Then, obtained the descriptors of all of these keypoints present in all reference images using the FREAK keypoint descriptor. All of these keypoints and their associated descriptors describing important local information are added into a database. This resulted in a bag-of-features, which contained features for all of the keypoints which were collected from all reference signature images. Once the bag-of-features was created, keypoints and descriptors are extracted for the query/questioned signature. Now a comparison was made between the query signature keypoints and the keypoints present in our bag-of-features for that particular author. The same process of detecting local area of interest using FAST and then descriptors by FREAK is applied to the query image. After that we compared each of the query keypoints with the keyponts present in the bag-of-features. Kept this process going until all the query signatures keypoints were traversed. Finally, the average was calculated by considering the total number of query keypoints and the query keypoints matched with the bag-of-features. This represents the average local features of the questioned signature that were present in the bag-of-features of that author. Now, if this average was greater than an empirically found threshold θ, (meaning, most of the questioned signature local features are matched with reference local features present in the bag-of-features), the questioned signature was classified as belonging to the authentic author, otherwise (meaning, there were only a few query keypoints for whom any match is found in the reference bag-of features), the query signature did not belong to the authentic author. Figure 1a shows an example reference (genuine) signature and Figure 1b shows the correspond-ing SURF-keypoints extracted from this reference (genuine) signature. Similarly Figure 1c shows a questioned (forged) signature and Figure 1d shows a ques-tioned (disguised) signature, respectively, with SURF-keypoints extracted. Here blue dots represent the original questioned keypoints and red dots represent the keypoints matching with the reference signature keypoints.

3.2   System 3

In this system, given a scanned image as an input, first of all binarization is performed. Second, the image is normalized with respect to skew, writing width and baseline location. Normalization of the baseline location means that the body of the text line (the part which is located between the upper and the lower baselines), the ascender part (located above the upper baseline), and the descender part (below the lower baseline) is vertically scaled to a predefined size each. Writing width normalization is performed by a horizontal scaling operation, and its purpose is to scale the characters so that they have a predefined average width.

To extract the feature vectors from the normalized images, a sliding window approach is used. The width of the window is generally one pixel and nine geometrical features are computed at each window position. Thus an input text line is converted into a sequence of feature vectors in a 9-dimensional feature space. The nine features correspond to the following geometric quantities. The first three features are concerned with the overall distribution of the pixels in the sliding window. These are the average gray value of the pixels in the window, the center of gravity, and the second order moment in vertical direction. In addition to these global features, six local features describing specific points in the sliding window are used. These include the locations of the uppermost and lowermost black pixel and their positions and gradients, determined by using the neighboring windows. Feature number seven is the black to white transitions present within the entire window. Feature number eight is the number of black-white transitions between the uppermost and the lowermost pixel in an image column. Finally, the proportion of black pixels to the number of pixels between uppermost and lowermost pixels is used. For a detailed description of the features see [21].

Gaussian Mixture Models [22] have been used to model the handwriting of each person. More specifically, the distribution of feature vectors extracted from a person's handwriting is modeled by a Gaussian mixture density. For a

D-dimensional feature vector denoted as x, the mixture density for a given writer (with the corresponding model A) is defined as:

$$p(x\|A) = \sum_{i=1}^{m} w_i p_i(x)$$

In other words, the density is a weighted linear combination of M uni-modal Gaussian densities, $p_i(x)$, each parameterized by a $D \times 1$ mean vector, and D*D covariance matrix. For further details refer to [23], and [24].

4   Evaluation

4.1   Dataset

We used the test set of the 4NSigComp2010 signature verification competition for evaluations. This is the first ever publicly available dataset containing disguised signatures. The collection contains only offline signature samples. The signatures are collected by forensic handwriting examiners and scanned at 600 dpi resolution. The collection contains 125 signatures. There are 25 reference signatures by the same writer and 100 questioned signatures by various writers. The 100 questioned signatures comprise 3 genuine signatures written by the reference writer in her/his normal signature style and 7 disguised signatures written by the reference writer where s(he) tried to disguise herself/himself (the reference writer provided a set of signatures over a five day period); and 90 simulated signatures (written by 34 forgers freehand copying the signature characteristics of the reference writer. The forgers were volunteers and were either lay persons or calligraphers.). All writings were made using the same make of ball-point pen and using the same make of paper.

4.2   Results

As mentioned above, our evaluation data contained 3 genuine, 7 disguised, and 90 forged signatures. This is not a problem for the evaluation since we computed the Equal Error Rates (EER), calculated when the False Reject Rate (rate at which genuine and/or disguised signatures are misclassified as forged by a system) is same as the False Accept Rate (rate at which forged signatures are misclassified as genuine by a system).

We performed three experiments for evaluating the efficiency and EER of the three systems explained above and also compared their performance against all the other participants of the 4NSigComp2010 signature verification competition (the participants were tested on the same data under the same conditions in [4]).

- Experiment 1 that focused the classification of disguised, forged, and genuine signatures using FAST Kepypoint detector and FREAK features.
- Experiment 2 that focused the same classification using SURF Kepypoint detector and FREAK features.

Table 1. Summary of the comparisons performed among the participants of the 4NSigComp2010 (from systems 1 to 7) and mentioned local features based systems

System	FAR	FRR	EER	Time (sec.)
1	1.1	90	80	312
2	41.1	90	58	1944
3	20.0	70	70	85
4	0.0	80	70	19
5	13.3	80	55	45
6	87.0	10	60	730
7	1.1	80	70	65
(SURF-FREAK)	30	30	30	12
(FAST-FREAK)	30	30	30	**0.6**
(Bunke-GMM)	20	20	**20**	100

- Experiment 3 that focused the same classification using Bunke [21] features and GMM classification.

The results of these experiments are provided in Table 1. As shown in the table, all of our proposed local feature based systems, i.e., SURF-FREAK, FAST-FREAK, and Bunke-GMM outperform all the participants of the 4NSig Comp2010 signature verification competition in terms of EER. The best system from the competition could achieve an EER of 55%, whereas, the Bunke features based system reached an EER of 20% and both the SURF-FREAK and FAST-FREAK systems achieve an EER of 30%.

Furthermore, Table 1 also presents the performance comparison of the said systems on the basis of time. The time is given in seconds and is actually the average time taken by any algorithm to report its result on the authenticity of one questioned signature. For reporting this result, the system has to process the questioned as well as 25 reference signatures. Both of the proposed systems again outperformed all the participants. Specially the FAST-FREAK method is extremely time efficient. It succeeds from the other nine methods by a times of (520, 3240, 141, 31, 75, 1216, 108, 166, and 20 respectively). We performed all the tests at a machine with the following specifications.

- Processor: Intel Dual Core 1.73 GHz
- Memory: 1GB
- OS: WinXP Professional

A general drawback of most of the local features based approaches is the enormous amount of time they take to compute results. In our experiments, most of the participating systems were relying on global features except the proposed systems, yet the execution of the proposed systems was fairly time efficient than other systems. This shows that, if utilized properly, local feature approaches show the potential of improving both performance and efficiency of classification.

5   Conclusion and Future Work

In this paper we have compared three of our part based forensic signature verification systems with each other and also with all the systems that participated in
the 4NSigComp2010 signature verification competition. We explicitly considered
the time required and equal error rate achieved by each system. We performed
three experiments with three different local feature sets. In the first system we
used a combination of SURF-FREAK, in the second: a combination of FAST-
FREAK, and in the third system we used the Bunke features. All of these local
features based systems outperformed the participants of the 4NSigComp2010
signature verification competition by achieving EERs of 30%, 30%, and 20%,
respectively. Whereas the EER of the best participant in the 4NSigComp2010
competition was 55%.

Furthermore, we have made a time efficiency comparison among the considered local features based systems and the participants of the 4NSigComp2010.
Here again our local features based systems out-performed other participants
and one of our systems (i.e., FAST-FREAK) outperformed all other systems
remarkably.

In future we plan to use larger data sets where disguised signatures from
large number of authors are present in the test set. Regarding the systems' outcomes, we plan to enable them produce likelihood ratios according to Bayesian
approach, which will make these systems even more useful in the real world
forensic casework. This, however, is a difficult task since respective likelihood
computation of multiple classes is required in this case.

References

1. Plamondon, R., Lorette, G.: Automatic signature verification and writer identification – the state of the art. Pattern Recognition 22, 107–131 (1989)
2. Plamondon, R., Srihari, S.N.: On-line and off-line handwriting recognition: A comprehensive survey. IEEE TPAMI 22, 63–84 (2000)
3. Impedovo, D., Pirlo, G.: Automatic Signature Verification: The State of the Art.
   IEEE Trans. on Systems, Man, and Cybernetics, Part C (Applications and Reviews) 38, 609–635 (2008)
4. Liwicki, M., van den Heuvel, C.E., Found, B., Malik, M.I.: Forensic signature
   verification competition 4NSigComp2010 - detection of simulated and disguised
   signatures. In: ICFHR 2010, pp. 715–720 (2010)
5. Malik, M.I., Liwicki, M., Dengel, A.: Evaluation of local and global features for
   offline signature verification. In: 1st Int. Workshop on Automated Forensic Handwriting Analysis (AFHA), pp. 26–30 (2011)
6. De Stefano, C., Marcelli, A., Rendina, M.: Disguising writers identification: an
   experimental study. In: IGS 2009, pp. 99–102 (2009)
7. Fiel, S., Sablatnig, R.: Writer Retrieval and Writer Identification Using Local Features. In: DAS 2012, pp. 145–149 (2012)
8. Zhiyi, Z., Lianwen, J., Kai, D., Xue, G.: Character-SIFT: A Novel Feature for Offline Handwritten Chinese Character Recognition. In: ICDAR, pp. 763–767 (2009)

9. Jin, Z., Qi, K.-Y., Chen, K.: SSIFT: An Improved SIFT Descriptor for Chinese Character Recognition in Complex Images. In: CNMT, pp. 1–5 (2009)
10. Song, W., Uchida, S., Liwicki, M.: Comparative Study of Part-Based Handwritten Character Recognition Methods. In: ICDAR 2011, pp. 814–818 (2011)
11. Ta, D.-N., Chen, W.-C., Gelfand, N., Pulli, K.: SURFTrac: Efficient tracking and continuous object recognition using local feature descriptors. In: IEEE C. S. Conf. on Computer Vision and Pattern Recognition, pp. 2937–2944 (2009)
12. Bay, H., Ess, A., Tuytelaars, T., Van Gool, L.: Speeded-Up Robust Features (SURF). Comput. Vis. Image Underst. 110(3), 346–359 (2008)
13. Jeong, K., Moon, H.: Object Detection Using FAST Corner Detector Based on Smartphone Platforms. In: First Int. Conf. on Computers, Networks, Systems and Industrial Engineering (CNSI), pp. 111–115 (2011)
14. Bilinski, P., Bremond, F., Kaaniche, M.B.: Multiple object tracking with occlusions using HOG descriptors and multi resolution images. In: ICDP 2009, pp. 1–6 (2009)
15. Diem, M., Sablatnig, R.: Recognition of Degraded Handwritten Characters Using Local Features. In: ICDAR 2009, pp. 221–225 (2009)
16. Rosten, E., Drummond, T.: Fusing points and lines for high performance tracking. In: 10th Int. Conf. on Computer Vision, pp. 1508–1515 (2005)
17. Lowe, D.G.: Object recognition from local scale-invariant features. In: 7th Int. Conf. on Computer Vision, pp. 1150–1157 (1999)
18. Harris, C., Stephens, M.: A combined corner and edge detector. In: 4th Alvey Vision Conf., pp. 147–151 (1988)
19. Alahi, A., Ortiz, R., Vandergheynst, P.: FREAK: Fast Retina Keypoint. In: CVPR 2012, pp. 510–517 (2012)
20. Otsu, N.: A threshold selection method from gray-level histograms. Automatica 111, 285–296 (1975)
21. Marti, U.-V., Bunke, H.: Using a statistical language model to improve the performance of an HMM-based cursive handwriting recognition system. IJPRAI 110(15), 65–90 (2001)
22. Marithoz, J., Bengio, S.: A comparative study of adaptation methods for speaker verification. In: Int. Conf. on Spoken Language Processing, pp. 581–584 (2002)
23. Liwicki, M.: Evaluation of Novel Features and Different Models for Online Signature Verification in a Real-World Scenario. In: 14th Conf. of Int. Graphonomics Society, pp. 22–25 (2009)
24. Schlapbach, A., Liwicki, M., Bunke, H.: A Writer Identification System for On-line Whiteboard Data. PR 41(7), 2381–2397 (2008)

Exploiting Stability Regions
for Online Signature Verification

Antonio Parziale, Salvatore G. Fuschetto, and Angelo Marcelli

Natural Computation Laboratory,
DIEM, University of Salerno
Via Ponte Don Melillo, Fisciano (SA), Italy
{anparziale,amarcelli}@unisa.it, sgfuschetto@gmail.com
http://nclab.diiie.unisa.it

Abstract. We present a method for finding the stability regions within a set of genuine signatures and for selecting the most suitable one to be used for online signature verification. The definition of stability region builds upon motor learning and adaptation in handwriting generation, while their selection exploits both their ability to model signing habits and their effectiveness in capturing distinctive features. The stability regions represent the core of a signature verification system whose performance is evaluated on a standard benchmark.

Keywords: online signature verification, stability region, handwriting generation, motor learning.

1 Introduction

Handwritten signatures are an interesting biometric characteristic, since they are largely used and accepted in daily life as proof of one individual's identity.

As any handwriting, they are obtained by concatenating elementary movements, or strokes, in such a way that their execution requests the minimum amount of metabolic energy. Such an optimization is learned along the years by repeated practice, so that signing becomes automated and can be performed, at least partially, without any proprioceptive feedback, as it was an elementary movement. When the signature has been completely learned, i.e. it becomes a distinctive feature of the subject, it is stored in the brain as a motor plan that incorporates both the sequence of target points, i.e. the points where two successive strokes join, and the sequence of motor command to be executed to draw the desired shape between them [1]. The encoding of such a motor plan, moreover, is independent of the actuator [2].

According to those findings, multiple executions of the signature by the subject may produce ink traces with different shapes only because of variations on both the psychophysical conditions of the subject and the signing conditions, since the motor plan remains the same [3,4]. It is also expected, however, that the variations in the signing conditions mentioned above may affect only some of the signature features, but not all of them. For this reason, one of the aspects

A. Petrosino, L. Maddalena, P. Pala (Eds.): ICIAP 2013 Workshops, LNCS 8158, pp. 112–121, 2013.
© Springer-Verlag Berlin Heidelberg 2013

around which is centered the research activity in the field of signature verification is the detection of stability regions, which are the traits of ink that are shared by different executions of the signature.

Signature stability can be estimated directly from the signature signal or indirectly on the set of features used for representing the signature [3]. Among the methods for directly estimating on-line signature stability, those using DTW to derive a local stability function [5,6], are the most similar to the one presented in this paper, in that the analysis of local stability is used to select the best subset of reference signatures.

In this work we present a method for the detection of stability regions in online signatures. The proposed method assumes as stability regions the longest common sequences of similar strokes between pairs of signatures. This assumption follows from the observation that, as discussed above, signing is the automated execution of a well-learned motor task, and therefore repeated executions should produce, at least ideally, the same movements and therefore ink traces with the same shapes. Because of the variations in the signing conditions, it happens that the ink traces are different, but because they results from the execution of the same motor plan, and because the effects of different initial conditions in signing attenuate quickly during writing, it is expected that only short sequences of strokes will exhibit different shapes. The longer the sequence of similar strokes the longer the time during which the same motor program is executed under the same conditions.

Once the stability regions of the genuine signatures have been found, the classification of a questioned signature as either genuine or forged is achieved by evaluating the longest common sequence of similar strokes between the ink trace of the questioned and those of the genuine containing the selected stability regions.

The remaining of the paper is organized as it follows. In section 2 we illustrate the method for finding the stability regions between a pair of signatures, and discuss how they can be used for selecting the reference signatures. The selected reference signatures and their associated stability regions are then used in a signature verification experiment reported in section 3. Eventually, in the conclusion we discuss the performance achieved by the proposed method and outline our future research.

2   Modeling Stability in Signatures

In a previous work we have introduced an earlier version of our method for finding stability regions between two signatures [7]. Here we introduce a new version of the method, that takes in account the existing correlation between consecutive strokes, and an alternative criterion for finding stability regions in a set of N signatures.

2.1   Searching for Stability Regions between Two Signatures

The proposed method assumes that the signature signal has been segmented into a sequence of strokes, each of which has been label as ascender, descender or normal, and the detection of the stability regions is achieved by an ink matcher that finds the longest common sequences of strokes with similar shapes between the ink traces of a pair of signatures. For deciding when two sequences are similar enough, i.e. when they match, the method exploits the concept of saliency that has been proposed to account for attentional gaze shift in primate visual system [8]. Accordingly, sequence of strokes that are "globally" more similar than other will stand out in the saliency map.

To implement such an approach one needs to define a scale space, to find a similarity measure to be adopted at each scale, to compute the saliency map, and eventually to select the matching pieces of ink. We have adopted as scale the number of strokes in the sequences whose similarity is being measured. Such a number will be referred in the following as the *length* of the sequence. Let us assume that the two sequences have N and M strokes, respectively. The number of scales corresponds to the length $K \leq min(N, M)$ of the longest common sequence of strokes. Note that the inequality sign holds because we assume that ascenders and descenders can match only themselves, not normal strokes. Thus, K represents the length of the longest common sequence of compatible strokes, i.e. strokes that can be matched. Successive scales are obtained considering sequences made of $k = K, K - 1, ..., 2$ strokes [9]. As similarity measure, we adopt the Weighted Edit Distance (WED), which measures the shape similarity between pair of strokes [10]. The shape similarity of a sequence is obtained by adding the WED of its strokes. After the shape similarity is evaluated at each scale, we compute its saliency as it follows. At each scale k, the most similar pair of sequence is selected and the saliency S_{ij}^k of all its strokes is computed as $S_{ij}^k = WED_{ij}/k$. Thus, the saliency map for a pair of inks made of N and M strokes, respectively, assumes the shape of an NxM array, whose elements are either 0, in case of incompatible strokes, or $\sum_K S_{ij}^k$. The saliency map is then thresholded, and the longest diagonal sequences of values S_{ij}^k greater than the threshold S_{th} are selected and they are named *invariants*.

As previously said, an ink trace is the result of a complex motor task that can be decomposed in elementary movements. It is important to point out that each stroke is not independent by the others but it is affected by the movements realized before it and by those that will be realized after it. It means that another parameter is needed to describing globally a strokes sequence and giving a reliability measure of the similarity evaluated before. For this purpose, given an invariant that goes from stroke T_1 to stroke T_2, we introduce another parameter named *compatibility*:

$$C = \sum_{t=T_1}^{T_2} WED_t * \beta_t \tag{1}$$

where β_t takes into account the difference of slope variation between two consecutive strokes in the reference and in the query signature.

Fig. 1. The segmentation points (dots) and the stability regions (bold) of two signatures

Therefore, the invariants with a compatibility greater than a threshold C_{th} are the stability regions between pair of signatures, as shown in (Fig. 1)

2.2   Searching for Stability Regions in a Set of N Signatures

In way of principle, one would expect that the stability regions appear in all the signatures of a subject, and therefore would define the stability regions of a set of N signatures as the longest common subsequences of the stability regions computed for every available pair of signatures. In practice, however, both the stroke segmentation and the ink matching may introduce errors in locating the segmentation points and/or in deciding when a sequence of strokes is similar to another, that may produce different stability regions for the set of signatures. For all these reasons, we must define how many and which are the most representatives signatures, hereinafter called *references*, of a given data set. As with regards to the number of references, we restrict our investigation to 2 and 3, because this is the number of genuine signatures generally available in real life applications. Therefore, given a set of N signatures we have $\binom{N}{2}$ and $\binom{N}{3}$ subsets of signatures respectively, and we need to find the most representative ones.

According to our basic assumption, longer stability regions correspond to longer sequence of elementary movements executed in a highly automated fashion. Because the level of automation is the result of the learning process described above, and because the learning is an individual feature, long stability regions are more subject-specific than short ones. Accordingly, we can select as *references* the signatures corresponding to the longest stability regions.

Another suitable criterion is to select as references the signatures that minimize the equal error rate on a verification experiment performed on the training set composed by genuine and forgery samples.

3   Experimental Validation

The detection of the stability regions and its effectiveness in a verification problem can be modulated by choosing the thresholds S_{th} and C_{th} of the ink matcher stage and the number of references. A set of experiments has therefore been executed for evaluating the effect of the value of those parameters on the performance.

3.1   The Datasets

The performance of the proposed method has been evaluated on the signatures of SVC2004 database [11] and on the signatures of the Blind subcorpus of the SUSIG database [12]. The first contains 20 genuine and 20 forgery signatures for each of 100 subjects, for a total of 40,000 specimen divided in training set, which is publicly available, and test sets that is not available. The second database contains 10 genuine and 10 forgery signatures for each of 60 subjects. The protocol proposed during the *First International Signature Verification Competition* [11] has been adopted during the test:

1. Skilled forgery detection: For each subject the genuine signatures are randomly divided in two disjoined subsets: 5 samples are used together with 5 forgery signature as training set, the remaining are added to the set of forgery signatures and used as test set.
2. Random forgery detection: the training set is built as before, whereas the test set includes as forgery 20 genuine signatures produced by 20 different subjects.

3.2   The Classification Rule

In this work we are interested in presenting and evaluating the method for the detection of the stability regions by means of a signature verification experiment. For this reason, we use a simple classification rule for showing that the obtained results mainly depend on the selection of the stability regions and not on the classification scheme. Each signature of the training set, either genuine or not, is mapped in a N dimensional space Γ, where N is the number of references, and whose dimensions are:

$$r_i = \frac{L_m(f, ref_i)}{L_s(ref_i)} \quad i = 1, ..., N \tag{2}$$

In equation 2, L_m is the length of the longest common sequence of strokes between the signature under verification f and the reference ref_i and L_s is the length of the stability region found in ref_i. Each r_i ranges between 0 and 1. For the sake of clarity, let's consider the case $N = 2$. In such a case, Γ assumes the shape of a square, whose vertices are (0,0), (0,1), (1,0) and (1,1). In such a space, genuine signatures should have a (long) match with the stability regions of both references, and therefore should be represented by points close to the vertex of coordinates (1,1). On the contrary, forged signatures should not have a (long) match with any of the stability regions of the references, and therefore should be represented by points near to the vertex of coordinates (0,0). Thus, it is possible to find two thresholds, T_g and T_f, by maximizing both the number of genuine signatures correctly classified whose distances from the vertex (1,1) is smaller than T_g, and the number of forgery correctly classified whose distances from the vertex (0,0) is smaller than T_f, as shown in figure 2. Then, the selected references and the value of T_g and T_f model the signing habit of the subject with respect to a given population of writers. The verification is eventually achieved by mapping the signatures under verification in Γ as above, and by computing the distances d_f and d_g between the point representing the signature and the two vertices (0,0) and (1,1), respectively. The decision criterion follows naturally from above:

```
if [(df >= Tf) AND (dg >= Tg) AND (df - Tf) < (dg - Tg)] OR
[(df < Tf) AND (dg >= Tg)] then
            forgery;
if [(df >= Tf) AND (dg >= Tg) AND (df - Tf) >= (dg - Tg)] OR
[(df >= Tf) AND (dg < Tg)] then
            genuine;
if [(df < Tf) AND (dg < Tg)] then
        if [(df - Tf) < (dg - Tg)] then
        forgery;
    else
        genuine;
```

3.3 Results

The classification rules are applied for different values of S_{th} and C_{th} in four different conditions:

1. ref2_H0: 2 genuine signatures with the longest stability region are selected as references by the training set;

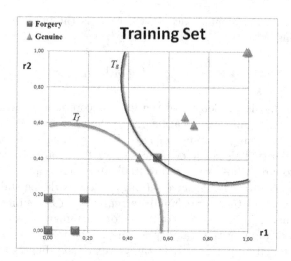

Fig. 2. The signatures from the training set and the decision region for genuine and forgery

2. ref2_H1: 2 genuine signatures that minimize the EER on the training set are selected as references;
3. ref3_H0: 3 genuine signatures with the longest stability region are selected as references by the training set;
4. ref3_H1: 3 genuine signatures that minimize the EER on the training set are selected as references.

In the experiments, S_{th} and C_{th} were chosen by using a grid search with $S_{th} = (0.70 \div 1.0)$ and $C_{th} = (0.40 \div 0.80)$. In the figures 3 and 4 we plot EER_{avg} as function of C_{th} for $S_{th} = 0.9$ in case when the test set includes skilled and random forgeries, respectively. The best results on the SVC2004 database were obtained using $S_{th} = 0.9$, $C_{th} = 0.75$ and selecting as references the two genuine signatures that minimize the EER on the training set. The test executed on the SUSig dataset confirmed that the best performance was obtained by selecting the references as above, whereas the best values for the parameters of the ink matcher stage were $S_{th} = 0.9$ and $C_{th} = 0.5$. In this case, a smaller value of compatibility is required because the signatures are shorter and segmented in a smaller number of strokes than the samples of the SVC2004 database and then shorter stability regions are obtained. Table 1 reports the performance of our method in its best configuration in comparison with those participating in the SVC2004 benchmark.

4   Conclusions

We have presented a model for describing the signature of a subject centered upon the concept of the stability regions. In particular, we have discussed about

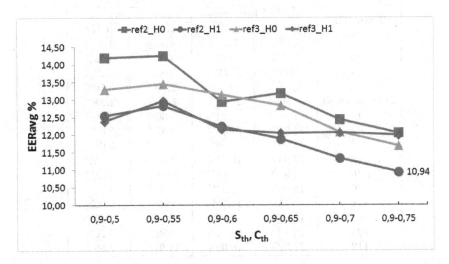

Fig. 3. Trials performed on the test set composed by genuine and skilled forgery signatures. EER_{avg} values are obtained with different scheme of references selection and different values of ink matching threshold $S_{th}\ C_{th}$.

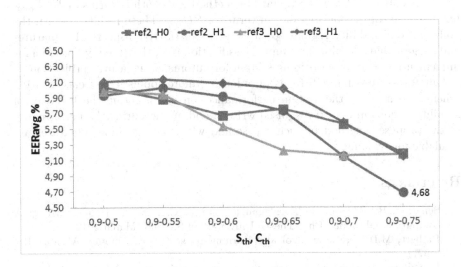

Fig. 4. Trials performed on the test set composed by genuine and random forgery signatures. EER_{avg} values are obtained with different scheme of references selection and different values of ink matching threshold $S_{th}\ C_{th}$.

Table 1. Results on SVC2004 database

Team ID	skilled forgeries		random forgeries	
	EERavg	**EERsd**	**EERavg**	**EERsd**
106	5.50%	7.73%	3.65%	4.80%
126	6.45%	10.41%	3.49%	4.53%
124	7.33%	7.71%	2.93%	3.72%
115	9.80%	13.90%	2.90%	3.60%
Our method	**10.94%**	**2.97%**	**4.68%**	**2.38%**
114	11.10%	11.11%	3.36%	4.36%
119c	11.98%	17.65%	2.87%	3.68%
119b	11.99%	17.66%	2.88%	3.68%
118	14.34%	16.11%	4.29%	5.45%
119a	14.91%	18.98%	2.90%	3.64%
116	15.67%	13.24%	2.89%	3.64%
117	16.45%	11.79%	4.66%	5.22%
104	18.99%	13.95%	11.57%	13.28%
103	25.83%	22.11%	6.58%	9.20%
112	31.32%	18.09%	11.67%	9.58%

how to select a limited number of signatures by a given set of N genuine signatures for finding the most robust stability regions for a subject. We have evaluated the effectiveness of the proposed definition of stability by performing a signature verification experiment based on a standard protocol and using two standard datasets of online signatures.

The results in Table 1 show that our method ranks 5th in terms of EER_{avg}, but it is the top performing one in terms of SD_{avg}. These results confirm the ability of our stability regions to capture the distinctive aspects of signatures and suggest that, despite the simple classification rule, they are a viable tool for implementing a good performing system for automatic signature verification.

Our future research will focus on adopting more sophisticated classification schemes to improve the system performance, on investigating the behavior of stability regions in case of disguised writers, and on measuring the performance of the proposed method in such a case and when only genuine signatures are available for training.

References

1. Senatore, R.: The role of Basal ganglia and Cerebellum in Motor Learning: A computational model. PhD Thesis, University of Salerno (March 2012)
2. Raibert, M.H.: Motor control and learning by state space model. AILab. MIT (1977)
3. Impedovo, D., Pirlo, G.: Automatic signature verification: the state of the art. IEEE Transactions on Systems, Man, and Cybernetics, Part C: Applications and Reviews 38(5), 609–635 (2008)
4. Impedovo, D., Pirlo, G., Plamondon, R.: Handwritten Signature Verification: New Advancements and Open Issues. In: 2012 International Conference on Frontiers in Handwriting Recognition (ICFHR), pp. 367–372. IEEE (September 2012)

5. Dimauro, G., Impedovo, S., Modugno, R., Pirlo, G., Sarcinella, L.: Analysis of stability in hand-written dynamic signatures. In: Eighth International Workshop on Frontiers in Handwriting Recognition, pp. 259–263. IEEE (2002)
6. Huang, K., Yan, H.: Stability and style-variation modeling for on-line signature verification. Pattern Recognition 36(10), 2253–2270 (2003)
7. Marcelli, A., Fuschetto, S.G., Parziale, A.: Modeling Stability in On-line Signatures. In: Proceedings of IGS 2013, pp. 135–138 (June 2013)
8. Itti, L., Koch, C., Niebur, E.: A model of saliency-based visual attention for rapid scene analysis. IEEE Transactions on Pattern Analysis and Machine Intelligence 20(11), 1254–1259 (1998)
9. De Stefano, C., Marcelli, A., Santoro, A.: On-line cursive recognition by ink matching. In: Phillips, J.G., Rogers, D., Ogeil, R.P. (eds.) Proceedings of IGS 2007, pp. 23–37 (2007)
10. De Stefano, C., Garruto, M., Lapresa, L., Marcelli, A.: Using strings for on-line handwriting shape matching: A new weighted edit distance. In: Roli, F., Vitulano, S. (eds.) ICIAP 2005. LNCS, vol. 3617, pp. 1125–1132. Springer, Heidelberg (2005)
11. Yeung, D.-Y., Chang, H., Xiong, Y., George, S., Kashi, R., Matsumoto, T., Rigoll, G.: SVC2004: First international signature verification competition. In: Zhang, D., Jain, A.K. (eds.) ICBA 2004. LNCS, vol. 3072, pp. 16–22. Springer, Heidelberg (2004)
12. Kholmatov, A., Yanikoglu, B.: SUSIG: an on-line signature database, associated protocols and benchmark results. Pattern Analysis and Applications 12(3), 227–236 (2009)

Stability of Dynamic Signatures:
From the Representation to the Generation Domain

Giuseppe Pirlo[1], Donato Impedovo[1], Rejean Plamondon[2], Christian O'Reilly[2],
A. Cozzolongo[1], R. Gravinese[1], and Andrea Rollo[1]

[1] Dipartimento di Informatica, Università degli Studi di Bari, Italy
[2] Ecole Polytecnique de Montreal, Canada
giuseppe.pirlo@uniba.it

Abstract. Stability analysis of handwritten signatures is very relevant for automatic signature verification. In this paper the analysis of stability is performed by considering the characteristics of the processes underlying signature generation. More precisely, the analysis of stability is performed by considering the Sigma-Lognormal parameters, according to the Kinematic Theory. The experimental tests, carried out using the SUSig database, demonstrate that the new technique can provide useful information both for a deep understanding of the processes of signature generation and for the improvement of the processes for automatic signature verification.

Keywords: Biometry, Automatic Signature Verification, Stability Analysis, Sigma-Lognormal.

1 Introduction

In the contemporary society, handwritten signature is a common trait for personal authentication and people are familiar with its use [1].

Unfortunately, a handwritten signature is a very complex trait. The rapid writing movement underlying handwritten signature generation is determined by a motor program stored into the signer's brain and implemented through the signer's writing system and writing devices (paper and pen type, etc.). Therefore, each handwritten signature strongly depends on a multitude of factors such as the psychophysical state of the signer and its social and cultural environment as well as the conditions under which the signature apposition acquisition process occurs [2,3]. Hence, it is not surprising that although there is a growing interest in the field of automatic signature verification, several basic aspects concerning the nature of this very special kind of biometric trait are still open to investigation. Indeed, research on automatic signature verification is a multifaceted field of research involving aspects from disciplines as wide ranging as human anatomy and engineering, neuroscience and computer sciences, and so on.

One of the basic aspects that is currently at the centre of a large debate concerns signature stability [4,5]. In fact, everyone is aware that his/her signature is never the

A. Petrosino, L. Maddalena, P. Pala (Eds.): ICIAP 2013 Workshops, LNCS 8158, pp. 122–130, 2013.
© Springer-Verlag Berlin Heidelberg 2013

same even if each of us generally learns to sign at an early age and practices constantly to produce similar signatures according to his/her specific and personal model. Hence, stability in handwritten signatures is a crucial characteristic for investigating the intrinsic human properties related to handwriting generation processes concerning human psychology and biophysics. In addition, its study can provide new insights for a more accurate treatment of signatures for verification purposes, hence contributing to the design of more effective signature verification systems. For these reasons, it is not surprising that the scientific community has been devoting much effort to the analysis of signature stability.

When considering dynamic signatures, many approaches estimate signature stability by the analysis of a specific set of characteristics. In general, these approaches have shown that there is a set of features which remain stable over long time periods, while others can change significantly in time [6,7]. More precisely, a comparative study of the consistency of certain features of dynamic signatures has demonstrated that position, velocity and pen inclination can be considered to be among the most consistent, when a distance-based consistency model is applied [6]. Other results based on personal entropy demonstrated that position is a stronger characteristic than pressure and pen inclination in both short and long-term variability. Moreover, although pressure may give better performance results in a short-term context, it is not recommended for signature verification in a long-term.

When static signatures are considered, the degree of stability of each region of a signature can be estimated by a multiple pattern-matching technique [8,9]. The basic idea is to match corresponding regions of genuine signatures in order to estimate the extent to which they are locally different. Of course, a preliminary step is used to determine the best alignment of the corresponding regions of signatures, in order to diminish any differences among them.

This paper presents a new technique for the analysis of local stability in dynamic signature. This technique applies Dynamic Time Warping (DTW) to match signatures in their generation domain according to the Sigma-Lognormal model. The organization of this paper is the following. Section 2 presents the Sigma- Lognormal model. Section 3 presents the new technique for the analysis of stability based on Dynamic Time Warping and Section 4 presents the experimental results, carried out on signatures of the SuSig database. Finally, section 5 presents the conclusion of the work.

2   Sigma-Lognormal Model

The kinematic theory of rapid human movement[10], relies on the Sigma-Lognormal model to represent the information of both the motor commands and timing properties of the neuromuscular system involved in the production of complex movements like signature [11,12].

The Sigma-Lognormal model considers the resulting speed of a single stroke j as having a lognormal shape Λ scaled by a command parameter (D) and time-shifted by the time occurrence of the command (t0):

$$\left| \vec{v}_j(t; P_j) \right| = D_j \Lambda(t - t_{0j}; \mu_j, \sigma_j^2) = \frac{D_j}{\sigma(t - t_{0j})\sqrt{2\pi}} \exp\left\{ \frac{\left[\ln(t - t_{0j}) - \mu_j\right]^2}{-2\sigma_j^2} \right\} \quad (1)$$

where $P_j = [D_j, t_{0j}, \mu_j, \sigma_j, \Theta_{sj}, \Theta_{ej}]$ represents the sets of Sigma-Lognormal parameters[11]:

- D_j : amplitude of the input commands;
- t_{0j} : time occurrence of the input commands, a time-shift parameter;
- μ_j: log-time delays, the time delay of the neuromuscular system expressed on a logarithmic time scale;
- σ_j: log-response times, which are the response times of the neuromuscular system expressed on a logarithmic time scale;
- Θ_{sj}: starting angle of the circular trajectories described by the lognormal model along pivot;
- Θ_{ej}: ending angle of the circular trajectories described by the lognormal model along pivot.

Additionally, from the hypothesis that every lognormal stroke represents the movement as happening along pivot, the angular position can be computed as [11]:

$$\phi_j(t; P_j) = \theta_{sj} + \frac{\theta_{ej} - \theta_{sj}}{D_j} \int_0^t \left| \vec{v}(\tau; P_j) \right| d\tau \quad (2)$$

In this context, a signature can be seen as the output of a generator that produces a set of individual strokes superimposed in time. The resulting complex trajectories can be modeled as a vector summation of lognormal distributions (being N_{LN} the total number of lognormal curves in which the handwritten trace is decomposed):

$$\vec{v}(t) = \sum \Lambda(t) = \sum_{j=1}^{N_{LN}} \vec{v}_j(t; P_j) \quad (3)$$

For each of the components of the signature, and then for each stroke, it can define some profiles that add information to those already expressed by the parameters of the Sigma-Lognormal [10]. For the aims of this paper, the most relevant profile is the velocity profile, that is expressed by this expression:

$$v_i(t) = \frac{D_i}{\sigma_i(t - t_{0i}\sqrt{2\pi})} e^{-\frac{1}{2\sigma_i^2}[\ln((t-t_{0i}))-\mu_i]^2} \quad (4)$$

Of course, expression (4) reaches its maximum for

$$t = t_0 + \exp(-\sigma^2 + \mu) \tag{5}$$

According to the Sigma-Lognormal model, in this paper a signature S^t is characterized in the generation domain by a sequence of couples

$$S^r = (z^r_1, z^r_2, z^r_3, \ldots z^r_j, \ldots, z^r_m) \tag{6}$$

where each couple $z^r_j = (t_j, v_j(t_j))$ describes synthetically the j-th lognormal curve in which the signature is decomposed (in eq. (6) it is supposed that a signature is decomposed in m lognormal curves).

3   Analysis of Stability by Dynamic Time Warping

Stability analysis is here performed by the DTW, that is used to match the sequences representing sets of genuine signatures. Precisely, a local stability function is here defined starting from a set $S = \{ S^r \mid r=1,2,\ldots,n \}$ of n hand-written signatures of the same writer. According to eq. (6) S^r is described as [13]:

$$S^r = (z^r_1, z^r_2, z^r_3, \ldots z^r_j, \ldots, z^r_m) \tag{7}$$

Let be S^r, S^t two signatures of S. A warping function between S^r and S^t is any sequence of couples of indexes identifying points of S^r and S^t to be joined:

$$W(S^r, S^t) = C^1, C^2, \ldots C^k \tag{8}$$

where $c^k=(i^k,j^k)$ (k,i^k,j^k integers, $1 \leq k \leq K$, $1 \leq i^k \leq M^r$, $1 \leq j^k \leq M^t$).
   Now, if we consider a distance measure

$$D(C^k) = d(z^r_{ik}, z^t_{jk}) \tag{9}$$

between points of S^r and S^t, we can associate to warping function in (9) the dissimilarity measure

$$D(W(S^r,S^t)) = \sum_{k=1}^{K} d(C^k) \tag{10}$$

The elastic matching procedure detects the warping function

$$W^*(S^r, S^t) = C^{*1}, C^{*2}, \ldots, C^{*K} \tag{11}$$

which satisfies the monotonicity, continuity and boundary conditions, and for which it results [4]

$$D(W*(S^r,S^t)) = \min{}_{W(S^r, S^t)} W*(S^r,S^t) \tag{12}$$

From the warping function in (11) we identify the Direct Matching Points (DMP) of S^r with respect to S^t [4,14].

In the generation domain, a DMP of a signature S^r with respect to S^t is a lognormal curve which has a one-to-one coupling with a lognormal curve S^t. In other words, let z^r_p be a curve of S^r coupled with z^t_q of S^t ; $z^r(p)$ is DMP of S^r with respect to S^t iff [14, 15, 16]:

- $\forall$ p' = 1,....,M^r, it results that $z^r_{p'}$ is not coupled with z^t_q;   (13a)
- $\forall$ q' = 1,....,M^t, it results that $z^t_{q'}$ is not coupled with z^r_p;   (13b)

Now, a DMP indicates the existence of a curve of the generation process of the r-th signature which is roughly similar to the corresponding curve of the t-th signature. Therefore, for each curve of index p of S^r, a score is introduced according to its type of coupling with respect to the corresponding index of S^t [17]:

- $Score^t(z^r_p) = 1$ if z^r_p is a DMP   (14a)
- $Score^t(z^r_p) = 0$ if z^r_p is not a DMP   (14b)

Of course, when the genuine signature S^t is matched against all the genuine signatures of the set (7), we can derive the local stability function of S^t for each lognormal curve, by averaging the scores obtained from eqs. (14) as follows :

$$L(z^t_i) = \frac{1}{n-1} \sum_{\substack{s=1 \\ s \neq r}}^{s} Score^i(z^t_i) \tag{15}$$

The global stability function for the signature S^t can be defined as:

$$G(z^t) = \frac{1}{m} \sum_{j=1}^{m} L(z^t_j) \tag{16}$$

4   Experimental Results

For the testing stage the signatures of the Visual SubCorpus of the SuSig database (developed at the Sabançi University – Turkey) were used. The Visual SubCorpus is composed by 10 genuine signatures and 10 forgery signatures, acquired by 94 authors, that are maximally students or associates of the Sabançi University, aged between 21 and 52 years [15].

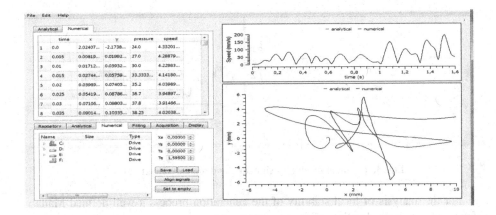

Fig. 1. An example of using ScriptStudio for parameter extraction

For each signature, Sigma-Lognormal parameters were extracted using Script Studio [11]. Figure 1 shows an example of parameter extraction for a signature of the SuSig database.

The parameters are modeled in a matrix, in which in each row contains the parameters of a Sigma-Lognormal curve of the signature, such as: stroke initial time; stroke amplitude; log time delay; log response time; initial angle; final angle.

Figures 2 and 3 show respectively the velocity profiles obtained by the Sigma-Lognormal curves for a genuine and a forged signature. It is worth noting that the analysis of the signatures in the generation domain (through the lognormal model) allows us to have a first indication of the authenticity of a signature. In fact, the number of curves underlying a forgery signature is generally higher than the number of curves that underlying the corresponding genuine specimen. This can be explained with the presence of additional strokes that are created by the forger in an attempt to imitate particularly complex traits of the genuine signature.

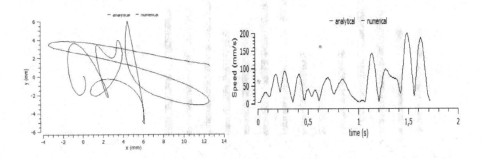

Fig. 2. Example of genuine signature and related velocity profile

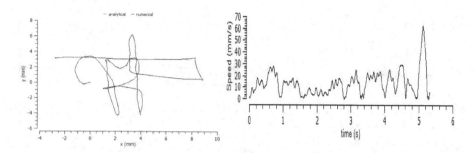

Fig. 3. Example of forgery signature and related velocity profile

For the analysis of local stability of the generation process a well-defined Matlab function was realized with the following purposes:

1. determine time and velocity profile for the target signature, that is first signature produced by author;
2. determine time and velocity profile for signatures that must be matched with the target signature;
3. determine the warping path using Dynamic Time Warping (TDW);
4. count the number of DMP for each stroke;
5. compute the local stability function (according to eq. (15));
6. compute the global stability for each signature (according to eq. (16))

Figure 4 shows the stability function for a genuine signature, when it is matched against other genuine specimens (genuine-genuine) and forgeries (genuine-forgeries).

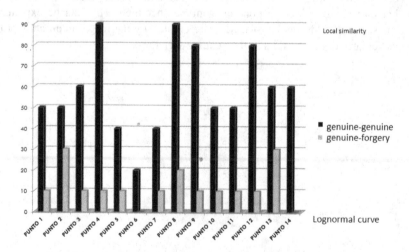

Fig. 4. An example of results obtained by analyzing local stability

The result shows that generally the local stability among genuine-genuine signatures is significantly greater than local stability among genuine-forgeries. In particular, some curves exist in which stability of genuine signatures is clearly superior to those of the forgeries signature (examples are curves 4 and 8), while for other curves the difference is not so evident (examples are curves 2 and 13).

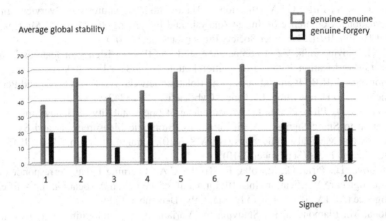

Fig. 5. An example of results obtained by analyzing global stability

As regards the global stability, figure 5 shows the results obtained by 10 authors, taken randomly from the 94 authors of Visual Subcorpus. For each author the averaged value of the global stability function of their signatures is reported, that provide an information about the stability of the signatures of each signer. In this case the result demonstrate that generally global stability of the signatures produced by the signer exceeds 60%, while global stability of the signatures produced by forgeries is just over 20%.

5   Conclusions

In this paper, a new approach for the analysis of local and global stability for online signatures was presented. This approach is based on Dynamic Time Warping algorithm applied to signatures modeled by speed profiles extracted from appropriate parameters of Sigma-Lognormal distributions. The experimental results demonstrate that the new approach can provide useful information about signatures that reveal some specific characters about signers' behaviors.

References

1. Vielhauer, C.: A Behavioural Biometrics. Public Service Review: European Union 9, 113–115 (2005)
2. Plamondon, R.: A Kinematic Theory of Rapid Human Movements: Part I: Movement Representation and generation. Biological Cybernetics 72(4), 295–307 (1995)

3. Impedovo, D., Pirlo, G., Plamondon, R.: Handwritten Signature Verification: New Advancements and Open Issues. In: XIII International Conference on Frontiers in Handwriting Recognition (ICFHR 2012), Monopoli, Bari, Italy, pp. 365–370 (September 2012)
4. Huang, K., Yan, H.: Stability and style-variation modeling for on-line signature verification. Pattern Recognition 36(10), 2253–2270 (2003)
5. Impedovo, S., Pirlo, G.: Verification of Handwritten Signatures: an Overview. In: 14th International Conference on Image Analysis and Processing, ICIAP 2007, Modena, Italy, pp. 191–196. IEEE Computer Society Press (September 2007)
6. Lei, H., Govindaraju, V.: A comparative study on the consistency of features in on-line signature verification. Pattern Recognition Letters 26, 2483–2489 (2005)
7. Schomaker, L.R.B., Plamondon, R.: The Relation between Axial Pen Force and Pen Point Kinematics in Handwriting. Biological Cybernetics 63, 277–289 (1990)
8. Impedovo, D., Pirlo, G.: On the Measurement of Local Stability of Handwriting - An application to Static Signature Verification. In: Biometric Measurements and Systems for Security and Medical Applications (BIOMS 2010), Taranto, Italy, pp. 41–44. IEEE Computer Society Press (September 2010)
9. Impedovo, D., Pirlo, G., Stasolla, E., Trullo, C.A.: Learning Local Correspondences for Static Signature Verification. In: 11th Int. Conf. of the Italian Association for Artificial Intelligence (AI*IA 2009), Reggio Emilia, Italy (December 2009)
10. Djioua, M., Plamondon, R.: Studying the Variability of Handwriting Patterns using the Kinematic Theory. Human Movement Science 28(5), 588–601 (2009)
11. O'Reilly, C., Plamondon, R.: Development of a Sigma-Lognormal Representation for On-Line Signatures. Pattern Recognition 42, 3324–3337 (2009)
12. Plamondon, R.: Strokes against stroke- Stroke for strides. In: 3rd ICFHR, Bari, Italy (September 2012), http://www.icfhr2012.uniba.it/ICFHR2012-Invited_I.pdf
13. Di Lecce, V., Dimauro, G., Guerriero, A., Impedovo, S., Pirlo, G., Salzo, A., Sarcinella, L.: Selection of Reference Signatures for Automatic Signature Verification. In: 5th Int. Conf. on Document Analysis and Recognition (ICDAR-5), Bangalore, India, pp. 597–600 (1999)
14. Congedo, G., Dimauro, G., Impedovo, S., Pirlo, G.: A new methodology for the measurement of local stability in dynamical signatures. In: 4th Int. Workshop on Frontiers in Handwriting Recognition (IWFHR-4), Taipei, Taiwan, pp. 135–144 (1994)
15. Impedovo, D., Modugno, R., Pirlo, G., Stasolla, E.: Handwritten Signature Verification by Multiple Reference Sets. In: 11th Int. Conf. on Frontiers in Handwriting Recognition, Concordia University, Montreal, Canada, pp. 125–129 (August 2008)
16. Di Lecce, V., Dimauro, G., Guerriero, A., Impedovo, S., Pirlo, G., Salzo, A.: A Multi-expert System for Dynamic Signature Verification. In: Kittler, J., Roli, F. (eds.) MCS 2000. LNCS, vol. 1857, pp. 320–329. Springer, Heidelberg (2000)
17. Impedovo, D., Pirlo, G.: On-line Signature Verification by Stroke-Dependent Representation Domains. In: 12th Int. Conf. Frontiers in Handwriting Recognition (ICFHR-12), Kolkata, India, pp. 623–627 (November 2010)
18. Yanikoglu, B., Kholmatov, A.: SUSIG: An online handwritten signature database, associated protocol and benchmark results. Pattern Anal. Applic. 12, 227–236 (2009)

SID Signature Database:
A Tunisian Off-line Handwritten Signature Database

Imen Abroug Ben Abdelghani[1] and Najoua Essoukri Ben Amara[2]

[1] Higher Institute of Applied Sciences and Technology of Kairouan,
UR: SAGE-ENISo, University of Sousse, Tunisia
abrougimen@yahooo.fr
[2] National Engineering School of Sousse, UR: SAGE-ENISo, University of Sousse, Tunisia
najoua.benamara@eniso.rnu.tn

Abstract. Our research works are concerned with checking the off-line handwritten signature. We propose a base of Tunisian static handwritten signatures. In this paper, we go through the phase of designing the SID-Signature database and its various features. Afterwards, we present the results obtained by this base as part of our system of handwritten-signature verification.

Keywords: off-line handwritten signature, SID-Signature database, Tunisian signature, Planar modeling signature.

1   Introduction

The biometric verification of the handwritten signature remains one of the main approaches to authenticating the identity, which are present in various fields of the modern society such as financial and legal transactions. The static handwritten signature has always been used by different social classes to authenticate and certify all sorts of official documents and make individuals aware of their commitments (contracts, financial and legal transactions, etc.).

The signature is a draw resulting from a more or less voluntary movement that is specific to each individual and which allows certifying the documents they append. The signing action existed for a very long time and has known a significant geometric variation since the Middle Ages. Indeed, to certify documents, people in the Middle Ages used the signatures, crosses or monograms, to which they could add initials or parts of their names [1]. Fig1 gives examples of signatures used at that era.

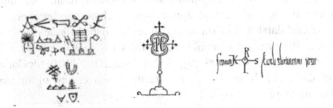

Fig. 1. .Sample signatures of the Middle Ages

A. Petrosino, L. Maddalena, P. Pala (Eds.): ICIAP 2013 Workshops, LNCS 8158, pp. 131–139, 2013.

The handwritten-signature morphology changes from one person to another as well as for the same one. In fact, the signatures of the same person may show shape variations depending on their age, physical and moral state, the material conditions, and the nature of the document (official or unofficial) [2-3].

However, according to the country's culture, signatures may be very different in their shape. The literature shows that we distinguish the classes of European, North American, Asian and Arabic signatures.

According to [4], the Arabic signatures have partly the characteristics of the cursive writing as well as those of the graphic initials, which makes them more complicated. In our case, we are interested in the Tunisian signatures. Table 1 shows some forms of signatures classified according to their origin.

Table 1. Examples of different-origin classified signatures

Origin/style	Samples		
North-Americans/ handwriting			
Europeans/ Graphical lines			
Asians/ Asian characters			
Arabs/ Graphics, writing			

In this context, several automatic systems of checking the handwritten signature have been proposed; the role of such a system is to determine the authenticity of a given signature by referring to a beforehand-conceived database. Various papers have run over the conducted research, [5-8].

In general, the systems checking the signature are learning-based, which requires to have a large database ideally representing the majority of the target population of the concerned application. The database samples must take into account all the possible variations in the real case of applications such as the intrapersonal variations. There are several databases of static signatures published for academic use and scientific research. We cite, for example the SIGMA [5], GPDS960 [6], GPDS960 Gray [7], MCYT-75 [8], SigComp09 [9], 4NSigComp2010 [10], SigComp11 [11] and 4NSigComp2012 [12] bases. We give in Table 2 an overview of the main features of some static signatures databases.

Table 2. The main characteristics of some static-handwritten-signature databases

Ref\ Base	Origin	Signatory Number		Type of signatures	Characteristics
[5] SIGMA	Malaysian	213			
[8] MCYT	Spanish	75			600dpi, 256 gray level
[6] GPDS960		960			300dpi, BMP
[7] GPDS960 gray		960 (881)		Simulated	600dpi, PNG
[9] SigCom09		App: 12	Test: 100		300dpi, 600dpi, PNG
[10] 4NSigComp2010 (Subset of GPDS960)	Spanish	400			300dpi, BMP
[11] SigCom11	Chinese Dutch	12			400 dpi, PNG
[12] 4NSigComp2012		2	3	Simulated Disguised	300dpi, BMP

As showing in the literature and Table 2, most databases contain particularly the type of forgery by simulation; it is always the most difficult case to solve. Similarly, the bases are more and more composed of a large number of signatories to be closer to the real situation of the applications. We also note that the different research teams set up their own databases to validate their signature verification / identification systems. This can be explained by the lack of databases of international static handwritten signatures and the need to have a database tallying with the population of the country concerned with the corresponding real application.

As part of our research works, we have been brought to build a database of North African offline handwritten signatures, taking into account the characteristics purely specific to the image of the North African signature. In this paper we are confined to the sub-base tallying with the Tunisian population; we present the SID-Signature database by exploiting it in the case of validating a planar modeling of the static handwritten signature. In the following section, we detail the phase of designing the database and its various features. Section 3 is devoted to the morphological study of the base. Section 4 presents the results of using this basis for validating a planar architecture of the handwritten signature. The conclusion and the perspectives are given in Section 5.

2   Design of the SID-Signature Database

To design this database we have proceeded by a collection of signature samples followed by a phase of digitizing and storing data. We describe in what follows the different adopted choices.

2.1   Collecting Signatures

The different signature samples have been affixed by means the same make of blue ballpoint pen on the same make of white A4 paper forms divided into 15 blocks of the same size. The choice of using 15 blocks to append the signatures has been the basis of studying a large number of signatures. The space reserved for appending is sufficient to draw different-sized signatures.

The database has currently 6,000 genuine signatures corresponding to 100 Tunisians with different ages and cultural and scientific levels. Each signatory has provided 60 samples, in different sessions, to avoid possible geometric variations related to the appending close to the time of signatures. Indeed, the signatory risks being tired from signing several times in succession or from being pressed to finish, which leads to significant variations in the form of their signature. Table 3 shows some statistics of the SID-Signature database.

Table 3. Some statistics of the SID-Signature database

SID-Signature Database	
Gender distribution	64% male / 36% female
Age distribution	10% (<18); 34% (18-25); 28% (25- 35); 21% (35-50); 7% (> 50)
Scientific level	17% employee; 46% student; 37% teacher

10 forgers (persons different from writers) have been solicited to collect the forged signatures. Each forger has provided, in different sessions, 2 simple forgeries and 2 ones by a skilled imitation of each signature class.

To produce a skilled imitation, we have provided the forger with different static images of the genuine signature to imitate, and he produce the skilled forgery without practicing imitation.

Table 4. Samples of the SID-Signature database

Signatory	Genuine	Skilled Imitation	Simple Forgery	Random signature
Name: Sahnoun Surname: Mohamed				
Surname:Wafa				
Surname: كريم				

The simple forgery corresponds to writing the surname and / or the name of the genuine signatory (which have been provided to them); this gesture is often adopted by the majority of this type of falsifiers (Table 4).

It should be noted that the scrutiny of the two forgery types takes into account the highly variable shape of the Tunisian signatures (writing, graphics, and a blend between the two).

The SID-Signature database is subdivided into a learning sub-base and a test one. The learning base is composed of 4,000 genuine signatures (40 first samples corresponding to each signatory). The test sub-base consists of 2,000 authentic signatures, 2,000 simple forgeries, 2,000 skilled-imitated forgeries, and 2,000 random signatures: The random signatures correspond to the authentic signatures belonging to other writers (20 samples for each type) (Table 5).

Table 5. Distribution of samples of the SID-Signature database for modeling evaluation

Sets of data	Number of samples	Type of signatures
Learning	4,000 (40x100)	Genuine
Test	2,000 (20x100)	Genuine
	2,000(20x100)	Random
	2,000(20x100)	Simple forgeries
	2,000(20x100)	Skilled-imitated forgeries

2.2   Signature Digitization

The different forms of the collected signatures have been digitized at a 300 dpi resolution with 256 gray levels. We have used for this three scanners: a HP 3200C, HP G2710 and EPSON DX4400.

Extracting the signatures of each form takes place automatically. To do this, we have developed a segmentation module based on exploring mainly the horizontal and vertical projections of the image of the considered form. The result images are stored in the SID-Signature database in a bitmap format in black and white (Fig 2). This database will be accessible to the public from the site http://www.sage-eniso.org/equipe/fr/1/SID-Signal-Image-et-Document.html

3   Morphologic Study of the Signature Database

The morphological study of the samples of the SID-Signature database shows the presence of the three signature styles previously mentioned in section 1: 14% of the

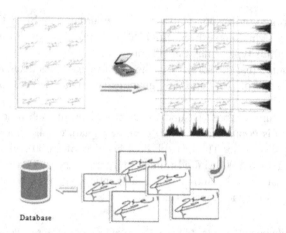

Fig. 2. Process of acquiring and extracting signatures database

signatories sign with writing (their surnames and / or forenames), 27% sign with pure-ly-random graphical forms, and the majority sign with a mixture parts of their sur-names and / or names linked to graphical lines.

We have noted an intrapersonal variation that is more or less important for all the signatories. This is a natural characteristic of the handwritten-signature drawing.

We have even noticed strong similarities between the shapes of some signatures classes, which can then bring about confusion during verification (Fig 3). The two dimensions of the various signatures of the base are highly diverse and range respec-tively from 86 to 670 and 137 to 812 (Table 6).

Table 6. Distribution of some characteristics of the SID-Signature database

Widths distribu-tion	3% (131.5-190) ; 35% (190-365) ; 36% (365-482) ; 22% (482-598) ; 4% (598-715)
Heights Distribution	7% (74-118) ; 38% (118-205) ; 41% (205-336) ; 14% (336-510.5)
Slant distribution	4% (< -12.2°) ; 16% (-12.2°... -1.35°) ; 35% (-1.35°... 9.54°) ; 38% (9.54°- 42.2°) ; 7% (> 42.2°)

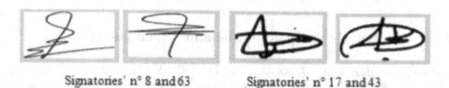

Signatories' n° 8 and 63   Signatories' n° 17 and 43

Fig. 3. Similarities between the shapes of signatures corresponding to different persons

4   Exploiting the Database by a Planar Architecture of the Handwritten Signature

Our research is about checking the handwritten signature by a planar modeling [13-14]. The choice of the planar modeling allows considering the two dimensions of the image in a simplified way. The signature image pre-processed beforehand (binarization, median-filtering, and size normalization) is segmented into three horizontal bands in order to bring the successive lines containing approximately homogeneous information together in the same band. The number of 'three' has been chosen following a study of the morphological changes in each class signature. Each band is modeled by a secondary modular MLP model. A vertical main modular MLP model ensures thereafter the correlation between the three secondary models. Thus, each signature class has been associated with a specific neuronal planar model.

We use two basic global feature types: geometric features and textural ones extracted from the application of the wavelet transform. Each secondary model has a six-characteristic input vector; these characteristics represent the number of black pixels and wavelet features of the corresponding band. As wavelet features, we retain the mean and the standard deviation of the approximation image and the standard deviation of the horizontal, vertical and diagonal detail images.

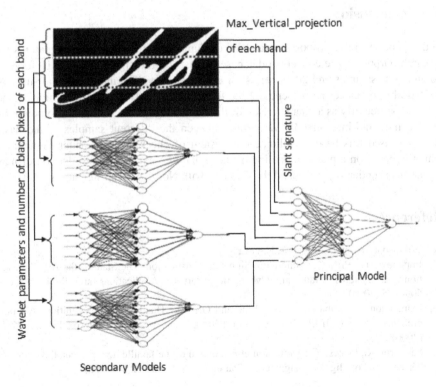

Fig. 4. The Planar model Architecture associated to the signatory n°100

The input vector of the principal model contains seven characteristics corresponding to the outputs of the three secondary models, the signature orientation, and the number of black pixels, in the highest line, of the vertical histogram for each band (Fig 4).

Several experiments have been carried out to determine the best parameters of each model tallying with each signatory (the number of hidden layers and hidden neurons of the principal and secondary models). We retain an MLP structure with three layers for both secondary and principal models. The number of hidden neurons varies according to the signatory class from 5 to 13. A particular learning procedure with the feed-forward-back propagation algorithm has been necessary [13-14]; we first carry out the learning of the three secondary models separately, and then we carry out the training of the principal model.

The training of the secondary models is carried out with an equal number of genuine and false samples (random genuine signatures of other persons) for each model. The training of the principal model is carried out in a particular way. In each algorithm iteration, the outputs of the three secondary models as well as the retained geometric features will then be injected as inputs for training the principal model. The experimentations give an FRR of 14.95%, a random FAR of 3.79%, a simple FAR of 1.25%, and a skilled FAR of 8.95%.

5   Conclusion

In this paper we have proposed a database of Tunisian static handwritten signatures for research purposes. The conceived database consists of 100 signatories and 10 forgers: 60 authentic samples and 20 forgeries for each signatory. The morphological study of the base has revealed the presence of the three signature styles (writing, graphics and hybrid), particularly as a characteristic of the Arabic signature. We have also noted the diverse intra-and-interpersonal variations between the different samples of the base. We have used this base to validate our system of checking handwritten signatures, which is based on a planar modeling of the signature image. The introduction of new signatures is underway to expand the database with North-African signatures.

References

1. Wikipedia, http://wikipedia.fr
2. Impedovo, D., Pirlo, G.: Automatic Signature Verification: The State of the Art. Transactions on Systems, Man, and Cybernetics, Part C: Applications and Reviews 38(5), 609–635 (2008)
3. Plamondon, R., Srihari, S.N.: On-Line and Off-Line Handwriting Recognition: A Comprehensive Survey. IEEE Transaction on Pattern Analysis and Machine Intelligence 22(1) (2000)
4. Sabourin, R., Genest, G.: Définition et évaluation d'une famille de représentations pour la vérification hors-ligne des signatures. Traitement du Signal 12(6) (1995)

5. Ahmad, S.M.S., Shakil, A., Ahmad, A.R., Agil, M., Balbed, M., Anwar, R.M.: SIGMA- A Malaysian Signatures Database. In: International Conference on Computer Systems and Applications, Doha, pp. 919–920 (2008)
6. Vargas, J.F., Ferrer-Aguilar, M., Travieso, C.M., Alonso, J.B.: Off-line Handwritten Signature GPDS-960 Corpus. In: The Ninth International Conference on Document Analysis and Recognition, Parana, Brazil, pp. 764–768 (2007)
7. Ferrer-Aguilar, M., Vargas, F., Morales, A., Ordoñez, A.: Robustness of Off-line Signature Verification based on Gray Level Features. IEEE Transactions on Information Forensics and Security 7(3), 966–977 (2012)
8. Ortega-Garcia, J., Fierrez-Aguilar, J., Simon, D., Gonzalez, J., Faundez-Zanuy, M., Espinosa, V., Satue, A., Hernaez, I., Igarza, J.-J., Vivaracho, C., Escudero, D., Moro, Q.-I.: MCYT baseline corpus: A bimodal biometric database. IEEE Proceedings Vision, Image and Signal Processing 150(6), 395–401 (2003)
9. Blankers, V.L., Van den Heuvel, C.E., Franke, K.Y., Vuurpijl, L.G.: The ICDAR 2009 signature verification competition. In: International Conference on Document Analysis and Recognition, Spain, pp. 1403–1407 (2009)
10. Blumenstein, M., Ferrer- Aguilar, M., Vargas, J.F.: The 4NSigComp2010 off-line signature verification competition: Scenario 2. In: 12th International Conference on Frontiers in Handwriting Recognition, Kolkata, India, pp. 721–726 (2010)
11. Liwicki, M., Blumenstein, M., Heuvel, E.V.D., Berger, C.E.H., Stoel, R.D., Found, B., Chen, X., Malik, M.I.: SigComp11: Signature Verification Competition for On- and Offline Skilled Forgeries. In: 11th International Conference on Document Analysis and Recognition, Beijing, China (2011)
12. Liwicki, M., Malik, M.I., Alewijnse, L., van den Heuvel, E., Found, B.: ICFHR 2012 Competition on Automatic Forensic Signature Verification (4NsigComp 2012). In: 13th International Conference on Frontiers in Handwriting Recognition, Bari, Italy, pp. 819–824 (2012)
13. Abroug, I., Essoukri Ben Amara, N.: A Neuronal Planar Modeling for Handwriting Signature based on Automatic Segmentation. International Journal of Computer Applications 49(8), 29–34 (2012)
14. Abroug Ben Abdelghani, I., Ghardallou Lasmar, A., Essoukri Ben Amara, N.: Planar Hidden Markov/Neural Networks Modelling for Off-line Signature Vérification. In: The International Arab Conferénce on Information Technology, Jordan, pp. 455–460 (2005)

A Two-Stage Approach for English and Hindi Off-line Signature Verification

Srikanta Pal[1], Umapada Pal[2], and Michael Blumenstein[1]

[1] School of Information and Communication Technology, Griffith University, Australia
[2] Computer Vision and Pattern Recognition Unit, Indian Statistical Institute, India
srikanta.pal@griffithuni.edu.au

Abstract. The purpose of this paper is to present an empirical contribution towards the understanding of multi-script off-line signature identification and verification using a novel method involving off-line Hindi (Devnagari) and English signatures. The main aim of this approach is to demonstrate the significant advantage of the use of signature script identification in a multi-script signature verification environment. In the 1st stage of the proposed signature verification technique a script identification technique is employed to know whether a signature is written in Hindi or English. In the second stage, a verification approach was explored separately for English signatures and Hindi signatures based on the script identification result. Different features like gradient feature, water reservoir feature, loop feature, aspect ratio etc. were employed, and Support Vector Machines (SVMs) were considered in our scheme. To get the comparative idea, multi-script signature verification results on the joint Hindi and English dataset without using any script identification technique is also computed. From the experiment results it is noted that we are able to reduce average error rate 4.81% more when script identification method is employed.

1 Introduction

Nowadays, civilized and advanced societies require secure means for personal authentication. Traditional authentication methods, which are based on knowledge (a password) and the utility of a token (photo ID cards, magnetic strip cards, keys) are less reliable because of forgetfulness, loss and theft. These issues direct substantial attention to biometrics as an alternative method for person authentication and identification. Consequently, handwritten signatures as a pure behavioral biometric are used widely and are well accepted as a personal authentication method.

On the basis of signature acquisition, signature verification methods can be categorized into two groups: static (offline) and dynamic (online) methods [1, 7]. Offline signature verification uses the shape of the signature to authenticate the signer [2]. Online signature verification uses dynamic characteristics of the signature (time-dependent signals) to authenticate the signer [3].

Although significant research has already been undertaken in the field of signature verification, particularly involving single-script signatures, conversely, less attention has

A. Petrosino, L. Maddalena, P. Pala (Eds.): ICIAP 2013 Workshops, LNCS 8158, pp. 140–148, 2013.

been devoted to the task of multi-script signature verification. Pal et al. [4] presented a bi-script signature identification technique involving Bangla (Bengali) and English off-line signatures based on background and foreground information. The purpose of that paper was to identify whether a claimed signature belongs to the group of Bengali or English signatures. In another contribution by Pal et al. [5], a multi-script off-line signature identification technique was proposed. In that signature identification scheme, the signatures involving Bangla (Bengali), Hindi (Devnagari) and English were considered for the identification process. An encouraging accuracy of 92.14% was obtained in those experiments. In another report by Pal et al. [6], multi-script off-line signature identification and verification involving English and Hindi signatures was presented. The verification phase considering multi-script signatures before the identification stage was not investigated, and it was the drawback of that technique. As a consequence, the comparison of experimental outcomes of two different verification stages (before identification and after identification) was not previously considered in that paper.

In this paper a two-stage approach is proposed for multi-script signature verification. In the 1st stage of the proposed signature verification technique a script identification technique is employed to know whether a signature is written in Hindi or English. In the second stage, a verification approach was explored separately for English signatures and Hindi signatures based on the script identification result. To get the idea about the advantage of this two-stage approach, multi-script signature verification results on the joint Hindi and English dataset without using any script identification technique is also computed and the diagram of such a system is shown in Fig.1.

2   Significance of Multi-script Signature Verification

In a multi-script and multi-lingual country like India, languages are not only used for writing/reading purposes but also applied for reasons pertaining to signing and signatures. In such an environment in India, the signatures of an individual with more than one language (regional language and international language) are essentially needed in official transactions (e.g. in a passport application form, an examination question paper, a money order form, bank account application form etc.). To deal with these situations, signature verification techniques employing single-script signatures are not sufficient for consideration. Therefore in a multi-script and multi-lingual scenario, signature verification methods considering more than one script are expressly needed. Consequently, the idea of the proposed multi-script signature verification technique considering Hindi and English signatures are significant.

Development of a general multi-script signature verification system, which can verify signatures of all scripts, is very complicated and it is not possible to develop such a system in the Indian scenario. The verification accuracy in such multi-script signature environments will not be desirable compared to single script signature verification. To achieve the necessary accuracy for multi-script signature verification, it is first important to identify signatures based on the type of script and then use an individual

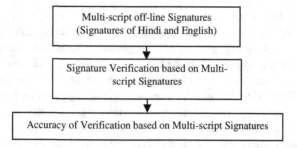

Fig. 1. Diagram of Signature Verification Considering Joint Dataset

single script signature verification system for the identified signature script. Based on this observation, in the proposed system the signatures of different scripts are separated to feed into the individual signature verification system. The diagram of such a system is shown in Fig.2. To the best of the authors' knowledge, a complete analysis of a multi-script signature verification technique, where signature identification factors affecting signature verification results with a large dataset, is still missing from the literature. This research work is the first important report towards such a direction in the area of signature verification.

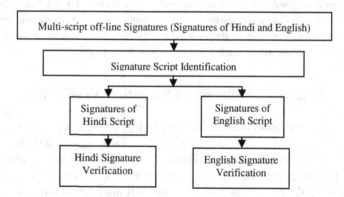

Fig. 2. Diagram of Multi-script Signature Identification and Verification Based on Hindi and English Signatures

3   Database Used for Experimentation

3.1   Hindi Signature Database

As there has been no public signature corpus available for Hindi script, it was necessary to create a database of Hindi signatures. This Hindi signature database consists of 100 sets. Each set consists of 24 genuine signatures and 30 skilled forgeries. From each individual, 24 genuine signatures were collected. A total number of 2400 genuine signatures from 100 individuals were collected. A total number of 3000 skilled forgeries were collected from the writers.

3.2   GPDS English Database

Another database consisting of 100 sets from GPDS-160 [8] was also utilised for these experiments. The reason 100 sets were used from the GPDS on this occasion, is due to the fact that the Hindi dataset described previously was comprised of 100 sets, and it was considered important to have equivalent signature numbers for experimentation and comparison between the two datasets.

4   Feature Extraction and Classifier Details

Before feature extraction, the signatures are extracted from the data collection form, and for this purpose some pre-processing is performed as follows. The signatures to be processed by the system needed to be in a digital image format. Each signature was handwritten on a rectangular space of fixed size of a white sheet of paper. It was necessary to scan all signature document pages. At the very beginning, the images were captured in 256 level grey-scale at 300 dpi and stored in TIFF format (Tagged Image File Format) for the purpose of future processing. In the pre-processing step, a histogram-based threshold technique was applied for binarization. Then the signature images were extracted from the signature-collecting document forms.

Feature extraction is a crucial step in any pattern recognition system. Three different types of feature extraction techniques such as: 576 dimensional gradient feature extraction (described in [9]), water reservoir-based technique (described in [10]), the aspect ratio-based technique [11] and the loop feature [12] are considered here.

Based on gradient feature, Support Vector Machines (SVMs) are applied as the classifier for verification experiments. Other features are used in a Tree classifier for signature script identification.

5   Experimental Settings

5.1   Settings for Verification Used Prior to Script Identification

In this experimental method of verification, skilled forgeries were not considered for training, and genuine signatures were considered for both training and testing purposes. For the experiments in the proposed research, the Hindi database developed and 100 sets from the GPDS described in Section 3, were used. For each signature set, an SVM was trained with 12 randomly chosen genuine signatures. The number of genuine samples (24) in a set was divided in two parts for training and testing purposes. The negative samples for training (random forgeries) were the genuine signatures of 199 other signature sets. Two signatures were taken from each set. In total, there were 199x2=398 random forgeries employed for training. For testing, the remaining 12 genuine signatures and 30 skilled forgeries of the signature set being considered were employed. The number of samples for training and testing for these experiments are shown in Table 1.

Table 1. No. of Signatures Used Per Set in 1st Phase of Verification

Table 2. No. of Signatures used per Set in the 2nd Phase of Verification

	Genuine Signature	Random Forgeries	Skilled Forgeries
Training	12	398	n/a
Testing	12	n/a	30

	Genuine Signature	Random Forgeries	Skilled Forgeries
Training	12	198	n/a
Testing	12	n/a	30

5.2   Settings for Verification Used after Script Identification

The same experimental settings were also used for this verification method, except the number of negative (random) samples used for the training phase. In total 99x2=198 negative samples for training were employed from 99 other genuine signature sets. The number of samples for training and testing for these experiments are shown in Table 2.

5.3   Script Identification Strategies

Feature set selection for signature script identification was decided based on the knowledge of observing the signature samples used during experimentation. As the physical characteristics and structural behaviours of the Hindi and English signatures were well known, the feature set selection for the script identification method was straightforward. Viewing the samples in the combined dataset it was noted that all the Hindi samples were written as full signatures and the English samples were written primarily as 'initial' signatures. As a consequence, the height of Hindi signature samples was smaller than the width of samples. Conversely, the height and width of most of the English signatures were nearly same. So, it was easy to apply the aspect ratio feature to identify those two different scripts of signatures. But there were a few samples that were not as easy to identify by the aspect ratio (H/W) feature. So, in the next stage, the top water reservoir (WR) (for details about this feature see [10]), number of loops (L) and reservoir height (RH) was further applied to identify those signatures. Applying these three simple feature sets, all the samples were correctly identified (100% accuracy). Naturally, these three heuristic features may not necessarily yield the same accuracy levels for identification using other datasets. Two signatures of Hindi and English with their existing top water reservoirs are shown in Fig.3 and Fig.4 respectively. The graphical representation of the script identification strategy is shown in Fig.5.

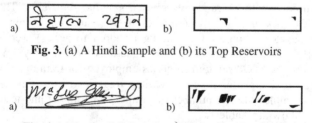

Fig. 3. (a) A Hindi Sample and (b) its Top Reservoirs

Fig. 4. (a) An English Sample and (b) its Top Reservoirs

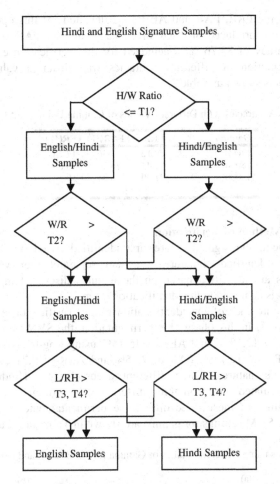

Fig. 5. Flow Chart of the proposed Identification Method (Here T1=4, T2=3, T3=7 and T4=30 are different threshold values obtained empirically)

6   Results and Discussion

6.1   Experimental Results

The experimental results of any signature verification system are evaluated based on FRR (False Rejection Rate), FAR (False Acceptance Rate) and the AER (Average Error Rate).

6.1.1   First Method of Verification(Without Script Identification)

In this experiment, 10800 signatures involving English and Hindi scripts were employed for training and testing purposes. Among these signatures, 4800 (24x200) samples were genuine and 6000 (30x200) samples were skilled forgeries. Using the gradient features, the FRR, FAR and AER are calculated. At this operational point, the SVM classifiers produced an FRR of 20.12 % and an FAR of 14.36 %. An encouraging accuracy of 82.76 % is achieved for this verification experiment. The graphical representation of different accuracies with different values of gamma settings for SVMs is shown in Table 3.

Table 3. Accuracies with Different Values of Gamma Using Joint Dataset

Gamma	FRR(%)	FAR(%)	AER(%)
17000	20.12	14.36	17.24
18000	21.44	16.24	18.84
19000	21.90	16.34	19.12

6.1.2   Second Method of Verification

For this experiment, the signatures are first identified based on their script and subsequently the identified signatures are sent separately for verification. All signature samples are identified based on the features discussed in Section 4. An accuracy of 100% is achieved at the identification stage.

Based on the outcomes of the identification phase, verification experiments are conducted as follows. In this phase of experimentation, the SVMs produced an FRR of 18.12 %, FAR of 12.18 % and AER of 15.15% using English signatures. On the other hand, an FRR of 12.17%, FAR of 7.25% and AER of 9.71% were achieved employing Hindi signatures. Three different accuracies for Hindi and English signatures are calculated based on three different values of gamma for the SVM classifier. The values of these three different experimental outcomes achieved for different values of SVM settings for gamma are shown in Tables 4 (a) and (b).

Table 4. Accuracies using Different Values of Gamma for (a) English and (b) Hindi Datasets

(a)

Gamma	FRR(%)	FAR(%)	AER(%)
19000	18.12	12.18	15.15
18000	18.66	12.20	15.43
17000	18.90	16.20	17.55

(b)

Gamma	FRR(%)	FAR(%)	AER(%)
19000	12.17	7.25	09.71
18000	12.65	7.85	10.25
17000	17.25	8.25	12.75

6.2   Comparision of Performance

From the experimental results obtained, it was observed that the performance of signature verification in the second method is very encouraging compared to signature verification using the first method. Table 5 demonstrates the accuracies achieved in the first and second methods discussed in sub-Sections 6.1.1 and 6.1.2.

For the second method of verification, the overall accuracy is 87.57 % (Avg. of 84.85 and 90.29) which is higher than the accuracy obtained from the first method.

Table 5. Accuracies for Different Methods

Verification Methods		Accuracy (%)
Stages	Dataset Used	
1st Method	English & Hindi	82.76
2nd Method	English	84.85
	Hindi	90.29

Table 6. Accuracies for Different Schemes

Verification Method	Accuracy (%)
Without Script Identification	82.76
With Script Identification	87.57

The comparison of these two accuracies is shown in Table 6. It can be noted from the table that the average error can be reduced 4.81% (87.57-82.76) when the script identification method is employed.

From the above table and chart it is easily understood that verification accuracy after script identification is much higher than before. This increased accuracy is achieved because of the proper application of the identification stage. Thus, this research clearly demonstrates the importance of using identification in multi-script signature verification techniques.

6.3   Error Analysis

Most of the methods used for signature verification generate some erroneous results. In the proposed approach, confusing signature samples obtained using the SVM classifier is shown in Fig.6 and Fig.7. Two categories of confusing samples are given by the classifier. The first category illustrates genuine signature samples treated as forged signature samples. The second one illustrates forged signature samples treated as genuine signature samples.

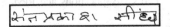   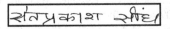

Fig. 6. Genuine Signatures Treated as Forgeries   **Fig. 7.** Forged Signatures Treated as Genuine

7   Conclusions and Future Work

This paper demonstrates an investigation of the excellent performance of a multi-script signature verification technique involving Hindi and English off-line signatures. Actually, the novel approach used in a multi-script signature verification environment with the combination of a large newly-prepared Hindi off-line signature dataset provides a substantial contribution in the field of signature verification. In such a verification environment, the proper utilization of a script identification phase, which substantially affects the verification accuracy, indicates an important step in the process. The comparatively higher verification accuracy obtained for the second method of experimentation (identification plus verification) is likewise a substantial contribution.

The gradient feature, water reservoir feature, loop feature and aspect ratio feature as well as SVM classifiers were employed for experimentation. To the best of the authors' knowledge, the idea of multi-script signature verification, which deals with an identification phase, has not previously been used for the task of signature verification, and hence this is the first important report detailing such a process in the area of signature verification. The proposed off-line multi-script signature verification scheme is a new investigation in the field of off-line signature verification. In the near future, we plan to extend our work considering further groups of signature samples, which may include different languages/scripts.

References

1. Madabusi, S., Srinivas, V., Bhaskaran, S., Balasubramanian, M.: On-line and off-line signature verification using relative slope algorithm. In: International Workshop on Measurement Systems for Homeland Security, pp. 11–15 (2005)
2. Kalera, M., Srihari, S., Xu, A.: Offline signature verification and identification using distance statistics. International Journal on Pattern Recognition and Artificial Intelligence, 1339–1360 (2004)
3. Plamondon, R., Lorette, G.: Automatic signature verification and writer identification - the state of the art. Pattern Recognition, 107–131 (1989)
4. Pal, S., Alaei, A., Pal, U., Blumenstein, M.: Off-line signature identification using background and foreground information. In: International Conference on Digital Image Computing, pp. 672–677 (2011)
5. Pal, S., Alaei, A., Pal, U., Blumenstein, M.: Multi-Script off-line signature identification. In: 12th International Conference on Hybrid Intelligent Systems, pp. 236–240 (2012)
6. Pal, S., Pal, U., Blumenstein, M.: Hindi and English off-line signature identification and verification. In: International Conference on Advances in Computing, pp. 905–910 (2012)
7. Impedovo, D., Pirlo, G.: Automatic Signature Verification: The State of the Art. IEEE Transactions on Systems, Man, and Cybernetics—Part C: Applications and Reviews 38, 609–635 (2008)
8. Ferrer, M.A., Alonso, J.B., Travieso, C.M.: Offline geometric parameters for automatic signature verification using fixed-point arithmetic. IEEE PAMI 27, 993–997 (2005)
9. Ito, T., Ohyama, W., Wakabayashi, T., Kimura, F.: Combination of signature verification techniques by SVM. In: International Conference on Frontiers in Handwriting Recognition, pp. 428–431 (2012)
10. Pal, U., Belaid, A., Choisy, C.: Touching numeral segmentation using water reservoir concept. Pattern Recognition Letters 24(1-3), 261–272 (2003)
11. Schafer, B., Viriri, S.: An off-Line signature verification system. In: International Conference on Signal and Image Processing Applications, pp. 95–100 (2009)
12. Tarafdar, A., Mandal, R., Pal, S., Pal, U., Kimura, F.: Shape code based word-image matching for retrieval of Indian multi-lingual documents. In: ICPR, pp. 1989–1992 (2010)

Improving Ancient Roman Coin Classification by Fusing Exemplar-Based Classification and Legend Recognition

Sebastian Zambanini, Albert Kavelar, and Martin Kampel

Computer Vision Lab, Vienna University of Technology, Austria
{zamba,kavelar,kampel}@caa.tuwien.ac.at

Abstract. In this paper we present an image-based classification method for ancient Roman Republican coins that uses multiple sources of information. Exemplar-based classification, which estimates the coins' visual similarity by means of a dense correspondence field, and lexicon-based legend recognition are unified to a common classification approach. Classification scores from both coin sides are further integrated to an overall score determining the final classification decision. Experiments carried out on a dataset of 60 different classes comprising 464 coin images show that the combination of methods leads to higher classification rate than using them separately.

1   Introduction

Numismatics deals with all forms of money and other payment media and its contemporary and historic aspects [9]. Along with studying use and production of historic money, cataloging or classifying coins is one of its major aspects. Coin hoards possibly comprise thousands of coins and therefore the classification of each individual coin is a time-consuming and cumbersome task, which up until now has to be carried out manually [9]. This is where numismatists could largely benefit from a fully-automated coin classification method. When the coins are registered in digital archives, their front *(obverse)* and back sides *(reverse)* are photographed using a digital camera and stored in a database along with textual descriptions. Hence, we suggest an image-based classification method since it does not require additional digitization steps which would cause extra work and costs and therefore would reduce the chances of such a system to be accepted by numismatists.

Several image-based coin classification systems for modern coins were developed in the past (e.g., Dagobert [16] and Coin-O-Matic [15]). However, the development of a fully-automated image-based coin classification system for ancient coins is still subject of ongoing research. One of the major reasons for this is that, as opposed to their modern counterparts, ancient coins show little inter-class variability and large intra-class variability (see Fig. 1) and thus pose different challenges to computer vision. The intra-class variability is related to the manufacturing process of ancient coins. They were cast or struck using manually engraved dies. The longer a die was used, the more worn down it became

A. Petrosino, L. Maddalena, P. Pala (Eds.): ICIAP 2013 Workshops, LNCS 8158, pp. 149–158, 2013.

(a)

(b)

Fig. 1. Examples of Roman Republican coins. (a) Low inter class-variability: three coins of different classes that show the same basic motive and only differ in the depicted legend (highlighted in red). (b) High intra-class variability: three coins of the same class.

and consequently the quality of the struck coins decreased over time. Hence, a die could only be used for a limited number of coins before they had to be replaced by a new one, which introduced additional variations. Moreover, the dies were not always centered and the relative alignment of obverse and reverse die on the *flan* (the raw piece of metal the coin is made of) shows inconsistencies.

In the past, promising approaches for recognizing ancient Roman coins including image matching [20] and the recognition of the coin legends [12] have been proposed. The former measures the visual similarity of coin images by the energy needed to establish a dense correspondence between them. This approach has the advantage that it is more independent on the number of images available from the same class, as no offline machine learning is performed. However, it also suffers from a low inter-class variability as different coin classes possibly depict the same central motive (e.g., a chariot or a god portrait) [5]. In such hard cases only minor sources of information like the legend can be exploited for differentiation [5].

In this paper, we present a way of fusing these methods which helps to improve the robustness of image-based coin classification. Legend recognition is based on a vocabulary which maps the words to coin classes and thus adds a different kind of background knowledge to the pure visual similarity of coins estimated from the dense correspondence. We also increase the level of robustness by exploiting both coin sides for classification.

The remainder of the paper is organized as follows: Section 2 reviews the state of the art in coin classification. Section 3 explains the proposed image matching and legend recognition algorithms and how they are combined. In Section 4 the experimental setup and test results are presented. Finally, Section 5 concludes this work.

2 Related Work

Fukumi et al. [8] were the first to use computer vision methods for coin classification. Their system can distinguish 500 yen from 500 won coins. After separating the coin from the background, it is divided into several ring segments by a log-polar grid; this separation ensures rotational invariance. For each segment, the sum of gray levels is computed and fed to a multilayered neural network. Nölle et al. [16] presented a powerful coin recognition system called Dagobert, which discerns 600 different coin types. Their method computes a binarized edge image from the coin input image which is compared to master images stored in a database. The coin is assigned to the class which gives the closest match using nearest neighbor classification. To reduce computation time, a pre-selection based on the measurements of two additional sensors, which capture the coin's diameter and thickness, is carried out beforehand. Bremananth et al. [4] proposed a method for the recognition of 1-, 2- and 5-rupee coins. After successful edge detection, the location of the numerals depicted on the coin is found via template matching. Next, Gabor features are computed for the subimage containing the numeral, which are then classified by a back propagation network. The COIN-O-MATIC system suggested by van der Maaten and Poon [15] relies on edge information, similar to the Dagobert approach. After computing an edge image from a coin input image, a histogram based on a log-polar grid, which captures the angle and distance distribution of the edge pixels, is calculated and classified using nearest neighbour classification. Finally, Reisert et al. [17] introduced another classification system for modern coins. Their approach segments the coin from the background using a generalized Hough transform [3]. Next, the segmented image is transformed to polar coordinates and gradients are computed. The gradients are quantized into different orientational bins and for each of which a binary image is constructed. The binary images serve as feature vectors and are classified using a nearest neighbor classification.

Kampel and Zaharieva were among the first to present an end-to-end recognition workflow for ancient coins [11]. They experimented with various interest point detectors and local image descriptors in order to determine the best combination. Recognition is performed by finding the nearest neighbour using the Euclidean distance. While Kampel and Zaharieva only considered three different coin types in their experiments, Arandjelovic [1] works with 65 classes. He introduced a new type of feature called *locally-biased directional histogram*, which captures geometric relationships between interest points found via the Difference-of-Gaussian detector [14]. Huber-Mörk et al. [10] extended the work of Kampel and Zaharieva [11] to coin identification by introducing an additional preselection step which exploits the coin's contour as a characteristic feature for single coin specimens. The contour is analyzed by intersecting rays cast from the coin's center of gravity with the coin border. The distances between the intersection points and a hypothetical perfect circle fit to the coin contour are measured and used to build a descriptor, which can be computed quickly and allows for an efficient preselection. Thus, the introduction of this step allows fast pruning and increases the recognition rate while the computation time of the coin recognition algorithm can be reduced. Arandjelovic recently introduced another coin classification method which exploits coin legends [2]. He focuses on Roman Imperial denarii, which have legends running along the coin border. This *a priori* assumption about the coin layout allows to align the legends horizontally by transforming the coin images to polar coordinates. The individual letters are then detected by a sliding window for which HoG-like features [6] are computed. This results in a likelihood for each letter and sliding window location, which is then combined to legend words using dynamic programming. The recognized legend is used to select a subset of matching coin types for which SIFT-based matching is performed in order to determine the final class.

Like in the work of Arandjelovic [2], we combine legend recognition with image matching for an improved classification. However, we are focusing on Roman Republican coins instead of Roman Imperial coins. Thus, legends in our case can be arbitrarily located on the coin and are not restricted to be circularly placed at the coin border [5]. Furthermore, instead of doing legend recognition on one side and image matching on the other, we apply both methods to both sides to achieve a more reliable and robust classification.

3   Methodology

The method we propose combines image matching with legend recognition in order to improve the classification rates the methods achieve separately. The general architecture of the fused methodology is depicted in Fig. 2. It takes two input parameters: an image showing the obverse of a coin and one of the corresponding reverse. For each of these images, image matching and legend recognition compute their separate probabilities $P_{s,c}^{M}$ and $P_{s,c}^{L}$ for each coin side $s \in \{1, 2\}$ and class $c \in C$. These values are then combined to an overall probability for each class, which finally allows the determination of the coin class to which the input image belongs.

3.1   Coin Classification by Image Matching

Coin classification by image matching [20] has the advantage that there is no need for a large amount of training data as no machine learning techniques with an offline straining stage are involved. Instead, classification is done by means of reference images per class whose visual similarity to an input image is estimated. This methodology has the benefit that we can cope better with the partially limited amount of available training data for ancient Roman coins [20].

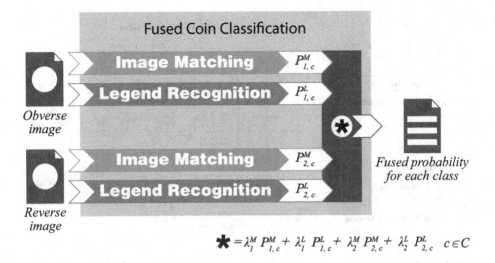

Fig. 2. The fused coin classification workflow

The challenge of high intra-class variance is thereby overcome by using a flexible model for dense correspondence that is able to handle the spatial variations of local structures between coins of the same class and is robust to image clutter.

Similar to the SIFT flow method proposed in [13], we use a dense field of SIFT features [14] to compute pixel-to-pixel correspondences between two images. Each SIFT feature provides a rotation-invariant description of its local neighborhood by means of gradient orientation distributions and thus the costs of matching two pixels can be computed by their Euclidean distance. This can be described in form of an energy term $E(\mathbf{w})$ with an additional regularization term to favor smoothness of the result:

$$E(\mathbf{w}) = \sum_{\mathbf{p}} \|S_1(\mathbf{p}) - S_2(\mathbf{p} + \mathbf{w}(\mathbf{p}))\|_2 \tag{1}$$

$$+ \sum_{(\mathbf{p},\mathbf{q})\in\Omega} \min(\alpha|u(\mathbf{p}) - u(\mathbf{q})|, d) + \min(\alpha|v(\mathbf{p}) - v(\mathbf{q})|, d) \tag{2}$$

where S_1 and S_2 are dense fields of SIFT features computed at every image point $\mathbf{p}$ of the two images to be compared, $\mathbf{w}(\mathbf{p}) = (u(\mathbf{p}), v(\mathbf{p}))$ describes the correspondences, Ω contains all four-connected pixel pairs and α and d control the influence of the regularization term.

As in the SIFT flow method [13], a dual-layer belief propagation [18] is used along with a coarse-to-fine matching scheme to minimize $E(\mathbf{w})$ and determine the optimal image matching. The resulting energy value is taken as measure of dissimilarity between the two coin images. Therefore, for a given input image class scores $\Psi_{s,c}^M$ are determined by comparing it to single reference images of all classes in the database.

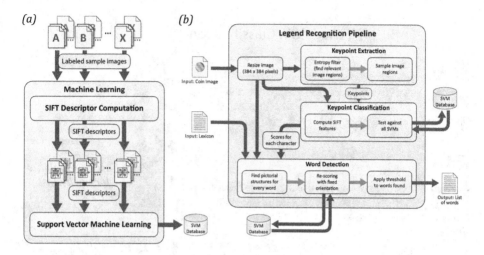

Fig. 3. Overview of the legend recognition methodology [12]. (a) Training of SVMs. (b) Legend recognition pipeline.

3.2 Coin Classification by Legend Recognition

The overall architecture of the legend recognition [12] method is depicted in Fig. 3. The method is classification-based and therefore requires an initial training step before the actual recognition can be performed.

Training. In order to teach the appearance of the individual legend letters to our system, we again use SIFT features [14] for letter representation (see Fig. 3(a)). The training set comprises 50 100 × 100 pixel-sized images per character class. The legends considered can be represented by 18 different capital letters. Since structures resembling the letter 'I' often occur in the depicted imagery, this letter is not trained. Due to high variations in the illumination conditions and heavy degradations related to wear and chemicals in the soil, some letters are barely visible and the respective edges in the image cannot be used for robust keypoint detection. Thus, only one descriptor which is centered and scaled according to the letter size is computed and used in the Support Vector Machine (SVM) training. Because both rotationally invariant and fixed SIFT descriptors are required in the recognition step, two different databases are created.

Legend Recognition. The legend recognition step is depicted in Fig. 3(b). Its input parameters are a coin image and a lexicon containing all legend words the image should be scanned for. Since the legend recognition results are more reliable for longer words, we do not consider words having less than five letters. After an initial downscaling of the image to a standard size of 384 × 384 pixel, the image is passed to the *Keypoint Detection* step where flat image regions are identified using an entropy filter and ignored for further processing. Next, a densely sampled grid is constructed in the remaining image regions which represents the *candidate character locations* (CCL) [19]. These locations serve as input for the *Keypoint Classification* step, in which a SIFT descriptor is computed for each of the CCLs. Every descriptor is tested against the 18 SVMs trained for rotationally invariant SIFT features and yields a score telling how likely it is to encounter a letter of the respective class at this location. Thus, every CCL is now associated with 18 scores. In the *Word Detection* step, the optimal configuration for every word of the input lexicon is found within the image using pictorial structures [7]. Finally, all words found are rescored. Since the individual character locations are known for a specific word hypothesis, the respective character orientations are known as well and can be used to compute SIFT descriptors aligned accordingly. This increases the confidence in the hypothesis since orientationally fixed SIFT descriptors lead to a better character recognition rate [12]. In the end, the output of the legend recognition pipeline is a list of words ordered by their scores. The respective coin classes are retrieved via a lookup table which maps the legend words to coin types, resulting in the class scores $\Psi_{s,c}^L$.

3.3   Combination of Image Matching and Legend Recognition

Both image matching and legend recognition provide class scores $\Psi_{s,c}^M$ and $\Psi_{s,c}^L$, respectively, which indicate the dissimilarity of the input coin's side $s \in \{1,2\}$ to class $c \in C$. In order to combine the individual class scores, we first transform them to the same range. More specifically, the class scores are transformed to pseudo probabilities $P_{s,c}^M$ and $P_{s,c}^L$ in such a way that the class score with lowest dissimilarity is mapped to the highest probability and $\sum_{c \in C} P_{s,c} = 1$. Furthermore, we define a parameter δ that describes the factor between the class with highest probability and the class with lowest probability, i.e., the class with lowest class dissimilarity has a probability δ times higher than the class with highest dissimilarity:

$$P_{s,c} = \frac{1}{\widetilde{\Psi}_{s,c} \cdot \sum_{c \in C} 1/\widetilde{\Psi}_{s,c}} \tag{3}$$

where

$$\widetilde{\Psi}_{s,c} = \frac{\Psi_{s,c} - \min_{c \in C}(\Psi_{s,c})}{\max_{c \in C}(\Psi_{s,c}) - \min_{c \in C}(\Psi_{s,c})}(\delta - 1) + 1. \tag{4}$$

For the final class decision we apply a weighted sum rule, since it allows for a flexible combination which accounts for the unequal recognition accuracies of the individual votes. Thus, a coin is finally classified to class c^* with

$$c^* = \arg\max_{c \in C}(\lambda_1^M P_{1,c}^M + \lambda_2^M P_{2,c}^M + \lambda_1^L P_{1,c}^L + \lambda_2^L P_{2,c}^L) \tag{5}$$

4   Experiments

The experiments were conducted on images of 232 coins from 60 classes. All coins are from the Roman Republican age and have been provided by the *Museum of Fine Arts* in *Vienna*. Class membership is defined by Crawford's standard

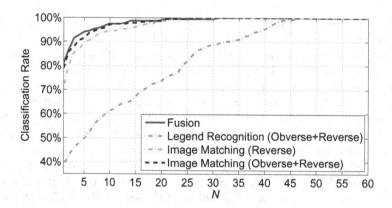

Fig. 4. Classification accuracy of legend recognition, image matching and our proposed fusion method for the top N classes

reference book [5]. For each coin, an image of obverse and reverse is present in the dataset; thus, an overall of 464 images was used. The lexicon of obverse and reverse words contains 21 and 41 words, respectively, since some classes have words in common and not all words present on the coins can be used: legend recognition is not robust enough for words with less than five letters because falsely classified letters have a stronger influence on the overall score for shorter words. The parameters for classifier combination have been empirically chosen as $\delta = 10$, $\lambda_1^M = \lambda_2^M = 0.4$ and $\lambda_1^L = \lambda_2^L = 0.3$. The weights of the legend recognition are lower due to the general worse performance of legend recognition compared to image matching.

In Fig. 4 the results for legend recognition, image matching and our proposed fusion method are compared. The plot shows the respective percentage of coins where the correct class is within the top N probabilities. First of all, it can be seen that combining both coin sides supports the classification, as for image matching only the classification rate is generally higher compared to the case where only the reverse side is considered (78.9% vs. 71.1% for $N = 1$). Legend recognition is more error-prone than image matching due to the challenging nature of the problem: in contrast to image matching only small coin parts are analyzed and thus this process is more affected by noise and the variation of the image data. Nonetheless, it is clearly shown that in combination with image matching legend recognition improves the classification rate, as for $N = 1$ the classification rate is increased from 78.9% to 81.0%. The highest gap between image matching only and the fused result is spotted at $N = 3$, where an improvement from 87.9% to 91.4% can be achieved.

The benefit of using legend information is also demonstrated by the two classification results shown in Fig. 5. By using image matching only, the coins are classified to the wrong class (Fig. 5(b)), since the reference images (Fig. 5(c)) are in a sub-optimal condition and the strong abrasions on the coin impede to establish the true correspondences. However, with the support of legend recognition the final decision is changed to the correct class.

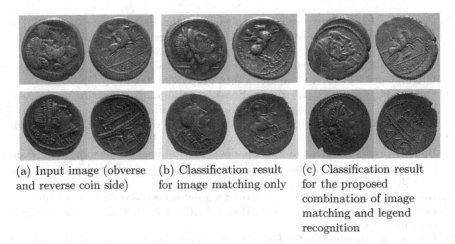

(a) Input image (obverse and reverse coin side)

(b) Classification result for image matching only

(c) Classification result for the proposed combination of image matching and legend recognition

Fig. 5. Two classification results comparing the use of image matching only and the proposed fusion method

5   Conclusion

In this paper, a novel way for the classification of ancient Roman Republican coins is proposed that combines image matching with legend recognition to improve the classification rates the methods achieve individually. The presented experiments carried out on 464 images prove the effectiveness of the fused approach as it outperforms both methods when applied separately. The proposed method is more flexible than state-of-the-art coin classification systems for ancient coins as it does not rely on a specific coin layout and legend alignment. However, for future research both methods, but especially the legend recognition, have to be further improved to provide a stronger benefit of combining both methods.

Acknowledgment. This research has been supported by the Austrian Science Fund (FWF) under the grant TRP140-N23-2010 (ILAC).

References

1. Arandjelovic, O.: Automatic attribution of ancient roman imperial coins. In: Conference on Computer Vision and Pattern Recognition, pp. 1728–1734 (2010)
2. Arandjelović, O.: Reading ancient coins: Automatically identifying denarii using obverse legend seeded retrieval. In: Fitzgibbon, A., Lazebnik, S., Perona, P., Sato, Y., Schmid, C. (eds.) ECCV 2012, Part IV. LNCS, vol. 7575, pp. 317–330. Springer, Heidelberg (2012)
3. Ballard, D.H.: Generalizing the hough transform to detect arbitrary shapes. Pattern Recognition 13, 111–122 (1981)
4. Bremananth, R., Balaji, B., Sankari, M., Chitra, A.: A new approach to coin recognition using neural pattern analysis. In: IEEE INDICON 2005, pp. 366–370 (2005)

5. Crawford, M.H.: Roman republican coinage. Cambridge University Press (1974)
6. Dalal, N., Triggs, B.: Histograms of oriented gradients for human detection. In: Conference on Computer Vision and Pattern Recognition, pp. 886–893 (2005)
7. Felzenszwalb, P.F., Huttenlocher, D.P.: Pictorial structures for object recognition. International Journal of Computer Vision 61, 55–79 (2005)
8. Fukumi, M., Omatu, S., Takeda, F., Kosaka, T.: Rotation-invariant neural pattern recognition system with application to coin recognition. In: Proceedings of the International Joint Conference on Neural Networks, vol. 2, pp. 1027–1032 (1991)
9. Grierson, P.: Numismatics. Oxford University Press (1975)
10. Huber-Mörk, R., Zambanini, S., Zaharieva, M., Kampel, M.: Identification of ancient coins based on fusion of shape and local features. Machine Vision Applications 22, 983–994 (2011)
11. Kampel, M., Zaharieva, M.: Recognizing ancient coins based on local features. In: Bebis, G., et al. (eds.) ISVC 2008, Part I. LNCS, vol. 5358, pp. 11–22. Springer, Heidelberg (2008)
12. Kavelar, A., Zambanini, S., Kampel, M.: Word detection applied to images of ancient roman coins. In: International Conference on Virtual Systems and Multimedia, pp. 577–580 (2012)
13. Liu, C., Yuen, J., Torralba, A.: Sift flow: Dense correspondence across scenes and its applications. IEEE Pattern Analysis and Machine Intelligence 33(5), 978–994 (2011)
14. Lowe, D.G.: Distinctive image features from scale-invariant keypoints. International Journal of Computer Vision 60(2), 91–110 (2004)
15. van der Maaten, L.J., Poon, P.: Coin-o-matic: A fast system for reliable coin classification. In: Muscle CIS Coin Competition Workshop, pp. 7–18 (2006)
16. Nölle, M., Penz, H., Rubik, M., Mayer, K., Holländer, I., Granec, R.: Dagobert - a new coin recognition and sorting system. In: 7th International Conference on Digital Image Computing - Techniques and Applications, pp. 329–338 (2003)
17. Reisert, M., Ronneberger, O., Burkhardt, H.: An efficient gradient based registration technique for coin recognition. In: Muscle CIS Coin Competition Workshop, pp. 19–31 (2006)
18. Shekhovtsov, A., Kovtun, I., Hlaváca, V.: Efficient mrf deformation model for non-rigid image matching. Computer Vision and Image Understanding 112(1), 91–99 (2008)
19. Wang, K., Belongie, S.: Word spotting in the wild. In: Daniilidis, K., Maragos, P., Paragios, N. (eds.) ECCV 2010, Part I. LNCS, vol. 6311, pp. 591–604. Springer, Heidelberg (2010)
20. Zambanini, S., Kampel, M.: Coarse-to-fine correspondence search for classifying ancient coins. In: 2nd ACCV Workshop on e-Heritage, pp. 25–36 (2013)

Stopwords Detection in Bag-of-Visual-Words: The Case of Retrieving Maya Hieroglyphs

Edgar Roman-Rangel and Stephane Marchand-Maillet

CVMLab, University of Geneva, Switzerland

Abstract. We present a method for automatic detection of stopwords in visual vocabularies that is based upon the entropy of each visual word. We propose a specific formulation to compute the entropy as the core of this method, in which the probability density function of the visual words is marginalized over all visual classes, such that words with higher entropy can be considered to be irrelevant words, i.e., stopwords. We evaluate our method on a dataset of syllabic Maya hieroglyphs, which is of great interest for archaeologists, and that requires efficient techniques for indexing and retrieval. Our results show that our method produces shorter bag representations without hurting retrieval performance, and even improving it in some cases, which does not happen when using previous methods. Furthermore, our assumptions for the proposed computation of the entropy can be generalized to bag representations of different nature.

Keywords: Bag-of-words, stopwords, retrieval, archaeology, hieroglyphs.

1 Introduction

The bag-of-visual-words (BOW) paradigm [9] stands among the most efficient representations of images for the purpose of classification and retrieval [5] [12]. Based upon an analogy with the representation of text documents, this approach models a given visual document (i.e., image) as the frequency histogram of its *visual words*. In practice, the BOW model consists in a single vector per image which corresponds to a global representation constructed from a set of local descriptors, often robust to a variety of transformations, e.g., rotation, scale, affine, etc. As such, the BOW representation enables the capabilities for efficient indexing of large datasets and fast comparison of documents, as opposed to the expensive point-to-point matching paradigm.

One important step to generate discriminative BOW models of text documents consists in removing all stopwords from the vocabulary, i.e., words that are of low relevance for the BOW representation, e.g., articles or prepositions. This step is relatively trivial as text documents have finite vocabularies that can be easily discovered by identifying all unique words within the dataset. However, this is not the case for visual documents whose local descriptors are vectors in the continuous feature space R^N, and whose vocabularies often need to be estimated by the unsupervised quantization of the local descriptors [5]. As a consequence of

A. Petrosino, L. Maddalena, P. Pala (Eds.): ICIAP 2013 Workshops, LNCS 8158, pp. 159–168, 2013.

this, it is rather difficult to associate visual words to lexical components such as nouns or verbs, and consequently, equally difficult to decide which visual words should be considered stopwords and removed from the vocabulary.

Following the analogy with text representations, many past works have defined lists of visual stopwords as those words occurring with the highest frequencies [1] [9]. However, there is neither empirical nor statistical evidence that all the popular words in a corpus correspond to stopwords. Furthermore, recent works have shown that removing frequent visual words can harm the classification performance [11] [12]. Fig. 1 shows one example of a frequent visual word that is of high relevance and therefore must not be removed from the vocabulary.

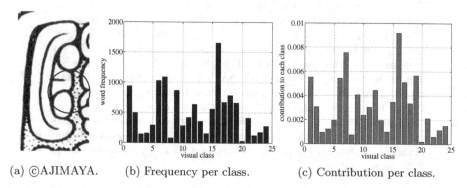

(a) ©AJIMAYA.   (b) Frequency per class.   (c) Contribution per class.

Fig. 1. Example of a frequent visual word in a vocabulary of 1000 words estimated for a dataset of Maya hieroglyphs. 1a shows a visual example of the word, i.e., the blue circle indicates the local feature computed using the HOOSC descriptor [6]; 1b shows the frequency of this word across 24 visual classes; and 1c shows the contribution of the word to each class, proportional to the rest of the vocabulary. Although this word presents high occurrence count in the dataset, it is relevant as it distributes differently among the visual classes, thus contributing to the discriminative potential of the BOW representations.

In this work, we propose to use the probability distribution of each word as an indicator of the relevance of each such a word. More specifically, we consider that irrelevant words are roughly equally present in all visual classes, i.e., their probability distribution is uniform, thus resulting in high entropy [7], and therefore they must be considered stopwords. We also propose a specific formulation to compute the entropy as the core of this method, in which the probability density function of the visual words is marginalized over all visual classes.

We evaluate our methods on a dataset of syllabic Maya hieroglyphs that exists in binary format. This is a dataset of great importance for archaeologists devoted to the study of the ancient Maya civilization, as it serves the purpose of catalog to compare an identify new symbols as they are discovered. This dataset contains instances from 24 visual classes, while there are almost 1000 Maya symbols that have been identified thus far [6]. Yet it posits many challenges for automatic retrieval. In practice, this dataset is a portion of a large corpus that is currently under construction, and that, in the long term, would benefit from automated methods that enable its efficient browsing and retrieval.

We compare our proposed approach with: (1) previous methods that simply consider stopwords those words having high or low frequency within a given dataset [1] [9]; and (2) a PCA-based method for dimensionality reduction [3] [2]. Our results show that different from these approaches, ours allows to remove up to 30% of visual words with almost no drop in the retrieval precision. Furthermore, it results in higher retrieval precision in some cases.

The rest of this document is organized as follows. Section 2 presents the related work in the detection of visual stopwords. Section 3 introduces our proposed approach. Section 4 explains the dataset and protocol followed to evaluate our proposed approach. Section 5 discusses our results. And section 6 presents our conclusions and potential future directions for this research.

2   Related Work

The most common approach to remove visual stopwords consists in simply excluding all the most frequent words from the vocabulary [1] [9]. This approach was devised based the analogy that text-stopwords have high frequencies over the whole corpus, e.g., articles and prepositions [9], and assuming that in the images they will point to local descriptors corresponding to background or simply to uninformative structures.

A more recent work [4] shows that the most frequent words are in fact not very informative, as the classification performance is not impacted by removing them. In addition, some new experiments show an increased performance after removing the most frequent words from the vocabulary [10]. However, some other recent explorations on this regard have shown that simply excluding the most frequent visual words may be harmful for the classification performance [12]. Furthermore there is not guarantee that all of the most frequent terms correspond to stopwords, and some claims have been raised in favor that frequent visual words are highly informative [11].

A related approach that pursuits dimensionality reduction of BOW representations is PCA [3]. This approach consists in projecting the BOW representations onto linear uncorrelated variables that are sorted according the amount of variance they are able to describe. These projected variables are called principal components, and a reduced BOW representation can be constructed by using only the N most principal components. However, this approach does not guarantee that the components excluded from the reduced representation correspond to stopwords. Also, the discussion regarding whether the loss in performance is acceptable or not remains open [2].

Upon an entropy-based approach, visual stopwords are automatically detected in a video corpus [13], where words correspond to actions and their distribution is conditioned to their occurence within each video. However, this approach suffers from two main drawbacks: (1) the list of actions (words) must be manually defined, which might be unfeasible when there are no labels associated to the visual content; and (2) the entropy of each visual word is sensitive to small variations in its density across videos.

Similar approaches to ours are used to remove stopwords from text corpora [14] [15] and web documents [8], with the difference that the distribution of words is conditioned directly over the documents rather than on the classes, thus these approaches are sensitive to intra-class variations. However, to the best of our knowledge, there are not previous works that detect visual stopwords for still images based on their entropy.

3   Identifying Stopwords

This section explains our proposed method to compute entropy for visual words.

The entropy [7] can be used as an indicator of information content for a given random variable X, in the sense that the entropy of this variable will be larger as its probability density function (PDF) tends to the uniform distribution. This follows after the observation that little information is represented when all the possible values of a random variable are equally probable, i.e., no information is acquired by knowing the value of the random variable. Based on this observation, we define a visual stopword as a word with high entropy.

The Shannon entropy [7] of the discrete random variable X, with possible values $\{x_1, x_2, \ldots, x_n\}$ is defined as,

$$H(X) = -\sum_{i=1}^{n} p(x_i) \log p(x_i), \tag{1}$$

where $p(x_i)$ denotes the PDF of the random variable X, i.e., the probability of the variable taking the value $X = x_i$.

For the case of visual words, we marginalize their PDF over all possible visual classes in the dataset. This is, we can consider each visual word as a random variable W that can take values $\{w_1, w_2, \ldots, w_n\}$,

$$w_i = P(W|c_i), \quad i = 1, \ldots, n, \tag{2}$$

where c_i denotes each of the n visual classes in the dataset, and $P(W|c_i)$ indicates the relevance of W given the i-th class.

In practice, we can compute the PDF of the random variable W directly by,

$$p(w_i) = \frac{f^W(c_i)}{\sum_i f^W(c_i)}, \tag{3}$$

where $f^W(c_i)$ denotes the frequency of the word in class c_i, and the normalization induced by the denominator corresponds to the summation over all the visual classes within the dataset, but independently for each visual word.

Therefore, for each visual word in the dataset, the entropy of its associated random variable W can be computed as,

$$H(W) = -\sum_{i=1}^{n} p(w_i) \log p(w_i). \tag{4}$$

After the entropy of each word is computed, we mark as stopwords all visual words with high entropy values, and remove them from the vocabulary.

4   Experiments

This section presents the dataset used to evaluate the proposed approach for detection of visual stopwords, and the experimental protocol we followed.

4.1   Dataset

The dataset consists of 24 visual classes of syllabic Maya hieroglyphs in binary format. Each class having 10 instances manually segmented from larger inscriptions that were collected by the AJIMAYA project [6], and that correspond to manual drawings traced upon photographies of stone monuments. This dataset also contains 25 synthetic variations that were randomly generated for each instance with the purpose of increasing the size of the dataset, thus accounting for 260 final instances per visual class.

The process to generate the synthetic data consisted in shifting the position of the bounding box containing the glyph of interest within the inscription that contains it, but without modifying its original size. During this process, the position was shifted at fixed intervals of $\{-16, -8, 0, 8, 16\}$ pixels from the original position, both in the horizontal and vertical axes. Therefore, the synthetic variant contain only sections of each original instances plus random visual structures that are present in the large inscription. Fig. 2 shows some examples the instances in the Maya dataset.

4.2   Experimental Protocol

We compare the performance of our proposed method against two approaches. Namely, (a) the traditional method that removes the most and less frequent visual words [1] [9], and (b) a PCA-based method [3] [2] for dimensionality reduction which assumes that the less principal components correspond to stopwords. Independently for each of these methods, we performed retrieval experiments to evaluate the proposed approach under the following protocol:

1. Compute local descriptors for all the images. We used the HOOSC descriptors [6] for the binary shapes.
2. Estimate a visual vocabularies of different sizes using a random subset of the descriptors and the k-means clustering algorithm.

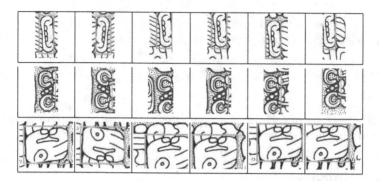

Fig. 2. Examples of Maya instances. The first element in each row is the initial segmented glyph, and the following elements are some of its synthetic variations. The glyph of interest is highlighted by a cyan rectangle in all cases. ©AJIMAYA

3. Estimate the BOW representation of each image, removing at each time, different portions of the vocabulary, i.e., the words that most likely are stopwords given the evaluated method.
4. Perform retrieval experiments under a leave-one-out full-cross validation, i.e., each of the instances in the dataset, one at the time, was considered as query, and the rest of the instances in the dataset were ranked according their visual similarity with respect to the current query. We use the Manhattan distance as ranking function, except for the PCA-based method that uses Euclidean distance since this metric is more suitable due to the Gaussian underlaying model and the orthonormality induced by the PCA projections.
5. Compute the mean Average Precision (mAP) of the retrieval experiment.

Note that the retrieval experiments were repeated several times, removing a different percentage of the visual vocabulary each time. All of our results are reported in terms of mAP.

5   Results

We start by evaluating the retrieval performance of the baseline approach that removes the most frequent visual words by varying the rate of words removed. Fig. 3a shows the mAP achieved by removing up to 30% of the most frequent words in dictionaries of different size. Note that the performance exhibits a slight degradation as more words get excluded, specially for the smaller dictionaries.

Similarly, Fig. 3b shows the mAP obtained after removing up to 30% of the visual words based on our method. Contrary to the frequency-based case, the performance only degrades for small dictionaries with the entropy-based approach, and provides a slight improvement for larger dictionaries. This result shows that it is possible to obtain compact dictionaries that not only hold good retrieval performance but also could improve it in some cases.

To validate the idea of considering words with low frequency to be stopwords as suggested by some previous works [1] [9] [10], we combined such an approach

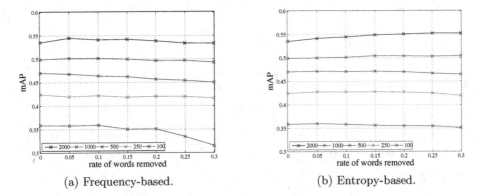

(a) Frequency-based.   (b) Entropy-based.

Fig. 3. mAP achieved by removing words from the BOW representations at different rates based on: 3a their high frequency; and 3b their high entropy. Each curve corresponds to a vocabulary of different size, i.e., 2000, 1000, 500, 250, and 100 visual words, respectively.

with both the baseline and our proposed approach. This is, we removed (a) words of high frequency and also words of low frequency first, and then (b) words of high entropy together with words of low frequency. Fig. 4a shows the degradation in the retrieval performance as more words of low frequency get removed from the BOW representations using the vocabulary of 2000 words, where each curve corresponds to a fix rate of words removed using the criteria of high frequencies. Note that all of these curves degrade as more words of low frequency are excluded. A very similar behavior is found when the approach of excluding the less frequent words is combined with the proposed approach based on high entropy, as shown in Fig. 4b. The curves obtained for the dictionaries of 1000, 500, 250, and 100 words all have similar behavior when removing words of low frequency (we do not show those curves here due to space limitations).

This consistent degradation in the performance suggests that words of low frequency do not correspond to stopwords. However, the performance is not drastically affected by removing up to 30% of these words. More specifically, by looking at the cyan curve in Fig. 4b[1], that corresponds to removing 30% of the words with higher entropy, we can see that it is also possible to remove up to 10% of the less frequent words without hurting the retrieval performance, thus 800 words in total. This means that there are roughly 1200 words that are of actual relevance for a vocabulary of 2000 visual words. Note that this does not imply that a direct estimation of a vocabulary of 1200 words would achieve the same performance, as this would change the structure of the vocabulary.

The final approach that we evaluated consists in a PCA-based dimensionality reduction. Fig. 5a shows the curves of the retrieval precision obtained after removing words that correspond to the less principal components. Note that

---

[1] Best viewed as pdf since the red curve overlaps the cyan curve.

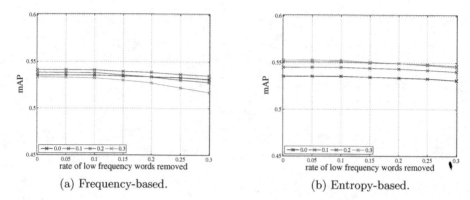

(a) Frequency-based.   (b) Entropy-based.

Fig. 4. *mAP* achieved by removing words of low frequency from the BOW representations at different rates, and using a fixed dictionary of 2000 visual words. Each curve corresponds to the approach that removes words based on: 4a their high frequency; and 4b their high entropy. Note that the two blue curves are the same, as they mean that words are excluded solely based on their low frequency.

in this case, removing more words results in better retrieval precision for the largest dictionaries, e.g., the best performance is achieved by using only 10% of the words from the dictionaries of 1000 and 2000 words (blue and green curves). In Fig. 5b, the retrieval precision of PCA is further compared with an entropy-based method that also uses the Euclidean distance for ranking, red and blue curves respectively. We can see that these two approaches achieve similar results up to 70% of the words are removed, and that PCA is more suitable that the entropy to produce very short representations, although at the price of a small drop in performance when compared with the entropy-based method that uses the L1 distance (green curve, which corresponds to the green curve also in Fig. 3b). Note that this comparison corresponds to the vocabulary of 1000 words, and that the behavior remains similar for vocabularies of different sizes.

In practice, the proposed entropy-based approach proves to be a suitable option for detection of visual stopwords, as it ensures that only those words that are irrelevant for a given visual vocabulary get excluded from the final BOW representations, i.e., words having a uniform distribution over the visual classes.

6   Conclusions

We presented a method to detect stopwords in visual vocabularies, and proposed a formulation to compute the entropy of visual words based upon their probability distribution, which is marginalized over all the visual classes but independent for each visual word.

We evaluated our proposed formulation on a dataset of syllabic Maya hiero-glyphs, which consist in complex shapes. The dataset we used represents but

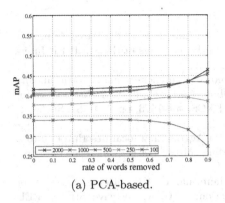

(a) PCA-based.

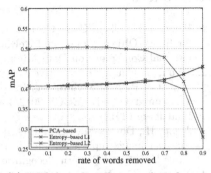

(b) PCA-based vs Entropy-based comparison for 1000 visual words.

Fig. 5. *mAP* achieved by removing words from the BOW representations at different rates based on the amount of variance they describe after applying PCA on the visual vocabulary

a portion of a potentially enormous corpus that its currently under construction, and which will require adequate representations for efficient indexing and automatic retrieval, thus the motivation for this research.

Our proposed formulation ensures that only those words that are irrelevant for a given visual vocabulary get excluded from the final BOW representations. This is those visual words having a uniform distribution over the visual classes, regardless of their distribution across a given document or their frequency within the whole dataset. In practice, our results demonstrate that the proposed formulation provides with shorter BOW representations of equal or higher discriminative power to retrieve complex shapes. Such shorter representations are equally capable of good retrieval results as the original representations constructed after simple quantization, and much more suitable than those found under a PCA-based dimensionality reduction approach. Furthermore, a slight improvement in the retrieval precision was possible in some cases.

It remain to be evaluated whether our findings will be true also for visual vocabularies of different nature, e.g., bag representations for intensity images, or based on other kind of local descriptors. However, we believe that our approach will be equally suitable for those cases, under the same assumption that the entropy can guide the detection of visual stopwords, as it previously did for the detection of text stopwords.

Acknowledgments. This works was supported by the Swiss NSF through the NCCR IM2.

References

1. Hsiao, J.-H., Chen, C.-S., Chen, M.-S.: A Novel Language-Model-Based Approach for Image Object Mining and ReRanking. In: Proceedings of the 8th IEEE International Conference on Data Mining (2008)
2. Jégou, H., Chum, O.: Negative evidences and co-occurences in image retrieval: The benefit of PCA and whitening. In: Fitzgibbon, A., Lazebnik, S., Perona, P., Sato, Y., Schmid, C. (eds.) ECCV 2012, Part II. LNCS, vol. 7573, pp. 774–787. Springer, Heidelberg (2012)
3. Jégou, H., Douze, M., Schmid, C., Pérez, P.: Aggregating local descriptors into a compact image representation. In: Proceedings of the IEEE Conference on Computer Vision and Pattern Recognition (2010)
4. Jiang, Y.-G., Yang, J., Ngo, C.-W., Hauptmann, A.G.: Representations of Keypoint-Based Semantic Concept Detection: A Comprehensive Study. IEEE Transactions on Multimedia 12(1), 42–53 (2010)
5. Quelhas, P., Monay, F., Odobez, J.-M., Gatica-Perez, D., Tuytelaars, T.: A Thousand Words in a Scene. IEEE Transactions on Pattern Analysis and Machine Intelligence 29(9), 1575–1589 (2007)
6. Roman-Rangel, E., Pallan, C., Odobez, J.-M., Gatica-Perez, D.: Analyzing Ancient Maya Glyph Collections with Contextual Shape Descriptor. International Journal of Computer Vision 94(1), 101–117 (2011)
7. Shannon, C.E.: A Mathematical Theory of Communication. Bell System Technical Journal 27(3), 379–423 (1948)
8. Sinka, M.P., Corne, D.W.: Towards Modernised and Web-Specific Stoplists for Web Document Analysis. In: Proceedings of the IEEE/WIC International Conference on Web Intelligence (2003)
9. Sivic, J., Zisserman, A.: Video google: A text retrieval approach to object matching in videos. In: Proceedings of the 9th IEEE International Conference on Computer Vision (2003)
10. van Zwol, R., Garcia Pueyo, L.: Spatially-aware indexing for image object retrieval. In: Proceedings of the 5th ACM International Conference on Web Search and Data Mining (2012)
11. Yang, J., Hauptmann, A.: A text categorization approach to video scene classification using keypoint features. CMU Technical Report (2006)
12. Yang, J., Jiang, Y.-G., Hauptmann, A.G., Ngo, C.-W.: Evaluating Bag-of-Visual-Words Representations in Scene Classification. In: Proceedings of the International Workshop on Multimedia Information Retrieval (2007)
13. Zhao, Z.: Towards a Local-Global Visual Feature-Based Framework for Recognition. PhD Thesis. Rutgers University (October 2009)
14. Zheng, L., Cox, I.J.: Entropy-Based Static Index Pruning. In: Boughanem, M., Berrut, C., Mothe, J., Soule-Dupuy, C. (eds.) ECIR 2009. LNCS, vol. 5478, pp. 713–718. Springer, Heidelberg (2009)
15. Zou, F., Wang, F.L., Deng, X., Han, S., Wang, L.S.: Automatic Construction of Chinese Stop Word List. In: Proceedings of the 5th WSEAS International Conference on Applied Computer Science (2006)

3D Object Partial Matching
Using Panoramic Views

Konstantinos Sfikas[1], Ioannis Pratikakis[1,2], Anestis Koutsoudis[1],
Michalis Savelonas[1], and Theoharis Theoharis[3,4]

[1] ATHENA Research and Innovation Center, Xanthi, Greece,
[2] Democritus University of Thrace, Department of Electrical & Computer
Engineering, Xanthi, Greece,
[3] Department of Informatics and Telecommunications,
University of Athens, Greece
[4] IDI, Norwegian University of Science and Technology (NTNU), Norway

Abstract. In this paper, a methodology for 3D object partial matching
and retrieval based on range image queries is presented. The proposed
methodology addresses the retrieval of complete 3D objects based on
artificially created range image queries which represent partial views.
The core methodology relies upon Dense SIFT descriptors computed on
panoramic views. Performance evaluation builds upon the standard measures and a challenging 3D pottery dataset originated from the Hampson
Archeological Museum collection.

Keywords: 3D object retrieval, partial matching, 3D pottery dataset.

1 Introduction

Generic 3D object retrieval has considerably matured and a number of accurate
and robust descriptors have been proposed in the literature [5, 14, 21, 22, 27].
However, there are still many challenges regarding the retrieval of 3D models
that originate from specific domains and/or exhibit special characteristics. One
such domain is Cultural Heritage (CH) which includes 3D models that are usually
deteriorate, due to aging, their shape is altered due to environmental factors and
in most cases only incomplete artefacts have been preserved.

The problem with the partial data is that it is not possible to effectively match
them against a full 3D model representation, since most of it may be missing.
The representation gap makes it difficult to extract a signature that will be,
at least partially, similar when presented with a complete 3D model and when
presented with a partial query of a similar object.

We have addressed this challenge by using a panoramic view representation
that is able to encode the 3D surface characteristics onto a 2D image map,
as well as range image representation which can be mapped to the panoramic
views through interest points correspondence. For the complete 3D models, we
compute a number of panoramic views on axes, which are perpendicular to
the faces of a dodecahedron. Each axis defines three panoramic view cylinders

A. Petrosino, L. Maddalena, P. Pala (Eds.): ICIAP 2013 Workshops, LNCS 8158, pp. 169–178, 2013.

(one for the axis itself and two more for any two axes in order to make up an orthonormal basis, along with the first one.). Then, we apply the Dense SIFT (DSIFT) algorithm [9, 18] to the points and calculate the corresponding descriptor. In the same spirit, for the partial objects, we initially compute a range image representation used as the query model for which the DSIFT algorithm is calculated.

The remainder of the paper is structured as follows. In Section 2, recent work on 3D model retrieval based on range image queries is discussed. Section 3 details the proposed method and Section 4 presents experimental results achieved in the course of the method's evaluation. Finally, conclusions are drawn in Section 5.

2   Related Work

Over the past few years, the number of works addressing the problems of partial 3D object retrieval has increased significantly. Although this task still remains non-trivial, very important steps have been made in the field.

Stavropoulos et al. [25] present a retrieval method based on the matching of salient features between the 3D models and query range images. Salient points are extracted from vertices that exhibit local maxima in terms of protrusion mapping for a specific window on the surface of the model. A hierarchical matching scheme based is used for matching. The authors experimented on range images acquired from the SHape REtrieval Contest 2007 (SHREC'07) *Watertight Models* [11] and the Princeton Shape Benchmark (PSB) standard [24] datasets. Chaouch and Verroust-Blondet [3] present a 2D/3D shape descriptor which is based on either silhouette or depth-buffer images. For each 3D model a set of six projections in calculated for both silhouette and depth-buffers. The 2D Fourier transform is then computed on the projection. Furthermore, they compute a relevance index measure which indicates the density of information contained in each 2D view. The same authors in [4] propose a method where a 3D model is projected to the faces of its bounding box, resulting in 6 depth buffers. Each depth buffer is then decomposed into a set of horizontal and vertical depth lines that are converted to state sequences which describe the change in depth at neighboring pixels. Experimentations were conducted on range images artificially acquired from the PSB dataset. Shih et al. [23] proposed the elevation descriptor where six depth buffers (elevations) are computed from the faces of the 3D model bounding box and each buffer is described by a set of concentric circular areas that give the sum of pixel values within the corresponding areas. The models were selected from the standard PSB dataset.

Experimenting on the SHREC'09 *Querying with Partial Models* [7] dataset, Daras and Axenopoulos in [6] present a view-based approach for 3D model retrieval. The 3D model is initially pose normalized and a set of binary (silhouette) and range images are extracted from predefined views on a 32-hedron. The set of features computed on the views are the Polar-Fourier transform, Zernike moments and Krawtchouk moments. Each query image is compared to all the extracted views of each model of the dataset. Ohbuchi et al. [20] extract features from 2D range images of the model viewed from uniformly sampled locations on a view sphere. For every range image, a set of multi-scale 2D visual features are computed using the Scale Invariant Feature Transform (SIFT) [18]. Finally, the features are integrated into a histogram using the Bag-of-Features approach [10]. The same authors enhanced their approach by pre-processing the range images, in order to minimize interfere caused by any existing occlusions,as well as by refining the positioning of SIFT interest points, so that higher resolution images are favored [9,19]. Their works have experimented on and have participated on both corresponding SHREC'09 *Querying with Partial Models* and SHREC'10 *Range Scan Retrieval* [8] contests. Wahl et al. [28] propose a four-dimensional feature that parameterizes the intrinsic geometrical relation of an oriented surface point pair (surflets). For a 3D model a set of surflet pairs is computed over a number of uniformly sampled viewing directions on the surrounding sphere. This work was one of the two contestants of the SHREC'10 *Range Scan Retrieval* track. Finaly, Koutsoudis et al. [16,17] presented a set of 3D shape descriptors designed for content based retrieval of complete or nearly complete 3D vessels. Their performance evaluation experiments were performed on a dataset that included among others a subset of Virtual Hampson Museum 3D collection [15].

In this work, we propose the use of a 3D model representation that bridges the gap between the 3D model and the range scan.

3   Methodology

The main steps of the proposed methodology for partial 3D object retrieval via range queries are: (i) shape descriptors extraction from each full 3D model of the dataset (off-line), (ii) range image computation of the partial query model, (iii) shape descriptor extraction from the range image query (on-line) and (iv) matching of the query descriptor against the descriptor of each 3D model of the dataset.

In the case of the full 3D models, a number of panoramic views of each model are extracted on viewpoint axes that are defined by a dodecahedron, thus extending the PANORAMA [21] method to multiple viewpoint axes. Each axis defines three panoramic view cylinders (one for the axis itself and two more for any two axes so that, along with the first one to make up an orthonormal basis). To obtain a panoramic view, we project the model to the lateral surface of a cylinder of radius R and height $H = 2R$, centered at the origin with its axis parallel to one of the coordinate axes (see Fig. 1a). We set the value of R to $2 * d_{max}$ where d_{max} is the maximum distance of the model's surface from its centroid. In the following, we parameterize the lateral surface of the cylinder using a set of points $s(\phi, y)$ where $\phi \in [0, 2\pi]$ is the angle in the xy plane, $y \in [0, H]$ and we sample the ϕ and y coordinates at rates B and $2B$, respectively (we set $B = 256$). Thus, we obtain the set of points $s(\phi_u, y_v)$, where $\phi_u = u * 2\pi/(2B)$, $y_v = v * H/(B)$, $u \in [0, 2B - 1]$ and $v \in [0, B - 1]$. These points are shown in Fig. 1b.

The next step is to determine the value at each point $s(\phi_u, y_v)$. The computation is carried out iteratively for $v = 0, 1, ..., B - 1$, each time considering the

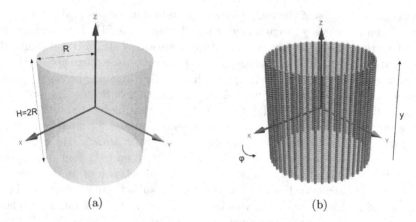

(a)   (b)

Fig. 1. (a) A projection cylinder for the acquisition of a 3D model's panoramic view and (b) the corresponding discretization of its lateral surface to the set of points $s(\phi_u, y_v)$

set of coplanar $s(\phi_u, y_v)$ points i.e. a cross section of the cylinder at height y_v and for each cross section we cast rays from its center c_v in the ϕ_u directions. To capture the position of the model surface, for each cross section at height y_v we compute the distances from c_v to the intersections of the model's surface with the rays at each direction ϕ_u.

Let $pos(\phi_u, y_v)$ denote the distance of the furthest from c_v point of intersection between the ray emanating from c_v in the ϕ_u direction and the model's surface; then $s(\phi_u, y_v) = pos(\phi_u, y_v)$. Thus the value of a point $s(\phi_u, y_v)$ lies in the range $[0, R]$, where R denotes the radius of the cylinder.

A cylindrical projection can be viewed as a 2D gray-scale image where pixels correspond to the $s(\phi_u, y_v)$ intersection points in a manner reminiscent of cylindrical texture mapping [26] and their values are mapped to the [0,1] range. In Fig. 2a, we show an example 3D model and in Fig. 2b the unfolded visual representation of its corresponding cylindrical projection $s(\phi_u, y_v)$.

Once the panoramic views have been extracted, the DSIFT descriptor is calculated on the cylindrical depth images. The first step of the DSIFT computation, is the extraction of a number of interest points, for which the DSIFT descriptors are calculated. The original implementation by Lowe, calculates these interest points through the Difference of Gaussians (DoG) method, which is geared towards enhancing the edges and other details present in the image. It has been experimentally found that the calculation of the DSIFT descriptors over the complete image for a large number of randomly selected points [1, 2, 9, 18] (frequently defined as Dense SIFT/ DSIFT, in the literature), instead of selecting a limited number of interest points, yields better results in terms of retrieval accuracy.

In the case of query models, range images are computed by taking the depth buffer projection. The selected size of sampling is 256×256 pixels and the DSIFT descriptor is computed directly on the range image. The histogram produced out of the total number of DSIFT descriptors is stored as the signature.

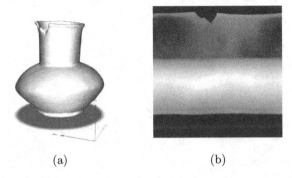

(a)   (b)

Fig. 2. (a) An example 3D model and (b) its corresponding cylindrical projection on the z-axis.

Finally, the descriptors for each interest point of the range image must be matched against the 3D model dataset descriptors. To this end, every DSIFT point of the range image is compared against every DSIFT point of a 3D model's panoramic views, for which the minimum is kept in terms of $L2$ distance. The average of these minimum distances is stored as the final distance of the query and the target model.

4 Evaluation

For the experimental evaluation we have use a dataset related to the cultural heritage domain which is a 3D pottery dataset originated from the Hampson Archeological Museum collection.

The Hampson Archeological Museum collection composes a major source of information on the lives and history of pre-Columbian people of the Mississippi river valley [12]. The Centre of Advanced Spatial Technologies - University of Arkansas worked on the digitisation of numerous artefacts from the Hampson museum collection using a Konica-Minolta Vivid 9i short-range 3D laser scanner. The digitisation was performed at a precision close to 0.2 mm. The 3D digital replicas are covered by the creative common 3.0 license and are offered for online browsing or downloading in both high (>1M facets) and low (<= 25K facets) resolutions [13].

As a testbed for content based retrieval and partial matching experiments, we have used 384 models of low resolution, that were downloaded from the website of the museum along with associated metadata information, as a testbed for content based retrieval and partial matching experiments. Initially the models were classified by the museum into six general classes (Bottle, Bowl, Jar, Effigy, Lithics and Others). As the current classification did not ensure similarities based on shape within a given class, we performed an extended shape-oriented classification. We initially organised the models into thirteen classes of different

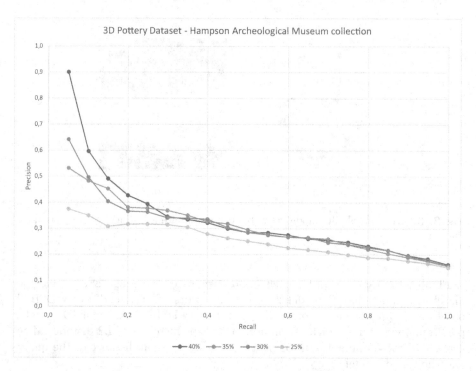

Fig. 3. Average P-R scores for the pottery dataset originating from the Hampson Archeological Museum collection. Illustrated is the performance of the presented method, obtained using queries with reduced surface (40% - 25%) with respect to the surface of the original complete 3D models.

populations (Bottles, Bowls 1 - 4, Figurines, Masks, Pipes, Tools, Tripod-Base Vessels, Conjoined Vessels, Twin Piped Vessels and Others).In the sequel five of these classes (all Bottle and Bowls classes) were further divided into 15 subclasses resulting in a total of 23 distinct classes.

Since this dataset does not contain any partial 3D object that can be used as query, we artificially created a set of 20 partial queries by slicing and cap filling an amount of complete 3D objects, originating from those classes that are densely populated. The partial queries comprise objects with a reduced surface compared to the original 3D object by a factor which ranges from 40% to 25% with a step of 5%.

Our experimental evaluation is based on Precision-Recall (P-R) plots and five quantitative measures: Nearest Neighbor (NN), First Tier (FT), Second Tier (ST), E-measure (E) and Discounted Cumulative Gain (DCG) [24] for the classes of the corresponding datasets. For every query model that belongs to a class C, recall denotes the percentage of models of class C that are retrieved and precision denotes the proportion of retrieved models that belong to class C

over the total number of retrieved models. The maximum score is 100% for both quantities. Nearest Neighbor (NN) indicates the percentage of queries where the closest match belongs to the query class. First Tier (FT) and Second Tier (ST) statistics, measure the recall value for the $(D-1)$ and $2(D-1)$ closest matches respectively, where D is the cardinality of the query class. E-measure combines precision and recall metrics into a single number and the DCG statistic weights correct results near the front of the list more than correct results later in the ranked list under the assumption that a user is less likely to consider elements near the end of the list [24].

In Figure 3 we illustrate the average P-R scores for the presented 3D model retrieval method using the artificially created partial queries of the complete pottery dataset. Results are presented for various amounts of partiality: Table 1 shows the corresponding five quantitative measures. Figure 4 illustrates query examples and the corresponding list of the retrieved 3D models.

Our experimental results show that the proposed method is able to handle quite well the problem of partial to complete matching and illustrates stability in its performance with respect to the percentage of partiality. Even at the high partiality levels where only one quarter of the surface of original model is available, the results are promising.

Table 1. Five quantitative measures for the presented 3D object retrieval methodology, using partial queries on the pottery dataset. All measures are normalized.

Method	NN	FT	ST	E	DCG
Proposed Method (25%)	0.23	0.227	0.388	0.185	0.587
Proposed Method (30%)	0.428	0.289	0.495	0.228	0.655
Proposed Method (35%)	0.619	0.372	0.536	0.327	0.713
Proposed Method (40%)	0.857	0.288	0.508	0.237	0.683

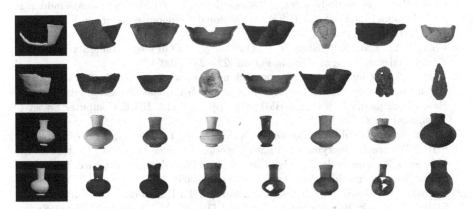

Fig. 4. Example retrieval results from the pottery dataset. At each row, a partial query (column 1) and a ranked list of the retrieved 3D objects (columns 2 - 8) are shown.

The proposed method was tested on a Core2Quad 2.5 GHz system, with 6 GB of RAM, running Matlab R2012b. The system was developed in a hybrid Matlab/C++/OpenGL architecture. The average descriptor extraction time for an 100,000 faces 3D model is about 5 seconds.

5 Conclusions

We have presented a method for partial matching based on DSIFT and panoramic views. This method is able to encode the continuous characteristics of the (partial) 3D models into a 2D representation, thus preserving model structure. The performance of the method is evaluated on a pottery dataset originated from the Hampson Archeological Museum collection of historical artefacts. We have shown that using the proposed methodology, we can attain retrieval results which are not severely affected by the reduction in 3D model surface. This work sets a baseline for methodologies addressing partial 3D object retrieval for cultural heritage datasets.

Acknowledgments. The research leading to these results has received funding from the European Union's Seventh Framework Programme (FP7/2007-2013) under grant agreement n° 600533 PRESIOUS.

References

1. Bosch, A., Zisserman, A., Muñoz, X.: Scene classification via pLSA. In: Leonardis, A., Bischof, H., Pinz, A. (eds.) ECCV 2006. LNCS, vol. 3954, pp. 517–530. Springer, Heidelberg (2006)
2. Bosch, A., Zisserman, A., Muñoz, X.: Image classification using random forests and ferns. In: ICCV 2007, pp. 1–8. IEEE (2007)
3. Chaouch, M., Verroust-Blondet, A.: Enhanced 2D/3D approaches based on relevance index for 3D-shape retrieval. In: SMI, p. 36. IEEE Computer Society (2006)
4. Chaouch, M., Verroust-Blondet, A.: A new descriptor for 2D depth image indexing and 3D model retrieval. In: IEEE International Conference on Image Processing, ICIP 2007, vol. 6, pp. 373–376 (2007)
5. Chen, D.Y., Tian, X.P., Shen, Y.T., Ouhyoung, M.: On visual similarity based 3D model retrieval. Comput. Graph. Forum, 223–232 (2003)
6. Daras, P., Axenopoulos, A.: A compact multi-view descriptor for 3D object retrieval. In: Proceedings of the 2009 Seventh International Workshop on Content-Based Multimedia Indexing, CBMI 2009, pp. 115–119. IEEE Computer Society, Washington, DC (2009)
7. Dutagaci, H., Godil, A., Axenopoulos, A., Daras, P., Furuya, T., Ohbuchi, R.: SHREC'09 track: Querying with partial models. In: Spagnuolo, M., Pratikakis, I., Veltkamp, R., Theoharis, T. (eds.) Eurographics Workshop on 3D Object Retrieval, pp. 69–76. Eurographics Association, Munich (2009)
8. Dutagaci, H., Godil, A., Cheung, C.P., Furuya, T., Hillenbrand, U., Ohbuchi, R.: SHREC'10 track: Range scan retrieval. In: Daoudi, M., Schreck, T. (eds.) Eurographics Workshop on 3D Object Retrieval, pp. 109–115. Eurographics Association, Norrköping (2010)

9. Furuya, T., Ohbuchi, R.: Dense sampling and fast encoding for 3D model retrieval using bag-of-visual features. In: Proceedings of the ACM International Conference on Image and Video Retrieval, CIVR 2009, pp. 26:1–26:8. ACM, New York (2009)

10. Geurts, P., Ernst, D., Wehenkel, L.: Extremely randomized trees. Machine Learning 36(1), 3–42 (2006)

11. Giorgi, D., Biasotti, S., Paraboschi, L.: SHape REtrieval contest 2007: Watertight models track (2007)

12. Hampson: The hampson archaeological museum state park, http://www.arkansasstateparks.com/hampsonmuseum/#.UahgmdJ8lRg (accessed on May 31, 2013)

13. Hampson: The virtual hampson museum project, http://hampson.cast.uark.edu (accessed on May 31, 2013)

14. Kazhdan, M., Funkhouser, T., Rusinkiewicz, S.: Rotation invariant spherical harmonic representation of 3D shape descriptors. In: Proceedings of the 2003 Eurographics/ACM SIGGRAPH Symposium on Geometry Processing, SGP 2003, pp. 156–164. Eurographics Association, Aire-la-Ville (2003)

15. Koutsoudis: A 3D pottery content based retrieval benchmark dataset, http://www.ipet.gr/~akoutsou/benchmark (accessed on May 31, 2013)

16. Koutsoudis, A., Chamzas, C.: 3D pottery shape matching using depth map images. Journal of Cultural Heritage 12(2), 128–133 (2011)

17. Koutsoudis, A., Pavlidis, G., Liami, V., Tsiafakis, D., Chamzas, C.: 3D pottery content-based retrieval based on pose normalisation and segmentation. Journal of Cultural Heritage 11(3), 329–338 (2010)

18. Lowe, D.G.: Object recognition from local scale-invariant features. In: Proceedings of the International Conference on Computer Vision, ICCV 1999, vol. 2, pp. 1150–1157. IEEE Computer Society, Washington, DC (1999)

19. Ohbuchi, R., Furuya, T.: Scale-weighted dense bag of visual features for 3D model retrieval from a partial view 3D model. In: 2009 IEEE 12th International Conference on Computer Vision Workshops (ICCV Workshops), September 27-October 4, pp. 63–70 (2009)

20. Ohbuchi, R., Osada, K., Furuya, T., Banno, T.: Salient local visual features for shape-based 3D model retrieval. In: Shape Modeling International, pp. 93–102. IEEE (2008)

21. Papadakis, P., Pratikakis, I., Theoharis, T., Perantonis, S.J.: PANORAMA: A 3D shape descriptor based on panoramic views for unsupervised 3D object retrieval. International Journal of Computer Vision 89(2-3), 177–192 (2010)

22. Sfikas, K., Pratikakis, I., Theoharis, T.: ConTopo: Non-rigid 3D object retrieval using topological information guided by conformal factors. In: Laga, H., Schreck, T., Ferreira, A., Godil, A., Pratikakis, I., Veltkamp, R.C. (eds.) 3DOR, pp. 25–32. Eurographics Association (2011)

23. Shih, J.L., Lee, C.H., Wang, J.T.: A new 3D model retrieval approach based on the elevation descriptor. Pattern Recognition 40(1), 283–295 (2007)

24. Shilane, P., Min, P., Kazhdan, M., Funkhouser, T.: The princeton shape benchmark. In: Proceedings of the Shape Modeling International 2004, SMI 2004, pp. 167–178. IEEE Computer Society, Washington, DC (2004)

25. Stavropoulos, T.G., Moschonas, P., Moustakas, K., Tzovaras, D., Strintzis, M.G.: 3D model search and retrieval from range images using salient features. IEEE Transactions on Multimedia 12(7), 692–704 (2010)

26. Theoharis, T., Papaioannou, G., Platis, N., Patrikalakis, N.M.: Graphics and Visualization: Principles & Algorithms. A. K. Peters, Ltd., Natick (2007)
27. Vranic, D.V.: DESIRE: A composite 3D-shape descriptor. In: ICME, pp. 962–965. IEEE (2005)
28. Wahl, E., Hillenbrand, U., Hirzinger, G.: Surflet-pair-relation histograms: A statistical 3D-shape representation for rapid classification. In: 3DIM, pp. 474–481. IEEE Computer Society (2003)

Reconstructing Archeological Vessels by Fusing Surface Markings and Border Anchor Points on Fragments

Fernand Cohen, Zexi Liu, and Zhongchuan Zhang

Electrical and Computer Engineering, Drexel University, Philadelphia, PA 19104, USA
fscohen@coe.drexel.edu, {zl54,zz57}@drexel.edu

Abstract. This paper presents a method to assist in the tedious process of reconstructing ceramic vessels from excavated fragments. The method exploits vessel surface marking information (models) supplied by the archaeologists along with anchor points on the fragment borders for reconstruction. Marking models are based on expert historical knowledge of the period, provenance of the artifact, and site location. The models need not to be identical to the original vessel, but must be within a geometric transformation of it in most of its parts. Marking matching is based on discrete weighted moments. We use anchor points on the fragment borders for the fragments with no markings. Corresponding anchors on different fragments are identified using absolute invariants, from which a rigid transformation is computed allowing the fragments to be virtually mended. For axially symmetric objects, a global constraint induced by the surface of revolution is applied to guarantee global mending consistency.

Keywords: 3D Weighted Moment, Mending, Archeological Shards, Ceramic Fragments, Global Constraint, Virtual Reconstruction.

1 Introduction

The mending of unearthed archeological ceramic shards to reconstruct vessels that the fragments once formed is currently a tedious and time-consuming process, and yet is a vital step in interpreting, understanding, and preserving cultural heritage. In this paper, we focus on virtually reconstructing/mending ceramic vessel fragments shown in Figure 1. They are scanned using Konica Vivid 910 3D scanner. Our contribution is that we develop a method that makes use of marking vessel models given by the experts and surface makings (of both fragments and marking models) to drive the reconstruction of the vessels from broken fragments via a novel set of weighted discrete moments, coupled with the use of fragment borders to mend them as a jigsaw puzzle game.

1.1 Related Work

Computer vision technology has been used to facility the image and document reassembly. Saharan and Singh [1] use the flood fill algorithm to obtain the closed

A. Petrosino, L. Maddalena, P. Pala (Eds.): ICIAP 2013 Workshops, LNCS 8158, pp. 179–187, 2013.

Fig. 1. Ceramic remains and digitized model

boundaries of fragmented images and calculate the local curvature of each boundary pixel which is stored into a string.

The fragment matching is then reduced to a string matching problem. Zhu et al. [2] propose to use turning-function-based partial curve matching to find the candidate matches and define the global consistency as the global criterion to do document reconstruction. The global match confidences are assigned to each candidate match and then these confidences are iteratively updated via the gradient projection method to maximize the criterion. Tsamoura and Pitas [3] instead pre-sent a color based approach to reassemble fragmented images and paintings. A neural network based color quantization approach for the representation of the image contour followed by a dynamic programming technique is employed to identify the matching contour segments of the image fragments. Aminogi et al. [4] utilize both the shape and the color characteristics of the image fragment contours for matching.

1.2   Marking Models

Archeologists usually possess a library that consists of excavated broken, unbroken, or mended artifacts, patterns of relief, color markings, and historical documents describing the shape and dimension of various artifacts. The creation of a set of marking models is a process that involves the archaeology experts who are assisted by graphics and computational engineers of rendering in 3D what the archaeology experts perceive and consider as possible representations for possible vessels in a given dig.

A raw template can be one of those unbroken or manually mended vessels. It is scanned and imported into any commercial 3D sculpture software such as Zbrush. When the unbroken/mended vessels are not available, we simply create a 3D template vessel in ZBrush with the information supplied by the archaeologists (e.g., height, neck size, belly size of a vase), and have them interactively modify the template in accordance with what they think are good marking models.

The creation of the marking models is also a dynamic process. If the marking models in one category have very few fragments aligned to them, the archeologists will make changes to the shape, the marking patterns, or the location of these patterns, creating new variations. An overview of the proposed system is shown in Figure 2.

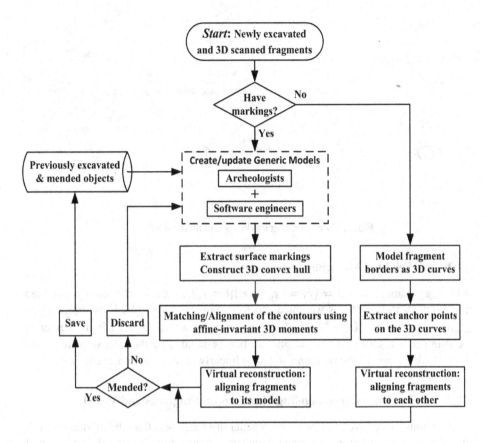

Fig. 2. System overview

2   Reconstruction of Archeological Vessels

2.1   Alignment Using Marking Models

Figure 3 shows the mending procedure based on the surface markings, the patterns drawn on a vessel and usually having different colors from most other parts of a vessel. The surface markings on the marking models and fragments are first extracted by thresholding the color information of the markings and/or the background. For each surface marking, a 3D convex hull is computed based on its containing points. Corresponding markings are established using the 3D convex hulls, based on which the transformation between a matched marking pairs is computed. The transformation giving the smallest alignment error is used to align a fragment to the marking model.

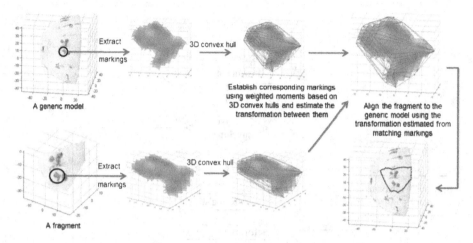

Fig. 3. Corresponding markings and their convex hull

2.1.1   Weighted Moments

With   a   data   set $R = \{r_i = (x_i, y_i, z_i) | i = 1, 2, ..., n\}$, and   an   s-weighted
tion $w(r_i, r_j, r_k)_s$, the s-weighted central moment is defined as $\mu(a, b, c)_s = \sum_{i=1}^{n}(x_i - \bar{x})^a (y_i - \bar{y})^b (z_i - \bar{z})^c \sum_{j=1}^{n} \sum_{k=1}^{n} w(r_i, r_j, r_k)_s$, where $(\bar{x}, \bar{y}, \bar{z})$ is the center of the data set. The choice of the weight function is dictated by the relative affine inva-riant which allows for the moments to factor linearly in the affine parameters.

2.1.2   Declaring Corresponding Markings on Fragment and Vessel

As the number of convex hull vertices is generally much less than the marking points, the computation load of the weighted moments is reduced when using the convex hull as a compressed representation of a surface marking. Since the volume of a convex hull is a relative invariant under the affine transformation $T = \{[L], B\}$, the s-weighted function is defined as $w(r_i, r_j, r_k)_s = |(r_i - r_0) \cdot [(r_j - r_0) \times (r_k - r_0)]|^s$, where r_i, r_j and r_k are 3 vertices on the convex hull, and r_0 is the centroid. If r_{ai} is the affine counterpart of r_i after the transform T, we have $r_{ai} = [L]r_i + B$. The zero[th] order s-weighted affine invariant central moments are related by $\mu_a(0,0,0)_s = |\det\{[L]\}|^s \mu(0,0,0)_s$, where $\mu(0,0,0)_s = \sum_{i=1}^{n} \sum_{j=1}^{n} \sum_{k=1}^{n} w(r_i, r_j, r_k)_s$ and $\mu_a(0,0,0)_s = \sum_{i=1}^{n} \sum_{j=1}^{n} \sum_{k=1}^{n} w_a(r_{ai}, r_{aj}, r_{ak})_s$. Absolute affine invariant (AAI) can be constructed from these relative invariants by using any two different weight factors s_0 and s_1 : $AAI(s_0, s_1) = \dfrac{\sqrt[s_1]{\mu_a(0,0,0)_{s_1}}}{\sqrt[s_0]{\mu_a(0,0,0)_{s_0}}} = \dfrac{\sqrt[s_1]{\mu(0,0,0)_{s_1}}}{\sqrt[s_0]{\mu(0,0,0)_{s_0}}}$, where $\mu_a(0,0,0)_{s_0}$, $\mu(0,0,0)_{s_0} \neq 0$ since $w_a(r_{ai}, r_{aj}, r_{ak})_s$, $w(r_i, r_j, r_k)_s > 0$. The AAI is used to es-tablish which convex hull of marking on the marking models corresponds to a given one on the fragment. Corresponding convex hulls (not markings) are declared if their AAIs are close enough. Once the convex hull correspondences are established, the

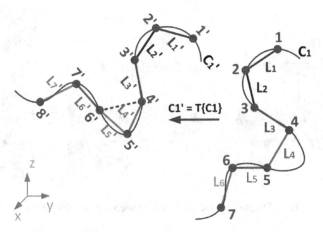

Fig. 4. Absolute invariants with anchor points with some possible missing. The algorithm in section 2.2.2 will always find the longest matching string.

affine transformation that maps the convex hull on the fragment onto its corresponding one on the vessel is computed as explained in 2.1.3.

2.1.3   Aligning Fragments against Marking Models

Given corresponding convex hull pairs determined using AAIs, we proceed to estimate the unique affine transformation $T = \{[L], \boldsymbol{B}\}$ that will align them. Towards that end, we use a set of first order s-weighted affine invariant central moments. To solve the transformation $[L]$ that has 9 unknowns, a set of 3 different s values is used to arrive at 9 equations with 9 unknowns. This results in the linear equation

$$[M_a] = [L][M] = [L]\begin{bmatrix} \mu(1,0,0)_{s1} & \mu(1,0,0)_{s2} & \mu(1,0,0)_{s3} \\ \mu(0,0,0)_{s1} & \mu(0,0,0)_{s2} & \mu(0,0,0)_{s3} \\ \mu(0,1,0)_{s1} & \mu(0,1,0)_{s2} & \mu(0,1,0)_{s3} \\ \mu(0,0,0)_{s1} & \mu(0,0,0)_{s2} & \mu(0,0,0)_{s3} \\ \mu(0,0,1)_{s1} & \mu(0,0,1)_{s2} & \mu(0,0,1)_{s3} \\ \mu(0,0,0)_{s1} & \mu(0,0,0)_{s2} & \mu(0,0,0)_{s3} \end{bmatrix} \tag{1}$$

And $[M_a]$ is the counterpart of $[M]$. The transformation $[L]$ is uniquely computed from (1). Once $[L]$ is found, the translation parameters $\boldsymbol{B}$ can be obtained from the centroids of the matched convex hull pair. To evaluate the goodness of the alignment we use the average distance error between all the 3D points (not just those on the marking) on the morphed fragment to their closest points on the vessel. The morphing of the fragment into the vessel coordinate space is done in accordance with the estimated affine transformation T.

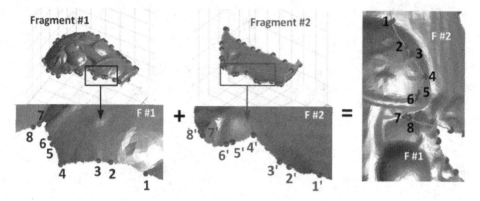

Fig. 5. Fragment mending based on anchor points (red dots)

2.2 Mending Fragments Using Anchor Points on Borders

When the fragments have no markings on them or if we want to use complementary information for mending, landmarks on fragment borders are used. The rigid transformation preserved landmarks used in this paper are inflection, corner, and zero-torsion points.

2.2.1 Constructing Absolute Invariants Using Anchor Points

Since length is preserved under 3D rigid maps and are absolute invariants, we can construct a sequence of absolute invariants by considering the sequence of length of lines between the two consecutive anchor points (e.g., lines between points #1-2, points #2-3, etc. as shown in Figure 4).

Although an anchor point is missing between points #4 and #5 on curve C_1, the matching is not affected. For a curve with n anchor points, the sequence of length is denoted by $I = (L_1, L_2, ..., L_{n-1})$. The transformed lines sequence has also the same number of elements $I' = (L'_1, L'_2, ..., L'_{n-1})$. And we need to find the sequences of elements in that invariant vectors in I and I' that correspond. Towards that end we introduce the "longest string search" technique, which is similar to the "list-matching algorithm" [5] for establishing the correspondence and declaring the match. To recover the rigid transformation at least 3 pairs of matched points is required, i.e., the minimum edge string length should be 2.

2.2.2 Longest String Match between Fragments

A set of two or more consecutive anchor points and their corresponding invariants are considered to be a "string" (e.g., the set $(i, i + 1, i + 2, ...)$ on one fragment and the set $(j, j + 1, j + 2, ...)$ on another fragment). We allow for a small error (2-5%) in the values of the invariants when declaring matching edges. i.e., the sets $(i, i + 1, i + 2, ...)$ and $(j, j + 1, j + 2, ...)$ of anchor points are declared as matching if $|I'(j) - I(i)| < 0.05\, I(i)$ for every pair in the two sets. In case that there are missing points,

Fig. 6. With/without global optimization

for example, in Figure 4, $L_4 \neq L_{4'}$, then the distance $L_{5'}$ will be discarded and the distance between points $4'$ and $6'$ will be calculated, then $L_4 = L_{4'6'}$. Generally speaking, if we encounter an "unmatched" segment, we will always jump over one point and check its next anchor point. As this process is recursive we can deal with more than one missing point. The rigid transformation $T = \{[R], t\}$ can be recovered from three pairs of matched points, or estimated from more matched anchor points using a least square error (LSE) estimation method [6]. Once the transformation parameters are found, the fragments are mapped into the same coordinates system by undoing the rigid transformation and the fragments are aligned.

2.2.3   Global Optimization

The mending described in the previous section and shown in Figure 5 is a pair wise mending process. It is conceivable that alignment errors will accumulate, rendering the reconstruction result less than satisfactory (See right hand side of Figure 6).

For vessels that are axially symmetric, this problem can be solved by adopting the surface of revolution as a global constraint. The surface of revolution is obtained by going through the following steps: 1) Extract the "profile curve" [7]; 2) Obtain the symmetry axis (revolution axis); 3) Rotate the profile curve about the axis; 4) Generate a rotation surface; 5) Use the surface as a global optimization "basis". Steps 1~2 are shown in Figure 7 left.

The lower rim and upper rim are obtained by fitting a circle to the fragment border segments. Of all the fragment border segments, the one with the smallest fitting error is the rim. The cross-section curve c is the profile curve. Steps 3~4 are shown in Figure 7 right. Here we rotate the profile curve about the revolution axis to generate a set of curves which constitute the rotation surface. This rotation surface is used in our mending process as a basis shape, where the fragments are not only aligned to each

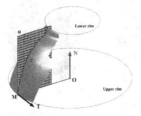

Fig. 7. Obtain profile curve, symmetric axis and generate a rotation surface

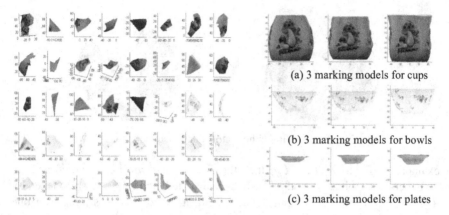

(a) 3 marking models for cups

(b) 3 marking models for bowls

(c) 3 marking models for plates

Fig. 8. 3D scanned fragments and marking models

other, but are also aligned to this surface. With this global optimization constraint, the result is improved as shown on the left hand side of Figure 6. Note that before a basis shape is found, fragments with no upper and lower rims are set aside, and only fragments that do possess both rims are found and possibly mended using the pair wise invariants approach. After we obtain a mended fragment with both upper and lower rims, we extract the profile curve and generate the rotation surface (steps 1-5). We then improve on the mending for all fragments using the basis shape as a global constraint.

3   Experiments

We test our methods on 62 fragments (40 of them have markings and are shown in Figure 8 left. The 22 fragments with no markings are mended later using the anchor point method. The fragments are from 3 types of vessels: cups, bowls and plates. The archaeologists provide 20 marking models for each type of vessel, hence a total of 60 possible marking models. We show 3 marking models for each category (cups, bowls and plates) in Figure 8 right.

The reconstruction results of the 62 fragments are shown in Figure 9. The fragments bounded by red boundaries are aligned using markings and marking models.

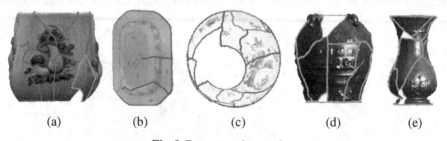

(a)   (b)   (c)   (d)   (e)

Fig. 9. Reconstruction results

The fragments bounded by green boundaries are mended using anchor points. We find that most fragments can be aligned against one marking model for each category of vessels. However, as the marking models are not exact, it's possible that parts of the best marking model are not close enough to the true vessel, which resulted in having a few fragments not aligned with the best marking model. Based on markings alone, 70% of fragments with markings (red boundaries in Figure 9) are aligned to the best models. This figure changes upward to around 90% if we consider the markings along with the anchor points in the mending. Finally, out of the 22 fragments that don't have any markings on, 18 (>80%) fragments are properly mended (see Figure 9 (d), (e)). The remaining 4 fragments had insufficient number of anchor points on their borders and hence couldn't be mended. In the end, 54 (>85%) out of the 62 fragments are successfully mended, when using markings plus anchor points for the first set and anchor points for the set with no markings on them.

4   Conclusions

We present novel complementary methods to reconstruct vessels virtually by aligning 3D scanned fragments against vessels based on surface markings and anchor points on borders. These methods weigh between expert opinion (with expected uncertainties), and total lack of prior knowledge. Building in uncertainties in the markings models allow for rotation, scaling, shifting, and shearing between markings on the marking vessels and their corresponding ones on the fragments. Whereas using anchors points as complementary information on fragment surfaces allows for a natural mending when expert prior information is lacking or as cross validation method. This paper shows the importance of using complementary information in the mending process for assisting in the tedious process of vessels reconstruction from fragments.

References

1. Saharan, R., Singh, C.V.: Reassembly of 2D fragments in image reconstruction. International Journal of Computer Applications 19, 41–45 (2011)
2. Zhu, L., Zhou, Z., Hu, D.: Globally consistent reconstruction of ripped-up documents. IEEE Transactions on Pattern Analysis and Machine Intelligence 30, 1–13 (2008)
3. Tsamoura, E., Pitas, I.: Automatic color based reassembly of fragmented images and paintings. IEEE Transactions on Image Processing 19, 680–690 (2010)
4. Amigoni, F., Gazzani, S., Podico, S.: A method for reassembling fragments in image reconstruction. Presented at the Proceedings of International Conference on Image Processing (2003)
5. Bratko, I.: Prolog Programming for Artificial Intelligence. Addison Wesley, London (1990)
6. Umeyama, S.: Least-Square Estimation of Transformation Parameters Between Two Point Patterns. IEEE Transactions on Pattern Analysis and Machine Intelligence 13, 376–380 (1991)
7. Willis, A., Orriols, X., Cooper, D.B.: Accurately Estimating Sherd 3D Surface Geometry with Application to Pot Reconstruction. In: CVPR Workshop: ACVA, Madison, WI, USA (2003)

Automatic Single-Image People Segmentation and Removal for Cultural Heritage Imaging

Marco Manfredi, Costantino Grana, and Rita Cucchiara

Università degli Studi di Modena e Reggio Emilia, Modena MO 41125, Italy

Abstract. In this paper, the problem of automatic people removal from digital photographs is addressed. Removing unintended people from a scene can be very useful to focus further steps of image analysis only on the object of interest, A supervised segmentation algorithm is presented and tested in several scenarios.

Keywords: people removal, segmentation, cultural heritage imaging, inpainting.

1 Introduction

Multimedia technologies find fruitful employment into tools and solutions for Cultural Heritage (CH) preservation and exploitation. Traditionally CH documents, reports and publications are created by few (expert) for many (e.g. users,tourists,etc...) based on expensive photographic and documentation campaigns. Instead, there is a huge heritage, especially in Italy and Europe, that is still only partially documented both for lack of economic support, and for terrible environmental changes (e.g. earthquakes), which change their conservation status and external aspects.

In this paper we address the problem of fully-automatic people removal from single images in order to create a privacy-compliant and de-personalized dataset of CH pictures, working on the huge picture footage coming from social networks and photo sharing sites. CHI fosters the development of technologies for digital capture and documentation of the worlds cultural, scientific, and artistic treasures, although most of the related techniques are up-to-now oriented to creating manual or semi-automatic tools both for experts and private users [15].

The "people removal" is a typical problem for digital documentation and consists in deleting humans from pictures to improve the quality or the semantic value of the picture. This is a useful feature of many graphic tools (e.g. GIMP), which is now also being provided for mobile devices[1] or as an online tool[2]. Indeed, people removal is a well-addressed problem on videos or image sequences, where multiple images differences [19,10] or structure prediction [21] are available, while robust automatic solutions for single images have not been presented yet.

---

[1] http://www.scalado.com/display/en/Remove
[2] http://www.snapmania.com/info/en/trm

A. Petrosino, L. Maddalena, P. Pala (Eds.): ICIAP 2013 Workshops, LNCS 8158, pp. 188–197, 2013.
© Springer-Verlag Berlin Heidelberg 2013

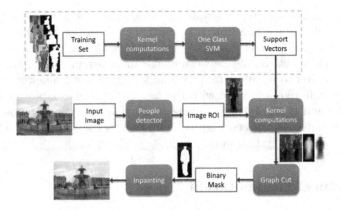

Fig. 1. Overview of the proposed system

Three steps are required to address the single-image people removal task: automatic target detection, person segmentation and highlighted area inpainting. While an automatic people detector can be used to initialize the system, in our solution the detection are manually supplied, so to correctly initialize the further steps. A supervised segmentation algorithm, able to accurately outline the people thanks to a structured machine learning approach is adopted. This step creates the mask to apply photo enhancing algorithms, such as inpainting [6] or Seam Carving [1], to remove people in the scene without any user input.

In this paper we describe the system workflow, focusing in particular on the structured segmentation algorithm, comparing with other segmentation algorithms and illustrate results on a common segmentation dataset and on web images.

2   Single-Image People Removal

Taking a clear picture of a cultural heritage site, a church, a statue in the middle of a crowded square can be an undertaking. Unintended people often clutter the scene, ruining the shot. Since inpainting has to add unreal but plausible image data, the less is added, the better it is. So, usually, manual selection of the removal areas should be provided, in order to have a perfectly segmented shape, without under-segmented areas and possibly with very small over segmented ones. In our case the problem of target removal becomes a problem of automatic target detection and segmentation.

Automatic people (or pedestrian) detection is a well-studied problem in computer vision, Enzweiler and Gavrila provide a thorough survey on the topic [8]. All of these approaches return the bounding box where the target is found, without a precise silhouette segmentation, which is a challenging problem, due to the high variability of people pose and scale, different lighting condition, low contrast between the selected person and the background and not uniform color and texture distribution within the shape. The main strength of this work is indeed the people segmentation step: a graph-cut [4] segmentation is employed, and the unary potentials are learned from a training set, weighting examples based on their similarity to the target image. We exploit One Class SVMs to describe the people class and Joint Kernels between image and mask pairs, to robustly learn an energy function to be minimized with an s/t graph cut framework.

This approach allows to cope with the fact that people shapes are found in several poses and postures, and walking pedestrians, chatting groups or other tourists have different aspects. Figure 1 summarizes the steps of the algorithm and describes the full system workflow.

3   Structural Segmentation

Structural prediction through SSVMs [18] proved to be effective in many computer vision tasks, such as object detection [12], tracking [13] and recently also image segmentation [16]. Structured segmentation describes the problem of learning a function $f : \mathcal{X} \to \mathcal{Y}$, where $\mathcal{X}$ is the space of samples (images) and $\mathcal{Y}$ is the space of structured labels (binary masks), from a segmented training set. SSVMs learn a scoring function $F(x, y)$ that matches a sample x with a label y, such that maximizing F through the label space gives the correct output label for sample x.

A common approach is to work in the dual formulation using positive definite joint kernels, so that the scoring function $F(x, y)$ can be written as:

$$F(x, y) = \sum_{y' \in \mathcal{W}} \alpha_{y'} \left(\frac{1}{n} \sum_{i=1}^{n} [K((x, y), (x_i, y_i)) - K((x, y), (x_i, y_i'))] \right),$$

(1)

where $\mathcal{W}$ is the set of the most violated constraints, α are the weights for the support vectors that are found solving the dual problem, and (x_i, y_i) are the training pairs. Given an input image x, we can find the output label by maximizing $F(x, y)$:

$$y^* = \arg\max_{y \in \mathcal{Y}} F(x, y).$$

(2)

This maximization can be done using graph cuts. Unfortunately, this formulation has two relevant performance issues:

- during training we have to construct the set of the most violated constraints $\mathcal{W}$: for each training sample, find k constraints (k depends on the desired accuracy), each with the size of the training set, and solve an inference step (graph cut maximization) for each element;
- during testing we have to compare a sample x with each support vector. A single support vector is composed of all training images and their corresponding most violated constraint (mask), as in (1).

The main idea behind the proposed model is to exploit one-class SVMs in a kernel space to learn a set of support vectors and their relative weights and to delete outliers from the training set, thus reducing the complexity at testing time. This idea was firstly introduced by Lampert et al. [14], with the name of Joint Kernel Support Estimation, and applied to object localization and sequence labeling. We want to use $f(x) = \arg\max p(x, y)$ for prediction, assuming that $p(x, y)$ is high only if y is a correct label for x. The support of $p(x, y)$ can be effectively obtained by a one-class support vector machine (OC-SVM), expressing $p(x, y)$ as a linear combination of a suitable joint kernel K that matches two sample-label pairs. The joint kernel can be an arbitrary Mercer kernel [20]. The output of the OC-SVM learning process becomes a linear combination of kernel evaluations with training samples, thus the prediction function can be formulated as:

$$f(x) = \arg\max_{y \in Y} \sum_{i=1}^{n} \alpha_i K\left((x, y), (x_i, y_i)\right). \tag{3}$$

The learning process can be done using standard existing implementations of OC-SVM, with the joint kernel matrix between sample-label pairs.

It is important to point out the difference between our approach and KSSVMs [2]: in the training phase we only have to construct the joint kernel matrix between training samples, and then train a standard non linear OC-SVM, no inference steps are required during training. As a consequence, the training time does not depend on the structure of the output space, but only on the size of the training set.

The similarity kernel for the task of people segmentation was formulated as the product of an image kernel and a mask kernel:

$$K((x_i, y_i), (x_j, y_j)) = \theta(x_i, x_j) \cdot \Omega(x_i, x_j, y_i, y_j), \tag{4}$$

where $\theta(x_i, x_j)$ measures the similarity of the objects depicted in x_i and x_j, and acts as a weight for the mask similarity kernel $\Omega(x_i, x_j, y_i, y_j)$. Consequently, if the two images are very different, the final similarity measure will be low, even if the masks are similar.

3.1 Image Similarity Kernel

The purpose of the image similarity kernel is to return high similarity values between images that contain very similar objects. We adopt a general purpose similarity measure between images, the comparison of HOG descriptors [7]. HOGs can be compared using standard similarity measures like Bhattacharyya distance. Since we are working with images of the same category (people), we employ a Gaussian kernel, capable of distinguishing between different images, due to the parameter σ, optimized for the specific dataset. The image similarity kernel between image x_i and image x_j becomes:

$$\theta(x_i, x_j) = \exp\left(-\frac{\|\rho(x_i) - \rho(x_j)\|^2}{2\sigma^2}\right), \tag{5}$$

where $\rho(x_i)$ is the feature vector extracted from image x_i. For the computation of the HOG descriptors we adopted rectangular HOG (R-HOG) [7], computing gradients on R,G, and B color channels and taking the maximum, then dividing the image with a 5×5 grid of cells (25 cells), and grouping them in 4 partially overlapped blocks of 3×3 cells each. Trilinear interpolation between histogram bins and cells was appropriately applied.

3.2   Mask Similarity Kernel

The mask similarity kernel takes into consideration both images and masks to extract knowledge about how comparable two segmentations are. The kernel is composed of a linear combination of three parts:

$$\Omega(x_i, x_j, y_i, y_j) = \sum_{k=1}^{3} \beta_k \Omega_k(x_i, x_j, y_i, y_j). \qquad (6)$$

The first kernel $\Omega_1(y_i, y_j)$ only depends on the binary masks, and directly compares the similarity between the two, by counting the number of corresponding pixels:

$$\Omega_1(y_i, y_j) = \frac{1}{P} \sum_{p=1}^{P} \delta(y_{ip}, y_{jp}), \qquad (7)$$

where P is the total number of pixels in the image, y_{ip} is the p-th pixel of image y_i, and $\delta(\cdot, \cdot)$ is an indicator function defined as:

$$\delta(y_{ip}, y_{jp}) = \begin{cases} 1 & \text{if} \quad y_{ip} = y_{jp} \\ 0 & \text{if} \quad y_{ip} \neq y_{jp} \end{cases} . \qquad (8)$$

The second and the third kernels exploit 3D color histograms computed in the RGB space. Let's define F_i^j and B_i^j as foreground and background histograms extracted from image x_i using mask y_j, and $P_r(x_p|H)$ as the likelihood of pixel x_p to match histogram H. We use negative log-likelihoods to express the penalties to assign a pixel to foreground or to background, as firstly introduced by [5]. Negative log-likelihoods are defined as:

$$L(x_p|H) = -log(P_r(x_p|H)). \qquad (9)$$

We can also define:

$$L(x_p|y_p, F, B) = \begin{cases} L(x_p|B) & \text{if} \quad y_p = \text{``obj''} \\ L(x_p|F) & \text{if} \quad y_p = \text{``bkg''}. \end{cases} \qquad (10)$$

To highlight the mutual agreement of two masks, the second kernel extracts an histogram from image x_i using mask y_j and evaluates it using y_i. Having F_i^j and B_i^j:

$$\Omega_2(x_i, y_i) = \frac{1}{P} \sum_{p=1}^{P} L(x_{ip}|y_{ip}, F_i^j, B_i^j). \qquad (11)$$

The third kernel exploits global features extracted from the entire training set to model the expected color distribution of foreground and background pixels. We define F_G and B_G as the global histograms extracted from training samples using their relative masks.

$$\Omega_3(x_i, x_j, y_i, y_j) = \Omega_{3i} \cdot \Omega_{3j} \tag{12}$$

where

$$\begin{aligned} \Omega_{3i} &= \frac{1}{P} \sum_{p=1}^{P} L(x_{ip}|y_{ip}, F_G, B_G) \\ \Omega_{3j} &= \frac{1}{P} \sum_{p=1}^{P} L(x_{jp}|y_{jp}, F_G, B_G) \end{aligned} \tag{13}$$

The histograms are quantized uniformly over the 3D color space using a fixed number of bins per channel, set at 16 by experimental evaluations (no smoothing is applied).

4   Graph Construction

It is worth noting that the previously defined kernels compare two image-mask pairs, while at testing time the test mask is obviously missing. Kernels must thus be reformulated so to return pixel-wise potentials, in order to perform the maximization reported in (3). This maximization is done using s/t graph cuts [5].

The problem can be formulated as a maximum a posterior estimation of a Markov Random Field, minimizing the energy function:

$$E(y) = R(y) + \lambda B(y), \tag{14}$$

where y is a binary vector of pixel labels and $R(y)$ is the unary term expressing the cost of assigning a pixel to the foreground or to the background. $B(y)$ is the smoothness term, formulated as proposed by Rother *et al.* [17]:

$$B(y) = \sum_{p,q \in \mathcal{N}} \delta(y_p, y_q) \frac{1}{dist(p,q)} \exp\left(-\frac{\|x_p - x_q\|^2}{2\sigma^2} \right) \tag{15}$$

where $\mathcal{N}$ is the set of neighboring pixels (8-connected), $\delta(\cdot, \cdot)$ is the indicator function defined in (8), $dist(p,q)$ is the distance between pixels and σ is the expectation of the euclidean distance in color space $\|x_p - x_q\|^2$. At classification time we have to compute the foreground and background potentials P_f and P_b corresponding to the unary term in the graph cut framework. They are the result of a linear combination of potentials P_{f_i} and P_{b_i} obtained from the comparison of the testing image x_j with each support vector (x_i, y_i), weighted by the corresponding α_i. The potentials at position p are:

$$\begin{aligned} P_{f_{ip}} &= \theta(x_i, x_j)(\beta_1 P_{f_{ip}}^1 + \beta_2 P_{f_{ip}}^2 + \beta_3 P_{f_{ip}}^3) \\ P_{b_{ip}} &= \theta(x_i, x_j)(\beta_1 P_{b_{ip}}^1 + \beta_2 P_{b_{ip}}^2 + \beta_3 P_{b_{ip}}^3) \end{aligned} \tag{16}$$

where $\theta(x_i, x_j)$ is the image similarity kernel defined in (5). The first kernel is strictly related to the mask y_i:

$$\begin{aligned} P_{f_{ip}}^1 &= y_{ip} \\ P_{b_{ip}}^1 &= 1 - y_{ip} \end{aligned} \tag{17}$$

The second kernel expresses the cost of assigning a pixel to foreground or to background, according to the histograms F_j^i and B_j^i, defined in Sec. 3.2:

$$\begin{aligned} P_{f_{ip}}^2 &= L(x_{jp}|B_j^i) \\ P_{b_{ip}}^2 &= L(x_{jp}|F_j^i) \end{aligned} \tag{18}$$

The third kernel expresses the cost of assigning a pixel to foreground or to background, given the global histograms F_G , B_G calculated on the training set:

$$\begin{aligned} P_{f_{ip}}^3 &= L(x_{jp}|B_G) \cdot \tfrac{1}{P}\gamma(x_i, y_i) \\ P_{b_{ip}}^3 &= L(x_{jp}|F_G) \cdot \tfrac{1}{P}\gamma(x_i, y_i) \end{aligned} \tag{19}$$

where

$$\gamma(x_i, y_i) = \sum_{p=1}^{P} L(x_{ip}|y_{ip}, F_G, B_G). \tag{20}$$

5   Experimental Evaluation

The experimental setup is thought to evaluate both the segmentation accuracy and the inpainting effectiveness, comparing the proposed approach with other segmentation algorithms. To test the segmentation accuracy we chose the Weizmann horse dataset [3], publicly available and commonly used in the segmentation community. We compared our results with GrabCut, initialized using the bounding boxes coming from a part based detector [11,9], or using the average of the masks of the k nearest image found with the object similarity of Eq. 5. We also report the results obtained by Bertelli *et al.* [2]. Their approach exploits Kernelized Structural SVMs, and reaches the best results (Table 2). The accuracy gap between our solution and the one proposed in [2] is noticeable, but To

Table 1. Image reconstruction results with different initializations

Inpainting Init.	MSE	SSIM
Our approach	57.24	0.469
GrabCut	67.55	0.391
Bounding Box	110.3	0.123

test the impact that different segmentations have on the inpainting procedure, we collected some images from the web, depicting CH sites with unintended people cluttering the scene. A qualitative comparison between our approach and GrabCut shows that in the 70% of cases we perform better

We created a dataset to test the impact that different segmentations have on the inpainting procedure. The dataset is composed of 60 photographs of churches and monuments, with several people cluttering the scene. For each photograph, a background image is provided. The inpainting algorithm [6], is initialized in three

Fig. 2. Visual comparison of the segmentation results. First column contains the original image with the detected people. The other columns show the area to be inpainted using the bounding box, the GrabCut and the proposed approach respectively.

different ways: directly using the bounding box of the people detection, using the binary mask provided by GrabCut and using the proposed approach. To evaluate the quality of the image reconstruction step we use Structural Similarity Index (SSIM). SSIM is commonly used for image quality assessment, and measures the changes in structural information given a couple of images. SSIM is chosen because more consistent human eye perception than MSE or PSNR.

Results are reported in Table 1. As expected, initializing the inpainting algorithm with the bounding boxes leads to the worst results, in particular, the accuracy of the reconstruction quickly worsen as the person size increases. Heterogeneous background is very difficult to reconstruct, but the precision of the segmentation mask considerably affect the reconstruction process. Some qualitative results are reported in Figure 2.

Some parameters of the proposed solution must be optimized over a validation set. These are the kernel weights $\beta_1, \beta_2, \beta_3$ and the parameter ν of the One Class SVM. As for training, the optimization step is done over the 3DPeS dataset, by means of a grid search over the parameter space.

Table 2. Performance comparison on the three datasets

Horses Dataset	$S_a(\%)$	$S_o(\%)$
KSSVM + Hog feature	93.9	77.9
Our method	**91.04**	**73.28**
GrabCut init. with BB	69.53	50.39
GrabCut init. with 1-NN mask	85.66	62.34
GrabCut init. with 5-NN masks	86.93	63.83
GrabCut init. with 10-NN masks	86.46	63.20

6   Conclusions

We proposed a novel segmentation approach based on one-class SVMs and joint kernels between image-mask pairs. The method exploits the ability of OC-SVMs to identify and ignore outliers in the training set, while reducing the number of kernel computations needed at classification time. The characteristics of this generative learning algorithm allow to deal with very large datasets, otherwise intractable using discriminative approaches like KSSVMs and increase the robustness to mislabeled or incomplete ground truths.

References

1. Avidan, S., Shamir, A.: Seam carving for content-aware image resizing. ACM Trans. Graph. 26(3) (July 2007), http://doi.acm.org/10.1145/1276377.1276390
2. Bertelli, L., Yu, T., Vu, D., Gokturk, B.: Kernelized structural SVM learning for supervised object segmentation. In: Proceedings of the 24th IEEE Conference on Computer Vision and Pattern Recognition, pp. 2153–2160 (June 2011)
3. Borenstein, E., Sharon, E., Ullman, S.: Combining top-down and bottom-up segmentation. In: Proceedings of the 17th IEEE Conference on Computer Vision and Pattern Recognition Workshops, p. 46 (June 2004)
4. Boykov, Y., Kolmogorov, V.: An experimental comparison of min-cut/max- flow algorithms for energy minimization in vision. IEEE Transactions on Pattern Analysis and Machine Intelligence 26(9), 1124–1137 (2004)
5. Boykov, Y., Jolly, M.P.: Interactive graph cuts for optimal boundary & region segmentation of objects in N-D images. In: Proceedings of the 8th IEEE International Conference on Computer Vision, vol. 1, pp. 105–112 (2001)
6. Criminisi, A., Perez, P., Toyama, K.: Object removal by exemplar-based inpainting. In: Proceedings of 16th IEEE Conference on Computer Vision and Pattern Recognition, vol. 2, pp. 721–728 (June 2003)
7. Dalal, N., Triggs, B.: Histograms of oriented gradients for human detection. In: Proceedings of the 18th IEEE Conference on Computer Vision and Pattern Recognition, vol. 1, pp. 886–893 (June 2005)
8. Enzweiler, M., Gavrila, D.: Monocular pedestrian detection: Survey and experiments. IEEE Transactions on Pattern Analysis and Machine Intelligence 31(12), 2179–2195 (2009)
9. Felzenszwalb, P.F., Girshick, R.B., McAllester, D., Ramanan, D.: Object detection with discriminatively trained part based models. IEEE Transactions on Pattern Analysis and Machine Intelligence 32(9), 1627–1645 (2010)

10. Flores, A., Belongie, S.: Removing pedestrians from google street view images. In: 2010 IEEE Computer Society Conference on Computer Vision and Pattern Recognition Workshops (CVPRW), pp. 53–58 (June 2010)
11. Girshick, R.B., Felzenszwalb, P.F., McAllester, D.: Discriminatively Trained Deformable Part Models, Release 5, http://people.cs.uchicago.edu/~rbg/latent-release5/
12. Girshick, R.B., Felzenszwalb, P.F., McAllester, D.A.: Object Detection with Grammar Models. In: Neural Information Processing Systems, pp. 442–450 (2011)
13. Hare, S., Saffari, A., Torr, P.: Struck: Structured output tracking with kernels. In: Proceedings of the 13th International Conference on Computer Vision, pp. 263–270 (November 2011)
14. Lampert, C., Blaschko, M.: Structured prediction by joint kernel support estimation. Machine Learning 77, 249–269 (2009)
15. Mudge, M., Ashley, M., Schroer, C.: A digital future for cultural heritage. In: Proceedings of the 21st CIPA Symposium, ISPRS Archives, vol. XXXVI-5/C53 (October 2007)
16. Nowozin, S., Gehler, P.V., Lampert, C.H.: On Parameter Learning in CRF-Based Approaches to Object Class Image Segmentation. In: Daniilidis, K., Maragos, P., Paragios, N. (eds.) ECCV 2010, Part VI. LNCS, vol. 6316, pp. 98–111. Springer, Heidelberg (2010)
17. Rother, C., Kolmogorov, V., Blake, A.: "GrabCut": interactive foreground extraction using iterated graph cuts. In: ACM SIGGRAPH 2004 Papers, SIGGRAPH 2004, pp. 309–314. ACM (2004), http://doi.acm.org/10.1145/1186562.1015720
18. Tsochantaridis, I., Joachims, T., Hofmann, T., Altun, Y.: Large margin methods for structured and interdependent output variables. Journal of Machine Learning Research 6, 1453–1484 (2005)
19. Uchiyama, H., Deguchi, D., Takahashi, T., Ide, I., Murase, H.: Removal of moving objects from a street-view image by fusing multiple image sequences. In: Proceedings of the 20th International Conference on Pattern Recognition, pp. 3456–3459 (August 2010)
20. Vapnik, V.: Statistical learning theory. Wiley (1998)
21. Wexler, Y., Shechtman, E., Irani, M.: Space-time completion of video. IEEE Transactions on Pattern Analysis and Machine Intelligence 29(3), 463–476 (2007)

An Early Framework
for Determining Artistic Influence

Kanako Abe, Babak Saleh, and Ahmed Elgammal

Department of Computer Science
Rutgers University
kanaabe,babaks@rutgers.edu,
elgammal@cs.rutgers.edu

Abstract. Considering the huge amount of art pieces that exist, there is valuable information to be discovered. Focusing on paintings as one kind of artistic creature that is printed on a surface, artists can determine its genre and the time period that paintings can belong to. In this work we are proposing the interesting problem of automatic influence determination between painters which has not been explored well. We answer the question "Who influenced this artist?" by looking at his masterpieces and comparing them to others. We pose this interesting question as a knowledge discovery problem. We presented a novel dataset of paintings for the interdisciplinary field of computer science and art and showed interesting results for the task of influence finding.

1 Introduction

How do artists describe their paintings? They talk about their works using several different concepts. The elements of art are the basic ways in which artists talk about their works. Some of the elements of art include space, texture, form, shape, color, tone and line [7]. Each work of art can, in the most general sense, be described using these seven concepts. Another important descriptive set is the principles of art. These include movement, unity, harmony, variety, balance, contrast, proportion, and pattern. Other topics may include subject matter, brush stroke, meaning, and historical context. As seen, there are many descriptive attributes in which works of art can be talked about.

One important task for art historians is to find influences and connections between artists. By doing so, the conversation of art continues and new intuitions about art can be made. An artist might be inspired by one painting, a body of work, or even an entire genre of art is this influence. Which paintings influence each other? Which artists influence each other? Art historians are able to find which artists influence each other by examining the same descriptive attributes of art which were mentioned above. Similarities are noted and inferences are suggested.

It must be mentioned that determining influence is always a subjective decision. We will not know if an artist was ever truly inspired by a work unless he or she has said so. However, for the sake of finding connections and progressing

A. Petrosino, L. Maddalena, P. Pala (Eds.): ICIAP 2013 Workshops, LNCS 8158, pp. 198–207, 2013.

Fig. 1. An example of an often cited comparison in the context of influence. Diego Velázquez's Portrait of Pope Innocent X (left) and Francis Bacon's Study After Velázquez's Portrait of Pope Innocent X (right). Similar composition, pose, and subject matter but a different view of the work.

through movements of art, a general consensus is agreed upon if the argument is convincing enough. Figure 1 represents a commonly cited comparison for studying influence.

Is influence a task that a computer can measure? In Computer Vision, there has been extensive research on the object-recognition in images, similarity between images.

Also there has been united research on automated classification of paintings [1,2,3,9,8]. However, there is very little research done on measuring and determining influence between artists ,e.g. [9]. Measuring influence is a very difficult task because of the broad criteria for what influence between artists can mean. As mentioned earlier, there are many different ways in which paintings can be described. Some of these descriptions can be translated to a computer. Some research includes brushwork analysis [9] and color analysis to determine a painting style. For the purpose of this project, we do not focus on a specific element of art or principle of art but instead we focus on finding new comparisons by experimenting with different similarity measures.

Although the meaning of a painting is unique to each artist and is completely subjective, it can somewhat be measured by the symbols and objects in the painting. Symbols are visual words that often express something about the meaning of a work as well. For example, the works of Renaissance artists such as Giovanni Bellini and Jan Van-Eyck use religious symbols such as a cross, wings, and animals to tell stories in the Bible. This shows the need for an object-based representation of images. We should be able to describe the painting from a list of many different object classes. By having an object-based representation, the image is described in a high-level semantic as opposed to low-level semantics such as color and texture. By using the Classemes [11] feature, we are able to capture both high-level and low-level semantics. For example, Figure 2 may not look like similar images, but when considering the objects placed in each of the paintings, similarity becomes clear. This comparison is a result from our experiments which we describe later.

Fig. 2. Frédéric Bazille's *Studio 9 Rue de la Condamine* (left) and Norman Rockwell's *Shuffleton's Barber Shop* (right). The composition of both paintings is divided in a similar way. Yellow circles indicate similar objects, red circles indicate composition, and the blue square represents similar structural element. The objects seen – a fire stove, three men clustered, chairs, and window are seen in both paintings along with a similar position in the paintings. After browsing through many publications and websites, we conclude that this comparison has not been made by an art historian before.

One important factor of finding influence is therefore having a good measure of similarity. Paintings do not necessarily have to look alike but if they do or have reoccurring objects (high-level semantics), then they will be considered similar. If influence is found by looking at similar characteristics of paintings, the importance of finding a good similarity measure becomes prominent. Time is also a necessary factor in determining influence. An artist cannot influence another artist in the past. Therefore the linearity of paintings cuts down the possibilities of influence.

By including a computer's intuition about which artists and paintings may have similarities, it not only finds new knowledge about which paintings are connected in a mathematical criteria but also keeps the conversation going for artists. It challenges people to consider possible connections in the timeline of art history that may have never been seen before. We are not asserting truths but instead suggesting a possible path towards a difficult task of measuring influence. The main contribution of this paper is proposing the interesting task of determining influence between artist as a knowledge discovery problem and proposing a new relevant dataset. To the best of our knowledge, Carneiro et al[4] recently published the "PRINTART" on paintings along with primarily experiments on image retrieval and genre classification. However this dataset contains only monochromatic artistic images. Our dataset have chromatic images and its size is about double the "PRINTART" dataset.

2   Dataset

Our novel dataset contains a total of 1710 works by 66 artists chosen from Mark Harden's Artchive database of fine-art. Each image is annotated with the artist's first name, last name, title of work, year made, and genre. The majority of the images are of the full work while a few are details of the work. We are primarily dealing with paintings but we have included very few images of sculptures as well. The artist with the most images is Paul Cézanne with 140 images and the artist with the least number of works is Hans Hoffmann with 1 image.

The artists themselves ranged from 13 different genres throughout art history. These include Expressionism (10 artists), Impressionism (10), Renaissance (12), Romanticism (5), Cubism (4), Baroque (5), Pop (4), Abstract Contemporary (7), Surrealism (2), American Modernism (2), Post-Impressionism (3), Symbolism (1), and Neoclassical (1). The number in the parenthesis refers to the number of artists in each genre. Some genres were condensed such as *Abstract Contemporary*, which includes works in the *Abstract Expressionism, Contemporary*, and *De Stijl* periods. The *Renaissance* period has the most images (336 images) while *American Modernism* has the least (23 images). The average number of images per genre is 132. The earliest work is a piece by Donatello in 1412 while the

Fig. 3. Examples of paintings from thirteen genres: Renaissance, Baroque, Neoclassical, Romanticism, Impressionism, Post-Impressionism, Expressionism, Cubism, Surrealism, Symbolism, American Modernism, Pop, and Abstract Contemporary.

most recent work is a self portrait by Gerhard Richter done in 1996. The earliest genre is the *Renaissance* period with artists like Titian and Michelangelo during the 14th to 17th century. As for the most recent genre, art movements tend to overlap more in recent years. Richter's painting from 1996 is in the *Abstract Contemporary* genre.

3   Influence Discovery Framework

Consider a set of artists, X. For each artist, X_i, we have a ground truth time period t_i that artist X_i has performed his work. Also consider a set of images I_i, for each artist X_i. We extract Classeme features [11] as visual features for each image and represent it by a vector called $C = [c_1, ..., c_N]$ where N represents the dimension of the feature space.

We represent the problem of influence as similarity following time. For the statement $X_i \Rightarrow X_j$ to be true, where the arrow indicates the left side influencing the right side, two requirements must be met. In the time constraint, time period t_i must be either come before or overlap t_j thus, we not only allow artists to be influenced by their past but also by people from an overlapping time period since this is generally true for influence within a genre.

For the second requirement, two artists in the the feature space should be similar $X_i \sim X_j$. For determining similarity, averaging of each artist X_i's image set I_i will not work. Doing so results in a loss of information. If an artist X_i has significantly less images in I_i than an artist X_j does in I_j, then X_j will have a larger variation of images. This may result in skewed information about the similarity between artists since it reflects each I's number of images. Therefore, a method that measures distance between sets is important. This way, artists can be represented by their entire work, yet still keep information about each individual painting. The goal is to avoid the risk of losing information about a painting while providing meaningful set distances.

We consider potential influence if it reflects ground-truth or artists are of similar genre. Our ground-truth is a collection of known influences and general consensus of influences.

Once a good similarity measurement is found, we can map artists into a space, and here knowledge discovery becomes prominent. Which artists are similar but have not been talked about before? How will different distance metrics lead to different conclusions about artists? This portion of the study is also important for contribution to the art world.

4   Experiments

4.1   Visual Features

We extracted the Classeme feature vector [11] as the visual feature for our experiments. Classeme features are output of a set of classifiers corresponding to a set of C category labels, which are drawn from an appropriate term list (defined in [11] and not related to our art content). For each category $c \in \{1 \cdots C\}$, a set of training images was gathered by issuing a query on the category label to an image search engine. After a set of coarse feature descriptors (Pyramid HOG, GIST) is extracted, a subset of feature dimensions was selected [11]. Considering this reduced dimension feature a one-versus-all classifier ϕ_c is trained for each category. The classifier output is real-valued, and is such that $\phi_c(x) > \phi_c(y)$ implies that x is more similar to class c than y is. Given an image x, the feature vector (descriptor) used to represent it is the classeme vector $[\phi_1(x), \cdots, \phi_C(x)]$. The Classeme feature is of dimensionality $N = 2569$.

4.2   Artist Similarity

To judge about similarity between paintings and consequently judge about similarity between artists we computed the Euclidean distance between Classeme features corresponding to each image in the dataset. The results showed some interesting cases, several of which have not been studied by art historians as a potential comparison before. Figure 2 is an example of this, as well as Figure 4 and Figure 5.

Fig. 4. Vincent van Gogh's *Old Vineyard with Peasant Woman* 1890 (left) and Joan Miro's *The Farm* 1922 (Right). Similar objects and scenery but different moods and style.

We researched known influences between artists within our dataset from multiple resources such as The Art Story Foundation and The Metropolitan Museum of Art. For example, there is a general consensus among art historians that Paul Cézanne's use of fragmented spaces had a large impact on Pablo Picasso's work.

We say there is a good artist-to-artist similarity if 1) it reflects the ground-truth artist influence list or 2) they are of similar genres. We include the genre as another indication of influence because the works of artists in the same genre tend to be influenced by the same people and also by each other. After computing distances, an affinity matrix of similar artists is made. To measure accuracy, we focus on the top 5 artists similar to each artist X and considered how many of them are correct based on annotation.

We tried several different methods for measuring the distance between two sets of artists. First, we used the Hausdorff distance [5] to measure the distance between sets of artists. We computed the distance between each artist set in a Euclidean space. Our result had an accuracy of 22.73%.

In another variation, we modified the Hausdorff distance to consider a subset of distances. Our modification only considers 90 percent of the paintings for every artist set. This would presumably eliminate 10 percent of the least similar images. The results were not very different from the previous case. Those artists which were affected had slightly better results than regular Hausdorff distance. This results held an accuracy of 23.03%

Next we tried modified Hausdorff distance (MHD) proposed by Dubuisson et al [5]. This adjusted version of Hausdorff distance is shown to work better for object matching. This result had an accuracy of 30%, which was our best result.

Fig. 5. Georges Braque's *Man with a Violin* 1912 (Left) and Pablo Picasso's *Spanish Still Life: Sun and Shadow* 1912 (Right).

Previously, we had tried using only symmetric measurements. If artists are influenced by each other (meaning they have overlapping t time periods), it may be important to describe which artist influences the other more. Further experiments were done on asymmetric and symmetric affinity matrices and those results are seen in Figure 8.

We also tried to see if we can reduce the feature dimensionality before computing the similarity or not. We applied various methods including PCA, MDS, LLE, Isomap, etc but got a worse results emphasizing classemes feature are optimized in terms of dimension.

4.3   Visualizing Influences - A Map of Artists

In order to visualize artists in a new space based on similarity, we used a non-linear dimension reduction approach, namely Locally Linear Embedding (LLE) [10]. With LLE, we map our high-dimensional data to an embedded space. The embedding provides relationships between artists in relation to the artist space as a whole.

First, we applied LLE to the affinity matrix computed previously down to one dimension. In this reduction, Modern and Abstract artists seemed to be grouping together while other artists were too clustered to determine groupings. In a different mapping, we use LLE to reduce the affinity matrix to two dimensions. Figure 6 visualizes this two dimension varying mapping in both the x and y axis. We color each artist name according to its genre (13 colors for 13 genres) to get a better sense of groupings.

In Figure 6 we can see a few *Expressionist* artists (in red) clustered together as well as *Abstract Contemporary* artists (in grey-blue). As seen, the artists at the bottom of the mapping are Lichtenstein, Hepworth, Malevich, Mondrian, Motherwell, O'Keffe, and Rothko who are all Modern and Abstract artists. Their genres differ slightly but all share some stylistic approaches and time period.

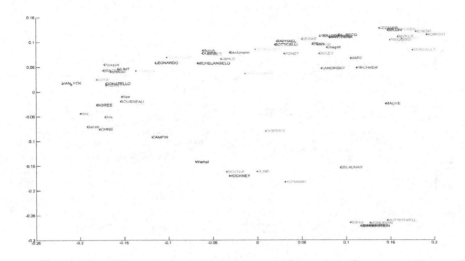

Fig. 6. Similar artists in two dimensions

However, this time we can see that the *Impressionists* and *Renaissance* artists seem to have similar values in one dimension but not the other. Other genres, such as *Romanticism*, seem to have a broader range of values.

Some artists in this mapping seem to cluster according to their genre, but in the context of influence, it is also important to think about the similarities between artists instead of the classification of genre. This is especially true as style varies in certain genres. This is yet another complication of the task of measuring influence.

Therefore, another way to analyze this graph is to disregard genre all together. We can wonder whether Richter and Hockney share a connection because they lie close to each other. Or we can wonder if Klimt was influenced by Picasso or Braque. In fact, both Picasso and Braque were listed as influences of Klimt in our ground-truth list. When comparing these close mappings to the ground truth influence, some are reasonable while others seem less coherent. In another example, Bazille lies close to Renoir and Delacroix who were both influences of Bazille. Renoir was also influenced by Delacroix according to our research and it is reflected in our mapping. Other successful mappings include Munch's influence on Beckmann, Pissarro's influence on Cezanne, Degas's influence on Caillebotte, Velazquez's influence on Manet, and so on. Caillebotte and Van Gogh are nearly mapped on top of each other. Although it is not reflected in our sparse ground-truth list, it is known that both Caillebotte and Van Gogh were influenced by an outside source, Japanese art and composition [6]

We try another mapping with a 3-dimensional reduced space. Figure 7 shows a 3-dimensional view of artists mapped using an asymmetric affinity matrix. Here, more of the genres seem to be clustering together. There is a clear band of Impressionists (green), Renaissance (blue), and Expressionist (red) artists. Other interesting pairs include Ruben's influence on Delacroix, Pissarro and

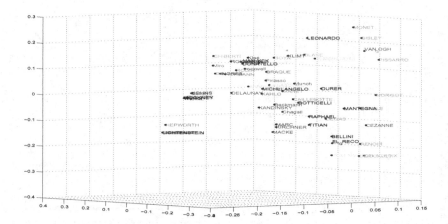

Fig. 7. Embedded mapping of artists in three dimensions using an asymmetric Hausdorff distance

Monet's influence on Van Gogh, Manet's influence on Munch, and the congestion of Modern and Abstract artists. This asymmetric 3 dimensional LLE mapping shows a better categorization of genres then any other mapping we tried.

We've tried other reduction methods besides LLE, e.g. PCA, MDS, etc. However we figure out that LLE dimension reduction is the best method for accuracy in the context of influence with accuracy 28.18 %.

Variation of Hausdorff distance Accuracy		
	Symmetric	Asymmetric
Hausdorff	22.73%	20.00%
Percentile Hausdorff	23.03%	20.30%
Modified Hausdorff	30.00%	26.36%

Fig. 8. Accuracy rates of asymmetric vs. symmetric affinity matrices for similarity measuring

5   Conclusion and Future Works

In this paper we presented a new dataset with diverse set of artists and wide range of paintings. This dataset will be publicly available and can be used for interdisciplinary tasks of Art and Computer Science. We also posed the interesting question of finding influence between painters as a knowledge discovery problem and showed interesting results for both of the qualitative and quantitative measurements.

Through our experiments we have found that Modified Hausdorff Distance (MHD) works well on image similarity. We also found that combining this with Locally Linear Embedding is the best technique for mapping into a low dimensional embedding space. Mapping results in lower accuracy than without the mapping but the trade-off is that we are able to visualize artists in relation to each other. MHD worked best for symmetric affinity matrices at 30% accuracy. However, applying LLE to an asymmetric matrix shows better accuracy than a symmetric one and it can be explained by the fact that LLE is graph based dimensionality reduction and asymmetric MHD will make more accurate directed graph to apply LLE on it.

References

1. Arora, R.S., Elgammal, A.M.: Towards automated classification of fine-art painting style: A comparative study. In: ICPR (2012)
2. Cabral, R.S., Costeira, J.P., De la Torre, F., Bernardino, A., Carneiro, G.: Time and order estimation of paintings based on visual features and expert priors. In: SPIE Electronic Imaging, Computer Vision and Image Analysis of Art II (2011)
3. Carneiro, G.: Graph-based methods for the automatic annotation and retrieval of art prints. In: ICMR (2011)
4. Carneiro, G., da Silva, N.P., Del Bue, A., Costeira, J.P.: Artistic image classification: An analysis on the PRINTART database. In: Fitzgibbon, A., Lazebnik, S., Perona, P., Sato, Y., Schmid, C. (eds.) ECCV 2012, Part IV. LNCS, vol. 7575, pp. 143–157. Springer, Heidelberg (2012)
5. Dubuisson, M.P., Jain, A.K.: A modified hausdorff distance for object matching. In: Pattern Recognition (1994)
6. Fell, D.: Van Gogh's Garden. Simon & Schuster (2001)
7. Fichner-Rathus, L.: Foundations of Art and Design. Clark Baxter
8. Graham, D., Friedenberg, J., Rockmore, D.: Mapping the similarity space of paintings: image statistics and visual perception. Visual Cognition (2010)
9. Li, J., Yao, L., Hendriks, E., Wang, J.Z.: Rhythmic brushstrokes distinguish van gogh from his contemporaries: Findings via automated brushstroke extraction. IEEE Trans. Pattern Anal. Mach. Intell. (2012)
10. Roweis, S.T., Saul, L.K.: Nonlinear dimensionality reduction by locally linear embedding. Science (2000)
11. Torresani, L., Szummer, M., Fitzgibbon, A.: Efficient object category recognition using classemes. In: Daniilidis, K., Maragos, P., Paragios, N. (eds.) ECCV 2010, Part I. LNCS, vol. 6311, pp. 776–789. Springer, Heidelberg (2010)

Identifying Vandalized Regions in Facial Images of Statues for Inpainting*

Milind G. Padalkar[1], Manali V. Vora[1], Manjunath V. Joshi[1],
Mukesh A. Zaveri[2], and Mehul S. Raval[1]

[1] Dhirubhai Ambani Institute of Information and Communication Technology,
Gandhinagar, India-382007
{milind_padalkar,manali_vora,mv_joshi,mehul_raval}@daiict.ac.in
[2] Sardar Vallabhbhai National Institute of Technology, Surat, India–395007
mazaveri@coed.svnit.ac.in

Abstract. Historical monuments are considered as one of the key aspects for modern communities. Unfortunately, due to a variety of factors the monuments get damaged. One may think of digitally undoing the damage to the monuments by inpainting, a process to fill-in missing regions in an image. A majority of inpainting techniques reported in the literature require manual selection of the regions to be inpainted. In this paper, we propose a novel method that automates the process of identifying the damage to visually dominant regions viz. eyes, nose and lips in face image of statues, for the purpose of inpainting. First, a bilateral symmetry based method is used to identify the eyes, nose and lips. Textons features are then extracted from each of these regions in a multi-resolution framework to characterize both the regular and irregular textures. These textons are matched with those extracted from a training set of true vandalized and non-vandalized regions, in order to classify the region under consideration. If the region is found to be vandalized, the best matching non-vandalized region from the training set is used to inpaint the identified region using the Poisson image editing method. Experiments conducted on face images of statues downloaded from the Internet, give promising results.

Keywords: texton, inpainting, vandalism, damage-detection, heritage.

1 Introduction

Heritage sites are essential sources of precious information. Cultural heritage conservation helps a community to preserve its history and gives a sense of continuity and identity. However, because of a variety of factors such as weather, antisocial elements, etc., monuments are sometimes ruined or vandalized. Renovating such sites is a very sensitive activity and requires great expertise. Renovation not only poses danger to the undamaged monuments but may also introduce changes in

---

* This work is a part of project sponsored by Department of Science and Technology (DST), Govt. of India (Grant No: NRDMS/11/1586/2009/Phase-II).

A. Petrosino, L. Maddalena, P. Pala (Eds.): ICIAP 2013 Workshops, LNCS 8158, pp. 208–217, 2013.

the damaged ones that notably deviate from the historical existence. An obvious solution that avoids physical contact is to digitally renovate these monuments, which may be accomplished using image restoration and inpainting techniques [2,3,10]. Image restoration refers to the recovery of an original image from its degraded version, while image inpainting refers to the process of modifying image contents imperceptibly, such as adding or removing object.

Image inpainting has been an active area of research for over a decade. A number of techniques have been proposed during this period. Notable among these works are those based on level lines [2,10], exemplar [3], solving Poisson's equation [12], global image statistics [9], multiple views of a scene [18], multiple images that are semantically similar [6], texture and structure information [1] and many more. All the above listed inpainting techniques are, however, not fully automatic i.e. they require the target regions for inpainting to be either known or selected manually. Work proposed in this paper addresses this issue by automating the region detection process for inpainting face images of damaged statues. Globally, it is observed that vandalism by humans is a major reason for statues being damaged. The facial regions like eyes, nose and lips are the visually the most dominant ones when one looks at a statue and are therefore more likely to get damaged when vandalized. A damage to such regions diminishes the attractiveness of the statues. Although other facial regions may be vandalized, the damage may not be as noticeable as that to the eyes, nose or lips, when it comes to visual attractiveness. We therefore intend to detect and inpaint any damaged eye, nose or lips in a given facial image of a statue.

Recently, Parmar et al. [11] proposed a method on similar lines. Their method relies on the use of edge based features and template matching to detect the damaged regions in frontal-face images of statues. However, the method is highly dependent on the scaling, rotation and pose in the facial images. Moreover, images of different statues may have different sizes and shapes of eyes and lip regions, while the templates used are of fixed size and shape, leading to unreliable results. Further, their method does not address the classification of nose regions. Our proposed approach also takes care of these limitations.

The motivation behind our proposed work is twofold. First, it can be a useful tool to continuously monitor the heritage site using a surveillance system and alert the authorities if any damage to monuments takes place. This damage may be unintentional due to the curiosity of visitors to know details or it may be intentional. After the alert is sounded, a corrective action can be initiated and monuments can be protected from further damage. Secondly, since our approach automatically detects the target regions for inpainting, the subjectiveness associated with the manual selection of target regions for inpainting will be eliminated. Results of an inpainting algorithm are highly influenced by selection of target regions. If the target regions are manually selected, a fair comparison of various inpainting algorithms might not be possible. Thus, a common automatically detected target region for inpainting may prove helpful here. Our work may be used to add up a new feature in digital cameras to create immersive navigation effect. The work can also be useful to replace the manual selection of regions by automatic detection in a photo editing software, for correcting / replacing a damaged part of a given photograph.

Texture analysis of several facial images of statues downloaded from the Internet [5] revealed that the texture of a damaged region is different from that of an undamaged region. This study motivated us to use texture as a feature for region classification. Textons, which are cluster centres in a filter response space, have been extensively used for texture classification [14,15]. In the proposed method, we try to identify a region being vandalized or non-vandalized by comparing its textons with those of a training set consisting of true vandalized and non-vandalized regions. Moreover, our method extracts these textons in a multi-resolution framework to characterize both the regular and irregular textures. The organization of this paper is as follows. Section 2 presents the proposed approach. In section 3, experimental results are shown and finally, we conclude in section 4.

2   Proposed Approach

Our approach for automatic inpainting the face images of monument is divided into following major steps viz. (a) extraction of potential regions of interest, (b) identification of vandalized regions and (c) inpainting vandalized regions.

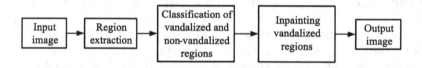

Fig. 1. Block diagram of the proposed approach

Figure 1 illustrates our proposed approach. Initially, major regions of interest from given face image are extracted using bilateral symmetry of gradient directions. Vandalized and non-vandalized regions are identified using the texture based method, out of which the vandalized regions are inpainted using Poisson image editing technique [12]. Here, we have considered eyes, nose and lips as the potential region of interest because of the tendency of human beings to target these regions while vandalizing. The inputs are assumed to be frontal face images. It may be noted that our algorithm works well even when there is slight deviation from the frontal pose. For large deviation due to complex distortions, one may think of using image registration as a preprocessing step. However, given a single image with complex distortions, registration itself is a difficult problem and involves pixel interpolation, affecting texture classification.

2.1   Extraction of Potential Regions of Interest

Given a face image of a statue, we intend to identify visually attractive regions like eyes, nose and lips. Such regions have a common property viz. symmetry.

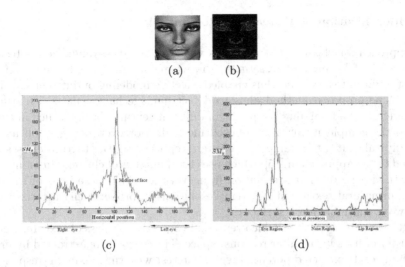

Fig. 2. To extract potential regions of interest; (a) input image, (b) image containing edges, (c) plot of symmetry measure SM_x, (d) plot of symmetry measure SM_y

A method to identify eyes, nose and lips that uses symmetry as a cue has been proposed by Katahara and Aoki [7]. In our approach, we use symmetry based method with noise removal as a preprocessing. This leads to better edge preservation and hence the potential regions are extracted with better accuracy. The use of single scale retinex (SSR) algorithm [16] makes our method invariant to illumination changes. Following are main steps of face region extraction.

(a) Make the input image illumination invariant using SSR algorithm [16].
(b) Apply Perona-Malik edge preserving diffusion [17] to smooth the image.
(c) Extract various outlines present in the smoothed image.
(d) Compute the symmetry measure of each pixel $b_m(x, y)$ [7].
(e) Project the symmetry measure onto X-axis, i.e. SM_x

$$SM_x = \sum_{j=1}^{M} b_m(j, x),$$ (1)

where, M is number of columns in an image and b_m represents symmetry measure around horizontal axis. Once SM_x is computed, its peak value is used to find mid-line about which the face is nearly symmetric.

(f) Project the symmetry measure onto Y-axis, i.e. SM_y

$$SM_y = \sum_{i=1}^{N} b_m(y, i),$$ (2)

where, N is number of rows in an image. The various peaks in SM_y are used to find eyes, nose and lips.

Figure 2. shows an input edge image and the plots of symmetry measure on the X and Y axis, respectively.

2.2   Identification of Vandalized Regions

Our approach for classifying a region as vandalized or non-vandalized is based on the work of Varma and Zisserman [15], where the materials to be classified were of uniform texture and thus enabled effective modeling of different texture classes. The proposed method aims to detect damage having natural texture. We therefore avoid building the model of different texture classes, which in turn reduces the complexity of the proposed method. Moreover, our method automatically calculates the number of clusters representing the texture classes as opposed to the approach in [15], which uses fixed number of clusters. In addition, our method explores multi-resolution framework to address the issue of irregularities in natural texture at different resolutions; a property characterized by stone-work and monument surfaces.

Textons are basic entities which represents a particular class of texture. They are cluster centres in the filter response space. The textons are extracted by first convolving each extracted potential region interest with the maximum-response-8 (MR8) filter bank [14]. The MR8 filter bank consists of 38 filters which include Gaussian, Laplacian of Gaussian, edge and bar filters, out of which 8 responses are considered [14]. Each pixel of the input region is now transformed into a vector of size 8 as there are 8 filter responses. K-means algorithm is then applied on these vectors where the K cluster centres are known as textons. In the proposed method, selection of K for K-means is done automatically as described later in section 2.3. The texton are extracted individually for each region of interest viz. eyes, nose and lips. Figure 3 illustrates extraction of textons from a nose region.

Since the face images of monuments have natural texture which is complex, it is difficult to extract any repetitive pattern at a single scale. However, irregular patterns and structures in nature have been successfully represented using fractals in computer modeling [4,8]. A fractal is a geometric pattern that is repeated at smaller scales to produce irregular shapes and surfaces that cannot be represented by classical geometry. This property of fractals motivated us to apply a multi-resolution framework for obtaining textons that would better represent the natural texture of the photographed monuments. In order to incorporate the multi-resolution framework, the procedure of texton extraction is repeated for two coarser scales as well. Thus, the actual region and the corresponding two coarser resolution versions are the three different scales at which the MR8 filter response is computed. To obtain coarser versions of an actual regions (i.e. extracted nose), the image is low-pass filtered before down sampling using Gaussian filter.

The training set that consists of true vandalized and non-vandalized regions is now used in a learning stage. This stage is used to extract textons that represent the true vandalized and non-vandalized regions. Thus, all the training images containing true vandalized eye are considered together to extract the textons representing vandalized eye. Similarly, textons for non-vandalized eye, vandalized and non-vandalized nose and lips are extracted from the training set. Figure 4 illustrates the learning of textons for vandalized nose region.

In the classification stage, the Euclidean distance between the textons of extracted regions of the test image and those from the corresponding vandalized

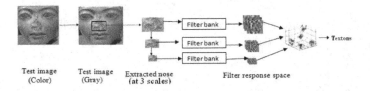

Test image   Test image   Extracted nose   Filter response space
(Color)   (Gray)   (at 3 scales)

Fig. 3. Extraction of textons using the MR8 filter bank

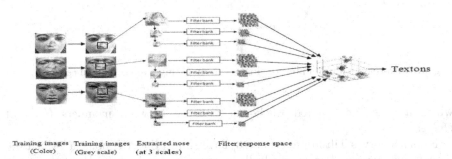

Training images   Training images   Extracted nose   Filter response space
(Color)   (Grey scale)   (at 3 scales)

Fig. 4. Learning of texton for vandalized nose region using the MR8 filter bank

and non-vandalized region of the training images is computed. The minimum distance criteria is used to classify the region as either vandalized or non-vandalized. It may be noted that for each extracted region, viz. eyes, nose and lips, classification is performed independently. This enables detection and inpainting of more than one damaged regions in an image simultaneously. Since the textons being robust features are used to represent the training images containing a variety of textures, the vandalized and non-vandalized regions in different statues can be successfully identified.

2.3   Automatic Selection of Number of Clusters

Many of the existing clustering algorithms require the number of clusters (i.e. textons represented as vectors) to be known in advance. However, it may not be possible to pre determine the number of clusters. In our work, we use an uncomplicated approach to estimate the number of clusters. Here, we obtain clusters by varying the value of K in the K-means algorithm. We then plot a two dimensional evaluation graph, where X-axis shows number of clusters (K) and Y-axis shows a function of the pooled within cluster sum of squares around the cluster means (W_k) calculated as follows [13],

$$W_K = \sum_{r=1}^{K} \left(\sum_{\forall i, i' \in C_r} d_{i,i'} \right) \tag{3}$$

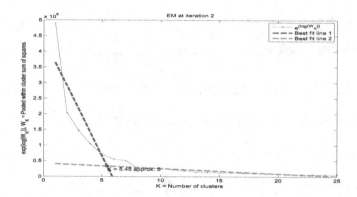

Fig. 5. Auto-selection of number of clusters K by fitting two straight lines to the data

where $d_{i,i'}$ is the squared Euclidean distance between members (i, i') of cluster C_r.

For such curves Tibshirani et al. [13] have shown that the point at which the monotonic decrease flattens markedly is taken as the best K. However, if the curve is smooth (like the one shown in figure 5) where it is difficult to determine where exactly the decrease flatters, then we have a challenging task to obtain the best value of K. To overcome this difficulty, we try to best fit two straight lines to the curve using expectation-maximization (EM) algorithm. The point of intersection of the two best fit lines then gives the approximate point at which the curve starts to flatten. We take this point to be the best K. This is illustrated in figure 5.

2.4   Inpainting

After the identification of vandalized and non-vandalized regions, final step is to inpaint vandalized regions using the corresponding non-vandalized regions from the same image or from different images available in the database. The source region that replaces the vandalized region is selected from the training set of true non-vandalized images. Here the selection criteria is the extent of similarity of the undamaged regions in the vandalized image with the true non-vandalized images. The extent of similarity is measured as the distance in the Euclidean space. Once the vandalized region and the non-vandalized source image are identified, we use Poisson image editing technique for seamless blending as described in [12].

Let f denote the test image, Ω denote the vandalized region in the test image and $\delta\Omega$ denotes the boundary of vandalized region. The minimization problem to be solved for replacing vandalized region with corresponding non-vandalized region can be written as

$$\min_f \iint_\Omega |\nabla f - \nabla f^*|^2 \; with \; f|_{\delta\Omega} = f^*|_{\delta\Omega}, \tag{4}$$

where, f^* represents the non-vandalized source, ∇ is the gradient operator.

3   Experimental Setup and Results

Our database consists of 40 facial images of statues having vandalized and non-vandalized regions. The inputs used are frontal face images downloaded from the Internet [5]. However, the proposed method can be extended for non-frontal faces by using homography with keypoints invariant to changes in scale, illumination and view point, which we intend to address in future. The spatial resolution of the images is adjusted such that all images are of the same size. A mean correction is applied to the images so that, they have the same average brightness. To select the source image from which the non-vandalized regions are chosen for inpainting, we use minimum of the squared distance between the non-vandalized regions of the test image and the database images. A manual selection of the non-vandalized source image would be required in case all the regions in the test image classified as vandalized. Figure 6-9 show results of our proposed approach.

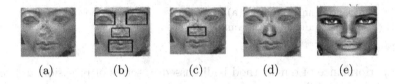

(a)   (b)   (c)   (d)   (e)

Fig. 6. Auto-inpainting on vandalized nose; (a) input image, (b) extracted potential regions of interest, (c) detected vandalized nose, (d) inpainted image, (e) source image.

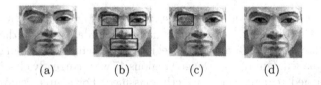

(a)   (b)   (c)   (d)

Fig. 7. Auto-inpainting on single vandalized eye; (a) input image, (b) extracted potential regions of interest, (c) detected vandalized eye, (d) inpainted image.

Training for the eyes, nose and lips regions was done independently. For training, we have used 10 images each for vandalized and non-vandalized regions. Testing was carried out on all the images from the database including those used for training. Results are shown in figures 6-9. In figure 7, the reflected version of non-vandalized left eye has been used to inpaint vandalized right eye. However, in figure 8, since both eyes are vandalized, the face image from the training set which gives minimum squared Euclidean distance for the non-vandalized regions when compared to the test image, is used as the source image. Figure 9 shows a result where our proposed work fails to detect vandalized region. As the input image contains nose having small, the corresponding textons match those of a non-vandalized nose. This happens due to the similarity in the extracted statistics of the vandalized and non-vandalized regions, and our method fails to differentiate the two regions.

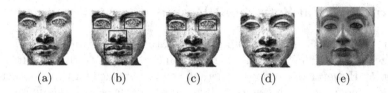

Fig. 8. Auto-inpainting on vandalized eyes; (a) input image, (b) extracted potential regions of interest, (c) detected vandalized eyes (d) inpainted image, (e) source image

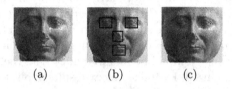

Fig. 9. Failed vandalism detection; (a) input image, (b) extracted potential regions of interest, (c) unable to detected the vandalized nose

The performance of our method is discussed in terms of precision and recall metrics defined as follows

$$Recall = \frac{|Ref \cap Dect|}{|Ref|}, \qquad Precision = \frac{|Ref \cap Dect|}{|Dect|}, \qquad (5)$$

where *Ref* are the regions declared to be damaged or undamaged by volunteers and *Dect* are the regions detected as damaged or undamaged by the proposed technique. From a set of 40 images, 50 regions were found to be damaged, while 50 were undamaged. Out of 50 damaged regions 47 were correctly classified, while all 50 undamaged regions were correctly classified. For source region selection 49 out of 50 regions were correctly selected in accordance to the volunteers. The performance in terms of these metrics is summarised in table 1.

Table 1. Performance evaluation

Region type	# regions	Recall	Precision
Damaged	50	0.9400	1.0000
Undamaged	50	1.0000	1.0000

The source selection method used in our approach in not comparable with content based image retrieval (CBIR) techniques. This is because for a large vandalized region, a CBIR system may not find adequate amount of non-vandalized content to retrieve the best match relevant for inpainting. The proposed method is developed for images of statues. However, since statues and natural face images, both have same facial characteristics, the method can certainly be effective for facial regions in natural images.

4   Conclusion

In this paper, we have presented a texture based approach to automatically detect vandalized regions in face images of statues for inpainting. The results show that facial regions viz. eyes, nose and lips in images can be effectively repaired. In future we aim to incorporate invariance to rotation, illumination and view point so that vandalized regions in non-frontal face images can also be inpainted. Also we would extend our work such that damage in non-facial region can be auto-detected for inpainting.

References

1. Bertalmio, M., Vese, L., Sapiro, G., Osher, S.: Simultaneous structure and texture image inpainting. Trans. Img. Proc. 12(8), 882–889 (2003)
2. Bertalmio, M., Sapiro, G., Caselles, V., Ballester, C.: Image inpainting. In: Computer graphics (SIGGRAPH 2000), pp. 417–424 (2000)
3. Criminisi, A., Pérez, P., Toyama, K.: Region filling and object removal by exemplar-based image inpainting. Trans. Img. Proc. 13(9), 1200–1212 (2004)
4. Emerson, C., Lam, N., Quattrochi, D.: Multi-scale fractal analysis of image texture and patterns. Photogrammetric Engg. and Remote Sensing 65(1), 51–62 (1999)
5. Google Images (March 2012), http://www.images.google.com
6. Hays, J., Efros, A.A.: Scene completion using millions of photographs. ACM Transactions on Graphics (SIGGRAPH 2007) 26(3) (2007)
7. Katahara, S., Aoki, M.: Face parts extraction windows based on bilateral symmetry of gradient direction. In: Solina, F., Leonardis, A. (eds.) CAIP 1999. LNCS, vol. 1689, pp. 489–497. Springer, Heidelberg (1999)
8. Legrand, P.: Local regularity and multifractal methods for image and signal analysis. In: Scaling, Fractals and Wavelets. Wiley (January 2009)
9. Levin, A., Zomet, A., Weiss, Y.: Learning how to inpaint from global image statistics. In: Int. Conf. on Computer Vision, vol. 1, pp. 305–312 (October 2003)
10. Masnou, S., Morel, J.M.: Level lines based disocclusion. In: Int. Conf. on Image Processing, vol. 3, pp. 259–263 (October 1998)
11. Parmar, C.M., Joshi, M.V., Raval, M.S., Zaveri, M.A.: Automatic image inpainting for the facial images of monuments. In: Proceedings of Electrical Engineering Centenary Conference 2011, December 14-17, pp. 415–420 (2011)
12. Pérez, P., Gangnet, M., Blake, A.: Poisson image editing. In: ACM SIGGRAPH 2003 Papers, SIGGRAPH 2003, pp. 313–318 (2003)
13. Tibshirani, R., Walther, G., Hastie, T.: Estimating the number of clusters in a data set via the gap statistic. Journal of Royal Stat. Soc., B 63(2), 411–423 (2001)
14. Varma, M., Zisserman, A.: A statistical approach to material classification using image patch exemplars. IEEE Trans. PAMI 31(11), 2032–2047 (2009)
15. Varma, M., Zisserman, A.: Classifying images of materials: Achieving viewpoint and illumination independence. In: Heyden, A., Sparr, G., Nielsen, M., Johansen, P. (eds.) ECCV 2002, Part III. LNCS, vol. 2352, pp. 255–271. Springer, Heidelberg (2002)
16. Štruc, V., Pavešić, N.: Illumination invariant face recognition by non-local smoothing. In: Proceedings of the BioID MultiComm., pp. 1–8 (2009)
17. Weickert, J.: Theoretical foundations of anisotropic diffusion in image processing. Computing, Suppl. 11, 221–236 (1996)
18. Whyte, O., Sivic, J., Zisserman, A.: Get out of my picture! internet-based inpainting. In: Proceedings of the 20th British Machine Vision Conference, London (2009)

Detection and Correction of Mistracking in Digitalized Analog Video

Filippo Stanco, Dario Allegra, and Filippo Luigi Maria Milotta

Dipartimento di Matematica e Informatica, University of Catania,
viale A. Doria no. 6, 95125 Catania
fstanco@dmi.unict.it, {darioalltalk,fmilotta}@gmail.com

Abstract. Nowadays video technology is basically digital, but in the last half century the most diffused devices have been analog magnetic tapes. Since this is an old storing technique, it is necessary to convert these data in digital form. Moreover, analog videos may be affected by particular defects, called *drops*. Despite there are many hardware to perform the digitalization, few implement the correction of drops. In this paper, the drop also known as "Mistracking" is focused. A method to detect and correct this artifact is developed.

Keywords: Mistracking, Tracking Error, Analog Video, Drop Out.

1 Introduction

Image processing techniques have been successfully applied in many fields related to cultural heritage [1–3] and can be also exploited in video storage and restoration as part of the "Archeomatica Project" [4]. Since 1950s videotapes are used as data storage, and nowadays there are huge archives which contain considerable information. Today the magnetic tapes are obsolete and replaced by digital devices. Hence, in order to preserve these data it is necessary to convert them in digital form. For example, TV networks have a lot of news report stored on magnetic tapes only. In particular, Italian public broadcasting company RAI (Radiotelevisione Italiana [5]), our partner in this research, needs to solve this problem by software.

Videotape technology is based on electromagnetism. In particular using an electric field to align magnetic domains on the material of tape so that they remain aligned, even in absence of it. In this way, thanks to electromagnetic induction principles, it is possible to retrieve information stored on the tape through the magnetic fields of domains. Usually, reader devices consist in mechanical heads and reels for winding the tape. Data information is not recorded longitudinally and it does not fill all tape surface, so a synchronization signal, usually called CTL (Control Track Longitudinal), is required. A wrong synchronization or general mechanical problems could introduce some defects during reading or writing video flow. The Fig. 2 shows some examples of these analog drops: Dropout, Head Clog, Tracking Error or Mistracking, Skew Error, Comets,

A. Petrosino, L. Maddalena, P. Pala (Eds.): ICIAP 2013 Workshops, LNCS 8158, pp. 218–227, 2013.
© Springer-Verlag Berlin Heidelberg 2013

Sync Loss, Tape Crease, Head Switching Noise, Dot Crawl, AC Beat. In this paper, a method to correct the Mistracking is presented. Mistracking error is one of the most common defect originated by CTL, and it is independent from video coding format (PAL or NTSC) [11]. In particular, we propose a method to detect and correct this artifact (Fig. 1).

In literature, at the best of our knowledge, there are not work related on Mistracking. However, there are many papers about film defects. A. Kokaram et al. [7,8] focused just in Dirt, Lines, Shake, Flicker or Noise. Also Buisson et al. [9] and Rosenthaler et al. [10] develop techniques to solve video restoration problems. Unfortunately, none of these algorithms can be applied to Mistracking.

The paper is organized as follow. Section 2 reports an overview on Mistracking. Then, Section 3 describes the detection phase and Section 4 the correction phase. Finally, experimental results are shown in Section 5. Conclusions ends the paper.

2   An Overview on Mistracking

Mistracking, also called Tracking Error, consists in random rows of noise in the frame, usually white or black (Figs. 6(a), 5(a)). It is caused by misreading of video tracks recorded on a tape for an error in synchronization signal (CTL). In this way video heads could read a wrong area of tape, which may contains no data or inconsistent information, like a previous subscribed record. When interlaced mode is used, each frame consists of two distinct fields (odd rows and even rows), and Mistracking could affect just one field or both of them (Fig. 4). In some cases is possible to solve Mistracking modifying synchronization analogically by device components, but if this is allowed by the device and CTL skew is uniform along all the track. Otherwise, if the video is already converted in digital form, some Image Processing technique is required to solve this problem.

3   Detection Phase

The Mistracking consists in a quick variation of luminance between close horizontal lines in a rectangular area. This property suggests a connection with edge detection filters, which may be implemented through convolution masks. A known example is Laplacian kernel, which allow to detect vertical and horizontal edges of the image [6]. Effectively if we use this approach, the result isn't bad. In fact, the damaged area, is highlighted exactly such as an edge, but unfortunately it can't be distinguished by other regular edges (Fig. 3(b)). This problem is slightly attenuated if we use an edge detection filter for horizontal edges only, as Prewitt or Sobel, but not enough to distinguish the tracking line by other edges. In some case, mainly in images with very few details, this approach could show satisfactory results, because the edge filters would detect less edges with respect to a typical detailed image, allowing the distinction. However, it is not a good solution. To solve this problem we propose a new filter, with kernel:

$$\begin{bmatrix} 1 & -1 & 1 \\ -1 & 1 & -1 \end{bmatrix} /6 \tag{1}$$

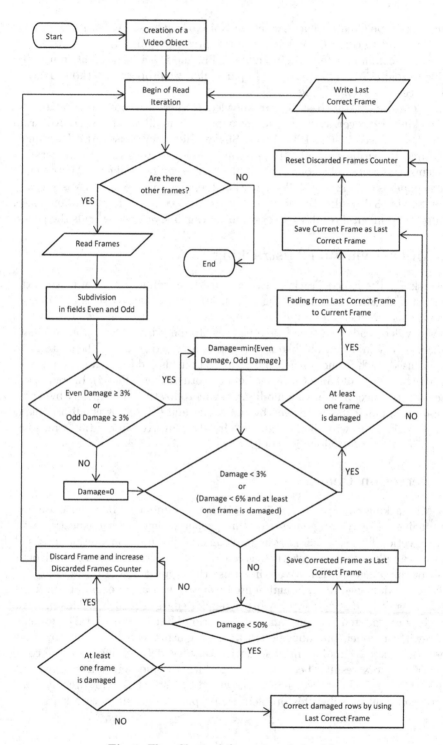

Fig. 1. Flow Chart of the proposed algorithm

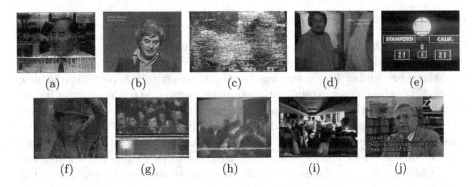

Fig. 2. Some examples of Analog Video Artifacts. (a) Head Clog: black or dark frame due to bad contact between heads and tape; (b) Drop Out: white and/or black lines of missing information in the picture; (c) Mistracking: horizontal lines of random noise; (d) Skew Error: frame hooked to the right or to the left; (e) AC Beat: bar of milky rolling luminance; (f) Comets: white or black dots with tail on the frame; (g) Sync Loss: loss of vertical hold during switching interval; (h) Tape Crease: horizontal rolling band of noise; (i) Head Switching Noise: loss of information in the lower border of the frame; (l) Dot Crawl: colored dots on horizontal borders.

This kernel, as well as detects horizontal edges only, sharpens above all the horizontal lines close together with marked luminance difference. Now, the filtered image consists in a grey scale frame with a great pixel value in the damaged area and a low value in other areas (Fig. 3(c)). The next step consists to find an index to describe the damage level. Our idea takes into account rectangular area whose length is the same as that of the image. The height depends on other criteria. Although this solution is definitely better than the previous proposals, it could fail when the image contains pattern similar at the tracking lines.

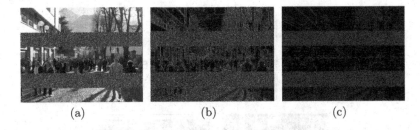

Fig. 3. (a) Input image; (b) Frame filtered with Laplacian kernel. (c) Frame filtered with the proposed kernel. The new kernel selects the corrupted lines but less details of the image. The figures (b) and (c) are gamma-modified to permit to see the not zero values.

3.1 Processing Filtered Image

Once we gain the filtered frame we have to establish a principle to determine which part of this one must be considered damaged or not. Due the convolution, now there are higher luminance values where an artifact appears in the new image. Since these areas extend horizontally from one side to the other of frame, is easy to see that the sum of luminance values of one or more damaged rows will be higher. Try to locate a damaged line using only the values of its pixels can be unreliable, but since the drop usually occurs on several consecutive rows, should also be considered for each row few lines adjacent to it, for a better estimation. We decided to analyze for each row the two upper and two lower, that is the same to use the values of the rectangle for each row r:

$$\Omega(r) = \{f(x,y) | 1 \leqslant x \leqslant c; r - 2 \leqslant y \leqslant r + 2\} \qquad (2)$$

where c is the number of all columns of the image. For each row r, the Equation (2) defines a set of luminance values where the average is the index related to row r.

3.2 Application Threshold

Indexes show the level of noise in each row so we have to decide which can be considered a correct line or not. The values obtained experimentally are always between 0 and 10 (theoretical values are between 0 and 64). Areas affected by other types of noise or containing details not have a value equal to 0, but in any case the value is still low, so is obtained experimentally that a good threshold value is between 1.5 and 3.5, according to the quality of the image. With the use of a low threshold we will have a most sensitive detection, on the other hand will be higher the chance of getting a false positive. A higher value would cause a failure detection of the drop.

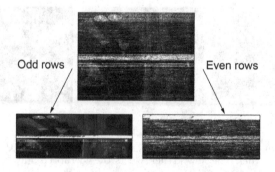

Fig. 4. Interlaced frame splitted in its two fields

4   Correction Phase

After the tracking lines have been detected, some property of video is used to allows to correct this problem (Fig. 1). Two main characteristics are considered:

- Two adjacent frames are very similar each other. This doesn't happen when there is a "scene transition".
- Each frame consists in two fields: pair rows and odd rows (height is half of the entire frame, Fig. 4).

There are two coding modes: progressive or interlaced. When interlacement is used each frame consists of two fields, stored in two distinct tracks. Devices read the tracks individually but the frame rate is high enough that a unique frame is perceived. In progressive mode, each frame is not splitted in two fields but there is just a single track.

Our solution uses the similar information in adjacent frames and in the most genuine field. The original video could be interlaced, while after the conversion, a progressive video is obtained. First we split each frame in correspondent two fields again (Fig. 4), and use it as input of detection algorithm. Basically, to repair damaged frames, the single tracking lines or the entire frame/field can be replaced. Now, there are three different cases:

1. Detection of a strongly damaged frame;
2. Detection of a slightly damaged frame or half-frame (field);
3. Detection of a correct half-frame.

We fix that when a frame has over 50% of tracking lines in both fields (even and odd), is "strongly damaged"; when at least one half-frame has between 3% and 50% of tracking lines, is "slightly damaged"; otherwise the frame is "correct". Moreover, a discarded frames counter is used for correction in case 3. When discarded frames counter has a value higher than 0 is not a good choice to correct the single lines of a "slightly damaged" frame because the last "correct" frame could be temporally incoherent with the current scene. In particular:

Case 1. This case happens when we detect at least 50% of tracking lines in the even field, and at least 50% of tracking lines in the odd field. In this condition is very difficult to restore the damaged area, because we have very few information. For this, the best solution is to remove the entire frame. We will explain how replaces this damaged frame in the third case. Finally, the counter for discarded frames is increased.

Case 2. When at least one of two fields has a number of tracking lines between 3% and 50%, it's possible try to correct it. First, the field with the lowest damage is chosen and restored. If the counter of discarded frames is 0, the damaged lines of chosen field is replaced with correspondent genuine lines in the last correct field. Finally, the new field is resized and becomes the "the last" corrected frame. Else, if the counter of discarded frames isn't 0, to replace the single lines isn't a good solution, because the last corrected frame could be temporally too far by the field under consideration. The result would be a bad image. To solve this,

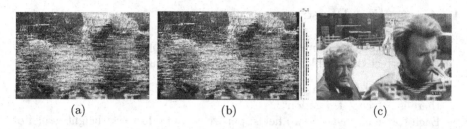

(a)   (b)   (c)

Fig. 5. Correction of Mistracking of frame called "Clint". (a) Original; (b) Detection on a non blurred frame, with several threshold values on the right; black lines under each value show which defected rows have been detected; (c) Restored frame using threshold equal to 1.5.

we do a further consideration: if the number of tracking lines is over 6%, we fall back in the case 1, else go to the case 3.

Case 3. In the last case if the percentage of at least one field is lower than 3% or is lower than 6% and the consecutive damaged frame counter is higher than 0, then we consider this field as a correct field. First of all we have to consider this frame (or field) as the new "correct frame" (or "correct field"). Then if the consecutive damaged frame counter is equal to d we have to correct previously discarded frame. To avoid an abrupt replacement of all these frames with the current correct frame, and the consequent effect of *freeze* frame, we use a fading transition that weights the previous correct frame (start) and the current one (end), based on the temporal position of appearance. The fading is described by the following process:

Let m be the consecutive damaged frame counter, a_i be the generic frame with $i = 0, 1, \ldots, m + 1$ and $k = 1, \ldots, m$, where "a_0" is the previous correct frame and a_{m+1} is the current correct frame; so each a_k frame of fading is obtained by:

$$a_k = a_0 \left(1 - \frac{k}{m+1}\right) + a_{m+1} \left(\frac{k}{m+1}\right) \tag{3}$$

Instead if the counter is equal to 0, than we don't make any correction operation. The choice of considering a frame as a "correct frame" even with a damage up to 6% due to the fact that if we find a slightly damaged frame after at least one strongly damaged one, then the slightly damaged frame will be discarded with a greater margin of error. In this way we avoid long sequence of fading, as seen in case 2. We must keep in mind that we can consider a "correct frame" or a "correct field". During the correction phase we have to compare the size of the damaged frame with the correct frame or correct field, so if these are different we have to resize the smallest vertically, or if these are equal we can correct them immediately, and only at the end if they were fields, resize the result to the size of a frame.

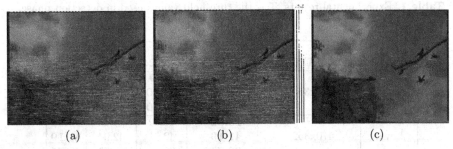

(a)   (b)   (c)

Fig. 6. Correction of Mistracking of frame called "Indy". (a) Original; (b) Detection on a blurred frame, with several threshold values on the right; black lines under each value show which defected rows have been detected; (c) Restored frame using threshold equal to 2.

5   Experimental Results

The proposed algorithm is tested on several videos. In some cases the Mistracking is properly generated to know percentage of total defect in each frame, in this way is possible to verify the correctness of detection algorithm.

From the Table 1 it can be seen that in almost all cases good results are obtained with a threshold value equal to 4. However, this threshold is not recommended because it does not take into account the correct rows adjacent to the damage. These rows often show a slight deterioration, so it is better to detect and correct them too. For this a threshold value such as 2.5, which also detects those lines, will provide better results. Very low threshold values, like 1.5, should be used in the case of very blurry images and poorly detailed, which are common in many analog video. In the Figs. 6(b) and 5(b) are reported two images taken from video affected by real Mistracking and are presented some results of the detection algorithm with threshold values from 1 to 2.5. The Fig. 6(c) and Fig. 5(c) shows results of the correction algorithm. Two restored videos can be found in [4].

5.1   Other Considerations about Correction Phase

The correction algorithm works well in most of the cases treated. However, there are situations in which the results do not coincide with those expected; the most significant cases are those in which:

- Many other types of drop are present in the same video;
- The content of the video is not homogeneous throughout the duration;
- There are undamaged horizontal lines identical to tracking lines;
- There are black bands in the sides of the frame.

When there are drops of other kinds, to detect mistracking can become difficult, and during the correction phase the areas affected by another defects could be used to make the replacement. Anyway, this usually enhances these drops. If

Table 1. Experimental results. T is the threshold values used in detection phase.

IMAGE	RESOLUTION	% DAMAGED	% T = 2.5	% T = 3.5	% T = 4
Geometric	416x330	**8.78**	**9.39**	7.87	7.87
		40.60	**40.90**	**40.30**	40.00
		60.30	**60.30**	60.00	60.00
Lawn	470x352	**13.92**	15.62	14.48	**13.92**
		41.19	42.61	42.04	**41.19**
		68.75	69.31	68.75	**68.75**
People	641x480	**18.95**	29.58	21.04	**19.79**
		32.29	42.91	32.70	**32.50**
		83.12	85.83	83.54	**83.33**
Text	400x320	**13.43**	16.25	13.75	**13.43**
		37.81	39.37	38.43	**37.81**
		61.25	63.43	**62.50**	**62.50**
Cartoon	720x576	**12.67**	14.40	**12.84**	12.50
		29.51	30.38	29.68	**29.51**
		62.15	**62.32**	61.97	61.97

the video quality is not uniform or there are very different scenes/contexts, it may happen that there is not a single threshold value suitable for the correct detection of each frame of video. In this case it is possible to split the video into several parts and correct them separately using different threshold. Among the other problems mentioned, there is the difficult identification of the tracking lines when the frames contain many lines similar in shape. This situation is very common in the case of cartoons, or video with a few shades of color or sharp lines. This usually results in false positives. Similar problems occur when the video presents the classic black bars to adapt to a certain aspect ratio. Their presence has different effects depending on the position. When these are located at the top or bottom of the frame, the percentages of the damage is altered. The "black" part of each frame always will be correct even if not contain any information. The case in which the bands are present in the right or left side will cause an incorrect calculation of the average of each rectangle described in detection algorithm, with the effect of false negatives. Moreover, in our implementation we use always a previous frame for the correction.

6   Conclusions

Although the analog technologies of recording and playback are intended to be completely replaced by digital ones, the development of algorithms for the correction of defects typical of analog media is required to ensure the preservation in the years ahead. Our experiments show that the proposed algorithm detects and corrects Mistracking in many cases. Moreover, some other drops like Tape Crease, Drop Out or Head Switching Noise, which have an error pattern similar to Mistracking one, are also partially corrected.

References

1. Stanco, F., Battiato, S., Gallo, G.: Cultural Heritage Preservation. Analysis, Restoration and Reconstruction of Ancient Artworks. Digital Imaging and Computer Vision. CRC Press (2011)
2. Stanco, F., Tanasi, D., Gallo, G., Buffa, M., Basile, B.: Augmented perception of the past. The case of hellenistic Syracuse. Journal of Multimedia 7(2), 211–216 (2012)
3. Stanco, F., Tenze, L., Ramponi, G.: Virtual restoration of vintage photographic prints affected by foxing and water blotches. J. Electronic Imaging 14(4), 043008 (2005)
4. Select "Analog video", http://www.archeomatica.unict.it/
5. RAI Radiotelevisione Italiana, www.rai.it
6. Gonzalez, R.C., Woods, R.E.: Digital image processing. Pearson Prentice Hall (2008)
7. Kokaram, A., Morris, R., Fitzgerald, W., Rayner, P.: Detection of missing data in image sequences. IEEE Transactions on Image Processing 4, 1496–1508 (1995)
8. Kokaram, A., Morris, R., Fitzgerald, W., Rayner, P.: Interpolation of missing data in image sequences. IEEE Transactions on Image Processing 4, 1509–1519 (1995)
9. Buisson, O., Besserer, B., Boukir, S., Helt, F.: Deterioration detection for digital film restoration. In: Proceedings of IEEE International Conference Computer Vision and Pattern Recognition, vol. 1, pp. 78–84 (June 1997)
10. Rosenthaler, L., Gschwind, R.: Restoration of movie films by digital image processing. In: Proceedings of IEEE Seminar on Digital Restoration of Film and Video Archives 2001 (2001)
11. Gupta, R.G.: Television Engineering and Video Systems. McGrawn-Hill Ed. (2005)
12. AV Artifact Atlas, http://preservation.bavc.org/artifactatlas/index.php

Using Various Types of Multimedia Resources to Train System for Automatic Transcription of Czech Historical Oral Archives

Josef Chaloupka, Jan Nouza, and Michaela Kucharova

Institute of Information Technology and Electronics, Technical University of Liberec
Studentska 2, 461 17 Liberec, Czech Republic
josef.chaloupka@tul.cz
https://www.ite.tul.cz/itee/

Abstract. Historical spoken documents represent a unique segment of national cultural heritage. In order to disclose the large Czech Radio audio archive to research community and to public, we have been developing a system whose aim is to transcribe automatically the archive files, index them and make them searchable. The transcription of contemporary (1 or 2 decades old) documents is based on the lexicon and statistical language model (LM) built from a large amount of recent texts available in electronic form. From the older periods (before 1990), however, digital texts do not exist. Therefore, we needed a) to find resources that represent language of those times, b) to convert them from their original form to text, c) to utilize this text for creating epoch specific lexicons and LMs, and eventually, d) to apply them in the developed speech recognition system. In our case, the main resources included: scanned historical newspapers, shorthand notes from the national parliament and subtitles from retro TV programs. When converted into text, they allowed us to built a more appropriate lexicon and to produce a preliminary version of the transcriptions. These were reused for unsupervised retraining of the final LM. In this way, we significantly improved the accuracy of the automatically transcribed radio news broadcast in 1969-1989 era, from initial 83 % to 88 %.

Keywords: historical audio archives, speech-to-text transcription, OCR, lexicon building, machine learning.

1 Introduction

Historical spoken documents represent a unique segment of national cultural heritage. They authentically illustrate events, ideas, language, personalities and atmosphere of the past and present. Usually they have form of audio (or audio-video) files originally recorded and stored on various types of fragile carriers. Therefore, for many years, their content was available only to a limited number of people. Due to the recent progress in information processing technology, namely digitization, speech-to-text transcription software and Internet, they can

A. Petrosino, L. Maddalena, P. Pala (Eds.): ICIAP 2013 Workshops, LNCS 8158, pp. 228–237, 2013.
© Springer-Verlag Berlin Heidelberg 2013

be disclosed to any interested researcher or even to public. Let us mention at least several examples of oral archives that have been made accessible, recently: the US National Gallery of the Spoken Word [1], the Dutch collection of historical oral records [2], audio-video library HistoryMakers [3], or international project MALACH [4]. The process of recording, preserving, processing, tagging, indexing and searching speech-based information has been described from several points of view in [5].

In 2011 we launched a large 4-year project supported by the Czech Ministry of Culture, whose aim is to disclose more than 100,000 spoken documents collected by the Czech Radio (and its predecessor Czechoslovak Radio) during its 90 years of broadcasting [6]. For this purpose, we have adapted our previously developed large-vocabulary continuous speech recognition (LVCSR) system to deal with broadcast recordings in Czech and Slovak and designed modules for speech indexation and search. During the first 18 months of the project, we have processed about 75,000 audio files (with total duration of 30,000 hours) and created a demo version of the web service that allows for smart search in the transcribed data [7].

The large amount of the data processed within the first two years was possible due to one main reason: So far, we have focused on the transcription of the files from the last two decades (1990 to present). Within that epoch, the Czech Radio archive covers hundreds of different broadcast programs, including main evening news, political debates, discussions, talk-shows, regional news, daily commentaries or read feuilletons. All are provided in good audio quality and their automatic transcription can benefit from the lexicon and statistical language model (LM) developed for contemporary Czech. However, when moving deeper to the history, we face two additional challenges: a lower signal quality and a language that differs from the recent one. The latter aspect is related to the fact that former Czechoslovakia belonged to the Soviet block (till 1989) where all official media was controlled by a strong communist regime. Most archive documents from that era are news and reports highly influenced by propaganda. Yet, these audio files reflect one important epoch in national history and their disclosure helps younger generations to understand it better.

The main difficulty with adapting the LVCSR system to the language of previous epochs consists in the fact that there are no texts available in digital form from those older periods. This complicates the creation of the epoch specific lexicons and LMs, which are necessary for the reliable performance of the transcription system. In this paper, we show our solution to the problem. We try to utilize less common resources, like scanned and digitized newspapers, subtitles from retro TV programs or shorthand parliament notes. When converted into electronic form, pre-processed and analyzed, these are a good source of epoch specific names, words and phrases. We describe the procedures used to build a representative corpus of historical texts, and to employ it for lexicon and LM adaptation. In experimental section, we show that this approach yields a significant improvement in the transcription accuracy.

2 Spoken Archive Transcription System and Its Linguistic Module

The speech transcription system is the most complex part of the Archive Processing and Accessing Platform (APAP). It converts audio recordings into text and provides detailed information on each processed document, each individual utterance (namely about speaker and language) and each word (including its pronunciation and exact time of occurrence). All these pieces of information are stored in a large database, they are indexed and made searchable. More technical details about the APAP can be found in [8]. In this contribution, we will focus mainly on its linguistic module.

The linguistic module consists of a lexicon (words with their pronunciations) and a statistical language model. Its version applicable for contemporary Czech has been based on a huge (11 GB) corpus of electronic texts, mainly newspapers published since 1990 to present. (This corpus will be referred to as *CPaper*.) A small subset of the corpus (2 GB) contains human made transcriptions of real speech, namely speech in selected major TV and radio programs broadcast during the last decade. (Let us denote it *CBroad*.) Recently, the size of the whole text corpus is 13 GB of data, and every year it increases by approx. 0.3 GB.

The corpus is regularly analyzed to identify the most frequent words that should be included in the lexicon. Its current version contains 551K lexemes (words, word-forms and multi-word expressions) that occurred at least 10 times in the corpus. In spite of the lexicon's large size, the Out-of-Vocabulary (OOV) rate is still about 1 %, mainly due to the fact that Czech belongs to the languages with a very high degree of inflection. The corpus also serves as a source data for computing the statistical (N-gram based) LM. In our system, we use a bigram LM, which is a compromise between memory usage, computation speed and performance accuracy. Again, more details can be found in [8].

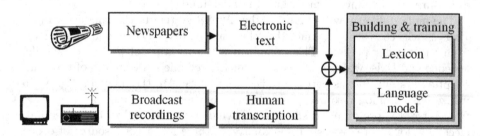

Fig. 1. Main resources used for building lexicon, and training statistical language model for speech recognition of contemporary Czech

3   Language Resources for Historical Document Transcription

As explained in Introduction, year 1990 makes an important milestone in the audio archive. Before 1990, the language of media was much influenced by the communist regime and propaganda. The crucial question is how to adapt the transcription system to the speech of that historical epoch, i.e. how to teach the system the words, phrases, names and language structure that are not covered by the above mentioned corpus. The only effective solution consists in building a similar corpus that will represent the language before 1990. Because almost no electronic texts from that period exist, they must be acquired first. So far, we have discovered three major sources: old newspapers (in paper form), shorthand notes from parliament sessions and audio-visual retro programs with subtitles. Each source and its specific way of processing is described below.

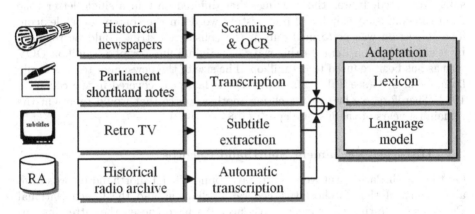

Fig. 2. Resources and procedures used to adapt the lexicon and language model to the period before 1990

3.1   Historical Newspapers and Their Processing

In the period of the communist regime (1948-1989), the main and the largest Czech newspaper was *Rude pravo*. It was the official press media of the Communist party. Recently, all its issues (with approx. 80 thousand pages) have been scanned by the Czech National Library. The same institution launched a project of their conversion (via an OCR software) into electronic texts. Up to now, years 1948 to 1983 have been processed. The OCR-based word error rates differ from page to page (typically in range 5 to 20 %), depending on the quality of the original copies. Unfortunately, many common methods used for OCR error reduction, like those based on statistical language modeling, could not been applied. It is logical, because a language model corresponding to that historical period does not exist, yet, and the application of the contemporary one would introduce irreversible loss in historical texts (e.g. changes in names or in spelling, replacements of epoch specific - and now obsolete - words by the modern ones, etc.)

To convert the raw OCR output to the text suitable for our purpose, we have performed the following steps:

Page Filtering. For each page we measured the number of OOV strings. If the OOV rate was larger than 15 % (the threshold found by the histogram analysis of the development data), the page was removed from the corpus, because either the original print or the scan were of very low quality.

Advertisement Blocking. To avoid repeated passages irrelevant for further linguistic analysis (namely advertisement, programs of TV, radio and theaters, etc) we have trained a simple key-word based classifier that identifies this type of unwanted text and removes it, too.

Safe Single-Letter-Error Correction. Using a small subset of OCRed texts we have detected the most frequent letter confusions (e.g. 'í' instead of 'i', 'l' instead of 'i', 'v' instead of 'y', 'é' instead of 'ě', etc). After that, we have compiled a list of the most frequent OOV strings that can be automatically and safely corrected. It was those strings that differed only in a single letter (one from the confusion pair list) from existing words in the contemporary lexicon. The correction was performed only if the considered string could be replaced by a unique lexicon item. In this way, the original number of 8.5 million OOV strings has been reduced to 6.4 million. The size of the newspaper texts is really large - 843 MB (see Table 1). However, the last year covered in the corpus is 1983. Therefore, we had to search for another source that would represent the remaining years of the historic epoch (1984 to 1989).

3.2   Historical Parliament Shorthand Records

On the Czech Parliament web [9] we have found official shorthand records from all sessions of the Czechoslovak Federal Parliament and the Czech National Council held during their entire existence. We have chosen the latter institution because its documents contain only Czech, while in the Federal Parliament, both Czech and Slovak occurred. The records written originally by stenographers and now available in electronic form describe 93 sessions within the 1969-1989 period and include verbatim transcriptions of all speeches. To get a text resource appropriate for our purpose, we wrote a script that extracted only the transcriptions of verbal communication and removed the description of formal acts, like session opening and management, voting protocols, etc. In spite of its relatively small size, the acquired text offers at least some coverage of names and major events from the period 1984 to 1989.

3.3   Subtitles from Retro TV Programs

Since 1990s Czech TV has been producing a retro document series named *25 years ago*. It is aired every day and contains a 5-minute-long selection of the most relevant news that were shown in TV exactly a quarter of century ago. In accord with the new public broadcast regulations, this type of program must be accompanied by subtitles. They can be downloaded from the Czech TV web site and used (with minimum additional effort) as another resource for the lexicon and LM adaptation. Their main advantage consists in the fact that they represent authentic broadcast speech in all its forms (read, planned and spontaneous) in the similar way as it occurred in the radio archive in that period.

4 Adapting Linguistic Module for 1969-1989 Period

One of the most interesting historical epochs in the radio archive is the 1969-1989 era. From this period, the archive offers a continual series of main (evening) news broadcast for 20 years. This is a unique collection of 7660 recordings (approx. 3800 hours of speech), valuable both from the historic as well as linguistic points of view. Its transcription and disclosure has been declared one of the top goals of the project and therefore we aimed at making a proper lexicon and language model fitted specially for this epoch.

Table 1. Statistics of text resources used for adaptation of lexicon and LM for 1969-1989 era

Resource	Covered period	Size [MB]	Size in words	Selected OOV words
Historical newspapers (*RP*)	1969-1983	942	132,772,115	5886
Parliament steno-notes (*Parl*)	1969-1989	23	3,359,474	2773
Retro TV (*Retro*)	1986-1988	5	626,767	1261
Transcribed radio archive (*RA*)	1969-1989	182	26,330,195	-

4.1 Adapting Lexicon

We took the pre-processed text data from the three sources described in section 3 and limited them to the 1969-1989 period. For each source, we compiled a frequency ordered list of those OOV strings that were not in the existing 551K lexicon. In case of the scanned newspapers, the list contained 1,779,756 strings, from which more than 90 % were error strings caused mainly by OCR. Even if we focused only on the terms with frequency higher than 20, we had to check more than 50,000 strings and manually pick up 5886 word candidates for addition to the lexicon. This tedious work could not be automated as most of the candidates were names of people, companies or institutions closely related to the given historical era. We often used Czech Wikipedia to verify the existence of these entities and their correct spelling. As to the other two sources, their processing was much easier, because they contained minimum typing or spelling errors. Here, we picked up the words with minimum frequency 2. Table 1 gives an overview of the relevant statistics on the three resources. The last column shows the numbers of lexicon candidates selected from each source. Because the three candidate lists had some overlap, the total number of added words was 7368. The meaning of the last row will be explained later.

4.2   Adapting Language Model

To compute an N-gram language model (a bigram LM in our case), we have to chose an appropriate text corpus and compute occurrence counts for all N-word sequences. Usually, a word which is not present in the corpus is removed from the lexicon. The sequences not seen in the corpus are assigned small probability values according to the applied smoothing method. In our system we prefer Knesser-Ney technique [10].

We have prepared and evaluated four different LMs based on the following corpora: a) *RP* only, b) *RP+Parl+Retro*, c) *CBroad+RP+Parl+Retro* and d) *CPaper+CBroad+RP+Parl+Retro*. The first two language models were computed entirely from the historical data, the remaining ones employed the contemporary texts, too. Their parameters and the results achieved with them are presented in Table 2.

4.3   Unsupervised LM Adaptation

In experiments described in section 5, we show that the transcription accuracy measured on the test set (made of selected archive documents from the 1969-1989 era) can go up to 87 %. This allows us to consider the application of an unsupervised LM adaptation scheme. In our case it means that we can try to use the automatically acquired transcriptions of the target archive documents as an additional text corpus. Obviously, it will always contain a certain type and amount of errors. In order to minimize their number and ensure the correct validation in tests, we applied the following strategy:

1. The data was transcribed by the system that had been set up for the optimal performance (in the same way as in experiment F in Table 2.
2. The speech segments in which the transcription system identified an increased amount of noise were removed from the corpus.
3. The utterances that were classified as Slovak by the language identification module [11] were removed.
4. The documents used in the test set were removed, too.

In this way we obtained a corpus (denoted as *RA*) whose size was 182 MB and that contained 26,330,195 words. Its statistics are shown in the last row of Table 1. The corpus was utilized together with all the other corpora for the LM adaptation.

5   Experiments and Performance Evaluation

All experiments have been done on a large test set. We randomly picked 13 complete radio news programs from the 1969-1989 period, transcribed them automatically and corrected manually. Utterances spoken in Slovak language were removed. The total duration of the audio data was 7.2 hours and the news contained 47,217 words.

In the experiments, we focused mainly on measuring the impact of lexicons and language models on transcription accuracy and also on the Out-of-Vocabulary rate. The accuracy was evaluated using the standard measure:

$$Acc = (H - I)/N \qquad (1)$$

where H represent the number of correctly recognized words (hits), I is the number of insertions and N is the total number of words in reference transcriptions.

The goal of the first experiment was to learn the baseline performance level of the system operating with the linguistic module trained for contemporary Czech (with the existing 551K lexicon). The accuracy was 82.95 % with the OOV rate 1.64 %.

In the second experiment we used the lexicon and language model built from the RP corpus (i.e. the scanned and OCRed historical newspapers). In spite of a much smaller amount of training data (compared to the corpus of modern Czech) and a smaller lexicon (454K words), the OOV rate decreased to 1.45 % and the accuracy improved to 84.58 %. This can be explained by a very tight match between the newspaper text and the speech used in official media, which was a typical feature during the communist regime. In the next series of experiments,

Table 2. Impact of text corpora used for creating lexicons and LMs on transcription accuracy of archive news from 1969-1989 period. Experiments were performed with 1-pass and 2-pass decoding schemes. (The latter used unsupervised speaker adaptation between the two passes.)

	Data used for creating lexicon and LM	Decoding scheme	Lexicon size	Acc [%]	OOV [%]
A	CPaper+CBroad	1-pass	551,771	82.95	1.64
B	RP	1-pass	454,074	84.58	1.45
C	RP+Parl+Retro	1-pass	455,031	84.84	1.34
D	CBroad+RP+Parl+Retro	1-pass	529,489	85.21	1.32
E	CPaper+CBroad+RP+Parl+Retro	1-pass	559,139	85.67	1.32
F	CPaper+CBroad+RP+Parl+Retro	2-pass	559,139	87.54	1.32
G	CPaper+CBroad+RP+Parl+Retro+RA	1-pass	559,139	86.23	1.32
H	CPaper+CBroad+RP+Parl+Retro+RA	2-pass	559,139	88.19	1.32

we were gradually increasing the size of the training data, by adding the other historical texts first and mixing them with contemporary resources later. The results are summarized in Table 2. The best performance with Acc=85.67 % was achieved when all the available test resources were employed.

So far, all the tests were done with the LVCSR system running in a 1-pass mode. It is possible, however, to set up the speech decoding engine so that it utilizes a 2-pass approach. It means that after the standard first pass, the system tries to segment the speech signal into parts spoken by different speakers, and for each one it utilizes the recognized phoneme sequences for an unsupervised adaptation of the acoustic model [12]. The speaker adapted model is used in the second pass. The transcription process gets slower (usually by factor 2 to 3), but the results are better. In our case, the accuracy increased from 85.67 % to 87.54 % (see experiments E and F).

This best performing system was used to transcribe automatically all archive documents from the 1969-1989 period and to create a domain specific text corpus (denoted as RA) described in details in section 4.3. When added to the other corpora, the accuracy reached 86.23 % in the first pass and 88.19 % after the second pass. At the moment, this is the best result we are able to achieve.

6   Conclusion and Future Work

In this paper, we present a system whose aim is to transcribe the historical archive of spoken documents collected by Czech and Czechoslovak Radio during the last 90 years. Within those 9 decades, the language has evolved substantially, mainly due to political and social changes in the society. The linguistic module of the transcription system has to follow this evolution, which means that the lexicon and language model must be adapted to each historical epoch. For contemporary speech, it was not that difficult because there exists a large amount of electronic texts representing modern written and spoken language.

For previous epochs, however, suitable and applicable language resources are hard to find. In our case, we utilized scanned and OCRed newspapers as the main source and complemented it by additional data, such as historical parliament files and subtitles from retro TV broadcasting. These resources helped us to adapt the lexicon and language model, which significantly improved the transcription accuracy. On the large test set representing radio news from 1969-1989 period, the accuracy got over 88 %, which is 5 % better than with the original linguistic module. We have also shown that at this level it is possible to utilize the automatically transcribed archive documents for unsupervised adaptation of the language model.

As the next step, we want to pick up about 100 news documents evenly representing the 1969-1989 period. Their automatic transcriptions will be manually checked and corrected by students collaborating on the project. These corrected texts will serve several purposes:

a) to identify broadcast specific OOV words (e.g. names of news editors, words and terms typical for radio speech, etc) which will be added to the lexicon,

b) to get a large development set on which we can optimize weighting factors applied for different corpora during the language model computation, and also

c) to retrain the existing acoustic model so that it better fits audio signal recorded 30 to 40 years ago.

Furthermore, we plan to use the proposed approach also for the previous historical epochs, i.e. 1948-1968 and 1923-1947.

Acknowledgments. The research was supported by the Czech Ministry of Culture - project no. DF11P01OVV013 in program NAKI.

References

1. Hansen, J.H.L., Huang, R., Zhou, B., Seadle, M., Deller, J.R., Gurijala, A.R., Kurimo, M., Angkititrakul, P.: SpeechFind: Advances in Spoken Document Retrieval for a National Gallery of the Spoken Word. IEEE Trans. on Speech and Audio Processing 13(5), 712–730 (2005)
2. Ordelman, R.J.F., de Jong, F.M.G., Huijbregts, M.A.H., van Leeuwen, D.A.: Robust audio indexing for Dutch spoken-word collections. In: 16th Int. Conference of the Association for History and Computing. Humanities, Computers and Cultural Heritage, Amsterdam, pp. 215–223 (2005)
3. Christel, M.G., Stevens, S.M., Maher, B.S., Richardson, J.: Enhanced exploration of oral history archives through processed video and synchronized text transcripts. In: Proceedings of the International Conference on Multimedia, pp. 1333–1342. ACM (2010)
4. Byrne, W., et al.: Automatic recognition of spontaneous speech for access to multilingual oral history archives. IEEE Trans. Speech Audio Process. 12(4), 420–435 (2004)
5. Goldman, J., et al.: Accessing the spoken word. International Journal on Digital Libraries 5(4), 287–298 (2005)
6. Nouza, J., Blavka, K., Bohac, M., Cerva, P., Zdansky, J., Silovsky, J., Prazak, J.: Voice Technology to Enable Sophisticated Access to Historical Audio Archive of the Czech Radio. In: Grana, C., Cucchiara, R. (eds.) MM4CH 2011. CCIS, vol. 247, pp. 27–38. Springer, Heidelberg (2012)
7. Nouza, J., Blavka, K., Zdansky, J., Cerva, P., Silovsky, J., Bohac, M., Chaloupka, J., Kucharova, M., Seps, L.: Large-scale processing, indexing and search system for Czech audio-visual cultural heritage archives. In: IEEE 14th International Workshop on Multimedia Signal Processing (MMSP), pp. 337–342 (2012)
8. Nouza, J., Blavka, K., Cerva, P., Zdansky, J., Silovsky, J., Bohac, M., Prazak, J.: Making Czech Historical Radio Archive Accessible and Searchable for Wide Public. Journal of Multimedia 7(2), 159–169 (2012)
9. Czech Parliament webpages, http://www.psp.cz
10. Kneser, R., Ney, H.: Improved backing-off for m-gram language modeling. In: Proc. of IEEE Int. Conf. on Acoustics, Speech and Signal Processing, Detroit, pp. 181–184 (1995)
11. Nouza, J., Cerva, P., Silovsky, J.: Dealing with Bilingualism in Automatic Transcription of Historical Archive of Czech Radio. In: Petrosino, A., Maddalena, L., Pala, P. (eds.) ICIAP 2013 Workshops. LNCS, vol. 8158, pp. 238–246. Springer, Heidelberg (2013)
12. Cerva, P., Palecek, K., Silovsky, J., Nouza, J.: Using Unsupervised Feature-Based Speaker Adaptation for Improved Transcription of Spoken Archives. In: Proc. of Interspeech 2011, Florence, pp. 2565–2568 (2011)

Dealing with Bilingualism in Automatic Transcription of Historical Archive of Czech Radio

Jan Nouza, Petr Cerva, and Jan Silovsky

Institute of Information Technology and Electronics, Technical University of Liberec
Studentska 2, 461 17 Liberec, Czech Republic
jan.nouza@tul.cz
https://www.ite.tul.cz/itee/

Abstract. One of the biggest challenges in the automatic transcription of the historical audio archive of Czech and Czechoslovak radio is bilingualism. Two closely related languages, Czech and Slovak, are mixed in many archive documents. Both were the official languages in former Czechoslovakia (1918-1992) and both were used in media. The two languages are considered similar, although they differ in more than 75 % of their lexical inventories, which complicates automatic speech-to-text conversion. In this paper, we present and objectively measure the difference between the two languages. After that we propose a method suitable for automatic identification of two acoustically and lexically similar languages. It is based on employing 2 size-optimized parallel lexicons and language models. On large test data, we show that the 2 languages can be distinguished with almost 99 % accuracy. Moreover, the language identification module can be easily incorporated into a 2-pass decoding scheme with almost negligible additional computation costs. The proposed method has been employed in the project aimed at the disclosure of Czech and Czechoslovak oral cultural heritage.

Keywords: oral archives, automatic speech-to-text transcription, language identification.

1 Introduction

In 2011 we launched works on an ambitious project supported by the Czech Ministry of Culture whose aim is to disclose the historical audio archive of Czech Radio (and its predecessor Czechoslovak Radio) to researchers (historians, media experts, linguists, phoneticians) as well as to wide public [1]. The archive contains several hundreds of thousands of spoken documents (with the total duration exceeding 100.000 hours) and covers 90 years of public broadcasting in Czechoslovakia and Czechia. During the last decade, the archive records have been digitized and now, within the project, they are to be transcribed, indexed and made accessible for search and listening via a special web portal.

For the transcription task, we have been adapting and enhancing a large-vocabulary continuous speech recognition (LVCSR) system developed previously

A. Petrosino, L. Maddalena, P. Pala (Eds.): ICIAP 2013 Workshops, LNCS 8158, pp. 238–246, 2013.
© Springer-Verlag Berlin Heidelberg 2013

in our lab. During the first two years of the 4-year project, we have implemented most of the required functionalities and utilized the system to process, transcribe and index more than 75.000 documents broadcast since 1993 to present [2]. That period did not pose a particular challenge for our research as we could employ the existing system trained for contemporary Czech.

When moving backwards in time, the situation becomes more complicated. Many older spoken documents contain not only Czech but also Slovak, as both the languages were the official ones in former Czechoslovakia (which split into the Czech and Slovak republics in 1993) and both were used in broadcasting. For example, in news programs, they were arbitrarily mixed as each speaker used his or her own native tongue. This may occasionally happen also in recently broadcast Czech Radio programs if there is an interview with a Slovak person.

Several years ago, we have adapted our LVCSR system also to Slovak [3]. Hence, the remaining problem to be solved is how to recognize automatically which language is spoken. This task is known as language identification (LID). One of its classic techniques is based on statistical modeling of phoneme sequences, which vary from one language to another (phonotactic approach, [4]). In this paper, we propose and evaluate a method that performs better, particularly for languages that are acoustically and lexically similar. The method is applicable if we already have a LVCSR system with lexicons and language models for each of the languages. In that case, instead of just phoneme sequences, the method takes into account words and word sequences. Moreover, the method can be made fast as only a smaller part of the lexicon from each language is really needed, which is shown in the experimental part.

2   Related Work

Recently, there has been an intensive research towards multilingual and bilingual LVCSR systems. The main reason for their use and development is the benefit of sharing resources, namely the data needed for training acoustic models [5]. Bilingual systems have been designed and tested both for pairs of tongues from different language families, e.g. English and Tamil [6], or English and Mandarin [7], as well as for those closely related, e.g. Spanish and Valencian [8], or Croatian and Slovenian [9]. In the last mentioned paper, the authors focused also on the automatic language identification task, though only in a narrow domain of weather forecast reports. For these two similar Slavic languages, the LID scheme based on identifying language-specific words performed better than the classic phonotactic approach. The limitations of the phonotactics (even if complemented by some recently proposed improvements) was demonstrated in the LID system evaluation campaign organized by NIST in 2011 [15], where Czech and Slovak were reported among the most confusable language pairs.

3   Czech and Slovak as Related Languages

Czech and Slovak belong to the West-Slavic branch of European languages. They are considered very similar and closely related because in the past both were the official languages used within one state. Anyway, since 1993, when Czechoslovakia split, a new generation of young people has grown in the succession states who have difficulties to understand the language of the other nation. This indicates that the difference is larger than it was commonly thought.

3.1   Difference in Lexical Inventories

To quantify the degree of difference, we compared two lexicons used in the Czech and Slovak versions of our LVCSR system. For each language, we created a subset made of 100,000 most frequent words. The two subsets contained 25,325 items with the same orthography, from which 2,802 differed in pronunciation. It means that only 23 % of the lexical inventory is exactly same in the two languages. In [3] we arrived at the same figure (also 23 %) by comparing several parallel corpora - EU documents published in Czech and Slovak.

Despite this 77 % difference in the lexicons, the perceptual level of dissimilarity will look not that high if we perform a more detailed comparison of corresponding word pairs. Many differ only in one or two letters, often in prefixes and suffixes.

3.2   Difference in Morphology

Czech and Slovak are languages with rich morphology and a high degree of inflection. There exist several thousands of words in the two languages that have the same lemma but differ in some inflected forms. Where Czech nouns take suffix -*em*, the Slovak ones would use -*om*, where Czech adjective use suffix -*ém*, the other language take -*om*, etc. In Table 1, we give several examples of these related morphological patterns. This phenomenon can be utilized, if we need to transfer a list of words (proper names, particularly) from one lexicon to the other.

Table 1. Examples of some regular differences between suffixes used in Czech and Slovak (demonstrated on proper name 'Barack' and adjective 'political')

Word type	Czech [CZ]	Slovak [SK]
Proper names	Barack*em*	Barack*om*
	Barack*ův*	Barack*ov*
	Barack*ova*	Barack*ovho*
Adjectives	politick*ém*	politick*om*
	politick*é*	politick*ej*
	politick*ou*	politick*ú*

3.3   Difference in Phonetics

In LVCSR systems, Czech phonetic inventory is usually composed of 41 basic phonemes, while the Slovak one uses 48. For their SAMPA symbols, see Table 2.

In [3] we have shown that for initial experiments with Slovak speech recognition and also for bootstrapping a Slovak acoustic model (AM) trained on speech records that are not phonetically annotated, we can map the Slovak specific phonemes on the closest Czech ones. The mapping proposed in [3] is useful also for a bilingual Czecho-Slovak LVCSR system as it can operate (if desired) with one phonetic inventory, which allows for fast and efficient switching between Czech, Slovak and Czecho-Slovak AMs.

Table 2. Czech and Slovak phonemes represented by their SAMPA symbols (language specific ones are printed in bold)

Groups	Czech [CZ]	Slovak [SK]
Vowels	a, e, i, o, u, a:, e:, i:, o:, u:, @ (schwa)	a, e, i, o, u, a:, e:, i:, o:, u:, {
Consonants	p, b, t, d, c, J\, k, g, ts, dz, tS, dZ, r, l, **Q**, **P** f, v, s, z, S, Z, X, j, h\, m, n, N, J, F	p, b, t, d, c, J\, k, g, ts, dz, tS, dZ, r, l, **r=**, **r=:**, **l=**, **l=:**, **L** f, v, s, z, S, Z, X, j, h\, **w**, **U_^**, **G**, **I_^** m, n, N, J, F

4 Speech Transcription System

The LVCSR system used for the transcription of archive documents employs a two-pass strategy. The output of the first decoder pass is used for a) segmentation to speech and non-speech parts, b) synchronization of speaker change detector with word and noise boundaries [10], c) speaker clustering [11], and d) speaker adaptation via the CMLLR technique [12]. The first pass is usually performed with a smaller lexicon to reduce computational costs and time. In the second pass, the decoder processes the already separated segments, uses the adapted acoustic model, and utilizes the full lexicon with the corresponding language model.

The acoustic front-end takes the archive data and converts them into 16 kHz, 16 bit, PCM WAV format. A signal is parameterized into a stream of 39 mel-frequency cepstral coefficient (MFCC) feature vectors computed every 10 ms in 25-ms-long frames. Using a 2-second long moving window, the MFCC features are normalized by the cepstral mean subtraction (CMS) technique. The final step is the HLDA (Heteroscedastic Linear Discriminant Analysis) transform performed by multiplying each feature vector by a 39 x 39 HLDA matrix determined during the acoustic model training procedure. These features are employed in all the following modules and in both the passes.

The acoustic model is a triphone-based one covering 41 phonemes and 7 types of noise. The Czech AM has been trained on 320 hours of (mainly broadcast) data. The amount of speech available for training the Slovak AM was smaller, 107 hours. In the experiments described in section 5, we used also a Czecho-Slovak (CZ+SK) AM trained on 120 hours of Czech and 107 hours of Slovak.

The lexicon for contemporary Czech contains 551K words. For Slovak, the lexicon is smaller (due to smaller text corpora), its size is 303K words. The language models are based on bigrams. However, as both the lexicons contain several thousands multi-word expressions (frequently collocated word strings), a significant part of bigrams covers sequences that are three-, four-, five- or even six-word long. This feature helps to improve the recognition rate by 2 %. The unseen bigrams are backed-off by the Kneser-Ney smoothing technique [13].

5   LID Scheme for Czech and Slovak

In the situation, when we need to distinguish between two closely related languages, for which we already have lexicons and LMs, the most reliable approach to language identification is to employ the existing LVCSR system. The scheme can be efficiently incorporated within the first pass.

5.1   LVCSR with Merged Lexicons and Language Models

The LID module has been designed in the following way: A Czecho-Slovak (CZ+SK) lexicon is created by merging L most frequent Czech words with the same number of words from the Slovak lexicon. (The total size of the merged lexicon is $2L$.) Each word gets a label saying whether the word is Czech or Slovak. Using the available text corpora we compute word-pairs counts separately for the Czech part of the merged lexicon and for the Slovak one. Before merging the two word-pair lists, we label their items in the same way as in the lexicon. (The only common item in the two lists is the $START$ symbol used for the beginning of an utterance.) After that, the CZ+SK LM is computed using the standard Kneser-Ney smoothing technique, which assigns some small probabilities also to transitions between Czech and Slovak words.

Now, the LID task can become a part of the first pass, without influencing the other goals required on that level. The only modification is that the LVCSR runs with the CZ+SK acoustic model and CZ+SK language model. The output of the recognizer contains words with either Czech (CZ) or Slovak (SK) labels. A special label (COM) is assigned to those Czech and Slovak words that share the same orthography and pronunciation. For each speech segment (determined by the speaker change point detector [10]), we get the numbers of recognized Czech words (N_{CZ}), Slovak words (N_{SK}) and the common ones (N_{COM}).The utterance in the segment is identified as Czech or Slovak according to the higher of counts N_{CZ} and N_{SK}.

The performance of the proposed scheme is illustrated in Table 3. It shows a transcription of an initial part of evening news where two speakers, a Czech and a Slovak one, talk. In the first row, there is the manual transcript that can be used for comparison. The second row shows the languages used. The third and fourth rows indicate the recognized words (from a joint CZ+SK lexicon) and their labels. In the last row, there is information from the speaker change detector that provides boundaries for speaker and language identification modules. We can see that the utterance of the first speaker included four words that are common to both the languages (i.e. N_{Com}=4). Anyway, it was identified as Czech because N_{CZ}=1 and N_{SK}=0. The second fragment would be labeled as Slovak since the Slovak specific words prevail.

Table 3. Illustration of the LID scheme performance on evening news. (English translation is: In Czech: Good evening, we broadcast radio news. In Slovak: We welcome listeners ...)

Manual	Dobrý	večer	vysíláme	rozhlasové	noviny	Pri	počúvaní	vítáme	posluchačov
Lang.	Czech					Slovak			
Auto	dobrý	večer	vysíláme	rozhlasové	noviny	pri	počúvaní	vítané	posluchačov
Label	COM	COM	CZ	COM	COM	SK	SK	COM	SK
Speaker	1	1	1	1	1	2	2	2	2

5.2 Experimental Evaluation

The proposed LID scheme has been evaluated on a test set that included 1000 Czech and 1000 Slovak speech segments. Their total duration was 228 minutes (31,214 words). In average, each utterance was 6.8 seconds long and contained 15.6 words. (The minimum length was 6 words).

Table 4. Language identification error and Real Time factor as function of lexicon size

Lexicon size [L words in each language]	LID error rate [%]	RT factor
L = 1,000	8.75	0.43
L = 5,000	3.03	0.51
L = 10,000	2.02	0.53
L = 20,000	1.51	0.56
L = 30,000	1.31	0.60
L = 40,000	1.31	0.64
L = 50,000	1.15	0.69

We conducted several experiments with different size of the merged lexicons. The results are summarized in Table 4. From the above results we can see, that if L is chosen 20,000 or higher, the two languages are identified with an acceptable error rate smaller than 1.6 % and the time required for processing and decision is slightly above one half (0.56) of the signal duration. The same lexicon size (20,000 words) was found sufficient also for the unsupervised speaker adaptation scheme proposed in [12]. This means that the inclusion of the LID module to the complete transcription system requires almost negligible additional computation costs.

We have also run a complementary series of experiments in which we investigated the influence of the *acoustic model* on the LID results. We compared the performance of the above described Czecho-Slovak (CZ+SK) AM with those trained only on Czech or Slovak speech data. From the diagram in Fig. 1 we can see, that the impact of the acoustic models becomes significantly smaller when the lexicon size increases. This confirms the strength of the information provided by the lexicon and LM in the task of discrimination between closely related languages.

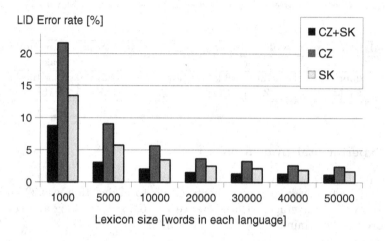

Fig. 1. Comparison of LID performance for increasing lexicons and 3 acoustic models

6   Evaluation of Complete Bilingual Transcription System

Recently, the proposed LID method has been tested on a set of archive documents representing the last eight years of Czech Radio broadcasting (2005-2012). We chose this particular period from which we have official transcripts provided by a media monitoring company for some relevant radio programs, like evening news or political talk-shows. This allows us to compare the human-made transcriptions with those achieved by our system in a fully automated way. For experimental evaluation we selected 24 complete news (3 from each year). The duration of each was 30 minutes.

The LID module worked with 40,000-word CZ+SK lexicon (i.e. L=20,000). It identified 58 segments spoken in Slovak whose total duration was 15.2 minutes (approx. 2 % of all audio data). That language was used by Slovak correspondents of the Czech Radio and by Slovak politicians who had been interviewed. One of the 58 found segments was wrongly labeled as Slovak. It was a short Czech utterance that contained Slovak proper names. From the same reason also an opposite error occurred when one Czech sentence was identified as Slovak. These results as well as those presented in section 5 seem much better the results reported for Czech and Slovak in [15].

The successful separation of the two languages in the first pass allowed for running the second pass with the proper (Czech or Slovak) full-size lexicon and the corresponding language model. The transcription accuracy of the Czech part of the news was 89.1 %. For the Slovak segments, it was lower, only 83.6 %. There were several reasons for the worse latter result: a) most Slovak utterances were recorded out of studio, b) they had a character of either planned or spontaneous (but not read) speech, and c) the Slovak lexicon is smaller (303K words) when compared to the Czech one (551K words) - due to a much smaller amount of text resources available for Slovak.

7   Conclusion and Future Work

In this paper, we present a LID method suitable for distinguishing between languages that are acoustically and lexically similar. The method utilizes a large-vocabulary speech recognition system operating with the merged lexicon and language model composed from size-optimized lexicons and LMs of the individual languages. Unlike the classic phonotactic technique, this approach takes into account real words and their N-gram probabilities and hence it provides a better discriminative strength. Moreover, the proposed LID module can be incorporated into a two-pass decoding scheme with minimum additional computation costs.

So far, the method has been tested on contemporary spoken documents from the Czech radio archive. It identified almost all utterances spoken in Slovak language and allowed for automatic switching between two language specific speech recognition modules.

Recently, we prepare its application also to the historical part of the archive, which is the main goal of the project. Especially before 1993 (i.e. in times of former Czechoslovakia) the Slovak language will occur more frequently. Before doing it, we have to adapt the lexicons so that they better fit speech of previous historical epochs. For Czech, it has been already done [14].

Acknowledgments. The research was supported by the Czech Ministry of Culture -project no. DF11P01OVV013 in program NAKI.

References

1. Nouza, J., Blavka, K., Bohac, M., Cerva, P., Zdansky, J., Silovsky, J., Prazak, J.: Voice Technology to Enable Sophisticated Access to Historical Audio Archive of the Czech Radio. In: Grana, C., Cucchiara, R. (eds.) MM4CH 2011. CCIS, vol. 247, pp. 27–38. Springer, Heidelberg (2012)
2. Nouza, J., Blavka, K., Zdansky, J., Cerva, P., Silovsky, J., Bohac, M., Chaloupka, J., Kucharova, M., Seps, L.: Large-scale processing, indexing and search system for Czech audio-visual cultural heritage archives. In: IEEE 14th International Workshop on Multimedia Signal Processing (MMSP), pp. 337–342 (2012)
3. Nouza, J., Silovsky, J., Zdansky, J., Cerva, P., Kroul, M., Chaloupka, J.: Czech-to-Slovak Adapted Broadcast News Transcription System. In: Proc. of Interspeech 2008, Australia, pp. 2683–2686 (2008)

4. Navratil, J., Zuhlke, W.: An efficient phonotactic-acoustic system for language identification. In: Proc. of ICASSP, Seattle, USA, vol. 2, pp. 781–784 (1998)
5. Uebler, U.: Multilingual speech recognition in seven languages. Speech Communication 35(1-2), 53–69 (2001)
6. Kumar, C.S., Wei, F.S.: A Bilingual Speech Recognition system for English and Tamil. In: Proc. of ICICS PCM, pp. 1641–1644 (2003)
7. Zhang, Q., Pan, J., Yan, Y.: Mandarin-English bilingual speech recognition for real world music retrieval. In: Proc. of ICASSP, Las Vegas, USA, pp. 4253–4256 (2008)
8. Alabau, V., Martinez, C.D.: A Bilingual Speech Recognition in Two Phonetically Similar Languages. Jordanas en Tecnologia del Habla, Zaragoza, pp. 197–202 (2006)
9. Zibert, J., Martincic-Ipsic, S., Ipsic, I., Mihelic, F.: Bilingual Speech Recognition of Slovenian and Croatian Weather Forecasts. In: Proc. of EURASIP Conf. on Video/Image Processing and Multimedia Communications, Zagreb, Croatia, pp. 957–960 (2000)
10. Silovsky, J., Zdansky, J., Nouza, J., Cerva, P., Prazak, J.: Incorporation of the ASR output in speaker segmentation and clustering within the task of speaker diarization of broadcast streams. In: Proc. of IEEE workshop on Multimedia Signal Processing (MMSP), Banff, Canada, pp. 118–123 (2012)
11. Silovsky, J., Prazak, J.: Speaker Diarization of Broadcast Streams using Two-stage Clustering based on I-vectors and Cosine Distance Scoring. In: Proc. of ICASSP, Kyoto, pp. 4193–4196 (2012)
12. Cerva, P., Palecek, K., Silovsky, J., Nouza, J.: Using Unsupervised Feature-Based Speaker Adaptation for Improved Transcription of Spoken Archives. In: Proc. of Interspeech 2011, Florence, pp. 2565–2568 (2011)
13. Kneser, R., Ney, H.: Improved backing-off for m-gram language modeling. In: Proc. of IEEE Int. Conf. on Acoustics, Speech and Signal Processing, Detroit, pp. 181–184 (1995)
14. Chaloupka, J., Nouza, J., Kucharova, M.: Using Various Types of Multimedia Resources to Train System for Automatic Transcription of Czech Historical Oral Archives. In: Petrosino, A., Maddalena, L., Pala, P. (eds.) ICIAP 2013 Workshop. LNCS, vol. 8158, pp. 228–237. Springer, Heidelberg (2013)
15. Brümmer, N., et al.: Description and analysis of the Brno276 system for LRE2011. In: Proc. of Speaker Odyssey Workshop, Singapur, pp. 216–223 (2012)

Passive Profiling and Natural Interaction Metaphors for Personalized Multimedia Museum Experiences

Svebor Karaman, Andrew D. Bagdanov, Gianpaolo D'Amico, Lea Landucci,
Andrea Ferracani, Daniele Pezzatini, and Alberto Del Bimbo

Media Integration and Communication Center (MICC)
University of Florence, Florence, Italy
{svebor.karaman,andrea.ferracani,daniele.pezzatini}@unifi.it,
{bagdanov,damico,delbimbo}@dsi.unifi.it, lea.landucci@gmail.com
http://www.micc.unifi.it/vim/people

Abstract. Museums must balance the amount of information given on individual pieces or exhibitions in order to provide sufficient information to aid visitor understanding. At the same time they must avoid cluttering the environment and reducing the enjoyment of the exhibit. Moreover, each visitor has different interests and each might prefer more (or less) information on different artworks depending on their individual profile of interest. Finally, visiting a museum should not be a closed experience but a door opened onto a broader context of related artworks, authors, artistic trends, etc. In this paper we describe the MNEMOSYNE system that attempts to provide such a museum experience. Based on passive observation of visitors, the system builds a profile of the artworks of interest for each visitor. These profiles of interest are then used to personalize content delivery on an interactive table. The natural user interface on the interactive table uses the visitor's profile, a museum content ontology and a recommendation system to personalize the user's exploration of available multimedia content. At the end of their visit, the visitor can take home a personalized summary of their visit on a custom mobile application. In this article we describe each component of our approach as well as the first field trials of our prototype system built and deployed at our permanent exhibition space at *Le Murate*[1] in the city of Florence.

Keywords: Computer vision, video surveillance, cultural heritage, multimedia museum, personalization, natural interaction.

1 Introduction

Modern museums are awash in physical and digital content that they struggle to catalog, to maintain, to manage, and – most importantly – to deliver in meaningful ways to the museum-going public. Each visitor would like to easily access different aspects of the massive amount of available information. To address this

---

[1] http://www.lemurate.comune.fi.it/lemurate/

A. Petrosino, L. Maddalena, P. Pala (Eds.): ICIAP 2013 Workshops, LNCS 8158, pp. 247–256, 2013.
© Springer-Verlag Berlin Heidelberg 2013

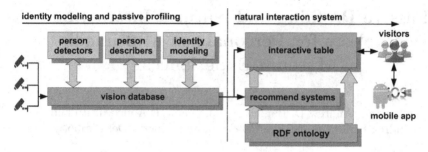

Fig. 1. An overview of the MNEMOSYNE architecture

issue most research has focused on providing personalized access through hand-held devices carried by visitors [1,5] and possibly offering some sort of augmented reality experience [11,3]. However, the use of mobile devices is intrusive to the museum experience as it changes the way the visitor behaves with respect to the museum. It also requires active participation of the user in front of each artwork of interest.

Museum exhibits are often designed out of the need to target a sort of "common denominator" visitor. This necessity arises from the difficulty in understanding *a priori* the interests of individual visitors in order to customize content delivery in a meaningful way. User interest modeling for personalization has been addressed in [12] where the user inputs his interests both on the museum website and inside the museum in order to create a "virtuous circle" of online and offline visits. In [8], the authors propose to model user interest based on his displacement in the museum environment in order to personalize audio content delivery via a specific audio guide given to each user. This last approach, like the MNEMOSYNE system we describe in this article, differs from the global trend as it does not require explicit input from the user.

MNEMOSYNE is a three-year research project [2] studying techniques for passively observing museum visitors [9] in order to build profiles of interest for personalizing multimedia content delivery (see figure 1). Aiding the delivery of multimedia content, an ontology that models museum content is used to infer connections between visitor interest and works on display, works located in other collections, and works of broader interest. This knowledge model, along with a statistical recommendation system, is used to drive a natural user interface on a large format interactive table. The user interface allows visitors to explore digital museum content personalized to their own interests, and a mobile application allows them to download content of interest they have explored during their visit to a smartphone or tablet.

In the next section we describe the passive profiling system in detail. In section 3.1 we detail the two types of recommendation systems we have experimented with, and in section 3.2 we describe the natural interaction user interface used to deliver personalized content. Finally, in section 4 we discuss the first field trials of our prototype system.

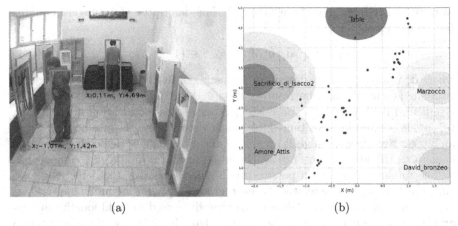

(a)   (b)

Fig. 2. (a) Example of frame with detections (b) Detection map with artwork sphere of influence for one visitor model

2 Passive Interest Profiling

Here we detail each step of the MNEMOSYNE passive visual profiling approach. First, a pre-processing step is performed to map the artistic content and physical properties of the museum. Then, fixed cameras are used to observe visitors as they visit the museum. Our aim is to maintain a record of what each visitor has observed during their visit and to build a profile of interest him.

2.1 Mapping the Physical Museum

Most museums are often already equipped with a set C of fixed cameras installed for surveillance purposes, and the MNEMOSYNE system is designed to exploit these already-installed cameras. We calibrate each camera c to a common ground plane. A simple tool allows an operator to estimate the homography $\mathcal{H}_c$ from each camera image plane to the ground plane with a few mouse clicks [7].

Given the homography $\mathcal{H}_c$, an operator can easily input the position on the ground plane of each artwork of interest by simply clicking once in the camera view where the artwork sits on the ground or on the position on the floor below the artwork. A sphere of influence is associated with each artwork, defined as a bi-dimensional Gaussian of mean equal to the ground position of the artwork and variances in x and y dimensions defined by the operator. These variances depend on the structure of the museum as well as the artwork scale.

2.2 Identity Modeling

On the video stream corresponding to camera $c \in C$, we run a pedestrian detector [4] in order to obtain a set of N person bounding boxes. The bounding boxes are then described with a number of visual, temporal and spatial descriptors (the

person describers module in figure 1). The descriptor of a person bounding box is defined as:

$$d_i = \left\{ \mathbf{d}_i^a, \mathbf{d}_i^s, d_i^t, d_i^c \right\}, \text{ for } i \in \{1, \dots, N\}, \tag{1}$$

where $\mathbf{d}_i^a$ is an appearance descriptor consisting of RGB and HS color histograms computed on overlapping horizontal stripes and the HoG (Histogram of Oriented Gradients) descriptor [6] as proposed for person re-identification in [10], $\mathbf{d}_i^s = (d_i^x, d_i^y)$ is the absolute position of the person detection on the ground plane, d_i^t is an integer timestamp, and d_i^c is an index indicating that the detecion comes from camera c. All video streams are synchronized so that d_i^t and d_j^t are comparable.

The fundamental step in passive profiling is associating the detections $D = \{d_i \mid i = 1 \dots N\}$ to one another to form groups representing individual visitors in the museum. Algorithm 1 details the procedure used to build identity models and to associate detections to them. This algorithm relies on the computation of the distance between a model cluster m_j and a detection description d_i which takes into account the appearance and all spatio-temporal information available. Precisely, the distance between a description d_i and model m_j is computed as:

$$\text{dist}(m_j, d_i) = (1 - \alpha - \beta) \times ||\mathbf{m}_j^a - \mathbf{d}_i^a||_2 \text{ (appearance contribution)} \tag{2}$$
$$+ \alpha \times \text{dist}_w(\mathbf{m}_j^s, \mathbf{d}_i^s, w_s) \quad \text{(spatial contribution)} \tag{3}$$
$$+ \beta \times \text{dist}_w(m_j^t, d_i^t, w_t) \quad \text{(temporal contribution)} \tag{4}$$

where $\text{dist}_w(x, y, w)$ is the windowed L2 distance:

$$\text{dist}_w(x, y, w) = \min(\frac{||x - y||_2}{w}, 1). \tag{5}$$

The parameters w_s and w_t are, respectively, the spatial and temporal window around observations. The weights α and β control the contribution of spatial and temporal distances, respectively, to the overall distance calculation and are defined such that $\alpha, \beta \in [0, 1]$ and $\alpha + \beta < 1$. A detection is associated with a model if its distance to the model is less than δ. The system must accumulate at least τ detections in a temporary model before promoting it to a real one. The appearance of a model $\mathbf{m}_j^a$ is computed as a running average of the detections associated to it, while the position and time information are those of the last matched detection. Whether a model is active is determined by the last associated detection time. Note that we also forbid multiple associations from one camera at the same timestamp to the same model.

2.3   Interest Profiling

Each visitor's interest profile is built on-the-fly when the visitor enters the interactive table area (see figure 2b) and is sent to the interactive table. Every detection associated with the visitor's model contributes to each artwork according to its proximity to the artwork sphere of influence. If the visitor leaves the interactive area, goes and sees some other artworks and comes back to the table, his interest profile will be updated.

Data: D, δ, τ
Result: Detection associations
$M_a \leftarrow$ getActiveModels()
$M_{temp} \leftarrow$ getTmpModels()
for $d_i \in D$ **do**
    dist $\leftarrow \{\text{dist}(d_i, m_j), \forall m_j \in M_a\}$
    if $\min(\textbf{dist}) \leq \delta$ **and** $M_a \neq \emptyset$ **then**
        $k \leftarrow \text{argmin}(\textbf{dist})$;
        $m_k.\text{associate}(d_i)$;
    else
        tmpDist $\leftarrow \{\text{dist}(d_i, m_j), \forall m_j \in M_{temp}\}$
        if $\min(\textbf{tmpDist}) \leq \delta$ **and** $M_{temp} \neq \emptyset$ **then**
            $k \leftarrow \text{argmin}(\textbf{tmpDist})$;
            $m_k.\text{associate}(d_i)$;
            if $m_k.\text{AssociationsCount} \geq \tau$ **then**
                $M_a = M_a + \{m_k\}$;
                $M_{temp} = M_{temp} \setminus \{m_k\}$;
            end
        else
            $M_{temp} = M_{temp} + \{d_i\}$;
        end
    end
end

Algorithm 1. Detection association algorithm

3 The Augmented Museum Experience

The second stage of the museum visit consists of entering an area equipped with an interactive tabletop display in which users can have a seamless multimedia experience and increase their knowledge of art and cultural heritage. Thanks to the natural interaction with the table, they can explore and select in-depth and related information about each artwork according to the suggestions given by the recommendation systems, further personalizing the profile of interest built passively during their visit. Their favorite artworks and related multimedia content can then be transferred to a mobile device via a dedicated application.

3.1 Recommendation Systems

The MNEMOSYNE prototype uses two solutions for generating content recommendations to users: a Knowledge-based and an Experience-based system. These modules have been developed as web servlets which expose several web services accessible via a Representational State Transfer (REST) interface.

Knowledge-Based Recommendation. As a use case we chose one of the most famous museums of Florence: the National Museum of Bargello. In particular, we focus on a subset of 8 monitored artworks from the 70 artworks displayed in the *Sala di Donatello*. The MNEMOSYNE Semantic Search Engine exploits the potential of the Semantic Web through an RDF (Resource Description Framework) ontology that models not only instances of these artworks, but also places, events, historical curiosities and other artworks from Florence and all over the world, and their relations to the 8 chosen artworks. Our ad-hoc ontology implements six different entities: artist, artwork, category, museum/place and story. Every artwork instance is equipped with information about its creator, meanings, materials, techniques and historical context (all represented by instances of their own). Each artwork entity is also accompanied by a variety of multimedia content and has different thematic links to other artworks or stories. SPARQL queries are used to query subgraphs of data from the ontology, providing different views on the data model: subgraphs of artwork data, stories related to artworks, and resources related by tags or stories.

Experience-Based Recommendation. The MNEMOSYNE Recommendation Engine uses two types of recommendation algorithms. Recommendation algorithms try to solve a problem of prediction and give the system the ability to suggest to users items that they are more likely to find interesting. The Recommender Engine implements metrics based on both user similarity and item similarity. The data model consists of preferences stored as triples in a database table containing the following fields: the user ID, the item ID, and a value, assigned by the MNEMOSYNE passive visual profiling module, expressing the strength of the user preference for the item. From this information we compute which users or items are more similar. Both similarity metrics, user based and item based, make use of the same components: a data model, a metric of similarity, a notion of proximity (i.e. a neighborhood of users or items) and an algorithm that predicts values of preference weighting them differently according to the similarity metric. The Recommendation Engine uses Euclidean distances: a greater distance indicates a lower similarity. The system makes use of the Mahout library[2], the state of the art for machine learning on big data.

3.2   The Natural Interaction Tabletop System

When a visitor approaches the table, he is detected by the camera which triggers the tabletop system and the computer vision system to exchange data about his profile of interest which had been built during their interaction with the physical artworks. Initially the display of the tabletop shows a language selector and then an interactive tutorial as a carousel of images.

The metaphor used for the user interface is based on the idea of the hidden museum waiting to be unveiled, an all-digital environment where visitors can go beyond the artworks level of the physical museum. The tabletop provides an augmented perspective of the museum thanks to the interest profile estimated by the computer vision system, the recommendation systems, and via the adoption of natural interaction paradigms. With the natural interaction interface visitors can discover new, interesting information and resources, and then collect them for future inspection. The main user interface adopts principles derived from

---

[2] http://mahout.apache.org

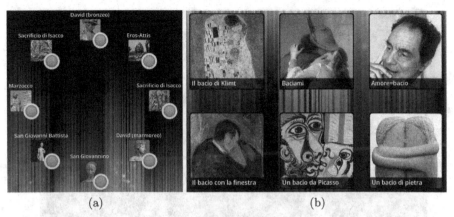

(a)   (b)

Fig. 3. (a) Detail of the artwork level: the artworks of the museum are represented with the original title, a thumbnail and a circular symbol visualizing the amount of interest showed by the current user during the visit. (b) Detail of the insights space in the related resources level: information related thematically to the selected artwork.

Information Visualization and consists of two levels of navigation: the *artworks* and the *related resources*.

The Artworks Level.   visualizes artworks of the museum for which the visitor has shown the highest level of interest (see figure 3a) based on the profile created by the computer vision system. When the user touches an artwork an animation starts in order to trigger the following actions: the space containing the unselected artworks moves up vertically off the screen, the selected artwork moves to the middle left and a new space of information comes up from the bottom.

The Related Resources Level.   follows the selection of an artwork and consists of a structured environment in which the visitor can navigate the multimedia content related to this artwork. Related resources are organized in four different spaces (*stories, secrets, recommendations, insights*) according to their relations to the artwork based on the recommendation system and the ontology structure:

- **stories:** stories directly related to the artwork in the ontology;
- **secrets:** resources related to the artwork and its related stories in the ontology according to the knowledge-based recommendation system;
- **recommendations:** similar artworks according to the experience recommendation system using the visitor profile;
- **insights:** resources related by tags or stories to the artwork according to the knowledge-based recommendation system.

The user can navigate these spaces via a textual menu at the bottom of the display. In each space details are represented in a different layout: the background color, shape and arrangement of interactive items are all adjusted in order to highlight the difference between the visualized data and to provide the user

Fig. 4. The information level: when the user selects an item from one space, multimedia content is displayed in the center of the screen. A *star* element can be touched in order to collect the item in the space at the bottom of the screen. The selected artwork is visualized on the left of the screen with its title, a thumbnail, location and level of visitor interest.

a pleasant experience while navigating in the information space. The *insights* space is illustrated in figure 3b. In each space, if the user touches one of the visible items an information window composed of several multimedia contents is triggered, see figure 4. The visitor is able to collect the most interesting resources for later use via the mobile system.

3.3   Mobile System

The main goal of the MNEMOSYNE mobile application, shown in figure 5, is to collect personalized digital content displayed in the interactive tabletop interface. Unlike [5,11], the mobile app is intended to be used at the end of the visit and not as an interactive device throughout the museum tour. It was developed using the Adobe AIR framework and can therefore be installed on devices running iOS (iPhone, iPad) or Android.

Once installed on the visitor's device, the application allows the user to scan a QR code displayed on the interface of the interactive table. This transfers the unique identifier of the user to the mobile device. The application queries the MNEMOSYNE database to retrieve the user's favorite artworks, generated both through the passive profiling module and from his interaction on the table-top surface. The user then has access to in-depth information about individual and related artworks or resources in the MNEMOSYNE dataset. In particular, the user can visualize a collection of points on a map of interest suggested by the recommendation system taking into account the user's profile and current geolocalization. The latter functionality allows us to extend the personalized user experience of the visit from an indoor to an outdoor scenario.

Fig. 5. The mobile application. Left: user's favorite artworks; Center: in-depth information on the artwork; Right: map of suggested points of interest.

4   Field Trials and Ongoing Work

We have installed a prototype of the MNEMOSYNE system in a permanent exhibition space at *Le Murate* in the historical center of Florence. For this installation, we printed four high resolution images of artworks from the Donatello Room and used a single surveillance camera to capture images of visitors observing the artworks as well as interacting with the table. Some detections obtained are shown in figure 2a. For this installation the parameters were set manually ($\alpha = \beta = 0.2$, $w_s = 5$m, $w_t = 80$ frames, $\delta = 0.75$ and $\tau = 10$), but given a training set of annotated detections they could be easily learned. Two critical issues were evident when running the system continuously for several hours: ensuring that the system does not lag and that profile messages are thus sent in a timely fashion; and limiting the confusion between visitors since, when observing for several hours, it is very likely that several persons will have similar appearance.

Lag is mostly due to the detection process which is computationally onerous, and we dedicated an 8-core computer to this task and limited the frame rate to 5 frames per second. Moreover, we implemented a lag monitor that considers a maximum allowed lag (set to 5 seconds) and discards frames until the lag falls within the allowed range. To limit confusion between visitors with similar appearance across several hours of observation we limit the association of detections to visitor models that were "active", i.e. ones with which at least one detection was associated in the previous 10 minutes. These proposed solutions are the first necessary steps towards bringing MNEMOSYNE to real museum.

5   Conclusions

In this paper we detailed our proposal to enhance and personalize museum visits. Our system makes use of passive observation to estimate each visitor's interest.

This interest profile is then used conjointly with a recommendation system to provide personalized content delivery through a natural interaction interface. MNEMOSYNE is operational and has been tested, but in order to determine the efficiency of the approach several aspects must be evaluated with further experiments, user studies, and also potentially on how the suggested resources impact visitor visits. We are also interested in using the mobile application as a bridge between different museums adopting MNEMOSYNE, by suggesting artworks of interest in other museums. These are our main objectives and we hope to deploy our system in museums of Florence in the near future.

References

1. Baber, C., Bristow, H., Cheng, S.L., Hedley, A., Kuriyama, Y., Lien, M., Pollard, J., Sorrell, P.: Augmenting museums and art galleries. In: Human-Computer Interaction, INTERACT, vol. 1, pp. 439–447 (2001)
2. Bagdanov, A.D., Del Bimbo, A., Landucci, L., Pernici, F.: MNEMOSYNE: Enhancing the museum experience through interactive media and visual profiling. In: Grana, C., Cucchiara, R. (eds.) MM4CH 2011. CCIS, vol. 247, pp. 39–50. Springer, Heidelberg (2012)
3. Bay, H., Fasel, B., Van Gool, L.: Interactive museum guide: Fast and robust recognition of museum objects. In: Proceedings of the First International Workshop on Mobile Vision (May 2006)
4. Bimbo, A.D., Lisanti, G., Masi, I., Pernici, F.: Person detection using temporal and geometric context with a pan tilt zoom camera. In: 2010 20th International Conference on Pattern Recognition (ICPR), pp. 3886–3889. IEEE (2010)
5. Bruns, E., Brombach, B., Zeidler, T., Bimber, O.: Enabling mobile phones to support large-scale museum guidance. IEEE MultiMedia 14(2), 16–25 (2007)
6. Dalal, N., Triggs, B.: Histograms of oriented gradients for human detection. In: IEEE Computer Society Conference on Computer Vision and Pattern Recognition, CVPR 2005, vol. 1, pp. 886–893. IEEE (2005)
7. Hartley, R.I., Zisserman, A.: Multiple View Geometry in Computer Vision, 2nd edn. Cambridge University Press (2004) ISBN: 0521540518
8. Hatala, M., Wakkary, R.: User modeling and semantic technologies in support of a tangible interface. Journal of User Modeling and User Adapted Interaction 15(3-4), 339–380 (2005)
9. Karaman, S., Bagdanov, A.D.: Identity inference: Generalizing person re-identification scenarios. In: Fusiello, A., Murino, V., Cucchiara, R. (eds.) ECCV 2012 Ws/Demos, Part I. LNCS, vol. 7583, pp. 443–452. Springer, Heidelberg (2012)
10. Karaman, S., Lisanti, G., Bagdanov, A.D., Del Bimbo, A.: From re-identification to identity inference: labelling consistency by local similarity constraints. In: Person Re-identification (to appear, 2013)
11. Kuflik, T., Stock, O., Zancanaro, M., Gorfinkel, A., Jbara, S., Kats, S., Sheidin, J., Kashtan, N.: A visitor's guide in an active museum: Presentations, communications, and reflection. Journal on Computing and Cultural Heritage (JOCCH) 3(3), 11 (2011)
12. Wang, Y., Stash, N., Sambeek, R., Schuurmans, Y., Aroyo, L., Schreiber, G., Gorgels, P.: Cultivating personalized museum tours online and on-site. Interdisciplinary Science Reviews 34(2-3), 2–3 (2009)

Recommending Multimedia Objects
in Cultural Heritage Applications

Ilaria Bartolini[1], Vincenzo Moscato[2], Ruggero G. Pensa[3], Antonio Penta[3],
Antonio Picariello[2], Carlo Sansone[2], and Maria Luisa Sapino[3]

[1] University of Bologna, DISI
i.bartolini@unibo.it
[2] University of Naples "Federico II", DIETI
{vmoscato,antonio.picariello,carlo.sansone}@unina.it
[3] University of Torino, DI
{pensa,penta,mlsapino}@di.unito.it

Abstract. Italy's Cultural Heritage is the world's most diverse and rich
patrimony and attracts millions of visitors every year to monuments, archaeological sites and museums. The valorization of cultural heritage
represents nowadays one of the most important research challenges in
the Italian scenario. In this paper, we present a general multimedia recommender system able to uniformly manage heterogeneous multimedia
data and to provide context-aware recommendation techniques supporting intelligent multimedia services for the users. A specific application
of our system within the cultural heritage domain is proposed by means
of a real case study in the mobile environment related to an outdoor
scenario, together with preliminary results on user's satisfaction.

1 Introduction

Italy's Cultural Heritage represents a worldwide resource of inestimable value,
attracting millions of visitors every year to monuments, archaeological sites and
museums. One of the most challenging and interesting research problems within
such a scenario is surely the valorization of such heritage. Indeed, it should be
important to provide a cultural environment with functionalities to represent
the related knowledge derived from current digital sources describing cultural
heritage, such as text descriptions, pictures, and videos, in order to allow a
tourist visiting a site to enjoy multimedia stories in real time so as to enrich
his/her cultural experience.

Our goal is to "extend" classical recommendation techniques (*content-based,
collaborative filtering* and *hybrid* strategies [11,13] usually exploited for facilitating the browsing of web large data repositories) to support useful services (e.g.
a multimedia touristic guide) that assist users visiting cultural environments
(indoor museums, archeological sites, old town center), containing several *cultural Points Of Interest* - POIs - (e.g. paintings of museum rooms, buildings in
ancient ruins or in an old town center, etc.) correlated with a large amount of
multimedia data.

A. Petrosino, L. Maddalena, P. Pala (Eds.): ICIAP 2013 Workshops, LNCS 8158, pp. 257–267, 2013.

The recommendation strategy should be able to provide users with the more relevant information depending on the *context* [14] (i.e. user preferences, user location, observed objects, weather and environmental conditions, etc. as in *Context Aware Recommendation Systems* - CARS [15]) and eventually linked with other on-line touristic information and services, which are usually customized for indoor envronments without taking into account the context information [4].

The majority of approaches to recommendation in the multimedia realm generally exploits *high level* metadata - extracted in automatic or semi-automatic way from *low level* features - that are in different manners correlated and compared with user preferences. These approaches suffer from several drawbacks: (i) it is not always possible to extract in automatic and effective way useful high level information from multimedia features; (ii) for some kinds of multimedia data there is not a precise correlation between high and low level information; (iii) there is not always available explicit and useful information (*knowledge*) about user preferences and feedbacks; (iv) in the recommendation process sometimes it is useful to take into account features of the objects (*context*) that user is currently observing as content information.

Here, we propose a different approach which tries to avoid such drawbacks: (i) analyzing in a separate way low and high level information, i.e. both contribute to determine the utility of an object in the recommendation process; (ii) exploiting system logs to implicitly determine information about users and the related community, considering their browsing sessions as a sort of "ratings"; (iii) considering as relevant content for the recommendation the features of the object that a user is currently watching together with user preferences and other context information. In particular, we present a general multimedia recommender system able to uniformly manage heterogeneous multimedia data and to provide context-aware recommendation techniques supporting intelligent multimedia services useful for the users. In addition, we describe a real case study in the mobile environment, related to an outdoor scenario, together with some preliminary results on user's satisfaction.

The paper is organized as follows. Section 2 presents at a glance a functional overview of our recommender system. Section 3 describes the techniques used for multimedia data management, while Section 4 details the proposed recommendation strategy. Section 5 outlines the chosen case study with the related implementation details and preliminary experiments. Finally, Section 6 reports some conclusions.

2   System Overview

Figure 1 describes at a glance a functional overview of the proposed system in terms of main components. The *Multimedia Data Management Engine* (MDME) is responsible for: (i) accessing by the *Data Indexing and Access* module to the media contents present in the different data sources (*Multimedia Data Repositories*), (ii) extracting by the *Feature Extraction* module from *Multimedia Data* high and low level features useful both for indexing and for the structured representation of the data itself (*Structural Description*).

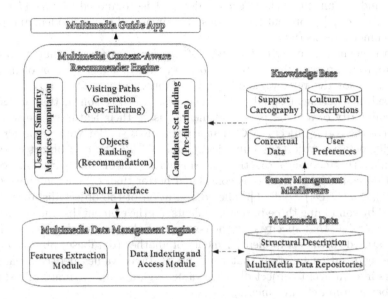

Fig. 1. System Overview

The *Sensor Management Middleware* is responsible for deriving, on the basis of information accessible via physical sensors (e.g. GPS, WSN), Web-services/API or wrapping techniques, the "knowledge" related to the context in which the user is located. In particular, the *Knowledge Base* is constituted by the *Contextual Data* (e.g. weather and environmental conditions registered for the considered place), *User Preferences* (explicitly or implicitly captured), *Cultural POI Descriptions* (in terms of multimedia information) and by a *Support Cartography* useful to geo-localize users and visualize their positions with respect to POIs.

The *MultiMedia Context-Aware Recommender Engine* provides a set of recommendation facilities for multi-dimensional and interactive browsing of multimedia data related to cultural POIs. In particular, on the basis of context information and user preferences the *Candidate Set Building* module selects a set of candidate objects for recommendation; successively, the *Objects Ranking* module performs a ranking of candidates exploiting a proper recommendation strategy (by *Users and Similarity Matrices Computation*). Eventually, the *Visit Paths Generation* module recommends to the users visit paths, providing all the support information (logistics, costs, services, etc..). Finally, each user device is equipped with a *Multimedia Guide App* that allows the fruition of multimedia contents (a questionnaire is submitted in order to capture his/her profile).

3   Management of Multimedia Data

Our data and retrieval models are inspired by the WINDSURF ones [5]. We have a database $\mathcal{O}$ of M multimedia objects, $\mathcal{O} = \{O^1, \ldots, O^M\}$, such as images, videos, and documents, where each objects O is composed of m_O *elements*, $O = \{o_1, \ldots, o_{m_O}\}$ representing, regions of an image, shots of a video, and parts of a document, respectively.

Each element o is described by way of *low level features* F that represent, in an appropriate way, the content of o (e.g., the color distribution of image's regions). As for the retrieval model, given a query object $Q = \{Q_1, \ldots, Q_m\}$ composed of m elements, and an element distance function δ, that measures the dissimilarity of a given pair of elements (using their features), we want to determine the top-k objects in $\mathcal{O}$ that are the most similar with respect to Q. Similarity between objects is numerically assessed by way of a object distance function d_F that combines together the single element distances into an overall value. Consequently, object O^a is considered better than O^b for the query Q iff $d(Q, O^a) < d(Q, O^b)$ holds [6]. The computation of the object distance d_F is obtained by combining three basic ingredients: (i) the element distance δ, (ii) the set of constraints that specify how the component elements of the query Q have to be matched to the component elements of another (database) object O, and (iii) the aggregation function that combines distance values between matched elements into an overall object distance value (e.g., a simple average of distance values between matched elements).

The efficient resolution of queries over features is ensured by the *Data Indexing and Access* module which supports indices built on top of elements (e.g., image regions, and video shots) based on the M-tree metric index [8].

In particular, images are first segmented into regions, where pixels included in a single region o share the same visual content (i.e., color/texture) [5]. Image regions are then compared according to their visual features using Bhattacharyya distance metric δ; region scores are opportunely matched by solving a one-to-one matching problem, where each element of a document can be only matched to at most one element of the other document, and vice versa. Then a "biased" average d_F is used to aggregate distance values of matched elements. Videos are first segmented into shots [9]. Then, each shot o is represented by a single representative key frame (e.g., the first frame of the shot), so that shots can be compared by means of the above image similarity function d_F. Each keyframe is first segmented into visually coherent regions, then color/texture features are extracted and stored for each keyframe region [5]. Whole videos are compared by aggregating the similarities between shots (i.e., their representative keyframes). Documents are modeled as follows: each element o is a page contained in the document O and we want to discover whether a new document Q is similar to some existing documents in our database $\mathcal{O}$. Comparison between pages is performed by taking into account relevant contained keywords by using the vector space model [7], so that features extracted from each page include keywords using $tf \times idf$ values after stopping & stemming.

In order to enrich data representation, objects are annotated with high level (semantic) descriptors S (e.g., labels describing what a video shot is related to). Such descriptors are in the form of keywords (or tags) and are semi-automatically assigned to objects by means of a multimedia annotator that, starting from a training set of pre-annotated objects, is able to predict sets of "good" tags able to effectively characterize the content of new untagged objects [10].

We define the universe of tags T as the union of all possible semantic descriptors to be associated to objects in $\mathcal{O}$, and the membership relation $R \subseteq \mathcal{O} \times T$ that indicates that an object O has assigned a tag in T. The annotation process is modelled as a nearest neighbors (NN) problem on object elements and turn into a set of graph-based problems. First, we try to discover affinities between tags and an unlabelled object, which is done using a *Random Walk with Restart* algorithm on a graph that models current annotations as well as elements' similarities. Then, we compute pairwise tag correlations. Again, this relies on the analysis of links in a (second-order) graph. Finally, we combine the results of the two steps to derive a set of terms which are both semantically correlated each other and affine to the new object. This final step amounts to solve an instance of the *Maximum Weight Clique Problem* on a small graph [10]. Note that, while for objects of type image tags are directly associated to images, when annotating videos, we are able to predict tags not only for shots but even for videos, by opportunely propagate tags at the shot level to the video level [9].

Given a user-provided set of tags, as query semantic concepts, objects are selected by the query processor by applying a $co-occurrence$-based distance function d_S on T. The search provides the set of objects (i.e., images, videos/shots, documents) that share at least one tag with the input set.

Both low level features and semantic descriptors concur to determine the *multimedia relatedness* $d(O^i, O^j)$ among two objects. In details, if O^i and O^j are of the same type (e.g., we are comparing two images), we define their global distance as the average between the contribution given by low level features and the one provided by semantics, that is: $d(O^i, O^j) = (d_F(O^i, O^j) + d_S(O^i, O^j))/2$; on the other hand, if we are comparing objects of different type (e.g., a document with a video), their multimedia relatedness equals to their semantic distance only, i.e., $d(O^i, O^j) = d_S(O^i, O^j)$.

4   Context-Aware Multimedia Recommendation Services

The basic idea behind our proposal is that when a user is near to a cultural POI, the related and personalized multimedia description is presented and the recommender system has to be able to: (i) determine a set of *candidate* objects for the recommendation, on the base of user needs and preferences (*pre-filtering stage*); (ii) automatically propose, when a user selects an object, other similar multimedia objects (*recommendation stage*); (iii) dinamically arranges the selected objects in apposite "visiting paths" considering other context information such as weather or environmental conditions (*post-filtering stage*).

Pre-filtering Stage. Each object subject to recommendation may be represented in different and heterogeneous feature spaces. For instance, the picture of a monument may be described by annotations concerning history of the monument, the materials it has been built with, low-level image features, experts' descriptions, visitors' descriptions and reviews, and so on. Each of these sets of features contributes to the characterization of the objects to different extents. Hence, it is important to consider congruently each type of descriptor during the recommendation process. The first step consists in clustering together "similar" objects, where the similarity should consider all (or subsets of) the different spaces of features. To this purpose, we employ high-order star-structured co-clustering techniques [12] to address the problem of heterogeneous data pre-filtering. In this context, the same set of objects is represented in different feature spaces. Such data represent objects of a certain type, connected to other types of data, the features, so that the overall data schema forms a star structure of inter-relationships. The co-clustering task consists in clustering simultaneously the set of objects and the set of values in the different feature spaces. In this way we obtain a partition of the objects influenced by each of the feature spaces and at the same time a partition of each feature space. The pre-filtering stage leverages the clustering results to select a set of candidate objects by using the user's profile, which is modeled as sets of descriptors in the same spaces as the objects' descriptors.

We now provide the formalization of our problem. Let $\mathcal{O} = O^1, \ldots, O^M$ be a set of M multimedia objects and $\mathcal{F} = \{F^1, \ldots, F^N\}$ a set of N feature spaces. A dataset can be viewed under the different views given by the different feature spaces F^k. Therefore, the view k is associated with each feature space F^k. Given a star-structured dataset $\mathcal{SD}$ over $\mathcal{O}$ and $\mathcal{F}$, the goal of the star-structured data co-clustering is to find a set of partitions $\mathcal{Y} = \{Y^1, \ldots, Y^N\}$ over the feature set $\mathcal{F} = \{F^1, \ldots, F^N\}$, and a partition $\mathcal{X}$ of the object set $\mathcal{O}$ by optimizing a certain objective function.

To solve the high-order star-structured co-clustering problem, several algorithms have been proposed based on different approaches. In this work, we adopt a parameter-less iterative algorithm that maximizes the Goodman-Kruskal τ, a statistical measure of association that automatically identifies a congruent number of high-quality co-clusters [12].

In our recommendation problem, a user is represented as a set of vectors $U = \{u^1, \ldots, u^N\}$ in the same N feature spaces describing the objects. Each vector u^k is updated each time the user visits (or re-visit) an object by considering the object features in each space at the instant of the visit. To provide a first candidate list of objects to be recommended, we measure the *cosine distance* of each user vectors associated to the k-th space, with the centroids of each object clusters in the k-th space. For each space, the most similar object cluster is chosen leading to N clusters $\{X_1^c, \ldots, X_N^c\}$ of candidate objects. Then, two different strategies can be adopted to provide the pre-filtered list of candidate objects $\mathcal{O}^c$: (i) *set-union strategy* - the objects belonging to the union of all clusters are retained, i.e., $\mathcal{O}^c = \bigcup_k X_k^c$; (ii) *threshold strategy* - the objects that appears in at least *ths* clusters ($ths \in \{1 \ldots N\}$) are retained.

The first strategy is suitable when user's vectors are associated to very small clusters (e.g., because the user likes very uncommon objects). In any other situation, the second strategy is the most appropriate. As a final step, objects already visited/liked/browsed by the user are filtered out. Notice that, thanks to this approach, users are not described by set of objects, but by sets of features that characterize the objects they visit, like or browse.

Recommendation Stage. In this stage we use a technique that combines several features of multimedia objects (low-level and semantics), eventual past behaviour of individual users and overall behaviour of the whole "community" of users to [2]. Our basic idea is to assume that when an object O_i is chosen after an object O_j in the same browsing session, this event means that O_i "is voting" for O_j. Similarly, the fact that an object O_i is very similar in terms of multimedia features to O_j can also be interpreted as O_j "recommending" O_i (and viceversa). Thus, we model a browsing system for the set of candidate objects $\mathcal{O}^c$ as a labeled graph (G,l), where $G = (\mathcal{O}^c, E)$ is a directed graph and $l : E \rightarrow \{pattern, sim\} \times R^+$ is a function that associates each edge in $E \subseteq \mathcal{O}^c \times \mathcal{O}^c$ with a pair (t, w), where t is the type of the edge which can assume two enumerative values (*pattern* and *similarity*) and w is the weight of the edge. We list two different cases: (i) a *pattern label* for an edge (O_j, O_i) denotes the fact that an object O_i was accessed immediately after an object O_j and, in this case, the weight w_j^i is the number of times O_i was accessed immediately after O_j ; (ii) a *similarity label* for an edge (O_j, O_i) denotes the fact that an object O_i is similar to O_j and, in this case, the weight w_j^i is the similarity between the two objects. Thus, a link from O_j to O_i indicates that part of the importance of O_j is transferred to O_i .

Such an importance is then measured by means the introduction of a recommendation grade $\rho(O)$, and in [1], it has been shown as the ranking vector $R = [\rho(O_1) \dots \rho(O_n)]^T$ of all the objects can be computed as the solution to the equation $R = C \cdot R$, where $C = \{w_j^i\}$ is an ad-hoc matrix that defines how the importance of each object is transferred to other objects. Such a matrix can be seen as a linear combination of a *local browsing matrix* $A_l = \{a_{ij}^l\}$ for each user u_l, a *global browsing matrix* $A = \{a_{ij}\}$ and a *multimedia similarity matrix* $B = \{b_{ij}\}$ such that $b_{ij} = \frac{1-d(O^i,O^j)_{ij}}{\Gamma}$ if $1 - d(O^i, O^j)_{ij} \geq \tau \ \forall i \neq j$, 0 otherwise ($\tau$ is a threshold and Γ is a normalization factors which guarantees that $\sum_i b_{ij} = 1$, see [1] for more details).

The final step is to compute customized rankings for each individual user. In this case, we can then rewrite previous equation considering the ranking for each user as $R_l = C \cdot R_l$, where R_l is the vector of preference grades, customized for a user u_l. We note that solving the discussed equation corresponds to find the stationary vector of C, i.e., the eigenvector with eigenvalue equal to 1. In [1], it has been demonstrated that C, under certain assumptions and transformations, is a real square matrix having positive elements, with a unique largest real eigenvalue and the corresponding eigenvector has strictly positive components. In such conditions, the equation can be solved using the *Power Method* algorithm.

Post-filtering Stage. Finally, the list of suggested items, which are selected as interesting by users, is organized in apposite visiting paths (considering the distances from user location): they are not fixed and are arranged on the base of weather and environmental situations. The recommendation grades of objects, which come from certain cultural POIs with a certain number of persons or with particular values of temperature or humidity, are penalized and such objects could be excluded from recommendation.

5   A Case Study

We consider as real case study the archeological site of *Paestum*, one of the major Graeco-Roman cities in the South of Italy. The main cultural attractions are represented by a set of ancient buildings; in particular, three main temples of Doric style (i.e. the first Temple of Hera, also called Basilica, the second Temple of Hera, also known as Temple of Neptune, and the Temple of Athena), the Roman Forum with several ruins, and the amphitheater, all surrounding by the remains of the city's walls. In addition, there is a museum near the ancient city containing many evidences of the graeco-roman life (e.g. amphorae, paintings and other objects). Thus, all the cited buildings will constitute cultural Points of Interest for our case study.

Users visiting ruins could be happy of having a useful multimedia guide able to describe the main cultural attractions (POIs) and to suggest automatically visiting paths containing multimedia objects of interest. In particular when a user is approaching to a cultural POI (e.g. Temple of Neptune), the related multimedia description is delivered on the user's mobile device. Successively, the recommendation services determine first the list of possible interesting objects (images of other Temples and of Roman Forum) in according to users' preferences (the user prefers to see only images) and then compute a visiting path, shown on a map. The paths have to take into account the current context (in terms of actual position – obtained by GPS – and the selected multimedia data), and to consider the weather and environmental conditions and the previous paths of other users, thus enhancing the visiting experience. Once acquired such kind of information, the path can dynamically change in the case of crowded or unfit to use areas (e.g. too high temperature/humidity or a closed area). Eventually, the visiting paths could be enriched with other touristic POIs (e.g. restaurants, hotels, etc.). A graphic user interface gives the detailed view of the suggested path on an proper cartography, reporting a preview of cultural POIs.

In the following, we report some implementation details concerning the developed prototype for Paestum ruins.

The Multimedia Data is constituted by a collection (managed by *PostegreSQL* DBMS) of about 10,000 images and texts coming from several multimedia repositories (e.g. Flickr, Panoramio, Facebook, Wikipedia, etc.) and related to all the main attractions of Paestum. We associated to each object a set of metadata and spatial information (managed by *PostGIS* spatial database extension), in according to the CIDOC-CRM model [1]. All the data are managed by the Multimedia Data Management Engine that is based on the *Windsurf* library[2]. The Sensor Management Middleware collects and manage sensors' messages from

---

[1] http://www.cidoc-crm.org/

[2] http://www-db.deis.unibo.it/Windsurf/

Table 1. Comparison between our system and no facilities

TLX factor	Experts		Medium Exp.		Not Experts	
	With rec.	Without	With rec.	Without	With rec.	Without
Mental demand	25.2	27.1	33.1	33.8	35	41
Physical demand	25	31	28	35	31.5	44
Temporal demand	27	32.5	29	35	30	35
Effort	24.8	31.2	33	42	35	50
Perfomances	71	68	71.8	71.2	73.5	73.1
Frustation	24	34	25.1	31.6	25	32

users' mobile devices. By means of apposite *JAVA* libraries and exploiting *GPS* facilities, it is able to capture user location and some environmental parameters (number of a persons in a given area). The Knowledge Base, realized using the *Sesame* Repository and *JENA* libraries, allows to map the observed context instances in the RDF linked open data format. From the other hand, the Multimedia Context-Aware Recommender Engine exploits proper *JAVA* libraries (developed for the systems presented in [2] and integrated with co-clustering libraries) to accomplish its tasks. Eventually for the support cartography, we decided to use *Google Maps*. Finally, a user can interact with our system using – at the moment – an *Android* Multimedia Guide App. The presentation logic is based on apposite widgets. The client requests are elaborated by *JAVA Servlets* and the results are sent to the client in form of XML data.

Wedesigned and carried out several preliminary experiments to investigate how helpful the recommendations offered by our system are, demonstrating that the introduction of such techniques can improve the tourists' experience.

In the training phase, we have chosen 10 users among graduate students that used for 2 days the system without recommendation facilities to capture their browsing sessions (GPS sensor of mobile devices were used to locate user positions) during their visit to build a consistent matrix A for the described collection. We then asked a different group of about 10 people (this group consisted of 5 not-expert users on graeco-roman art, 3 medium expert users and 2 expert users) to complete several visits (3 visits per user) of different complexity within the Paestum ruins and without any recommendation facility. After this test, we asked them to browse once again the same collection with the assistance of our recommender system and complete other tasks of the same complexity. In a similar manner, in a second time we asked another group of 10 people to browse the same collection first with the assistance of our recommender system completing other different tasks and then without any help.

We have subdivided browsing tasks in the following four broad categories: (i) *Low Complexity* tasks (T_1) - explore at least 5 POIs related to ancient buildings; (ii) *Medium Complexity* tasks (T_2) - explore at least 10 POIs related to graeco-roman *temples* or *amphitheaters* or *Roman forum buildings*; (iii) *High Complexity* tasks (T_3) - explore at least 15 POIs related to *Roman forum buildings* or *amphitheaters* or *city walls' gates*.

The strategy we used to evaluate the results of this experiment is based on NASA TLX (*Task Load Index factor*). To this aim, we then asked the users to express their opinion about the advantage of our system to provide an effective user experience in completing the assigned visitng tasks, with respect to use a simple museum map and a touristic guide. We also considered situations (that we have simulated during experimentation) in which an area is closed.

Thus, we obtained the average results scores for each of three categories of users reported in Table 1 (the lower the TLX score — in the range [0 − 100] — the better the user satisfaction).

Note that not-expert users find our system more effective than the other users' category in every sub-scale, because they consider very helpful the provided suggestions. Instead, for expert and medium expert users' opinion, our system outperforms a classical touristic guide in every sub-scale except for *mental demand and performances*: this happens because an expert user considers sometimes not useful the automatic suggestions just because they know what they are looking for.

6   Conclusions

In this paper we proposed a novel recommender platform in the Cultural Heritage domain. We realized a system for Paestum ruins, providing to tourists personalized visiting paths. Then we investigated the effectiveness of the proposed approach in the considered scenario, based on the browsing effectiveness and users satisfaction. Experimental results showed that our approach is quite promising and encourages further research.

References

1. Albanese, M., d'Acierno, A., Moscato, V., Persia, F., Picariello, A.: Modeling recommendation as a social choice problem. In: Proc. of ACM RecSys 2010, Barcelona, Spain, pp. 329–332. ACM (2010)
2. Albanese, M., d'Acierno, A., Moscato, V., Persia, F., Picariello, A.: A multimedia semantic recommender system for cultural heritage applications. In: Proc. of ICSC 2011, Palo Alto, CA, USA, pp. 403–410. IEEE (2011)
3. Hart, S.G., Staveland, L.E.: Development of NASA-TLX (Task Load Index): results of empirical and theoretical research. Human Mental Workload 1, 139–183 (1988)
4. Kabassei, K.: Personalisation systems for cultural tourism. In: Multimedia Services in Intelligent Environments, Springer, pp. 101–111. Springer (2013)
5. Bartolini, I., Ciaccia, P., Patella, M.: Query processing issues in region-based image databases. Knowl. Inf. Syst. 25(2), 389–420 (2010)
6. Ilyas, I.F., Beskales, G., Soliman, M.A.: A survey of top-k query processing techniques in relational database systems. ACM Comput. Surv. 40(4) (2008)
7. Salton, G.: Automatic text processing: the transformation, analysis, and retrieval of information by computer. Addison-Wesley, Reading (1989)
8. Ciaccia, P., Patella, M., Zezula, P.: M-tree: An efficient access method for similarity search in metric spaces. In: Proc. of VLDB 1997, Athens, Greece, pp. 426–435 (1997)
9. Bartolini, I., Patella, M., Romani, C.: SHIATSU: tagging and retrieving videos without worries. Multimed. Tools Appl. 63(2), 357–385 (2013)

10. Bartolini, I., Ciaccia, P.: *imagination*: Exploiting link analysis for accurate image annotation. In: Boujemaa, N., Detyniecki, M., Nürnberger, A. (eds.) AMR 2007. LNCS, vol. 4918, pp. 32–44. Springer, Heidelberg (2008)

11. Bartolini, I., Zhang, Z., Papadias, D.: Collaborative filtering with personalized skylines. IEEE Trans. Knowl. Data Eng. 23(2), 190–203 (2011)

12. Ienco, D., Robardet, C., Pensa, R.G., Meo, R.: Parameter-less co-clustering for star-structured heterogeneous data. Data Min. Knowl. Discov. 26(2), 217–254 (2013)

13. Ricci, F., Rokach, L., Shapira, B., Kantor, P.B. (eds.): Recommender Systems Handbook. Springer (2011)

14. Dourish, P.: What we talk about when we talk about context. Personal and Ubiquitous Computing 8(1), 19–30 (2004)

15. Karatzoglou, A., Amatriain, X., Baltrunas, L., Oliver, N.: Multiverse recommendation: n-dimensional tensor factorization for context-aware collaborative filtering. In: Proc. of ACM RecSys 2010, Barcelona, Spain, pp. 79–86. ACM (2010)

Model-Driven Generation of Collaborative Virtual Environments for Cultural Heritage

Alberto Bucciero[1] and Luca Mainetti[2]

[1] National Council of Researches, Institute of Archaeological and Monumental Heritage,
Rome, Italy
alberto.bucciero@cnr.it
[2] University of Salento, Department of Innovation Engineering, Lecce, Italy
luca.mainetti@unisalento.it

Abstract. Collaborative Virtual Environments are experiencing a large interest in cultural heritage field mostly due to the strong opportunity given by novel augmented reality applications. There are already several examples of collaborative augmented visit to museums or historical sites. Anyway the traditional and static approach to computer graphics is very limiting because it often requires the development of a Virtual Environment for every new application.

In this paper, we propose a technique for model-driven generation of mixed reality virtual environments, where every modification in contents, visit path and in interactions with the physical surrounding environment don't require a great re-coding effort, enabling fast deployment of collaborative virtual environments for cultural explorations only providing new contents and a small set of parameters.

Keywords: collaborative virtual environment, conceptual design, conceptual map, mixed reality, multi-user virtual environment, 3D virtual world.

1 Introduction

Collaborative Virtual Environments (CVE) are becoming more and more important in many areas; their use goes from military training and simulation, to sharing of scientific data between scientists or decision-makers (CSCW), from support for innovative teaching paradigms, to support for collaborative e-learning (CSCL). Also, they are becoming one of the most promising multimedia technologies used to preserve and explore cultural goods [1].

One of the traditionally and oldest application field of CVE is virtual reconstruction of real or imaginary places for cultural heritage, for example in [2] a multi-user 3D world supports users in virtually visiting the Qumran museum to overcome the difficulties due to the geographic region where it is located.

Another interesting example is in [3] where users interact in real time from remote locations with 3D archaeological models through a shared virtual environment using tele-immersive technology.

A. Petrosino, L. Maddalena, P. Pala (Eds.): ICIAP 2013 Workshops, LNCS 8158, pp. 268–277, 2013.

Starting from a definition, a CVE (Collaborative Virtual Environment) is a virtual 3D place representation, in which users, being represented with graphical embodiments called avatars, share the same experience, working and interacting with the same set of virtual objects. In this case users see the same representation of shared workspace (i.e. a 3D world) and the effects on the users' or objects' actions are also the same for all. This paradigm is known as WYSIWIS ("What you see is what I see").

The availability of mobile location aware technologies on consumer devices encourages researchers to consider how to join the classic desktop CVE paradigm with a newer one based on mobile devices, in a mixed reality oriented fashion. Then the paradigm is not anymore "WYSIWIS", like a classic Collaborative Virtual Environment, but WYSINWIS ("What you see is NOT what I see"): users see different representation of the same workspace (both environment and objects).

Such systems are called CMVRs (Collaborative Mobile Virtual Reality systems) in which avatars in the virtual world and mobile players in the real world share the same experience, aiming to a common goal even if provided with different devices, with different capabilities and then with different views of the same workspace.

Mixed and augmented system involving 3D visualizations and mobile units are extensively used in virtual archeological reconstructions (e.g. ARCHEOGUIDE [4] and MUSE [5]) and collaborative exploration of museum exhibitions (see e.g. [6]). The equipment used typically involves HMD (head-mounted display [6]), wearable laptops and tablet PCs [4, 5, 6] and PDAs [4, 6]. The positioning of the user is determined by direct user input, recognition of images of corresponding landmarks taken by wearable camera [4] or GPS [6].

The design of such application is however very difficult, because on the one hand the interactions between users and workspace in the 3D environment are substantially different from those that could be supported by mobile devices, on the other hand it is very important being able to design environment, interactions and contents of both 3D and mobile 2D without loosing sight of the main goal of the collaborative session (oriented to learning, gaming, virtual visit, etc.).

Even if CVEs are more and more widespread and technologically advanced, they are often still developed starting from the environmental container, tightly coupled with them. The development of the 3D environment, that represents the stage where the action and interaction takes place, often lead designers to define action/interaction rules on the basis of the environment facilities offered by it, and not the exact contrary as it should be. In CMVRs this cannot happen because the shared workspace is not homogeneous, typically it is partially 3D (on traditional workstation) and partially 2D (on mobile devices). Then it is needed a design approach that let the designers free themselves from technicalites and that let them focus the attention over the goals that the collaborative session is aiming.

In this paper we present a technique for model-driven generation of mixed reality virtual environments, where every modification in contents, visit path and in interactions with the physical surrounding environment don't require a great re-coding effort. The paper is structured as follows: section 2 reports essential related work. Section 3 provides readers with an introduction of our model-driven approach to CVEs, stating the design problem, the proposed conceptual solution, and a real case study in the cultural heritage domain. Finally, in section 4 the conclusions summarize our key messages and sketch future research directions.

2   Related Work

In the international scientific panorama there are many examples of research works related to the CVE and, in particular, of those oriented to the cultural heritage. We present here an overview of the approaches to the design of the virtual environment and we focus on the conceptual layer of design: all these approaches demonstrate that even if CVEs are widespread, the problem of their conceptual design is far to be solved.

The traditional virtual environment design techniques are based on real world concepts and the usual approach is to design just the real situation, translating physical concepts in a 3D virtual world.

Collaborative Virtual Real Environment (CVRE) [7] was developed by the Universidad du Chile and it models the virtual environment using the concepts of the real world such as rooms, auditorium and so on.

Another approach to the conceptual design is Process Modeling Language (PML) [8]. It is derived by UML and has two levels: High Level UML-Based Diagram (in which it uses P-activity to design the activities and P-class to design objects) and Low Level Process Language, an Object-Oriented language that provides a representation of the classes defined in the P-class using methods defined in the P-activity. The output of the Low Level Process Language may be used in the graphical engine to create the 3D environment.

NiMMiT (Notation for Modeling Multimodal Interaction Techniques) [9] is another technique to design the computer human interaction. It is based on a state chart graphical notation, oriented to virtual environments.

Considering the semantic gap between designers and developers of CVE, a new technique was thought: the InTML (Interaction Techniques Markup Language) [10]. It is a domain specific language made to define several aspects of a virtual environment (device, objects, interactions). InTML uses a dataflow architecture where objects and device are part of the flow, and are linked each other.

Whereas these approaches provide technical designers (mainly engineers) with support for modeling the graphical or behavioral aspects of 3D virtual worlds, they lack in characterizing the semantics of the user interaction and collaboration in CVEs. To cope this lack, we propose to extend the semantic perspective to establish a common ground between designers of collaborative experiences and CVEs engineers, and to provide guidance in particular for cultural heritage domain experts.

3   Mixed CVE Conceptual Design

3.1   The Design Problems

The problem of the conceptual modeling of virtual environments has been traditionally faced, as described in the state of the art, using an approach that forces the designer to learn technical formalisms, distracting him from the aspects more related to the specific conceptual modeling. Therefore, domain experts (archaeologists, historians, sociologists, etc.) are forced to acquire some technical skills just to be able to give requirements to developers and 3D graphic designers.

To enable directly domain experts to model CVEs, the number of elements the designer must keep under control must be reduced, focusing on those that are related to the goal of the collaboration and social interaction. In other words, it is needed to add the conceptual perspective to CVE design. The approach must be easy and intuitive, simply understandable also for the virtual environment designers and from which a formal representation can be derived, to can be used to generate CVEs. The best strategy to define a conceptual level is, in our opinion, to think to a metaphor (intended as "a figure of speech and or phrase that one word as being or equal to a second object in some way"). This metaphor should be able to represent the conceptual primitives for the CVE modeling and should be abstract enough to be used in several contexts.

Moreover defining adequate general concepts, abstract from technology-specific details, we can devise a representation of a CVE independently from the specific technical platform used, and we can think to create a sort of "compiler" that would translate the unique abstract representation to a concrete implementation ready to be deployed on specific classes of devices (workstations, smartphones, tablets, etc.).

In order to reach this goal, we carried out an experiment capturing the concepts that underlie the theatre domain and representing them with a concept map.

3.2   Proposed Solution: The Map of Concepts

Evolving our virtual world engine WebTalk [11] and its mobile version [12] during past six years – in collaboration with the HOC-Lab of Politecnico di Milano under the L@E, S@L, L@SS, and L4A (Learning for All) projects –, we faced a number of issues trying to make highly configurable our technology. To rise in generality, we have been driven by the need to capture all the relevant abstractions embodied in CVEs for several domains (education, cultural heritage, and sport ethic). These would have been a clear guideline to design the software architecture. The abstraction process has been the result of several iterations that involved on the one hand technical experts and on the other hand conceptual modeling and domain experts in analyzing CVEs and 3D virtual worlds.

The result is presented in the "concept map" presented in Fig. 1. The concept map is a diagram showing the relationships among CVE's recurring concepts. In Fig. 1 concepts are represented as nodes, while relationships are symbolized as labeled arrows. Labels express the informal semantics of relationships. As readers can see, we identified two different sets of concepts: static concepts (white nodes) and dynamic concepts (dark nodes). They capture in a separate layer two aspects of CVEs: (1) the world appearance and its spatial organization, (2) the interaction among users and between user and the word. Analyzing Fig. 1, readers can observe the presence of some fundamental concepts in CMVR design, that in the following are described as theatre concepts:

- *Theatre*: a building (i.e. a finite space) where a performance takes place.
- *Stage*: a large platform on which actors can stand and can be seen by an audience.
- *Scenography*: a description of a stage that illustrates the environment organization in term of space, set, costume, sound, lighting, etc.
- *Script*: the written text of a stage play.
- Act: a segment of a performance of a theatrical work; it is an organizational part.
- *Scene*: a division of an act presenting continuous action in one place. It is the shortest autonomous (semantic) unit in the script.
- *Actor*: a theatrical performer, i.e. a person who interprets a dramatic character or personality.
- *Director*: a person who oversees and orchestrates the theatre production usually with responsibility for action, lighting, music, and rehearsals.
- *Scene director*: a person who is responsible for the stage set up. He/she can modify the original configuration.
- *Prompter*: a person who assists (one acting or reciting) by suggesting or saying the next words of something forgotten or imperfectly learned. He/she gives the actors the opening words of each phrase a few seconds early.
- *Stage whisper*: a loud whisper by an actor that is audible to the spectators but is supposed for dramatic effect not to be heard by one or more of the actors.

Actors have a central role, because they are the protagonists of the virtual environment many other concepts are related to this one.

The *Curtain* is the entry point of the *Stage* the virtual environment is composed of. When *Actors* access a *Curtain*, they must be identified; then, depending on their *Roles*, the environment configures itself consequently.

Moreover, a relationship between *Curtain* and *Script* has been considered: the *Curtain* could change the *Script* that, in turn, is related to the *Actors*.

It is important to note the presence of a *Director* for the specific virtual space. A *Director* is a particular *Actor* who acts as a guide or a tutor for other users during the virtual sessions. In other words, a *Director* is a staff member that make sure that the action is moving along predefined lines, taking care of the collaborative mixed experience goal.

3.3   Case Study: The SIBECS Project

To test the approach we used the SIBECS project scenario. SIBECS was a project founded between 2007 and 2009 by Apulia region that aimed carrying out, experimenting and promoting innovative fruition services to access (and at the same time to preserve) the cultural heritage. One of its results was to develop a mixed reality walk-through between the modern city of Lecce and its ancient core, Lupiae, discovering "Points Of Interest" (POIs) near their visit path. In this collaborative experience, standard users log on a tridimensional environment in which they can access the contents in collaboration with other connected users, both standard and mobile ones.

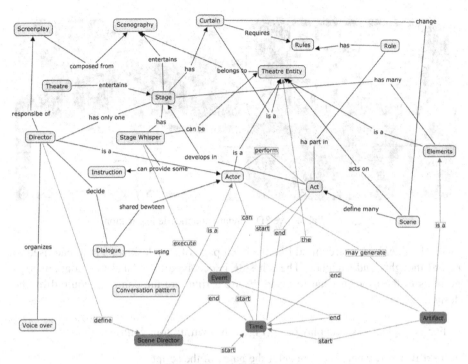

Fig. 1. Map of CVE concepts

Users, showed in the 3D environment (Fig. 2) as avatars, can discover new details about a POI using this the 3D channel. On the other hand, the users equipped with a smartphone can browse the tours using a geo-referred map (Fig. 3). When a POI is near the user, its detailed description will appear automatically on the display. Standard and mobile users share a conceptual workspace: standard users walk in a 3D reconstruction of the city while mobile users are really there in the same time, and can interact to each other chatting, raising events (for example the first who arrives in a place force a video to be played on all other devices), discovering POIs, etc.

When we first worked at the SIBECS project (2007-2009), the deployment of a collaborative session was still hand coded. After having developed our generative approach (starting from 2010), an experiment has been carried out re-writing (re-modeling and generating) the SIBECS cultural application. Every concept has been expressed exploiting the theatre metaphor and, thank to an ad hoc editor (see Fig. 4), the CVE model of the SIBECS environment has been translated (mapped) in the configuration script that has been provided as input to the WebTalk engine.

3.4   Architecture of the CVE Configuration Editor

In order to simplify the configuration phase, the CVE editor has been designed as wizard whose steps drive the users in the definition of each concept of the conceptual

Fig. 2. Collaborative 3D standard and mobile application

map. The interface is structured like the open page of a moleskine, a note pad used to record thoughts and sketches. The left side is occupied by a label that contains suggestions to the user on what to do in the front right are the controls required by the design.

For example, the screenplay page (Fig. 4) has within four controls:

1. Text Box n.1, where you can enter the name of the script
2. Text Box n.2, where you can enter the plot of the opera
3. Numerical textbox with arrows to automatically change the value entered, to set the number of acts
4. Validation control that displays in real time the errors and diagnostic messages for their correction

The wizard is developed in Microsoft Silverlight and its architecture can be divided in the following modules:

1. Model
2. Wizard logic
3. Views
4. XMI serializer
5. Webservice access

The software modules composing the system architecture can be logically arranged into three distinct functional layers:

1. Presentation
2. Business logic
3. Communication

The Presentation layer contains all the classes that interact with the end user, their goal is to show the data obtained from the model and to process user input. These

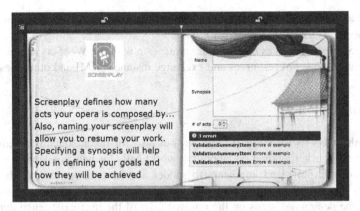

Fig. 3. A screenshot of the editor of CVEs based up on the theatre metaphor - screenplay interface

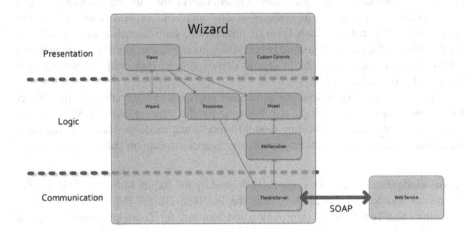

Fig. 4. Wizard software architecture in the large

classes are included in the Views module, and can use extensions to user controls in Silverlight Controls defined in the module.

The Business Logic layer contains all the classes that manage instances of conceptual map and the inner workings of the software. Other significant modules are:

1. Resources, which manages the resources associated with the elements of theater (stage, size, ...).
2. Wizard, which provides live validation of the concepts instantiated and gives feedbacks to the user.

The communication layer is responsible for access and communication with the server, it is composed of modules:

1. Serializer, which provides the serialization of models in XMI to allow interchange with the WebService.
2. TheatreServer, who takes care of communication with the WebService the purpose of receiving the set of resources and exchange instances XMI and other messages.

4   Conclusion

The growth of CVEs for cultural heritage (but also for other domains as education, entertainment, marketing, and collaborative work) calls for new conceptual tools that enable domain experts and engineers to model and keep under control the design complexity unleashed by innovative 3D virtual worlds, and carefully consider the impact of the design decisions on the optimal flow of the user experience during on-line sessions. To meet this challenge, we devised a set of concepts organized in a conceptual map that we used instantiate our mixed collaboration engines: WebTalk and Mobile Webtalk. The case study carried out in the cultural heritage domain demonstrated the promising advantages of our approach: expressiveness to capture collaborative features at a high level of abstraction, semi-formality to facilitate the establishment of a common ground between designers of educational experiences and CVEs engineers, and guidance to enable non-experts to cope with all the relevant aspects of a 3D virtual world.

In the future we will evolve our generative approach to CVE adopting the Object Management Group technology, i.e. formalizing the concept map as Meta Object Facility meta-model and exploiting model-to-model and model-to-code (e.g. Acceleo) techniques to configure virtual environments instances to support cultural exploration.

Acknowledgment. The work is partially funded by the Italian Ministry of Education, University and Research (MIUR) under the PON4a2 DICET-INMOTO (LivingLab on Culture and Technology - Information and Mobility for Tourism) national research project.

References

1. Cucchiara, R., Grana, C., Borghesani, D., Agosti, M., Bagdanov, A.D.: Multimedia for Cultural Heritage: Key Issues. In: Grana, C., Cucchiara, R. (eds.) MM4CH 2011. CCIS, vol. 247, pp. 206–216. Springer, Heidelberg (2012)
2. Di Blas, N., Bucciero, A., Mainetti, L., Paolini, P.: Multi-User Virtual Environments for Learning: Experience and Technology Design. IEEE Transactions on Learning Technologies 4(5), 349–365 (2012)
3. Kurillo, G., Forte, M., Bajcsy, R.: Teleimmersive 3D Collaborative Environment for Cyber-rarchaeology. In: Computer Vision and Pattern Recognition Workshops (CVPRW), pp. 23–28. IEEE Press, New York (2010)
4. Vlahakis, V., et al.: Archeoguide: first results of an augmented reality, mobile computing system in cultural heritage sites. In: 2001 Conference on Virtual Reality, Archeology, and Cultural Heritage, pp. 131–140. ACM, New York (2001)

5. Corlàita, D., et al.: Exciting understanding in Pompeii through on-site parallel interaction with dual time virtual models. In: 2001 Conference on Virtual Reality, Archeology, and Cultural Heritage, pp. 83–90. ACM, New York (2001)
6. Hall, T., et al.: The visitor as virtual archaeologist: explorations in mixed reality technology to enhance educational and social interaction in the museum. In: 2001 Conference on Virtual Reality, Archeology, and Cultural Heritage, pp. 91–96. ACM, New York (2001)
7. Guerrero, L.A., Collazos, C.A., Pino, J.A., Ochoa, S.F., Aguilera, F.: Designing collaborative virtual environments based on real spaces to promote community interaction. In: First Latin American Web Congress, pp. 58–65 (2003)
8. Rossi, D., Turrini, E.: Using a process modeling language for the design and implementation of process-driven applications. In: ICSEA 2007, Cap Esterel, France, pp. 55–55 (2007)
9. Vanacken, D., De Boeck, J., Raymaekers, C., Coninx, K.: NiMMiT: A notation for modeling multimodal interaction techniques. In: International Conference GRAPP 2006, Setúbal, Portugal, pp. 224–231 (2006)
10. Di Blas, N., Poggi, C., Torrebruno, A.: Collaboration and Playful Competition in a 3D Educational Virtual World: The Learning@Europe Experience. In: World Conference on Educational Multimedia, Hypermedia and Telecommunications, pp. 1191–1198. AACE, Chesapeake (2006)
11. Barchetti, U., Barbieri, T., Bucciero, A., Mainetti, L., Santo Sabato, S.: WebTalk04: a Framework to Support 3D Collaborative e-Learning. In: WBE 2006 - 5th IASTED International Conference on Web-based Education, Puerto Vallarta (Mexico), pp. 13–18 (2006)
    Barchetti, U., Bucciero, A., De Benedittis, T.A., Macchia, F., Mainetti, L., Tamborino, A.: MoWeT: A Configurable Framework to Support Ubiquitous Location-Aware Applications. In: The Sixth International Conference on Ubiquitous Computing and Intelligence, Brisbane, Australia, pp. 75–82 (2009)

Enhancing End User Access
to Cultural Heritage Systems:
Tailored Narratives and Human-Centered Computing

Maristella Agosti[1], Marta Manfioletti[1], Nicola Orio[2], and Chiara Ponchia[2]

[1] Department of Information Engineering, University of Padua, Italy
{agosti,manfioletti}@dei.unipd.it
[2] Department of Cultural Heritage, University of Padua, Italy
nicola.orio@unipd.it, chiara.ponchia.1@studenti.unipd.it

Abstract. This paper reports on the results of a study that aims to support end users of a multimedia system that manages a digital cultural heritage collection. The system is provided with automatic tools that simulate the behavior of the research method adopted by professional users when they interact with the multimedia application. The experimental results have been obtained using a multimedia application that manages the digital representation of historical botanical manuscripts.

Keywords: Cultural heritage systems, multimedia systems, human-centered computing, history of art research method, digital archives, illuminated manuscripts, historical botanical manuscripts, recommendation.

1 Introduction

Advanced cultural heritage systems are often digital applications that manage multimedia content for diversified categories of users, ranging from professional researchers to interested members of the general public. To this end, these systems have to be adapted to the user needs of such a diversified user range. One major challenge for system designers is thus to allow the general public to take advantage of the automatic tools created to support professional research while at the same time exploiting scholars' knowledge about the digital collections. The dissemination of cultural heritage can be fostered when end users are able to actively interact with the system, discover the professional knowledge and have a rewarding experience that would not otherwise be possible.

This paper presents the findings of a study that aims to support end users of a multimedia system that manages the digital representation of historical botanical manuscripts. The system is provided with automatic methods that are based on the research method of the professional users of history of art.

The paper is structured as follows. An initial section presents the context that gave rise to the study. This is followed by a section that presents the basic characteristics of the research method used by history of art professional users when they identify

A. Petrosino, L. Maddalena, P. Pala (Eds.): ICIAP 2013 Workshops, LNCS 8158, pp. 278–287, 2013.

correspondences and similarities between images in manuscripts that may have been written over the centuries and/or in different geographical areas. After having identified and presented the essential characteristics of the methodological tools used by history of art experts, we present the process adopted to define and enrich the digital representations of botanical manuscripts with useful metadata representations that are used with a proposed method for automatically discovering similarity between images. At the end we make some final remarks together with some suggestions for future work.

2   Context

The findings presented in the paper originated in the CULTURA project, a European project that aims at increasing user engagement with cultural heritage digital collections through the development of a new adaptive and dynamic environment[1]. To fulfill the challenging goal of the project, continuous interaction with different categories of end users is required to understand the needs, wishes and desires CULTURA has to address. As an exemplary cultural heritage digital collection, we used the digital archive containing the digital representations of illuminated manuscripts identified and chosen in the context of the IPSA (*Imaginum Patavinae Scientiae Archivum*) project.

The IPSA digital archive was created at the University of Padua for professional researchers in History of Illumination to allow them to compare the illuminated images held in the collection and to examine in depth certain aspects of scientific illustration in Italy[2]. The approach adopted in designing the IPSA multimedia system was focused on the user with the aim of developing a real human-centered multimedia application [1].

Due to involvement in the CULTURA project, we had to face the stimulating task of opening up such a specialist collection to new user categories with different interests toward the IPSA collection and History of Art in general. In fact, a subset of the IPSA collection was selected to be imported in the CULTURA environment for use as a case study to test the new environment and its functions. This new environment was named IPSA@CULTURA to underline that the IPSA content was being used with tools and services of the CULTURA environment[3]. CULTURA provides a service-oriented architecture, where the user can interact with a number of functions that have been developed and are maintained by partners of the project; the portal was developed using Drupal by the research group of the Trinity College Dublin [2].

With our involvement in the design and development of IPSA@CULTURA, we have come to the conviction that a valuable way to catch the attention of new users is to give them the basic critical tools and information to approach the collection and to involve them in the research paths of professional users. This would then help them to develop their own research method and have a more satisfactory interaction with the system.

Therefore, we prepared a *narrative* to guide users through the collection, and we presented them with both the IPSA@CULTURA contents and the main functions.

---

[1] http://www.cultura-strep.eu/
[2] http://ipsa.dei.unipd.it/en_GB
[3] http://kdeg.cs.tcd.ie/ipsa/

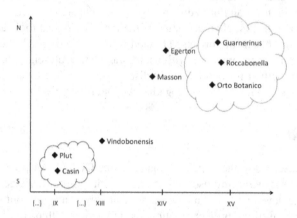

Fig. 1. Graphical representation of the three groups of manuscripts used in the study

Up to now art historians have developed the recommendations to create the narrative, but we decided to investigate how they are related to features that can be directly computed from metadata descriptors and multimedia content.

3   Art Historical Research Method Recommendations

The main functions of IPSA@CULTURA include enabling the final user to follow different paths through the collection thanks to the use of narratives. With the term narrative we mean short lessons that allow the user to become acquainted with the collection and to obtain a clearer idea of the research that can be carried out in IPSA@CULTURA. Illuminations are presented to the user according to their interest toward the collection: a beginner or user with a low level of interest would only be shown the basic resources of the narrative. A mid-level user would be shown more information, whereas a person with a high level of interest is shown all the documents. However, it is possible for a beginner to see additional resources from the higher levels if they are so interested.

Let us see a narrative in detail. Since the IPSA collection includes a rich group of illuminated herbals, it was considered very significant to create a narrative on the development of botanical illustrations in Italy from the early centuries of the Middle Ages until the XV century. Therefore, not only can the user follow the history of this particular kind of illustration, but they are also given a quick and simple overview of some of the main medieval periods that are relevant from an art-historical point of view.

Art historians employ a number of methods in their research into the qualities, nature and history of objects. They examine works of art through an analysis of form (i.e. the use of line, shape, color, texture and composition, and iconographic analysis) that takes account of the particular design elements. Art historians are able to assign a date to different works of art by studying their style and making comparisons with other images (frescos, illuminations, jewelry decoration and so on) whose realization time is unknown. For example, if an illumination presents the same stylistic and iconographic feature of the Scrovegni Chapel frescoes in Padua, which were painted by Giotto between 1303 and 1305[4], it can reasonably be assumed that the illumination was painted at the beginning of the XIV century, maybe by a Paduan illuminator or by an illuminator that visited Padua.

Table 1. Catalog information on the IPSA manuscripts used in the study

Call Number	Label	Century	Provenance
Montecassino, Archivio della Badia, Casin. 97	Casin	IX	Montecassino
Firenze, Biblioteca Medicea Lauren-ziana, ms. Plut. 73.41	Plut	IX	Montecassino
Wien, Osterreichische Nationalbiblio-thek, Codex Vindobonensis 93	Vindobonensis	XIII	Southern Italy
Paris, Bibliothèque de l'Ecole des Beaux-Arts, ms. Masson 116	Masson	XIV (1370-1380)	Northern Italy
London, British Library, ms. Egerton 2020	Egerton	XIV (1390-1404)	Padua
Venezia, Biblioteca Nazionale Mar-ciana, Cod.Lat.VI 59	Roccabonella	XV (1445-1448)	Venice
Padova, Biblioteca Orto Botanico, ms Ar. 26 n. 1283	Orto Botanico	XV	Veneto
Bergamo, Biblioteca Civica Angelo Mai, ms MA 592 (già Lambda 1.3)	Guarnerinus	XV (1441)	Feltre

According to this methodology, the IPSA herbal collection can be divided into three main groups of manuscripts that were produced roughly at the same time and that present illuminations with the same stylistic features and sometimes with similar iconographic elements. These three groups constitute three main steps in the development of botanical illustrations: (1) the Montecassino group, which includes very early botanical manuscripts produced in Southern Italy between the VIII and IX centuries [3], (2) the Federico II group, constituted by manuscripts produced at the court of Federico II in Southern Italy during the XIII century, and (3) the Veneto group, which consists of herbals produced in the Veneto region during the XIV and XV centuries and characterized by very realistic images. In Figure 1 the three mains groups of manuscripts are represented in a graph where the vertical axis represents the geographic areas of provenance of the manuscripts, where N stands for North of Italy and

---

[4] http://www.cappelladegliscrovegni.it/index.php/en/

S stands for South of Italy, and the horizontal axis represents the time, from the IX to the XV century.

Once users start to access the narrative, they are shown an introductive page with instructions on how to use the lesson functions. In one lesson they can use the "Lesson Block", which is located on the left hand side of the screen of the IPSA@CULTURA application, to read their tasks and to navigate through the lesson. While in the middle of course, they can move from one page to the next by simply clicking on the "Next" button, or in some cases they can choose between the "Next" button and the "See extra resource related to this one" button to access more detailed information on the issue.

In this narrative lesson, users are firstly shown an illumination of the Rosmarinum plant belonging to a manuscript of the Montecassino group. Then, users can decide whether to view the illumination of another manuscript of this group ("See extra resource related to this"), thus obtaining more knowledge of the manuscript production and botanical illustration of this period, or whether to skip to the second important moment of botanical illustration in Italy, the production of the Federico II manuscripts ("Next").

All the illuminations are accompanied by detailed explanations of the subject of the manuscript they belong to as well as their historical and art-historical context, as can be seen in Figure 2.

The narrative proceeds by guiding users through the centuries until the period of Veneto herbal production, a highly important point in the history of botanical illustration in Italy. In fact, whereas illuminated herbals during the Middle Ages presented very simple and highly schematic illustrations, illuminations of the Veneto herbal group have in common a marked search for realism. The first herbals with highly realistic illustrations of plants were produced in Padua in the XIV century, thanks to the scientific research undertaken in the University of Padua, particularly by Pietro d'Abano. The new scientific studies had a deep influence on the development of contemporary painting, which became increasingly more faithful to nature [4]. Users can verify this sea-change by comparing two illuminations of the rosemary plant and two illuminations of the "Mandragora". The Mandragora is an imaginary plant, thought to be half human and half vegetable. Users are invited to view its different representations to gain a better understanding of how the style developed, as it is easier to verify this evolution by comparing images of the human body rather than images of plants.

4   Thematic Paths Starting from Metadata

Originally the IPSA archive was designed for expert users, scholars and researchers with a particular interest in history of illumination. Users of such a sample typically have a broad knowledge of the archive content and interested scholars usually already have detailed knowledge of the whole collection of images. With the opening of the IPSA collection to the general public, in the context of the CULTURA project, the system needed to be redesigned to fulfill not only professional requirements, but also the needs of the general public. One of the most important aspect which needed improvements to satisfy user requirements is the metadata corpus, and for this reason a challenging task was undertaken on the metadata that describe the collection.

Lesson Block

Rosmarinum chain of derivation

We are now looking at the Rosmarinum catalogue file. This page presents the most common layout of herbals pages: the different names of the plant are presented at the top of the page, and short information about the plant are offered, but the real protagonist is the representation of the plant. In this case, we can appreciate a very high quality representation by a skilful illuminator. For example, look at the leaves, each of them is painted with at least two different shadows of green that suggest the third dimension and the presence of real light.

If you find interesting content in CULTURA, you can always save a reference to the page by clicking the "Bookmark Page" button at the very bottom of the screen. View your saved bookmarks by clicking "My Bookmarks" at the top of the page. Please bookmark this page and then click 'NEXT' to proceed with your tour.

2 of 10

<--PREVIOUS

NEXT-->

See extra resource
related to this one

rosmarinum - rosmarinus officinalis - rosemary, rosmarino, rosmarinum, rosmarinus,

(Previous Illustration) (Next Illustration)

Call Number: Padova, Biblioteca Orto Botanico, ms Ar. 26 n. 1283

Title: De herbarum virtutibus

Author: Pseudo Apuleio

Subject: rosmarinum

Scientific Name: rosmarinus officinalis

Names: rosemary, rosmarino, rosmarinum, rosmarinus,

Technique:

Sheet: 95v

Illuminator:

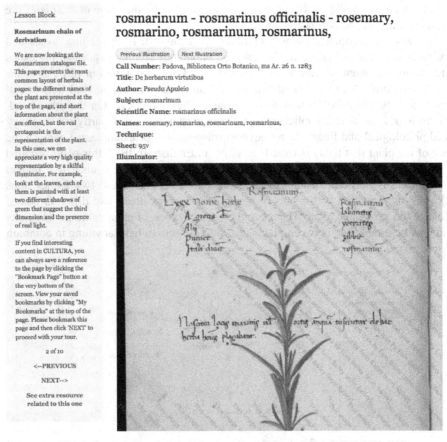

Fig. 2. Screen shot of a step of a narrative lesson in IPSA@CULTURA

IPSA@CULTURA contains nine digitized manuscripts for a total of more than 3000 digital images representing about 1000 different plants, since it is common that the same plant is contained in more than one manuscript. Each manuscript is described by 25 fields which specify physical description of the manuscript (dimension, binding, etc.), historical information (century, dating, provenance, etc.) and side notes (bibliography, observations, etc.). In addition, each image contained in a manuscript has a specific description that consists of 10 fields.

Since IPSA gathers illuminations of botanical manuscripts, the main issue regarding metadata concerns plant names. In medieval times plants did not have a standard classification as they do today, nor had an orthographic standard been established. As a consequence, the very same plant could be called by different names, and at the same time, these names could be written using different orthographic variations. Therefore, normalization of the plant names was critically needed to guarantee a correct and complete functioning of the research tool. In fact, when a user looks for a specific plant, the system should present all the images in the result list which represent that specific plant, and not only those which present the identical written shape of the query.

This outcome is possible only if the metadata that describe the name of the plants are rendered uniform and normalized.

The work of normalization was entrusted to a linguist. Both spelling issues and lexical issues were solved using phonetic and phonology studies, historical linguistics and etymology: what we call today "*camphor*" in English is found in IPSA as "*canfora*", "*camfora*", "*canphora*" and "*camphora*", and there is no explicit link between all these variants, even though they look similar to the human eye. On the other hand, lexical issues are more complicated to solve than spelling issues, partly because they need philological and linguistic research to solve them. For example, we can use the case of the plant that today is called "*alkanet*" in English. In IPSA this plant is called "*buglossa*" in one manuscript and "*lingua bovis*" in another. It is clear that human intervention is needed to establish an explicit link between these two names, thus allowing users to find both plants in a single query since these two different names indicate the very same plant. Thanks to the normalization of plant names, many links can now be established between plants that did not seem to have anything in common before.

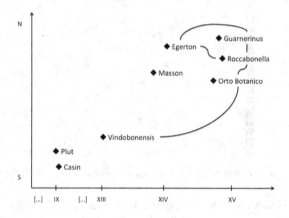

Fig. 3. Graphical representation of possible paths across the collection based on the co-occurrence of illustrations in manuscripts

Additional recommendations can be made, including computing the similarity between manuscripts based on the overlap in their visual content. In fact, it is likely that when one manuscript inspired the development of another, the choice of the plants to be represented was influenced as well. This situation is exemplified by the relation between Egerton and Roccabonella, because the former largely inspired the development of the latter, and in fact two thirds (66%) of the subjects represented in Egerton are also represented in Roccabonella. Another piece of evidence is the relation between Orto Botanico and Vindobonensis. As described in the narrative reported in Section 3, historians of art believe that the former was influenced by previous models developed at the court of Federico II. This result is also reflected by the overlap between the two manuscripts, since all the illustrations of Vindobonensis that are common to at least one other manuscript (one third of the total, about 35%) are also depicted in Orto Botanico.

The analysis of overlapping images also highlights a group of manuscripts that have in common a large number of illustrations: Egerton, Roccabonella, Guarnierinus and Orto Botanico. As can be seen in Figure 1, they share the same provenance and they were created in the same historical period, meaning that automatic analysis can provide relevant hints about the relations between these manuscripts.

Figure 3 shows the presence of possible thematic paths which were computed by starting from metadata content, as an automatic alternative to the narratives provided by scholars.

5   Visual Similarity as Evidence for Alternative Paths

Another kind of analysis can be carried out on image content. Visual descriptors have become a popular tool for content-based information retrieval, in particular in the context of MPEG-7[5]. Although these descriptors were not developed for historical illustrations, they capture some characteristics that can be relevant also from the point of view of an art historian. In particular, according to a joint analysis with an expert in illuminated manuscripts, we selected three of the standard MPEG-7 descriptors:

- *Color Structure Descriptor* (CSD): providing that some normalization is carried out to compensate for the background color of the parchment, this takes into account the color palette used by the illustrator. In particular, the artistic quality of the manuscript and the choice of a realistic representation versus a simplified one are likely to be correlated with the color structure of the illustration.
- *Edge Histogram Descriptor* (EHD): this is correlated with the process of creating illuminations. In fact, depending on stylistic choices, some illustrators decided to highlight the contours with black ink, while others created a pencil sketch and did not delete the pencil drawing after painting. Sometimes, they covered the whole pencil sketch with colors, so we do not have any evidence of the existence of underdrawing. Hence, edges can be of many different types, colors and dimensions.
- *Region Shape Descriptor* (RSD): this is correlated with the choice on how the illustration is integrated with the text of the manuscript. Typically, the illustrations were made after the calligrapher wrote the manuscript, using the available space that was left on the page.

We carried out an initial evaluation of how visual similarity can be correlated with the relations highlighted in the narratives, using the plants that were common to almost all the manuscripts in the collection. To this end we manually cropped the images from the full manuscript pages contained in IPSA and we computed the similarity using the cosine distance between images of the same subject. We then qualitatively analyzed the individual effect of each descriptor.

---

[5] http://mpeg.chiariglione.org/standards/mpeg-7

The relation between Egerton and Roccabonella, which present a high level of stylistic resemblance, is also highlighted by visual descriptors. When an illustration from Roccabonella is used as a query, the corresponding illustration from Egerton had the highest rank for both CSD and EHD, while it was among the first two for RSD. Similarly, also the relation between Vindobonensis and Orto Botanico (described in the previous section) is correlated with their visual similarity: using illustrations from Orto Botanico as queries gave the corresponding illustrations of Vindobonensis at top rank. Using both CSD and EHD the two manuscripts created in Montecassino showed the highest similarity, although this result is not surprising considering that the illustrations in both case are monochromatic. Similarly, the more recent manuscripts in the IPSA collection tended to cluster together, with Guarnierinus very close to Roccabonella and Orto Botanico. This characteristic is particularly evident using RSD.

We think that these initial results can be an interesting starting point for the development of computer-aided narratives. Clearly, the experience of art historians cannot be simulated by the use of these general-purpose descriptors, yet we believe it is interesting that some correlation exists between different sources of evidence. An example of these paths is shown in Figure 4.

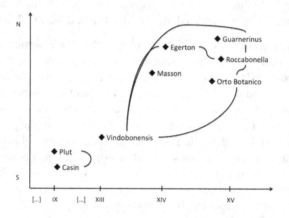

Fig. 4. Graphical representation of possible paths across the collection based on visual similarity

6   Conclusions and Future Work

In this paper we presented different possible approaches for engaging users with a digital collection. On the one hand, the experience of scholars can be used to create narratives through a collection of manuscripts in order to present relevant content to the general public. On the other hand, automatic analysis of metadata, and visual descriptors can be used as an alternative way to recommend new items to end users. In this way, users can access digital cultural heritage both following the paths prepared by experts in the domain and exploring content preselected by automatic methods. As an additional feature, users could be taught not only with the content of the collection but also they would get to know art historian research methodologies, expecially the way they analyze and compare images.

Further experiments are underway to see if some support to narratives can be automatically prepared by using the results of the visual similarity computed on the enriched metadata available in the cultural heritage environment in use in the project.

Acknowledgements. The work reported has been partially supported by the CULTURA project (reference: 269973) within the Seventh Framework Programme of the European Commission.

References

1. Elgammal, E.: Human-centered multimedia: representations and challenges. In: Proc. of the 1st ACM Int. Workshop on Human-Centered Multimedia (HCM 2006), pp. 11–18. ACM, New York (2006)
2. Hampson, C., Lawless, S., Bailey, E., Yogev, S., Zwerdling, N., Carmel, D., Conlan, O., O'Connor, A., Wade, V.: CULTURA: A Metadata-Rich Environment to Support the Enhanced Interrogation of Cultural Collections. In: Dodero, J.M., Palomo-Duarte, M., Karampiperis, P. (eds.) MTSR 2012. CCIS, vol. 343, pp. 227–238. Springer, Heidelberg (2012)
3. Adacher, S.: La trasmissione della cultura medica a Montecassino tra la fine del IX secolo e l'inizio del X secolo. In: Atti del II convegno di studi sul medioevo meridionale. Montecassino. Dalla prima alla seconda distruzione. Momenti e aspetti di storia cassinese (secc. VI-IX), pp. 385–400. Pubblicazioni cassinesi, Montecassino (1987)
4. Mariani Canova, G.: Per Cultura: le immagini dei manoscritti della scienza a Padova dal Medioevo al Rinascimento. Atti e Memorie dell'Accademia Galile-iana di Scienze, Lettere ed Arti, vol. CXXIV, pp. 81–90 (2011-2012)

Modeling and Visualization of Drama Heritage

Vincenzo Lombardo[1] and Antonio Pizzo[2]

[1] University of Torino - Dip. Informatica - CIRMA
{vincenzo.lombardo,antonio.pizzo}@unito.it
[2] University of Torino - Dip. Studi Umanistici - CIRMA

Abstract. This paper presents a multimedia system for the modeling and visualization of drama heritage. The system consists of an ontology based annotation schema for the dramatic metadata of the cultural heritage artifacts (in textual or audiovisual form), a web–based platform for the introduction of the metadata, and a module for the visualization and exploration of such metadata. The system was tested on the cross–media studies of drama.

Keywords: narrative audiovisual, ontological representation, information visualization, film heritage.

1 Introduction

In the last decade, the notion of cultural heritage has been extending from the tangible to the intangible heritage, i.e. heritage that is "not closely linked to the physical consistency" [20]. Often this heritage presents artifacts that are digitized, although there is a general agreement about the lack of resources for "cataloguing" the collections and "make them accessible to the tradition bearers and the general public" [9]. Quite often the focus of cultural heritage cataloguing has been put on the audiovisual resources and the safeguarding activity has been coinciding with the preservation of the physical storage of the data, in both analogical and digital formats. Although there are a number of examples where the physical support (film and tape) has been augmented with metadata in order to preserve/represent information otherwise lost, yet there is not a shared system to represent the symbolic features. On the one hand, the efforts of digitisation of Cultural Heritage are providing common users with access to large amount of materials (see, e.g., Europeana[1]), on the other, the amount of metadata is very restricted, items come with very short descriptions and lack contextual information. Complying with the UNESCO *Convention for the Safeguarding of Intangible Cultural Heritage*, we can stress the "cultural" side, henceforth pointing at the social and symbolic values [16].

There are a number of approaches for enriching cultural heritage items with metadata. Some authors have resorted to Wikipedia, which offers in-depth descriptions and links to related articles, and is thus a natural target for the automatic enrichment of CH items (see, e.g., [1]). Other approaches come from the

---

[1] http://www.europeana.eu/

A. Petrosino, L. Maddalena, P. Pala (Eds.): ICIAP 2013 Workshops, LNCS 8158, pp. 288–297, 2013.
© Springer-Verlag Berlin Heidelberg 2013

field of video indexing, where semantic descriptors are automatically associated with videos. Semantic descriptors have been growing from a few tens of the first TRECVid conferences to a few thousands[2], and individual concepts are connected through the creation of semantic relations and ontological organization: for example, LSCOM is an ontology of concepts targetedly designed for a corpus of broadcast news [13] and the MediaMill dataset relies on a set of 101 semantic descriptors that are best suited for that repository [17]. Finally, a relevant source are the user–generated metadata, such as the tags that are freely inserted by users to annotate the items contained in public repositories. With reference to the audiovisual CH items, [10] report an informal survey carried out on the clips extracted from the feature film from *North by Northwest* (the famous 1959 MGM–Hitchcock's movie), contained in the YouTube repository. The survey reveals that of the 183 unique tags, split manually, into eleven different categories (Title, Actor, Director, Production, Editing, Publish, Genre, Character, Object, Environment, Action), following grounded–theory based analysis [18], only 32 could be interpreted as content metadata (such as, e.g., auction, boulevard), with most tags referring to characters ("Roger", "mother") or their qualities ("blonde", "dress"). The other tags all concern the resource itself (actors, director, ...) and could be retrieved from other sources, such as IMDB.

In this paper we address CH items that have a narrative form, i.e. they tell a story about characters who perform live actions. The fruition of this cultural heritage mostly focuses on *enjoying* the *story* rather than appreciating the aesthetic features, although the latter are appraised by professionals and knowledgeable users. The notion of "story" is widely acknowledged as the construction of an incident sequence [3], that, abstracting from the cinematographic properties, is motivated by the cause–effect chain [15]; this chain results from a complex interplay among agents, events, and environments, well known in playwriting techniques [6]. We propose an annotation relying on user tagging, driven by a narration model that is encoded in an ontology and an access that takes advantage of a visualization tool that reveals interesting properties of the item. Hence, the multimedia application we present is designed to model, annotate, and visualize the dramatic values of the narrative heritage (such as film, video and drama), and provides a cross–media, abstract representation of a narration sequence (a timeline of incidents) and of the complex interplay.

The structure of the paper is the following. In the next section we sketch the CADMOS (Character-based Annotation of Dramatic Media Objects) suite, which, relying on the computational ontology Drammar, provides an interface for annotating the dramatic features of a narrative heritage item and visualizes the structure to the benefit of drama scholars and narration enthusiasts. Then we run a classic example, a scene extracted from Shakespeare's *Hamlet* to illustrate how the CADMOS suite works. Finally, we discuss the contribution of the representation in analyzing the differences between the original Shakespeare's screenplay and Olivier's film adaptation, a topic of much interest for drama scholars. Conclusions end the paper.

---

[2] http://www.lscom.org

2   CADMOS Suite for the Annotation of Metadata

CADMOS suite is a set of applications built around a computational ontology of
the notion of story, called Drammar (see [4] for details). Based on the Drammar
ontology, we have introduced an annotation schema, which is employed for the
construction of a repository of drama items enriched with metadata, and a visualization tool, for the exploration of the metadata in the interest of scholars and
enthusiasts. The Figure 1 illustrates the workflow of the CADMOS suite. Given
an audiovisual item[3] the annotator, being her/him an expert or a visitor, splits
the item into units (CADMOS segmentation phase), and defines a timeline of
incidents as perceived from the movie. Then, he/she annotates the metadata for
each unit, encoding the character's intentional behaviors in terms of goal, plans
and achievement states, also with the support of the information from Shakespeare's text (CADMOS annotation phase). Timeline incidents, actions, goals,
and plans are encoded according to the Drammar ontology. Finally, the encoding is displayed by matching the timeline incidents with the actions and plans
assigned to the characters, to reveal the structure of the story plot (CADMOS
vistool).

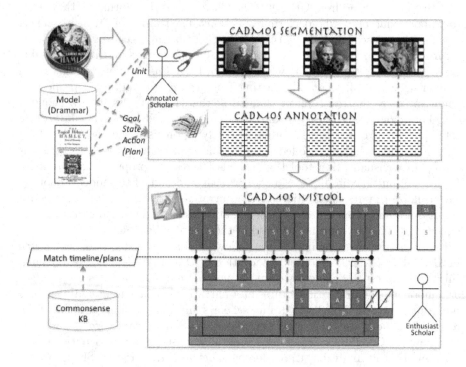

Fig. 1. The CADMOS suite workflow for metadata annotation and exploration

---

[3] In the figure, we have used the CH item *Hamlet*, the film directed by Laurence
Olivier, UK, Two Cities Film production, 1948.

Now we introduce the ontology, the web–based application for annotating the metadata, and eventually the visualization tool.

2.1   Ontology Drammar

The Drammar ontology describes the content and structure of a story in terms of Units (the incidents of a story are grouped in segments), Entities (i.e., Agents, Objects and Environments of the story incidents), and Actions/States (that relate the entities one another). Drammar generalizes over the specific format by which a story is expressed (novel, screenplay, etc.) and the medium through which it is conveyed. Following the paradigm of linked data[8], the ontology refers to external resources for the description of facts that are common to other domains: the large–scale commonsense ontologies SUMO (Suggested Upper Merged Ontology [14]) and YAGO (Yet Another Great Ontology [19]), merged into YAGO–SUMO [5], which provide very detailed information about millions of situations, including entities and process concepts; the lexical resources WordNet [12] and FrameNet [2], providing the means for an annotation interface based on linguistic terms and describing incidents and states through semantic templates expressed in terms of predicates and roles played by the participating elements; design patterns provided by other descriptive ontologies, such as DOLCE [7].

As an example of ontological encoding, we describe the annotation of a story incident (see Figure 2), driven by the Time Indexed Situation design pattern. This incident is extracted from the "nunnery scene" in the Third Act of Shakespeare's *Hamlet*. In this scene, Ophelia is sent to Hamlet by Polonius and Claudius to confirm the assumption that his madness is caused by his rejected love. According to the two conspirers, Ophelia should induce him to talk about his inner feelings. The girl is ready to return the love gift received by the prince, and hence hopes to induce him to confess his love and his suffering. Figure 2 shows the representation of the incident in which Ophelia is returning the gift to Hamlet.

The whole story is a sequence of incidents arranged on a timeline. Incidents are motivated by the achievement of agents' goal that are functional to the story advancement. Each agent features a library of plans that link the agents' goals with the actions they are committed to for the achievement of their goals. Actions then become actual incidents on the timeline, though some remain unrealized in favor of the realization of other agents' plans, who act in conflict with them. The plan structure is the following:

$P[Goal] = PreConditions(A) \ A \ Effects(A)$

$P[Goal] = +_{i=1}^{M} PreConditions(P) \ P_i \ Effects(P)$

A base plan for the achievement of some goal consists of an action A and its Precondition and Effect states, respectively. States are ontological structures similar to processes (see Figure 2). A generic plans is then recursively defined as a sequence of (sub)plans, with Precondition and Effect states again (+ is the concatenation operator). Preconditions can be mental states, i.e. goals (G) and beliefs (B), and states of affairs in the story world (SOA). A base plan annotated for the agent Ophelia in the previous example is the following:

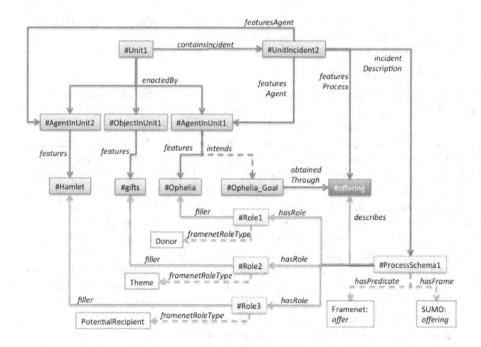

Fig. 2. The annotation of the incident where Ophelia offers the gift back to Hamlet, with instances (#) of Unit (#Unit1), Agent (#Hamlet, #Ophelia), and Object #gift). The action/process #offering (a SUMO concept) is connected to the role fillers (Framenet frame *offer*): #Ophelia is the *Donor*, #Hamlet the *PotentialRecipient*, gift the *Theme*.

$$P_{b1}^{Ophelia}[G : Ophelia\ wants\ Ophelia\ interact\ with(Hamlet)] =$$

SOA : *Ophelia neglected*
A : *Ophelia returning gift to(Hamlet)*
SOA : *Hamlet have gift*

   In this example, Ophelia, convinced by Claudius and Polonius, tries to induce Hamlet to reveal his deeper feelings. She use the gift once received as love signs as a means to provoke the prince. Thus, the action of returning gift is motivated by Ophelia's goal of having an interaction with Hamlet and because of the preconditional state of affairs that she is neglected; the effect should be that Hamlet is in possess of the gift (but this state will remain unrealized).

2.2   CADMOS Annotation and Mapping

Within the CADMOS project we have developed a web based interface and annotation tool (see Figure 3), that was designed to carry out the annotation without the load of formality on the annotator. The annotation process starts by identifying the meaningful units of the item, by marking its boundaries through a video player interface (Figure 3, above right); then, selecting the appropriate tabs, the annotator introduces the metadata for the story entities (agents, objects, environments); finally, the annotator retrieves the incident templates (a similar template concerns actions, events, and states), with roles that are filled with the story elements (the M–e–s tab concerns the mise–en–scène properties of the scene, i.e. camera movements, camera angle, type of shot, staging of actors). The annotation of actions also include their motivations, namely goals and plans, with precondition and effect states. The appropriate metadata are identified through natural language words that are used to retrieve the formal terms in the lexical and commonsense knowledge ontologies.

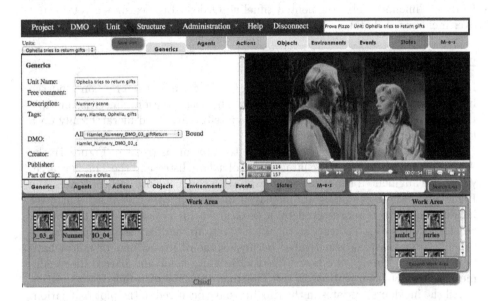

Fig. 3. The Cadmos Web Application for the segmentation and the annotation phases

The mapping of plan actions over timeline incidents is useful to visualize the motivations underlying agents' actions. First, we analyze the plans, and discover the actions that match (i.e., motivate) the incidents of the timeline; then, we point out successes and failures of characters' behaviors, i.e. we evaluate what plans can be fully realized or what plans fail; finally, we project the states required by the plan, as preconditions or effects of the plan actions, onto the timeline incidents.

This mapping is realized in the ontology by 1) modeling the timeline and the plans as sketched above, 2) defining the incident mapping through SWRL (Semantic Web Rule Language) IF–THEN rules, and 3) augment the timeline with states through an off–line algorithm. Both Timeline and Plan classes modeling relies on the generic class *OrderedList*, that represents the incidents' positions. An instance of Process or State refers to some position (relation *refersToTimeline*) in the Timeline or in a Plan, respectively. Based on the representation above, the reasoner infers that some ordered list of incidents in the timeline belongs to some plan. The reasoner works with inferences of an ontological nature and with a SWRL rule that validates the mapping of some incident to some plan action. Finally, the timeline of the incidents is augmented through an off–line algorithm that takes as inputs the timeline, the plans, and the incident mapping, and returns as output an OrderedList named Augmented Timeline that contains the incidents of the Timeline, in the same partial order as in the Timeline, interspersed with states (agglomerated into story world states) as projected from the plans. So, if a state S is a precondition of the action A in the plan P, and the action A is mapped the incident I in the Timeline, then a state S', that is the same as S is inserted in the Timeline before I (and after the incident preceding I in the Timeline). The augmented timeline OrderedList features a total order over incidents and states.

2.3   CADMOS Visualization Tool

In this section we describe the design, both interface and interaction, and the implementation of the visualization tool. The visualization concerns multiple trees of characters' intentions (or plans), possibly arranged hierarchically on a tree that spans a timeline of events.

The whole visualization space is split into three areas (refer to Figure 4): the Agents area (top), where the characters involved are listed and the Timeline area, where the augmented timeline is displayed with the incidents and the states, the Plans area, where the plans are displayed in hierarchical order. Each narrative incident or state is represented by a box (green for actions, yeller for events, red for states). White boxes in the Plans area are actions not mapped in the timeline, but the plan is activated because some of it's actions or states have been mapped. Finally, the boxes filled with white color and barred diagonally means have not been realized in the Timeline, thus the plan failed.

All the incidents or states in the timeline have occurred in the plot realization. The timeline incidents pivot the horizontal alignment: each realized plan action is aligned with the matching timeline incident; at the same time states of the plans are projected onto the timeline to represent the story world state between adjacent units. The incidents that occur in a unit are considered in parallel, though we decided to assign them an individual position to allow for a visible alignment with the plan action. The plan label is an horizontal box that spans all the states and actions that belong to it.

In figure 4 there is the visualization of the excerpt of "nunnery scene" described above. As an example of mapping, consider the actional incident I_OLI_0016 ("Ophelia returning gift to(Hamlet)"), mapped onto the plan action A_0005 ("Ophelia returning gift to(Hamlet)"). A plan participates to the mapping and the augmentation of a timeline when the order of the incidents on the timeline respects the order of the mapped actions in the plan. In our example, since we have the mapping I_OLI_0016–A_0005, and the subsequent mapping I_OLI_0017 (Hamlet denying gift)–A_1112(Hamlet refuse gift), the plan $P\_P\_0003^{Ophelia}$ can participate to mapping (notice that the last part of the plan

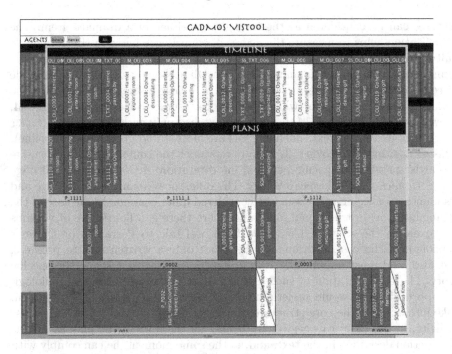

Fig. 4. Augmenting timeline with states projected from plans, with an enlargement in the middle area

is not mapped then). If the sequence of incidents does not respect the order exhibited by the mapping actions in some plan, that plan is not activated for contribution to mapping.

We augment the timeline with the states that hold between adjacent incidents on the timeline. States are taken from the preconditions and effects that are associated with the actions in the plans. So, in the case of A_0005 ("Ophelia returning gift to(Hamlet)"), we will have $SOA : Ophelia\ neglected$ as precondition, and $SOA : Hamlet\ have\ gift$ as effect.

3 Discussion and Conclusion

In order to validate our approach, we tested the differences between the original text and one specific mise-en-scène, a much appreciated topic for drama scholars. The matching of the plans over the augmented timeline shows the relation between the description of the agents' behaviors and intentions, as implied by the text *Hamlet* and the factual representation of those behaviors in the mise-en-scène (i.e. the actors' displayed actions). The latter can be considered a sort of translation that converts the information provided by the written text into the performance, transcoding the "dramatic text" into the "performance text" [11]. In a drama, the most important aspects of the translation are the dramatic features of the text (e.g. characters, intentions, conflicts, emotions). These features can be considered as the intangible heritage of a dramatic item. The visualization helps to measure the degree of equivalence between this intangible cultural heritage and a specific form of representation. In our example, the beginning of the so called "nunnery scene" in Olivier's movie shows a high grade of conformity with the drama, albeit there is a clear discrepancy regarding the Hamlet's plan P_1111_1 for which we have to resume to the text, I_TXT_0004, as well as in the plan P_1114 that can be matched only with I_TXT_0017 (I_TXT are facts stated in the text timeline; I_OLI are facts stated in the movie timeline). This means that the movie fails to fully represent the content of the drama, i.e. the artist provides a specific personal interpretation of the intangible heritage called *Hamlet*, the Shakespeare's play. The differences among such heritage and its numerous mise-en-scène's can be considered quite common in the case of the intangibility, as in traditional folk fable where there is a flourishing of versions (for example the story of *Cinderella* from oral tale to Perrault's or Disney's versions). In the case of drama, we have not only a written text to preserve, but also, and most importantly, the dramatic features that shape the specific story. The representation of such features must go beyond the mere philological approach (that would undermine the quality of the performance), and can take into account the core structure of the heritage. In other words, the artist (Olivier, in our case) can neglect to display all the lines of the play as well as each action described in the text, and, in the same moment, he can comply with the drama. For example, Olivier's rendering of Hamlet's character seems to add actions that weren't clearly stated in the text (the white boxes in the timeline representation - Figure 4), but nevertheless they fulfill the plan as devised in the original behaviors in the play.

In this paper, we have presented a tool for acquiring the metadata of intangible cultural heritage, specifically drama heritage. Our proposal relies on a computational ontology that encodes the major facts about drama and provides a web-based application for annotators to contribute. After computed the mapping between the agents' intentions and the actions they carry out, the alignment is displayed through a visualization tool for study and access purposes. The approach has been tested on a study of the text/mise-en-scène differences on Hamlet's nunnery scene.

References

1. Agirre, E., Barrena, A., de Lacalle, O.L., Soroa, A., Fernando, S., Stevenson, M.: Matching cultural heritage items to wikipedia. In: Calzolari, N., Choukri, K., Declerck, T., Doğan, M.U., Maegaard, B., Mariani, J., Odijk, J., Piperidis, S. (eds.) Proceedings of the Eight International Conference on Language Resources and Evaluation (LREC 2012). European Language Resources Association (ELRA), Istanbul (2012)
2. Baker, C., Fillmore, C., Lowe, J.: The berkeley framenet project. In: Proceedings of the 36th Annual Meeting of the Association for Computational Linguistics and 17th International Conference on Computational Linguistics, vol. 1, pp. 86–90. Association for Computational Linguistics (1998)

3. Bordwell, D., Thompson, K.: Film art: An introduction. McGraw Hill, Boston (2006)
4. Cataldi, M., Damiano, R., Lombardo, V., Pizzo, A., Sergi, D.: Integrating commonsense knowledge into the semantic annotation of narrative media objects. In: Pirrone, R., Sorbello, F. (eds.) AI*IA 2011. LNCS, vol. 6934, pp. 312–323. Springer, Heidelberg (2011)
5. De Melo, G., Suchanek, F., Pease, A.: Integrating yago into the suggested upper merged ontology. In: 20th IEEE International Conference on Tools with Artificial Intelligence, ICTAI 2008, vol. 1, pp. 190–193. IEEE (2008)
6. Egri, L.: The Art of Dramatic Writing. Simon and Schuster, New York (1946)
7. Gangemi, A., Presutti, V.: Ontology design patterns. In: Handbook on Ontologies, pp. 221–243 (2009)
8. Heath, T., Bizer, C.: Linked data: Evolving the web into a global data space. Synthesis Lectures on the Semantic Web: Theory and Technology, pp. 1–136 (2011)
9. Kurin, R.: Safeguarding intangible cultural heritage in the 2003 UNESCO convention: A critical appraisal. Museum International 56(1/2), 66–77 (2004)
10. Lombardo, V., Damiano, R.: Commonsense knowledge for the collection of ground truth data on semantic descriptors. In: Proceedings of the 2012 IEEE International Symposium on Multimedia (ISM 2012), pp. 78–83. IEEE Computer Society (2012)
11. Marinis, M.D.: The Semiotics of Performance. Indiana University Press (1993)
12. Miller, G.: Wordnet: a lexical database for english. Communications of the ACM 38(11), 39–41 (1995)
13. Naphade, M., Smith, J.R., Tesic, J., Chang, S.F., Hsu, W., Kennedy, L., Hauptmann, A., Curtis, J.: Large-scale concept ontology for multimedia. IEEE MultiMedia 13, 86–91 (2006)
14. Pease, A., Niles, I., Li, J.: The suggested upper merged ontology: A large ontology for the semantic web and its applications. In: Working Notes of the AAAI-2002 Workshop on Ontologies and the Semantic Web (2002)
15. Rimmon-Kenan, S.: Narrative Fiction: Contemporary Poetics. Routledge (1983)
16. Smith, L., Akagawa, N.: Intangible Heritage. Key Issues in Cultural Heritage. Taylor & Francis (2008), http://books.google.it/books?id=voanOESUzgAC
17. Snoek, C.G., Worring, M., van Gemert, J.C., Geusebroek, J.M., Smeulders, A.W.: The challenge problem for automated detection of 101 semantic concepts in multimedia. In: Proceedings of ACM Multimedia, Santa Barbara, USA, pp. 421–430 (October 2006)
18. Strauss, A., Corbin, J.: Basics of qualitative research: grounded theory procedures and techniques. Sage Publications, Newbury Park (1990)
19. Suchanek, F., Kasneci, G., Weikum, G.: Yago: a core of semantic knowledge. In: Proceedings of the 16th International Conference on World Wide Web, pp. 697–706. ACM (2007)
20. Vecco, M.: A definition of cultural heritage: From the tangible to the intangible. Journal of Cultural Heritage 11(3), 321–324 (2010), http://www.sciencedirect.com/science/article/pii/S1296207410000361

An Intellectual Journey in History: Preserving Indian Cultural Heritage

Anupama Mallik[1], Santanu Chaudhury[1], T.B. Dinesh[2], and Chaluvaraju[3]

[1] Indian Institute of Technology, Delhi
{ansimal,chaluvaraju.hampi}@gmail.com, santanuc@ee.iitd.ac.in
[2] International Institute for Art, Culture and Democracy, Bengaluru, India
dinesh@iiacd.org
[3] Kannada University, Hampi, India

Abstract. Heritage preservation requires preserving the tangibles (monuments, sculpture, coinage, etc) and the intangibles (history, traditions, stories, dance, etc). Besides these artefacts, there is a huge amount of background knowledge that correlates all these resources and establishes their context. In this work, we present a new paradigm for heritage preservation – 'an Intellectual Journey into the past', which is more advanced than physical explorations of heritage sites and virtual explorations of monuments and museums. This paradigm proposes an experiential expedition into a historical era by using an ontology to inter-link the digital heritage artefacts with their background knowledge. A multimedia ontology encoded in the Multimedia Web Ontology Language (MOWL) is used to illustrate this paradigm by correlating the digital artefacts with their history as well their living context in today's world. The user experience of this paradigm involves a virtual traversal of a heritage site, with an ontology guided navigation through space and time and a dynamic display of different kinds of media.

1 Introduction

Heritage is not just an accumulation of tangible artefacts and intangible knowledge, preserved by presenting these resources to people to view, explore and analyse. To understand heritage, one must take a journey down several paths in history and experience the various events in their historical and cultural context. This journey can be carried out in space and time with the help of technology. It can be augmented by intellectual inputs from a collection of beliefs, customs and knowledge, and audio-visual inputs of digitized resources, placed in context and correlated by an ontology. In this work[1], we propose a new research paradigm in the domain of cultural heritage preservation, which entails an intellectual journey of an era, allowing a person to explore a heritage site virtually and experience the heritage in its past and current context.

---

[1] This research work has been funded by the heritage project entitled "Managing Intangible Cultural Assets through Ontological Interlinking" of the Department of Science and Technology of the Government of India.

A. Petrosino, L. Maddalena, P. Pala (Eds.): ICIAP 2013 Workshops, LNCS 8158, pp. 298–307, 2013.

While exploring a heritage site, what if one has immediate access to all the information about every monument, sculpture, art or mural painting that one looks at; information which is audio-visual and dynamic. Imagine being able to view the video of a dance performance portraying the dance posture depicted in a sculpture, or read the text of a narrative portrayed in a mural painting on a temple ceiling; or compare with images of other mural paintings at other sites, depicting the same narrative. What if besides hearing a recorded history of a monument on an audio-guide, one could watch videos of rituals which take place at the same site in current times, as well as hear recordings of different views given by various experts. This kind of experiential exploration is proposed in our paradigm which we illustrate with the help of an interactive user interface described in this paper. The *intellectual journey* that we propose here, is much more informative and advanced than physical exploration of heritage sites or the walk-throughs and virtual tours currently offered by online museums and websites [2],[6]. Other related works in cultural heritage preservation like [5] make use of augmented and virtual reality, but fail to present artefacts in context with background knowledge. A similar ontology-based framework for the digital exploration of cultural heritage objects has been used in [1], but authors have not looked at traversal over time possible through correlation of classical and historical narratives with living traditions and folk-lore.

The rest of the paper is organized as follows: Section 2 discusses *Intellectual Journey* paradigm, and details the architecture of the ontology based framework. In section 3, we discuss the advantage of using a MOWL encoded multimedia ontology in a heritage domain. Section 4 details the ontology-based annotation of the digital artefacts which is required for providing their semantic inter-linkages. Section 5 gives an overview of the ontology based interlinking of digital artefacts. In section 6 we illustrate our paradigm and framework with a web-based application in the domain of Indian Heritage. In section 7, we conclude our findings and discuss future work.

2 Architecture of Ontology Based Intellectual Journey

In this section, we discuss the proposed ontology-based heritage preservation scheme, offering an *Intellectual journey into history*, which correlates and presents various aspects of cultural heritage linked with the user context. Figure 1b shows the space and time traversal of heritage resources, offered by our ontology-based framework. The tangibles and intangibles in cultural heritage can belong to different eras, but can broadly be classified into belonging to the *Present* and *Past* times. Digital archiving of the various artefacts is done in different ways and the outputs are multimedia collections in different modalities, with different modes of perusal, as shown here:

1. Visualization of present day tangibles - monuments, coins, sculpture, inscriptions as they exist today.

2. Digitization of present day intangibles - recording of live events like festivals, craft traditions, dance and music, as they happen in current times.

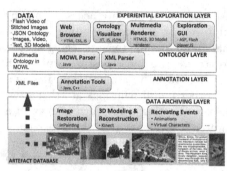 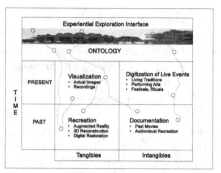

(a) Software Architecture   (b) Space-Time Exploration

Fig. 1. Ontology-based *Intellectual journey* paradigm

3. Recreation of the tangibles, as they existed in the past. This utilises techniques such as 3D modelling, augmented reality, visual reconstruction and image restoration for reconstructing the tangibles as they were, before their temporal degeneration.

4. Documentation of the intangibles. This involves documenting events of the past by collecting facts from recorded history like scriptures, and through making of historical movies, documentaries, etc. that recreate the images and events of an era.

Figure 1a shows the software architecture of the framework that offers the intellectual exploration experience using an ontology. The different layers in this architecture are:

Digital Archiving Layer: This layer consists of all the technical modules for capturing and recreating the digital artefacts. The output of this layer are digital collections of the artefacts of different modalities, i.e. image, text, 3D, video and audio collections.

Annotation Layer: It consists of annotation tools required for annotating and labelling the documents in artefact collections. This step assumes that a multimedia ontology for the domain has been acquired and semantic labels associated with domain concepts in the ontology are available for labelling the artefacts. Depending on the type of document (image, audio, video, text), different tools are required to identify artefacts within that document, For e.g. image cropping, selection, demarcating video segments, identifying individual video frames, etc. Semantic annotation involves labelling each artefact with one or more ontology concepts. This layer produces an MPEG-7 based XML file per document in the collections, with annotations for multiple artefacts in the document.

Ontology Layer: This layer consists of the language parsers - for the ontology as well as for the XML files. The ontology is parsed and web-compatible visualization graph is produced. The XML files are parsed to produce sets/chains of artefacts which are linked through common ontology concepts. Thus the ontology not only correlates the concepts through domain knowledge, it also produces data linkages which serve the purpose of an ontology-based exploration and cross-modal access of media.

Experiential Exploration Layer: This layer is composed of web-based graphic user interfaces for exploring a heritage site, for ontology visualization and for presenting or rendering the digital artefacts. The user interfaces with this layer to carry out an *Intellectual Journey* as proposed by our paradigm.

2.1 Space and Time Traversal

The Experiential exploration interface allows a complete space traversal of a heritage site, with entry points leading to the interior of different monuments, and option to exit and return to a central location, as desired by the user. Thus the user can move along several *spatial* paths in the site, as per her choice. This space traversal is augmented by a time-traversal in history, with the help of an interactive interface. *Clickable icons* placed on tangible artefacts visible in the structure, allow the user to access digital media related to the artefact. This access occurs through data linkages provided by an underlying ontology. The user-click maps to a concept node in the ontology graph. The XML files with artefact annotations are searched to produce the set of digital artefacts which have their semantic annotation matching this concept. The various image, video, 3D and text rendering modules are triggered to present these artefacts as a correlated set to the user as part of the exploration interface. Besides the space and time traversal in the heritage experience, our system also enables a perusal of the heritage resources *on demand* by the user, through interactions with the ontology, which allow selection of concepts and/or their relations and attributes.

A user of this system can explore a heritage site virtually, recreated using actual site images. Here are two examples of the different paths she can take in space and time with ontology-guided navigation. **Path1:** User clicks on a temple icon on screen. It maps to a concept in the ontology. XML annotation files are searched for annotations pertaining to this concept. This search produces a set of images of the temple as it exists now, a text detailing its history and a video of a tour of its premises, and a 3D model of the temple as it was built originally. These are presented to the user. **Path2:** User views the video of a weekly market or Bazaar (*present intangible*) as it happens at a temple site today. Then she selects a time-period (15th century) in history through the ontology. The system retrieves an animation movie (*past intangible*) which recreates the Bazaar as it used to happen in the 15th century in that temple. Figure 1b shows these paths as threads.

3 Multimedia Ontology and Its Representation

An ontology encoded in a traditional ontology language, e.g. OWL, uses text to express the domain concepts and their properties, and thus can be used for semantic text processing. Semantic processing of multimedia data, however, calls for ontology primitives that enable modeling of domain concepts with their observable media properties. This kind of modeling is called **Perceptual Modeling**, which needs to encode the inherent uncertainties associated with media properties of concepts as well. Traditional ontology languages do not support these capabilities. We have used the Multimedia Web Ontology Language (MOWL) [4] for representing the multimedia ontology used in our heritage experiments. In [7], authors had proposed an ontology-based scheme based on MOWL, for preserving the intangible heritage of Indian classical dance. Techniques of annotation and concept recognition detailed in [7] have been reused here, but the interlinking of heritage artefacts across media formats using MPEG-7 based metadata, and the experiential exploration and browsing interface for historical narratives is a novel paradigm that we have introduced in this paper.

A multimedia ontology helps encode media properties of the semantic concepts. For our illustration, we have used a MOWL encoded Indian heritage ontology to associate media properties of the multimedia segments with ontology concepts. As MOWL representation allows collection-independent modelling of the domain, different kinds of media - images, text, video and audio can also be associated with the concepts, which aid in perceptual modelling of the concepts. This also helps in building semantic conceptual linkages between different modalities, and can be used to provide inter-linking of the digital artefacts which are part of the heritage collection.

4   Artefact Annotation

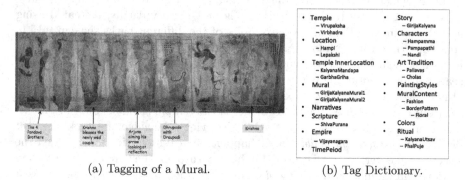

(a) Tagging of a Mural.   (b) Tag Dictionary.

Fig. 2. Annotation of `GirijaKalyanaMural`

Domain knowledge derived from experts and other sources, is used to create a *tag dictionary* which contains different tags that can be used for labelling different aspects of the artefacts. A sample of such a tag dictionary is shown in figure 2b. Typically the tag dictionary contains abstract domain concepts, some of which for a heritage domain are story, narrative, scripture, characters, rituals, location, temple, time period, technique, artistic style, color, etc. The tag dictionary when used for actual tagging of the artefacts, contains the data instances of these concepts - i.e. names of the characters, temples, rituals, scriptures, patterns, art style, colors used, etc.

An ontology expert analyses the tag dictionary, and generates an ontology of the domain. The ontology is enriched with media data from the collections as media segments are associated with appropriate semantic concepts in the ontology. This process is semi-automated, as it utilises machine learning of the associations between media content and semantic concepts, to generate automatic labels for media segments, but needs to be curated by a domain expert. Using the *tag dictionary*, the domain experts also provide tags and labels for different segments of the heritage collection. The digital artefacts belong to different media collections of text, audio, images and videos. The tag dictionary is used as the basis for providing tags for image segments, video shots, audio tracks and text segments in the digital collection. An example of tagging of a mural painting is shown in figure 2a. Different annotation tools used for tagging of different kinds of media, produce XML annotation files in a standard format which is based on MPEG-7 based media descriptions.

5   Ontology Based Interlinking of Digital Artefacts

In this section, we show how the multimedia ontology, by its collection-independent modelling of the domain, provides a robust basis for a semantic inter-linking of the digital artefacts collected in repositories stored in different media formats. XML files produced from the annotation of artefacts contain semantic labels linked with media segment descriptions. Thus media segments with same conceptual labels can be hyper-linked for access as required in retrieval through textual search queries or through a graphic user interface which provides an image or icon to click for retrieval of associated multimedia documents. The algorithm which shows how retrieval of media from different media collections is made possible through ontology-based interlinking is shown in algorithm 1.

Algorithm 1. MM Retrieval through ontology-based interlinking

---

Inputs: a) Search term set $\mathcal{T}$ or clicked image $\mathcal{K}$. b) Bayesian Network Ω of the relevant MOWL ontology segment. c) Set $\mathcal{X}$ of MPEG-7 compatible XML files.

Output: Concept $\mathcal{C}$ and associated set $\mathcal{I}, \mathcal{V}, \mathcal{T}$ of images, videos and text

1: Look up the mapping table which contains the mapping $\mathcal{K}, \mathcal{C}$ to get the concept $\mathcal{C}$ for image $\mathcal{K}$, and go to step 4.
2: Instantiate the leaf nodes in Ω, which match the search terms in $\mathcal{T}$.
3: Carry out Belief Propagation in the BN Ω.
4: Obtain set of concepts which have posterior probability $P(\mathcal{C}_i) >$ threshold. $\mathcal{C}$ is the concept with highest posterior.
5: **for** $i = 1$ to $|\mathcal{X}_r|$ **do**
6:     Search for the media segment descriptions with $\mathcal{C}$ as label.
7:     Add the corresponding media segment to set $\mathcal{I}, \mathcal{V}$ or $\mathcal{T}$ depending upon its media type
8: **end for**
9: Return the set $\mathcal{I}, \mathcal{V}, \mathcal{T}$

---

6 Intellectual Journey in Indian Heritage Domain

To demonstrate the Intellectual Journey paradigm, using our ontology-based framework, we have chosen the Indian heritage domain related to the UNESCO World heritage site of Hampi, in Karnataka, India. The framework is generic and extensible to preserve any heritage site in the world for which background knowledge and heritage resources are available. Hampi site comprises of the ruins of Vijayanagara city, former capital of the powerful Vijayanagara Empire, which flourished in South India during 14th to 17th century. Several dynasties which ruled during this period, patronised art and culture, built several new temples and renovated and enlarged many old ones. Festivals and rituals involving community participation were encouraged, and in fact still take place at the site.

We further focus on the **theme of** GirijaKalyana from our knowledge-base of the Hampi heritage. GirijaKalyana refers to the marriage between goddess Hampamma (also known as Uma, Parvati or Shakti) and male Hindu god Pampapathi (also known as Shiva, Shankara or Rudra). The concept manifests in both tangible and intangibles of Hampi as well as some other Vijayanagara sites like Lepakshi in Andhra Pardesh, India. The tangible manifestations include mural paintings depicting the marriage on the walls of ancient temples in Hampi and Lepakshi; sculptures and bronzes characters in the story, found in temples and museums, and so on. There is a story attached to the concept, text of which is found in certain ancient scriptures like the ShivaPurana. Certain aspects of this mythological story are also found in narratives in old inscriptions, memorial stones and manuscripts. Narratives of some performing arts like folk dance, theatre and puppetry in areas around Hampi and Lepakshi abound in references to the marriage of Shiva and Parvati.

GirijaKalyana context has a living heritage. Every year the marriage is celebrated in the ancient temple of Hampi. Communities from nearby areas congregate to attend the two famous rituals of KalyanaUtsava (the wedding), preceeded by Phalpuje (the engagement). Priests actually conduct a wedding of the deities in the temple, and people make offerings to please the Gods. Traditional crafts like making puppets, toys, wooden door-frames and wall-paintings are still

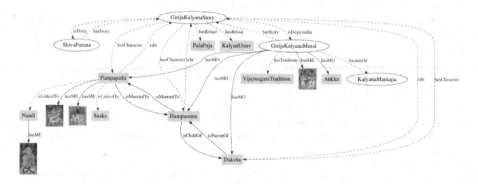

Fig. 3. Indian heritage ontology snippet with focus on GirijaKalyana concept

being practised in locations around Hampi. Many of these replicate images and patterns from the `Girijakalyana` concept. It is a fashion in local communities to get *tattos* depicting some `GirijaKalyana` patterns drawn on their person.

6.1 Resource Compilation

For our demo, we collected digitized versions of the tangible artefacts such as mural paintings, sculptures, crafts and manuscripts, related to `GirijaKalyana`, as well as audio-visual recordings of the intangibles such as the story, craft traditions, rituals and folk narratives. After segmenting, labelling and tagging of the images, there were 654 image segments. The other repository is of 126 stories from Indian mythology and folk-lore, with 3 different versions of each story on an average. The text segments after labelling and tagging for different characters, episodes, locations, etc. are approximately 1000. Our cultural teams were able to collect about 12 hours of video recordings of the various site visits, ritual celebrations and craft traditions. These media files were segmented into 95 video shots of varying length, which were then tagged and annotated with domain concepts in the ontology, as detailed in section 4.

Background knowledge about the concept was provided to the ontology expert by our group of domain experts – mainly art and cultural historians who specialise in the study of the Vijayanagara empire with a focus on the Hampi world heritage. We also collected facts and resources from books [8] written about Hampi and its art and archaeology. This knowledge along with the tag dictionary was then used in creating the Indian heritage ontology, which has approximately 156 concepts, 83 of which have media examples and patterns associated with them. Our cultural and ontology teams undertook 3 months of discussion, validations and corrections to produce the final version of the ontology, and 4 months to label and tag the artefacts with the semantic concepts. Part of annotation was semi-automatic as discussed in section 4, which was then curated by the experts.

A multimedia ontology snippet of the `GirijaKalyana` context, after its creation from the tag-dictionary in figure 2b, is shown in the figure 3. We focus on the `GirijaKalyanaStory` with characters `Hampamma` and `Pampapathi`, with its depictions in mural paintings, rituals and current traditions. A Mural painting depicting the `GirijaKalyanaStory` also has some other content besides the depiction of the story or narrative, like floral or geometric patterns, some fashion patterns like hair-styles and jewellery.

6.2 Experiential Exploration Interface

Once the annotated repositories are available, and the multimedia ontology has been generated, we allow the user to virtually explore a heritage site, using an interactive graphic user interface, which has an ontology-guided navigation and a dynamic display of associated digital artefacts. This is an intellectual journey around the `GirijaKalyana` manifestation in Hampi heritage. User experience of this journey involves a traversal of the stitched image sequence of the Hampi

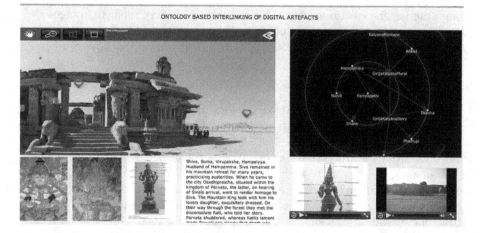

Fig. 4. Screen shot with `Pampapathi` concept selected

heritage site with a window view of the related ontology snippet as a frame of reference. Navigation is ontology guided where socio-cultural context of the frame is portrayed through a dynamic display of media and narratives.

Figures 4 is a screen shot of our GUI, which has a main pane, showing a 360 degree photo-realistic stereo view of the heritage site, created by stitching of actual images of the site. The user is allowed to explore the site virtually, with intelligent interactions, using mouse buttons to move left, right and other navigation controls for zooming and auto-rotating. The right pane shows an animated graphic view of the ontology, with a node in the center, which reflects the current context of the user selection. This visualization of the ontology graph is created by using the *weighted graph* animation tools of the Javascript Infovis Toolkit [3], with a JSON structure of the ontology. The frames at the bottom display images, text and videos associated with the concept node at the center of the ontology. If another concept node is selected by clicking on it in the ontology pane, the visualization perspective changes to center this node.

While moving around virtually, the user has an option to click on certain visual cues in order to alter a visual display of image, text and videos of the artefacts as well as change the perspective of the ontology visualization shown in a parallel window on screen. As the user context changes dynamically, so does the display of artefacts and the view of the ontology. User also has an option to navigate to a chosen concept in the ontology window by clicking on it. This too alters the set of artefacts displayed on screen. User evaluation of this interface is planned in near future and is not part of this work.

7   Conclusion

Physical or virtual tours of heritage sites need to be augmented with readily available contextual information to the tourist. Mere perusal of audio guides and visual cues is not sufficient to completely satisfy the information need. In this paper, we have proposed a new paradigm for a exploring heritage. The proposed paradigm offers an *Intellectual journey* into a heritage site, with readily available tools to traverse in space and time and access e-Heritage artefacts in context and on demand. We have illustrated this paradigm with a graphic user interface which offers ontology-guided navigation and dynamic display of artefacts in context of the theme of `GirijaKalyana` related to the World heritage site of `Hampi` in India. Such an ontology-based framework can easily be extended to offer cross-modal access to heritage resources preserved in different digital media formats.

References

1. Aliaga, D.G., Bertino, E., Valtolina, S.: Decho - a framework for the digital exploration of cultural heritage objects. J. Comput. Cult. Herit. 3, 12:1–12:26 (2011), http://doi.acm.org/10.1145/1921614.1921619
2. ASI-India: Archaeological survey of india – home, http://www.asi.nic.in/index.asp
3. Belmonte, N.G.: Javascript infovis toolkit, http://philogb.github.io/jit/index.html
4. Ghosh, H., Chaudhury, S., Kashyap, K., Maiti, B.: Ontology Specification and Integration for Multimedia Applications. In: Ontologies: A Handbok of Principles, Concepts, and Applications in Information Systems. Springer (2007)
5. Ikeuchi, K., Oishi, T., Kagesawa, M., Banno, A., Kawakami, R., Kakuta, T., Okamoto, Y., Lu, B.V.: Outdoor gallery and its photometric issues. In: Proceedings of the 9th ACM SIGGRAPH Conference on Virtual-Reality Continuum and its Applications in Industry, VRCAI 2010, pp. 361–364. ACM, New York (2010), http://doi.acm.org/10.1145/1900179.1900254
6. Louvre: Museum website, http://www.louvre.fr/llv/commun/home.jsp?bmLocale=en
7. Mallik, A., Chaudhury, S., Ghosh, H.: Nrityakosha: Preserving the intangible heritage of indian classical dance. JOCCH 4(3), 11 (2011)
8. Verghese, A., Dallapiccola, A.L. (eds.): South India under Vijayanagara: Art and Archaeology. Oxford University Press (2011)

'A Is for Art' – My Drawings, Your Paintings

Min Zhang[1], Sarah Atkinson[2], Natasha Alechina[3], and Guoping Qiu[3]

[1] Horizon Doctoral Training Centre, School of Computer Science, University of Nottingham,
Nottingham NG8 1BB, UK
psxmz1@nottingham.ac.uk
[2] Human Factors Research Group, Department of Mechanical, Materials and Manufacturing
Engineering, University of Nottingham, Nottingham NG7 2RD, UK
sarah.atkinson@nottingham.ac.uk
[3] School of Computer Science, University of Nottingham, Nottingham NG8 1BB, UK
{natasha.alechina,guoping.qiu}@nottingham.ac.uk

Abstract. The booming development of digital technologies has significant effects on the way that human see and feel this world. The digitalization of artworks raises a set of interesting topics with the aim of making the artworks accessible to anyone with an Internet connection. In this paper, an Android Mobile App 'A is for Art' was developed to help the general public to find paintings using free-hand drawings, with the aim of involving more people with the Visual Art in an interesting way, particularly the paintings from the Tate Collection[1]. A focus group for usability evaluation was conducted, and several design principles were drawn from the phases of development and evaluation.

Keywords: Digital Engagement, Visual Art, Mobile App, Image Retrieval, Painting, Free-hand Drawing, Design.

1 Introduction

In recent years, the advanced development of digital technology has changed people's life a lot. With broadband speed increasing [4] and a wide variety of devices capable of supporting many different media and connecting to the network [5], the artistic paintings in museums and galleries are digitized by high-quality equipment, the public now have more opportunities to appreciate the artworks by visiting online art libraries or galleries. Moreover, several other factors, such as the widely disseminated digital camera and the popularity of the social network, make *"arts comes to you, you no longer need to go to it"* [1]. This offers the chance to touch the works of art, thus appreciate and get familiar with the authentic replica before they visit the real one in the art museum or gallery.

Arts can have a highly great positive impact on a person's life. Great art could help people to develop thinking and imagination [2]. As the writer Blake Morrison said, *"Art can do many things: entertain, instruct, console, inspire, enrage, transform.*

---

[1] http://www.tate.org.uk/about/our-work/collection/about-the-collection

A. Petrosino, L. Maddalena, P. Pala (Eds.): ICIAP 2013 Workshops, LNCS 8158, pp. 308–317, 2013.
© Springer-Verlag Berlin Heidelberg 2013

It teaches us things we can't be taught in any other way and makes us see things we wouldn't otherwise see. It allows us the illusion of escaping our daily lives while simultaneously taking us deeper inside ourselves." [3]

However, arts do not make any impact on the world if few people see or hear what artists are trying to say. We did a survey on how often people went to art museums/galleries on average. From 134 survey responses, as shown by Fig. 1, around half (47.83%) of the subjects went to art museums/galleries less than once a year, 27.83% of them had never visited art museums/galleries.

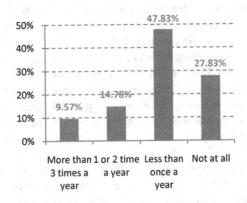

Fig. 1. 'How often, on average, you go to art museums to see paintings there?'

The motivation of our research is to explore some new and interesting ways to encourage more people to engage in the visual arts digitally.

The rest of this paper is structured as follows: section 2 introduces current related work, followed by section 3 which proposes a system overview of '*A is for Art*'. Section 4 describes the usability evaluation of the system, after analysing the study results, we propose several design principles for mobile app and plan for the following-up work in Section 5.

2   Related Work

Current digital museum participation includes visiting websites with aim of viewing the online museum/gallery collections, taking a virtual tour, searching for information about opening hours or buying tickets; on the other hand, the public use mobile device apps developed by museums or art organizations as a marketing tool, to enhance the participative arts experiences. For example, the '*Social Interpretation*' project [7] drew on the social media models to make museum visitors interact with other visitors via the Quick Response (QR) codes located near to Imperial War Museum (IWM) objects.

There are more and more museums and art institutes who digitize their art archives increasingly and provide free online access and other interactions. Google Art project[2] offers thousands of artwork pieces from 230 art collections or galleries, and the viewers can view the piece thematically and share the piece by posting onto social network sites or emailing to a friend. In December 2012, the Public Catalogue Foundation (PCF) and the British Broadcasting Corporation (BBC) launched 'Your Paintings'[3] website which allows the public to access and tag 212,000 United Kingdom's oil paintings online. The Rijksmuseum[4] (Dutch) released more than 125,000 high resolution works to the public on April 2013, the visitors can touch and zoom the masterpieces to reveal the details and they are allowed to download or create (crop and edit the artworks)   and print out their favorite ones on postcards, shirts or other materials.

Along with the booming mobile Internet, more and more smartphone users access the Internet via their mobile devices rather than their computers[5]. According to the latest mobile usage statistics from GPMD[6], in 2012 there are more mobile phones in the UK than people, and 52% of UK mobile phone users own a smartphone; the smartphone sales overtook the PC sales and will continue to grow. From comScore[7], 82% of mobile time is consumed via mobile Apps until April 2013. Therefore, we decided to seize this opportunity to foster a new way of consuming the visual artworks during users' fragmented time by means of exploring and developing mobile Apps.

However, the current mobile Apps are built by specific art museums/institutes, with the same functionalities of their websites. In the case of people who have pictures in mind but cannot remember the title or artist of the pieces, they could not search the exact paintings they expect by keywords. We developed a free-hand drawing mobile App, 'A is for Art', which allows people to find out the painting by drawing the sketch or rough colored objects in their memory.

A number of studies aimed to build the correspondence between sketches and the natural photographs [17], e.g., Sketch2Photo [6], Sketch-to-Image Matching [18], MindFinder [20]. Hu et al. [19] demonstrate a photo montage application based on sketches. To our best knowledge, we have not found any studies which are specifically focused on searching the paintings by free-hand drawn sketches.

3   'A is for Art' System Overview

With the consideration of fast response to user's query, our system adopted the Client-Server mode: users draw some sketches on the mobile phone (Client side), the

---

[2] http://www.googleartproject.com/
[3] http://www.bbc.co.uk/yourpaintings
[4] https://www.rijksmuseum.nl/
[5] http://www.emarketer.com/Article/How-Smartphone-
   PC-Internet-Users-Different/1009589
[6] http://www.gpmd.co.uk/blog/2012-mobile-internet-statistics/
[7] http://www.comscore.com/Insights/Press_Releases/2012/5/
   Introducing_Mobile_Metrix_2_Insight_into_Mobile_Behavior

searching procedure run on our Windows Azure server (Server side). We used the Jacobs et al.'s "Fast Multi-resolution image querying" algorithm [8] to do the image matching between the colour drawings and the paintings; the Inner-distance Shape Context [9-10] algorithm was implemented for searching the matched painting of the line drawings.

The current database for the painting searching engine was collected from the Tate website[8], which includes 748 abstract paintings, 91 portrait paintings and 95 others for line-drawing retrieval. We only show the matched paintings on the first version App, and the additional information of the paintings will be added in the later versions.

The interface of our Android App 'A is for Art' allows users to use touch-based drawing to search the painting search:

1) The user draws a character/object, such as a sketch or a color drawing on the mobile phone App user interface;
2) After finishing the drawing, the user can press the 'search' button and choose one of two options: 'Using line drawing' or 'Using colour drawing';
3) The system will retrieve the images through the search engine on the server and send the relevant paintings back to the mobile phone screen;
4) Then the user could select the most matched painting and zoom in/out to see more details by a double tap the image.

The workflow of the system is shown as Fig. 2 and Fig. 3.

Fig. 2. 'A *is for Art*' system workflow of searching '*Using line drawing*'

4   Usability Evaluation

Usability is defined as the "extent to which a product can be used with effectiveness, efficiency and satisfaction in a specified context of use" by ISO 9241-11 standard

---

[8] http://www.tate.org.uk

[11]. The usability testing of the mobile App might be slightly different from the traditional usability evaluation [12-13], because of the unique feature of the mobile devices. Therefore we conducted a focus group mainly by means of observing behavior and partly encouraging 'think-aloud' [14].

Fig. 3. 'A *is for Art*' system workflow of searching '*Using colour drawing*'

4.1   Participants

Four participants from the University of Nottingham Human Factors Research Group, volunteered to take part in the study. Levels of expertise were classified as expert in usability research.

4.2   Equipment

Four Nexus 4 phones were used with '*A is for Art*' installed. Google Nexus 4 phone offers relatively large displays (768×1280 pixels) and a high quality capacitive multi-touch touch screen, and built-in graphics processing unit (GPU), making it possible to create rich, visual interfaces such as zooming or touch-based manipulation.

The participants were recorded with one video camera (Canon Legria HF S21) and one webcam (Logitech C210) during the whole process of the focus group, with the purpose of later analysis.

4.3   Procedure

Participants were first welcomed to the room, the purpose of the study was explained clearly and the consent forms were signed before undertaking the tasks. Participants were asked to complete the following three tasks (shown as Fig. 4), and they were encouraged not to worry about the experiment or their performance, they could ask the observer for help if they got into difficulties. No instruction about how to use our system was provided. The participants could write notes about their experience during the action to make sure they could remember the details for the group discussion afterwards. The experiment lasted about one hour.

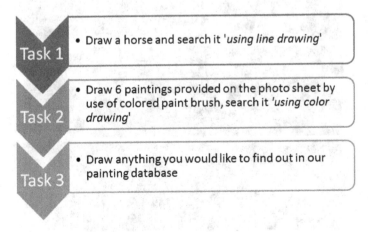

Fig. 4. Focus group tasks

4.4   Results and Discussions

There were no significant problems with accessing to the device, but most participants were confused about how to go back, because the Nexus 4 phone does not have any physical back button, home key and soft menu key, and some participants were not Android phone users. The participants' drawings are shown as Fig. 5 and Fig. 6.

Fig. 5. Colour Drawings from Participants A, B, C, D (individually each column) and the original paintings provided on a sheet as reference (last column)

Fig. 6. Horse line drawings from Participants A, B, C, D individually each column (Left) and the free-drawings from Participants A, B, C, D individually each row (Right)

92.8% of the tasks were completed (finding the paintings on the task sheet by free-hand drawings). One participant did not find the horse in Task 1; one participant failed to find the second paintings in Task 2.

Users were observed when using the mobile App in unexpected ways. From Task 1 (Fig. 6, left), two participants drew the horse in landscape orientation, which was not expected by our searching algorithm.

From undertaking task 2 (Fig. 5), several interface issues were reported:

- No instruction about what icons can do;
- No indication of the size & colour of the brush chosen;
- The size and colour of brush are set to a default size after clearing the canvas;
- The size of both the brush and eraser are not wide enough, and users can not choose the size continuously;
- No tutorial about how to choose colour on the colour picker;
- Top menu of App can be confused with the Android Notification because of the full-screen mode;
- Undo icon doesn't always highlight when only one point dropped;
- No 'save' function;
- Inconsistent interface for displaying the matching result of line-drawing and colour-drawing;
- No intuitive colour saving mode (e.g. saving the used colour in the way of first-used-first-saved).
- Need more pre-set colour.

Although there was a learning curve for the new user to explore the features of the system, the participants reported that they enjoyed using the system. One participant preferred the drawer-like way of displaying the result, so she could pull up and down to compare the matched painting and her own drawing.

During the discussion, some participants reported that they would like to find the particular painting by both free-hand drawing and text information, e.g., the year the painting was made or the name of the artist. Some participants thought taking photos of the painting or selecting one photo from the phone gallery to do the retrieval would be their preferred choice.

5   Conclusion

According to Flurry[9], the future is an App world. We predict that the digital participation will keep increasing.

Participants in the focus group informed the refinement of the design. Nickerson's Overimputation theory [15] indicates that it is difficult for the designer to put themselves in the position of a real user who has none of their specialist knowledge. So it is important to involve real users during the product development. There are several design principles learned from the usability study:

— Keep the user interface as simple and intuitive as possible;
— Always keep users informed about what they are doing and where they are;
— Provide the option to recover from mistakes;
— Increase the consistency between the mobile devices and application features, and keeping internal consistency [16] will make users to use the same way of thinking throughout the interaction;
— Applying the existing icons to make the functions easy to understand, so the metaphors could be transferred from other products and experiences;
— Making good use of users' prior knowledge.

The next stage of work will be refining and improving the system 'A is for Art', followed by field-work evaluation. Meanwhile, we plan to increasingly develop our painting database, and to build the new database of relevant text information about the paintings.

Acknowledgements This work is sponsored by Horizon Doctoral Training Center, The University of Nottingham and Tate Collection. The first author is supported by the Horizon Doctoral Training Centre at the University of Nottingham (RCUK Grant No. EP/G037574/1).

References

1. Berger, J.: Ways of Seeing. BBC and Penguin Books, London (1972)
2. Art Council England, Achieving great art for everyone (2010)

---

[9] http://blog.flurry.com/bid/95723/Flurry-Five-Year-Report-It-s-an-App-World-The-Just-Web-Lives-in-It

3. Morrison, B.: Achieving Great Art For Everyone: A Strategic Framework for the Arts, p. 10. Arts Council England, London (2010)
4. Ofcom: The Consumer Experience: Research report. Ofcom, London (2007)
5. Keaney, E.: The digital world: A review of the evidence (May 2009)
6. Chen, T., Cheng, M.-M., Tan, P., Shamir, A., Hu, S.M.: Sketch2photo: internet image montage. ACM Trans. Graph. 28 (2009)
7. Digital R&D Fund for the Arts: The Imperial War Museum's Social Interpretation Project (January 2013)
8. Jacobs, C.E., Finkelstein, A., Salesin, D.H.: Fast Multiresolution Image Quering. In: Proceedings of the 22nd Annual Conference on Computer Graphics and Interactive Techniques (1995)
9. Ling, H.B., Jacobs, D.W.: Using the Inner-Distance for Classification of Articulated Shapes. In: IEEE Conference on Computer Vision and Pattern Recognition (CVPR), vol. II, pp. 719–726 (2005)
10. Ling, H.B., Jacobs, D.W.: Shape Classification Using the Inner-Distance. IEEE Trans on Pattern Anal. and Mach. Intell. (PAMI) 29(2), 286–299 (2007)
11. ISO 9241-11 International Standard on Ergonomic Requirements for office work with visual display terminals (VDT), Part 11: Guidance on Usability, ISO (1997)
12. Stoica, A., Fiotakis, G., Cabrera, J.S., Frutos, H.M., Avouris, N., Dimitriadis, T.: Usability evaluation of handheld devices: A case study for a museum application. In: Proceedings PCI 2005, Volos (2005)
13. Zhang, D.S., Adipat, B.: Challenges, Methodologies, and Issues in the Usability Testing of Mobile Applications. International Journal of Human-Computer Interaction 18, 293–308 (2005)
14. Someren, M.W., Barnard, Y.F., Sandberg, J.A.C.: The Think Aloud Method: A Practical Guide to Modeling Cognitive Processes. Published by Academic Press, London (1994)
15. Nickerson, R.S.: How we know—and sometimes misjudge—what others know: imputing one's own knowledge to others. Psychological Bulletin 125(6), 737–759 (1999)
16. Kellogg, W.A.: The Dimensions of Consistency. In: Nielsen, J. (ed.) Coordinating User Interfaces for Consistency, pp. 9–20. Academic Press, Inc., San Diego (1989)
17. Jain, A., Vailaya, A.: Shape-Based Retrieval: A Case Study with Trademark Image Databases. Pattern Recognition 31(9), 1369–1390 (1998)
18. Shrivastava, A., Malisiewicz, T., Gupta, A., Efros, A.A.: Data-driven Visual Similarity for Cross-domain Image Matching. In: SIGGRAPH Asia (2011)
19. Hu, R., Barnard, M., Collomosse, J.: Gradient Field Descriptor for Sketch based Retrieval and Localization. In: International Conference on Image Processing, ICIP (2010)
20. Cao, Y., Wang, C., Zhang, L., Zhang, L.: Edgel Inverted Index for Large-Scale Sketch-based Image Search. In: CVPR (2011)

Identification of Protein Interaction Partners from Shape Complementarity Molecular Cross-Docking

Elodie Laine[1,2] and Alessandra Carbone[1,2]

[1] Université Pierre et Marie Curie, UMR 7238, Equipe de Génomique Analytique, 15 rue de l'Ecole de Médecine, 75006 Paris, France
[2] CNRS, UMR 7238, Laboratoire de Génomique des Microorganismes, Paris 75006, France
elodie.laine@upmc.fr, Alessandra.Carbone@lip6.fr

Abstract. There is a growing interest in using efficient shape complementarity docking algorithms to analyze protein-protein interactions at a large scale. We have realized complete cross-docking of several tens of enzyme/inhibitors proteins. On the one hand, we demonstrate that docking score distributions for the known complexes are not distinguishable from those for the non-interacting pairs. On the other hand, we show that the knowledge of the experimental interfaces applied to the docking conformations permits to retrieve true interaction partners with high accuracy. We further identify the determinants of the molecular recognition between true interactors compared to non-interacting proteins.

1 Introduction

Protein-protein interactions (PPI) regulate virtually all aspects of cell biology. The identification of protein interaction partners is thus of crucial importance to control signaling pathways in physio-pathological contexts. Computational methods such as molecular docking have proven to be valuable tools for the prediction of the native conformations of known protein-protein complexes [2,4]. Recent studies have also suggested that molecular docking could help retrieve true interacting partners among a set of non-interactors with high accuracy [9,10,6]. Wass *et al.* reported that score distributions produced by shape complementarity docking could be used to distinguish 56 known interactors among a diverse background of 922 non-interacting proteins [10]. We have shown that the combination of cross-docking simulations and experimental knowledge of protein interfaces successfully identifies known partners within a set of 168 proteins from various functional classes [6]. Our cross-docking simulations employed a refined molecular mechanics energy function and were highly time consuming compared to shape complementarity docking which uses a crude scoring scheme.

In the present work, we investigated whether rigid-body docking using a shape complementarity scoring function only or in combination with experimental knowledge could be used to efficiently identify protein interaction partners

A. Petrosino, L. Maddalena, P. Pala (Eds.): ICIAP 2013 Workshops, LNCS 8158, pp. 318–325, 2013.
© Springer-Verlag Berlin Heidelberg 2013

within a set of 46 enzyme/inhibitors proteins. In the following we report the effectiveness of the two strategies, we discuss the limitations of the docking algorithm we used and the associated scoring function, and we further characterize the conformational ensemble produced by docking.

2   Results

2.1   Docking Score Distributions

Complete cross-docking (CC-D) was realized on the Enzyme-Inhibitors dataset (46 proteins) of the Mintseris Benchmark 2.0 [7] from unbound conformations. Every one of the 46 unbound structures was docked to all the protein structures in the dataset by the very efficient rigid-body docking algorithm Hex [8]. Each calculation explored about 3 billions candidate ligand-receptor orientations. These were then evaluated and ranked by the Hex scoring function which estimates the shape complementarity between receptor and ligand. The 500 best scores were retained and their statistical distribution was computed. For each protein, the docking score distributions with the known interactor and the other 45 non-interacting proteins were compared using the Wilcoxon rank-sum test [11]. At the 1% significance level, none of the known true partner's score distributions has significantly better scores than false Enzyme-Inhibitors partners distributions (Table 1, *Single* column). Less than 10 proteins' known true partners lie within the top 20% score distributions and slightly more than 50% of the 46 proteins have their true partner score distribution in the best half of all 46 dataset distributions. We conclude that scores produced by Hex do not carry sufficient information to correctly distinguish known partners from non-interactors within the enzyme-inhibitors dataset considered here.

Table 1. Statistical significance of known true complex docking score distributions

Top %	# top proteins	Enzyme/inhibitors (%)	
		Single	Macro
1	1	0 (0)	0 (0)
5	2	3 (7)	1 (2)
10	5	4 (9)	3 (7)
15	7	6 (13)	6 (13)
20	9	9 (20)	7 (15)
30	14	17 (37)	10 (22)
40	18	21 (46)	17 (37)
50	23	25 (54)	24 (52)

2.2   Using Knowledge of the Interfaces

As pointed out in previous works [9,6], combining docking scores with the knowledge of the experimental interfaces should help retrieve true interacting partners. This was shown for coarse-grain docking algorithms and we show here that the same holds true for shape complementarity docking. We use a predictive PPI index (NII) as an estimator of the probability of two proteins to interact. For every protein pair $P_1 P_2$, we determine an optimal interaction index (II) [6]:

$$II_{P_1,P_2} = min(FIR_{P_1,P_2} * E_{P_1,P_2}) \tag{1}$$

where FIR (Fraction of Interface Residues) is the overall fraction of the docking interface composed of residues belonging to the experimentally identified interfaces for the receptor and the ligand: $FIR = FIR_{rec} * FIR_{lig}$, and E is the docking score. The minimum is defined over all the docking conformations considered. To compare interaction indexes computed over different pairs, a normalized interaction index, called NII, is computed, that models the symmetric role played by ligand and receptor. NII is defined in Lopes et $al.$ [6].

The calculation of the NII index for every protein pair of the Enzyme-Inhibitors dataset enabled to draw a receiver operating curve (ROC) from which known interacting protein pairs could be predicted with an area under the curve (AUC) of 0.81 (Table 2, $Single$ line). This result indicates that the knowledge of the experimental interfaces can be successfully used to evaluate shape complementarity docking conformations and retrieve true interactors. However in practice experimental interfaces are not known and one would wish to replace them by predictions. How precise shall the predictions be to ensure high performance ?

Table 2. AUC values for the prediction of known true partners, using complete (all) or partial (S: support, C: core, R: rim) knowledge of the experimental interfaces

Interaction index	Docking protocol	All	SUC	CUR	SUR	C	S	R
II	Single	0.81	0.79	0.75	0.73	0.76	0.73	0.62
	Macro	0.68	0.71	0.60	0.62	0.64	0.66	0.59
II_{cov}	Single	0.69	0.71	0.65	0.62	0.66	0.65	0.61
	Macro	0.63	0.67	0.59	0.60	0.64	0.60	0.55
$II_{FIROnly}$	Single	0.80	0.79	0.73	0.76	0.73	0.75	0.64
	Macro	0.73	0.74	0.65	0.68	0.67	0.68	0.60

2.3   Relative Contributions of Interface Sub-regions

In order to determine whether some interface residues contributed more than others to the discrimination of true partners from non-interactors, we defined three sub-regions of the interface depending on residue burial: support, core and rim (Fig. 1). Previous studies highlighted the specific amino acid compositions and the evolutionary conservation profiles of these sub-regions [5,1]. Using this structural definition of PPI interfaces, we investigated the importance of each sub-region for the prediction of true interacting partners. The AUC value was found similar when discarding information about the rim (0.79 in Table 2). By contrast AUC values significantly decreased down to 0.75 or 0.73 when ignoring support or core in the definition of the experimental interface. Moreover the knowledge of the core alone led to an AUC value of 0.76 as high as that obtained when using both core and rim (0.75). The knowledge of the support alone gave an AUC value of 0.72 similar to that obtained when using both support and rim. The sole knowledge of the rim led to a drastically lower AUC value of only 0.62.

These results show that the core and the support contain more relevant information than the rim for the identification of true interacting partners in the Enzyme-Inhibitors dataset. As a consequence, strategies to predict protein interfaces should concentrate on these two sub-regions. We shall note that this observation may not necessarily hold true for other functional classes of proteins.

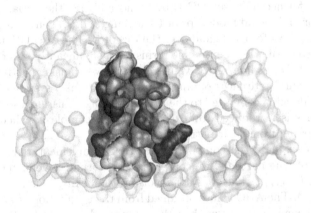

Fig. 1. Example of an enzyme/inhibitor complex (PDB code: 1AVX) from the Mintseris Benchmark 2.0 depicting the three interface sub-regions. The two partners are displayed in transparent light grey surface. The support, core and rim residues are displayed as opaque surface and colored in red, green and cyan respectively.

2.4 Positive Predictive Value vs Sensitivity

We also investigated whether it is more important for a docking interface to cover a large part of the experimental interface or be restricted to the residues that truly compose the experimental interface. The FIR computed to determine the interaction index II represents the overall fraction of the docking interface that is composed of residues belonging to the experimentally identified interface (Eq. 1). This formula is different from that employed in [9], where the fraction considered was that of the experimental interface covered by the docking interface, which we refer as FIR_{cov}. Here we also computed the corresponding alternative interaction index II_{cov}. The AUC values obtained from the calculation of II_{cov} are systematically lower than those obtained from II (Table 2). In particular when considering complete knowledge of the interface, the AUC value drastically decreased down to 0.69.

These results indicate that to be able to discriminate true from false partners it is more crucial to consider the portion of the docking interface that matches the experimental interface rather than the portion of the experimental interface that is covered by the docking interface. Consequently, methods designed to predict PPI should aim at maximizing positive predictive value rather than sensitivity.

2.5   Conformational Ensemble Generation and Selection

In the following we explored the robustness of the docking results and the contribution of the scoring function. To perform CC-D, we used the initial PDB files representing the 3D coordinates of the 46 proteins studied in unbound forms, superimposed on the bound conformations in the 23 native complexes. In order to investigate whether these initial locations and orientations could bias the results, we performed unbiased CC-D by (i) normalizing the initial distance between receptor and ligand models prior to docking and (ii) generating five initial docking orientations for the ligand over the receptor. The calculation of II from the obtained conformational ensemble furnished a significantly lower AUC value of 0.68 (Table 2, *Macro* line). AUC values obtained when using partial knowledge of the experimental interfaces or/and using II_{cov} are also systematically lower for the *Macro* docking compared to the *Single* docking. This suggests that indeed a favorable bias is introduced towards true known complexes when docking is performed starting from their native conformations.

In order to evaluate the contribution of Hex complementarity score to the identification of true partners, we computed an alternative version of the interaction index $II_{FIROnly}$ that does not incorporate docking scores : $II_{FIROnly} = max(FIR_{P_1,P_2})$. The AUC values obtained from the calculation of $II_{FIROnly}$ are similar to and sometimes better than those obtained from II for *Single* docking and they are systematically better for *Macro* docking (Table 2). This suggests that the contribution of the docking score is minor in the discrimination of the true complexes from the non-interacting protein pairs and that taking it into account can even deteriorate performance.

2.6   Characterization of Docking Conformations

In Fig. 2 we show the distributions of the docking conformations score-based ranks corresponding to three different intervals for the coverage FIR_{cov} of the support, core and rim. Only conformations whose global FIR is greater than 0.4 are considered. First we observe that docking conformations displaying high coverage of the experimental interface are not ranked first by the scoring function of Hex. Ranks are distributed rather uniformly whatever the value of the FIR_{cov}

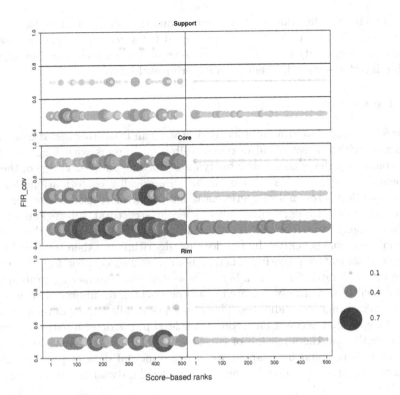

Fig. 2. Comparison of docking conformations for known true complexes (on the left) and non-interacting protein pairs (on the right). Among the 500 best-scored conformations of each docking experiment, those whose FIR is greater than 0.4 are plotted with respect to FIR_{cov} (y-axis) and score-based ranks (x-axis) for each of the three interface sub-regions: support, core and rim. The y-axis is defined with respect to three main intervals, $[0:4; 0:6]$, $(0:6; 0:8]$ and $(0:8; 1:0]$, and the x-axis varies between 1 and 500. Each interval on the y-axis is associated to a distribution of ranks, where a bin in the distribution corresponds to 5 consecutive ranks. Bins are represented as circles, their sizes are normalized and vary from 0.1 to 0.7 % of the total number of conformations. Grey levels are redundant with sizes.

and this is true for the three sub-regions. This agrees with the observed poor and even deleterious contribution of the docking score to the identification of true partners. Second, the comparison of docking conformations for known true complexes (Fig. 2, left panels) and for non-interacting protein pairs (Fig. 2, right panels) clearly shows that the coverage of the three sub-regions is greater for the known true complexes. Third, the comparison of the three sub-regions indicates that the coverage of the core region is much larger than those of the rim and support regions. This is in agreement with the central position of the core in the interface. Residues from the rim, which lie at the periphery are the least covered.

Finally, we shall notice that the conformations considered ($FIR > 0.4$) represent a small portion of the total number of docking conformations, respectively

4.5% and 3.0% for the known true complexes and the non-interacting pairs. Similar fractions (4.1% and 3.1%) were computed for *Macro* docking. This reveals that the large majority of conformations generated and selected by Hex display docking interfaces very different from experimental interfaces.

3   Discussion

Our work showed that true interacting partners can be distinguished from non-interactors within a set of 46 enzyme/inhibitors proteins with high accuracy when combining shape complementarity cross-docking and knowledge of the experimental interfaces. This is possible because docking conformations for the known complexes resemble experimental interfaces more that those for non-interacting pairs. In particular, some specific structural sub-regions of the interface largely contribute to the discrimination. The quality of the conformational ensemble generated by the docking algorithm and then selected by the shape complementarity scoring function is an essential element for the performance of our strategy. In a number of cases the true interacting protein pair was not identified as the best match from the docking results but lied in a certain top percentage of candidates. This observation calls for the development of methodologies that account for a confidence level in the determination of potential interacting partners instead of considering only the best one. The method we propose here could be adapted when experimental data of proteins' interfaces are lacking, for example by combining molecular dynamics simulations and ensemble-based docking.

4   Methods

Complete Cross-Docking. CC-D was realized on the 46 Enzyme-Inhibitors proteins of the Mintseris Benchmark 2.0 (http://zlab.bu.edu/benchmark2/) from unbound conformations, leading to 2116 docking experiments. Docking was performed with Hex v6.3 [8] using the shape complementarity scoring function. The precision of the molecular representation was defined from 18 and 25 expansion orders for the initial and final search steps. Unbiased CC-D was realized by positioning the receptor and ligand models at a distance of 100 Å from one another prior to docking. Moreover, five starting positions were defined using Hex Macro-Sampling module and were used to generate initial docking orientations for the ligand over the receptor and to derive appropriate local coordinate frames. Among all conformations explored during docking search, the 500 best-scored ones were retained for analysis.

Statistical Testing. Score distributions for the known complexes and the non-interacting protein pairs were compared following a protocol similar to that reported in [10]. For each known true complex, 45 individual one-sided Wilcoxon rank-sum tests [11] were performed, to determine if the ranked set of docking scores from that complex was significantly better (less) than (at P-value < 0.01) the ranked set of docking scores from each of the false complex docking.

Support-Core-Rim Definition. The three interface sub-regions were defined based on the per-residue relative accessible surface areas ($rasa$), computed by NACCESS 2.1.1 [3], with a probe size of 1.4 Å. For crystallographic structures, interface residues are those displaying any variation $\Delta rasa$ between bound (b) and unbound (u) conformations. The support is composed of residues buried in both conformations ($rasa_u < 0.25$, $rasa_b < 0.25$). The core contains exposed residues that become buried upon binding to the partner ($rasa_u \geq 0.25$, $rasa_b < 0.25$). The rim is defined by residues exposed in both unbound and bound conformations ($rasa_b \geq 0.25$, $rasa_b \geq 0.25$). For docking conformations, residues are considered at the interface when they display a change of at least 10% decrease in accessible surface area compared to the unbound protein.

Acknowledgements. The MAPPING project (ANR-11-BINF-0003), supported by the Excellence Programme "Investissement d'Avenir", supported this analysis.

References

1. Andreani, J., Faure, G., Guerois, R.: Versatility and invariance in the evolution of homologous heteromeric interfaces. PLoS Comput. Biol. 8, e1002677 (2012)
2. Gray, J.J.: High-resolution protein-protein docking. Curr. Opin. Struct. Biol. 16, 183–193 (2006)
3. Hubbard, S., Thornton, J.: NACCESS. Tech. rep., Computer Program, Dept of Biochemistry and Molecular Biology, University College London (1993)
4. Janin, J.: Protein-protein docking tested in blind predictions: the CAPRI experiment. Mol. Biosyst. 6, 2351–2362 (2010)
5. Levy, E.D.: A simple definition of structural regions in proteins and its use in analyzing interface evolution. J. Mol. Biol. 403, 660–670 (2010)
6. Lopes, A., Sacquin-Mora, S., Dimitrova, V., Laine, E., Ponty, Y.: Protein-protein interactions in a crowded environment via cross-docking and evolutionary information (submitted, 2013)
7. Mintseris, J., Wiehe, K., Pierce, B., Anderson, R., Chen, R., Janin, J., Weng, Z.: Protein-Protein Docking Benchmark 2.0: An update. Proteins 60, 214–216 (2005)
8. Ritchie, D.W., Kemp, G.J.: Protein docking using spherical polar Fourier correlations. Proteins 39, 178–194 (2000)
9. Sacquin-Mora, S., Carbone, A., Lavery, R.: Identification of protein interaction partners and protein-protein interaction sites. J. Mol. Biol. 382, 1276–1289 (2008)
10. Wass, M.N., Fuentes, G., Pons, C., Pazos, F., Valencia, A.: Towards the prediction of protein interaction partners using physical docking. Mol. Syst. Biol. 7, 469 (2011)
11. Wilcoxon, F.: Individual comparisons by ranking methods. Biometrics Bull. 1, 80–83 (1945)

A Supervised Approach to 3D Structural Classification of Proteins

Virginio Cantoni[1], Alessio Ferone[2],
Alfredo Petrosino[2], and Gabriella Sanniti di Baja[3]

[1] University of Pavia, Department of Electrical and Computer Engineering,
Via A. Ferrata, 1, 27100, Pavia, Italy
virginio.cantoni@unipv.it
[2] University of Naples Parthenope, Department of Applied Science, Centro
Direzionale Napoli - Isola C4, 80143, Napoli, Italy
{alessio.ferone,alfredo.petrosino}@uniparthenope.it
[3] Institute of Cybernetics "E. Caianiello" - CNR - Naples - Italy
g.sannitidibaja@cib.na.cnr.it

Abstract. Three dimensional protein structures determine the function of a protein within a cell. Classification of 3D structure of proteins is therefore crucial to inferring protein functional information as well as the evolution of interactions between proteins. In this paper we propose to employ a recently presented structural representation of the proteins and exploit the learning capabilities of the graph neural network model to perform the classification task.

Keywords: Concavity Tree, Graph Neural Network, Structural Classification of Proteins, Protein Function.

1 Introduction

There are currently more than 90,000 experimentally determined three dimensional (3D) structures of protein deposited in the Protein Data Bank (PDB) [25]. 3D structures of a protein are determined by the amino acid sequence and define the protein functions. The study of structural building blocks is very important in order to study the evolution and the functional annotation, and has yielded many methods for their identification and classification in classes of known structure.

There are several commonly used DBs for structural classification of proteins, such as Structural Classification Of Proteins (SCOP) [22] and Class Architecture Topology and Homologous super families (CATH) [23]. CATH and SCOP are primary and secondary structure based classifications which rely on experts to manually check the classifications. Such classifications organize protein structures into families. Another well-known DB is Families of Structurally Similar Proteins (FSSP), which is purely automatic [11].

Most of the existing classification methods are based on shapes, by means of suitable distances, such as RMSG [2]. Consequently, they have to deal with tens of thousands of structures for each protein. These approaches consume significant computation space. Machine learning methods to cluster and classify

A. Petrosino, L. Maddalena, P. Pala (Eds.): ICIAP 2013 Workshops, LNCS 8158, pp. 326–335, 2013.
© Springer-Verlag Berlin Heidelberg 2013

protein structures have recently become a very active area of research. Statistical methods include Shape Histograms proposed by Anskerst [16], Shape Distribution by Osada [24], meanwhile Ohbuchi put forward Shape Function and eigen-CSS proposed by Mark. In [17], authors use a statistical method as feature vectors to classify the protein structures. Since the statistics methods are based on overall feature extractions, the adoption statistical methods has a high robustness of the boundary noise as well as good performance for rough classification. In particular artificial neural networks (ANN) have been employed to develop a comprehensive view of protein structures to infer protein functional information.

The problem of structural representation of a protein until now has been tackled by specific descriptors, usually point-based and not suited for management and processing. Among these we can quote: spin image [26], [4], context shape [13], harmonic shape [14] and PGI [7]. Following [8], in this paper we propose to model the 3D structure of each protein employing its concavities and organize them in a hierarchical structure, the Protein Concavity Tree (PCT), that represents its concavity tree ([1]). For the learning task needed to classify proteins represented in such a way, we propose to employ the Graph Neural Network (GNN)[27] model that is particularly suited for learning in the structured domain. Graph classification techniques have been successfully employed in many applications fields. Borgwardt et al. [6] applied the graph kernel method to classify protein 3D structures. It outperformed classical alignment-based approaches. Karklin et al. [20] built a classifier for non-coding RNAs employing a graph representation of RNAs.

The remainder of the paper is as follows. In Section 2 the PCT data structure is presented. In Section 3 the Graph Neural Network model is introduced, while in Section 4 experimental results are presented. Section 5 concludes the paper.

2   Protein Concavity Tree

The concavity tree data structure is used for describing non-convex two and three dimensional shapes. It is a rooted tree in which the root represents the convex hull of the object and each node describes the set of objects obtained by subtracting the object from the convex hull. A leaf of the tree corresponds to a convex shape. Each node in a concavity tree stores information related to a concavity and to the tree meta-data (i.e. the level of the node, height, number of nodes, and number of leaves in the subtree rooted at the node, etc.).

In order to employ such structure to describe a protein, it is necessary to introduce some molecular models of a protein. The simplest model represents atoms as hard spheres whose radius, namely the van der Waals radius (VDWR), indicates the largest distance at which an atom repels its neighbors. The union of these hard spheres is called van der Waals volume and the resulting enclosing surface is termed the van der Waals surface (VDWS). The Solvent Accessible Surface (SAS) is the locus of the centers of a spherical probe that rolls over the molecular system. Geometrically, it coincides with the VDWS of the system where VDWR is increased by the size of the radius of the probe. The Solvent Excluded Surface (SES), often identified with the Molecular Surface, separates the volume accessible to a finite size solvent probe from the inaccessible one. This definition, based on a hard sphere model of both the solute and the solvent, was suggested by Lee and Richards [18]. An example of the surfaces, in the 2D case, is showed in Fig. 1.

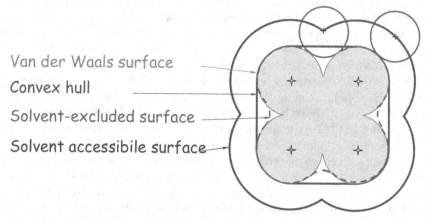

Van der Waals surface

Convex hull

Solvent-excluded surface

Solvent accessibile surface

Fig. 1. Examples of molecular models of a protein in 2D

In the discrete space the protein and its convex hull (CH) are defined in a 3D grid of dimension $L \times M \times N$ voxels. The grid is extended one voxel beyond the minimum and maximum coordinate of the SES in each orthogonal direction, so that both the SES and the CH are inside the grid. Let us call R the volume of the concavity [5] between the CH and the SES

$$R = CH \cap \overline{SES} \tag{1}$$

where $\overline{SES}$ identifies the complement of the SES. Let B_{CH} the set of the border voxels of CH

$$B_{CH} = CH - [CH \bullet K] \tag{2}$$

where $\bullet$ represents the erosion operator of mathematical morphology and K the discrete unit sphere (in the discrete space a $3 \times 3 \times 3$ cube). Starting from the voxels in B_{CH}, the propagation algorithm proposed in [9] computes the connected components A of R that represent both pockets and tunnels. In order to separate the different pockets and tunnels, A is partitioned into a set of disjoint segments $P_{SES} = \{P_1, \ldots, P_j, \ldots, P_N\}$ such that

$$P_i \cap P_j = \emptyset \qquad i \neq j \tag{3}$$

$$\bigcup_{i=1}^{n} P_i = A \tag{4}$$

In order to retain the topological relationships between the partitioned segments, we introduce a novel structural description of the protein called Protein Concavity Tree. The PCT of a given protein is computed by recursively applying the segmentation process, where at each stage, exact measures of the remaining concavities can be computed. Once the complex shape is segmented into a set of pockets, each pocket can be subsequently decomposed into simpler regions. The process continues until all regions are convex. In this way, the complete description is given in terms of the region's features and their spatial relationship.

The concavities at each level of the PCT can be analyzed and described using many different features (computed in terms of the voxels belonging to the concavities). In this paper we have selected the following discriminative features: Pocket Volume [19], given by the number of voxels belonging to the pocket; Pocket Surface-to-Volume Ratio, where the pocket surface is computed as the number of SES voxels belonging to the pocket; Skewness and Kurtosis of Height Distribution, that compute the asymmetry of the surface of the pocket and its deviation from an ideal bell–shape surface, respectively; Mouth Aperture of the pocket, computed as the ratio between the perimeter and the area of the aperture; Travel Depth [10], computed as the shortest path from the CH to the surface of the pocket. For a detailed description of these features, the reader is referred to [8].

As an example of the described process, Figures 2 and 3 show the protein 1MK5 and its concavity tree, respectively.

Fig. 2. Protein 1MK5

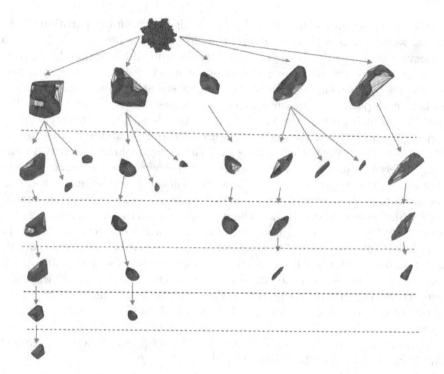

Fig. 3. Concavity Tree of protein 1MK5. In order to highlight the details a scaling factor is applied increasing the representation level.

3   Graph Neural Networks

In the recent years, many powerful machine learning methods have been developed to deal with one dimensional data, even though more complex data structures can be employed to obtain a better representation of data and possibly a better solution to a given problem. Neural methods are an example of techniques that evolved to handle structured data, where the original connectionist models have been modified to process sequences [29], trees and graphs models [15][3].

A more general supervised neural network model, is called Graph Neural Network (GNN). GNN extends Recursive Neural Network (RNN) [12] [28] since it can process a more general class of graphs including cyclic, directed, and undirected graphs, and it can deal with node-focused applications without any preprocessing steps.

The basic idea behind GNNs is the information diffusion mechanism, i.e. a graph is processed by a set of units, one for each node of the graph, connected following the graph connectivity. This representation of the graph, called encoding network, is unfolded through the structure of the input graph. At each step, all the units compute their states using information of the adjacent nodes, until stable state is reached

$$\begin{cases} x_n = f_w(l_n, l_{cp[n]}, x_{ne[n]}, l_{ne[n]}) \\ o_n = g_w(x_n, l_n) \end{cases} \tag{5}$$

where l_n is the label of node n, $l_{cp[n]}$ are the labels of its edges, $x_{ne[n]}$ are the states of the nodes in the neighborhood of n, $l_{ne[n]}$ are the labels of the nodes in the neighborhood of n, and x_n is the state of node n, i.e. it represents the concept denoted by node n. This value, along with the label l_n, is used to produce the output o_n, i.e. the decision about the concept.

The diffusion mechanism is constrained in order to ensure that a unique stable equilibrium always exists. Although this mechanism has been already used in cellular neural networks and Hopfield neural network, the one used in GNN allows the processing of more general classes of graphs. Also in [27] it is proved that GNNs show a sort of universal approximation property and they can approximate most of the practically useful functions on graphs.

4   Experimental Results

This section presents preliminary results of the proposed approach. In this paper, we use data from the spatial structures of Structural Classification of Proteins (SCOP) databases which are based on the similarities of their amino acid and three-dimensional structures [21]. This database includes fold classification family that are connected to sequence similarity. In particular, the employed dataset

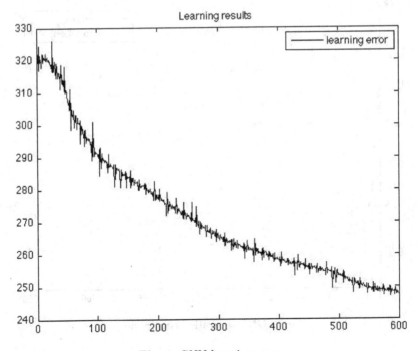

Fig. 4. GNN learning error

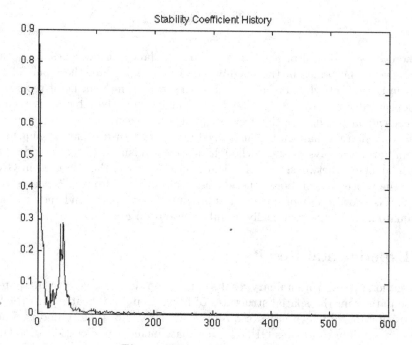

Fig. 5. GNN stability coefficient

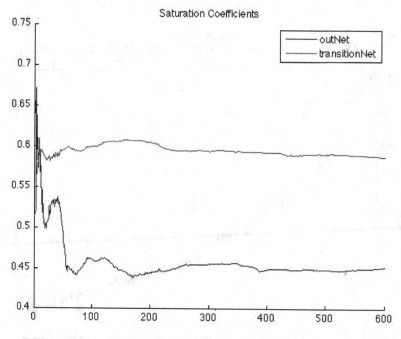

Fig. 6. GNN saturation coefficients

is composed by 70 proteins belonging to 4 classes (all alpha, all beta, alpha/beta and alpha+beta). The training set contains 90% of the samples and the testing set includes 10% of the samples, randomly selected from the whole dataset. We employed the Matlab GNN toolbox[1] using default parameters. The obtained mean accuracy is 69.93%. Although tests have not been performed on the whole SCOP database and hence comparisons with other methods have not been conducted, it is important to note how the performance of the proposed approach is very promising considering that only geometrical features have been selected. This consideration is also supported by the learning capabilities of the GNN that can be observed in the plot of the learning error, shown in Figure 4. Moreover, as can be seen in Figures 5 and 6, the low stability coefficient and the stable saturation coefficients clearly indicate that the network is able to converge.

5   Conclusions

In this paper, we have described a novel approach to classify protein structures. The proposed approach exploits the novel idea of representing a protein by means of its Protein Concavity Tree where concavities at each level are characterized by geometrical features. In order to classify proteins represented in this way, we propose to use the Graph Neural Network model that is able to exploit the topological structure induced by the concavities hierarchy. The experimental results show that our method achieves 69.93% accuracy on protein structure classification. Future works will be devoted to further analysis, more extensive experimentation and comparisons with other techniques.

References

1. Arcelli, C., Sanniti Di Baja, G.: Polygonal covering and concavity tree of binary digital pictures. In: Proceeding International Conference MECO, vol. 78, pp. 292–297 (1978)
2. Berman, H., Henrick, K., Nakamura, H.: Announcing the worldwide Protein Data Bank. Nature Structural Biology 10(12), 980–980 (2003)
3. Bianchini, M., Maggini, M., Sarti, L., Scarselli, F.: Recursive neural networks for processing graphs with labelled edges: Theory and applications. Neural Networks - Special Issue on Neural Network and Kernel Methods for Structured Domains 18, 1040–1050 (2005)
4. Bock, M.E., Garutti, C., Guerra, C.: Spin image profile: a geometric descriptor for identifying and matching protein cavities. In: Proc. of CSB, San Diego (2007)
5. Borgefors, G., Sanniti Di Baja, G.: Methods for hierarchical analysis of concavities. In: Proceedings of the Conference on Pattern Recognition (ICPR), vol. 3, pp. 171–175 (1992)
6. Borgwardt, K.M., Ong, C.S., Schönauer, S., Vishwanathan, S.V.N., Smola, A.J., Kriegel, H.-P.: Protein function prediction via graph kernels. Bioinformatics 21(suppl. 1), i47–i56 (2005)

---

[1] Available online at http://www.dii.unisi.it/~franco/Research/GNN.php

7. Cantoni, V., Ferone, A., Oliva, R., Petrosino, A.: Protein Gaussian Image (PGI): A protein structural representation based on the spatial attitude of secondary structure. New Tools and Methods for Pattern Recognition in Complex Biological Systems, Nuovo Cimento C 35(5, suppl. 1) (2012)

8. Cantoni, V., Gatti, R., Lombardi, L.: Proteins Pockets Analysis and Description. Bioinformatics, 211–216 (2010)

9. Cantoni, V., Gatti, R., Lombardi, L.: Analysis of geometrical and topological aptitude for protein-protein interaction. Nuovo Cimento della Società Italiana di Fisica. C, Geophysics and Space Physics 35 C, 81–88 (2012)

10. Coleman, R.G., Sharp, K.A.: Travel Depth, a New Shape Descriptor for Macromolecules: Application to Ligand Binding. Journal of Molecular Biology 362(3) (2006)

11. Day, R., Beck, D.A., Armen, R.S., Daggett, V.: A consensus view of fold space: combining SCOP, CATH, and the Dali Domain Dictionary. Protein Sci. 12(10), 2150–2160 (2003)

12. Frasconi, P., Gori, M., Sperduti, A.: A general framework for adaptive processing of data structures. IEEE Trans. on Neural Network 9(5), 768–786 (1998)

13. Frome, A., Huber, D., Kolluri, R., Bülow, T., Malik, J.: Recognizing Objects in Range Data Using Regional Point Descriptors. In: Pajdla, T., Matas, J. (eds.) ECCV 2004. LNCS, vol. 3023, pp. 224–237. Springer, Heidelberg (2004)

14. Glaser, F., Morris, R.J., Najmanovich, R.J., Laskowski, R.A., Thornton, J.M.: A Method for Localizing Ligand Binding Pockets in Protein Structures. PROTEINS: Structure, Function, and Bioinformatics 62, 479–488 (2006)

15. Gori, M., Maggini, M., Sarti, L.: A Recursive neural network model for processing directed acyclic graph with labeled edges. In: Procedings of the International Joint Conference on Neural Networks, vol. 2, pp. 1351–1355 (2003)

16. Holm, L., Kaariainen, S., Rosenstrom, P., Schenkel, A.: Searching protein structure databases with DaliLite. Bioinformatics 3, 24(23), 2780–2781 (2008)

17. Li, H., Liu, C., Burge, L., Southerland, W.: Classification of Protein 3D Structures Using Artificial Neural Network. International Journal of Machine Learning and Computing 2(6), 791–793 (2012)

18. Lee, B., Richards, F.M.: The interpretation of protein structures: Estimation of static accessibility. J. Mol. Biol. 55, 379–400 (1971)

19. Laskowski, R., Luscombe, N.M., Swindells, M.B., Thornton, J.M.: Protein clefts in molecular recognition and function. Protein Sci., 2438 (1996)

20. Karklin, Y., Meraz, R.F., Holbrook, S.R.: Classification of non-coding RNA using graph representations of secondary structure. In: Pac. Symp. Biocomput., pp. 4–15 (2005)

21. Marsolo, K., Parthasarathy, S., Ding, C.: A multi-level approach to SCOP folds recognition. In: Proc. Fifth IEEE Symposium on Bioinformatics and Bioengineering, pp. 57–64. IEEE Computer Society, Washington, DC (2005)

22. Murzin, A.G., Brenner, S.E., Hubbard, T., Chothia, C.: SCOP: A structural classification of proteins database for the investigation of sequences and structures. J. Mol. Biol. 247, 536–540 (1995)

23. Orengo, C.A., Michie, A.D., Jones, S., Jones, D.T., Swindells, M.B., Thornton, J.M.: CATH-a hierarchic classification of protein domain structures. Structure 5(8), 1093–1108 (1997)

24. Osada, R., Funkhouser, T., Chazelle, B., Donkin, D.: Shape Distributions. ACM Transactions on Graphics 21(4), 807–832 (2002)

25. Protein Data Bank, http://www.pdb.org/

26. Shulman-Peleg, A., Nussinov, R., Wolfson, H.: Recognition of Functional Sites in Protein Structures. J. Mol. Biol. 339, 607–633 (2004)
27. Scarselli, F., Gori, M., Tsoi, A.C., Hagenbuchner, M., Monfardini, G.: The Graph Neural Network Model. IEEE Trans. on Neural Networks 20(1), 61–80 (2009)
28. Sperduti, A., Starita, A.: Supervised neural networks for the classification of structures. IEEE Trans. Neural Network 8(2), 429–459 (1997)
29. Werbos, P.J.: Backpropagation through time: what it does and how to do it. Proceedings of the IEEE 78(10), 1550–1560 (1990)

SVM-Based Classification of Class C GPCRs from Alignment-Free Physicochemical Transformations of Their Sequences

Caroline König[1], Raúl Cruz-Barbosa[2,3], René Alquézar[1], and Alfredo Vellido[1]

[1] Univ. Politècnica de Catalunya. Barcelona Tech, 08034, Barcelona, Spain
{ckonig,alquezar,avellido}@lsi.upc.edu
[2] Univ. Tecnológica de la Mixteca, 69000, Huajuapan, Oaxaca, México
rcruz@mixteco.utm.mx
[3] Institut de Neurociències. Univ. Autònoma de Barcelona, 08193, Barcelona, Spain
raul.cruz@uab.es

Abstract. G protein-coupled receptors (GPCRs) have a key function in regulating the function of cells due to their ability to transmit extracellular signals. Given that the 3D structure and the functionality of most GPCRs is unknown, there is a need to construct robust classification models based on the analysis of their amino acid sequences for protein homology detection. In this paper, we describe the supervised classification of the different subtypes of class C GPCRs using support vector machines (SVMs). These models are built on different transformations of the amino acid sequences based on their physicochemical properties. Previous research using semi-supervised methods on the same data has shown the usefulness of such transformations. The obtained classification models show a robust performance, as their Matthews correlation coefficient is close to 0.91 and their prediction accuracy is close to 0.93.

Keywords: pharmaco-proteomics, G-Protein coupled receptors, homology, transformation, supervised learning, support vector machines.

1 Introduction

G protein-coupled receptors (GPCRs) are cell membrane proteins with a key role in regulating the function of cells. This is the result of their ability to transmit extracellular signals, which makes them relevant for pharmacology. This has led, over the last decade, to active research in the field of proteomics.

The functionality of a protein depends widely on its 3-D structure, which determines its ability for certain ligand binding. Currently, the 3-D structure is only fully determined for approximately a 12% of the human GPCR superfamily [7]. As an alternative, when the information about the 3-D structure is not available, the investigation of the functionality of a protein can be achieved through the analysis of its amino acid sequence, which is known and available in several public curated databases.

A. Petrosino, L. Maddalena, P. Pala (Eds.): ICIAP 2013 Workshops, LNCS 8158, pp. 336–343, 2013.
© Springer-Verlag Berlin Heidelberg 2013

Much research on sequence analysis has focused on the quantitative analysis of their aligned versions, although, recently, alternative approaches using machine learning techniques for the analysis of alignment-free sequences have been proposed. In this paper we focus on the alignment-free analysis of class C GPCRs, which have become an important research target for new therapies for pain, anxiety and neurodegenerative disorders.

The reported experiments concern a publicly available GPCR dataset that was analyzed, in a previous study, with semi-supervised techniques [3] as a strategy for GPCR deorphanization. Here, we extend this work through the use of a supervised multi-class classification approach. In this previous work, the analysis of the alignmnent-free sequences entailed a transformation of the symbolic sequences into real-valued feature vectors on the basis of the physicochemical properties of their constituent amino acids. In this study, the same transformations are used, including the Auto-Cross Covariance (ACC) transformation [15] and a more simple one: the amino acid composition (AA). To these, we add the Mean Transformation [10]. Some of these transformations have been used in previous research, such as in [10], where they were used to classifiy the five major GPCR classes using Partial Least Square Regression, and in [9], to classify a benchmark protein database using SVMs.

As previously mentioned, the current study uses primarily SVMs as the supervised classification model of choice for each of the transformed datasets. SVMs have been reported to be a top-performing method for protein classification [6,9] and are often attributed a high discriminating power due to their ability to use non-linear kernel functions to separate the input data in higher dimensional spaces. Nevertheless, some studies [2] report better results using more simple models such as Decision Trees (DTs) and Naive Bayes (NB). For this reason, these two techniques are compared with SVMs in the current study.

The obtained SVM classification models show a robust performance in the reported experiments. This is assessed using multi-class accuracy and Matthews Correlation Coefficient (MCC). The best results are obtained with the ACC-transformed dataset, achieving an MCC close to 0.91 and a prediction accuracy close to 0.93. GPCR subtype-specific results are also reported.

2   Materials

2.1   Class C GPCRs

GPCRs are cell membrane proteins with the key function of transmitting signals through it. Therefore, they are of special relevance in pharmacology. The GPCRDB [4], a popular database of GPCRs, divides the GPCR superfamily into five major classes (A to E) based on the ligand types, functions, and sequence similarities. The current study concerns class C of these receptors. This class has become an increasingly important target for new therapies, particularly in areas such as pain, anxiety, neurodegenerative disorders and as antispasmodics. They are also important from structural and mechanistic grounds. Whereas all GPCRs are characterized by sharing a common seven transmembrane helices

(7TM) domain, responsible for G protein activation, most class C GPCRs include, in addition, an extracellular large domain, the Venus Flytrap (VFT) and a cystein rich domain (CRD) connecting both [11].

Class C is further subdivided into seven types: Metabotropic glutamate (mGluR), Calcium sensing (CaSR), GABA-B, Vomeronasal (VN), Pheromone (Ph), Odorant (Od) and Taste (Ta). The investigated dataset consists of class C GPCR sequences obtained from GPCRDB[1], version 11.3.4 as of March 2011. A total of 1,510 sequences belonging to the seven types included: 351 *mGluR*, 48 *CaSR*, 208 *GABA-B*, 344 *VN*, 392 *Ph*, 102 *Od* and 65 *Ta*. The lengths of these sequences varied from 250 to 1,995 amino acids.

3 Methods

In this paper we use first of all SVMs for the classification of the alignment-free amino acid sequences and compare the results with those obtained by less complex techniques (DTs and NB). As the amino acid sequences have a variable length, one may apply sequence kernels to use them with SVMs or transform the sequence data to fixed-size vectors in order to use them with any supervised classifier, including non-kernel methods such as DTs and NB. The second approach has been followed in this work, which allows a comparison among different classifiers and also among different transformation methods.

3.1 Alignment-Free Data Transformations

- **Amino Acid Composition Transformation**: This transformation reflects the amino acid composition (AA) of the primary sequence, that is, the frequencies of 20 amino acids are calculated for each sequence (i.e., a $N \times 20$ matrix is obtained, where N is the number of items in the dataset).
- **Mean Composition Transformation**: This transformation applied in [10] first translates the amino acid sequence into physico-chemical descriptions, i.e. each amino acid is described by five z-scores [13]. In order to obtain a fixed-length representation of the sequence the average value of each z-score is calculated. This transformation generates a $N \times 5$ matrix.
- **Auto Cross Covariance Transformation**: The ACC transformation [8,15] is a more sophisticated transformation, which captures the correlation of the physico-chemical descriptors along the sequence. First the physico-chemical properties are represented by means of the five z-scores of each amino-acid as described by [13]. Then the Auto Covariance (AC) and Cross Covariance (CC) variables are computed on this first transformation. These variables measure respectively the correlation of the same descriptor (AC) or the correlation of two different descriptors (CC) between two residues separated by a lag along the sequence. From these, the ACC fixed length vectors can be

---

[1] http://www.gpcr.org/7tm/

obtained by concatenating the AC and CC terms for each lag up to a maximum lag, l. This transformation generates a $N \times (z^2 \cdot l)$ matrix, where $z = 5$ is the number of descriptors. In this work we use the ACC transformation for a maximal lag $l = 13$, which was found to provide the best accuracy for this dataset in [3].

3.2 Supervised Classification Techniques

Support Vector Machines (SVMs) [14] are complex classifiers with an ability to find a linear separation of instances in a higher dimensional space. DTs [12] predict class membership by examining the discriminative power of the attributes, whereas NB classifiers are probabilistic classifiers [5] that work under a simplifying assumption: attribute independence, that leads to efficient computation.

SVMs are based on the statistical learning theory first introduced in [14]. SVMs may map the feature vectors $x_i, i = 1, \ldots, N$, where $x_i \in \mathbb{R}^n$ and N is the number of instances, into possibly higher dimensional spaces by means of a function ϕ . The objective is to find a linear separating hyperplane, which separates the feature vectors according to its class label with a maximal margin and minimizing the classification error ξ. The use of non-linear kernel functions allows SVMs to separate input data in higher dimensional spaces, which would not be separable with linear classifiers in the original input space.

The radial basis function (RBF) kernel, specified as $K(x_i, x_j) = e^{(-\gamma||x_i - x_j||)}$, is a popular non-linear kernel. Using it, the SVM needs to adjust two parameters through grid search: the error penalty parameter C and the parameter γ of the RBF function. Since our aim is to separate the seven subclasses of the class C GPCRs, this requires to extend the original two-class classification approach of SVMs to a multi-class classification approach. To that end, we have chosen the "one-against-one" approach to build the global classification model, which is implemented in the LIBSVM[2] library [1].

3.3 Criteria and Performance Measures

Two different measures were used to evaluate the test performance of the multi-class trained classifiers, namely the Accuracy (Accu), which is the proportion of correctly classified instances, and the MCC, which indicates how predictable the target variable is knowing the other variables: its value ranges from -1 to 1, where 1 corresponds to a perfect classification, 0 to a random classification and -1 to complete misclassification.

For the individual (binary) classification of each subtype, we report the MCC and two common measures: Precision and Recall. The former is the ratio of cases belonging to a class that are correctly classified to the cases predicted to belong to such class, whereas the later is the ratio of cases belonging to a class that are correctly classified to the cases that actually belong to that class.

---

[2] http://www.csie.ntu.edu.tw/~cjlin/libsvm/

4   Experiments

4.1   SVM Model Selection

The SVM classification models are built upon the three transformed data sets. and involve the following processing steps:

1. Preprocessing of the dataset: Standardization of the data so that the mean is 0 and standard deviation is 1.
2. Splitting of the dataset into 5 stratified folds and applying 5-fold cross validation (5-CV) for the following steps:
   (a) Use the current training set for a parameter grid-search varying the parameters C and γ in a given range.
      i. For each combination of C and γ, determine the average classification accuracy using an inner 5-CV and update the parameters C and γ providing the best result.
      ii. Train an SVM model using the selected parameters C and γ and the current training set.
   (b) Classify the current test set with the SVM model obtained in the previous step recording the classification metrics aforementioned.
3. Calculate the mean value of the classification metrics recorded during step 2.b over the five outer iterations.

In our experiments we measure the Accuracy and MCC at the global level and the Precision, Recall and MCC at class level. The reported measures are the mean values of the respective metric over the five iterations of the (outer) 5-CV. At each iteration the aforementioned metrics are recorded for the SVM trained with the best parameters C and γ found in the corresponding grid search.

4.2   Model Selection Results

Table 1 shows details, for the three transformed datasets, of the grid searches conducted to find the optimal parameters C and γ of the RBF-SVM: the range of the tested parameters C and γ, the combination of parameters found to have the best performance, and the corresponding mean accuracy and MCC values on the test sets. The reported results of the grid search in Table 1 were confirmed with subsequent grid searches in smaller ranges of the parameters.

Table 1. Model selection results

DATA	RANGE C	RANGE γ	PARAMETERS	Accu	MCC
AA	1 to 16 (step +1)	2^{-5} - 2^{5} (step ×2)	C=[2,8] , $\gamma=2^{-4}$	0.88	0.84
MEAN	1 to 16 (step +1)	2^{-5} - 2^{5} (step ×2)	C=2 , $\gamma=1$	0.68	0.59
ACC	1 to 16 (step +1)	2^{-10} - 2^{5} (step ×2)	C=[2,8] , $\gamma=2^{-9}$	0.93	0.91

4.3   Results and Discussion

The best classification results are found for the ACC transformed dataset using SVM classifiers (see Table 2 for a summary), achieving an accuracy of 0.93 and an MCC value of 0.91. The results obtained both for the ACC and the AA transformed datasets are consistent with those obtained with semi-supervised techniques in [3], where the ACC dataset also outperformed the AA dataset. Regarding classifier selection, SVM clearly outperforms DTs and NB for all three datasets (see Table 2 and Figure 1 for a comparison).

Table 2. Accuracy and MCC according to dataset and classifier

	SVM		DT		NB	
DATA	**Accu**	**MCC**	**Accu**	**MCC**	**Accu**	**MCC**
AA	0.88	0.84	0.74	0.67	0.72	0.65
MEAN	0.68	0.59	0.61	0.51	0.58	0.46
ACC	0.93	0.91	0.7	0.63	0.84	0.80

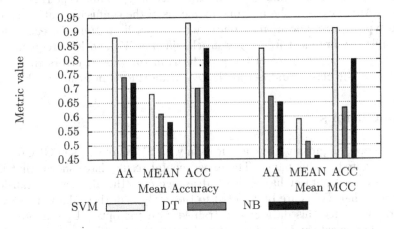

Fig. 1. Graphical representation of accuracy and MCC per dataset and classifier

Table 3 shows the classification results for the ACC-transformed dataset and the SVM classifier with greater detail at the per class level (these results correspond to a model with parameters $C=2$, $\gamma=2^{-9}$). The MCC value shows that classes $mGluR$, $CaSR$, $GABA$-B and Ta are very accurately discriminated from the other classes, having an MCC between 0.93 and 0.99. The prediction power of the classifier for classes VN, Ph and Od is clearly lower, with MCC values that range from 0.79 to 0.89.

As for the quality of the classifier, measured by the precision, it can be seen that it provides the most exact results for classes $CaSR$, $GABA$-B and Ta, as

Table 3. Per class results of SVM with the ACC data set

Class	MCC	Precision	Recall	Type I error	Type II error
mGluR	0.956	0.945	0.988	low	-
CaSR	0.933	1.000	0.877	-	high
GABA-B	0.986	0.990	0.985	-	-
VN	0.893	0.912	0.924	medium	medium
Ph	0.864	0.896	0.903	high	medium
Od	0.799	0.889	0.744	high	high
Ta	0.991	1.000	0.984	-	-

its precision gets very close to its maximum possible value. This metric shows that for classes *mGluR, Vn, Ph* and *Od* some type I classification errors (false positives) happen. Regarding the completeness of the classifier, measured by the recall, we see that it is most complete for classes *mGluR, GABA-B* and *Ta*, which means that nearly all real positives are correctly predicted. Classes *CaSR, Vn* and *Ph* have a lower recall, meaning that some type II errors (false negatives) happen for these classes. Class *Od* has a significantly lower recall than the other classes, what means that this class is most difficult to recognize.

Table 3 also shows an estimation of the quantity of type I and type II errors for each class. An analysis of these errors, by means of the confusion matrix, shows that the type II errors occur recurrently with a specific pattern for each class. For example, *Ph* are most frequently misclassified as *Vn* and less frequently as *mGluR* or *Od*. The existence of those patterns in the type II errors encourage an analysis of the class C dataset at the biochemical level in future work.

5   Conclusions

The supervised, alignment-free classification with SVMs of Class C GPCRs has been investigated in this paper. The experimental results have shown that the ACC transformed dataset has a clear advantage over the alternative transformations and that SVMs are best suited to the analysis of these data. The SVM classifiers built with this dataset and trained with the optimal parameters resulted highly accurate and discriminative. The per class results have shown some differences regarding the prediction power for some subclasses, which encourage the analysis of the less distinctive classes and the related classification errors in a future work at the biochemistry level.

Acknowledgments. This research is partially funded by Spanish research projects TIN2012-31377, SAF2010-19257, Fundació La Marató de TV3 (110230) and RecerCaixa 2010ACUP 00378. R. Cruz-Barbosa acknowledges Mexican council CONACYT for his postdoctoral fellowship.

References

1. Chang, C., Lin, C.: LIBSVM: A Library for Support Vector Machines. ACM Trans. Intell. Syst. Technol. 2(3), 27:1–27:27 (2011)
2. Cheng, B., Carbonell, J., Klein-Seetharaman, J.: Protein classification based on text document classification techniques. Proteins: Structure, Function, and Bioinformatics 58(4), 955–970 (2005)
3. Cruz-Barbosa, R., Vellido, A., Giraldo, J.: Advances in semi-supervised alignment-free classification of G protein-coupled receptors. In: Procs. of the International Work-Conference on Bioinformatics and Biomedical Engineering (IWBBIO 2013), pp. 759–766 (2013)
4. Horn, F., Bettler, E., Oliveira, L., Campagne, F., Cohen, F., Vriend, G.: GPCRDB: An information system for G protein-coupled receptors. Nucleic Acids Res. 26, 294–297 (1998)
5. John, G., Langley, P.: Estimating Continuous Distributions in Bayesian Classifiers. In: Proceedings of the Eleventh Conference on Uncertainty in Artificial Intelligence, pp. 338–345. Morgan Kaufmann (1995)
6. Karchin, R., Karplus, K., Haussler, D.: Classifying G-protein coupled receptors with support vector machines. Bioinformatics 18(1), 147–159 (2002)
7. Katritch, V., Cherezov, V., Stevens, R.C.: Structure-Function of the G Protein Coupled Receptor Superfamily. Annual Review of Pharmacology and Toxicology 53(1), 531–556 (2013)
8. Lapinsh, M., Gutcaits, A., Prusis, P., Post, C., Lundstedt, T., Wikberg, J.E.S.: Classification of G-protein coupled receptors by alignment-independent extraction of principal chemical properties of primary amino acid sequences. Protein Science 11(4), 795–805 (2002)
9. Liu, B., Wang, X., Chen, Q., Dong, Q., Lan, X.: Using Amino Acid Physicochemical Distance Transformation for Fast Protein Remote Homology Detection. PLoS ONE 7(9) (2012)
10. Opiyo, S.O., Moriyama, E.N.: Protein Family Classification with Partial Least Squares. Journal of Proteome Research 6(2), 846–853 (2007)
11. Pin, J.P., Galvez, T., Prezeau, L.: Evolution, structure, and activation mechanism of family 3/C G-protein-coupled receptors. Pharmacology & Therapeutics 98(3), 325–354 (2003)
12. Quinlan, J.R.: C4.5: Programs for Machine Learning by J. Ross Quinlan. Machine Learning 16(3), 235–240 (1993)
13. Sandberg, M., Eriksson, L., Jonsson, J., Sjöström, M., Wold, S.: New Chemical Descriptors Relevant for the Design of Biologically Active Peptides. A Multivariate Characterization of 87 Amino Acids. Journal of Medicinal Chemistry 41(14), 2481–2491 (1998)
14. Vapnik, V.N.: Statistical Learning Theory. Wiley-Interscience (1998)
15. Wold, S., Jonsson, J., Sjörström, M., Sandberg, M., Rännar, S.: DNA and peptide sequences and chemical processes multivariately modelled by principal component analysis and partial least-squares projections to latent structures. Analytica Chimica Acta 277(2), 239–253 (1993)

Structural Investigation of Supercooled Water Confined in Antifreeze Proteins: Models' Performance Evaluation between Coarse Grained and Atomistic Simulation Models

Nghiep H.V.[1], Hung P.N.[2], and Ly L.[1,2,*]

[1] School of Biotechnology, International University – Vietnam National University, HCMC, Vietnam
[2] Institute for Computational Science and Technology at Ho Chi Minh City, Vietnam
ly.le@hcmiu.edu.vn

Abstract. Antifreeze proteins (AFPs) play an important role as inhibitors of ice crystal growth in the body fluid of living organisms. Nonetheless, the exact mechanism of ice growth inhibition is still poorly understood to experimentally analyze the molecular-scale which strongly requires computer simulation for AFPs' binding site to certain planes of ice crystal. In this research, Coarse-Grained simulation using MARTINI force field was utilized to evaluate stability of helix/β-helix restraints of *M. americanus, L. perenne, M. primoryensis* and *C. Fumiferana* were collected on the Protein Data Bank using high resolution of X-ray diffraction because the β-helix/helix in AFPs' structure play an important role to face ice-binding residues with ice cluster, as receptor and ligand interactions. In results, the root mean square deviations have shown high identity of RMSF between AA-MD and CG-MD simulation in 1HG7 and 3P4G, exceptionally, 1N4I and 3ULT that can be further studied in detail using all-atoms molecular dynamics simulation (AA-MD).

Keywords: Antifreeze protein, Coarse-Grained simulation, helix/beta-helix, MARTINI force field, AA-MD.

1 Introduction

Once the temperature below sub-zero temperatures, ice crystals quickly grow then burst cells. This danger, ice formation, is a big problem for organisms in cold climates however a wide variety of organisms: plants (1,2), fish (3, 4, 5), insects (6, 7, 8) and bacteria (9) avoid damages of growth of ice crystals by producing antifreeze proteins (AFPs) or antifreeze glycoproteins (AFGPs) (10) to protect themselves as under zero temperatures. Fish can be lived at subzero temperature in the presence of specialized antifreeze protein substances in their blood, rather than the presence of salts or

---

* Corresponding author.

A. Petrosino, L. Maddalena, P. Pala (Eds.): ICIAP 2013 Workshops, LNCS 8158, pp. 344–355, 2013.
© Springer-Verlag Berlin Heidelberg 2013

additional substances (3, 10, 11). Studies revealed that these antifreeze proteins were isolated substance, which get specific function to protect the fish cold damages.

Up to date, the exact mechanism of AFPs are not jet fully understood but which have open many regards to freeze tolerance, they can survive with the formation of extracellular ice in their bodies, and freeze avoidance in organisms, food processing, pharmaceutical, cryopreservation and ice slurries (12, 13,14, 15). In food industries, the proteins can be significantly used additive compound to improve quality of product, such as making a better texture of ice cream and keeping longer shelf life of fruits and vegetables in supermarkets. Beside, antifreeze proteins can be introduced into yeast, fish, fruits and vegetables to give new beneficial properties to these organisms by genetic modification in cold climate areas. (16, 17).

Although antifreeze proteins function as inhibitors of ice formation at a certain point, they do not stop the growth of ice crystals. Size and shapes of ice crystals are controlled under different types of AFPs (18), known as ice-structuring proteins. According to a difference between melting point and freezing point, the activity of antifreeze proteins can be evaluated as thermal hysteresis (TH) which is currently focusing on complementary between binding regions of an AFP surface and specific ice cluster planes lead to high affinity protein binding to the ice surface, as receptor-ligand interactions (19). The size of the ice surface also affects directly to thermal hysteresis. On bigger ice crystals, the AFP cannot work as well as smaller ice crystals by inhibition of ice growth because of breaking the binding surface of AFP. Besides, the concentration and the type of AFP also effect to thermal hysteresis. The moderate AFP and the hyperactive AFP are two main types used to classify their activity in which the moderate is between 1 and 1.5^0C in fish AFP's and $0.1\text{-}0.5^0C$ in plant AFP's. Further, hyperactive AFP is at almost 5^0C in insect AFPs that base on the residues make up ice binding regions observing the difference in helical AFPs with different numbers of repeats to give more efficiency on the thermal hysteresis using nanoliter osmometer and a microscope in experiment (20).

Many theoretical studies have been proposed for understanding the unclear mechanisms of AFPs, which basically focus on hydrogen bonds to the surface of the ice crystals through a wide variety of folding motifs and are classified into five types based on their structure (Fig. 2). The independently AFP's active isoforms seem to be an important role in the forming hydrogen bonds between Threonine (Thr) residues array on one face of the protein and possible bonding places by their alignment on ice surface, to optimize their efficiency (10). The effect of differing numbers of coils has also been confined in the β-helical insect AFPs (20, 21) in in vitro determination by NMR and X-ray crystallography. However, in the study of flounder AFP, has shown no difference of AFP activity in comparison between blocked hydrogen bonds and non-blocked hydrogen bonds (23). After, computer simulation provided more experimental evidences to prove hydrogen bonds do not play a key role in AFP's inhibition of ice growth. (15). Following that way, the mechanism based on biomolecular structure, kinetics and thermodynamics of antifreeze proteins have been invested in dynamics behavior simulation in which all of computational calculations were done by all atoms molecular dynamics simulation (AA-MD) method (18). Molecular dynamics (MD) have become a major routine research tool. In the restricted time and equipment of my thesis, the coarse grained multi-point model was applied instead AA-MD that decreased computational complexity of MD simulation. Specially, feasible time with CG simulation occurring on microsecond or even millisecond timescale is at least four to six orders of magnitude smaller than AA-MD simulation which contains hundred thousands of atoms in a system for observing rearrangement upon ligand binding and folding, occur on microsecond or even the milliseconds timescale to β-helix AFPs stability, which can afford with desktop computers or limited cores in the high performance computer system.

In this study, CG simulation was employed as a new method of the ocean pout (*Macrozoarces americanus*), called globular type III AFP and three AFPs include perennial ryegrass (*Lolium perenne*), marine bacteria (*Marinomonas primoryensis*) and spruce budworm (*Choristoneura fumiferana*), have not classified type yet which have a same β-helix motif of insect AFP for molecular simulation to evaluate stability of β-helix/helix structures which showed activity at the beginning will be proportional to length or added repeats but decreasing activity come from lengthening the protein beyond nine repeats in type III AFP of ocean fish (24). Therefore, the stability evaluation of AFPs structure is very important in β-helix/helix motif presumably due to amino acid residues and ALA/Thr repeats accumulating steric mismatch with the ice cluster faces for further AA-MD simulation to understand AFPs mechanism in details that hypothesis for increasing thermal hysteresis by direct interaction between binding region and ice/water for a long time up to millisecond by using MD simulations.

2   Materials and Methods

2.1   Coarse Grained Simulation

In a wide variety of resources for data of structural AFPs collection, the Research Collaboratory for Structural Bioinformatics Protein Data Bank (RCSB PDB) has been invested in tools and resources of antifreeze proteins (25). In this research, there are five structural antifreeze proteins which was clarified based on four main strategies. Firstly, the research focus on diversity mechanisms of antifreeze proteins base on discrete structure from different species that involve plant, bacteria, insect and fish were collected in PDB-101. 1HG7 is a PDB entry which belongs to type III antifreeze protein of *Macrozoarces americanus* which eelpout ocean is common name, corresponding to the protein sequence code P19614 and the 1HG7 PDB high-resolution X-ray diffraction refined at 1.15Å resolution from individual anisotropic temperature factors parameter. In order, 3ULT, 3P4G and 1N4I entries of antifreeze protein structures were collected from Prennial ryegrass (*Lolium perenne*) with 1.4Å in resolution of plant, with 1.7Å in resolution of Antarctic bacterium (*Marinomonas*), spruce budworm (*Choristoneura fumiferana*), respectively. All of PDB entries were collected for molecular dynamic simulation using X-ray diffraction for structural constructing.

Martini coarse-grained protein force field, specifically, martinize version 2.3, February 13 2013 and martini v2.1_aminoacids.itp, containing 21 amino acids coarse grained force field, were applied to convert (all-atoms) atomistic antifreeze proteins structure existing as PDB format files into one Coarse Grained (CG) beads, with my

CG protein models, each amino acid is modeled by one or two beads according to their sizes in which can be classified into two broad categories: backbone bead and side-chain bead. The side chain and backbone beads can be denoted as SCi (i = ARG, GLN, GLU, HIS, ILE, LYS, MET, PHE, TRP, TYR) and BBi (i = ALA, ASN, ASP, CYS, GLY, LEU, PRO, SER, THR, VAL), respectively. Some small side-chains of amino acids are avoided due to only existing of one backbone bead while others were modeled by one uniform backbone bead and one distinct side-chain bead each residue has one backbone bead and zero or more side-chain beads depending on the amino acid type.

In the next steps, the CG-AFPs were introduced into the box would be solvate with full coarse grained water molecules which represented as polar type in the MARTINI force field using equilibrated water at 1 atm and 300k and time step of 40 femtosecond. Lennard Jones and Coulomb interactions were calculated very step for atoms within 1.2nm according t of neighbor list which updated every 10 steps. Then, all simulations were performed a short energy minimization before starting production run with for solvated box files using a same standard input options for martini 2.0/2.1 which describe the parameter for running the simulation, including distance step equals 1 femtosecond for 10000000 steps, electrostatics and Van der waals were set at 1.2Å, temperature coupling at 271K using Berend thermostat in equation 1 (spc water model) which approximately about -2°C based on Berendsen thermostat, and pressure at 1 atm during 10 ns. Besides, atomistic simulation were running using TIP5P water model to provide more detailed information.

$$\frac{dT}{dt} = \frac{T_0 - T}{\tau} \tag{1}$$

The Berendsen thermostat is an algorithm to re-scale the velocities of particles in molecular dynamics simulations to control the simulation temperature (T) in which the temperature of the system (T) is corrected such that the deviation exponentially decays with some time constant τ.

Further in data analysis, the root means square deviation (RMSD) was used to measure stable in structure of four types of antifreeze proteins follow RMSD equation which was calculated by least-square fitting the structure to the reference structure ($t_2 = 0$) and subsequently calculating the RMSD in equation 2:

$$RMSD(t_1, t_2) = \left[\frac{1}{M} \sum_{i=1}^{N} m_i \| \mathbf{r}_i(t_1) - \mathbf{r}_i(t_2) \|^2 \right]^{\frac{1}{2}} \tag{2}$$

Where $M = \sum_{i=1}^{N} m_i$ and $r_i(t)$ was the position of atom i at time t. In this thesis, carbon alpha was used as computing units for RMSD. Additionally, the radius of gyration (R_g) was applied to measure the size and compactness of AFPs base on equation 3:

$$R_g = \frac{1}{N} \sum_{k=1}^{N} (r_k - r_{mean})^2 \tag{3}$$

With N is number of coarse-graining atoms and r_k is the root mean square standard deviation of k atom(s). To ensure the state of coarse-graining water beads in box existing as an icy, the radial distribution function (RDF) or pair correlation function $g_{AB}(r)$ Between the particles of type A and B is defined by the following equation 4:

$$g_{AB}(r) = \frac{\langle \rho_B(r) \rangle}{\langle \rho_B \rangle local} = \frac{1}{\langle \rho_B \rangle local} \frac{1}{N_A} \sum_{i \in A}^{N_A} \sum_{i \in B}^{N_B} \frac{\delta(r_{ij}-r)}{4\pi r^2} \qquad (4)$$

$$\text{Or} \quad g(r) = n(r)/(\rho 4\pi r^2 \delta r)$$

With $\langle \rho_B(r) \rangle$ the particle density of type B at a distance r around particles A, and $\langle \rho_B \rangle local$ the particle density of type B averaged over all spheres around A with radius r_{max} which was half of the box length. The averaging was also performed in time. In alternative $g(r)$ formula, $n(r)$ is the number of atoms in a shell δr is shell thickness at r shell radius and ρ is the system density, (Fig. 1).

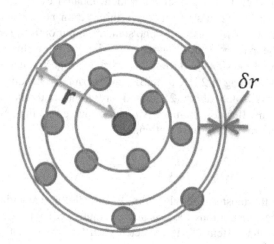

Fig. 1. Radial distribution function of the blue atoms around the red atom with r shell radius and δr shell thickness

2.2   Coarse-Grained Force Field

With the details mentioned antifreeze protein Coarse-Grained models, all internal interactions of a protein can be simplified under the CG force field which can be formulated as equation 5:

$$U = U_{bond} + U_{angle} + U_{torsion} + U_{vdw} + U_{elec} \qquad (5)$$

Where U_{bond}, U_{angle} and $U_{torsion}$ are the stretching potential energy of a virtual bond, the potential of a virtual angle bending and the potential function of a dihedral angle are about a rotating bond, respectively, which describe the bonded interactions between CG beads. U_{vdw} and U_{elec} describe the non-bonded interactions, which are the energy of van der Waals interactions and electrostatic interactions respectively. The virtual stretching interaction between two bonded cg beads can be described as a harmonic potential (equation 6):

$$U_{bond} = \sum \frac{1}{2} K_{bond} (1 - L_{bond})^2 \tag{6}$$

In which K_{bond} and L_{bond} are the force constant and the equilibrium stretching length of a bond, respectively, which would be determined by fitting the energy distribution of the virtual bond. Due to the coarse-graining, U_{angle} and $U_{torsion}$ curves become more complex and irregular when compared with those in AA force field, and they are described with Gaussian distribution function:

$$U_{angle/torsion} = \sum_{i=1}^{N} a_i \exp \left[-\left(\frac{x - b_i}{c_i} \right)^2 \right] \tag{7}$$

Where N, a_i, b_i, c_i are Gaussian parameters need to be determined in the parameterization process.

One of important equations of constructing CG-MD force field is the non-bonded potential. As in a classic AA force field, the non-bonded interaction can be divided into two categories, involving van der Waals interaction (U_{vdw}) and electrostatic interaction (U_{elec}). They can be formulated as sums of pairwise potential energy:

$$U_{vdw} = \sum_{i<j} 4\varepsilon_{ij} \left(\frac{c_{ij}^{12}}{r_{ij}} - \frac{c_{ij}^{6}}{r_{ij}^{6}} \right)$$

$$U_{elec} = \sum_{i<j} \frac{Q_i Q_j}{4\pi\varepsilon_0 \varepsilon_r r_{ij}} \tag{8}$$

Where c_{ij} is the van der Waals interaction parameter, r_{ij} is the distance between CG beads i and j, and Q_i and Q_j are the charges of i and j. The strength of the van der Waals interaction is determined by the value of well depth ε_{ij} which depends on the types of the interacting CG beads and can be determined in the force field parameterization process for all the 20 types of CG beads. In the coarse-graining, a group of atoms is treated as a single bead, and the relative positions of these atoms are fixed, but in reality, their relative positions vary in all the time.

3   Result and Discussion

3.1   Stability of Antifreeze Proteins

As the very first step to evaluate result's simulation that was relevant was based on for further data analysis, the popular root means square deviation, which used to evaluate structural similarity follow equation 2 by least-square fitting the structure to the reference structure ($t_2 = 0$) and subsequently calculating the RMSD of different types of antifreeze proteins were utilized for comparing positions of coarse grained atoms and atomistic simulation of a set of initial positions, Carbon-alpha with Carbon-alpha beads of trajectories simulated files.

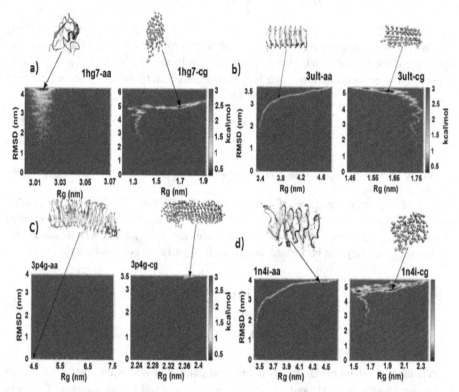

Fig. 2. The root means square deviation, radius of gyration (R_g) and free energy for protein folding. These figure shows the root means square deviation (RMSD) of back-bone carbon of (a) ocean pout (*M. Americanus*) type III antifreeze protein (1HG7) was equilibrium around about 4.5 nm in AA-MD and 5nm in CG-MD that results was higher than (b) antifreeze protein of perennial ryegrass (*L. perenne*, 3ULT) 3.2 nm and 5nm. Two remained antifreeze proteins of (c) marine bacteria (*Marinomonas primoryensis*, 3P4G) and (d) antifreeze protein of spruce budworm (*Choristoneura fumiferana*, 1N4I) which have high similarity in structure, were stable at 0.1nm and 3.5nm, at 4nm and 5nm for equilibrium, respectively.

In RMSD results, the CG-MD gave high 1 nm in average by reducing the number of atoms in AFPs' structure while the AA-MD used to keep the original structures due to the increasing number of atoms (N) of radius of gyration (R_g) equation (Eq. 3), it was larger about double times in all of case between AA-MD and CG-MD, at 4.5nm for AA-MD and 2.3nm for CG-MD in 1N4I; 4.5nm and 2.38nm in 3P4G; 3nm and 1.7nm in 1HG7 and 3.2nm and 1.65nm in 3ULT, respectively. In contrast, the folding energy were not dramatically different in AA/CG simulation arrange from 0.5 to 1 kcal/mol.

3.2   Ice Formation

All of water molecules existed as beads in Coarse Grained simulation, which cannot be evaluated ice formation based on using g_energy analysis tools in Gromacs package 4.6 to plot the bulk density of the system as a function of time of NPT simulations from bond details of atoms to atoms. By that reason, radial distribution function, called g(r), was calculated to ensure all of water beads in system that were ice. The non-periodic between ρ system density and $n(r)$ number of atoms found on shell caused to variety values of $g(r)$ in which two water beads of 1HG7 system was about 5 $\mathring{A}$, following that value was 3ULT, 3P4G and 1N4I (Fig. 8). All of water beads in four systems got a long range structural ordering that gave out the solid state of water beads which were ice clusters.

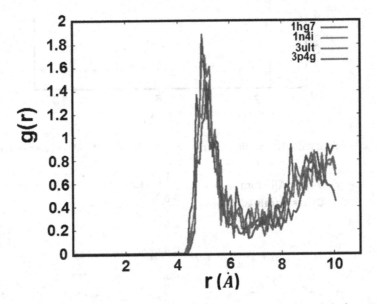

Fig. 3. Result of radial distribution function of coarse-graining water beads in four systems

Firstly, at short separations about $r < 4.3\mathring{A}$ the radial distribution function (Fig. 8) was zero that indicated the effective width of the CG water beads, since they cannot approach any more closely. Secondly, the peak appear, which indicated that the CG water beads distance between two coarse graining water beads pack around each other in shell radius that was 5 $\mathring{A}$ of distance (r) for all of four antifreeze proteins. The long ranges of the occurrence of peaks were a high degree of ordering while at -2^{0}C they were very sharp which were in crystalline where atoms are strongly confined in their positions. At very long range, CG water beads had dramatically fluctuated because the radial distribution function describes the average density in this range. In contrast, AA-MD, the short separation about $r < 1.7\mathring{A}$ for all of antifreeze proteins that showed reduced thermal dynamics of TIP5P water molecules in low temperature because the TIP5P freezing point is lower than water freezing point in ambient condition. So, the water molecules in atomistic level still remained liquid phase (Fig. 9).

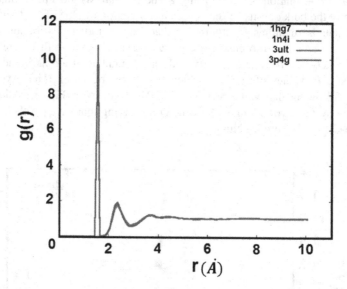

Fig. 4. Result of radial distribution function of TIP5P water molecules in four systems

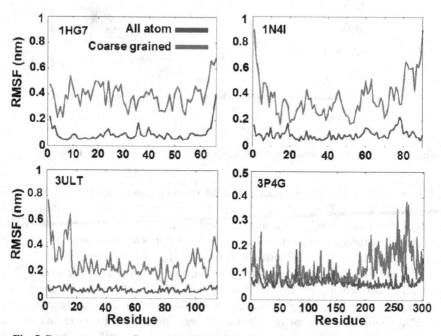

Fig. 5. Root mean square fluctuation of CG/AA models of 1HG7, 1N4I, 3ULT and 3P4G

3.3   Residues Fluctuation of AFPs

By comparing between CG-models and AA-models, the root mean square fluctuation (RMSF) of CG models frequently vibrate in a wide range from 0.2nm to 0.5nm in 1HG7; 0.2nm to 0.9nm in 1N4I; 0.2nm to 0.8nm in 3ULT and 0.15nm to 0.4 in 3P4G against a little change of atomistic simulation in Fig. 10. The main mobility in 1HG7 belong to freely movement of tail from residue 60 to 66 (MET, VAL, LYS, TYR, ALA and ALA) and was the same in a long tail of 3P4G from residue 270 to 300 (TYR, ASN, ASN, SER, SER, ASP, LEU, ARG, ASN, ARG, VAL, ALA, ASN, PHE, GLU, HIS, ILE, ARG, VAL, SER, ASP, GLY, VAL, VAL, LYS, GLY, SER, SER, PRO, ALA, ASP, PHE)   while three remained structure had differ to coupling results between CG and AA models occurred in two tail of 3ULT and 1N4I.

4   Conclusion and Recommendation

By studying antifreeze protein from four different types of antifreeze proteins in both all atoms and coarse grained models, the results are first drawing about fluctuation residues by RMSD that is ALA and ALA residues at position 65 and 66 belong to longest tail of 1HG7, the long tail including more than 30 residues in protein sequence of 3ULT which do not play crucial role in ice binding side that regularly arrange on beta-helix motif. Specifically, 1N4I and 3ULT have been stable in binding site which kept beta sheet structure during molecular dynamics simulation running. Although, the mismatch between CG and AA was not relevant for 1N4I and 3ULT came from reducing many potential in details.

5

This study recommends to build a new hybrid simulation between all-atoms and coarse grained molecular simulation will be applied to certain residues for optimized computing complex by reducing the number of atoms in 1HG7 and 3ULT systems that will at least hundred times faster than all-atoms molecular dynamic. Besides, the coarse grained simulation needs to be studied further for 3P4G and 1N4I systems by fluctuated residues which may be affected to ice bind sites. Additionally, molecular simulation cannot stand alone without the experiment up to date but it is utilized to support narrow understood of experiment, as small as picoseconds in interactions between waters and antifreeze proteins.

Acknowledgements. The work was funded by the Department of the Navy, Office of Naval Research under grant number N62909-12-1-7121. Computing resources and support by the Institute of Computational Science and Technology at the Ho Chi Minh City is gracefully acknowledged.

References

1. Atıcı, O., Nalbantoglu, B.: Antifreeze proteins in higher plants. Phytochemistry 64, 1187–1196 (2003)
2. Griffith, M., Yaish, M.W.F.: Antifreeze proteins in overwintering plants: a tale of two activities. Trends Plant Sci. 9, 399–405 (2004)
3. DeVries, A.L., Komatsu, S.K., Feeney, R.E.: Chemical and physical proper-ties of freezing-point depressing glycoproteins from antarctic fishes. J. Biol. Chem. 245, 2901–2908 (1970)
4. Davies, P.L., Hew, C.L., Fletcher, G.L.: Fish antifreeze proteins: physiology and evolutionary biology. Can. J. Zool. 66, 2611–2617 (1980)
5. Marshall, C.B., Fletcher, G.L., Davies, P.L.: Hyperactive antifreeze protein in a fish. Nature 429, 153 (2004)
6. Hew, C.L., Kao, M.H., So, Y.-P., Lim, K.-P.: Presence of cystine-containing antifreeze proteins in the spruce budworm, Choristoneura fumirana. Can. J. Zool. 61, 2324–2328 (1983)
7. Schneppenheim, R., Theede, H.: Isolation and characterization of freezing-point depressing peptides from larvae of Tenebrio molitor. Comp. Biochem. Phys. B. Biochem. Mol. Biol. 67, 561–568 (1980)
8. Duman, J.G., Bennett, V., Sformo, T., Hochstrasser, R., Barnes, B.M.: Anti-freeze proteins in alaskan insects and spiders. J. Insect Physiol. 50, 259–266 (2004)
9. Muryoi, N., Sato, M., Kaneko, S., Kawahara, H., Obata, H., Yaish, M.W.F., Yeh, Y., Feeney, R.E.: Antifreeze proteins: structures and mechanisms of function. Chem. Rev. 96, 601–618 (1996)
10. Yeh, Y., Feeney, R.E.: Antifreeze proteins: structures and mechanisms of function. Chem. Rev. 96, 601–618 (1996)
11. Ewart, K.V., Lin, Q., Hew, C.L.: Structure, function and evolution of antifreeze protein. Cellular and Molecular Life Sciences (CMLS) 55(2) (1999)
12. Bale, J.S.: Insects and Low Temperatures: From Molecular Biology to Distri-butions and Abundance. Biological Sciences 357(1423), 849–862 (2002)
13. Block, W.: To Freeze or Not to Freeze? Invertebrate Survival of Sub-Zero Temperatures. Functional Ecology 5(2), 284–290 (1991)
14. Duman, J.G., Wu, D.W., Xu, L., Tursman, D., Olsen, T.M.: Adaptations of In-sects to Subzero Temperatures. The Quarterly Review of Biology 66(4) (1991)
15. Dalal, P., Knickelbein, J., Haymet, A.D.J., Sönnichsen, F.D., Madura, J.D.: Hydrogen bond analysis of Type 1 antifreeze protein in water and the ice/water interface. Physical Chemistry Communications 7, 1–5 (2001)
16. Griffith, M., Lumb, C., Wiseman, S.B., Wisniewski, M., Johnson, R.W., Ma-rangoni, A.G.: Antifreeze Proteins Modify the Freezing Process in Planta. Plant Physiology 138(1), 330–340 (2005)
17. Hightower, R., Baden, C., Penzes, E., Lund, P., Dunsmuir, P.: Expression of antifreeze proteins in transgenic plants. Plant Molecular Biology 17, 1013–1021 (1991)
18. Hiroki, N., Yoshinori, F.: Antifreeze proteins: computer simulation studies on the mechanism of ice growth inhibition. Polymer Journal 44, 690–698 (2012)
19. Jia, Z.C., Davies, P.L.: Antifreeze proteins: An unusual receptor-ligand interaction. Trends Biochem. Sci. 27, 101–106 (2002)
20. Chao, H., Hodges, R.S., Kay, C.M., Gauthier, S.Y., Davies, P.L.: A natural variant of type I antifreeze protein with four ice-binding repeats is a particularly potent antifreeze. Protein Sci. 5, 1150–1156 (1996)

21. Leinala, E.K., Davies, P.L., Doucet, D., Tyshenko, M.G., Walker, V.K., Jia, Z.C.: A beta-helical antifreeze protein isoform with increased activity—Structural and functional insights. J. Biol. Chem. 277, 33349–33352 (2002)
22. Marshall, C.B., Daley, M.E., Sykes, B.D., Davies, P.L.: Enhancing the activity of a beta-helical antifreeze protein by the engineered addition of coils. Biochemistry 43, 11637–11646 (2004)
23. Haymet, A.D., Ward, L.G., Harding, M.M., Knight, C.A.: Valine substituted-winter flounder 'antifreeze': preservation of ice growth hysteresis. FEBS Lett. 3(430), 301–306 (1998)
24. Nolan, B.H., Yoshiyuki, N., Sakae, T., Frank, D.S.: Activity of a two-domain antifreeze protein is not dependent on linker sequence. Biophysical Journal 92, 541–546 (2007)
25. Rose, P.W., Bi, C., Bluhm, W.F., Christie, C.H., Dimitropoulos, D., Dutta, S., Bourne, P.E.: The RCSB Protein Data Bank: new resources for research and education. Nucleic Acids Res. 41(Database issue), D475–D482 (2013)
26. Gilbert, J.A., Christine, P.J., Dodd, E.R., Layborn-Parry, J.: Demonstration of Antifreeze Protein Activity in Antarctic Lake Bacteria. Microbiology 150, 171–180 (2004)

Comparison of GHT-Based Approaches to Structural Motif Retrieval

Alessio Ferone[1] and Ozlem Ozbudak[2]

[1] University of Naples Parthenope, Department of Applied Science,
Centro Direzionale Napoli - Isola C4, 80143, Napoli, Italy
alessio.ferone@uniparthenope.it
[2] Istanbul Technical University, Department of Electronics and Communication
Engineering, 34469, Istanbul, Turkey
ozbudak@itu.edu.tr

Abstract. The structure of a protein gives important information about its function and can be used for understanding the evolutionary relationships among proteins, predicting protein functions, and predicting protein folding. A *structural motif* is a compact 3D protein block referring to a small specific combination of secondary structural elements which appears in a variety of molecules. In this paper we present a comparison between few approaches for motif retrieval based on the Generalized Hough Transform (GHT). Performance comparisons, in terms of precision and computation time, are presented considering the retrieval of motifs composed by three to five SSs for more than 15 million searches. The approaches object of this study can be easily applied to the retrieval of greater blocks, up to protein domains, or even entire proteins.

Keywords: Hough transform, Protein motif retrieval, Protein structure comparison.

1 Introduction

Proteins are central molecules in biological phenomena because they form the functional and structural cell components of every organisms and their function is determined, to a large extend, by their spatial structures. Starting from the linear sequence of amino acid given in Protein Data Bank (PDB) [1], two basic regular 3D structures can be envisaged [11], called SSs: *helices and sheets*. Small specific combinations of SSs, which appear in a variety of molecules, are called *motifs*, and can be considered as super-SSs [12].

Several motifs are packed together to form compact, local, semi-independent units, i.e. with more interactions within it than with the rest of the protein, called *domains*. As consequence, a structural domain forms a compact 3D structure, independently stable, and can be determined by two characteristics: its compactness and its extent of isolation.

From the quantitative view-point, a structural motif is a 3D structural block appearing in a variety of molecules and usually consists of just a few SSs, each

A. Petrosino, L. Maddalena, P. Pala (Eds.): ICIAP 2013 Workshops, LNCS 8158, pp. 356–362, 2013.

one with an average of approximately 5 and 10 residues for sheets and helices respectively. The size of individual structural domains varies from about 25 up to 500 amino acids, but the majority (90%) has less than 200 residues with an average of approximately 100 residues. A protein in the average has 15 SSs or equivalently about 300 residues [10].

2   GHT-Based Approaches to Protein Structural Analysis

In recent years, many investigations have been made to analyze proteins at various structural levels [2,9,14], for more details see [3]. In particular, we developed various approaches for retrieving a structural block (a motif, or a domain, or ..., or an entire protein) within a protein or within the entire (PDB), by a 3D structure comparisons based on traditional pattern recognition techniques [7].

A central strategy is to exploit the Generalized Hough Transform (GHT) to implement blocks (of various sizes) retrieving through an exhaustive matching of structural elements. The searched block (let us call it model and m the number of its SSs) is in general decomposed in primitives consisting of a suitable subset of SSs. The subset can contain one, two, three, ..., up to m the entire block to be searched. The barycenter of the block model is usually assigned as Reference Point (RP) and the problem is the detection and the location of the RP in the macromolecule under scrutiny. The basic process is then a GHT voting process on the Parameter Space (PS) which is the 3D protein space.

In this work we compare the performance of four subsets consisting of the following primitive aggregates [5]: the single SS, the SS couples of the model, the SS triplets of the model and the entire model.

These subsets of primitive aggregates of the model are compared with all equivalent instances in the macromolecule or protein. For every correspondence, a vote is given to the candidate barycenter location, which is figured out with a special mapping rule determined from the RP position referred to the matched primitive aggregate of the model.

After the voting process, the points in PS which have the expected number of votes are candidate as location(s) of the RP(s) of the searched motif. Note that it is known the expected peak intensity: the number of occurrences of the primitive aggregates in the motif. In Tab. 1 a program sketch is given for searching all possible motifs in a set of M proteins.

2.1   Single Secondary Structure (SSS)

This method [13] adopts as primitive for the voting process the single SS. The SS being an helix or a sheet is represented by a straight segment on the regression line from all the C_α atoms of the segment. The extremes are determined by the projection of the terminal C_α atoms. The selective component of the Reference Table (RT) consists of two parameters, ρ and θ; ρ is the segment length between RP and SS midpoint A, and θ is the angle between SS axis and the segment $\overrightarrow{A - RP}$. The mapping rule which determines the candidate RP locations, for

Table 1. Algorithm for the retrieval of all possible r motifs contained in a set of M proteins. v is equal to 2 and 3 for couples and triplets respectively. p and p' are Md, Ad and φ for couple and direct matching, meanwhile are l_1, l_2, l_3 for triplets. r and s are respectively m and p for couples and terns and q and m for direct matching.

	Input : Protein .nss files; N_i: number of protein SSs; m: number of motif SSs
	Output : Locations of candidate motifs in the accumulator A_{RP}, representing the
	parameter space.
1	for i=1 to M do
2	Calculate all m combinations of N_i: $P_q = C(N_i, m)$
3	for j=1 to P_q do
4	Find the motif barycenter RP
5	Calculate the number of motif primitives: $P_r = C(m, v)$
6	Calculate the number of protein primitives: $P_s = C(N_i, v)$
7	for k=1 to P_r do
8	Compute the three parameters:p_1, p_2, p_3 //RT constituents
9	for l=1 to P_s do
10	Compute the three parameters: p'_1, p'_2, p'_3
11	for k=1 to P_r do
12	if (p_1, p_2, p_3) matches with (p'_1, p'_2, p'_3) then $A_{RP_l} = A_{RP_l} + 1$
13	Compute the peaks in HS
14	Assign the position with the expected votes as candidate RP

a given SS, is a circle on a plane perpendicular to the axis of the SS, with radius $r = \rho \sin \theta$, having the center along the SS axis and with a displacement $d = \rho \cos \theta$ from midpoint A. Each SS of the protein under scrutiny contributes on a circular locus on the PS. The candidate RP locations are detected as the points of intersections of these circles and, in ideal conditions, the number of intersection is just S_1.

2.2   Secondary Structure Couple Co-occurrences (SSCC)

An SS couple setup a local reference system, having the origin in the middle point of the first SS, the y-axis on its SS axis, and the x-axis on the plane defined by the y-axis and the mid-point of the second SS, then the z-axis is orthonormal to the previous two. In this reference system, the motif RP coordinates are determined, and for each couple of SSs of the protein under scrutiny that matches a motif couple, the candidate RP location is uniquely fixed [3].

The number of motif couples and protein couples is given by 2-combinations of m and N respectively: $C(m, 2)$, and $C(N, 2)$.

For every couple in the motif, a tuple is introduced in the RT where the selective component that characterizes the couple co-occurrence is composed by three parameters [10]: Md, the Euclidean distance between the middle points of the two SSs; Ad, the shortest distance between the two SSs axis; φ, the angle between the two SSs translated to present a common extreme. For each motif couple the mapping rule is reduced to a single location.

2.3   Secondary Structure Triplet Co-occurrences (SSTC)

In 3D, middle points of three SSs can be joined and an imaginary triangle is composed. So, through the SS triplets a local reference system is setup [6], e.g. having the origin in the triangle barycenter, the y-axis passing through the farthest vertex, the x-axis laying on the triangle plane and orthonormal to y-axis, and the z-axis following the triangle plane normal. With this reference system the motif RP coordinates are determined, and also in this case for each triplet of SSs of the protein under scrutiny that matches a motif triplet, the candidate RP location is uniquely fixed [4].

For every triplet in the motif, a tuple is introduced in the RT where the selective component that characterizes the triplet is composed by three parameters represented by the lengths of the triangle edges. For each motif triplet the mapping rule is reduced to a single location. The numbers of motif triplets and protein triplets are given by 3-combinations of m and N respectively: $C(m,3)$, and $C(N,3)$.

2.4   Entire Motif

This approach [8] consists on an exhaustive Motif Direct Matching (MDM) among the motif and all possible blocks (B) of the biomolecule under scrutiny having the same number of motif SSs. Let N and P_q be the number of SSs in the macromolecule and the cardinality of B respectively, i.e. P_q is the m-combinations in N, computed as $P_q = C(N,m)$. Each element of B must be compared with the motif.

So, for each couple of SSs in both biomolecule and motif, the terns Md, Ad and φ are computed. As in SSCC the RT tuples are composed for the discriminant component of the quoted set of motif terns, combined to the relative RP location as mapping rule. For every correspondence between an SS motif couple and a couple of the candidate block, a vote is given to the location of the candidate block barycenter.

3   Experimental Results

The aim of these experiments is the evaluation of precision and computation time of the proposed approaches. A set of proteins has been randomly selected among the PDB 91939 structures having a number N_i of SSs ranging from 14 to 46 (a number of residue from 174 to 496). All possible structural blocks with m equal to three, four and five, have been retrieved for the SSCC and SSTC approaches. For the MDM approach, due to high computation time, the experimentation has been limited to just one thousand randomly cases selected. Due to the evident poor performance regarding both computation time and precision the SSS has been experimented just in a few cases. Table 2 reports the number of experiments for the SSCC and SSTC cases $\sum_{i=1}^{M} C(N_i, m)$ (column three: $C(N_i, m)$) and the cumulative and average time performances.

Table 2. Performances and protein parameters of the experimented set

Number of motif SSs: m	Number of motifs: P_q	Average search time and range per motif for SSCS (msec)	Average search time and range per motif for SSTS (msec)	Average search time and range per motif for MDM(msec)
3	105971	1.1 [0.6-1.5]	7.3 [0.9-11.7]	21.1 [2.5-42.7]
4	918470	1.4 [0.5-1.8]	11.2 [1.2-16.9]	310.1 [9.1-1039.6]
5	6455009	1.7 [0.5-2.2]	17.3 [1.4-24.4]	10647.5 [36.7-69353.3]

In all the nearly 15 million cases, the matching of candidates motifs with the RT tuples has been verified with a tolerance in the comparison parameters of $\epsilon = 1\%$. Figure 1 shows just an example of search of a motif composed by mixed helices and strands on the protein 7FAB containing 46 SSs. In all cases, the collected RP locations had exactly the expected number of votes/contributions (three, six and ten respectively for three, four and five SSs per motif). Moreover, no spurious peaks have been detected for the SSCC and SSTC cases; meanwhile for MDM case the detected spurious peaks follow the above mentioned rules. In details, the sets of second peaks have a ratio with the first peak of 1/3, 1/2, and 3/5 as expected.

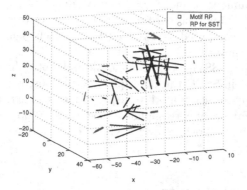

Fig. 1. Results obtained on searching a five SSs motif on the 7FAB protein. Red lines are α-helices and blue lines are β-strands. Bold lines form the five-SS motif (three α-helices and two β-sheets). RP and Max. vote coordinates are coincident.

No displacement from the true RP position could be measured: the motif location (just the one where the model was defined) perfectly coincided to the detected RP location.

From the computational time point of view the two worst solutions are the SSS and the MDM. This is certainly due, in the first case, to the cumbersome mapping rule which complicates both the voting process and the peaks detection on the PS. For the MDM instead, being an exhaustive matching, the number of comparisons grows with the polynomial complexity given above.

From the precision point of view we get good performances by the SSCC and SSTC, and also MDM, and the worst cases for the SSS that in the few experiment location precision, it was under 0.32%.

4 Conclusion

Important functionalities of proteins are determined by their 3D structure, so protein structures comparison and motif retrieving are areas of increasing interest in structural biology. This paper aims at comapring GHT-based approaches for retrieving a structural block on the basis of the 3D distribution of SSs.

All the analyzed approaches result effective for protein motif matching and retrieval. The approaches of SSCC and SSTC to compare motif and protein represented by SSs are simple to implement, robust, computationally efficient, and very fast with respect to the other implementations, even with GHT approach.

References

1. http://www.rcsb.org/pdb/
2. Camoglu, O., Kahveci, T., Singh, A.K.: Psi: indexing protein structures for fast similarity search. Bioinformatics 19(suppl. 1), i81–i83 (2003)
3. Cantoni, V., Ferone, A., Ozbudak, O., Petrosino, A.: Motif retrieval by exhaustive matching and couple co-occurrences. In: 9th International Meeting on Computational Intelligence Methods for Bioinformatics and Biostatistics, CIBB (2012)
4. Cantoni, V., Ferone, A., Ozbudak, O., Petrosino, A.: Search of protein structural blocks through secondary structure triplets. In: 3rd International Conference on Image Processing Theory, Tools and Applications, IPTA (2012)
5. Cantoni, V., Ferone, A., Ozbudak, O., Petrosino, A.: Structural analysis of protein secondary structure by ght. In: 2012 21st International Conference on Pattern Recognition (ICPR), pp. 1767–1770 (2012)
6. Cantoni, V., Ferone, A., Ozbudak, O., Petrosino, A.: Protein motifs retrieval by ss terns occurrences. Pattern Recognition Letters 34(5), 559–563 (2013)
7. Cantoni, V., Ferone, A., Ozbudak, O., Petrosino, A.: Protein structural motifs search in protein data base. In: Proceedings of the 13th International Conference on Computer Systems and Technologies, CompSysTech 2012, pp. 275–281. ACM, New York (2012)
8. Cantoni, V., Ferone, A., Ozbudak, O., Petrosino, A.: Searching structural blocks by SS exhaustive matching. In: Peterson, L.E., Masulli, F., Russo, G. (eds.) CIBB 2012. LNCS, vol. 7845, pp. 57–69. Springer, Heidelberg (2013)
9. Chionh, C., Huang, Z., Tan, K., Yao, Z.: Augmenting sses with structural properties for rapid protein structure comparison. In: Proceedings of the Third IEEE Symposium on Bioinformatics and Bioengineering, pp. 341–348. IEEE (2003)
10. Dror, O., Benyamini, H., Nussinov, R., Wolfson, H.: Mass: multiple structural alignment by secondary structures. Bioinformatics 19(suppl. 1), i95–i104 (2003)
11. Eisenberg, D.: The discovery of alpha-helix and beta-sheet, the principal structural features of principal structural features of proteins. Proc. of the National Academy of Sciences of the United States of America 100, 11207–11210 (2003)

12. Singh, M.: Predicting Protein Secondary and Supersecondary Structure. Computer and Information Science Series. Chapman & Hall CRC (2005)
13. Cantoni, V., Mattia, E.: Protein structure analysis through hough transform and range tree. Biological Systems, Nuovo Cimento C 35(suppl. 1), 39–45 (2012)
14. Zotenko, E., Dogan, R., Wilbur, W., O'Leary, D., Przytycka, T.: Structural footprinting in protein structure comparison: The impact of structural fragments. BMC Structural Biology 7, 53 (2007)

CCMS: A Greedy Approach to Motif Extraction

Giacomo Drago, Marco Ferretti, and Mirto Musci

University of Pavia, Via Ferrata 1, 27100 Pavia, Italy
marco.ferretti@unipv.it,
{mirto.musci01,giacomo.drago01}@ateneopv.it

Abstract. Efficient and precise motif extraction is a central problem in the study of proteins functions and structures. This paper presents an efficient new geometric approach to the problem, based on the General Hough Transform. The approach is both an extension and a variation of the Secondary Structure Co-Occurrences algorithm by Cantoni et al. [1-2]. The goal is to provide an effective and efficient implementation, suitable for HPC. The most significant contribution of this paper is the introduction of a heuristic greedy variant of the algorithm, which is able to reduce computational time by two orders of magnitude. A secondary effect of the new version is the capability to cope with uncertainty in the geometric description of the secondary structures.

Keywords: Motif Extraction, Secondary Structures, SSC, Hough Transform, Algorithm Optimization, Greedy Algorithm.

1 Introduction

The study of proteins is a crucial aspect of the biological field, as they are essential elements of every living cell. Often, the function of a given protein is tightly tied to its geometric structure. Thus, protein structure analysis is an important issue with multiple applications. For example, the ability of a protein to bind other proteins or ligands and the estimation of evolutionary distances between families of proteins are both based on their spatial structure. A key part in the geometric description of a protein is played by the structural motif, a 3D group of secondary structures (SS) which appears in a variety of molecules. Thus, precise and efficient motif identification or extraction is a much requested application in the biological community.

The simplest approach to motif extraction is the entire motif search (EMS). It is used to identify the location of each possible motif (defined by a set of properties, e.g. its spatial dimension) in a given protein. The EMS has been thoroughly analyzed [3], with special regard to its parallel implementation.

However, the most interesting approach to the problem is one that we can call "*cross motif search*" (CMS). In this case every possible motif in a given source protein, is searched in each protein of a given set. A CMS run is composed of multiple iterations: defining the cardinality of a motif as the number of SS in that motif, the n-th iteration of a CMS run tries to extract, from the protein set, all the motifs with cardinality n.

A. Petrosino, L. Maddalena, P. Pala (Eds.): ICIAP 2013 Workshops, LNCS 8158, pp. 363–371, 2013.

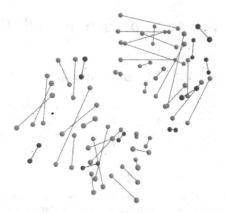

Fig. 1. Protein 7fab displayed as a cloud of segments using our ad-hoc visualizer software. *Segments*: SSs. *Spheres*: endpoints. *Dots*: barycenter. *Red*: alpha helices; *Blue*: beta sheets.

In the most generalized variant, a complete CMS (CCMS) searches for every possible motif of every source protein in any other protein in the set.

Of course, as the entire Protein Data Bank [4] contains about 90,000 proteins, a CCMS may require an extremely high computational time.

In this paper we will present the CCMS algorithm and show an efficient implementation, suitable for HPC. The algorithm is based on an existing approach, the Secondary Structure Co-Occurrences (SSC) [1-2], which is itself based on the General Hough Transform technique [5]. The key idea is to ignore the biological significance on the motifs as much as possible, and to focus on the geometric description of the structures which could be simply viewed as vectors in a 3D space.

First, we briefly describe the original SSC algorithm (sec. 2). Then we discuss an extensive set of modifications to the original algorithm, including an efficient greedy variant which is able to reduce the computational times down by two orders of magnitude (sec. 3). Finally, we present a few benchmarks (sec. 4).

2   The Base SSC Algorithm

Given a set of oriented segments in a 3D space (the source), and a search space consisting of a certain number of oriented segments, the SSC algorithm [1-2] is able to determine whether the source is present in the search space or not, independently of translations and rotations of the source.

The key idea underlying the algorithm is that any relevant secondary structure (SS) in a protein can be easily modeled as an oriented segment. A segment is obtained from a least-square approximation of all the relevant amino-acid positions, as defined in the DSSP description of a SS [6]. Every segment is simply identified by a barycenter, two endpoints and an orientation (fig. 1). Thus a DSSP file describing an entire protein can be transformed into a list of segments and their properties, and easily described by a simple XML file.

Thanks to this simplified model, the SSC algorithm is able to determine whether a given motif of SSs is present in a given protein or not. Of course, the SSC algorithm can be used as the base element of both the EMS and the CMS algorithms.

2.1   Using the GHT to Extract Motifs

The Generalized Hough Transform describes a *geometric pattern* by selecting a *reference point* (RP) in a coordinate system local to the pattern and a set of *features elements* (points, segments, etc.) that make up the pattern and that are geometrically referenced to this point. This structural description is encoded in a *reference table* (RT in the following).

The transform (*voting rule*) consists of producing, for each feature element in the *search space* (the object under scrutiny), a number of candidates for the RP of the geometric pattern; these candidates are collected in a *voting space* where evidence of occurrences of candidates are accumulated.

An analysis of the *voting space* looking for peaks of accumulated occurrences allows identifying places where there exist instances of the looked-for geometric pattern.

This method is often used in pattern recognition. Its computational complexity can be quite relevant, since it depends on the numbers of feature elements used to describe the geometric pattern (i.e., the cardinality of the RT), on the number of feature elements present in the search space, and on the resolution at which the voting space is quantized.

SSC is based on a modified GHT, which searches for motifs (*geometric patterns*) of SSs (*feature elements*) inside a given protein (*search space*). In the SSC approach, the basic feature elements are couples (or co-occurrences) of SSs, instead of single SSs as it would be expected. In this way it is possible to be both orientation- and translation-agnostic during the search.

The voting rule is defined using only the geometric features of the SSs vectors. In the case of SSC, it is a change-of-basis matrix.

Each row of a motif RT consists of a set of relevant geometric parameters for a single couple of SSs taken from that motif, and the relative transformation matrix.

A given feature element can meaningfully produce a vote (using the matrix) only if its geometric parameters *match* against the parameters contained inside at least one row of the RT. In general, this *matching phase* can be used to reduce the number of votes, thus reducing both the possibility of false positives and the execution time. The idea is to identify a certain number of properties that the feature elements in both source and search space must possess and check for them before voting.

In ideal conditions (without false positives and spurious votes), if a motif is present in the protein, the voting process produces a peak of votes with intensity exactly equal to the number of rows of the reference table or $\binom{c}{2}$, where c is the motif cardinality.

A step-by-step analysis of the SSC algorithm is outside the scope of this paper. For a more detailed discussion, see [1-2].

3   Extending the SSC: CCMS

3.1   Optimizations

As the goal of this paper is to produce an efficient implementation of the CMS algorithm, several optimizations have been introduced into the original SSC algorithm. Here we discuss only the most significant ones.

In a naïve implementation, geometric parameters associated to each couple of SSs are calculated *just-in-time*, i.e. each time that a couple is considered. Therefore, some computations are repeated uselessly multiple times. It is possible to save a significant amount of time if one stores the geometric parameters associated to each couple in a special purpose cache. The cache is filled in completely, for each protein, before the actual search on that protein.

It is also possible to linearize the cache, so that the algorithm reads it in sequence, thus ensuring both space and time locality. The key idea is to associate a set of contiguous natural number to the couples, and is based on the combinatorial number system by D. Knuth [7].

3.2   Tolerance Parameters

To adapt SSC for CMS, we need to make it account for tolerance in the geometric features. The first three features to consider are the ones used to construct the reference table, namely the barycenter distance, the line distance and the angle between the two SSs in the couple.

Moreover, it is extremely important to allow for adequate *peak tolerance* during the finding phase of the algorithm, as even extremely similar motifs can produce votes in a spread of a few angstroms. Thus, CMS employs an exact procedure to extract accumulation of votes from the search space, based on the *MaxCliqueDyn* algorithm by Konc et al. [8].

We also implemented two additional checks during the *matching* (see sec. 2.1) between a row in the RT and a couple of SSs in the search space. The first check is biological in nature: two geometrical affine couples can match only if both have the same biological types (e.g. two alpha helices can match only with two other alpha helices). The second check is based on the size of the SSs. Two couples can match only if they are comparable in size.

Accounting for tolerance during the matching phase yields two kinds of different false positives (i.e. accumulations of voting points which cannot be considered valid search hits):

1. Random accumulations of voting points, cast from completely unrelated couples;
2. Accumulations of voting points that are only due to a portion of the searched motif.

Note that random accumulations become more frequent as the number of cast votes increase.

In order to reduce the impact of this problem, one can eliminate all the clearly invalid accumulations points. Thus, peaks with cardinality lower than expected[1] and peaks which are too far away from their predicted reference points are filtered away.

Additionally, a third kind of spurious result is possible: an accumulation of votes referring to a valid motif, plus one or more spurious secondary structures. However, results of this kind cannot be filtered as they may contain peaks which were otherwise not considered.

3.3   The Orientation Problem

The base SSC algorithm defines the voting rule for each couple as a change-of-basis matrix (see sec.1), which transforms the coordinates of the motif reference point from the source protein reference system to a reference system which depends only on the geometric properties of that couple. As the SSs are modeled as oriented segments, and each couple defines an internal order of SSs, it is possible to define a procedure to identify a unique reference system for each couple. For more details, see again [1].

For performance reasons, it is not affordable to consider inverse couples (i.e. couple which are made of the same SSs, but taken in the inverse order) as different couples. This would double both the number of comparisons and the size of the cache. Moreover, we noticed that the orientations of the SS segments are dependent on their DSSP description, which can differ even for very similar motifs, leading to geometrically valid matches being discarded due to their opposite orientation.

Thus, an orientation-agnostic approach is needed to ensure correctness, i.e. to avoid losing potential matches.

Given two segments in a 3D space, there are at least four different ways to construct a local reference system, which is completely independent of the external context. Each of them depends on the orientations of the segments and their relative order. Thus we modified the way in which the RT is constructed: each row carries four different voting rules, i.e. four different matrices. This means that each match produces four votes, not one. In this way the core of the algorithm remains the same, it is still possible to exploit linear accesses to the cache and correctness is ensured. The increased cost, of course, is due to the extra time needed to process a single vote and the fact that the number of votes increases by a factor of four. Fortunately the filters help in greatly reducing the number of votes.

To avoid useless recalculation, all the inverse matrices are also stored in a cache, initially empty. Each entry is written only when needed, using appropriate synchronization. In this way the application would be safe from race conditions if it were to be run in parallel.

3.4   An Efficient Greedy Variant (Greedy-CCMS)

The CCMS algorithm can be implemented in a straightforward way, which leads to a *brute-force* approach. Each iteration (with increasing motif cardinality, see sec. 1) is

---

[1]   i.e. $\binom{c}{2}$, where c is the motif cardinality. See sec. 2.1.

performed independently from one another and has a complexity of $O\left(\frac{N^c}{c!}\right)$ where N is the number of SSs in the search protein and c is the cardinality of the motif [3].

Fortunately, it is possible to greatly reduce the *average complexity* of the CCMS algorithm. Note, however, that the asymptotic complexity remains the same.

Given two motifs S and M, we say that S is a sub-motif of M if the SSs in S are a proper subset of the SSs in M. The key idea is that a motif of dimension n is present in the search space only if all its sub-motifs of dimension $n-1$ are also present. Starting from this observation it is possible to define a constructive algorithm:

1. The first step consists of a fast brute-force iteration, where motifs of the source protein having a cardinality of three[2] are searched inside the search protein.
2. All found peaks, before being filtered (see sec. 3.2), are collected in a set (called *unfiltered*).
3. The peaks are filtered and saved in another set (*results*), as they are indeed valid.
4. From the next iteration onward, the algorithm constructs new source motifs in the following way: for each peak in the *unfiltered* set *of the previous iteration*, and for each SS s in the source protein, add s to the motive associated to the peak.
5. Search the so-constructed source motifs inside the search protein.
6. The algorithm terminates when the *unfiltered* set of the previous iteration is empty.

There are two main advantages related to the greedy approach. The first is the extremely lower execution times (up to two orders of magnitude) if compared to the brute-force approach (see sec. 4). The second one is that the approach is feasible even for motifs having a high cardinality, as opposed to the brute-force approach. In fact, Greedy-CCMS can efficiently extract motifs up to the maximum cardinality N, even identifying whole tertiary structures.

4   Benchmarks

In this section we will present some benchmarks for both the brute-force and the greedy variant of the CCMS.

As stated in sec. 1, a CCMS on a protein set implies comparing each protein in the set against each other, in order to extract all the common motifs.

The small protein dataset described in [2] has been used for the benchmarks. As the dataset contains 20 proteins, the total number of protein pairs to be processed is exactly $20^2 - 20 = 380$. The maximum cardinality for the source motifs was set to 5.

The results reported in Table 1 clearly show the performance improvement of the greedy variant of the algorithm over the brute-force one. The speed-up of the greedy variant is about 75.6 using strict tolerance parameters and 42.3 using loose parameters. Both implementations take advantage from the optimizations described in sec. 3. For higher cardinalities of the source motifs the speedup of the greedy variant is expected to be even better.

---

[2] The smallest significant dimension for a motif is three, as dimension one is nonsense, and dimension two is trivial.

Table 1. CCMS run on the test database (max. cardinality 5): execution times

CCMS variant	Tolerance	Total exec. time (sec.)	Avg. exec. time for a single pair of proteins (sec.)
brute-force	strict[3]	2,756.84	7.255
brute-force	loose[4]	2,821.06	7.424
greedy	strict	36.51	0.096
greedy	loose	66.62	0.175

It is worth mentioning that as the tolerance parameters become looser, the greedy variant tends to the same performance of the brute-force variant. The reason is that the higher number of matches for motifs of low cardinality (3 and 4) increases the number of motifs to be processed in the steps 4 and 5 of the Greedy-CCMS (see sec. 3.4).

Exploiting the high performance of the greedy variant, we repeated the benchmark, setting the maximum cardinality to 10. The number of matches, even on a very small dataset, is quite impressive (see Table 2) [5]. Fig. 2 depicts an example of match with cardinality 10.

Table 2. CCMS run on the test database (max. cardinality 10): histogram of the matches

Tolerance	Total exec. time (sec.)	Motif cardinality	Number of matches
strict	47.25	3-4	4,551
		5-8	2,313
		9-10	0
loose	119.33	3-4	5,007
		5-8	3,966
		9-10	611

Fig. 2. CMS between proteins 2qx8 (*source*) and 2qx9 (*search*). Example of match with cardinality 10.

---

[3] Barycenter distance: 0.5 Å; line distance: 0.5 Å; angle: 5°; peak: **1.0** Å.

[4] Barycenter distance: 0.5 Å; line distance: 0.5 Å; angle: 5°; peak: **1.5** Å.

[5] Numbers may include the same motifs matching more than one time. Moreover, items like 2qx8 and 2qx9 represent variants of the same protein, thus producing a large number of matches.

5   Conclusions and Future Work

In this paper we have presented a new algorithm, called CCMS, which is based on an extension of the pre-existent SSC algorithm. Benchmarks show that Greedy-CCMS is extremely more efficient than the straightforward brute-force implementation, so that the CCMS is indeed feasible in terms of execution times.

The number of extracted motifs is impressive. However, the current implementation is unable to automatically exclude duplicate results, to discriminate the most relevant results from a biological point of view, or to perform a statistic analysis of the matches. Addition of efficient data-mining is the main line of work for the next extension of the algorithm.

Moreover, it may be interesting to analyze a different variant of the original algorithm, by the same authors, called SS Tern [9]. The base feature element for the SST is a triplet of SSs, and not a couple as in the SSC. Using terns, it is easier to unambiguously identify a local reference system, thus decreasing the size of a single row in the reference table, even if the SST has a higher complexity.

Eventually it could be possible to implement a new CMS variant using as its base elements modified versions of both SSC and SST.

Finally, as it was noted previously, CCMS can be very computationally expensive, even in the greedy variant. An MPI implementation of the algorithm is in the workings; the goal is to process the entire PDB (or at least the most relevant SCOP fields [10]) on the CINECA supercomputing facilities [11].

References

1. Cantoni, V., Ferone, A., Ozbudak, O., Petrosino, A.: Structural analysis of protein secondary structure by GHT. In: 21st International Conference on Pattern Recognition, ICPR 2012, Tsukuba, Japan, November 11-15, pp. 1767–1770. IEEE Computer Society Press (2012)
2. Cantoni, V., Ferone, A., Ozbudak, O., Petrosino, A.: Motif Retrieval by Exhaustive Matching and Couple Co-occurrences. In: 9th International Meeting on Computational Intelligence Methods for Bioinformatics and Biostatistics, CIBB 2012, Texas, July 12-14 (2012)
3. Ferretti, M., Musci, M.: Entire Motifs Search of Secondary Structures in Proteins: A Parallelization Study. In: International Workshop on Parallelism in Bioinformatics EUROMPI 2013, Madrid, Spain, September 17 (in printing, 2013)
4. Protein Data Bank, http://www.rcsb.org/pdb
5. Ballard, D.: Generalizing the Hough Transform to Detect Arbitrary Shapes. Pattern Recognition 13(2), 111–122 (1981)
6. Kabsch, W., Sander, C.: Dictionary of protein secondary structure: pattern recognition of hydrogen-bonded and geometrical features. Biopolymers 22, 2577–2637 (1983)
7. Knuth, D.E.: Generating All Combinations and Partitions. In: The Art of Computer Programming, vol. 4, Fascicle 3, pp. 5–6. Addison-Wesley (2005)
8. Konc, J., Janežič, D.: An improved branch and bound algorithm for the maximum clique problem. MATCH Communications in Mathematical and in Computer Chemistry 58(3), 569–590 (2007)

9. Cantoni, V., Ferone, A., Ozbudak, O., Petrosino, A.: Protein motifs retrieval by SS terns occurrences. Pattern Recognition Letters 34, 559–563 (2012)
10. Structural Classification of Proteins and ASTRAL (January 2013), http://scop.berkeley.edu
11. CINECA supercomputing center (9th in top500.org as of May 2013), http://www.cineca.it

Structural Blocks Retrieval in Macromolecules: Saliency and Precision Aspects

Virginio Cantoni[1] and Dimo T. Dimov[2]

[1] Department of Industrial and Information Engineering, Pavia University, Italy
virginio.cantoni@unipv.it
[2] Inst. of Inf. & Comm. Tech., Bulgarian Academy of Sciences, Sofia, Bulgaria
dtdim@iinf.bas.bg

Abstract. A structural *motif* is a compact 3D block of a few secondary structural elements (SSs) – each one with an average of approximately 5 and 10 residues for sheets and helices respectively – which appears in a variety of macromolecules. Several motifs pack together and form compact, semi-independent units called *domains*. The domain size varies from about 25 up to 500 amino acids, with an average of approximately 100 residues. This hierarchical makeup of molecules results from the generation of new sequences from preexisting ones, in fact motifs and domains are the common material used by nature to generate new functionalities. Structural biology is concerned with the study of the structure of biological macromolecules like proteins and nucleic acids, and it is expected to give more insights in the function of the protein than its amino acid sequence. In this paper we propose and analyze a possible performance of a new approach for the detection of structural blocks in large datasets such as the Protein Data Base (PDB).

Keywords: protein motif retrieval, protein structure comparison, protein secondary structure, protein data bases, secondary structure saliency, error analysis.

1   Introduction

In the last decade many approaches have been developed for retrieving a block (a motif, or a domain, …, up to an entire protein) within a protein, or within the entire PDB, by using 3D structural comparison [1-3].

As an example, starting from a traditional pattern recognition techniques – the Generalized Hough transform (GHough) [4] – a family of new approaches have been proposed on the basis of the 'primitives' complexity from which the voting process can rise. The smallest aggregate can be the single SS [5]; at another more effective level we adopted the occurrences of pairs of SSs [6]; in alternative we proposed terns of SSs occurrences [7]; up to the entire motif of m SSs, $m{\geq}3$, for a complete exhaustive matching [8]. All these techniques are similar for what refers the basic process, and adopt the same Parameter Space (PS) – the protein volume – but differ consistently about the voting process and consequently in performances [9]. Nevertheless, in all

A. Petrosino, L. Maddalena, P. Pala (Eds.): ICIAP 2013 Workshops, LNCS 8158, pp. 372–380, 2013.

these methods, in the PS, after the voting process, the points which have the expected number of votes are candidates as Reference Point (RP) locations of the searched motif. Note that, it is known the expected peak intensity and the composition: the number of occurrences of each SSs types in the motif model.

The computational complexity of the quoted GHough approach is limited, e.g. for the pairs (and terns) co-occurrences, being N the number of SSs of the macromolecule under analysis, the computational complexity is $O(N^2 m^2)$: the number of protein SS pairs is $O(N^2)$ and the number of model motif SS pair is $O(m^2)$ and each protein pair is to be compared to each motif pair to eventually give a vote in the correspondent displacement of the RP location.

Nevertheless, for searching all the presences of a given motif in a large PDS, this approach is considered slow and thus impractical – even if, in the average, a three-SSs motif is detected in a given protein in about 5 μs! So, in this paper we proposed a new approach, derived by the quoted ones, but exploiting other than the 3D SSs distribution, also salient biochemical information on the SS composition. In this way we implement a new planning strategy in order to reduce consistently the computing time, but without losing the precision performance.

2   Our New Strategy

The SSs are usually represented as oriented linear segments, e.g. the axis for the α-helix and the best fit segment for a β-strand. The determination of the SSs of a protein is usually given by programs designed to standardize the SS assignment, such as the DSSP [10], or the STRIDE [11], which are both considered sufficiently precise (even if on the average 4.8% of the target residues were differently assigned). These programs support a rich information, such as: i) the total number of residues, ii) the number of chains, iii) the total number of hydrogen bonds, iv) the sequential residue number, v) the amino acid sequence, vi) a SS summary, vii) the type of helix (of 3-4-5 turns) or of β-bridge or the sheet label, moreover, viii) geometrical bend, ix) chirality, x) solvent accessibility, etc.

In our approach, the basic idea is initially to refer just to one SS, selected in the model motif for its saliency on the basis of the above detailed information. As for the GHough methods, it is also convenient to limit the displacement of analysis for a trivial reason related to precision, and thus to select the main SS as close as possible to the barycenter of the model motif. We will call S_0 this reference SS of the motif model hereinafter.

Also in this new approach, as for the mentioned GHough approaches, it is necessary to set up a Local Reference System (LRS) for the model representation, and it is convenient that the LRS origin is to be as close as possible to the barycenter. A suitable point for that is the midpoint of S_0. Moreover, it is convenient to put the y-axis of the LRS on the axis of S_0, meanwhile the x-axis is located on the plane defined by the y-axis and the midpoint of a second SS, in this connection the z-axis is obviously orthogonal (see figure 3). For the same reason of precision robustness, it is convenient that also this second SS would be well characterized and situated as far as possible from S_0, and as more as possible tilted with respect to S_0. Note that, the higher the distance the higher also the searching space for this second SS. We will call S_1 this second SS of reference for the motif.

For this SS pair (S_0, S_1), which characterizes the motif and fix the LRS, two parameters are discriminant: ρ_1, the Euclidean distance between the midpoints of the two SSs; φ_1, the angle between the axis of S_0 and the midpoint of S_1, as shown in figure 1.

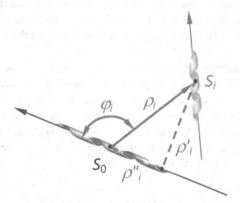

Fig. 1. The (ρ, φ) parameters definition of the main motif SSs-pair (S_0, S_i), $i=1$

The general target is to detect all possible instances of the motif in the given protein, or in a set of proteins, or in the whole PDB.

A preliminary search is devoted to look for all possible SSs, which have the same peculiarities (SS type, number of residues, amino acid sequence, etc.) of S_0, where we locate the origin of the LRS. Being n, $n \leq N$, the number of protein SSs, which match S_0, it would be necessary to analyze all the n-neighborhood $NB(n)$ to validate the possible existence of the motif.

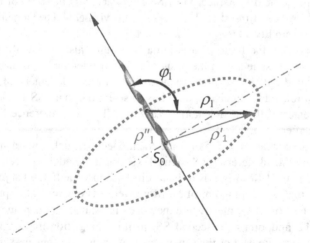

Fig. 2. The locus of candidate S_1 positions is a circle in PS, which is orthogonal to reference S_0 and centered on S_0 axis

In a second phase we have to introduce the LRS of the candidate motif in each NB(n). For this purpose we need to identify the possible locations of S_1. Obviously, these instances of S_1 must be compatible with the two parameters (ρ_1, φ_1), shown in figure 1, referred to S_0, other than compatible to the peculiarities of S_1 (its SS type, number of residues, amino acid sequence, etc.). From the geometrical point of view the locus of the candidate positions of the midpoints of S_1 is a circle belonging to a plane, normal to the axis of S_0, and having the center on this axis at a distance $\rho.\cos(\varphi)$ from the midpoint of S_0. Figure 2 details this locus. For each point of the dashed circle the possible existence of S_1 must be validated.

Let us call n_1 the number of compatible pairs (S_0, S_1) that are extracted in the above way, obviously $n_1 \leq n$. It is now necessary to examine the existence of all the other SSs of the motif in the proper locations of neighborhoods NB(n_1).

For this purpose all the SSs of the motif model are described in a Reference Table (RT) by their displacements (x, y, z) referred to LRS. The cardinality of the RT equals (m-2). In each of these m-2 positions, a SS of the motif must be located. Beside this geometrical validation, obviously, also the biochemical validation is better to be done (as usual in terms of SS type, number of residues, amino acid sequence, etc.). Figure 3 illustrates this process for the simple case of a motif model composed of just three SSs.

Saliency and precision of these matches is analyzed in the sequel.

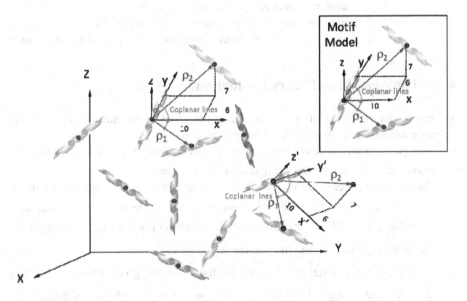

Fig. 3. Top-right: a 3 SSs motif model description. The local reference system is defined as follows: the y-axis coincides with the axis of S_0, the (x,y)-plane is defined by this axis and the midpoint of S_1. The motif existence confirmation process for two cases, in which the main pair (S_0, S_1) of helices is detected, is illustrated: top-left the complete motif is present; bottom-right the 3rd SS (S_2) of the motif is missing.

3   The Algorithm

A protein structure of N segments and a motif of $m, 0 < m \le N$ are considered. Each segment is determined in a 3D space by its start and end points, i.e. the directions are known. Additionally, the midpoints of the all segments are also considered known.

For next formula simplicity we will introduce $k, k = m-1$, $0 < k < N$. Thus, the algorithm on the proposed strategy can be briefed as follows:

1   Choose a reference SS S_0. Consequently choose S_1 to build the LRS of the motif. Referring to LRS build the model motif description on the RT, containing the information of all the remaining SS: ρ and φ parameters, the displacement (x, y, z), and the biological information.

2   Detect all the reference segment candidates in the protein structure under analysis. The search rule is – each candidate should have similar biological characteristics like the motif reference segment. Let the number of the reference candidates is $n, n \le N$.

3   For each protein reference candidate, do
   -    look for a reference SS candidate S_1. Let the number of the these reference candidates is $n_1, n_1 \le N$.
   -    look for a k-long series protein SSs compatible to ρ and φ and other biological and/or geometrical parameters like in the motif.

4   End and result: a number l of appearances (instances) of the motif are found in the given protein, $0 \le l \le n_1$, where $l=0$ is the worst case of nothing found.

4   The Algorithm Errors Evaluation

We can model the errors of an appearance of the given motif into the given protein structure following the strategy described above, namely:

-    The given motif consists of $k+1$ number of segments, $S_i, i = 0,1,...k$, where S_i plays for both, the segment itself and for its midpoint.

-    As the initial (referencing) segment S_0 is already chosen, the midpoint of all the rest of segments $S_i, i = 1,...k$ determines the respective couple (ρ_i, φ_i), $\rho_i = D(S_0, S_i)$, $D(.,.)$ is the Euclidian distance operator, and φ_i is the angle between the segment S_0 and the line-cut $\overline{S_0, S_i}$.

-    A few reference instances $\tilde{S}_0$ can be found in the given protein, such that $\tilde{S}_0 \sim S_0$, and to dispatch the task we will consider as $\tilde{S}_0$ only one of them. Thus, each segment $\tilde{S}_i, i = 1,...k$ of the motif appearance in the protein will determine the respective couple $(\tilde{\rho}_i, \tilde{\varphi}_i)$.

-    For the errors between the motif and its appearance we can write down as follows: $\Delta\varphi_i = |\tilde{\varphi}_i - \varphi_i|$ and $\Delta\rho_i = |\tilde{\rho}_i - \rho_i|$, $i = 1,...k$,   as   well   as:

$\Delta_i = \max\{\rho_i \sin(\Delta\varphi_i), \Delta\rho_i\} \approx \max\{\rho_i \Delta\varphi_i, \Delta\rho_i\}$, where Δ_i, $i = 1,...k$ is the respective distance error modeled by a sphere of radius Δ_i and center $\tilde{S}_i$, $i = 1,...k$, see also figure 4.

Additionally, considering that each midpoint $\tilde{S}_i$, $i = 1,...k$, is chosen independently from the other ones, we can evaluate the maximal error Δ of choosing an appearance of the motif as follows:

$$\Delta = \max_{i=1,...k}\{\Delta_i\} = \max_{i=1,...k}\{\max\{\rho_i\Delta\varphi_i, \Delta\rho_i\}\} = \max\left\{\max_{i=1,...k}\{\rho_i\Delta\varphi_i\}, \max_{i=1,...k}\{\Delta\rho_i\}\right\} \leq$$

$$\leq \max\left\{\max_{i=1,...k}\{\rho_i\}\Delta\varphi, \Delta\rho\right\} = \max\{P.\Delta\varphi, \Delta\rho\};$$

$$(1)$$

where $P = \max_{i=1,...k}\{\rho_i\}$ can be calculated preliminary, while $\Delta\varphi$ is the admissible angle error, and $\Delta\rho$ is the admissible distance error, both of them to be given outside, see also figure 5.

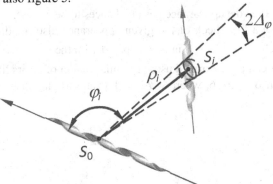

Fig. 4. Errors model of choosing the midpoint of a segment

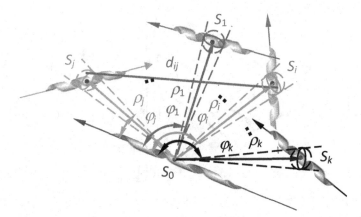

Fig. 5. Errors model of choosing the all segment midpoints of a motif

- We can rewrite (1) as follows:

$$\Delta = \max\{P.\Delta\varphi, \Delta\rho\} \iff \Delta = \begin{cases} \Delta\rho, & \Delta\varphi \le \Delta\varphi_0 \\ P.\Delta\varphi, & \Delta\varphi > \Delta\varphi_0 \end{cases}, \tag{2}$$

where $\Delta\varphi_0 = \dfrac{P}{\Delta\rho} = \max_{i=1,...k}\{\rho_i\}/\Delta\rho$.

Besides, $\Delta\varphi$ should be given in radians, while $\Delta\rho$ should be given relatively to the size of the pixels (voxels) in the searching algorithm (see sections 2 and 3).

- Additionally, we can use the error evaluation (1) to check the precision of the given appearance of the motif, considering the triangle distance inequality among each triplet of points $(S_0, S_i, S_j), 1 \le i < j \le k$ (see also figure 5):

$$\left| D(\tilde{S}_i, \tilde{S}_j) - D(S_i, S_j) \right| \le \Delta \tag{3}$$

If (3) is fulfilled for every couple $(\tilde{S}_i, \tilde{S}_j), 1 \le i < j \le k$, i.e. $k(k-1)/2$ number of check-ups, then the appearance has all chances to be correct.

- To accomplish a full check of the given appearance also the directions and the lengths of each $\tilde{S}_i, i = 1,...k$ can be compared with the respective S_i of the motif. And the latter can be performed using a similar model of errors like the above described, see also figure 6, where $d_i/2$ and γ_i are to play instead of ρ_i and φ_i, $i = 1,...k$.

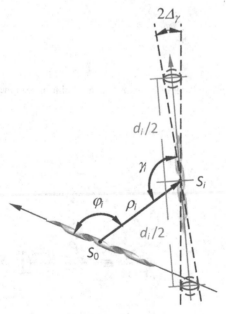

Fig. 6. Errors model of checking the direction and length of a segment

5   Conclusions

The spatial protein structure determines to a large extend the protein functionalities. It is thus very important to learn the structure-function relationship of proteins, and to compare their structures for retrieving of recurrent structural blocks such as motifs, domains, and units.

This paper aims to motif retrieval in single protein and in protein dataset, up to the whole PDB.

In order to retrieve motifs many approaches have been proposed in literature. In this paper we discussed a new tool that supports a planning strategy, targeting efficient analysis and robustness to error.

The efficiency is related to the capability to exploit the salient data, usually supported and made available, beside their geometrical features – such as the length of the structure in terms of number of amino acids, the biochemical properties, the sequence of the amino, etc., by known reliable programs like DSSP and STRIDE. Robustness is analyzed on the basis of a predefined maximum tolerable error, and on a rigorous analysis of the consequence of this constraint.

We are now planning an intensive quantitative analysis of the effectiveness of this new approach for practical problems such as alignment and structural block retrieval at different level of complexity: from basic motifs composed of a few SSs, up to entire units.

Moreover, in a more application oriented paper, we will analyze the motif modeling exactness or flexibility, with the opportunity of introducing a suitable metric for standard protein motifs (that is for structural blocks belonging to various protein families). Thus the focus will be on common components for a set of proteins that perform similar function, and will not relate to a metric block model extracted from a given protein as we experimented up to now.

Acknowledgements. This research is partly supported by the project AComIn "Advanced Computing for Innovation", grant 316087, funded by the FP7 Capacity Programme (Research Potential of Convergence Regions).

References

1. Zotenko, E., Dogan, R.I., Wilbur, W.J., O'Leary, D.P., Przytycka, T.M.: Structural footprinting in protein structure comparison: The impact of structural fragments. BMC Structural Biology 7(1), 7–53 (2007)
2. Camoglu, O., Kahveci, T., Singh, A.: PSI: Indexing protein structures for fast similarity search. Bioinformatics 19(1), 81–83 (2007)
3. Chionh, C.H., Huang, Z., Tan, K.L., Yao, Z.: Augmenting SSEs with structural properties for rapid protein structure comparison. In: The Third IEEE Symposium on Bioinformatics and Bioengineering, pp. 341–348. IEEE Press (2003)
4. Illingworth, J., Kittler, J.: A Survey of the Hough Transform. Comp. Vision, Graphics, and Image Proc. J. 44, 87–116 (1988)

5. Cantoni, V., Mattia, E.: Protein Structure Analysis through Hough Transform and Range Tree. Nuovo Cimento della Società Italiana di Fisica. C. Geophysics and Space Physics 35, 39–45 (2012)
6. Cantoni, V., Ferone, A., Ozbudak, O., Petrosino, A.: Motif Retrieval by Exhaustive Matching and Couple Co-occurrences. In: Computational Intelligence Methods for Bioinformatics and Biostatistics, Houston, Texas, USA, June 12-14 (2012)
7. Cantoni, V., Ferone, A., Ozbudak, O., Petrosino, A.: Protein Motifs Retrieval by SS Terns Occurrences. Pattern Recognition Letters 34, 559–563 (2013)
8. Cantoni, V., Ferone, A., Ozbudak, O., Petrosino, A.: Searching Structural Blocks by SS Exhaustive Matching. In: Peterson, L.E., Masulli, F., Russo, G. (eds.) CIBB 2012. LNCS, vol. 7845, pp. 57–69. Springer, Heidelberg (2013)
9. Cantoni, V., Ferone, A., Ozbudak, O., Petrosino, A.: Structural Analysis of Protein Secondary Structure by GHT. In: The Int. Conf. on Pattern Recognition, Tsukuba, Japan, November 11-15, pp. 1767–1770. IEEE Computer Society (2012)
10. Kabsch, W., Sander, C.: Dictionary of Protein Secondary Structure: Pattern Recognition of Hydrogen-bonded and Geometrical Features. Biopolymers 22, 2577–2637 (1983)
11. Heinig, M., Frishman, D.: STRIDE: a Web Server for Secondary Structure Assignment from Known Atomic Coordinates of Proteins. Nucl. Acids Res. 32, W500–W502 (2004)

Discovering Typical Transcription-Factors Patterns in Gene Expression Levels of Mouse Embryonic Stem Cells by Instance-Based Classifiers

Francesco Gagliardi and Claudia Angelini

Istituto per le Applicazioni del Calcolo 'Mauro Picone' — CNR,
via Pietro Castellino, 111 — 80131 Napoli, Italy
fnc.ggl@gmail.com, claudia.angelini@cnr.it

Abstract. The development of high-throughput technology in genome sequencing provide a large amount of raw data to study the regulatory functions of transcription factors (*TFs*) on gene expression. It is possible to realize a classifier system in which the gene expression level, under a certain condition, is regarded as the response variable and features related to *TFs* are taken as predictive variables. In this paper we consider the families of *Instance-Based (IB)* classifiers, and in particular the *Prototype exemplar learning classifier (PEL-C)*, because IB-classifiers can infer a mixture of representative instances, which can be used to discover the typical epigenetic patterns of transcription factors which explain the gene expression levels. We consider, as case study, the gene regulatory system in mouse embryonic stem cells (*ESCs*). Experimental results show IB-classifier systems can be effectively used for quantitative modelling of gene expression levels because more than *50%* of variation in gene expression can be explained using binding signals of *12* TFs; moreover the *PEL-C* identifies nine typical patterns of transcription factors activation that provide new insights to understand the gene expression machinery of mouse *ESCs*.

Keywords: Knowledge Discovery, Instance-Based Learning, High-throughput Sequencing, ChIP-Seq, RNA-Seq.

1 Introduction

High-throughput genome-sequencing technologies are now routinely being applied to a wide range of important topics in biology and medicine, often allowing researchers to address important biological questions that were not possible before [1] [2]. The recent development of RNA sequencing (RNA-Seq) technology holds the promise to provide more accurate gene expression measurements than traditional microarray. Meanwhile, chromatin immunoprecipitation (ChIP) coupled with sequencing technologies (ChIP-Seq) have been developed to identify whole-genome localization of protein–DNA binding sites [3][4]. Applications of techniques belongs to fields of Machine Learning (ML) [5][6] and Knowledge Discovery in Databases (KDD) [7] can be useful to make an integrative analysis of these data and providing us an insightful view of genome functions. Predictive modeling (such as the training of a

A. Petrosino, L. Maddalena, P. Pala (Eds.): ICIAP 2013 Workshops, LNCS 8158, pp. 381–388, 2013.

classifier system) is a machine learning strategy to predict an outcome from one or more variables (predictors). In the study of gene regulation, a classifier system can be constructed in which the gene expression levels under a certain condition is regarded as the response variable and various features related to transcription factors (TFs) are taken as the variables. A classifier system can have two mayor purposes: to predict class of new observations and to extract knowledge [7] from past experiences. In this work we choice to use instance-based (IB) classifiers in order to extract the typical patterns and internal structure in data obtained from sequencing of RNA (RNA-Seq) and of chromatin immunoprecipitation (ChIP-Seq) regarding the gene-expression regulatory-system in mouse embryonic stem cells (ESCs).

2   Instance-Based Classifier Systems

Instance-based (*IB*) classifier systems [5] [6] constitute a family of classifiers which main distinctive characteristic is to use the instances themselves as classes representation. *IB* classification relies on the similarity between the new observation to be classified and instances chosen as representative of the learnt class. Within this family we can identify two sub-families [6]: the first is based on prototype methods and the second on nearest-neighbours. The prototype methods build representative instances as centroids of classes or sub-classes, often using iterative clustering algorithms; conversely the nearest-neighbours methods use exemplars filtered from dataset as representative instances. The *IB* based classifiers and in particular the *k-Nearest Neighbour Classifier* (*k-NNC*) achieve such performances to be used in real-life problems, but they are not used in situations where an explanation of the output of the classifier is useful, because it is commonly assumed that *"instances do not really «describe» the patterns in data"* [5, p.79].

Some recent developments show that some hybrid *IB* classifiers, such as the *Prototype exemplar learning classifier* (*PEL-C*) [8] and the *Total recognition by adaptive classification experiments* (*T.R.A.C.E.*) [9], which generalize both prototype-based and exemplar-based classifiers, can be used to discover the "typicality structure" of learnt category, detecting how the class is decomposable in subclasses and their typicality grade within the class. The representative instances obtained from these classifiers are composed of a mixture of instances varying from prototypical ones to atypical ones, which form the so-called *"gradient of typicality"* [10].

We focus on the learning algorithm introduced in [9] (see Algorithm 1 in the following) because it has particular formal characteristics which are explained in detail in [9; sect. 3]. In particular it is possible to demonstrate (theorem 3.2 in [9]) that the representative-instance set inferred by this learning algorithm can vary from that of the Nearest Prototype Classifier (*NPC*), which is completely based on prototypes, to one of the Nearest Neighbour Classifier (*NNC*), which is completely based on exemplars according to the number of learning iterations and to the particular dataset.

We present in the following the learning algorithm[1]; we indicate *TS* as the training set, *RI* as the representative instances set and C_k as the items of the *k-th* class:

---

[1] A similar version of this algorithm can be found in [9, p.481].

Algorithm 1. Learning algorithm of hybrid instance-based classifiers

```
1. Initialize RI with the barycentres of the classes C_k
2. WHILE NOT (Termination Condition)
%%(Find a new candidate representative instance)
   2.1 Calculate the distances between every instance of TS and every
       instance of RI
   2.2 Among the misclassified instances of TS, find the instance which
       is the farthest from the nearest instance of RI belonging to its
       own class. Call it X and assume that it belongs to the class C_k
   2.3 Add X to RI.
%%(Update RI)
   2.4 Consider only instances of RI and TS belonging to C_k Call them as
       RI_k and TS_k, respectively
   2.5 Update the positions of RI using the k-means clustering algorithm
       applied only to TS_k with starting conditions RI_k:
       2.5.1 Apply the NN-rule to the items of TS_k respect to the RI_k
       2.5.2 Iteratively re-calculate the locations of instances of RI_k
             by updating the barycentres calculated respect to the
             subclasses determined with the NN-rule.
3. END
```

The behaviour of these classifier systems can vary from the one of the *NPC* to the one of *NNC* in an adaptive way and according to the chosen termination condition and to the particular classification problem. In intermediate cases the number and the kind of the representative instances is dynamically determined as a combination of prototypes, exemplars and representative instances of an intermediate abstraction level. We call these classifiers "hybrid" to refer to the type of representative instances set which can be inferred and it does not refer to a kind of classifier obtainable with a simple joining of classifiers *NPC* and *NNC*. In general, we can think about different possible termination conditions for the Algorithm 1, such as the following:

• *Training accuracy.* The accuracy percentage in classification of the training set is fixed and it can be equal to or less than *100%*. In the case it is set to *100%*, the system is forced to classify correctly all the training set, and the obtained classifier is the one proposed by Nieddu and Patrizi [9] and it is known as *T.R.A.C.E.*
• *Predictive accuracy.* The system can estimate its own performance on new instances by using a technique of cross validation [5, p.149] as varying the number of iterations. Therefore, the system is able to find the minimum number of iterations to obtain the maximum capability of generalizing (predictive accuracy on new instances). This termination condition is the one used by the *Prototype exemplar learning classifier* (*PEL-C*) [8], which usually [8][10] infers a number of representative instances definitely lower than both the *T.R.A.C.E.* and the *k-NNC.*

3   The Case-Study in Mouse Embryonic Stem Cells

We consider the gene regulatory system in mouse embryonic stem cells (ESCs) as investigated firstly in [3]. The study of this type of cellular line is fundamental in molecular biology because ESCs can maintain self-renewal and pluripotency, i.e., having the ability to differentiate to any adult cell type. The considered genes are extracted from the *NCBI Reference Sequence database* (RefSeq) which is an open access, annotated and curated collection of publicly available nucleotide sequences (http://www.ncbi.nlm.nih.gov/refseq/). In order to predict gene expression, we use the ChIP-Seq data of *12* Transcription Factors (TFs): E2f1, Mycn, Zfx, Myc, Klf4, Tcfcp2l1, Esrrb, Nanog, Oct4, Sox2, Stat3, Smad1. The gene expression values of the sequencing data were calculated by the RPKM definition (the number of reads per kilobase of exon region per million mapped reads) based on a RNA-sequencing data. The reference genome used for *Mus musculus* is the *UCSC mm8* (http://genome.ucsc.edu/).

3.1   The Dataset

Following Ouyanga *et al.* [3] we consider 18936 RefSeq genes for the mouse and for each of them we define a feature vectors composed of *12* attributes (one for each TF) called *TF Association Strength* (TFAS); TFAS are computed using a weighted summation of TF binding peaks where those with higher reads intensity or location proximity to the transcription start site (TSS) were given higher weights.

Formally, the association strength of TF_j on gene i is a weighted sum of intensities of all of the peaks of TF_j:

$$a_{ij} = \sum_k g_k e^{-d_k/d_0}$$

where: g_k is the intensity (number of reads) of the *k-th* binding peak of the TF_j, d_k is the distance (number of nucleotides) between the TSS of gene i and the *k-th* binding peak, and d_0 is a constant, posed equal to 500 bps for E2f1 and 5000 bps for other TFs because E2f1 tends to be closer to TSSs [3]. Gene-expression classes are defined in the following *2* step procedure. First, we apply a logarithmic rescaling to the raw expression values (RPKM) based on mapped mRNA sequencing data for mouse ESCs; as usual, to avoid taking the logarithm of zero, a small positive constant is added; formally:

$$Log_{10}(RPKM + 0.01)$$

Then we apply a 5-classes equal-width binning, to transform the continuous variable of expression level into a categorical one with 5-values. Each class represents an intervals of equal size. The five classes are labelled as following: C_1 – '*Very Low*', C_2 – '*Low*', C_3 – '*Middle*', C_4 – '*High*', C_5 – '*Very High*'.

Summarizing, the used dataset[2] has *18936* rows (one for each gene), *12* features (one for each transcription factor) considered as predictive variables and 5 classes (one for each gene-expression level) regarded as the response variable to be predicted.

---

[2] The original version of the dataset is available as supplementary material of [3]; the dataset used in this work is available on request.

4   Experimental Results and Discussions

4.1   Experimental Procedure

We use an experimental procedure, to evaluate the classifier systems, composed of 3 steps: training, validation, and testing. In the training phase we train the classifier systems on data and in the validation phase we estimate how good the classifiers has been trained to select the best performing parameters, such as the value of k for the k-NNC or the number of learning iterations for the PEL-C. Because accuracy computed on the data used for training or also for validation are optimistically biased to predict real classification capabilities of the systems[3], in the testing phase we compute the accuracy of the previously tuned classifiers on a different data.

According to this procedure the dataset is divided in a sample-dataset, used for training and validation, and a test-dataset, used for testing. The sample-dataset is iteratively split in the training set and validation according to a cross-validation procedure. The sample is composed of 1000 genes randomly selected from the entire dataset with no stratified sampling; so we have a sample set which have $N >> p$ (N is 2 order of magnitude higher than $p = 12$).

We carried out different cross-validation runs applied to sample dataset for every classifier system considered: NPC, NNC, k-NNC, T.R.A.C.E. and PEL-C. Each run on sample set was prepared by using the leave-one-out procedure as a cross-validation technique.

4.2   Experimental Results

We show here the comparison of the experimental results obtained applying the different classifier systems to the above problem of classification.

The k-NNC is applied to sample-dataset by varying k between 1 and 25. The best accuracy is obtained for $k=16$. In order to analyze the behaviour of the PEL-C the iterative learning algorithm (see Algorithm 1) is applied to sample-dataset by varying the number of iterations between 1 and 16. The PEL-C obtains the maximum accuracy on the test set after 5 iterations and finds 9 representative instances, while 457 iterations are needed so that the learning algorithm converge to the stop condition of T.R.A.C.E, and it finds 461 representative instances. To compare classification performance and the kind of class representations obtained by different IB classifiers we have considered the following indexes: the accuracy on sample-set (computed by leave-one-out), the number of representative instances and the accuracy on the test-set (see Table 1).

We observe that PEL-C is outperformed in classification performance only by the k-NNC, that has the k optimized in order to maximize performances, but PEL-C obtains a classes representation composed with only 9 instances against the 1000 of the k-NNC. The NPC uses only 5 instances, which are all pure prototypes, but its accuracy is lower than PEL-C and k-NNC. The k-NNC and NNC use a classes representation entirely composed of exemplars, which are the 1000 instances of the whole sample-dataset.

---

[3] In fact accuracy on sample-set is also called *resubstitution rate* or also *apparent accuracy*.

Table 1. Performance indexes obtained by different classifier systems

	NPC	PEL-C	T.R.A.C.E.	NNC	k-NNC $(k_{best}=16)$
Representation:	Prototype-based	*Hybrid*		*Exemplar-based*	
Accuracy on test set (%)	46.36	54.40	49.29	53.23	63.84
Accuracy on sample set (%)	48.45	52.07	47.31	49.59	59.02
Representative instances	5	9	461	1000	1000

To analyse the behaviour of a classifier system to discriminate among different classes in a multiclass problem is often useful to compute the confusion matrix between actual classes and predicted ones; because the actual classes in our problem is obtained by a binning procedure from a continuous values we show (see Figure 1) the box-plot of log values of actual gene expression levels for each predicted classes by the *PEL-C*.

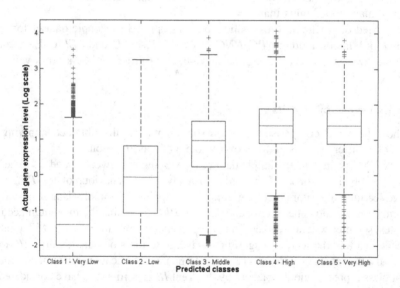

Fig. 1. Actual gene expression values *versus* the gene expression class predicted by *PEL-C*

4.3   Knowledge Extraction

Knowledge discovery has been defined as *"a non-trivial process of identifying valid, novel, potentially useful and ultimately understandable patterns from collections of data"* [7]; its main aim is to reveal some new and useful information from the data.

The most interesting and useful representative instances inferred by *IB* classifiers are the ones obtained by *PEL-C*, which extracts a representation of classes very concise, regarding the number of instances (only 9 patterns), and expressive, because is composed of a mixture of prototypical instances, with graded abstraction.

In Figure 2 on the left we show the heatmap [11] of typical patterns inferred by *PEL-C*, whereas on the right we reports the representativeness for each pattern inside their own class. This latter index is computed as the ratio between the number of observations assigned to a class using a given representative instance of that class and the total of the instances assigned to that class. The inferred representative instances are the typical patter that explain different level of gene expression. Moreover, these typical patterns is useful to detect how the classes are decomposable in some subclasses and their typicality grade within the own class, in fact we observe that the classes descriptions vary from classes totally based on a prototype (Classes 2 and 5) to classes based on a mixture of prototypes with graded representativeness (Classes 1, 3 and 4).

Representative Instances		Number of genes (sample set)	Representativeness (sample set)	Number of genes (test set)	Representativeness (test set)	
	1) Class_1	300	71.26	5113	69.80	
	2) Class_1	121	28.74	2212	30.20	
	3) Class_2	81	100.00	1436	100.00	Full Prototype
	4) Class_3	117	39.13	2285	42.54	
	5) Class_3	102	34.12	1687	31.40	
	6) Class_3	80	26.76	1400	26.06	
	7) Class_4	79	57.66	1424	53.35	
	8) Class_4	58	42.34	1245	46.65	
	9) Class_5	52	100.00	842	100.00	Full Prototype

Heatmap columns (left to right): E2f1, Mycn, ZFx, Myc, Klf4, Tcfcp2l1, Esrrb, Nanog, Oct4, Sox2, Stat3, Smad1. Scale 0.086 to 3.1.

Fig. 2. The heat map of typical patterns inferred by *PEL-C* and their representativeness

5   Concluding Remarks

We have utilized ChIP-seq and RNA-seq data to explore the relationship between the pattern of *TF* binding activity and gene expression. We show that *IB* classifier systems can be used for quantitative modelling of gene expression levels from binding location data. For the embryonic stem cell, more than 52% of variation in gene expression can be explained using binding signals of *12* transcription factors (*TFs*).

As expected only the *TFs* do not explain all the variability of gene expression levels and we should consider other feature definitions criteria or other new features to improve both performances and explanation of gene expression machinery.

Hybrid classifiers as the *PEL-C* are also useful as tool for knowledge discovery providing us the typical patterns of epigenetic factors which explain a considerable part of variability in gene expression. We identify nine typical patterns of transcription factors activation for *5* levels of gene expression (varying from *zero* or *very low* to *very high*). These results provide new potential insights into transcriptional control of gene expression level for embryonic stem cell.

Acknowledgments. This research is supported by *"Italian Flagship Project Epigenomic"* of the Italian Ministry of Education, University and Research and the National Research Council (http://www.epigen.it/).

References

1. Soon, W.W., Hariharan, M., Snyder, M.P.: High-throughput sequencing for biology and medicine. Molecular Systems Biology 9, Article number:640 (2013)
2. Hawkins, R.D., Hon, G.C., Ren, B.: Next-generation genomics: an integrative approach. Nature Review Genetics 11(7), 476–486 (2010)
3. Ouyanga, Z., Zhoub, Q., Wongc, W.H.: ChIP-Seq of transcription factors predicts absolute and differential gene expression in embryonic stem cells. PNAS 106(51), 21521–21526 (2009)
4. Young, M.D., Willson, T.A., Wakefield, M.J., Trounson, E., Hilton, D.J., Blewitt, M.E., Oshlack, A., Majewski, I.J.: ChIP-seq analysis reveals distinct H3K27me3 profiles that correlate with transcriptional activity. Nucleic Acids Research 39(17), 7415–7427 (2011)
5. Witten, I.H., Frank, E.: Data Mining: Practical Machine Learning Tools and Techniques with Java Implementations, 2nd edn. Morgan Kaufmann, San Francisco (2005)
6. Hastie, T., Tibshirani, R., Friedman, J.: Prototype Methods and Nearest-Neighbors. In: The Elements of Statistical Learning. Data Mining; Inference; and Prediction, 2nd edn., pp. 459–484. Springer, New York (2009)
7. Fayyad, U., Piatetsky-Shapiro, G., Smyth, P., Uturusamy, R.: Advances in Knowledge Discovery and Data Mining. MIT Press, Cambridge (1996)
8. Gagliardi, F.: Instance-based classifiers applied to medical databases: diagnosis and knowledge extraction. Artificial Intelligence in Medicine 52(3), 123–139 (2011)
9. Nieddu, L., Patrizi, G.: Formal methods in pattern recognition: A review. European Journal of Operational Research 120, 459–495 (2000)
10. Gagliardi, F.: Instance-Based Classifiers to Discover the Gradient of Typicality in Data. In: Pirrone, R., Sorbello, F. (eds.) AI*IA 2011. LNCS, vol. 6934, pp. 457–462. Springer, Heidelberg (2011)
11. Pavlidis, P., Noble, W.S.: Matrix2png: A Utility for Visualizing Matrix Data. Bioinformatics 19(2), 295–296 (2003)

Motif-Based Method for the Genome-Wide Prediction of Eukaryotic Gene Clusters

Thomas Wolf, Vladimir Shelest, and Ekaterina Shelest*

Leibniz Institute for Natural Product Research and Infection Biology e. V.
Hans-Knöll-Institute (HKI),
Research group Systems Biology / Bioinformatics,
Beutenbergstrasse 11a, 07745 Jena, Germany
ekaterina.shelest@hki-jena.de

Abstract. Genomic clustering of functionally interrelated genes is not unusual in eukaryotes. In such clusters, co-localized genes are co-regulated and often belong to the same pathway. However, biochemical details are still unknown in many cases, hence computational prediction of clusters' structures is beneficial for understanding their functions. Yet, in silico detection of eukaryotic gene clusters (eGCs) remains a challenging task. We suggest a novel method for eGC detection based on consideration of cluster-specific regulatory patterns. The basic idea is to differentiate cluster from non-cluster genes by regulatory elements within their promoter sequences using the density of cluster-specific motifs' occurrences (which is higher within the cluster region) as an additional distinguishing feature. The effectiveness of the method was demonstrated by successful re-identification of functionally characterized clusters. It is also applicable to the detection of yet unknown eGCs. Additionally, the method provides valuable information about the binding sites for cluster-specific regulators.

Keywords: eukaryotic gene clusters, transcription regulation, secondary metabolites, transcription factor binding sites.

1 Introduction

Genomic clustering (co-localization) of functionally interrelated genes in conjunction with co-regulation, although less present than in prokaryotes, has been found in a great variety of eukaryotic species, from yeast to vertebrates [1,2].

The term "gene cluster" can imply various interpretations. In this work, we consider as clusters the sets of co-localized and co-regulated genes, the products of which are presumably functionally connected (e. g., they can belong to the same biochemical or signaling pathway). Thus, the co-localization and co-regulation are the main characteristics of such eGCs and they form the basis of our approach.

---

* Corresponding author.

A. Petrosino, L. Maddalena, P. Pala (Eds.): ICIAP 2013 Workshops, LNCS 8158, pp. 389–398, 2013.

Clusters of co-expressed genes have been found in higher eukaryotes, such as drosophila and human [3,4]. It has been shown that genes belonging to the same metabolic pathways are localized significantly closer to each other than it can be expected by chance [2]. This was demonstrated for diverse metabolic pathways from the KEGG database. A relatively well investigated class of eGCs represent the clusters of secondary metabolite genes, which are found in fungi, plants, and protists [5]. Secondary metabolites (SMs) are pharmaceutically important substances (e. g., antibiotics, antimycotics, toxins). The genes responsible for their synthesis, modifications, transport, etc., are often organized in clusters [6]. These clusters are characterized by modest sizes (normally not more than 20 genes) and tight co-localization: the genes are immediately adjacent to each other, although the insertions of non-cluster genes are also possible. The expression of SM clusters is often governed by specific regulators [7] and in many cases the specific transcription factor (TF) is embedded in the cluster [8]. Moreover, non-cluster specific (broad) TFs are also involved in the regulation of SM clusters [9] (Fig. 1).

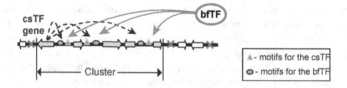

Fig. 1. Regulation of a gene cluster by cluster specific and broad function transcription factors (csTF and bfTF, correspondingly)

There are several ways to predict eGCs genome-wide. One of the first methods was suggested by Lee and Sonnhammer [2] who linked the gene annotations from KEGG with the localization information. The same approach was used in some follow-up works, e. g., in [10], where the authors suggested a method to identify all possible clusters of genes annotated to the same GO term. These methods predict any clusters regardless to their functions and specific features. In the particular cases, like SM clusters, such approaches will give imprecise predictions, mostly because the assignments of genes to pathways are partly or completely unknown.

Another group of cluster-detection methods relies on expression data (microarrays, etc.) [11]. These methods are reliable as long as the data is good, as they provide relatively solid evidence for co-regulation. However, many eGCs, for instance, in fungal genomes are silent under laboratory conditions [6] and it is challenging to experimentally determine the conditions for the cluster induction. Thus, the application of such methods to cryptic clusters is limited.

Some methods have been developed specifically for particular cluster types, e. g., for the SM clusters. Most of the methods developed so far for the detection of SM clusters are similarity based [12,13,14]. Due to the limited number of known clusters that can serve as a template, and also to the possible incorrect assignments of genes to clusters, similarity based methods are error-prone and tend to overestimate the clusters' lengths. Additionally, these methods do not differentiate closely located (adjacent) eGCs, interpreting them as a single cluster.

These limitations could be circumvented by consideration of sequence characteristics of the cluster regions: GC content and averaged DNA curvative profile [15]. However, not all clusters are characterized by a conserved curvative pattern, which means that a substantial part of them would be skipped by the method if applied to a genome-wide search.

We suggest a novel approach to predict gene clusters based on the density of transcription factor binding site (TFBS) occurrences. In contrast to related tools, our method is not similarity-based. The main idea is that the cluster-specific TFBSs should be enriched in the cluster in comparison to other parts of the genome. Yet, their occurrence outside the cluster is not excluded. We characterize promoters by cluster-specific motif occurrences and consider the density of the motifs as the main feature of the cluster region. The method is applicable to any clusters of co-regulated genes. We demonstrate its usefulness on the example of SM clusters.

2   Results

The presumable co-regulation of the cluster genes presupposes that their promoters share at least one common motif to bind the regulating TF. Ideally, this common motif should be specific to the cluster but not to the surrounding genes (since they are not co-regulated). As the cluster-specific TF (csTF) is assumed not to have ubiquitous functions, its TFBSs should not be widely distributed across the genome. On the other hand, the cluster genes are not necessarily adjacent; "alien" genes inside the cluster may occur (e. g., in [11]). Thus, our requirements for the cluster genes are the following: (i) genes are co-localized; (ii) promoters share at least one common motif; (iii) there can be "gap" genes that do not share the common motif with the rest of the cluster. These requirements allow us to formulate the algorithm to find clusters in a genomic sequence. We call our approach the motif density method (MDM).

2.1   Motif Density Method

The basic idea of the method is that the binding sites for csTFs are enriched in the region of the cluster. Note that we do not exclude their occurrence outside the cluster. Most important, the cluster-specific motifs should be observed in consecutive promoters.

To start the cluster predictions, we need to specify the so-called "anchor" genes. These can be the genes that are already assigned to the pathway in question. In the case of the SM clusters, polyketide synthases (PKSs) or non-ribosomal peptide synthetases (NRPSs) can serve as the anchor genes. PKSs and NRPSs are characterized by a specific set of domains and large size, which makes them relatively easy to detect in genomes.

Step 1: Motif Search. On the first step, all anchor genes are searched and marked in the genomes. Next, an interim set of genes around the anchor gene of interest is selected. Since we do not know how the anchor gene is located relative to the presumable cluster (in the middle or on the edge), we consider several gene sets around the anchor gene not to miss the correct motif: 4/6/8 genes upstream, 4/6/8 genes downstream, and 2 genes up- and downstream the anchor gene. The common motifs are predicted by MEME [16] in the corresponding promoter sequences ($-1000/+50$ bp around the transcription start site or the whole intergenic region if it is shorter than 1000 bp). Occurrence in the anchor gene promoter is the prerequisite for the further consideration. The best-scoring motif (the one with the lowest score as defined by MEME) out of all considered promoter sets is then searched in all promoter sequences genome-wide.

Step 2: Transforming the Genomic Sequence into the Sequence of Promoters. Counting Occurrences in Frames. On this step, we switch to consideration of promoters as units characterized by the number of occurrences of a particular motif. The order of units follows the order of the corresponding promoters in the genomic sequence. Now instead of the real genomic sequence we consider a string of numbers, which represent the motifs' occurrences in a unit. For instance, if 1 motif was found in the first promoter, 2 motifs in the second, and 0 in the third and fourth promoters, the string will be 1-2-0-0. This number string is scanned by a sliding window (frame) with the step of one unit counting the cumulative number of found motifs per frame. The highest number of occurrences per frame should be obtained for the window coinciding with the cluster. Consideration of different frame lengths allows us to determine the real cluster length.

Step 3: Scoring. To select the optimal frame we apply a scoring system. As the "gap" genes are allowed in the cluster, we allow gaps ("empty" promoters) in the frames but introduce a gap penalty. In this way, we do not forbid the occurrence of small gaps, which are indeed common in clusters, but larger gaps are scored with a penalty that is growing depending on the gap length. The promoters with motifs, on the contrary, add a positive value to the score depending on the number of motifs found.

Let us consider a frame with the length l. In this frame, each promoter i is characterized by the number of found motifs m_i. The consecutive promoters without motifs ($m_i = 0$) form a gap, which is characterized by its length d, the number of gaps in the frame being n.

Then the score S of a frame is calculated as:

$$S = \sum_{i=1}^{l} m_i - \sum_{j=1}^{n} P^{d_j} , \tag{1}$$

where P is the gap penalty and is an adjustable parameter.

The scores are calculated for different frame lengths (normally from 3 to 30, because this is the usual size of the known clusters).

Step 4: Visualization and Selection of the Optimal Frame. The frames are characterized by their score, position, and length. To visualize all characteristics at once, we apply the heat maps (Fig. 2).

2.2 Effectiveness of the Approach

To demonstrate the effectiveness of MDM, we applied it to the re-identification of several functionally characterized SM clusters with known borders. We selected two clusters with characterized regulatory patterns (TFBSs) in order to see if our motif predictions match the real motifs. These chosen examples are the aflatoxin cluster in *Aspergillus flavus* and violaceol cluster in *Aspergillus nidulans*. The latter was also of special interest because it is located in close vicinity to another eGC (orsellinic acid cluster). It was tempting to see if our method is able to separate the two clusters.

The other examples are clusters with characterized products and different patterns of regulation. For instance, the asperfuranone is subject to inter-cluster cross-talk (see Discussion for more details). For all clusters, we compared the predictions of MDM to those of the SMURF tool (Table 1). The gap penalty was set to 1.3 for all examples.

Aflatoxin Cluster in *A. flavus*. Aflatoxin is produced by different Aspergilli [17] and its production is regulated by the csTF AflR, along with several broad function TFs (depending on conditions). The binding sites for AflR have the consensus sequence $TCG(N_5)CGA$. In *A. flavus*, the cluster spans 21 genes with 15 promoters (AFL2G_07210 to AFL2G_07230). The analysis was run on the genomic sequence from the Broad Institute website [18].

The motif search was performed from scratch in order to confirm the ability of the algorithm to re-identify the real (known) motif. Seven interim sets of promoters around the anchor gene ALF2G_07228 *pksA* (in different arrangements) were submitted to MEME for motif prediction. For each set we could get

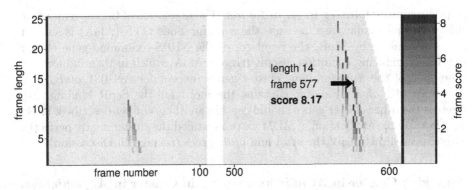

Fig. 2. Heat map for the re-identified aflatoxin cluster (right) and the sub-cluster (left), both on contig 7

common motifs. The motif in the set "8 promoters upstream *pksA*" scored the best and thus was submitted to the genome-wide search. Remarkably, this motif coincided with the AflR TFBS. The AflR motif correctly identified the cluster region with high precision: from AFL2G_07211 to AFL2G_07230 (Fig. 2). The predictions made by the other (non-AflR-like) motifs were much more noisy and failed to detect the cluster.

Violaceol Cluster in *A. nidulans*. The violaceol cluster was described recently [19] and its regulation is yet not well investigated. However, the potential binding sites for the cluster specific regulator were proposed in [19]. MDM was applied to the re-identification of this cluster in the same way as to the aflatoxin cluster, starting with the motif prediction from scratch. The genomic sequence was downloaded from Aspergillus genome database [20]. MDM successfully detected the correct motif (CYCGGAGWWWC) and the correct cluster location (Fig. 3). The length of the cluster is two genes longer than the reported one due to the high number of the csTFBSs in the promoters (Fig. 3). We return to this in the Discussion section. As expected, the orsellinic acid cluster, which is located only five genes apart from the violaceol cluster and which is not regulated by the violaceol csTF, was not detected. In this way, we show the specificity of MDM and its ability to separate closely located clusters.

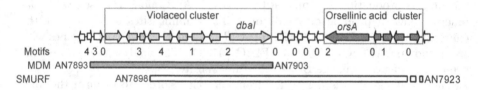

Fig. 3. Re-identification of the violaceol cluster with MDM and SMURF. Coordinates of the real cluster: AN7896 to AN7903.

Asperfuranone Cluster in *A. nidulans*. The regulation of the asperfuranone cluster is a particular case, because the asperfuranone csTF (AfoA) is subject to the regulation by ScpR, the regulator of the NRPS-containing gene cluster *inp*. Under inducing conditions, ScpR triggers AfoA, which in turn induces the expression of the asperfuranone cluster genes (except for AN1031 *afoB*) [21]. Therefore, the *afoA* promoter contains the motif for the ScpR binding [21], whereas the other cluster genes should contain another, not yet described TFBS for AfoA. By the application of MDM we re-identified the cluster nearly perfectly, with expected missing of the *afoA* and *afoB* genes (see also in Discussion).

Aspyridon Cluster in *A. nidulans*, Gliotoxin Cluster in *A. fumigatus*, and WYK-1 cluster in *A. oryzae*. We applied MDM to the re-identification of three more clusters. In all three cases we detected the clusters, although

Table 1. Comparision of SM gene cluster predictions beetween SMURF and MDM

Method	Cluster		Reference
	Start	End	
Aflatoxin *(Aspergillus flavus)*			
Experimental	AFL2G_07210	AFL2G_07230	[17]
MDM	AFL2G_07211	AFL2G_07230	
SMURF	AFL2G_07219	AFL2G_07248	
Asperfuranone *(Aspergillus nidulans)*			
Experimental	AN1029	AN1036	[21]
MDM	AN1032	AN1036	
SMURF	AN1029	AN11288[1]	
Aspyridon *(Aspergillus nidulans)*			
Experimental	AN8408	AN8415	[22]
MDM	AN8401	AN8421	
SMURF	AN8415	AN9243	
Gliotoxin *(Aspergillus fumigatus)*			
Experimental	AFU6G_09630	AFU6G_09745	[23]
MDM	AFU6G_09630	AFU6G_09785[2]	
SMURF	AFU6G_09580	AFU6G_09740	
Violaceol *(Aspergillus nidulans)*			
Experimental	AN7896	AN7903	[19]
MDM	AN7893	AN7903	
SMURF	AN7898	AN7923	
WYK-1 *(Aspergillus oryzae)*			
Experimental	AO090001000009	AO090001000019	[24]
MDM	AO090001000009	AO090001000018	
SMURF	AO090001000009	AO090001000031	

not ideally. The results are presented in Table 1 and discussed in detail in the Discussion section.

3 Discussion

Computational prediction of eukaryotic clusters is especially important when precise information about the corresponding pathways is missing. In such cases, the predicted cluster's structure can point at the involvement of particular enzymes in the pathway and thus be beneficial for the understanding of the pathway's functioning.

Neither of the so far published tools has used the promoter information for the cluster prediction. Since the co-regulation is the basic idea of the cluster

---

[1] AN11288 is located 2 genes upstream AN1036.

[2] AFU6G_09785 is located 4 genes upstream AFU6G_09745.

definition, we consider the neglect of the promoter information as an oversight. We developed an approach that not only allows to reliably predict the eGCs but also provides information about the potential regulators of the cluster (by description of their TFBSs).

We compared the performance of our method with that of SMURF, the most prominent similarity based approach to SM cluster predictions. SMURF fails to detect the correct borders for most of the clusters and mixes the violaceol cluster with the orsellinic acid cluster reporting them as a single eGC (Fig. 3). MDM gives better or comparable predictions for all examined eGCs and solves the problem of the two adjacent clusters. In the aflatoxin cluster prediction, only one gene of 21 (AFL2G_07210) is missing because the bidirectional promoter between AFL2G_07210 and AFL2G_07209 does not contain the AflR TFBS. This may be reasonable, as AFL2G_07209 does not belong to the cluster and AFL2G_07210 has no assigned cluster function [17]. In the violaceol cluster, two promoters upstream the cluster also shared the specific motif. This does not contradict the experimental data, as the corresponding genes show slight expression under cluster-inducing conditions [19]. In fact, their involvement in the cluster under some specific conditions is not excluded and the function of the csTFBSs deserves additional examination. It remains problematic how to predict clusters with such mosaic regulation. We aim to address this problem in the next versions of MDM.

As mentioned above, the asperfuranone cluster is an interesting case, because its regulator AfoA is induced by a csTF of another cluster. AfoA is shown to induce all cluster genes except for *afoB* [21]. Our findings confirm this experimental result, since the promoter of *afoB* apparently does not contain the AfoA binding motif.

The prediction of the aspyridon cluster by MDM is not perfect, however, it covers the whole cluster, although adding several extra genes up- and downstream of it. Given that SMURF does not find the cluster at all, we consider this result rather good. For the gliotoxin cluster, the left border is found perfectly but on the right side MDM predicts four more genes as cluster members. In such cases (when the promoters have a potential TFBS for a cluster-specific regulator) we cannot exclude a possibility that the cluster is actually longer and those genes can be expressed under some specific conditions. This could be a subject of further experimental investigation. The MDM prediction of the WYK-1 cluster is missing one gene. However, compared to the SMURF result (12 genes more) the prediction of the MDM is closer to the real cluster borders.

The results of the re-identification of the known clusters show that there is space for the improvement of our approach. In many cases, MDM predictions are not perfect. Yet, in the great majority they are better than those made by the similarity-based method, which underscores the higher potential of the motif-based approach.

The genome-wide detection of the csTFBSs can help to discover other genes and even additional clusters regulated by the csTF. Regulatory cross-talk between the clusters has already been described in fungi [21]. In our examples, we could detect a second peak on the heat map for the AflR motif (Fig. 2). The peak corresponds to a frame in a distant location on the same contig. There is no SM synthase gene in this cluster-like stretch, however, the genes are typical for SM clusters (monooxygenases, methyltransferase, MFS transporters, etc.). There can be two explanations for that: either this is a sub-cluster that is in some way involved in the aflatoxin biosynthetic pathway, or these are the remainings of a damaged cluster that has lost the synthase. In any case, this intriguing sub-cluster deserves further investigation.

To our knowledge, MDM is the first attempt to consider the promoter information in the eGC prediction. We show the high potential of this approach on the examples of the SM clusters, however, the method can be applied to the detection of any eGCs analogous to the SM clusters.

Acknowledgements. This work was financially supported by the Pakt für Wissenschaft und Forschung (2009-2012) and by the International Leibniz Research School for Microbial and Molecular Interactions (ILRS), as part of the excellence graduate school Jena School for Microbial Communication (JSMC), supported by the Deutsche Forschungsgemeinschaft.

References

1. Blumenthal, T.: Gene clusters and polycistronic transcription in eukaryotes. Bioessays 20, 480–487 (1998)
2. Lee, J.M., Sonnhammer, E.L.: Genomic gene clustering analysis of pathways in eukaryotes. Genome Res. 13, 875–882 (2003)
3. Caron, H., van Schaik, B., van der Mee, M., Baas, F., Riggins, G., van Sluis, P., Hermus, M.C., van Asperen, R., Boon, K., Voute, P.A., Heiqsterkamp, S., van Kampen, A., Versteeg, R.: The human transcriptome map: Clustering of highly expressed genes in chromosomal domains. Science 291, 1289–1292 (2001)
4. Spellman, P.T., Rubin, G.M.: Evidence for large domains of similarly expressed genes in the Drosophila genome. J. Biol. 1, 5 (2002)
5. Sasso, S., Pohnert, G., Lohr, M., Mittag, M., Hertweck, C.: Microalgae in the postgenomic era: a blooming reservoir for new natural products. FEMS Microbiol. Rev. 36, 761–785 (2012)
6. Brakhage, A.A., Schroeckh, V.: Fungal secondary metabolites - strategies to activate silent gene clusters. Fungal Genet. Biol. 48, 15–22 (2011)
7. Keller, N.P., Hohn, T.M.: Metabolic Pathway Gene Clusters in Filamentous Fungi. Fungal Genet. Biol. 21, 17–29 (1997)
8. Brakhage, A.A.: Regulation of fungal secondary metabolism. Nat. Rev. Microbiol. 11, 21–32 (2013)
9. Hoffmeister, D., Keller, N.P.: Natural products of filamentous fungi: enzymes, genes, and their regulation. Nat. Prod. Rep. 24, 393–416 (2007)
10. Yi, G., Sze, S.H., Thon, M.R.: Identifying clusters of functionally related genes in genomes. Bioinformatics 23, 1053–1060 (2007)
11. Schroeckh, V., Scherlach, K., Nützmann, H.W., Shelest, E., Schmidt-Heck, W., Schuemann, J., Martin, K., Hertweck, C., Brakhage, A.A.: Intimate bacterial-fungal interaction triggers biosynthesis of archetypal polyketides in *Aspergillus nidulans*. Proc. Natl. Acad. Sci. USA 106, 14558–14563 (2009)

12. Khaldi, N., Seifuddin, F.T., Turner, G., Haft, D., Nierman, W.C., Wolfe, K.H., Fedorova, N.D.: SMURF: Genomic mapping of fungal secondary metabolite clusters. Fungal Genet. Biol. 47, 736–741 (2010)

13. Medema, M.H., Blin, K., Cimermancic, P., de Jager, V., Zakrzewski, P., Fischbach, M.A., Weber, T., Takano, E., Breitling, R.: antiSMASH: rapid identification, annotation and analysis of secondary metabolite biosynthesis gene clusters in bacterial and fungal genome sequences. Nucleic Acids Res 39, W339–W346 (2011)

14. Fedorova, N.D., Moktali, V., Medema, M.H.: Bioinformatics approaches and software for detection of secondary metabolic gene clusters. Methods Mol. Biol. 944, 23–45 (2012)

15. Do, J.H., Miyano, S., The, G.C.: window-averaged DNA curvature profile of secondary metabolite gene cluster in *Aspergillus fumigatus* genome. Appl. Microbiol. Biotechnol. 80, 841–847 (2008)

16. Bailey, T.L., Boden, M., Buske, F.A., Frith, M., Grant, C.E., Clementi, L., Ren, J., Li, W.W., Noble, W.S.: MEME SUITE: tools for motif discovery and searching. Nucleic Acids Res. 37, W202–W208 (2009)

17. Amaike, S., Keller, N.P.: Aspergillus flavus. Annu. Rev. Phytopathol. 49, 107–133 (2011)

18. Aspergillus Comparative Sequencing Project, Broad Institute of Harvard and MIT, http://www.broadinstitute.org/

19. Gerke, J., Bayram, O., Feussner, K., Landesfeind, M., Shelest, E., Feussner, I., Braus, G.H.: Breaking the silence: protein stabilization uncovers silenced biosynthetic gene clusters in the fungus *Aspergillus nidulans*. Appl. Environ. Microbiol. 78, 8234–8244 (2012)

20. Arnaud, M.B., Chibucos, M.C., Costanzo, M.C., Crabtree, J., Inglis, D.O., Lotia, A., Orvis, J., Shah, P., Skrzypek, M.S., Binkley, G., Miyasato, S.R., Wortman, J.R., Sherlock, G.: The Aspergillus Genome Database, a curated comparative genomics resource for gene, protein and sequence information for the Aspergillus research community. Nucleic Acids Res. 38, D420–D427 (2010)

21. Bergmann, S., Funk, A.N., Scherlach, K., Schroeckh, V., Shelest, E., Horn, U., Hertweck, C., Brakhage, A.A.: Activation of a silent fungal polyketide biosynthesis pathway through regulatory cross talk with a cryptic nonribosomal peptide synthetase gene cluster. Appl. Environ. Microbiol. 76, 8143–8149 (2010)

22. Bergmann, S., Schümann, J., Scherlach, K., Lange, C., Brakhage, A., Hertweck, C.: Genomics driven discovery of PKS-NRPS hybrid metabolites from *Aspergillus nidulans*. Nat. Chem. Biol. 3, 213–217 (2007)

23. Gardiner, D.M., Howlett, B.: Bioinformatic and expression analysis of the putative gliotoxin biosynthetic gene cluster of *Aspergillus fumigatus*. FEMS Microbiol. Lett. 248, 241–248 (2005)

24. Imamura, K., Tsuyama, Y., Hirata, T., Shiraishi, S., Sakamoto, K., Yamada, O., Akita, O., Shimoi, H.: Identification of a Gene Involved in the Synthesis of a Dipeptidyl Peptidase IV Inhibitor in *Aspergillus oryzae*. Appl. Environ. Microbiol. 78, 6996–7002 (2012)

An Approach to Identify miRNA Associated with Cancer Altered Pathways

Giovanna Maria Ventola[2], Antonio Colaprico[2], Fulvio D'Angelo[2],
Vittorio Colantuoni[1], Giuseppe Viglietto[3],
Luigi Cerulo[1,2], and Michele Ceccarelli[1,2]

[1] Dep. of Science and Technology, University of Sannio, Benevento, Italy
[2] BioGeM, Institute of Genetic Research "G. Salvatore", Ariano Irpino, AV, Italy
[3] Dep. of Experimental and Clinical Medicine, University of "Magna Graecia",
Catanzaro, Italy

Abstract. MicroRNAs play an important role in the regulation of gene expression by binding mRNA targets causing their degradation or blocking their translation. Several genes has been found to be implicated as miRNA targets in different types of malignant tumors suggesting their involvement in cancer pathogenesis. Detecting direct miRNA–targets associations is not straightforward as in principle targets expressions are not altered except when they are completely repressed by the degradation complex.

In this paper we propose an approach to identify direct miRNA–targets associations hypotheses by means of indirect association measures such as mutual information. Indirect regulons of miRNA and Transcription Factors (TFs) are compared with the Fisher's exact test to identify potential co-regulations which may constitute potential miRNA–TF direct associations.

We apply the method on two cancer datasets, Colon and Lung, drawn from the Cancer Genome Atlas (TGCA) obtaining promising results.

Keywords: miRNA, reverse engineering, gene regulatory networks.

1 Introduction

MicroRNAs (miRNAs) are small noncoding, endogenous, single-stranded RNA molecules of approximately 22 nucleotides. They play an important role in the regulation of gene expression by binding mRNA targets causing mRNA degradation or blocking mRNA translation. About 5300 human genes are found to be implicated as targets of miRNAs and have function in various human diseases [1]. In particular, deregulation of miRNAs in different types of malignant tumors suggests their involvement in the pathogenesis of cancer. Similarly to oncogenes the over-expression of miRNAs may contribute to tumor formation if they bind to tumor suppressor genes, instead, they act as onco-suppressors if they bind oncogenes slowing down cancer progression [15]. Such a behavior makes the study of miRNA regulation associations crucial in cancer diagnosis, prognosis and therapy. For instance, Calin *et al.* found that two genes, coding

A. Petrosino, L. Maddalena, P. Pala (Eds.): ICIAP 2013 Workshops, LNCS 8158, pp. 399–408, 2013.

for *miR-15* and *miR-16*, are located within a 30 kb region of loss in chronic lymphocytic leukemia and that both genes are deleted or down-regulated in the majority of cases [6]. The repression activity modulated by miRNAs depends on the recognition of binding sites located mainly on the 3' untranslated regions of target mRNAs [1]. In order to understand the role of miRNAs in biological processes, it is important to identify their gene targets and which conditions make such binding pivotal. In addition to experimental techniques to identify miRNA-target interactions, several computational algorithms have been developed to predict putative targets [16]. The most common prediction algorithms identify miRNA targets using sequence–based approaches and rank the candidate targets by considering the sequence complementarity between miRNA seeds and genes 3'–UTRs. Such algorithms yield usually a very high number of false positives. On the other hand, these tools, tested against the available experimentally validated miRNA-target pairs, are not able to predict every known gene target them (false negatives) [3]. Alternative approaches exploit reverse engineering algorithms to reconstruct miRNA–gene regulatory networks. For instance, Zhao *et al.* analyzed the *feed-forward loop* consisting of miRNAs, transcription factors (TFs) and genes to construct a miRNA-TF regulatory network in glioblastoma and identified miRNA components involved in the Notch signaling pathway [20]. Genovese *et al.* adopted a network-modeling algorithm to compute pairwise measures of associations and identified some important miRNA, such as miR-34a proposed as a novel regulator of TGF-β signaling [8]. The algorithm evaluates the mutual information of miRNA-mRNA pairs. This analysis resulted in the identification of some putative interactions, whose only the minimal proportion (0.17%) was predicted to be direct.

In this paper we propose an approach inspired by the work of Genovese *et al.* to identify potential miRNA–TF associations in cancer altered pathways. In principle the expression of miRNA's targets is not altered except when they are completely repressed by the degradation complex. Thus expression correlation methods, such those adopted by Genovese *et al.*, are not able to identify such direct relationships. To avoid such a limitation we adopt an indirect approach. The regulons of both miRNA and TF are computed through the mutual information of their expression profiles. Such regulons, that comprises both direct and indirect associations, are then compared by means of Fisher's exact test to identify miRNA–TF co-regulations. We show on two cancer datasets that such a computed co-regulation is a valuable criterion to suggest direct miRNA–TF associations. We test our approach on two datasets of common malignant tumors, colon adenocarcinoma (COAD) and lung squamous cell carcinoma (LUSC), obtaining a relevant number of strong literature confirmed interactions, such as *miR-17/miR-20a* → *BCL2* [4,10,14].

The paper is organized as follows. The next Section covers material and methods detailing the proposed approach and defining the evaluation procedure adopted. Section 3 reports and discusses the results obtained by applying the approach on two datasets. Section 4 draws conclusions and outlines future directions.

2   Material and Methods

2.1   Datasets

We test our approach on two datasets drawn from The Cancer Genome Atlas (TCGA) portal (http://cancergenome.nih.gov/): Colon Adenocarcinoma (COAD) and Lung Squamous cell Carcinoma (LUSC). The COAD dataset contains the expression levels of 1046 miRNAs in 187 tumor samples obtained with Illumina Genome Analyzer miRNA Sequencing and the expression level of 20531 genes in 193 tumor and 18 normal samples obtained with IlluminaHiSeq RNASeqV2. The LUSC dataset contains the expression levels of 1046 miRNAs in 213 tumor and 45 normal samples obtained with Illumina HiSeq miRNASeq and the expression level of 20531 genes in 259 tumor and 35 normal samples obtained with IlluminaHiSeq RNASeqV2.

2.2   The Proposed Approach

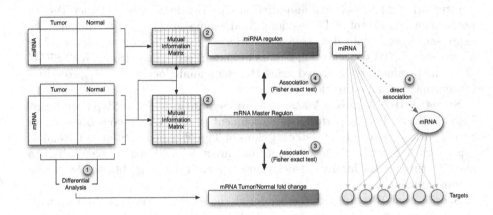

Fig. 1. The proposed analysis workflow

Our aim is to identify hypothesis of association between miRNAs and targets in the context of cancer altered pathways. We adopt the workflow shown in Figure 1 which consists of 5 steps detailed below:

Step1: Differential expression analysis. To determine whether a gene is differential expressed, we apply a test of hypothesis and the fold-change between two conditions, e.g. tumor and normal. In particular we adopt the quantile-adjusted conditional maximum likelihood (qCML) method for experiments with single factor, implemented in the edgeR package from Bioconductor [17]. Compared against several other estimators, qCML is the most reliable in terms of bias on a wide range of conditions and specifically performs best in the situation of many small samples with a common dispersion. The p-values generated from the analysis sorted in ascending order, are corrected using the Benjamini-Hochberg procedure for multiple testing correction.

Step2: miRNA and TF regulon estimation. Network inference, which is the reconstruction of biological networks from high-throughput data, can provide valuable information about the regulation of gene expressions in cells. Several methods have been proposed in literature [19]. Among all we adopt mutual information implemented in the parmigene R package, as it is particular efficient for large dataset. The mutual information provides us with an index of dependence between miRNAs and genes and between TFs and genes. We estimate an appropriate threshold with a permutation test to filter out non significant dependences and thus obtaining the set of genes regulated (directly or indirectly) by miRNAs and TFs.

Step3: Transcription factor master regulon estimation. Master Regulators are those transcription factors whose targets are enriched for a particular gene signature (e.g. differentially expressed genes). The enrichment is evaluated using a statistical test, such as Fishers Exact Test. The objective is to place the signature genes within a regulatory context and identify the Master Regulators responsible for coordinating their activity, thus highlighting the regulatory apparatus driving phenotypic differentiation [7]. We adopt Fisher's Exact Test to perform an enrichment of TF-regulons obtained in step 2 respect to differentially expressed genes obtained in step 1, identifing the TFs master regulators. The known list of 1503 transcription factors in human is obtained from TRANSFAC [22]. The p-values are corrected using the Benjamini-Hochberg (BH) procedure for multiple testing correction.

Step4: miRNA–mRNA association estimation. As for Step 3 we adopt Fisher's Exact Test to perform an enrichment of miRNA-regulons obtained in Step 2 with respect to the master regulons of TFs obtained in Step 3. This analysis let us to identify the most significant direct associations between miRNAs and TFs through the indirect associations with their regulons obtained by means of mutual information.

Step5: post-filtering. To further enrich the set of associations obtained with the previous steps we propose two post-filtering steps:

1. *Directional interaction.* The association of a miRNA with a TF could determine or not the degradation of the TF mRNA. Consequently the TF expression could be down-regulated, in the case of degradation, or at least unchanged, when mRNA degradation does not occur, allowing mRNA stability and accumulation. To this aim we filter out up-regulated TFs as they are non representative of the canonical functioning of miRNA regulation.

2. *Tool prediction.* The association of a miRNA with a TF should be supported by the complementarity of miRNA seed sequence with the 3' UTR mRNA. To support such a condition we adopt a representative set of tools provided by miRWalk [5], such as: DIANA-mT, miRanda, miRDB, miRWalk, RNAhybrid, PICTAR4, PICTAR5, PITA, RNA22, and TargetScan. We consider associations predicted by at least 3 tools in at least 5 TF.

2.3   Evaluation against the Literature

To evaluate miRNA–mRNA association hypotheses we conduct a survey to test to which extend such hypotheses are confirmed in literature. To this aim we adopt the miRWalk database [5] (http://www.umm.uni-heidelberg.de/apps/zmf/mirwalk/) and IPA®, (Ingenuity Pathways Analysis, http://www.ingenuity.com). The miRWalk database provides experimentally verified miRNA interaction information obtained from literature. The database, last updated on 15th March 2011, is build semi-automatically through text mining approaches and may provides false positives when for instance the names of miRNAs and TFs co-appears in the article text but are in fact not directly correlated. We assess manually the set of miRWalk validated associations by performing a manual inspection of the referred article and annotate the associations with: *text co-occurrence* for terms co-occurrence in the published article; *expression pattern evidence* for less strong validations by high-throughput gene expression experiments, such as microarrays, which not necessarily demonstrate if the miRNA causes the changed expression patterns directly or not; and *direct interaction evidence* for strong experimental evidence by western blot, qPCR or luciferase reporter assay which accurately validate miRNA target genes. IPA®, is a tool able to identify biological and molecular networks by mapping gene expression data into relevant pathways based on their functional annotation and known molecular interactions. Annotation information comes from published, peer-reviewed scientific publications and is continuously updated. For our purpose we adopt the following IPA enrichment analyses: *Biological Functions*, that allows for the identification of the biological functions that are most significantly enriched for a given set of genes; *Canonical Pathways*, that identifies molecular pathways from the IPA library that are significantly associated to a given set of genes; and *Network enrichment*, that generates regulatory networks of a given set of genes based on their literature known connectivity and constructs networks that optimize for both inter-connectivity and number of focus genes under the constraint of maximal network size.

3   Results and Discussions

3.1   COAD

Starting from the expression values of 20531 genes and applying specific filters, we found 1944 deregulated genes between cancer and normal colon tissues. Among the 1046 miRNAs in COAD dataset, we selected the 105 top expressed miRNAs in cancer condition. The expression data of both genes and miRNAs were then analyzed to calculate their mutual information and estimate the gene regulon for each miRNA. Similarly, we computed the mutual information between the expression profiles of genes and TFs identifying 482 TF master regulators (p-value < 0.01), *i.e.* those that are enriched with differentially expressed genes. By comparing miRNA and master regulons we obtained 61738 significantly associated miRNA-TF pairs (BH corrected p-value < 1.0×10^{-2}). Those

Table 1. miRWalk confirmed associations on COAD dataset

miRNA	TF	FDR	No. of tools	PubMed	Notes
hsa-mir-15b	CD36	$1.06 \ 10^{-26}$	1	17379065	text co-occurence
hsa-mir-181a-1	CD36	$8.35 \ 10^{-4}$	0	17379065	text co-occurence
hsa-mir-22	CD36	$5.72 \ 10^{-25}$	0	17379065	text co-occurence
hsa-mir-28	CD36	$1.95 \ 10^{-3}$	1	17379065	text co-occurence
hsa-let-7c	KIT	$1.54 \ 10^{-10}$	3	18068232	text co-occurence
hsa-mir-17	KIT	$1.49 \ 10^{-24}$	3	18068232	text co-occurence
hsa-let-7c	MEIS1	$3.48 \ 10^{-70}$	1	18308931	text co-occurence
hsa-let-7i	MEIS1	$1.33 \ 10^{-9}$	0	18308931	text co-occurence
hsa-mir-29a	MEIS1	$8.35 \ 10^{-3}$	0	18308931	text co-occurence
hsa-mir-141	FOXF1	$1.05 \ 10^{-61}$	0	18698484	text co-occurence
hsa-mir-200a	FOXF1	$1.22 \ 10^{-103}$	0	18698484	text co-occurence
hsa-mir-200c	FOXF1	$1.16 \ 10^{-90}$	6	18698484	text co-occurence
hsa-mir-429	FOXF1	$2.82 \ 10^{-36}$	6	18698484	text co-occurence
hsa-mir-20a	BCL2	$3.21491 \ 10^{-7}$	5	18941111	direct interaction evidence
hsa-mir-17	MEIS1	$3.23 \ 10^{-187}$	0	19155294	text co-occurence
hsa-mir-17	BCL2	$5.48908 \ 10^{-7}$	5	19666108	direct interaction evidence
hsa-let-7c	MEF2C	$4.28 \ 10^{-34}$	2	19897480	text co-occurence
hsa-mir-143	KLF4	$7.82 \ 10^{-3}$	1	20089806	text co-occurence
hsa-mir-27a	MEF2C	$3.64 \ 10^{-3}$	6	20736237	expression pattern evidence
hsa-mir-27b	MEF2C	$3.54 \ 10^{-3}$	7	20736237	expression pattern evidence
hsa-mir-183	HMOX1	$7.68 \ 10^{-14}$	0	21147878	text co-occurence
hsa-mir-19b-2	BCL2	$5.7447 \ 10^{-8}$	1	21883694	text co-occurence
hsa-let-7c	CLU	$3.57 \ 10^{-20}$	0	22749186	text co-occurence
hsa-let-7i	CLU	$6.53 \ 10^{-4}$	0	22749186	text co-occurence
hsa-mir-143	CLU	$6.04 \ 10^{-114}$	0	22749186	text co-occurence
hsa-mir-200b	FOXF1	$8.4858 \ 10^{-117}$	6	23022474	text co-occurence

represents the potential relationships between miRNAs and TFs that could explain the molecular alterations observed in colon cancer. We examined the 672 most interesting miRNA–TF associations by applying the filters explained in Section 2.2. These associations contains 32 unique miRNAs associated in average with 20 TFs. Among the selected miRNA-TF pairs, 27 out of 672 associations corresponded to miRWalk validated miRNA-targets (Table 1).

One of the most interesting result is observed for *miR-17* and *miR-20a*, which share the same group of TFs, thus belonging to the same family. In literature they are widely reported to be up-regulated in colon cancer tissues [4,10,14], promoting cell proliferation, tumour growth and cell cycle progression [14]. In our study, *miR-17* resulted significantly associated to 31 TFs, 9 of which are predicted by at least 3 tools among DIANAmt, miRanda, miRWalk, and TargetScan. One of such associations (*miR-17/miR-20a* → *BCL2*) has been biologically demonstrated by Beveridge *et al.* [2]. The fact that such an association is predicted by 5 sequence prediction tools let us suppose for a strong direct target binding association.

We investigated the enrichment in Biological Functions and Canonical Pathways for *miR-17* associated TFs with IPA. Cellular proliferation and differentiation, gene expression and cancer are the most significant biological function categories (BH corrected p-value $< 1.0 \times 10^{-6}$). Interestingly, in the cancer biological function the first annotations are "metastatic colorectal cancer" and "colorectal tumor", suggesting that the central role of *miR-17* in colon tumorigenesis could be mediated by its associated TFs. Moreover, "glucocorticoid receptor signaling" is the only significantly affected canonical pathway suggesting cortisol synthesis in a non-endocrine tumor as recently reported by Sidler *et al.* [18]. To show the putative regulatory network associated with *miR-17/miR-20a* we adopted the IPA network analysis tool that allows for reconstructing the literature known connections among a group of molecules. Figure 2A shows the most significant minimal connected network based on Ingenuity curated annotations and constructed from the set of 31 TFs significantly associated with *miR-17/miR-20a*. The network reports a total of 35 connected molecules 9 of which are comprised in the initial 31 set and whose principal functions are cell death and survival, cancer, and cell-mediated immune response.

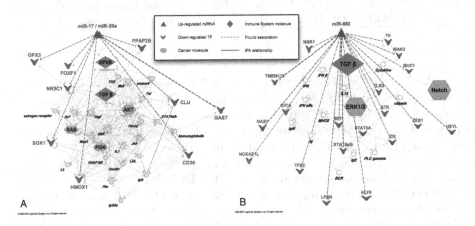

Fig. 2. Enriched biological networks obtained with IPA tool: A) COAD miR-17/miR-20a; B) LUSC miR-663

Other interesting associations have been found for *miR-200c*, *miR-221*, and *miR-429* [9,21,11] but not described due to space limitation.

3.2 LUSC

The differential expression analysis of LUSC data resulted in 3380 and 274 deregulated genes and miRNAs respectively. Then, we calculated their mutual information to define the gene regulons for miRNAs and we identified 558 TF master regulators (p-value < 0.01). miRNA and TF regulons were compared by Fisher exact test and 11125 miRNA–TF associations resulted significant (BH corrected

Table 2. miRWalk confirmed associations on LUSC dataset

miRNA	TF	FDR	No. of tools	PubMed	Notes
hsa-mir-200c	ZEB1	$2.85\ 10^{-10}$	2	18376396	direct interaction evidence
hsa-mir-196b	TLR4	$2.32\ 10^{-4}$	0	18291670	text co-occorrence
hsa-mir-205	ZEB1	$2.12\ 10^{-3}$	2	18376396	direct interaction evidence
hsa-mir-429	ZEB1	$5.28\ 10^{-28}$	0	18381893	direct interaction evidence
hsa-mir-141	ZEB1	$2.62\ 10^{-21}$	0	18483486	direct interaction evidence
hsa-mir-429	TBX2	$3.39\ 10^{-7}$	6	18698484	text co-occorence
hsa-mir-141	TBX2	$1.37\ 10^{-4}$	3	18698484	text co-occorence
hsa-mir-205	TBX2	$2.42\ 10^{-6}$	6	18698484	text co-occorrence
hsa-mir-96	ZEB1	$7.47\ 10^{-13}$	0	19167416	text co-occorence
hsa-mir-9-1	TLR4	$1.71\ 10^{-4}$	5	19289835	text co-occorrence
hsa-mir-9-1	TLR2	$1.52\ 10^{-3}$	2	19289835	text co-occorrence
hsa-mir-9-2	TLR4	$1.09\ 10^{-4}$	1	19289835	text co-occorrence
hsa-mir-9-2	TLR2	$1.15\ 10^{-3}$	6	19289835	text co-occorrence
hsa-mir-142	TLR4	$8.39\ 10^{-7}$	2	21037424	text co-occorrence
hsa-mir-369	ZEB1	$1.62\ 10^{-4}$	1	21125666	text co-occorrence
hsa-mir-429	WNT2	$1.30\ 10^{-10}$	2	21130073	text co-occorence
hsa-mir-200a	ZEB1	$7.95\ 10^{-10}$	2	18376396	direct interaction evidence
hsa-mir-200b	ZEB1	$5.02\ 10^{-5}$	6	22261924	direct interaction evidence
hsa-mir-7-1	TLR4	$2.95\ 10^{-4}$	0	23135998	text co-occorrence

p-value $< 1.0 \times 10^{-2}$). The identified miRNA–TF associations were further analyzed applying the filters described in Section 2.2. We focused on 1136 associations composed by 38 miRNAs that were associated in average with 30 TFs. Comparing the results with literature, 17 out of 1136 miRNA-TF associations were found already described in several studies (Table 2).

Very interesting miRNA-TF associations, for elucidating the role of miRNAs in lung tumorigenesis, were found for *miR-663*. The overexpression of *miR-663* in lung cancer was already reported in a recent study where the authors demonstrated it regulates cancer cell proliferation and apoptosis through targeting TGFβ [13]. In our study, we confirmed *miR-663* is highly up-regulated in LUSC, and it resulted significantly associated to 34 TFs, 9 of which are predicted by at least 3 tools (such as miRanda, miRWalk, TargetScan, PICTAR5). IPA analysis was performed to evaluate the enrichment in Biological Functions for *miR-663* associated TFs. The most significant Biological Function (BH corrected p-value $= 6.0 \times 10^{-9}$) is differentiation of cells which was predicted significantly decreased (z-score $= -2.844$) by IPA algorithm. This biological annotation represents also the top function of a proposed regulatory network built through IPA network analysis tool (Figure 2B). Starting from *miR-663* associated TFs, this regulatory network shows the known relationships between 35 connected molecules, 17 of which are included in the initial 34 set.

Other remarkable result is observed for *miR-141* and *miR-200c*, which share 37/44 associated TFs and, as expected, belong to the same miRNA family. Interestingly, they were recently reported as novel serum biomarkers associated to poor prognosis in LUSC [12]. Their associated TFs resulted enriched for cellular differentiation, cell death and immune cell trafficking (BH corrected p-value $< 1.0 \times 10^{-6}$) through IPA Biological Functions analysis.

4   Conclusions and Future Work

We proposed a method to identify potential associations between miRNAs and Transcription Factors playing a central role in altered cancer pathways. The algorithm is able to identify potential direct relationships where other methods, based on pure correlation measures, may fail. It is still affected by false positives thus heuristics able to filter out not relevant associations are necessary. We proposed two filtering heuristics, one based on interaction directionality and another that exploits sequence bases prediction tools.

We test the method on two cancer datasets, Colon Adenocarcinoma (COAD) and Lung Squamous cell Carcinoma (LUSC), showing important literature confirmed associations. Result obtained with this study consolidate the potential involvement of miRNAs in colon and lung cancerogenesis but further studies are necessary to examine all suggested interactions and to elucidate their role in cancer.

Acknowledgements. This work was supported by a research project funded by MiUR (Ministero dell'Università e della Ricerca) under grant FIRB2012-RBFR12QW4I.

References

1. Bartel, D.P.: MicroRNAs: genomics, biogenesis, mechanism, and function. Cell 116, 281–297 (2004)
2. Beveridge, N., Tooney, P., Carroll, A., Tran, N., Cairns, M.: Down-regulation of mir-17 family expression in response to retinoic acid induced neuronal differentiation. Cell Signal 21(12), 1837–1845 (2009)
3. Coronello, C., Benos, P.: Comir: combinatorial microRNA target prediction tool. Nucleid Acid Research (2013)
4. Diosdado, B., van de Wiel, M.A., Terhaar Sive Droste, J.S., Mongera, S., Postma, C., Meijerink, W.J., Carvalho, B., Meijer, G.A.: MiR-17-92 cluster is associated with 13q gain and c-myc expression during colorectal adenoma to adenocarcinoma progression. British Journal of Cancer 101(4), 707–714 (2009)
5. Dweep, H., Sticht, C., Pandey, P., Gretz, N.: miRWalk–database: prediction of possible miRNA binding sites by "walking" the genes of three genomes. Journal of Biomedical Informatics 44(5), 839–847 (2011)
6. Calin, G.A., et al.: Frequent deletions and down-regulation of micro- RNA genes miR15 and miR16 at 13q14 in chronic lymphocytic leukemia. Proceedings of the National Academy of Sciences of the United States of America 99(24), 15524–15529 (2002)
7. Lefebvre, C., et al.: A human B-cell interactome identifies MYB and FOXM1 as master regulators of proliferation in germinal centers. Molecular Systems Biology 6 (June 2010)

8. Genovese, G., et al.: MicroRNA regulatory network inference identifies miR-34a as a novel regulator of TGF-β signaling in glioblastoma. Cancer Discovery 13 (2012)

9. Hur, K., Toiyama, Y., Takahashi, M., Balaguer, F., Nagasaka, T., Koike, J., Hemmi, H., Koi, M., Boland, C., Goel, A.: Microrna-200c modulates epithelial-to-mesenchymal transition (emt) in human colorectal cancer metastasis. Gut (2012)

10. Earle, J.S., Luthra, R., Romans, A., Abraham, R., Ensor, J., Yao, H., Hamilton, S.R.: Association of microrna expression with microsatellite instability status in colorectal adenocarcinoma. J. Mol. Diagn. 12(4) (2010)

11. Li, J., Du, L., Yang, Y., Wang, C., Liu, H., Wang, L., Zhang, X., Li, W., Zheng, G., Dong, Z.: Mir-429 is an independent prognostic factor in colorectal cancer and exerts its anti-apoptotic function by targeting sox2. Cancer Lett. 329(1), 84–90 (2013)

12. Liu, X., Zhu, W., Huang, Y., Ma, L., Zhou, S., Wang, Y., Zeng, F., Zhou, J., Zhang, Y.: High expression of serum mir-21 and tumor mir-200c associated with poor prognosis in patients with lung cancer. Med. Oncol. (2011)

13. Liu, Z.Y., Zhang, G.L., Wang, M.M., Xiong, Y.N., Cui, H.Q.: Microrna-663 targets tgfb1 and regulates lung cancer proliferation. Asian Pac. J. Cancer Prev. 12(11), 2819–2823 (2011)

14. Luo, H., Zou, J., Dong, Z., Zeng, Q., Wu, D., Liu, L.: Up-regulated mir-17 promotes cell proliferation, tumour growth and cell cycle progression by targeting the rnd3 tumour suppressor gene in colorectal carcinoma. Biochem. J. 442(2), 311–321 (2012)

15. Nohata, N., Hanazawa, T., Kinoshita, T., Okamoto, Y., Seki, N.: MicroRNAs function as tumor suppressors or oncogenes: Aberrant expression of microRNAs in head and neck squamous cell carcinoma. Auris Nasus Larynx (2012)

16. Reyes-Herrera, P.H., Ficarra, E.: One Decade of Development and Evolution of MicroRNA Target Prediction Algorithms. Genomics, Proteomics & Bioinformatics 10(5), 254–263 (2012)

17. Robinson, M.D., McCarthy, D.J., Smyth, G.K.: edgeR: a Bioconductor package for differential expression analysis of digital gene expression data. Bioinformatics 26(1), 139–140 (2010)

18. Sidler, D., Renzulli, P., Schnoz, C., Berger, B., Schneider-Jakob, S., Flück, C., Inderbitzin, D., Corazza, N., Candinas, D., Brunner, T.: Colon cancer cells produce immunoregulatory glucocorticoids. Oncoimmunology 1(4), 529–530 (2012)

19. Smet, R.D., Marchal, K.: Advantages and limitations of current network inference methods. Nature Reviews Microbiology 8(10), 717 (2010)

20. Sun, J., Gong, X., Purow, B., Zhao, Z.: Uncovering microRNA and transcription factor mediated regulatory networks in glioblastoma. PLoS Computational Biology (2012)

21. Sun, K., Wang, W., Zeng, J., Wu, C., Lei, S., Li, G.: Microrna-221 inhibits cdkn1c/p57 expression in human colorectal carcinoma. Acta Pharmacol Sin. 32(3), 375–384 (2011)

22. Wingender, E., Dietze, P., Karas, H., Knüppel, R.: TRANSFAC: A Database on Transcription Factors and Their DNA Binding Sites. Nucleic Acids Research 24(1), 238–241 (1996)

Performance Comparison of Five Exact Graph Matching Algorithms on Biological Databases

Vincenzo Carletti, Pasquale Foggia, and Mario Vento

DIEM - University of Salerno
{vcarletti,pfoggia,mvento}@unisa.it
http://mivia.unisa.it

Abstract. Graphs are a powerful data structure that can be applied to several problems in bioinformatics. Graph matching, in its diverse forms, is an important operation on graphs, involved when there is the need to compare two graphs or to find substructures into larger structures. Many graph matching algorithms exist, and their relative efficiency depends on the kinds of graphs they are applied to. In this paper we will consider some popular and freely available matching algorithms, and will experimentally compare them on graphs derived from bioinformatics applications, in order to help the researchers in this field to choose the right tool for the problem at hand.

Keywords: Graph matching, Benchmarking, Graph methods in Bioinformatics.

1 Introduction

Graphs are a powerful and flexible data structure that can be used for the representation of several kinds of data in many applicative fields [9] [5] [7]. Among these, bioinformatic applications play a very important role. For instance, molecular structures can be represented using a graph whose nodes corresponds to atoms and whose edges represent chemical bonds. The secondary structure of a protein can be represented by a graph with aminoacids as nodes, and edges used for encoding the contact s between adjacent and non adjacent nodes (e.g. hydrogen bonds); a similar representation can be used for other large biomolecules. Also, graph structures have been recently used to represent information describing networks of relations. For instance, the biologists are collecting huge quantities of data related to the interactions between the activities of different proteins in a given species. The resulting data are interaction networks, i.e. graphs whose nodes represent proteins, and whose edges represent interactions; by comparing the interaction networks of different species, it is possible to predict unknown interactions, or to discover functionally equivalent groups of proteins that perform a specific activity.

Given this wide number of cases where biological information is represented by means of (possibly large) graphs, it is important to have some graph-based methods and techniques to extract information from graphs. *Graph Matching*,

A. Petrosino, L. Maddalena, P. Pala (Eds.): ICIAP 2013 Workshops, LNCS 8158, pp. 409–417, 2013.
© Springer-Verlag Berlin Heidelberg 2013

in its different meanings, plays a major role within such techniques. The simplest form of Graph Matching, *Graph Isomorphism*, can be used to determine if two graphs have the same structure, regardless the order of the nodes. *Graph-Subgraph Isomorphism* can be used to establish if a smaller graph is completely contained within a larger one as a subgraph, for example for searching all the graphs in a database that contain a certain desired substructure. *Monomorphism* is a weaker form of Graph-Subgraph Isomorphism, suitable when the desired substructure can be characterized by the presence of some relations, but not by their absence. Finally, the *Maximum Common Subgraph* (MCS) matching is aimed at finding common substructures within larger graphs. In the bioinformatics field, a substructure within a larger structure is often called a *motif*; *motif search* and *motif discovery* are considered problems of primary importance, since it is often a reasonable conjecture to assume that a motif common to different structures may have a perhaps undiscovered biological significance.

In the literature, hundreds of Graph Matching algorithms have been proposed in the last 40 years for the problems mentioned above. Still, none of them has proved to be the most effective in all situations. Different algorithms have different advantages and disadvantages, that can make them more or less suited for a particular kind of graphs. While in some cases a theoretical analysis is sufficient to exclude some algorithms, for the most commonly used ones there is an insufficient theoretical characterization of their computational cost. So, benchmarking is the only viable option to choose the right algorithm for a given problem; and this benchmarking has to be done using graphs with the same characteristics as the ones the will be encountered in the chosen application domain.

This paper aims at presenting the results of such a benchmarking activity using graphs from the bioinformatics research field. Of course, such an experimentation cannot reasonably aspire to be comprehensive and complete, given the large number of existing algorithms and of existing kinds of graph structures. However, it is our opinion that even within this limitations, this activity may provide useful information to the bioinformatics researchers looking for a graph matching algorithm, especially considering that we have included well known algorithms, for which stable and reliable implementations are freely available; such algorithms are very often the first choices for a researcher that views graph matching as a tool, and not as the goal of his research activity.

In the following, after a brief overview of the literature, we will present the chosen algorithms and the databases used for this experimentation. Then we will show and analyze the obtained results, especially the computation time, and draw some final conclusions.

1.1   Related Works

Several existing works [12] [14] [16] [1] point out the possibility of using graph based representations for bioinformatics data and problems; some of them specifically refer to particular kinds of graph matching, while others advocate a plurality of techniques without focusing onto one in particular. In the following we will present some important papers, without any claim of comprehensiveness. Kuhl et al. [13] present one of the earliest applications of graph matching to bioinformatics, namely the MCS problem is used for the prediction of the ligaind-protein binding. Gifford et al. [10] apply graph matching to the prediction of biological activity of a molecule. The paper by Milo et al. [15] discusses the analysis of network motifs (i.e. subgraphs) within complex networks from genomics, proteomics and other fields of bioinformatics, besides other application domains. Tian et al. [19] propose the use of subgraph isomorphism for searching for protein complexes in protein-protein interaction networks. The paper by Aittokallio and Schwikowski [1] presents several graph-based techniques, including graph matching, that can be applied for the analysis of cell networks in cellular biology. In the literature several papers have already appeared comparing and contrasting several graph matching algorithms, mostly from a theoretical point of view, and without a reference to a particular application. In Conte et al. [4], a comprehensive survey of graph matching techniques used in Pattern Recognition is provided, presenting the different kinds of exact and inexact graph matching problems and discussing for each problem the most important approaches. While this paper does not cover methods published in the last few years, it remain an essential reference to understand the different approaches to the problem, and most of the well known and proven algorithms. The paper [16] by Raymond and Willet presents a more focused survey for MCS algorithms, with specific reference to their application to 2D and 3D molecular data. Bonnici et al. in a recent paper [3], besides presenting a subgraph isomorphism algorithm called RI, describe an experimental evaluation of several algorithms for the same problem using different databases of graphs obtained from chemical and biological applications.

This latter paper is the closest in its conception to the present article. While both the papers share the focus on the importance of a quantitative evaluation of graph matching on graphs directly derived from bioinformatics applications, the present article considers a broader range of matching problems, including isomorphism and MCS, and as a consequence different algorithms have been used for the experimental comparison.

2   Benchmarking

2.1   The Compared Algorithms

In this work we compare five graph matching algorithms on four different biological databases, focusing our attention on three kinds of matching problems [4]: Graph Isomorphism, Subgraph Isomorphism and MCS. The five considered algorithms are not applicable to all the three problems; usually each algorithm is developed for a single problem and may be extended to a second similar problem with few changes. So, in the experiments we will not present all the 15 combinations between the five algorithms and the three problems; however we have ensured that for each problem there are at least two different algorithms to be compared.

Thus, in our experimentation we have used VF2 [6], Ullmann [20], RI [3] and LAD [18] for Graph Isomorphism; VF2, Ullmann, RI, LAD for Subgraph Isomorphism; and VF2 and DPC2 [8] for MCS. Of these algorithms, Ulmann, DPC2 and VF2 are widely known and widely used algorithms, for which stable implementations are available, while RI and LAD are newer entries, that should be representative of the most recent ideas on exact graph matching. In the following a short overview of each algorithm is provided.

VF2. The VF2 algorithm by Cordella et al. [6] uses a state space representation and is based on a depth-first strategy with a set of rules to efficiently prune the search tree. The algorithm can be used both for graph isomorphism, subgraph isomorphism and MCS selecting a suiteble set of rules for the cosidered problem. VF2 is an extension of the previous VF matching algorithm, and is characterized by the use of suitably designed data structures for reducing the amount of information that has to be replicated when passing from a state to its descendants, so reducing both the memory occupation and the computation time.

Ullmann. The Ullmann algorithm [20] is among the most commonly used algorithms for exact graph matching [4]. It is based on a depth-first search like VF2, and use a complex, iterative heuristic for pruning the search space, that significantly reduces the number of visited states, at the expense of the memory and time spent for each state. This algorithm can be used both for Graph Isomorphism and for Subgraph Isomorphism.

DPC2. The DPC2 algorithm by Durand and Pasari [8] uses a well known theoretical result that connects the MCS problem to the search of the Maximum Clique (i.e. complete subgraph) of a suitably defined *association graph* [2]. DPC2 solves the Maximum Clicque problem with a state-space representation, adopting a depth-first search algorithm with a heuristic criterion to prune some unfruitful search paths. This algorithm, by its definition, can only be used for the MCS problem.

LAD. The LAD algorithm [18] by C. Solnon is also based on a state space representation with depth-first search, and uses a formulation of the matching as a Constraint Satisfaction Problem (CSP) to derive a criterion for pruning the search space. Namely, LAD uses the constraint that the mapping between the nodes of the two graphs must be injective and edge-preserving, and after each node assignment it propagates iteratively this constraint to unmatched nodes until convergence. Thus the LAD algorithm can be used both for Graph Isomorphism and for Subgraph Isomorphism.

RI. Like VF2, also the RI algorithm [3] by Bonnici et al. during the matching the algorithm performs heuristic checks that are very fast to execute, thus requiring a short time for each visited search state. However, a preprocessing is performed, resulting in a reordering of the nodes of each graph; this reordering is aimed at ensuring that the nodes that involve more constraints are matched first, so as to reduce as early as possible the search space by means of those contraints. RI can be used for both Graph Isomorphism and Subgraph Isomorphism.

2.2   Test Databases

The benchmarks have been performed using graphs obtained by several databases from bioinformatics applications, namely molecular and protein databases. The choice of the databases is based on the paper by Bonnici et al. [3], whose authors provide six databases already converted into a common graph format.

The databases have been structured for the monomorphism problem, so each one is composed of very large graphs, called target, from which have been extracted a set of not induced subgraphs, called pattern, and so grouped by three densities: 1, 0.5 and 0.25. The aim of the authors is to use pattern graphs as queries on the target graph. We do not use all the six databases, but the following tree:

AIDS. This is molecular database containing 40000 graphs, from 4 to 256 nodes, representing the topological structure of a chemical compound tested for evidence of anti-HIV activity.

Graemlin. The Graemlin database contains 10 target graphs having up to 6726 nodes, extracted from 10 microbial networks.

PPI. The Protein-Protein interaction networks contains 10 network graphs, from 5720 to 12575 nodes, describing known protein interactions of 10 organisms. This is composed of more dense and big graphs than those in Graemlin.

The Graemlin and PPI databases have nodes with no labels. Since graph matching algorithms usually employ label information to reduce the computational costs, the matching times on unlabeled graphs are very long. For this reason, following [3], we have attached labels to the nodes of the graphs. The labels have been generated using random integer values. We have generated 5 labeled version of each database, varying the number of possible label values (128, 256, 512, 1024 and 2048 values have been used). For graph isomorphism we have generated two new databases, extracting random node-induced subgraphs from the target graphs in Graemlin and PPI; for each graph, 10 random permutations of the nodes have been computed to obtain isomorphic pairs of graphs. In order to test isomorphism algorithms on dense graphs, we have also added extra edges at random. So finally we have two isomorphism databases having 700 pairs, varying from 8 to 512 nodes.

3   Experimental Results

Experiments have been run employing of the implementations provided into VFlib for VF2, Ullmann and DPC2 algorithms, while for RI and LAD we used the code distributed by the respective authors [11] [17]. The experimental results

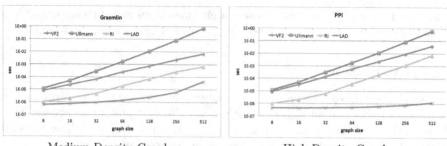

Fig. 1. The matching time, in logarithmic scale, of VF2, Ullmann, RI, LAD, algorithms on Isomorfism Databases, as a function of graph size

have been obtained on an Intel i3-2100 3.1 Ghz, with 2 cores and 3 Mb cache, equipped with 4 GB of RAM and running a Linux OS with kernel 3.2.0. We have not used multithreading to avoid caching problems. Moreover, for isomorphism and MCS we set a 30 minutes time out.

Graph Isomorphism. In this experimentation we have used the VF2, Ullmann, RI and LAD algorithms on two databases, with distinct densities, generated as described in 2.2. Fig. 1 shows the results on this problem. As it can be seen, RI perfoms better than VF2 and Ullman, altough the difference with VF2 seems to be a constant, and so these two algorithms have a very similar asymptotic behavior. However, on isomorphism the best algorithms seems to be LAD, especially on very dense graphs. The reason may be due the CSP approach used by LAD, that makes a better pruning of unfruitful matches when nodes have several constraints.

Induced Subgraph Isomorphism. The experiments on induced subgraph isomorphism involved the VF2, Ullmann and RI algorithms on the Graemlin and PPI databases. Tests have been run for five different uniform node label distributions, from 128 to 2048 values, but we only show a reduced set of results. RI always outperfoms both VF2 and Ullmann, as shown in Fig. 2. The distance, in execution time, between RI and VF2 seems to be the same for all considered cases, irrespective of label distribution or target graph size and density.

MCS. MCS experimentation only involved VF2 and DPC2 algorithms, because the others do not deal with this problem. Tests have been run using AIDS database, by choosing random pairs of graphs and computing their MCS. As shown in Fig. 3 VF2 outperforms DPC2, even though there is significant variance in the matching times. This is caused by the fact that the graphs in the database have all different number of nodes, and so the resulting times are not mediated over a large number of cases.

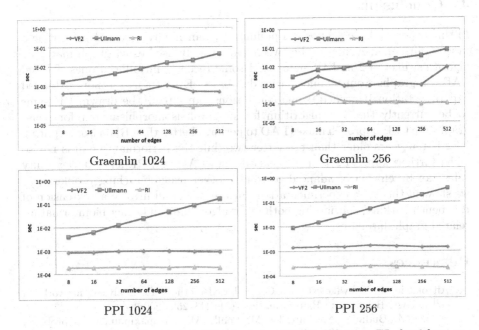

Fig. 2. The matching time, in logarithmic scale, of VF2, Ullmann, RI algorithms on Graemlin ad PPI Databases, as a function of query graph edges

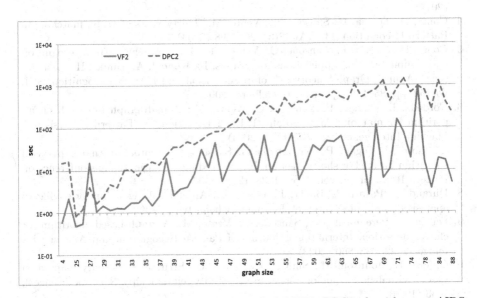

Fig. 3. The matching time, in logarithmic scale, of VF2, DPC2 algorithms on AIDS Dataset, as a function of graph size

4   Conclusions

In this paper we have proposed a preliminary banchmark aimed at presenting a first performance evaluation beetween some widely used exact graph matching algoritms, like VF2 and Ullmann, and some recently introduced ones, RI and LAD, on graphs from bioinformatics databases. Even though a more extended experimentation is needed, some conclusions can already be drawn. RI seems to be currently the best algorithm for subgraph isomorphism, but for dense graphs the CSP approach makes LAD to perform better than RI on isomorphism. VF2 is ten years older than the latter two, but the performance gap is not so wide; furthermore, VF2 is more general than LAD and RI, since its feasibilty rules can be efficiently adapted to resolve other exact matching problems, as we show in the MCS experimentation. Future work will involve an extension of this benchmarking, considering both other algorithms and other bioinformatics-related graph databases.

References

1. Aittokallio, T., Schwikowski, B.: Graph-based methods for analysing networks in cell biology. Briefings in Bioinformatics 7(3), 243–255 (2006)
2. Bomze, M., Budinich, M., Pardalos, M., Pelillo, M.: The maximum clique problem. Handbook of Combinatorial Optimization 4 (1999)
3. Bonnici, V., Giugno, R., Pulvirenti, A., Shasha, D., Ferro, A.: A subgraph isomorphism algorithm and its application to biochemical data. BMC Bioinformatics 14 (2013)
4. Conte, D., Foggia, P., Sansone, C., Vento, M.: Thirty years of graph matching in Pattern Recognition. IJPRAI 18(3), 265–298 (2004)
5. Conte, D., Foggia, P., Sansone, C., Vento, M.: How and why pattern recognition and computer vision applications use graphs. In: Kandel, A., Bunke, H., Last, M. (eds.) Applied Graph Theory in Computer Vision and Pattern Recognition. SCI, vol. 52, pp. 85–135. Springer, Heidelberg (2007)
6. Cordella, L., Foggia, P., Sansone, C., Vento, M.: A (sub)graph isomorphism algorithm for matching large graphs. IEEE Transactions on Pattern Analysis and Machine Intelligence 26, 1367–1372 (2004)
7. De Santo, M., Foggia, P., Percannella, G., Sansone, C., Vento, M.: An unsupervised algorithm for anchor shot detection. In: Proceedings - International Conference on Pattern Recognition, vol. 2, pp. 1238–1241 (2006)
8. Durand, P., Pasari, R., Baker, J., Tsai, C.C.: An efficient algorithm for similarity analysis of molecules. Internet Journal of Chemistry 2 (1999)
9. Foggia, P., Percannella, G., Sansone, C., Vento, M.: A graph-based algorithm for cluster detection. International Journal of Pattern Recognition and Artificial Intelligence 22, 843–860 (2008)
10. Gifford, E., Johnson, M., Smith, D., Tsai, C.C.: Structure-reactivity maps as a tool for visualizing xenobiotic structure-reactivity relationships. Network Science 2, 1–33 (1996)
11. Giugno, R.: Ri website, `http://ferrolab.dmi.unict.it/ri/ri.html`
12. Huan, J., et al.: Comparing graph representations of protein structure for mining family-specific residue-based packing motif. Journal of Computational Biology (2005)

13. Kuhl, F.S., Crippen, G.M., Friesen, D.K.: A combinatorial algorithm for calculating ligand binding. Journal of Computational Chemistry 5(1), 24–34 (1984)
14. Lacroix, V., Fernandez, C., Sagot, M.: Motif search in graphs: Application to metabolic networks. Transactions on Computational Biology and Bioinformatics (December 2006)
15. Milo, R., Shen-Orr, S., Itzkovitz, S., Kashtan, N., Chklovskii, D., Alon, U.: Network motifs: Simple building blocks of complex networks. Science 298(5594), 824–827 (2002)
16. Raymond, J., Willett, P.: Maximum common subgraph isomorphism algorithms for the matching of chemical structures. Journal of Computer-Aided Molecular Design 16(7), 521–533 (2002)
17. Solnon, C.: Lad website, http://liris.cnrs.fr/csolnon/LAD.html
18. Solnon, C.: Alldifferent-based filtering for subgraph isomorphism. Artificial Intelligence 174(12-13), 850–864 (2010)
19. Tian, Y., McEachin, R.C., Santos, C., States, D.J., Patel, J.M.: Saga: A subgraph matching tool for biological graphs. Bioinformatics 23(2), 232–239 (2007)
20. Ullman, J.R.: An algorithm for subgraph isomorphism. J. Assoc. Comput. Mach. 23, 31–42 (1976)

Pardiff: Inference of Differential Expression at Base-Pair Level from RNA-Seq Experiments

Bogdan Mirauta[1], Pierre Nicolas[2], and Hugues Richard[1]

[1] Génomique des microorganismes, UPMC and CNRS UMR7238, Paris, France
{bogdan.mirauta,hugues.richard}@upmc.fr
http://www.lgm.upmc.fr/parseq
[2] Mathématique Informatique et Génome, INRA UR1077, Jouy-en-Josas, France
pierre.nicolas@jouy.inra.fr

Abstract. In the field of RNA-Seq transcriptomics, detecting differences in expression levels between two data-sets remains a challenging question. Most current methods consider only point estimates of the expression levels, and thus neglect the uncertainty of these estimates. Further, testing for differential expression is often done on predefined regions. Here, we propose Pardiff, a method that reconstructs the profile of differential expression at a base-pair resolution and incorporate uncertainty via the use of a Bayesian framework. This method is built on our approach, Parseq, to infer the transcriptional landscape from RNA-seq data.

A program, named Pardiff, implements this strategy and will be made available at: http://www.lgm.upmc.fr/parseq/.

1 Introduction

Various technologies allowing genome wide profiling of the transcriptional activity have emerged in the last two decades. The microarray technology first monitored those types of changes at the gene, and then down to the exon level [7], [6]. More recently, the surge in throughput from sequencing technologies, like Illumina or SOLiD, has raised this resolution to the basepair. Deep sequencing of the transcriptome (RNA-Seq) consists in random shearing of transcripts, followed by amplification and sequencing of the RNA population. An RNA-Seq experiment produces millions of reads which, after alignment to the reference genome, serve to estimate the expression landscape [15].

One traditional question is, starting from two or more controlled experiments, to identify the set of elements that exhibit differential expression (DE). Answering this question is an important step towards formulating a biological hypothesis or for instance deriving disease biomarkers. In statistical terms, the question translates into detecting significant changes of expression level, after accounting for the sources of experimental and biological variability. However, this traditional statistical standpoint does not consider the magnitude of the effect, and authors proposed to overcome this limitation by directly testing whether fold change is above a given level [13].

A. Petrosino, L. Maddalena, P. Pala (Eds.): ICIAP 2013 Workshops, LNCS 8158, pp. 418–427, 2013.
© Springer-Verlag Berlin Heidelberg 2013

The analysis of DE usually starts from predefined units of possible change, such as genes, exons or transcript isoforms. In this case, after cumulating counts at unit level, one can estimate the statistical significance of differences [1], [17], [18]. Replicating the data sets permits the control of expression variability and mitigates the incertitude on expression level estimation. A challenging problem arises when these units of potential DE are not known. In this case, one faces the problem of having to jointly delineate the boundaries of the DE regions and estimating the magnitude of the DE.

Approaches to tackle this problem group in two categories. The first category consists of estimating the transcript structures from the different datasets (used separately or jointly) and then applying DE detection methods on predefined units. The second category computes the DE profile from the read coverage in the two conditions and then segment this profile into DE regions. The first option is made possible by several methods [11], [14], [19] that deal with transcript reconstruction. In this case, the DE units are derived from the estimated transcript structure and DE changes within those units remain invisible. Inferring DE regions directly from the DE profile provide a more detailed view of DE landscape but may raise problems concerning the correspondence to previous annotation. A work in progress belonging to this second category of approaches is presented in [10] where, from multiple replicates, coverage difference at position resolution are used to reconstruct DE regions. When replicates are not available alternative ways to control the incertitude should be considered.

Here we propose another method that also belongs to the second category of approaches and provides at base-pair resolution, both the regions whose expression changed above a given fold and an estimate of the change magnitude. Our approach builds upon a statistically sounded model, Parseq [14], for the analysis of the transcriptional landscape whose inference recovers the posterior distribution of expression levels for each genomic position. We complement this information by inferring regions which are statistically differentially expressed at a minimal fold change. After a description of the Parseq model, we will present our method, Pardiff which detects DE regions at a given fold change from RNA-Seq data. Then we will illustrate the relevance of such a strategy on semi-synthetic data-sets derived from an RNA-Seq experiment conducted on *S. cerevisae*.

2 Methods

2.1 Reconstruction of Transcriptional Profiles with Parseq

Given an RNA-Seq experiment, after alignment of the reads to the genome, we observe at each position t the counts y_t of reads starting at this position. We denote the transcription level by u_t (u_t and v_t in the case of two conditions). This level is by construction proportional to the expectation of y_t.

Our aim is to reconstruct the trajectory $\mathbf{u} = (u_t)_{t \geq 1}$, i.e. estimate expected values and credibility intervals along the genome and identify breakpoints from the sequence of read counts $\mathbf{y} = (y_t)_{t \geq 1}$. For this purpose we consider a State Space Model where u_t is a hidden variable taking values on the real half line

$[0; +\infty)$ whose distribution depends on u_{t-1} via a Markov transition kernel and y_t is an observation whose emission distribution depends on u_t. This framework allows accounting for the longitudinal dependency between the u_t's and provides great flexibility in the modeling of y_t given u_t. However, parameter inference and trajectory reconstruction is more challenging than in a classical HMM where only discrete values are considered for the hidden variable.

We recall shortly the characteristics of the Markov transition kernel and emission model underlying Parseq, more details are provided in [14].

Longitudinal model of transcriptional level Following the work of [16] on tiling array data, the Markov transition writes as a mixture of different change types, aiming at differentiating expressed ($u_t > 0$) and non expressed ($u_t = 0$) regions:

$$k(u_t; u_{t-1}) = \mathbf{1}_{\{u_{t-1}=0\}}\left[(1 - \eta)\delta_0(u_t) + \eta f(u_t)\right]$$
$$+ \mathbf{1}_{\{u_{t-1}>0\}}\left[\alpha\delta_{u_{t-1}}(u_t) + \beta f(u_t) + \beta_0\delta_0(u_t) + \gamma\, g(u_t; u_{t-1}, \lambda)\right],$$

where $\mathbf{1}$ denotes the indicator function indicating the expression status at $t-1$, and δ_x denotes the Dirac delta function with mass at point x that serves to give a non-zero probability for unchanged expression and for changes to 0 at t. The parameters $\eta \in (0,1)$ and $(\alpha, \beta, \beta_0, \gamma) \in (0,1)^4$ with $\alpha + \beta + \beta_0 + \gamma = 1$ define the probabilities of the different types of moves. The terms $f(u_t; \zeta)$ and $g(u_t; u_{t-1}, \lambda)$ are probability densities for the transcription level u_t, at the beginning of a transcribed region (occurring with probability η when $u_{t-1} = 0$) or after a shift (probability β when $u_{t-1} > 0$), and after a drift (probability γ when $u_{t-1} > 0$) respectively. The density $f(u_t; \zeta)$ corresponds to an exponential distribution of rate ζ and the parameter λ defines the average relative change caused by drifts.

Read count emission model Due to the sampling nature of the RNA-Seq experiment, we model the distribution of the counts y_t as a negative binomial distribution with expectation that depends on u_t. Previous analysis have revealed protocol-specific effects that influence the scale of the observed counts. Thus, we integrate two types of effect: (1) a position scaling term ν_t related to the effect of k-mer composition [12] and (2) a short range correlation term s_t modeled by a second sequence of Markov-correlated hidden variables with mean 1 [14]. Integrating the variability sources and adding the possibility of outliers, our read count emission model is:

$$y_t \mid u_t, s_t \sim (1 - \varepsilon_b - \varepsilon_o)\mathcal{NB}(\phi, u_t s_t \nu_t) + \varepsilon_b \mathcal{P}_{-\{0\}}(a\nu_t) + \varepsilon_0 \mathcal{U}(0\ldots b),$$

where the parameters $(\varepsilon_b, \varepsilon_0) \in (0,1)^2$ and $\varepsilon_b + \varepsilon_0 \leq 1$ correspond to the probability of two different types of outliers, $\mathcal{NB}(\phi, u_t s_t \nu_t)$ is the negative binomial distribution with mean $u_t s_t \xi_t$ and overdispersion ϕ, $\mathcal{P}_{-\{0\}}(a)$ is the zero-truncated version of the Poisson distribution with mean a and $\mathcal{U}(0\ldots b)$ is the discrete uniform distribution over $(0\ldots b)$. In practice a and b are respectively set to the mean and the maximum values of the observed read counts.

Characterizing $u|y$ For the expression reconstruction, we use a recent Sequential Monte Carlo method known as Particle Gibbs (PG) that makes possible to obtain exact joint samples of the hidden trajectory and parameters given the data [2].

The result of the PG algorithms consists in trajectories drawn from $\mathbf{u} \mid \mathbf{y}$ and give access, for each position to $u_t \mid y$ through a sample of N particles $(u_t^{(i)})_{i=1}^N$

Note on Normalization. When we consider more than one condition, the depth of sequencing (e.g. the total number of reads produced) will directly affect u_t, the inferred transcription level. Under a perfectly controlled experiment, u_t is expected to scale linearly with the depth, and thus people proposed to scale u_t accordingly. However, [4] highlighted that in most transcriptomes a small fraction of the genes makes up most of the molecular mass, and thus simple scaling could lead to very unstable normalization. Following classical strategy for microarray data, we can perform scalar or quantile normalization on the set of expression levels [3]. The analysis of semi-synthetic data-sets that served here to compare the perfomance of the methods did not necessitate a normalization step.

2.2   Statistics to Detect Differential Expression

We want to provide a statistically sounded way of estimating the fold change and calling regions exhibiting DE above a given fold change level c between two data-sets. We base our method on the separate estimation of the expression level on each sample, denoted $\mathbf{u} = (u)_{t \geq 1}$ and $\mathbf{v} = (v)_{t \geq 1}$, with Parseq algorithm. Our goal is to estimate the fold change at a base-pair resolution, that is to estimate the change between u_t and v_t where t is the position on the genome. For this reason, all our variables refer to the position resolution and we often omit to write the position index t.

The ratio distribution has already attracted attention in sample survey and many other areas. Multiple approximation were proposed, either from large sample or hypothesizing a Gaussian distribution of the variables. A more general approach was also proposed [9] to derive confidence intervals.

A direct point estimate is provided by the ratio of posterior means $\hat{r}_{\text{RM}} = \frac{\bar{u}}{\bar{v}}$ where $\bar{u}$ and $\bar{v}$ are expectations of the posterior distributions of the expression levels u and v in the two conditions as sampled with Parseq MCMC algorithm. To incorporate the information on uncertainty embeded in the posterior distribution we also considered fold-change estimate based on the posterior distribution of the ratio $r = \frac{u}{v}$. A natural way of doing it is to consider the empirical distribution of the sample $(r)_{1 \leq i \leq N^2} = (\frac{u^{i_u}}{v^{i_v}})_{1 \leq i_u \leq N, 1 \leq i_v \leq N}$ where N is the sample size drawn from each posterior using Parseq MCMC algorithm and i_u and i_v the corresponding sample indexes.

Here, we also analyzed the results obtained with another approximation of the posterior distribution of the ratio $r = \frac{u}{v}$ build on the hypothesis that the posteriors on expression levels u and v can be well approximated by a gamma distribution. Namely, $l \sim \gamma(\kappa_l, \theta_l)$, $l = \{u, v\}$, where the parameters κ_l and θ_l represent the shape and the scale parameters of the gamma distribution. In practice, examination of the posterior distributions suggest that this assumption is roughly justified for all of our experiments. Rescaling v by $\frac{\theta_u}{\theta_v}$ brings the two gamma distributions to the same scale while keeping the shapes unchanged allowing an explicit form of the ratio distribution. The ratio $\tilde{r} = \frac{u}{v} \cdot \frac{\theta_v}{\theta_u}$ has a Beta prime distribution $\mathcal{B}'(\kappa_u, \kappa_v)$ with density

$$\pi(\tilde{r}) = \frac{\tilde{r}^{\kappa_u - 1} \cdot (1 + \tilde{r})^{-(\kappa_v + \kappa_u)}}{\beta(\kappa_u, \kappa_v)} \tag{2.1}$$

where β refers to the beta function.

The parameters κ and θ can be estimated for each individual posterior using the method of the moments or by maximum likelihood. By default we use the moment estimates of κ and θ which gives $\hat{\kappa}_l = \bar{u}_l^2/\hat{\sigma}_l^2$ and $\hat{\theta}_l = \hat{\sigma}_l^2/\bar{u}_l$, where $\hat{\sigma}_l^2$ is the sample estimate for the variance.

Estimating Fold Change and Differential Expression. We approximate the fold change and the differential expression above a given threshold c by using these three estimation methods:

1. **RM** - the point estimate based on the ratio of posterior means $\hat{r}_{\mathrm{RM}}$
2. **DR-e** - the posterior distribution of the ratio r as approximated by its empirical distribution;
3. **DR-β'** posterior distribution of the ratio r as derived from the Beta prime approximation $\tilde{r} \sim \mathcal{B}'(\kappa_u, \kappa_v)$.

We derive the DE at a given fold change c from the cumulative probability above c (tail function). In each method we obtain the complementary cumulative probability as follows:

$$\textbf{RM: } \mathbf{1}_{\{\hat{r}_{\mathrm{RM}} \geq c\}}; \quad \textbf{DR-e: } \frac{1}{N^2} \sum_{i_{u,v}}^{1:N^2} \mathbf{1}_{\{\frac{u^{i_u}}{v^{i_v}} \geq c\}} \text{ and } \textbf{DR-}\beta\textbf{': } \int_{c\frac{\theta_v}{\theta_u}}^{\infty} \mathcal{B}'_{\kappa_u, \kappa_v}(r)\,\mathrm{d}r.$$

Also, we determine positions having a given fold change c. We define a precision level and for this level build a precision interval $[c_1, c_2]$ around the target fold value. We then identify positions with point estimators in this interval or with a cumulative probability $P(c_1 \leq r \leq c_2)$ greater than a probability threshold.

Annotation of Differentially Expressed Regions. Read coverage variability induces uncertainty in the estimation of the expression level, which in turn can lead to discontinuities in the annotation of DE regions. In order to cluster positions, we used a local score approach, defined by the classical recurrence relation:

$$s_t = \max\{s_{t-1} + \log z_t - m, 0\},$$

where, in the context of DE region detection, $z_t = \pi(r_t \geq c)$ and the score s_t is the signal in which we search enriched regions. The penalty m is set higher than the average of z_t, in practice at 0.5. We selected regions with positive score from the first positive value to the maximum local score in the region. The score was set back to a null value after the end position of each of these segments to avoid overlooking downstream high scoring segments.

3   Results

The difficulty raised by evaluating our strategy on real data motivated the use of semi-synthetic datasets. The relevance on real cases is shown in the paragraph on detection of DE positions.

We started from a RNA-Seq experiment which was published in a study on regulatory non-coding RNAs in *S. cerevisae* [8] and sequenced on a SOLiD platform (Short Read Archive identifier SRR121907). Currently available RNA-Seq simulators (simNGS, Flux simulator) do not account for coverage variability as we observe on real datasets. Thus, we decide to generate synthetic data by taking real transcript expression values and generating counts according to a dispersion estimated by Parseq on real datasets.

We simulated data for the first 6 chromosomes of *S. cerevisiae* using transcripts from the SGD annotation [5]. For the "wild" data set (**v**) we set the expression level for each transcript to the value computed from real data. This value is obtained by averaging the counts of reads corresponding to each transcript. For the "mutant" data set (**u**) we used the same expression levels but we over expressed randomly 15% of the transcripts (corresponding to 200 transcripts) with folds change values of $1/4, 2, 4$ or 8. To augment resemblance to real data we integrated in both cases local coverage alterations (s) as estimated on the real data. Conditioning on the expression profile and local alterations we sampled read counts: $y_l \mid l, s_l, l \in \{u, v\}$ according to a Negative Binomial distribution. We used mean ($\mu = l \cdot s_l$) and over-dispersion (ϕ) parametrization. The parameter ϕ was set to 2.9, a value estimated by Parseq on the real dataset. We then ran Parseq to estimate the expression profile for both data sets and obtained 2 samples of expression trajectories u^i and v^i, i=1:N. For each condition we run 2200 Parseq sweeps with a thinning step of 10 and we discard the 200 sweeps burn-in. Results using Parseq estimates were systematically compared with the estimation based on a sliding 100 bp window average of the read counts (SW). In order to avoid border effect, the SW estimate was constrained to the regions covered by at least one read.

For comparison at bp level we considered those positions where Parseq estimated average levels and SW values are above a background value (here 0.01 reads / bp). Reconstruction of DE regions included all values and we set to the background value all expression values below it. Estimation of parameters for the fold change distribution is done as described in the methods. However in some cases, degeneracy of the particles can lead to underestimate of the variance. We bound the coefficient of variation c_v to the maximum between 1‰low quantile $c_{v_{1‰}}$ and 0.001 and then recalculate the variance: $\hat{\sigma}_{lt} = l_t \cdot c_{v_{1‰}}$.

Given a level of fold change c, the results are assessed from three different standpoints: detection of positions with c fold change, of positions with at least c fold change, and the detection of DE regions of level c or above.

Results are reported in terms of sensitivity and positive predictive values (PPV) i.e. the fraction of true positives identified $\frac{TP}{TP+FN}$ and the percentage of positives from total predictions $\frac{TP}{TP+FP}$. Of main relevance, the comparison of results obtained using (1) RM, (2) DR-e and (3) DR-β' will motivate the choice of having sample estimates of expression level.

Table 1. Detection of change magnitude at position resolution. Synthetic data results. Positions expressed in any dataset lower than 0.01 reads/bp were disregarded. We show sensitivity and positive predictive values. Three fold values (2, 4, 8) were evaluated with a precision of $\pm$ 25% ; the threshold for the cumulative probability was set to 0.3.

	DR-e		DR-β'		RM		SW	
Fold	Sens.	PPV	Sens.	PPV	Sens.	PPV	Sens.	PPV
2	0.93	0.08	0.75	0.13	0.51	0.18	0.34	0.09
4	0.86	0.44	0.73	0.55	0.46	0.61	0.32	0.31
8	0.89	0.52	0.70	0.63	0.45	0.70	0.35	0.51

Fold Change Estimation. We consider a $\pm$ 25% precision around the correct fold change. Considering the theoretical cumulative betaprime function, for this precision interval, we threshold the cumulative probability (% of ratio values falling in the precision interval) at 0.3. Increasing this threshold will provide very high PPV but with significant sensitivity loss while, in reverse, at lower thresholds sensitivity reaches 1 but with very low PPV. All results based on Parseq expression level estimations are significantly better in both sensitivity and PPV that those obtained using SW (table 1). While DR-e and DR-β' show high sensitivity values for a moderate PPV decrease comparing to RM, the DR-β' seems to mediate better the trade-off between these two indicators.

Differential Expression. Estimation was done at bp precision for thresholds ranging from 2-fold to 8-fold. RM method performs better than SW mainly in terms of positive predictions (figure 1). DR-e and DR-β' results depend on the probability threshold. High sensitivity values are obtained by lowering the cumulative probability threshold to 0.25 with the cost of having PPV values similar to the SW method. We observe that, lowering the sample size, the PPV loss comparing to RM diminishes in the sensitivity - PPV trade. It is important to notice is the similar behavior of the DR-e and DR-β' sustaining the choice of the gamma distributions in modeling the expression level.

Differential Expression on Real Data. We analyzed the DE at position resolution on data from the study on regulatory non-coding RNAs, Xrn1-sensitive unstable transcripts (XUTs), in *S. cerevisae* [8]. XUTs accumulate in the mutant condition and their loci thus correspond to DE regions. As in [8], we scaled the reconstructed mutant expression profile so that levels of tRNA and snoRNA is equal between the two data sets and we excluded already annotated regions [5] from the DE analysis. To minimize the detection of UTRs we also excluded an additional 100 bp on both sides of each annotated gene. For DE thresholds ranging from 2 to 8 we compute the sensitivity and PPV in detecting XUT positions as annotated in the study. Results are shown in figure 2. As for the synthetic data, DR-e and DR-β' methods allow a good control of sensitivity with slight PPV changes.

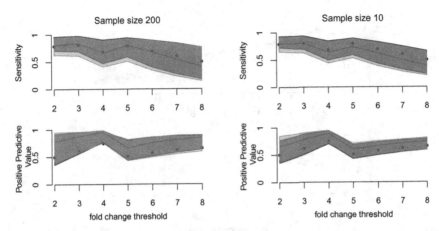

Fig. 1. Detection of DE at position level. X-axis: DE threshold. Y-axis: Sensitivity (top) and PPV (bottom). Sample size 200 (left) and 10 (right). Methods: DR-e (blue band), DR-β' (green band), RM (red line) and SW (black dots). Borders for DR-e and DR-β' bands: Sensitivity - top and low represent the 0.25 and 0.75 cumulative probability thresholds; PPV - top and low represent 0.75 and 0.25 thresholds.

Table 2. Accuracy in 5' End detection of DE regions. Results are shown for 3 values of DE thresholds. Estimated DE regions below 100 bp were discarded.

	DR-e		DR-β'		RM		SW	
Fold	Sens.	PPV	Sens.	PPV	Sens.	PPV	Sens.	PPV
≥ 2	0.72	0.20	0.72	0.25	0.69	0.25	0.66	0.12
≥ 4	0.57	0.43	0.58	0.39	0.54	0.39	0.63	0.26
≥ 8	0.43	0.39	0.48	0.38	0.38	0.35	0.44	0.23

Detection of DE Regions. To evaluate DE region detection we compared borders of regions estimated as having a fold change at least the DE threshold against those of transcripts with simulated fold change above the same threshold. The absence of noise and of longitudinal bias in the synthetic datasets allowed a high detection of transcript and DE regions borders. Sensitivity reaches values above 50% for all methods and most DE thresholds (table 2). Parseq based approaches have a net improvement in PPV with DR-e and DR-β' having slightly higher sensitivity results than RM.

4   Conclusion

This paper describes a method to reconstruct the regions having significant changes in expression between 2 conditions without recurring to predefined annotation and data sets replicates. This method is based on estimates of DE at position level and mitigates the lack of replicates by accounting for the incertitude in expression level estimation.

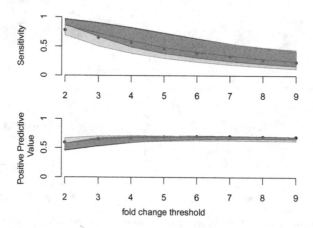

Fig. 2. Detection of XUTs at position level. Detection sensitivity and PPV computed on the whole repertoire of XUTs are shown as a function of the fold change threshold. Symbols are the same as in figure 1: DR-e (blue band), DR-β' (green band), RM (red line) and SW (black dots); the DR-e and DR-β' bands are delimited by the 0.25 and 0.75 cumulative probability thresholds.

Parseq, a probabilistic model for inferring expression profiles provides posterior estimates at position resolution which can be used to describe, directly or by approximation with a Betaprime distribution, the fold change distribution. Within this framework, we show improvements in the accuracy of predictions for methods based on empirical and betaprime approximation of ratio distribution, mainly for the estimation of the fold change.

This probabilistic model opens the way to more sophisticated approaches for the delineation of regions with constant a fold change, contributing to a better characterization of differences in expression.

References

1. Anders, S., Huber, W.: Differential expression analysis for sequence count data. Genome Biology 11(10), R106 (2010), http://genomebiology.com/2010/11/10/R106
2. Andrieu, C., Doucet, A., Holenstein, R.: Particle markov chain monte carlo methods. Journal of the Royal Statistical Society: Series B (Statistical Methodology) 72(3), 269–342 (2010)
3. Bolstad, B., Irizarry, R., Åstrand, M., Speed, T.: A comparison of normalization methods for high density oligonucleotide array data based on variance and bias. Bioinformatics 19(2), 185–193 (2003)
4. Bullard, J., Purdom, E., Hansen, K., Dudoit, S.: Evaluation of statistical methods for normalization and differential expression in mRNA-Seq experiments. BMC Bioinformatics 11(1), 94 (2010), http://www.biomedcentral.com/1471-2105/11/94
5. Cherry, J.M., Hong, E.L., et al.: Saccharomyces genome database: the genomics resource of budding yeast. Nucleic Acids Res 40(Database issue), D700–D705 (2012), http://dx.doi.org/10.1093/nar/gkr1029

6. Clark, T., Schweitzer, A., et al.: Discovery of tissue-specific exons using comprehensive human exon microarrays. Genome Biology 8(4), R64 (2007)
7. DeRisi, J., Bittner, M.: Use of a cDNA microarray to analyse gene expression patterns in human cancer. Nat. Genet. 14(4), 457–460 (1996)
8. van Dijk, E.L., Chen, C.L., et al.: Xuts are a class of xrn1-sensitive antisense regulatory non-coding rna in yeast. Nature 475(7354), 114–117 (2011), http://dx.doi.org/10.1038/nature10118
9. Fieller, E.C.: Some problems in interval estimation. Journal of the Royal Statistical Society. Series B (Methodological) 16(2), 175–185 (1954)
10. Frazee, A., Jaffe, A., Sabunciyan, S., Leek, J.: Differential expression analysis of rna-seq data at base-pair resolution in multiple biological replicates. Biostatistics (under revision)
11. Guttman, M., Garber, M., Levin, J.Z., Donaghey, J., Robinson, J., Adiconis, X., Fan, L., Koziol, M.J., Gnirke, A., Nusbaum, C., Rinn, J.L., Lander, E.S., Regev, A.: Ab initio reconstruction of cell type-specific transcriptomes in mouse reveals the conserved multi-exonic structure of lincRNAs. Nature Biotechnology 28(5), 503–510 (2010), http://www.nature.com/doifinder/10.1038/nbt.1633
12. Li, J., Jiang, H., Wong, W.H.: Modeling non-uniformity in short-read rates in RNA-Seq data. Genome Biol. 11(5), R25 (2010)
13. McCarthy, D.J., Smyth, G.K.: Testing significance relative to a fold-change threshold is a TREAT. Bioinformatics 25(6), 765–771 (2009)
14. Mirauta, B., Nicolas, P., Richard, H.: Parseq: transcriptional landscape reconstruction from rna-seq data based on state-space models (submitted, 2013)
15. Mortazavi, A., Williams, B.A., et al.: Mapping and quantifying mammalian transcriptomes by RNA-Seq. Nature Methods 5(7), 621–628 (2008), http://www.nature.com/doifinder/10.1038/nmeth.1226
16. Nicolas, P., Leduc, A., et al.: Transcriptional landscape estimation from tiling array data using a model of signal shift and drift. Bioinformatics 25(18), 2341–2347 (2009)
17. Robinson, M.D., McCarthy, D.J., Smyth, G.K.: edgeR: a bioconductor package for differential expression analysis of digital gene expression data. Bioinformatics 26(1), 139–140 (2010), http://bioinformatics.oxfordjournals.org/content/26/1/139.abstract
18. Trapnell, C., Hendrickson, D.G., Sauvageau, M., Goff, L., Rinn, J.L., Pachter, L.: Differential analysis of gene regulation at transcript resolution with RNA-seq. Nat. Biotech. 31(1), 46–53 (2013), http://dx.doi.org/10.1038/nbt.2450
19. Trapnell, C., Williams, B.A., Pertea, G., Mortazavi, A., Kwan, G., van Baren, M.J., Salzberg, S.L., Wold, B.J., Pachter, L.: Transcript assembly and quantification by RNA-Seq reveals unannotated transcripts and isoform switching during cell differentiation. Nat. Biotech. 28(5), 511–515 (2010), http://dx.doi.org/10.1038/nbt.1621

Environmental Risk Assessment of Genetically Modified Organisms by a Fuzzy Decision Support System

Francesco Camastra[1], Angelo Ciaramella[1], Valeria Giovannelli[2],
Matteo Lener[2], Valentina Rastelli[2], Antonino Staiano[1],
Giovanni Staiano[2], and Alfredo Starace[1]

[1] Dept. of Science and Technology, University of Naples Parthenope,
Centro Direzionale Isola C4, I-80143, Napoli, Italy
{camastra,angelo.ciaramella,staiano}@ieee.org, alfredo.starace@gmail.com
[2] Nature Protection Dept., Institute for Environmental Protection and Research
(ISPRA), via v. Brancati 48, 00144 Roma
{valeria.giovannelli,matteo.lener,valentina.rastelli,
giovanni.staiano}@isprambiente.it

Abstract. Aim of the paper is the development of a Fuzzy Decision
Support System (FDSS) for the Environmental Risk Assessment (ERA)
of the deliberate release of genetically modified plants. The evaluation
process permits identifying potential impacts that can achieve one or
more receptors through a set of migration paths. ERA process is often
performed in presence of incomplete and imprecise data and is generally
yielded using the personal experience and knowledge of the human experts. Therefore the risk assessment in the FDSS is obtained by using a
Fuzzy Inference System (FIS), performed using jFuzzyLogic library. The
decisions derived by FDSS have been validated on real world cases by
the human experts that are in charge of ERA. They have confirmed the
reliability of the fuzzy support system decisions.

Keywords: Fuzzy Support Decision Systems, Risk Assessment, Genetically Modified Organisms, Fuzzy Control Language, jFuzzyLogic library.

1 Introduction

The development of genetic engineering in the last years produced a very high
number of genetically modified organisms (GMOs). Whereas in USA the use
of GMOs is widely spread in agriculture, in Europe there are discordant poli-
cies w.r.t. GMOs. For instance, commercialization of food and feed containing
or consisting of GMOs is duly approved in European Community (EC), while
cultivation of new genetically modified crops are not adopted. The maize MON
810, approved by the old EC legislation framework, is currently the unique GMO
cultivated in the EC (e.g., Czech Republic, Poland, Spain, Portugal, Romania
and Slovakia). According to EC, the environmental release of GMOs is ruled
by Directive 200118EC and Regulation 18292003EC. The Directive refers to the

A. Petrosino, L. Maddalena, P. Pala (Eds.): ICIAP 2013 Workshops, LNCS 8158, pp. 428–435, 2013.

deliberate release into the environment of GMOs and sets out two regulatory regimes: Part C for the placing on the market and Part B for the deliberate release for any other purpose, i.e. field trials [16]. In both legislations the notifier, i.e., the person who requests the release into the environment of GMO, must perform an Environmental Risk Assessment (ERA) on the issue. The ERA is formally defined as "the evaluation of risks to human health and the environment, whether direct or indirect, immediate or delayed, which the deliberate release or the placing on the market of GMOs may pose". ERA should be carried out case by case, meaning that its conclusion may depends on the GM plants and trait concerned, their intended uses, and the potential receiving environments. The ERA process should lead to the identification and evaluation of potential adverse effects of the GMO, and, at the same time, it should be conducted with a view for identifying if there is a need for risk management and it should provides the basis for the monitoring plans. The aim of this work is the development of a decision system that should advise and help the notifier in performing the ERA about the cultivation of a specific genetically modified plant (GMP). ERA process is often performed in presence of incomplete and imprecise data. Moreover, it is generally yielded using the personal experience and knowledge of the notifier. Therefore the usage of fuzzy reasoning in the ERA support decision system is particularly appropriate as witnessed by the extensive application of fuzzy reasoning to the risk assessment in disparate fields [1,2,6,7,8,9,11,13,15,17]. Having said that, the fuzzy support decision system, object of the paper, is inspired by the methodological proposal of performing ERA on GMP field trials [16]. The methodology would allow to describe the relationships between potential receptors and the harmful characteristics of a GMP field trial, leading to the identification of potential impacts. The paper is organized as follows: In Section 2 the methodological proposal that has inspired the system is described; The FDSS structure of the Fuzzy System is discussed in Section 3; Section 4 describes how the system validation has been performed; Finally some conclusions are drawn in Section 5.

2   The Methodological Approach

The methodological proposal, that has inspired the system object of the paper, is based on a conceptual model [16]. The schema, shown in Figure 1, illustrates the possible paths of the impact from a specific source to a given receptor through disparate diffusion factors and migration routes. The model implies that the notifier fills an electronic questionnaire. The notifier answers are collected in a relational database management system and, in a second time, become input of a fuzzy decision support engine that is the system core and provides to the notifier the overall evaluation of risk assessment related to a specific GM plant. The questionnaire can be grouped in specific sets of questions where each set corresponds to a specific box of the diagram of the conceptual model. For each block the potential effects are calculated by using fuzzy concepts and a fuzzy reasoning system. The questions can be of two different types, e.g., qualitative

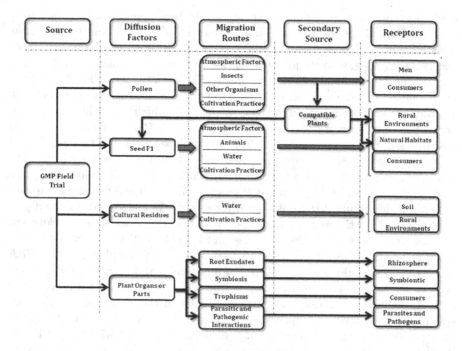

Fig. 1. Conceptual model

and quantitative. The former is typically descriptive and it is not used by fuzzy decision support system in the reasoning process. On the contrary, the latter is used by the fuzzy engine and can be an item chosen within a limited number of possible replies or a numeric or a boolean value.

3   The Fuzzy Decision Support System

The FDSS, object of the paper, has the same architecture of a Fuzzy Logic Control System. Moreover, the Fuzzy Inference System (FIS) of FDSS has been implemented using the jFuzzyLogic library. Therefore the section is organized in two subsections. In the former subsection we discuss the architecture of a generic Fuzzy Logic Control System and, hence, of our system. In the latter subsection jFuzzyLogic is described, in detail.

3.1   A Fuzzy Logic Control System

A Fuzzy Logic Control (FLC) system incorporates the knowledge and experience of a human operator, the so-called expert, in the design of a system that controls a process whose input-output relationships are described by a set of fuzzy control rules, e.g., IF-THEN rules. We recall that the *antecedent* is the part of rule delimited by the keywords IF and THEN. Whereas the *consequent* is the part of

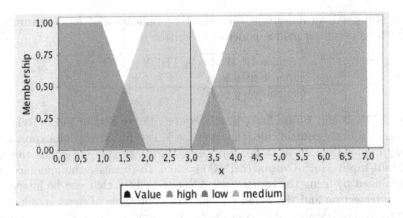

Fig. 2. Membership functions of the linguistic variable *number of insert copies*

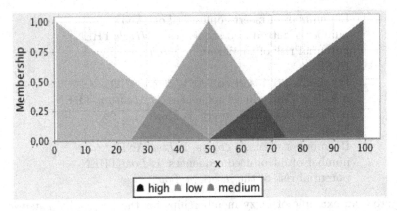

Fig. 3. Membership functions of the linguistic variable *potential risk of the insert*

the rule that follows the keyword THEN. The rules involve linguistic variables (*LV*s) that express qualitative high level concepts. A typical FLC architecture is composed of four principal components: a *fuzzifier*, a *fuzzy rule base*, an *inference engine* and a *defuzzifier* [12]. The fuzzifier has the task of transforming crisp measured data (e.g., *number of insert copies* is 1) into suitable linguistic values, namely the data becomes, for instance, *number of insert copies* is *low*. The fuzzy rule base stores the operation knowledge of the process of the domain experts. The inference engine is the FLC core, and it can simulate human decision making process by performing approximate reasoning in order to achieve a desired control strategy. The defuzzifier is used for yielding a control action inferred by the inference engine. In the inference engine the generalized modus ponens [12] plays an important role. For the application of fuzzy reasoning in FLCs, the generalized modus ponens can written as

Premise 1: IF x is A THEN y is B
Premise 2: x is A'
_____
Conclusion y is B'

where A, A', B and B' are fuzzy predicates i.e., Fuzzy Sets or Fuzzy Relations. In general, a fuzzy control rule, e.g., premise 1, is a fuzzy relation expressed by a fuzzy implication. In most general cases, the fuzzy rule bases has the form of a Multi-Input-Multi-Output (MIMO) system. In this case the inference rules are combined by using the connectives AND and ELSE that can be interpreted as the intersection and the union for different definitions of fuzzy implications, respectively. For instance, if we consider the LV *number of insert copies* as shown in Figure 2, the fuzzy inference system of the LVs *number of insert copies* and *number of introduced sequences* could be represented by:

IF number of insert copies is *Low* AND
number of introduced sequences is *High* THEN
potential risk of the insert is *High*
ELSE
IF number of insert copies is *High* AND
number of introduced sequences is *Medium* THEN
potential risk of the insert is *High*
ELSE
IF number of insert copies is *Low* AND
number of introduced sequences is *Low* THEN
potential risk of the insert is *Low*

In Figure 3 an example of fuzzy memberships for the output LV *potential risk of the insert* is presented. Finally, a crisp (i.e., non fuzzy) output is obtained considering a *Center of Area* defuzzifier [12].

3.2   jFuzzyLogic

jFuzzyLogic [4] is an open source software library for fuzzy systems which allows to design Fuzzy Logic Controllers supporting the standard *Fuzzy Control Programming* [10], published by the International Electrotechnical Commission. The library is written in Java and permits FLC design and implementation, following IEC standard for Fuzzy Control Language (FCL). The standard defines a common language to exchange portable fuzzy control programs among different platforms. The aim of jFuzzyLogic is to bring the benefits of open source software and standardization to the researchers and practitioners of fuzzy systems community, namely:

- *Standardization*, which reduces programming work.
- *Extensibility*, i.e., the object model and the Application Programming Interface (API) allow to create a wide range of different applications.

– *Platform independence*, that permits the software development on whatever hardware platform and operating system supporting Java.

Moreover, jFuzzyLogic allows to implement a *Fuzzy Inference System* (FIS). A FIS is usually composed of one or more *Function Blocks* (FBs). Each FB has variables (input, output or instances) and one or more *Rule Blocks* (RBs). Each RB is composed of a set of rules, as well as Aggregation, Activation and Accumulation methods. Having said that, jFuzzyLogic is based on *ANTLR* [14] that generates a lexer and a parser based on a FCL grammar defined by the user. The parser, written in Java, uses a left to right leftmost derivation recursive strategy, formally known as *LL(*)*. Using the lexer and the parser generated by ANTLR, it can parse FCL files by creating an *Abstract Syntax Tree* (AST), a well known structure in compiler design. The AST is converted into an *Interpreter Syntax Tree* (IST), which is capable of performing the required computations. This means that the IST can represent the grammar, in a similar way of AST, but it is also capable of performing computations. Moreover, all methods defined in the IEC norm are implemented in jFuzzyLogic. It should be noted that jFuzzyLogic fulfills the definitions of Aggregation, Activation and Accumulation as defined in [10]. Aggregation methods define the *t-norms* and *t-conorms* correspond to the familiar AND, OR and NOT operators [3]. These can be *Minimum*, *Product* or *Bounded difference* operators. Each set of operators fulfills *De Morgan's* laws [5]. The Activation method establishes how rule antecedents modify the consequent. Activation operators are Minimum and Product. Finally, accumulation methods determines the way the consequents from multiple rules in the same RB are combined. Accumulation methods defined in the IEC norm include: Maximum, Bounded sum, Normed sum, Probabilistic OR and Sum [10]. Only two membership functions are defined in the IEC standard, i.e., *singleton* and *piece-wise linear*. jFuzzyLogic implements other membership functions such as *trapezoidal, sigmoidal, gaussian, generalized bell, difference of sigmoidal*, and *cosine*, too. Moreover, jFuzzyLogic permits making arbitrary memberships by means of a combination of mathematical functions. Thanks to the flexibility in defining membership functions that can be sampled in a fixed number of points, called samples. The number, that is by default one thousand, can be modified on the basis of the precision-speed trade-off required for a specific application. Inference is performed by evaluating membership functions at these samples. To perform the sampling, the domain, called *universe*, of each variable, must be estimated. The variable universe is defined as the range where the variable assumes non-negligible value. For each variable, both membership function and term are considered during the universe computation. After the examination of all rules is terminated, the accumulation for each variable is complete. The last step in the evaluation of a FIS is the *defuzzification* [12]. The value for each variable is computed by means of the defuzzification method selected by the user within the following set: *Center of gravity, Rightmost Max, Center of area, Leftmost Max, Mean max* (for the continuous membership functions), or *Center of gravity* (for the discrete membership functions).

4   System Validation

The FDSS, object of the work, has a knowledge base organized in 123 FBs and it consists of 6215 rules of the type described in Section 3. FDSS was tested producing about 150 ERAs related to GM plants (e.g., Bt-maize[1] and Brassica napus). The ERAs, yielded by FDSS, were submitted to a pool of ISPRA[2] experts, not involved in the FDSS knowledge base definition, in order to assess the consistency and completeness of FDSS evaluations. For instance, we present two ERAs taken from the 150 ERAs produced by FDSS. The former estimates that all risks about GMP cultivation (see Tab 1, scenario 1) are negligible. Instead, the latter identify some risks that are potentially high (see Tab 1, scenario 2). FDSS has been developed as a Web Application and uses MySql database to store the data required to perform the ERA process. FDSS is implemented in Java2EE under Linux UBUNTU on a PC with Intel dual core 2.6GHz, 2GB RAM. It requires a CPU time lower than 2 sec to perform the whole ERA.

Table 1. Estimation of the risks for two scenarios. Value is in the $[0, 100]$ interval and LV are the Linguistic Variables.

Risk	Scenario 1 value	Scenario 1 LV	Scenario 2 value	Scenario 2 LV
Molecular aspect	0.0	low	50.0	medium
Potential expression of the inserts	50.0	medium	50.0	medium
Potential risk of the insert	0.0	low	0.0	low
Potential risks of the sequences	0.0	low	100.0	high
Potential risk of toxicity	0.0	low	0.0	low
Surface involved	0.0	low	100.0	high

5   Conclusions

In this paper a FDSS for the ERA of the deliberate release of GMPs has been presented. The evaluation process permits identifying potential impacts that can achieve one or more receptors through a set of migration paths. The risk assessment in the FDSS is obtained by using a FIS, implemented by means of jFuzzyLogic library. The decisions yielded by FDSS have been validated on real world cases by the human experts of ISPRA, confirming, in this way, the FDSS reliability. In the next future we plan to develop machine learning algorithms that allow to learn automatically the knowledge base of FDSS.

Acknowledgements. This research has been partially funded by the LIFE project MAN-GMP-ITA (Agreement n. LIFE08 NAT/IT/000334).

---

[1] Maize modified by using a Bt toxin (Bacillus thuringensis) [16].

[2] ISPRA is the institute governed by the Italian Ministery of the Environment that is in charge of GMO risk estimation.

References

1. Chen, Y.-L., Weng, C.-H.: Mining fuzzy association rules from questionnaire data. Knowledge-Based Systems 22, 46–56 (2009)
2. Chen, Z., Zhao, L., Lee, K.: Environmental risk assessment of offshore produced water discharges using a hybrid fuzzy-stochastic modeling approach. Environmental Modelling & Software 25, 782–792 (2010)
3. Ciaramella, A., Tagliaferri, R., Pedrycz, W.: The genetic development of ordinal sums. Fuzzy Sets and Systems 151(2), 303–325 (2005)
4. Cingolani, P., Fdez, J.A.: jFuzzyLogic: A Robust and Flexible Fuzzy-Logic Inference System Language Implementation. In: Proceedings of IEEE World Congress on Computational Intelligence 2012 (2012)
5. Cormen, T.H., Leiserson, C.E., Rivest, R.L., Stein, C.: Introduction to Algorithms, 3rd edn. The MIT Press (2009)
6. Davidson, V.J., Ryks, J., Fazil, A.: Fuzzy risk assessment tool for microbial hazards in food systems. Fuzzy Sets and Systems 157, 1201–1210 (2006)
7. Guimara, A.C.F., Lapa, C.M.F.: Fuzzy inference to risk assessment on nuclear engineering systems. Applied Soft Computing 7, 17–28 (2007)
8. Kahraman, C., Kaya, I.: Fuzzy Process Accuracy Index to Evaluate Risk Assessment of Drought Effects in Turkey. Human and Ecological Risk Assessment 15, 789–810 (2009)
9. Karimi, I., Hullermeier, E.: Risk assessment system of natural hazards: A new approach based on fuzzy probability. Fuzzy Sets and Systems 158, 987–999 (2007)
10. International Electrotechnical Commission technical committee industrial process measurement and control2. IEC 61131 - Programmable Controllers. Part 7: Fuzzy Control Programming. IEC 2000 (2000)
11. Li, W., Zhou, J., Xie, K., Xiong, X.: Power System Risk Assessment Using a Hybrid Method of Fuzzy Set and Monte Carlo Simulation. IEEE Transactions on Power Systems 23(2) (2008)
12. Lin, C.-T., Lee, C.S.: Neural Fuzzy Systems: A Neuro-Fuzzy Synergism to Intelligent Systems. Prentice Hall (1996)
13. Ngai, E.W.T., Wat, F.K.T.: Design and development of a fuzzy expert system for hotel selection. Omega 31, 275–286 (2003)
14. Parr, T.J., Quong, R.W.: Software: Practice and Experience 25(7), 789–810 (1995)
15. Sadiqa, R., Husain, T.: A fuzzy-based methodology for an aggregative environmental risk assessment: A case study of drilling waste. Environmental Modelling & Software 20, 33–46 (2005)
16. Sorlini, C., Buiatti, M., Burgio, G., Cellini, F., Giovannelli, V., Lener, M., Massari, G., Perrino, P., Selva, E., Spagnoletti, A., Staiano, G.: La valutazione del rischio ambientale dell' immissione deliberata nell' ambiente di organismi geneticamente modificati. Tech. Report (2003) (in Italian), http://bch.minambiente.it/EN/Biosafety/propmet.asp
17. Wang, Y.-M., Elhag, T.M.S.: An adaptive neuro-fuzzy inference system for bridge risk assessment. Expert Systems with Applications 34, 3099–3106 (2008)

Recognition of Human Actions
from RGB-D Videos Using a Reject Option

Vincenzo Carletti, Pasquale Foggia, Gennaro Percannella,
Alessia Saggese, and Mario Vento

Dept. of Information Eng., Electrical Eng. and Applied Mathematics (DIEM),
University of Salerno, Italy
{vcarletti,pfoggia,pergen,asaggese,mvento}@unisa.it

Abstract. In this paper we propose a method for recognizing human actions by using depth images acquired through a Kinect sensor. The depth images are represented through the combination of three sets of well-known features, respectively based on Hu moments, depth variations and the $\mathfrak{R}$ transform, an enhanced version of the Radon transform. A GMM classifier is adopted and finally a reject option is introduced in order to improve the overall reliability of the system. The proposed approach has been tested over two datasets, the Mivia and the MHAD, showing very promising results.

1 Introduction

The need for security in different applications fields, ranging from surveillance to patient monitoring systems, has led to a growing interest in those applications able to automatically interpret human behaviors. In this field, human action recognition is among the most challenging tasks.

According to [11], an action can be represented following two different approaches: local representation and global representation. Local representation is based on a bottom-up approach: the spatio-temporal interest points are extracted from the entire scene and local descriptors are then computed and combined into a final representation. For instance, a Microsoft Kinect sensor is used in [18] and [14]: the former proposed a novel 4D local spatio-temporal feature which combines both intensity and depth information; in the latter the features are based on human pose and motion, as well as on image and point-cloud information. Furthermore, the authors create a two-layer Maximum Entropy Markov strategy for modeling an activity as a set of sub-activities and exploit a dynamic programming approach for the inference. In [6] an unsupervised feature learning is proposed: the spatio-temporal features are learnt directly from unlabeled video data by means of an extension of the Independent Subspace Analysis algorithm. The main success of all these methods based on local features is that any kind of pre-processing methods, such as motion segmentation and tracking, can be avoided. Furthermore, such methods are invariant to changes in viewpoint, person appearance and partial occlusions. The main lack, however, lies in their computational burden: these techniques are usually very slow, and their applicability to real-time systems is not really feasible. For instance, in [6] the computation needs 0.44 seconds for each frame, 0.10 seconds only if the implementation is optimized for a GPU.

A. Petrosino, L. Maddalena, P. Pala (Eds.): ICIAP 2013 Workshops, LNCS 8158, pp. 436–445, 2013.
© Springer-Verlag Berlin Heidelberg 2013

On the contrary, in global representation based approaches the visual observation focuses on a Region of Interest (ROI): the person is located in the scene by applying background subtraction or tracking techniques; the descriptors in this case are usually derived from silhouettes, edges or optical flow. For instance, in [2] and [17] a Radon transform and an extended version, the $\mathfrak{R}$ transform, have been respectively adopted. In particular, the $\mathfrak{R}$ transform is invariant to scale and translation and, as experimentally demonstrated in [17], outperforms methods using silhouette-based moment descriptors (like, for instance, Invariant Moments, Zernike Moments, Pseudo-Zernike Moments and Wavelet Moments) without increasing the computational cost. In [9] each action is represented by its 3D volume (two spatial and one temporal dimensions); the characterization of this volume is performed by geometrical moments based on Hu moments [1]. In [8] RGB-D images are considered. Such approaches significantly improve the extraction of the silhouette, being insensitive to the typical problems of the detection phase (like, for instance, illuminance conditions changes or camouflage). However, the main problem in the approaches based on global representations lies in the fact that such techniques are sensible to noise, partial occlusions and variations in viewpoint. In order to overcome these limitations, global representations are often enriched by a grid-based approach: the ROI is partitioned into cells in order to also obtain local information about the part of the objects in the scene.

The proposed method belongs to the last category: RGB-D images acquired by a Kinect are processed in order to extract the moving object silhouette. A first original aspect of the method is the use of a combination of three well-known different sets of features, respectively based on the $\mathfrak{R}$ transform, depth variations and Hu moments. The first set is good at capturing properties related to the alignment of subregions of the image, while the second set describes in a more global way the overall distribution of the pixels; thus they are quite complementary in their nature, and their combination improves the discriminant ability with respect to each set taken separately. Also note that both sets are based on integral criteria, and so are quite robust with respect to noise.

The classification is performed by means of a Gaussian Mixture Model (GMM) classifier. A second major novelty of the method is the addition, after the classifier, of a module that estimates the reliability of the single classification response. This module is able to reject (i.e. refrain from recognizing an action) when observing a sample whose reliability is low. In this way the system avoids issuing erroneus action reports for ambiguous or unstable situations, such as during the transition between two different actions, thus improving the classification performance.

2   The Proposed Method

This section will detail the proposed method: two main phases can be identified, as shown in Figure 1: a *low-level* phase (colored in orange in the figure), aimed at extracting features starting from the analysis of raw data, and a *high-level* phase (in blue in the figure), devoted to identify the actions of the object of interest, by analyzing the extracted features. More details about each module will be provided in the following.

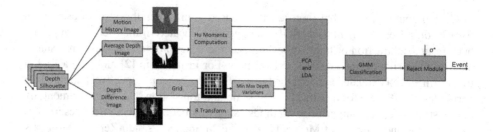

Fig. 1. Overview of the proposed method

2.1 Low-Level Phase

This phase includes acquisition of the images, their representation, and feature extraction. Each of these steps is described in the following.

Acquisition: The raw images are acquired using a Kinect, an affordable (under $150) input device produced by Microsoft, that provides both a RGB image and a depth image obtained by means of an infrared image sensor combined with a structured infrared light source.

Representation: The depth image D is processed to obtain three different representations, the *Motion History Image* (MHI), the *Average Depth Image* (ADI) and the *Depth Difference Image* (DDI); these three representations will be used as the basis for feature extraction. The *Motion History Image* MHI [4] is used to capture into a single and static image the sequence of motions. The value of MHI at time t and position (x, y) is updated as follows:

$$MHI(x, y, t) = 255 \qquad (1)$$

if point (x, y) passed from background to foreground at time t, and

$$MHI(x, y, t) = max\{M(x, y, t - 1) - \tau, 0\} \qquad (2)$$

otherwise; τ is a constant.

Given an observation window of N temporally adjacent images, the *Average Depth Image* $ADI(x, y, t)$ [8] is the average depth at position (x, y) over the images at times $t - N + 1, \ldots, t$.

Finally, the *Depth Difference Image DDI* [8] is used to evaluate the motions changes in the depth dimension:

$$DDI(x, y, t) = D_{max}(x, y, t) - D_{min}(x, y, t), \qquad (3)$$

where $D_{max}(x, y, t)$ and $D_{min}(x, y, t)$ are respectively the maximum and minimum depth for position (x, y) over the images at times $t - N + 1, \ldots, t$.

It is worth pointing out that N in our experiments is set to one second, corresponding to 25 frames. Furthermore, in [8] it has been experimental evaluated that the optimal value of τ is $(256/N) - 1$.

Features Extraction: Once obtained the derived images, three different kinds of features have been extracted. In particular, Hu moments [1] have been chosen to represent the MHI and ADI, while the DDI is represented through two different kinds of features: the $\Re$ transform [15] and the Min-Max Depth Variations [8]. The former is an extended Radon transform; its main advantages lie in its low computational complexity and its geometric invariance: in particular, such a descriptor is robust with respect to the errors of the detection phase, such as disjoint silhouettes and holes in the shape. The latter is obtained by hierarchical partitioning the box containing the silhouette into cells of equal size and by computing the maximum and the minimum values in each cell (see Figure 2).

It is worth pointing out that the features extraction step results in a vector composed by 303 features: 14 for the Hu moments, 181 representing the $\Re$ transform and 108 encoding the Min-Max Depth Variations over the grid.

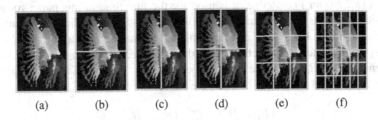

    (a)   (b)   (c)   (d)   (e)   (f)

Fig. 2. Min Max Depth Variations Features extracted with hierarchical grids

2.2   High-Level Phase

The high-level phase is composed by feature reduction, classification and reject module, described below.

Feature reduction: In order to improve the performance of the system, both in terms of overall accuracy and computational cost, a Principal Component Analysis (PCA) and a Linear Discriminant Analysis (LDA) are used for reducing the dimensionality of the feature vectors. This combination has been often used for face recognition applications (the reader can refer, for instance, to [7]), showing a significant improvement in the overall accuracy of the methods.

Classification: Once obtained the reduced features vector, a Gaussian Mixture Model (GMM) classifier is used for the final step. During the training step, the distribution of each class is estimated by maximizing the likelihood. During the classification phase, the likelihood for each class is computed; before assigning the observation to the class for which the likelihood is maximum, the system computes the estimation of the reliability of the obtained results ψ. If ψ is below a given threshold σ^*, then the sample will be rejected. According to the method proposed in [5], ψ can be computed as the combination of two different terms, ψ_a and ψ_b, that account for the typical situations that usually make low the reliability of a classifier: (a) the sample significantly differs from those present in the training set; (b) the point representing the sample in the features space lies at the boundary between two classes. In particular, for the GMM classifier ψ_a can be computed as

$$\psi_a = O_{win}, \tag{4}$$

being O_{win} the maximum likelihood computed. Similarly, ψ_b can be computed as

$$\psi_b = O_{win} - O_{2win} \tag{5}$$

where O_{2win} is the likelihood of the second best class. In conclusion, for the GMM classifier,

$$\psi = min\{O_{win}, O_{win} - O_{2win}\} = \psi_b. \tag{6}$$

Reject Module: This step compares the reliability indicator ψ with a threshold σ, and rejects the sample if it is below the threshold. The reject option has been successfully used in other application fields, ranging from audio-surveillance [3] to biomedical analysis [13]. At our knowledge, it is used for the first time in this paper for actions recognition purposes. The method for choosing an optimal threshold σ^* is described in [5]. The main idea is that σ^* can be computed by maximizing a function P, which measures the classification effectiveness in the considered application domain, in terms of recognition rate R_c, error rate R_e and reject rate R_r. Assuming a linear dependence for P on R_c, R_e and R_r, P can be computed as follows:

$$P = C_c \cdot (R_c - R_c^0) - C_e \cdot (R_e - R_e^0) - C_r \cdot R_r, \tag{7}$$

being R_c^0 and R_e^0 respectively the recognition rate and the error rate at 0-reject. Furthermore, C_e, C_r and C_c respectively represent the cost of each error, of each rejection and the gain of each correct classification. Of course, such costs strongly depend on the particular application domain.

It should be clear that R_c, R_e and R_r depend on σ. It means that also P is a function of the reject threshold. Since this function is not available in analytic form, the optimal threshold σ^* has to be experimentally evaluated by means an exhaustive search among the tabulated values of $P(\sigma)$.

3   Experimental Results

In the last years, a lot of datasets for action recognition have been proposed. However, they usually have two limitations with respect to the needs of our experimentation: first, the RGB-D images are not available [12] or, if available, the background is not included in the dataset [16]. This issue is justified by the fact that a lot of methods are not based on background subtraction strategies, since they directly extract the objects skeletons from the images. The second limitation depends on the typology of the extracted data: as a matter of fact, we are mainly interested in actions with a high semantic level (eating, drinking etc.). Most of the available datasets, instead, mainly focus on actions with low semantic level, like running, sitting down, standing up and so on. For the above mentioned reasons, we built our own dataset, from now on denoted as the Mivia Dataset;

however we also used an existing dataset, for making our results easier to compare with other. Thus, the used datasets were:

Mivia Dataset: it has been acquired in the Mivia lab and it is available at the following link: *http://mivia.unisa.it/datasets/video-analysis-datasets/mivia-action-dataset/*. It is composed by 7 high-level actions performed by 14 subjects (7 males and 7 females). All the subjects performed 5 repetitions of each action, so resulting in about 500 repetitions; the approximated length of each action is reported in Table 1.

Berkeley Multimodal Human Action Detection (MHAD) [10]: it contains 11 low-level actions performed by 7 male and 5 female subjects. All the subjects performed 5 repetitions of each action, yielding about 660 action sequences which correspond to about 82 minutes of total recording time.

Table 1 summarizes the actions recorded in each dataset, while Figure 3 shows some examples.

Table 1. Description of the Berkeley MHAD (a) and of the Mivia (b) Datasets

ID	Action	Length per Recording
A1	Bending - hands up all the way down	12 secs
A2	Clapping hands	5 secs
A3	Jumping in place	5 secs
A4	Jumping jacks	7 secs
A5	Punching (boxing)	10 secs
A6	Sit down	2 secs
A7	Sit down then stand up	15 secs
A8	Stand up	2 secs
A9	Throwing a ball	3 secs
A10	Waving - one hand (right)	7 secs
A11	Waving - two hands	7 secs

(a)

ID	Action	Length per Recording
B1	Opening a jar	2 sec
B2	Drinking	3 secs
B3	Sleeping	3 secs
B4	Random Movements	11 secs
B5	Stopping	7 secs
B6	Interacting with a table	3 secs
B7	Sitting	3 secs

(b)

For each dataset, two different experimentations has been conducted: in the first case, we did include the person to be tested in the training set; namely, one of the repetitions of each action performed by the person being tested was included in the training set, together with all the repetitions by all the other persons; the test has been repeated for all the persons in the database, and the average performance has been reported. This case represents the situation in which the person whose actions have to be recognized is known to the system, a situation that occurs in many applications (e.g. home monitoring of an elderly person). In the second case, the person to be tested is not included in the training set, which is formed by the actions of all the other persons. This case models the situation in which the actions of unknown persons have to be recognized, that occurs in applications like surveillance of public places.

The results, in terms of true positive rate, for the different sets of features (in particular $\Re$ features, used in [2], depth-based features (Hu Moments and Min-Max Depth Variation), used in [8], and their combination, first introduced in this paper) are shown in Tables 2 for the Mivia (a)(b) and the MHAD dataset (c)(d) respectively.

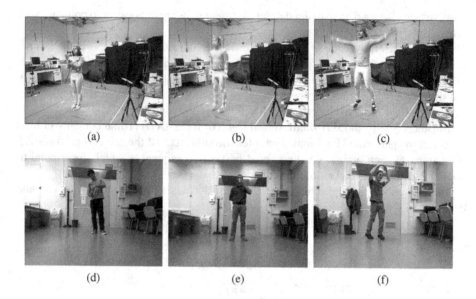

(a)   (b)   (c)

(d)   (e)   (f)

Fig. 3. Some examples of the Berkeley MHAD Dataset (A2 (a), A3 (b), A4 (c)) and of the Local Dataset (B1 (e), B2 (f), B4 (g))

On the Mivia dataset, the absolute performance for all the methods is quite high for the case of the test person included in the training set and (as expected) slightly worse for the case of the test person excluded. On the other hand, the performance on MHAD is lower; it is worth pointing out that the MHAD is a very challenging dataset: actions like, for instance, *Sit down* and *Sit down then stand up* are very similar to each other (the first two seconds are exactly the same). However, the interesting point is that in both the test cases, and for both the datasets, the proposed method results in a measurable improvement of the classification accuracy; the improvement is usually between 2% and 3%, but for some actions it is quite larger (e.g. for action A5 of the MHAD database, in the unknown person scenario, the accuracy improvement is 18%).

Finally, we evaluated the impact of the reject option on the classifier performance, by comparing the error rates of a zero-reject classifier with the error and reject rates of a classifier using the optimal reject threshold previously defined (for this experiment we set the costs as $C_r = 2$, $C_e = 5$ and $C_c = 1$).

Table 3 shows the obtained results. As it can be seen, for the Mivia Dataset the improvements were negligible. However, on the more difficult MHAD Dataset the reject option is able on the average to reduce the error rate by an additional 2.3%, thus confirming its usefulness.

Finally, as for the computational cost, we verified that the proposed method is able to run at 10 fps on a MacBook Pro equipped with Intel Core 2 Duo running at 2.4 GHz, so confirming its applicability in real frameworks.

Table 2. Recognition rates over the Mivia dataset (a)(b) and over the Berkeley MHAD dataset (c)(d) with a different feature set (ℜ Features, Depth Features and the combination of both), with and without the person under test in the training set

	The test person is in the training set		
	ℜ Features	Depth Features	Proposed Method
B1	47.453	91.491	**93.340**
B2	39.068	93.825	**94.660**
B3	97.913	99.986	**99.987**
B4	85.858	**98.809**	98.709
B5	89.225	98.791	**99.222**
B6	35.400	98.475	**98.950**
B7	65.596	98.756	**98.808**

(a)

	The test person is NOT in the training set		
	ℜ Features	Depth Features	Proposed Method
B1	33.574	82.604	**83.677**
B2	23.356	**77.794**	73.967
B3	80.297	97.694	**99.893**
B4	85.234	**98.023**	97.526
B5	85.532	**91.533**	88.287
B6	23.442	96.360	**98.033**
B7	43.529	93.090	**94.753**

(b)

	The test person is in the training set		
	ℜ Features	Depth Features	Proposed Method
A1	56.462	83.829	**86.483**
A2	82.999	94.405	**95.195**
A3	43.124	72.556	**83.223**
A4	84.020	88.273	**91.518**
A5	46.405	87.504	**88.999**
A6	24.020	66.612	**75.456**
A7	34.110	**81.843**	80.327
A8	38.912	**84.854**	81.829
A9	24.985	77.894	**81.038**
A10	80.270	95.823	**96.726**
A11	71.628	83.208	**89.233**

(c)

	The test person is NOT in the training set		
	ℜ Features	Depth Features	Proposed Method
A1	49.282	69.942	**74.974**
A2	44.101	54.580	**58.969**
A3	22.971	41.651	**47.450**
A4	**77.814**	69.151	67.886
A5	33.051	52.447	**70.201**
A6	12.540	32.554	**35.468**
A7	21.803	**66.086**	59.943
A8	19.130	47.467	**48.957**
A9	6.407	**58.167**	57.384
A10	44.783	78.271	**79.512**
A11	56.996	62.380	**64.903**

(d)

Table 3. Performance of the system over the Mivia and the MHAD datasets, in terms of Error Rate (with and without reject) and Reject Rate

Mivia Dataset			
Class	Error Rate without reject	Error Rate with reject	Reject rate
B1	6.66	5.53	2.49
B2	5.34	4.35	1.83
B3	0.01	0.01	0.01
B4	1.29	1.20	0.14
B5	0.78	0.52	0.63
B6	1.05	0.89	0.17
B7	1.19	1.16	0.04
Total	2.33	1.95	0.76

MHAD Dataset			
Class	Error Rate without reject	Error Rate with reject	Reject rate
A1	13.52	11.39	2.99
A2	4.80	3.66	1.40
A3	16.78	13.22	5.32
A4	8.48	7.36	1.64
A5	11.00	9.99	1.47
A6	24.54	21.94	5.06
A7	19.67	17.82	3.41
A8	18.17	15.11	4.84
A9	18.96	16.22	4.35
A10	3.27	2.58	1.16
A11	10.77	8.56	3.01
Total	15.25	12.90	3.59

4 Conclusions

In this paper we proposed a framework for recognizing human activities by analyzing depth images extracted from a Kinect sensor. The experimental results show that the combination of the three sets of features, respectively based on Hu moments, depth variations and $\Re$ transform, consistently improved the performance of the system. The overall reliability is further enhanced by introducing a reject option, which has been exploited for the first time in this paper in the field of action recognition.

Acknowledgment. This research has been partially supported by A.I.Tech s.r.l. (a spin-off company of the University of Salerno, www.aitech-solutions.eu).

References

1. Bobick, A.F., Davis, J.W.: The recognition of human movement using temporal templates. IEEE Trans. Pattern Anal. Mach. Intell. 23(3), 257–267 (2001), http://dx.doi.org/10.1109/34.910878
2. Chen, Y., Wu, Q., He, X.: Human action recognition based on radon transform. In: Lin, W., Tao, D., Kacprzyk, J., Li, Z., Izquierdo, E., Wang, H. (eds.) Multimedia Analysis, Processing and Communications. SCI, vol. 346, pp. 369–389. Springer, Heidelberg (2011)
3. Conte, D., Foggia, P., Percannella, G., Saggese, A., Vento, M.: An ensemble of rejecting classifiers for anomaly detection of audio events. In: 2012 IEEE Ninth International Conference on Advanced Video and Signal-Based Surveillance (AVSS), pp. 76–81 (September 2012)
4. Davis, J.: Hierarchical motion history images for recognizing human motion. In: Proceedings of the IEEE Workshop on Detection and Recognition of Events in Video, pp. 39–46 (2001)
5. Foggia, P., Sansone, C., Tortorella, F., Vento, M.: Multiclassification: reject criteria for the bayesian combiner. Pattern Recognition 32(8), 1435–1447 (1999), http://www.sciencedirect.com/science/article/pii/S0031320398001691
6. Le, Q., Zou, W., Yeung, S., Ng, A.: Learning hierarchical invariant spatio-temporal features for action recognition with independent subspace analysis. In: 2011 IEEE Conference on Computer Vision and Pattern Recognition (CVPR), pp. 3361–3368 (June 2011)
7. Li, J., Zhao, B., Zhang, H.: Face recognition based on pca and lda combination feature extraction. In: 2009 1st International Conference on Information Science and Engineering (ICISE), pp. 1240–1243 (2009)
8. Megavannan, V., Agarwal, B., Babu, R.: Human action recognition using depth maps. In: 2012 International Conference on Signal Processing and Communications (SPCOM), pp. 1–5 (July 2012)
9. Mokhber, A., Achard, C., Qu, X., Milgram, M.: Action recognition with global features. In: Sebe, N., Lew, M., Huang, T.S. (eds.) HCI/ICCV 2005. LNCS, vol. 3766, pp. 110–119. Springer, Heidelberg (2005)
10. Ofli, F., Chaudhry, R., Kurillo, G., Vidal, R., Bajcsy, R.: Berkeley mhad: A comprehensive multimodal human action database. In: IEEE Workshop on Applications on Computer Vision (WACV). IEEE (2013)
11. Poppe, R.: A survey on vision-based human action recognition. Image Vision Comput. 28(6), 976–990 (2010), http://dx.doi.org/10.1016/j.imavis.2009.11.014
12. Schuldt, C., Laptev, I., Caputo, B.: Recognizing human actions: a local svm approach. In: Proceedings of the 17th International Conference on Pattern Recognition, ICPR 2004, vol. 3, pp. 32–36 (August 2004)

13. Soda, P., Iannello, G., Vento, M.: A multiple expert system for classifying fluorescent intensity in antinuclear autoantibodies analysis. Pattern Anal. Appl. 12(3), 215–226 (2009), http://dx.doi.org/10.1007/s10044-008-0116-z
14. Sung, J., Ponce, C., Selman, B., Saxena, A.: Unstructured human activity detection from rgbd images. In: ICRA, pp. 842–849. IEEE (2012)
15. Tabbone, S., Wendling, L., Salmon, J.P.: A new shape descriptor defined on the radon transform. Comput. Vis. Image Underst. 102(1), 42–51 (2006), http://dx.doi.org/10.1016/j.cviu.2005.06.005
16. Wang, J., Liu, Z., Wu, Y., Yuan, J.: Mining actionlet ensemble for action recognition with depth cameras. In: 2012 IEEE Conference on Computer Vision and Pattern Recognition (CVPR), pp. 1290–1297 (June 2012)
17. Wang, Y., Huang, K., Tan, T.: Human activity recognition based on r transform. In: IEEE Conference on Computer Vision and Pattern Recognition, CVPR 2007, pp. 1–8 (June 2007)
18. Zhang, H., Parker, L.: 4-dimensional local spatio-temporal features for human activity recognition. In: 2011 IEEE/RSJ International Conference on Intelligent Robots and Systems (IROS), pp. 2044–2049 (September 2011)

Weakly Aligned Multi-part Bag-of-Poses for Action Recognition from Depth Cameras

Lorenzo Seidenari, Vincenzo Varano, Stefano Berretti,
Alberto Del Bimbo, and Pietro Pala

University of Firenze, Firenze, Italy
lorenzo.seidenari@unifi.it
http://www.micc.unifi.it

Abstract. In this work, we propose an efficient and effective method to recognize human actions based on the estimated 3D positions of skeletal joints in temporal sequences of depth maps. First, the body skeleton is decomposed in a set of kinematic chains, and the position of each joint is expressed in a locally defined reference system, which makes the coordinates invariant to body translations and rotations. A multi-part bag-of-poses approach is then defined, which permits the separate alignment of body parts through a nearest-neighbor classification. Experiments conducted on the MSR Daily Activity dataset show promising results.

Keywords: depth camera, action recognition, nearest-neighbor classification.

1 Introduction

Recently, the use of RGB-D map sequences (sequences of synchronized and aligned RGB and depth images) is receiving an increasing attention in various applications, including recognition of human actions and gestures [2], human pose reconstruction and estimation [10,1,5], scene flow estimation [6], face super-resolution [3]. Approaches proposed for recognition of human actions and gestures are relevant in very different domains ranging from biomedicine (e.g., monitoring and analysis of patient movements for supervised rehabilitation), to video-surveillance and social behavior analysis (e.g., indicators of shame and embarrassment based on human gestures) [11]). These approaches can be grouped into three main categories: *skeleton based*, that estimate the positions of a set of joints in the human skeleton from the depth map, and then model the pose of the human body in subsequent frames of a sequence using the position and the relations between joints; *depth map based*, that extract volumetric and temporal features from the overall set of points of the depth maps in a sequence; and *hybrid* solutions, which combine information extracted from both the joints of the skeleton and the depth maps.

Skeleton based approaches have become popular thanks to the work of Shotton et al. [10], where a real-time method is defined to accurately predict 3D positions of 16 body joints in individual depth map without using any temporal information. Relying on the joints location provided by Kinect, in [13] an approach for human action recognition is proposed, which computes histograms of the locations of 12 3D joints as a compact representation of postures. The histograms computed from the action depth

A. Petrosino, L. Maddalena, P. Pala (Eds.): ICIAP 2013 Workshops, LNCS 8158, pp. 446–455, 2013.

sequences are then projected using LDA and clustered into k posture visual words, which represent the prototypical poses of actions. The temporal evolutions of those visual words are modeled by discrete HMMs. Results were provided on the Microsoft Research (MSR) Action3D dataset [7]. In [14], human actions recognition is obtained by extracting pair-wise differences of joint positions in the current frame, between the current and the preceding frame, and between the current frame and the initial frame of the sequence (assumed as neutral). PCA is then used to reduce redundancy and noise in the feature and to obtain a compact *EigenJoints* representation for each frame. Finally, a naïve-Bayes nearest-neighbor classifier is used for multi-class action classification on the MSR Action3D dataset. With respect to the other classes of approaches, skeleton based solutions have the main merit in being simple and efficient, which is of paramount importance in real-time action recognition.

In this work, we propose a *skeleton based* solution for human action recognition from sequences of depth maps acquired with a Kinect camera. The key idea of our approach is to use joint positions to align multiple-parts of the human body using a bag-of-poses solution applied in a nearest-neighbor framework. We develop on the human body representation model proposed in [9], which is based on four kinematic chains. The coordinates of each joint in a chain are expressed in a local reference system, which is defined at the preceding joint. In this way, the coordinates are invariant to translation and rotation of the body, and each part of the body is modeled separately, to allow each part to be aligned independently. Hence, if the full body feature is noisy, the classifier can still obtain a strong score by aligning sub-parts of the body. Experimental results evidence competitive results in comparison to existing *skeleton based* solutions.

The rest of the paper is organized as follows: In Sect. 2, the proposed skeletal representation of the human body is described. This representation is then exploited in a multi-part nearest-neighbor classifier to perform action classification, as discussed in Sect. 3. Results obtained using the proposed framework on the MSR Daily Action 3D dataset are reported in Sect. 4. Finally, discussion and conclusions are drawn in Sect. 5.

2   Skeletal Representation

The proposed action recognition system relies on a skeletal based representation of the human body. This is provided by the Kinect platform that outputs a wireframe skeleton at a rate of 30 fps for each human body recognized in the acquired RGB-D datastream. Each skeleton part — forearm, upper arm, torso, head, etc. — is modelled as a rigid body. The position of the skeleton joints are provided as (x, y, z) coordinates in an absolute reference system that places the Kinect device at the origin with the positive z-axis extending in the direction in which the device is pointed, the positive y-axis extending upward, and the positive x-axis extending to the left. However, this absolute representation is highly inefficient and redundant since the coordinates of joints are mutually correlated. A much more convenient and generally adopted solution models the movements of the human body using kinematic chains, the root of the kinematic tree being the torso (base body) and the position of each joint being expressed relative to its parent joint. We adopt the same representation model proposed in [9] and assume the relative position of joints of the human torso — composed of the left and right shoulders, the base of the neck and the left and right hips — does not change over time. Thus, the entire torso is modeled as a rigid part and the remaining joints are classified into *first* and *second* degree joints. The first degree joints are those adjacent to the torso: the *elbows* and the *knees*. The second degree joints are the children of the first degree joints in the four kinematic chains: the *wrists* and the *feet*.

The position of each first degree joint is expressed in a coordinate system which is derived from the *torso frame*. This is a 3D orthonormal basis $\{u, r, t\}$ resulting from the PCA of the positions of the torso joints. The torso frame is translated so as to express the coordinates of the first degree joints (see Fig. 1). Coordinates $[u, r, t]_0$ of the left elbow joint are expressed in the torso frame coordinate system translated so as to center the origin at the left shoulder joint. Coordinates $[u, r, t]_1$ of the left knee joint are expressed in the torso frame coordinate system translated so as to center the origin at the left hip joint. Similarly, coordinates of the right elbow and knee are expressed in a torso frame coordinate system centered at the right shoulder and hip, respectively: $[u, r, t]_3$ and $[u, r, t]_2$. It should be noticed that this solution differs from the one proposed in [9] where two angular variables are used to represent the first degree joints in polar coordinates. Differently, we represent the coordinates of the first degree joints in Cartesian coordinates $[u, r, t]$, which makes the representation system immune to the well known "gimbal lock" problem.

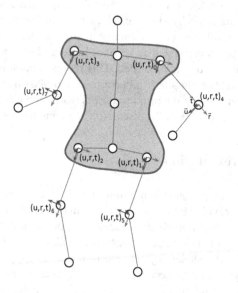

Fig. 1. The body skeleton and the first and second degree coordinate systems

The position of each second degree joint is expressed in a coordinate system that is derived from the coordinate system used to represent the position of its parent joint. Given a second degree joint, the $\{u, r, t\}$ system with origin centered at the root of its kinematic chain is rotated and translated so as to center its origin at the parent first degree joint. The applied rotation is such that the direction of r matches the direction of the link between the root of the kinematic chain and the parent first degree joint. In this way, four new coordinate systems $[u, r, t]_k$, $k = 4, \ldots, 7$ are created with origin at the left elbow, left knee, right knee and right elbow, respectively (see Fig. 1). Based on this representation system, a generic body pose is represented by a 24-dimensional feature vector $h = [u_0, r_0, t_0, \ldots, u_7, r_7, t_7]$ measuring the coordinates of the first and second degree joints in their coordinate systems. All of the vectors $v_j = [u_j, r_j, t_j]$ are L2-normalized in order to obtain robustness to the body size of different people and to the noise in estimating 3D joint position due to distance from the sensor.

3   Action Classification

State of the art methods for image classification are based on parametric classifiers, like SVM, Boosting, etc., which require an intensive learning/training stage. In contrast, non-parametric Nearest-Neighbor (NN) based classifiers have some favorable properties [4]: Naturally deal with a large number of classes; Avoid the overfitting problem; Do not require parameters learning.

Following this idea, in our approach a Naïve-Bayes Nearest-Neighbor (NBNN) classifier is applied for action recognition. For each frame in a sequence of depth maps, a feature vector is computed and used without quantization as frame descriptor, as detailed in Sect. 2. Considering M classes of actions to be recognized C_k, $k = 1, \ldots, M$, a number of labelled sequences per class is used as "training" set. Actually, this step does not include any learning/training of parameters, but the frame descriptors of these labelled sequences just serve as prototypes of a class.

According to this, given a depth frame f_i of a query sequence and its descriptor h_i, for each class C_k the training frame is searched which minimizes the distance:

$$d_i^{C_k} = \|h_i - NN^{C_k}(h_i)\|^2, \tag{1}$$

where $NN_{C_k}(h_i)$ is the NN-descriptor of h_i in the training frames of class C_k. Repeating this step for each frame $f_i, i = 1, \ldots, S$ of the query sequence, a set of M class-reconstructed sequences are derived, each comprising the NN-frames in the class C_k. Based on the distance between a query frame descriptor and its NN-frame descriptor, a goodness value is then associated to each of the class-reconstructed sequences:

$$G^{C_k} = \frac{1}{S} \sum_{i=1}^{S} g_i^{C_k} = \frac{1}{S} \sum_{i=1}^{S} \exp(d_i^{C_k}/\sigma^2). \tag{2}$$

3.1   Weak Temporal Alignment of Bag of Poses

The goodness value computed between two sequences does not account for their temporal ordering. Due to this, frames in the class-reconstructed sequences could have a meaningless temporal ordering when compared to the query sequence. So, in order to account for the temporal correlation between two sequences, we found beneficial to add an extra feature to the feature vector obtaining $h = \left[u_0 \, r_0 \, t_0, \ldots, u_7 \, r_7 \, t_7, \, \beta \frac{s}{S}\right]$, where s is the frame index and S is the sequence length in frames. The constant β ensures that

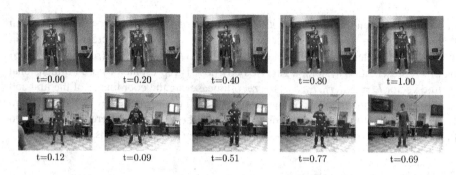

t=0.00   t=0.20   t=0.40   t=0.80   t=1.00

t=0.12   t=0.09   t=0.51   t=0.77   t=0.69

Fig. 2. Weak alignment between query (top) and (bottom) reconstructed sequence from the correct class with the normalized time-stamps

the weight of the temporal feature is not discarded because of the high dimensionality of the vector and it is selected by cross-validation. To encode short time temporal relationships, we also add to vector h temporal derivatives $[du_j \ dr_j \ dt_j]$. The final feature set is $h = \left[u_0 \ r_0 \ t_0, \ du_0 \ dr_0 \ dt_0, \dots, \ \beta \frac{s}{S}\right]$. Adding the normalized timestampe $\beta \frac{s}{S}$ makes frame in the same relative position in a sequence closer; this perform a weak alignment of sequences.

For efficiency reasons, the frame descriptors of the training sequences of a class are stored in a KD-tree (a total of M trees are constructed). Using a KD-tree, the *class-reconstructed* sequence of a query with S frames is constructed with S searches, each search having a logarithmic cost in the number of frames in the tree. As it can be observed in Fig. 2, our approach performs an implicit *sequence-to-class* alignment procedure picking for each query frame the best exemplar without taking into account the sequence, but only the relative positioning. Dynamic Time Warping (DTW) instead, performs a *sequence-to-sequence* alignment; thus our method can leverage a lot more data since virtually any combination of frames from a class can be used to reconstruct the query sequence.

3.2 Multi-part Models

Following the approach proposed in [12] based on learning relevant depth and joint features for each action class, we improve our model by combining multiple local body descriptors computed hierarchically. Let δ_p be a binary vector representing a selector for part p, that picks a subset of the features such that $\delta_p \circ h = \left[u_p \ r_p \ t_p, \ \beta \frac{s}{S}\right]$; we simply zero all features except the one not belonging to the part and the normalized frame. To define a higher order feature it is sufficient to OR two selectors: $\delta_{LA} = \delta_{LE} \vee \delta_{LH}$, where LA, LE and LH indicate the left arm, elbow and hand, respectively. The legs, torso and lower body selector can be obtained as such. This procedure also applies to derivatives separately. For a multi-part model the NBNN classifier becomes:

$$C_{NBNN} = \arg\max_{C_k} \frac{1}{S} \sum_{p \in P} \sum_{i=1}^{S} \exp\left(\|\delta_p \circ h_i - NN^{C_k}(\delta_p \circ h_i)\|^2 / \sigma_p^2\right), \quad (3)$$

given a set of parts P. We estimate the σ_p value as:

$$\sigma_p = \frac{1}{S(S-1)/2} \sum_{i \in D} \sum_{j \in D} \|\delta_p \circ h_i - \delta_p \circ h_j\|, \forall i < j \in D, \quad (4)$$

with a sample of the training data D. The value σ_p is fixed for each part and does not depend on the category. The same approach is used to tune the σ in (3). Note that we are not learning the feature representation, but the key idea is to align separately meaningful body parts by seeking the best sequence able to independently align the sub-parts. As an example, if the full body feature is noisy, the classifier can still obtain a strong score from aligning the torso or the arms in actions such as *drinking* or *eating*.

4 Experimental Results

The proposed method has been evaluated on the Microsoft Research (MSR) Daily Activity 3D dataset [12]. Results scored by our approach on this benchmark were also compared against those reported by state of the art solutions on the same benchmark.

The Daily Activity 3D dataset was captured at MSR using a Kinect device [12]. There are 16 activities: *drink, eat, read book, call cellphone, write on a paper, use laptop, use vacuum cleaner, cheer up, sit still, toss paper, play game, lie down on sofa, walk, play guitar, stand up, sit down*. There are 10 subjects in the dataset. Each subject performs each activity twice, once in "standing" position, and once in "sitting on sofa" position. The total number of the activity samples is $16 \times 2 \times 10 = 320$. This dataset has been designed to cover humans daily activities in a living room. As a consequence, when the user stands close to the sofa or sits on the sofa, the 3D joint positions extracted by the skeleton tracker are very noisy. In addition, most of the activities involve humans-object interactions, thus making this dataset quite challenging.

Experiments have been conducted using a cross-actor training/testing setup. Specifically, we left out each actor from the training set and repeated an experiment for each of them (leave-one-actor-out). The confusion matrix obtained using the multi-part variant of our approach is reported on Fig. 3. It can be noted as the most critical actions to classify correspond to the cases where subjects interact with external objects, rather than to pose variations alone. Our algorithm occupy a very tiny time-slot (<10 ms) with respect to the user detection and tracking. For a single user, our system runs at 20 fps on standard hardware.

4.1 Comparative Evaluation

Results of a comparative analysis of the proposed approach to alternative solutions are reported on Table 1. The first investigation aims to evidence accuracies obtained by using the different variants of our solution. In particular, in the Table we indicate our base solution with "NBNN", its variants adding separately time and parts as, respectively, "NBNN+parts" and "NBNN+time," and the solution which accounts for time and parts together as "NBNN+parts+time". Results obtained on the DailyActivity3D datasets show that the "time" feature is as relevant as the part based modeling in improving the performance of the NBNN base approach; both cues combined together

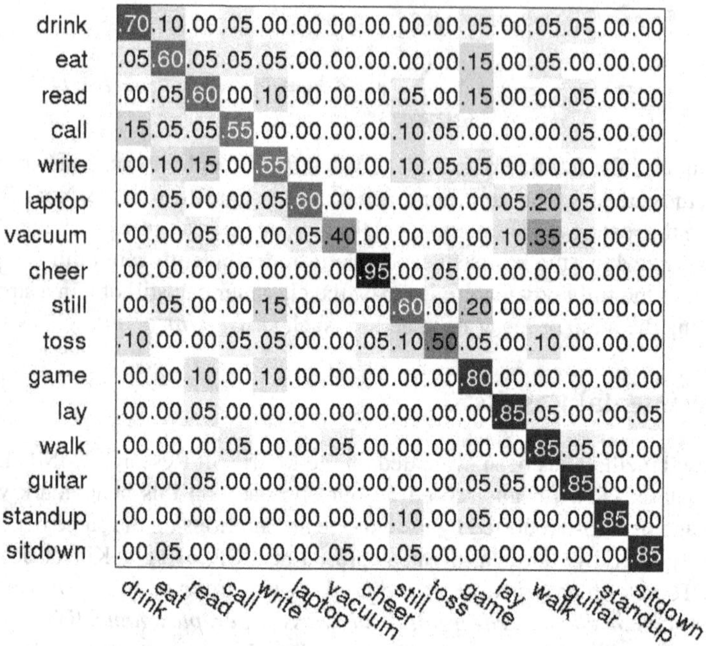

	drink	eat	read	call	write	laptop	vacuum	cheer	still	toss	game	lay	walk	guitar	standup	sitdown
drink	.70	.10	.00	.05	.00	.00	.00	.00	.00	.00	.05	.00	.05	.05	.00	.00
eat	.05	.60	.05	.05	.05	.00	.00	.00	.00	.00	.15	.00	.05	.00	.00	.00
read	.00	.05	.60	.00	.10	.00	.00	.00	.05	.00	.15	.00	.00	.05	.00	.00
call	.15	.05	.05	.55	.00	.00	.00	.00	.10	.05	.00	.00	.00	.05	.00	.00
write	.00	.10	.15	.00	.55	.00	.00	.00	.10	.05	.05	.00	.00	.00	.00	.00
laptop	.00	.05	.00	.00	.05	.60	.00	.00	.00	.00	.05	.20	.05	.00	.00	
vacuum	.00	.00	.05	.00	.00	.05	.40	.00	.00	.00	.00	.10	.35	.05	.00	.00
cheer	.00	.00	.00	.00	.00	.00	.00	.95	.00	.05	.00	.00	.00	.00	.00	.00
still	.00	.05	.00	.00	.15	.00	.00	.00	.60	.00	.20	.00	.00	.00	.00	.00
toss	.10	.00	.00	.05	.05	.00	.00	.05	.10	.50	.05	.00	.10	.00	.00	.00
game	.00	.00	.10	.00	.10	.00	.00	.00	.00	.00	.80	.00	.00	.00	.00	.00
lay	.00	.00	.05	.00	.00	.00	.00	.00	.00	.00	.00	.85	.05	.00	.00	.05
walk	.00	.00	.00	.05	.00	.00	.05	.00	.00	.00	.00	.00	.85	.05	.00	.00
guitar	.00	.00	.05	.00	.00	.00	.00	.00	.00	.00	.05	.05	.00	.85	.00	.00
standup	.00	.00	.00	.00	.00	.00	.00	.00	.00	.10	.00	.05	.00	.00	.85	.00
sitdown	.00	.05	.00	.00	.00	.00	.05	.00	.05	.00	.00	.00	.00	.00	.00	.85

Fig. 3. MSR Daily Activity 3D dataset: Confusion matrix

yield state of the art results. On the MSR Daily Activity 3D dataset, we also compared our approach with the solutions obtained with [8] and [12] reported in [12]. The solution in [8] uses Dynamic Temporal Warping (DTW) to match the 3D joint positions to a template, and action recognition can be done through a NN-classification method. The method in [12], instead, uses the estimated 3D joint positions and a Local Occupancy Pattern as local feature for human body representation. Since our method only exploits the joints positions, for a fair comparison in the Table we report the results of [12] obtained only using the joints positions, as given by the authors. On the MSR Daily Activity, we can observe a diffused confusion in the upper left quadrant of the confusion matrix relative to {*drink, eat, call, eat, write*}. Also, since we are not employing features other than the joints representation, our approach has not very high accuracy on actions mainly defined by the presence of an object, like *vacuum, laptop, read* or *write*.

In Tab. 2 we also report the accuracy scored by individual body parts. In particular, "ubody" and "lbody" include, respectively, joints in the arms and joints in the legs, with "dubody" and "dlbody" indicating the differential features computes on the "ubody" and "lbody" parts. The rightmost columns report the accuracy resulting by combining together all the parts and their differential components (all parts), and that of the complete approach that also explicitly includes the temporal feature (all parts+time). From the Table, it can be observed as for some actions, like lay or walk, the lower part of the body provides more accuracy, whereas for other actions, like cheer, read and

Table 1. Recognition accuracy comparison. For the method in [12], results obtained using only the joints position are reported

Method	MSR Daily
NBNN + parts + time	**0.70**
NBNN + time	0.62
NBNN + parts	0.60
NBNN	0.53
Actionlets [12]	0.68
DTW [8]	0.54

guitar, is the upper part to provide significantly better results. Noticeably, in some cases (bold-underlined in the table) individual parts perform better than their combination.

Finally, in Fig. 4 we report the variation of the recognition accuracy as a function of the β parameter, which weights the mutual relevance of the spatial and temporal component in the feature vector (Sect. 3.1). Values are reported for both the cases in which the parts are used or not. The accuracy gain using the temporal cue can be appreciated.

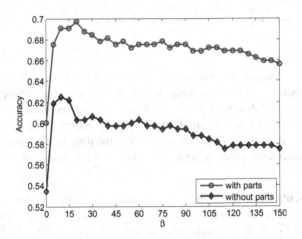

Fig. 4. Recognition accuracy as a function of β (for $\beta = 0$ no temporal information is used)

5   Conclusions

In this work, we proposed a method for human action recognition, which is based on weakly aligning the 3D coordinates of joints in multiple parts of the skeleton. First, four kinematic chains, each modeling a limb of the human body are defined, then the 3D coordinates of each joint in a chain are expressed in a locally defined reference system, which permits coordinates invariance with respect to rotations and translations. The coordinates of the joints, the temporal derivatives of the coordinates as well as a temporal

Table 2. Accuracy per class and body part (in bold the best part accuracy). In some cases (underlined values), the best part accuracy is better than the accuracy scored by all the parts+time

	ubody	lbody	dubody	dlbody	all parts	all parts + time
drink	**0.65**	0.20	0.60	0.30	0.65	0.70
eat	**0.55**	0.15	0.35	0.30	0.60	0.60
read	0.60	0.30	**_0.70_**	0.25	0.45	0.60
call	**0.40**	0.10	0.10	0.00	0.30	0.55
write	**_0.60_**	0.40	0.25	0.05	0.45	0.55
laptop	0.25	**0.40**	0.00	0.15	0.50	0.60
vacuum	0.40	**_0.45_**	0.30	0.40	0.50	0.40
cheer	0.95	0.35	**1.00**	0.40	0.95	0.95
still	0.40	0.10	**_0.65_**	0.45	0.55	0.60
toss	**0.45**	0.00	0.35	0.05	0.45	0.50
game	**0.70**	0.45	0.25	0.05	0.70	0.80
lay	0.80	**_0.90_**	0.80	0.80	0.70	0.85
walk	0.55	0.75	0.45	**_0.90_**	0.70	0.85
guitar	**0.85**	0.10	0.20	0.00	0.70	0.85
standup	0.60	**0.70**	0.50	0.65	0.70	0.90
sitdown	0.50	0.70	0.25	**0.75**	0.75	0.85
mean	0.58	0.38	0.42	0.34	0.60	0.70

feature are used as feature vector representing the human body in each frame. In order to make the approach robust to noise, a part based solution has been also deployed, which permits alignment of sub-sets of the joints. A sequence-to-class nearest-neighbor classifier has been used to score the similarity of a query action. Experiments carried out on a benchmark dataset support the applicability of the proposed solution, also showing competitive performance when compared to other skeletal- based solutions.

Acknowledgments. This research is carried out in the context of the RIS project that is funded with support from the *Programma Operativo Regionale* co-funded by FESR for the objective *Competitivitá regionale e occupazione* years 2007-2013.

References

1. Baak, A., Muller, M., Bharaj, G., Seidel, H.P., Theobalt, C.: A data-driven approach for real-time full body pose reconstruction from a depth camera. In: Proc. of Int. Conf. on Computer Vision, Barcelona, Spain, pp. 1092–1099 (November 2011)
2. Bagdanov, A.D., Del Bimbo, A., Seidenari, L., Usai, L.: Real-time hand status recognition from RGB-D imagery. In: Proc. of Int. Conf. on Pattern Recognition, Tsukuba, Japan, pp. 2456–2459 (November 2012)

3. Berretti, S., Del Bimbo, A., Pala, P.: Superfaces: A super-resolution model for 3D faces. In: Proc. of Work. on Non-Rigid Shape Analysis and Deformable Image Alignment, Florence, Italy, pp. 73–82 (October 2012)
4. Boiman, O., Shechtman, E., Irani, M.: In defense of nearest-neighbor based image classification. In: Proc. of IEEE Conf. on Computer Vision and Pattern Recognition, Anchorage, Alaska, USA, pp. 1–8 (June 2008)
5. Girshick, R., Shotton, J., Kohli, P., Criminisi, A., Fitzgibbon, A.: Efficient regression of general-activity human poses from depth images. In: Proc. of Int. Conf. on Computer Vision, Barcelona, Spain (November 2011)
6. Hadfield, S., Bowden, R.: Kinecting the dots: Particle based scene flow from depth sensors. In: Proc. of Int. Conf. on Computer Vision, Barcelona, Spain, pp. 2290–2295 (November 2011)
7. Li, W., Zhang, Z., Liu, Z.: Action recognition based on a bag of 3D points. In: Work. on Human Communicative Behavior Analysis, San Francisco, California, pp. 9–14 (June 2010)
8. Muller, M., Röder, T.: Motion templates for automatic classification and retrieval of motion capture data. In: ACM SIGGRAPH/Eurographics Symp. on Computer Animation, Vienna, Austria, pp. 137–146 (September 2006)
9. Raptis, M., Kirovski, D., Hoppe, H.: Real-time classification of dance gestures from skeleton animation. In: ACM SIGGRAPH/Eurographics Symp. on Computer Animation, Vancouver, Canada, pp. 147–156 (August 2011)
10. Shotton, J., Fitzgibbon, A., Cook, M., Sharp, T., Finocchio, M., Moore, R., Kipman, A., Blake, A.: Real-time human pose recognition in parts from single depth images. In: IEEE Conf. on Computer Vision and Pattern Recognition, Colorado Springs, Colorado, pp. 1–8 (June 2011)
11. Vinciarelli, A., Pantic, M., Bourlard, H.: Social signal processing: Survey of an emerging domain. Image and Vison Computing 27(12), 1743–1759 (2009)
12. Wang, J., Liu, Z., Wu, Y., Yuan, J.: Mining actionlet ensemble for action recognition with depth cameras. In: IEEE Conf. on Computer Vision and Pattern Recognition, Providence, Rhode Island, pp. 1–8 (June 2012)
13. Xia, L., Chen, C.C., Aggarwal, J.K.: View invariant human action recognition using histograms of 3D joints. In: Work. on Human Activity Understanding from 3D Data, Providence, Rhode Island, pp. 20–27 (June 2012)
14. Yang, X., Tian, Y.: Eigenjoints-based action recognition using naive-bayes-nearest-neighbor. In: Work. on Human Activity Understanding from 3D Data, Providence, Rhode Island, pp. 14–19 (June 2012)

Space-Time Pose Representation
for 3D Human Action Recognition

Maxime Devanne[1,2,3], Hazem Wannous[1], Stefano Berretti[3], Pietro Pala[3],
Mohamed Daoudi[2], and Alberto Del Bimbo[3]

[1] University of Lille 1 - LIFL (UMR Lille1/CNRS 8022)
[2] Institut Mines-Telecom
[3] University of Firenze

Abstract. 3D human action recognition is an important current challenge at the heart of many research areas lying to the modeling of the spatio-temporal information. In this paper, we propose representing human actions using spatio-temporal motion trajectories. In the proposed approach, each trajectory consists of one motion channel corresponding to the evolution of the 3D position of all joint coordinates within frames of action sequence. Action recognition is achieved through a shape trajectory representation that is learnt by a K-NN classifier, which takes benefit from Riemannian geometry in an open curve shape space. Experiments on the MSR Action 3D and UTKinect human action datasets show that, in comparison to state-of-the-art methods, the proposed approach obtains promising results that show the potential of our approach.

Keywords: 3D human action, activity recognition, temporal modeling.

1 Introduction

Imaging technologies have recently shown a rapid advancement with the introduction of consumer depth cameras with real-time capabilities, like Microsoft Kinect or Asus Xtion PRO LIVE. These new acquisition devices have stimulated the development of various promising applications, including human pose reconstruction and estimation, scene flow estimation, hand gesture recognition, face super-resolution. Encouraging results shown in these works have been made possible also thanks to the advantages that depth cameras have in comparison to conventional cameras, such as an easier foreground/background segmentation, and a lower sensitivity to lighting conditions.

In this context, an increasing attention has been directed to the task of recognizing human actions using depth map sequences. To this end, several approaches have been developed in the last few years that can be categorized as: *skeleton based*, that estimate the positions of a set of joints in the human skeleton from the depth map, and then model the pose of the human body in subsequent frames of a sequence using the position and the relations between joints; *depth map based*, that extract volumetric and temporal features from the overall set of points of the depth maps in a sequence; and *hybrid* solutions, which combine information

A. Petrosino, L. Maddalena, P. Pala (Eds.): ICIAP 2013 Workshops, LNCS 8158, pp. 456–464, 2013.
© Springer-Verlag Berlin Heidelberg 2013

extracted from both the joints of the skeleton and the depth maps. Following this categorization, existing methods for human action recognition with depth cameras are shortly reviewed below.

1.1 Related Work

Skeleton based approaches have become popular thanks to the work of Shotton et al. [5], where a real-time method is defined to accurately predict 3D positions of body joints in individual depth map without using any temporal information. In that work, prediction accuracy results are reported for 16 joints, but the Kinect tracking system developed on top of this approach is capable to estimate 3D positions for 20 joints of the human skeleton. Relying on the joints location provided by Kinect, in [12] an approach for human action recognition is proposed, which computes histograms of the locations of 12 3D joints as a compact representation of postures. The histograms computed from the action depth sequences are then projected using LDA and clustered into k posture visual words, which represent the prototypical poses of actions. The temporal evolutions of those visual words are modeled by discrete Hidden Markov Models (HMMs). Results were provided on a proprietary dataset and on the public Microsoft Research (MSR) Action3D dataset [4].

In [13], human actions recognition is obtained by extracting three features for each joint which are based on pair-wise differences of joint positions: differences between joints in the current frame; between joints in the current frame and in the preceding frame; and between joints in the current frame and in the initial frame of the sequence that is assumed to approximate the neutral posture. Since the number of these differences results in a high dimensional feature vector, PCA is used to reduce redundancy and noise in the feature, and to obtain a compact *EigenJoints* representation for each frame. Finally, a naïve-Bayes nearest-neighbor classifier is used for multi-class action classification on the MSR Action3D dataset.

Methods based on depth maps, do not rely on fitting a humanoid skeleton on the data, but use instead the entire set of points of depth map sequences to extract meaningful spatiotemporal descriptors. Several approaches are used for action recognition like 3D silhouettes [4], *Comparative Coding Descriptor* [2], or *Histogram of Oriented Gradient* (HOG) on *Depth Motion Maps* (DMM) [14]. Other methods represent the action sequence as a 4D shape and extract *Spatio-Temporal Occupancy Pattern* features (STOP) [9], or *Random Occupancy Pattern* features (ROP) [10].

Hybrid solutions try to combine positive aspects of both skeleton and depthmap based methods. The approach in [11] proposes a *Local Occupancy Pattern* (LOP) around each 3D joint as local feature for human body representation.

Relying on the observation that most human gestures can be recognized using only the shape of the skeleton of the human body, most of the human action approaches focus on the positions of 3D joints as features for recognition. The most important advantage of these features is that they are easy to extract with new depth cameras. Except that, the choice of good features to model the shape of the human body is not the only issue in human action recognition. Even if accurate 3D joints positions are available, action recognition task is still difficult due to significant spatial and temporal variations in an action for different, or even the same, actor. Feature space representation and similarity metric are also important factors for recognition effectiveness.

1.2 Proposed Approach

In this paper, we explore the joint positions as gesture representation and we model the dynamics of the full skeleton as a trajectory using shape analysis on Riemannian manifolds for human actions recognition. Our proposal in this work is motivated by: (1) The fact that many features in computer vision applications lie on curved space due to the geometric nature of the problems; (2) The shape and dynamic cues are very important for modeling human activity and their effectiveness have been demonstrated in several works in the state-of-the-art [8,1]; (3) Using such manifold offers a wide variety of statistical and modeling tools for gesture and action recognition.

The rest of the paper is organized as follows: Sect. 2 describes our approach including the spatio-temporal representation of action, the elastic metric used to compare action sequences and the recognition method used for classification; Sect. 3 discusses about the experimental results; Sect. 4 concludes the paper also prospecting future research directions.

2   Spatio-temporal Representation

In this work, 3D human actions are represented by spatio-temporal motion trajectories of pose vectors in an Euclidian space. Trajectories are represented as curves in the Riemannian manifold of open curve shape space in order to model the dynamics of temporal variations of pose as the action progresses. The shape of each trajectory is viewed as a point on the shape space of open curves and, hence, the similarity between two trajectories is qualified by an elastic distance between their corresponding points in shape space. Finally, a classification process is performed on shape space manifold. This approach is schematized in Fig. 1.

2.1 Space of Trajectories

Using the Kinect, we can easily obtain in real-time the 3D location of body parts, called joints. In each frame, the 3D positions of 20 joints are available. As there are 20 joints and each has 3 coordinates, the whole body pose at each frame can be represented by a vector in a 60-dimensional space (*pose space*). An instance of action will be regarded as a *trajectory of poses* or an open curve in the Euclidian space. Each trajectory consists of one motion channel corresponding to the evolution of all 3D joint coordinates. This is summarized on the left of

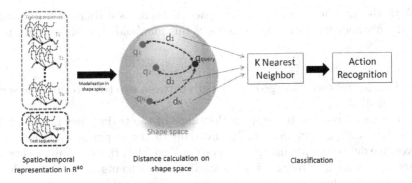

Fig. 1. Overview of our approach

Fig. 1, where each action is represented by a curve (for visualization, curves are shown in 2D, but they actually lie in a 60-dimensional space).

For each action sequence, we have a corresponding trajectory in a space of 60 dimensions. As the 3D position of each joint is represented by 3 different dimensions among the 60 dimensions, we are interested in the evolving shapes of these trajectories (curves) during actions. This motivated us to analyze the shape of the trajectories in order to compare action sequences. For this purpose, a measure representing the distance between the shape of two curves is needed. Since the actions are not realized at the same speed, and do not start and finish at the same time, the distance should be invariant to the temporal elasticity.

2.2 Trajectory Projection in Shape Space

In order to analyze human action trajectories independently to the elasticity (speed, time), we employ an elastic metric within a Riemannian shape space. Since a manifold is considered as a topological space which is locally similar to an Euclidean space, it can be seen as a continuous surface lying in a higher dimensional Euclidean space [3].

We can therefore represent the trajectory by $\beta : I \to \mathbb{R}^{60}$, for an interval I = [0,1]. To analyze the shape of β, we shall represent it mathematically using a square-root representation. We define its square-root velocity function (SRVF) $q : I \to \mathbb{R}^{60}$, given by:

$$q(t) \doteq \frac{\dot{\beta}}{\sqrt{\|\dot{\beta}\|}} \tag{1}$$

where $q(t)$ is a special function introduced in [3] that captures the shape of β and is particularly convenient for shape analysis. Its effectiveness has been shown in [6] for human body extremal curves in $\mathbb{R}^3$ in order to compute poses similarities. Our goal is to extend its use to spatio-temporal trajectories in $\mathbb{R}^n$.

As shown in [3], the $\mathbb{L}^2$ norm represents the elastic metric to compare the shape of two curves, under the SRVF representation. We define the set of curves:

$$\mathcal{C} = \{q : I \to \mathbb{R}^{60} | \|q\| = 1\} \subset \mathbb{L}^2(I, \mathbb{R}^{60}). \tag{2}$$

With the $\mathbb{L}^2$ norm on its tangent space, $\mathcal{C}$ becomes a Riemannian manifold and the distance between two elements of this manifold, q_1 and q_2, is given by:

$$d_c(q_1, q_2) \doteq cos^{-1}(\langle q_1, q_2 \rangle) \tag{3}$$

This distance measures the geodesic length between two trajectories represented in the manifold $\mathcal{C}$.

In our case, we need to compare the shape of the trajectories independently of the elasticity. So, we need to be invariant to the re-parametrization of the curves. We define the parametrization group Γ which is the set of all orientation-preserving diffeomorphisms of I to itself. The elements $\gamma \in \Gamma$ are the re-parametrization functions. For a curve $\beta : I \to \mathbb{R}^{60}$, $\gamma \circ \beta$ is a re-parametrization of β. As shown in [7], the SRVF of $\gamma \circ \beta$ is given by $\sqrt{\dot{\gamma}(t)}(q \circ \gamma)(t)$. We define the equivalent class containing q as:

$$[q] = \{\sqrt{\dot{\gamma}(t)}(q \circ \gamma)(t)|\gamma \in \Gamma\}. \tag{4}$$

The set of such equivalence classes is called the shape space of elastic curves, noted $\mathcal{S}$. In practise, dynamic programming is performed for optimal re-parametrization.

The shortest geodesic path between $[q_1]$ and $[q_2]$ in the shape space of open curves $\mathcal{S}$ is given by:

$$\alpha(\tau) = \frac{1}{\sin(\theta)} \left(\sin((1 - \tau)\theta)q_1 + \sin(\theta\tau)q_2^* \right) , \tag{5}$$

where $\theta = d_s([q_1], [q_2]) = d_c(q_1, q_2^*)$.

In the above equations, q_2^* is the optimal element associated with the optimal re-parametrization γ^* of the second curve q_2. This defined distance allows comparing the trajectories shape regardless to elastic deformation.

2.3   Recognition Algorithm

Let $\{(X_i, y_i)\}$, $i = 1, \dots, N$, be the training set with respect to class labels, where $X_i \in \mathbb{M}$, $y_i \in \{1, \dots, N_c\}$, where N_c is the number of classes and $\mathbb{M}$ is a Riemannian manifold. We want to find a function $F(X) : \mathbb{M} \longmapsto 1, \dots, N_c$ for clustering data lying in different submanifolds of a Riemannian space, based on the training set of labeled items of the data. To this end, we propose a K-Nearest-Neighbor classifier on the Riemannian manifold, learned by the trajectories modeled on the open curve shape space. Such learning method exploits geometric properties of the open curve shape space, particularly its Riemannian metric. This indeed relies only on the computation of the (geodesic) distances to the nearest neighbors of each data point of training set.

The action recognition problem is reduced to classification in Riemannian space. More precisely, given a set of training trajectory samples $X_i : i = 1, \dots, N$, they are represented by the underlying points $q_i : i = 1, \dots, N$, which map trajectories on the shape space manifold (see the mapping between trajectories and the shape space sphere in the middle of Fig. 1). Then, for any trajectory query sample X_q, a point representation q_q is obtained by mapping on the shape space manifold. Finally, a geodesic-based classifier is performed to find the K-closed trajectories of the query samples and to label X_q using the elastic metric computed via tangent spaces as given in Eq. (3).

3   Experimental Results

The proposed approach has been evaluated on two different datasets: MSR Action 3D and UTKinect. For each dataset, we compare our approach with state of the art methods which have been evaluated on these datasets.

3.1   MSR Action 3D Dataset

The MSR Action 3D dataset is a public dataset [4] on which many methods have been evaluated. This dataset includes 20 actions performed by 10 persons facing the camera. Each action is performed 2 or 3 times. In total, 567 sequences are available. For each sequence, the dataset provides depth information, color information and skeleton information. In our case, we only use the skeleton data. As reported in [11], 10 actions are not used in the experiments because the skeletons are either missing or too erroneous. For our experiments, we use 557 sequences.

In order to fairly compare our method with the state of the art, we follow the same experimental protocol as the works evaluated on MSR Action 3D. The sequences are split into three different subsets.

For each subset, we performed three different tests: Test One, Test Two, and Cross Subject Test. In Test One, 1/3 of the subset is used as training and the rest as testing. In Test Two, 2/3 of the subset is used as training and the rest as testing. In Cross Subject Test, one half of the subjects is used as training and the second half is used as test. The Cross Subject Test is more challenging because the subjects used as training are different from those used as testing. It is therefore more representative of a real case. In all our experiments, the data was randomly split into training and test sets. The random split was repeated 10 times and the average classification accuracy is reported here. Table 1 shows a comparison with the most significant state of the art methods on MSR Action 3D. Each comparison between a training action and a test action takes 45ms. The computation time to recognize a test action is 45ms multiplied by the number of training sequences.

We obtain an average accuracy of 93.1 for the Test One, 95.3 for the Test Two, and 92.8 for the Cross Subject Test. As shown in Tab. 1, we obtain competitive accuracies in the Test One and the Test Two, compared to the methods of the state of the art. In Cross Subject Test, we outperform existing methods.

First, we can see that for each test, we obtain better results with the Action Subset 3. Indeed, the actions in this subset are very different while most of the actions in subset 1 and subset 2 are quite similar. For example, we found actions

Table 1. MSR Action 3D: We compare our method with HO3DJ [12], EigenJoints [13], STOP [9], HOG [14], and Actionlet [11]. The method obtaining the best result in each experiment is evidenced in bold.

	HO3DJ	EigenJoints	STOP	HOG	Our Method
AS1 One	**98.5**	94.7	98.2	97.3	90.3
AS2 One	**96.7**	95.4	94.8	92.2	91.0
AS3 One	93.5	97.3	97.4	**98.0**	**98.0**
AS1 Two	98.6	97.3	**99.1**	98.7	93.4
AS2 Two	97.9	**98.7**	97.0	94.7	93.9
AS3 Two	94.9	97.3	**98.7**	**98.7**	98.6
AS1 CrSub	88.0	74.5	84.7	96.2	**90.1**
AS2 CrSub	85.5	76.1	81.3	84.1	**90.6**
AS3 CrSub	63.5	96.4	84.8	94.6	**97.6**

using hands or feet in subset 3 like *high throw* and *forward kick*. In subset 1 and 2, most of the actions are using only the hands, and especially only the left hand like *hammer, draw circle, forward punch*, or *draw X*.

We can also notice that we obtain similar accuracies for each subset regardless the test performed. Even if the subject who is performing the action is not present in the training set, we obtain good accuracies. Indeed, thanks to our spatio-temporal representation, an action performing by two different subjects are represented by similar trajectories in term of the shape. In real case, the subject performs an action for the first time in front of the recognition system. The Cross Subject Test is therefore the most representative test of a real case.

Finally, we observed that the accuracies are very low for some actions like *hammer* and *hand catch*, compared to the other actions. This can be explained by the fact that the way of performing these two actions varies a lot depending on the subjects. For example, some subjects repeat two or three times these actions while other subjects performs each action only once.

3.2 UTKinect Dataset

In order to confirm the effectiveness of our approach, we also evaluate the proposed method on a second dataset: UTKinect [12]. In this dataset, 10 subjects perform 10 different actions two times, for a total of 200 sequences. The actions include: *walk, sit-down, stand-up, pick-up, carry, throw, push, pull, wave* and *clap-hand*. The dataset provides color information, depth information, and skeleton information. This dataset presents three main challenges: First, the action sequences are registered from different views; Second, there is human-object interaction for some actions; Third, another difficulty is added by the presence of occlusions, caused by human-object interaction or by the absence of some body parts in the field of view.

To be comparable to the work in [12], we follow the same experimental protocol. We use the Leave One sequence Out Cross Validation method (LOOCV).

For each iteration, one sequence is used as test and all others sequences are used as training. The operation is repeated such that each sequence is used once as testing. We obtain an accuracy corresponding to the mean value of the accuracies obtained in each iteration. We also compute a mean accuracy obtained for each action separately (see Tab. 2).

Table 2. UTKinect dataset: We compare our method with HO3DJ [12]

Action	Walk	Sit	Stand	Pickup	Carry	Throw	Push	Pull	Wave	Clap	Overall
HO3DJ	**96.5**	91.5	93.5	97.5	**97.5**	59.0	81.5	92.5	**100**	**100**	90.9
Our	90.0	**100**	**100**	**100**	68.4	**95**	**90**	**100**	**100**	80.0	**91.5**

As we can see in the Tab. 2, we obtain an accuracy similar to the work in [12]. We remark that most of the wrongly classified sequences are due to actions that include human-object interaction. As our skeleton based approach is not able to detect objects, we expect these sequences to be the main source of error for our method. To investigate this point, we manually removed sequences with human-object interaction (*pick-up, carry, throw*) and repeated the classification experiments on this reduced dataset. We can see in Tab. 3 that removing actions with human-object interaction substantially improve the accuracy.

Table 3. Reduced version of UTKinect: Comparison of our method with HO3DJ [12]

Action	Walk	Sit	Stand	Push	Pull	Wave	Clap	Overall
HO3DJ	96.5	91.5	93.5	81.5	92.5	100	100	90.9
Our 100	100	100	95	100	100	100	80.0	**96.4**

4 Conclusions

We have proposed an effective human action recognition method by using a spatio-temporal motion trajectory representation. We take as input the 3D position of each joint of the skeleton in each frame of the sequence and use them to compute a corresponding trajectory. To compare the shape of the trajectories, we compute a distance between the projected trajectories in a shape space. Finally, we use a K-Nearest-Neighbor method to classify the action sequences which takes benefits from Riemannian geometry in open curve shape space. The experimental results on MSR Action 3D and UTKinect demonstrate that our approach outperforms the existing state-of-the-art in some cases. As future work, we plan to investigate other descriptors based on both depth and skeleton information to manage the problem of human-object interaction. We also plan to analyse and deal with specific cases where our method gives lower accuracies, like in sequences where actions are performed more than once. Finally, we would like to explore different applicative contexts and other available datasets.

References

1. Abdelkader, M.F., Abd-Almageed, W., Srivastava, A., Chellappa, R.: Silhouette-based gesture and action recognition via modeling trajectories on riemannian shape manifolds. Computer Vision and Image Understanding 115(3), 439–455 (2011)
2. Cheng, Z., Qin, L., Ye, Y., Huang, Q., Tian, Q.: Human daily action analysis with multi-view and color-depth data. In: Proc. of Work. on Consumer Depth Cameras for Computer Vision, Florence, Italy, pp. 52–61 (October 2012)
3. Joshi, S.H., Klassen, E., Srivastava, A., Jermyn, I.: A novel representation for riemannian analysis of elastic curves in rn. In: Proc. IEEE Comput. Soc. Conf. Comput. Vis. Pattern. Recognit., July 16 (2007)
4. Li, W., Zhang, Z., Liu, Z.: Action recognition based on a bag of 3D points. In: Proc. of Work. on Human Communicative Behavior Analysis, San Francisco, California, USA, pp. 9–14 (June 2010)
5. Shotton, J., Fitzgibbon, A., Cook, M., Sharp, T., Finocchio, M., Moore, R., Kipman, A., Blake, A.: Real-time human pose recognition in parts from single depth images. In: Proc. of IEEE Conf. on Computer Vision and Pattern Recognition, Colorado Springs, Colorado, USA, pp. 1–8 (June 2011)
6. Slama, R., Wannous, H., Daoudi, M.: Extremal human curves: a new human body shape and pose descriptor. In: 10th IEEE International Conference on Automatic Face and Gesture Recognition, Shanghai (2013)
7. Srivastava, A., Klassen, E., Joshi, S.H., Jermyn, I.: Shape analysis of elastic curves in euclidean spaces. IEEE Trans. Pattern Anal. Mach. Intell. 33, 1415–1428 (2011)
8. Turaga, P., Veeraraghavan, A., Srivastava, A., Chellappa, R.: Statistical computations on grassmann and stiefel manifolds for image and video-based recognition. IEEE Transactions on Pattern Analysis and Machine Intelligence 33(11), 2273–2286 (2011)
9. Vieira, A.W., Nascimento, E.R., Oliveira, G.L., Liu, Z., Campos, M.F.: Stop: Space-time occupancy patterns for 3d action recognition from depth map sequences. In: 17th Iberoamerican Congress on Pattern Recognition, Buenos Airies (2012)
10. Wang, J., Liu, Z., Chorowski, J., Chen, Z., Wu, Y.: Robust 3D action recognition with random occupancy patterns. In: Fitzgibbon, A., Lazebnik, S., Perona, P., Sato, Y., Schmid, C. (eds.) ECCV 2012, Part II. LNCS, vol. 7573, pp. 872–885. Springer, Heidelberg (2012)
11. Wang, J., Liu, Z., Wu, Y., Yuan, J.: Mining actionlet ensemble for action recognition with depth cameras. In: Proc. of IEEE Conf. on Computer Vision and Pattern Recognition, Providence, Rhode Island, USA, pp. 1–8 (June 2012)
12. Xia, L., Chen, C.C., Aggarwal, J.K.: View invariant human action recognition using histograms of 3D joints. In: Proc. of Work. on Human Activity Understanding from 3D Data, Providence, Rhode Island, USA, pp. 20–27 (June 2012)
13. Yang, X., Tian, Y.: Eigenjoints-based action recognition using naive-bayes-nearest-neighbor. In: Proc. of Work. on Human Activity Understanding from 3D Data, Providence, Rhode Island, USA, pp. 14–19 (June 2012)
14. Yang, X., Zhang, C., Tian, Y.: Recognizing actions using depth motion maps-based histograms of oriented gradients. In: Proc. of ACM Int. Conf. on Multimedia, Nara, Japan, pp. 1057–1060 (October 2012)

Human Body Language Analysis: A Preliminary Study Based on Kinect Skeleton Tracking

Danilo Avola[1], Luigi Cinque[2], Stefano Levialdi[2], and Giuseppe Placidi[1]

[1] Department of Life, Health and Environmental Sciences, University of L'Aquila
Via Vetoio Coppito 2, 67100, L'Aquila, Italy
{danilo.avola,giuseppe.placidi}@univaq.it
http://www.univaq.it/en/section.php?id=262
[2] Department of Computer Science, Sapienza University
Via Salaria 113, 00198, Rome, Italy
{cinque,levialdi}@di.uniroma1.it
http://w3.uniroma1.it/dipinfo/english/index.asp

Abstract. The nonverbal communication can be informally defined as the communicative process between two or more entities (e.g., persons) which achieving an informative exchange without using the semantic meaning of the words. This process can be accomplished by using one or more language forms, including the body language (i.e., movements, gestures, and postures) which in turn can be composed by voluntary and involuntary behaviours. The analysis and interpretation of these behaviours can infer different internal states of persons (e.g., feelings, attitudes, emotions) which in turn can support the development of a wide range of automatic applications in different fields, such as: rehabilitation, security, people identification, human behaviour analysis, biometric.

In recent years, we have focused our efforts in developing a first implementation of Kinematic, a novel multimodal framework designed to support advanced human-machine interfaces. The purpose of the framework is to provide a tool to analyze and interpret verbal and nonverbal human-to-human communication in order to transfer this ability to the human-machine interaction. In this paper we face a specific aspect of the framework regarding the first calibration phase of the numerical measures related to the Kinect skeleton used to analyze and interpret the body language. The numerical measures was obtained analyzing the movements of the skeleton during individual and social contexts. A preliminary qualitative and quantitative study has been reported and discussed.

Keywords: nonverbal communication, body language, human-machine interfaces, skeleton, numerical measures.

1 Introduction

The term communication derives from Latin *communicare* which means "to share" or "to make common". Over the centuries, this term has taken on increasingly heterogeneous meanings, representing material/immaterial as well as

A. Petrosino, L. Maddalena, P. Pala (Eds.): ICIAP 2013 Workshops, LNCS 8158, pp. 465–473, 2013.
© Springer-Verlag Berlin Heidelberg 2013

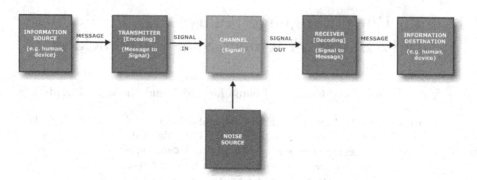

Fig. 1. Schematic Diagram of a General Communication System

concrete/abstract aspects of the interpersonal and social interaction processes. Subsequently, the term has been progressively focused on defining the incorporeal and conceptual information exchange between people and/or devices. In this context, a main contribute was provided from [16], where the authors formalized the basic theoretical aspects of communication. Their work, as shown in Fig. 1, consisted in providing an abstraction of the general steps involved in a communication process which can be summarized as follows:

Information Source: which produces a message or sequence of messages to be communicated to the receiving terminal.

Transmitter: which operates on the message to produce a signal suitable for transmission over the channel.

Noise Source: which represents the possible noise within the communication channel.

Receiver: which ordinarily performs the inverse operation of that done by the transmitter, reconstructing the message from the signal.

Information Destination: which represents the "entity" (e.g., person, device) to whom the message or sequence of messages are intended.

Two elements remain implicity defined in the schema:

Channel: representing the medium used to transmit the signal from transmitter to receiver.

Code: representing the set of symbols (e.g. words, sings, gestures) and related rules (i.e. to combine them) adopted to define a specific language.

The proposed definition has been subject of many variants and interpretations [12,11]. In our context, we adopt the steps of general communication system both to study the human-to-human communication processes and to develop the related human-machine interactions. In particular, we consider both "information source"/"transmitter", and 'receiver"/"information destination" belonging to two different combined entities: human and device, respectively. As shown in [7], the communication concept can be further characterized according to the following classification:

Nonverbal Communication: which represents the information exchange with the use of spoken language.

Verbal Communication: which represents the information exchange without the use of spoken language.

In particular, the **Nonverbal Communication** can be further classified as follows:

Paralinguistic System: which represents the set of sounds of the vocal (nonverbal) communication system (independently from the meaning of the words). It takes into account several aspects, such as: *tone* (which is influenced from different aspects: age, gender, and so on), *frequency* (which is tied to the general contexts and events), and *rhythm* (which is driven by specific contexts and social status).

Kinesic System: which represents two different classes of "movements". The first class considers the *body movements*, including: gestures (such as: hands, legs or arms movements), and posture (i.e., pose of the whole body or parts of it). The second class considers *facial expressions*, including: eyes movements, emotions, and so on.

Proxemics: which represents the study of the space use during a communication process. In particular, it explains that each person divides the surrounding space in four classes: *intimate zone* (from 0 to 50 centimeters), *personal zone* (from 50 cm to 1 meter), social zone (from 1 m to 3/4 m), *public zone* (over 4 m).

Haptic: which represents the relationship between the communication process and the physical contact. Also in this case, according to the specific "action" (e.g., handshake, hug) it is possible to derive peculiar information about the nature of the informative exchange.

The previous items have voluntary and involuntary aspects that highlight intrinsic behaviours of the human according to events, situations and personal internal states. Lately, we have intensified our efforts in developing a first implementation of Kinematic [3,4], a novel multimodal framework, based on Kinect [15], designed to support advanced human-machine interfaces. The purpose of the framework is to provide a tool to analyze and interpret verbal and nonverbal human-to-human communication in order to transfer this ability to the human-machine interaction. In this paper we face a specific aspect of the framework regarding the calibration phase and the first numerical measures related to the Kinect skeleton used to analyze and interpret the gesture class belonging to the kinesic system (i.e., body language).

This paper is structured as follows. Section 2 introduces some basic works supporting this preliminary measuring phase. Section 3 shortly presents an overview of the framework. Section 4 summarizes the calibration phase of the numerical measures related to the Kinect skeleton. Finally, Section 5 concludes the paper and introduces the current developments.

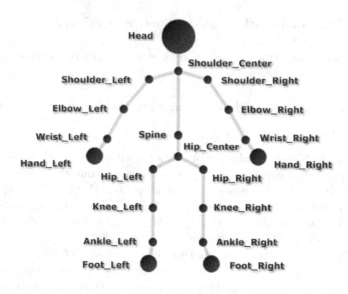

Fig. 2. Kinect Skeleton Model

2   Background

This section introduces some basic works supporting the set of numerical measures adopted to perform the first calibration phase related to the Kinect skeleton. As shown in Fig. 2 the kinect skeleton model of a human can be represented with a stickman having up to 20 joints (according to the Microsoft joint classification [17]), which can be used to analyze pose and tracking of the subject. Our intuition was to study the spatial movements over the time of the joints using well known numerical measures inherited from handwriting and freehand drawing analysis. The concept is that the spatial-temporal evolution of each joint, during a common activity (e.g., interpersonal or social interactions), tends to form "graphical shapes" which can be analyzed with usual mathematical and/or geometrical measures (e.g., curvature measure) to infer human behavioural patterns. In our context, we just wanted to classify the "disorder level" of the joints movement. The "disorder level" can be seen as the accuracy through which each "graphical shape" related to each joint (within a time interval) is drawn. In other words, the "disorder level" expressed by a set of joints during a specific interaction of the human subject can characterize a class of gestures and/or behaviours (e.g., social behaviour classification, emotion detection).

From an abstract point of view different works confirm our intuition. For instance, advanced works in graphology [8,6] show as the handwriting analysis can be used to evaluate and predict some basic aspects of the human personality. On the same direction, we analyze the graphic over the time composed by the tracking of the joints during a user interaction activity. To reach this task we were inspired by specific handwriting/freehand drawing measures related to the sketch recognition activity. A first interesting work is shown in [2], where the authors describe an intelligent framework able to automatically distinguish, in on-line way, freehand drawing from handwriting. Their approach takes into account only the mathematical features belonging to the sketch performed by users during interaction activity. In particular, their framework adopts a set of numerical measures (i.e., a feature vector) to analyse an object composed of a set of strokes in order to classify it as text or drawing. A similar work is presented in [1], where a gesture recognition system is introduced. Their system acquires freehand gestures performed by users which manage a led pen. A color tracking algorithm analyzes in real time the sequential frames and extracts the center of gravity of the blob on each of them. These centers, combined to form a sketch, are interpreted by means of mathematical features which identify the related gesture. Other basic works are presented in [10,9], where a set of geometrical features and a fuzzy logic approach to classify elementary geometric shapes, combined with an extensible set of heuristics is presented. Both works introduce a recognizer able to identify elementary geometrical shapes (e.g., triangles, diamonds, circles) which are recognized independently of changes in rotation, size or number of individual strokes. These last aspects play a key role in our context since the tracking of the joints can be influenced by this kind of issues. Another remarkable method is shown in [5], where a system to separate textual from graphical domain is presented. In their approach the authors set out first to find the single logically coherent feature which distinguishes shape from text. The authors observed that, when using any general set of coordinate equations, handwritten text symbols are more difficult to describe than common shapes (which are geometrically simpler). In that sense, text strokes are more randomly structured. For this reason, the measure of the degree of randomness of text strokes (high) compared with shape strokes (low) can be considered an accurate criterion of classification. We have applied a similar measure to support the characterization (concurrently with other measures) of the "graphical shapes" derived from the tracking of the joints. Other works were considered in relation to the used approach. A first example is described in [14], where the authors combine two algorithms for application to the recognition of unconstrained isolated handwritten numerals. The first algorithm employs a modified quadratic discriminant function utilizing direction sensitive spatial features of the numeral image. The second algorithm utilizes features derived from the profile of the character in a structural configuration to recognize the numerals. While both algorithms yield very low error rates, the authors combine the two algorithms in different ways to study the best polling strategy and realize very low error and rejections rates. In a similar way, we have analyzed the correlation among our selected features. A last remarkable work is presented in [13], where the authors adopt a Genetic Algorithm (GA) for solving the off-line handwriting recognition issue. Their basic idea is to use the GA both to combine various styles of writing a character and to generate new styles. In other words, the authors tried to transfer the ability of the human mind in understanding new character style (seen for the first time) within an application. They obtained excellent results. In similar way, we have tried to classify a set of general behavioural patterns by observing a sub-set of them. During our research

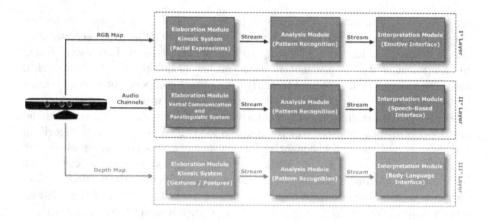

Fig. 3. The Framework Architecture

we have considered several measures, in this work we will show a restricted set of them since here our purposes is to define the basic calibration phase related to the Kinect skeleton.

3   The Framework Architecture

In order to provide a complete overview of the Kinematic framework, in Fig. 3 the whole simplified architecture is provided. As shown, it is composed by three parallel layers which elaborate the different input coming from the Kinect device: RGB Map, Audio Channels, and Depth Map. As previously discussed, in this work we are only interested in studying and providing preliminary results related to the Kinect skeleton model (i.e., third layer) according to a set of specific interactions. To achieve this result we have implemented (within the analysis module) three main mathematical features: *curvature*, *entropy*, and *homogeneity*.

Each feature treats the abstract "graphical shapes" drawn by each joint during the interpersonal or social activity as a set of strokes. The *curvature feature* measures the speed with which a stroke changes its trajectory. This task is achieved by dividing each stroke (when possible) in different sub-strokes according to the direction changes depending on the tracing direction, and by analyzing each of them by means of its spatial derivative. The computation of the distances among maximum and minimum points of all derivatives can be considered a characterizing measure of the main stroke. The *entropy feature* measures the stochastic distribution of the pixels composing a stroke. This task is achieved by considering the pixel disposition above and below the horizontal line of symmetry of the bounding box containing the stroke and by comparing their degree of randomness. Also in this case the computation of the absolute difference between the two sub-distributions can be considered a distinguishing measure of the stroke. The *homogeneity feature* measures both interception and closeness of the strokes

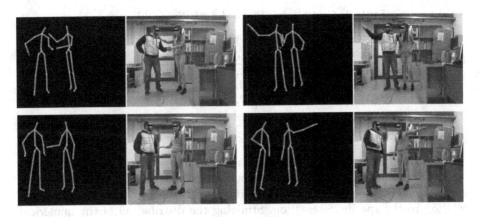

Fig. 4. Examples of Social Interaction

coming from the different joints. In particular, this last measure tend to identify spatial relationship among six groups of joints:

- $group_1$ (head, shoulder center),
- $group_2$ (spine, hip center),
- $group_3$ (shoulder left, elbow left, wrist left, hand left),
- $group_4$ (hip left, knee left, ankle left, foot left),
- $group_5$ (shoulder right, elbow right, wrist right, hand right),
- $group_6$ (hip right, knee right, ankle right, foot right).

In our context, the interpretation of the three measures according to specific interpersonal or social interaction can support the classification of different human behavioural patterns.

4   Experimental Results

With the aim to evaluate the degree of randomness related to the movements of the joints we have planned three activities: in the first, 5 subjects had to drawn on the air graphical and alphabet symbols using one or both hands; in the second, the same subjects had to explain a research paper using gestures (with hands and/or body); in the last, they were encouraged to perform a free exchange of opinions (e.g., social interaction) on free arguments (e.g., politics, sport). The screenshots in Fig. 4 show some examples related to the last activity.

Table 1 summarizes the basic intervals of values related to the three features in consideration of each specific group of joints. Within each group we have computed an average value (i.e., maximum and minimum) to provide a single interval. Although the obtained results are preliminary and rough, a careful analysis of the Table 1 has allowed us to extract some useful information. First of all, we have observed that all the joints can be numerically characterized within

Table 1. Case Study - Planned Activities and Features

Features/Groups	$Group_1$	$Group_2$	$Group_3$	$Group_4$	$Group_5$	$Group_6$
Curvature	[10,5..25,9]	[10,1..13,2]	[12,4..60,5]	[10,8..64,8]	[23,6..40,3]	[25,2..42,4]
Entropy	[22,1..33.2]	[20,3..25,5]	[30,4..65,2]	[28,4..68,5]	[28,6..45,8]	[26,6..44,7]
Homogeneity	[75,0..88,0]	[70,0..82,0]	[77,0..89,0]	[78,0..90,0]	[79,0..90,0]	[78,0..91,0]

a well-defined numerical interval. This means that we can hope to be able to classify human behavioural patterns according to the different activities. Moreover, we have observed consistent differences between the numerical values in relation to the specific interaction. Studying the distribution of the numerical values, we have also noted a direct relationship between *curvature* and *entropy*, and an inverse relationship between *curvature* and *homogeneity*. These last aspects highlight that the measures have a satisfactory degree of correlation which will be useful for detailing the intervals of classification according to the different activities. Finally, we have also tested that some gestures/interactions not belonging to the three introduced activities do not fall within the fixed intervals.

5   Conclusions

The verbal and nonverbal human-to-human communication can be analyzed and interpreted in order to transfer this ability to the human-machine interaction. In this way, a wide range of automatic applications in different fields (e.g., rehabilitation, security, people identification, human behaviour analysis) can be supported. In recent years, we have focused our efforts in developing a first implementation of Kinematic, a novel multimodal framework, based on Kinect sensor, designed to support advanced human-machine interfaces. A basic step of the framework regards the discrimination of the degree of randomness related to the movements of the kinect skeleton model with respect the ordered one. This target was achieved by implementing and evaluating three mathematical feature (*curvature*, *entropy*, and *homogeneity*) working on the joint movements.

References

1. Avola, D., Bottoni, P., Dafinei, A., Labella, A.: Color-based recognition of gesture-traced 2d symbols. In: Proceedings of the 17th International Conference on Distributed Multimedia Systems, DMS 2011, pp. 5–6. Knowledge Systems Institute, Convitto della Calza (2011), http://dblp.uni-trier.de
2. Avola, D., Del Buono, A., Del Nostro, P., Wang, R.: A novel online textual/Graphical domain separation approach for sketch-based interfaces. In: Damiani, E., Jeong, J., Howlett, R.J., Jain, L.C. (eds.) New Directions in Intelligent Interactive Multimedia Systems and Services - 2. SCI, vol. 226, pp. 167–176. Springer, Heidelberg (2009), http://dx.doi.org/10.1007/978-3-642-02937-0_15

3. Avola, D., Cinque, L., Levialdi, S., Placidi, G.: Kinematic: A kinect based framework to support advanced human-machine interfaces - ver. i. In: Internal Technical Report in Human-Computer Interfaces, ITR-HCI 2012, pp. 1–85. Sapienza University and Univeristy of L'Aquila (2012), http://dblp.uni-trier.de

4. Avola, D., Cinque, L., Levialdi, S., Placidi, G.: Kinematic: A kinect based framework to support advanced human-machine interfaces - ver. ii. In: Internal Technical Report in Human-Computer Interfaces, ITR-HCI 2013, pp. 1–158. Sapienza University and Univeristy of L'Aquila (2013), http://dblp.uni-trier.de

5. Bhat, A., Hammond, T.: Using entropy to distinguish shape versus text in hand-drawn diagrams. In: Proceedings of the 21st International Jont Conference on Artifical Intelligence, IJCAI 2009, pp. 1395–1400. Morgan K. Publishers Inc., USA (2009), http://dl.acm.org/citation.cfm?id=1661445.1661669

6. Champa, H., AnandaKumar, K.: Automated human behavior prediction through handwriting analysis. Integrated Intelligent Computing 1(1), 160–165 (2010)

7. Charbonnier, M.: The understanding of nonverbal communication in bilingual children. Ph.D. Thesis in Developmental and Social Psychology, XIX Cycle, pp. 1–126. University of Padova, Padova (2008), http://paduaresearch.cab.unipd.it/290/

8. Coll, R., Fornes, A., Llados, J.: Graphological analysis of handwritten text documents for human resources recruitment. In: International Conference on Document Analysis and Recognition, vol. 2(3), pp. 1081–1085 (2009)

9. Fonseca, M., Pimentel, C., Jorge, J.: Cali: An online scribble recognizer for calligraphic interfaces. In: AAAI 2002 Spring Symposium, AAAI 2002, pp. 51–58 (2002), http://dx.doi.org/10.1007/978-1-84882-812-4_7

10. Fonseca, M.J., Jorge, J.A.: Experimental evaluation of an on-line scribble recognizer. Pattern Recognition Letters 22(12), 1311–1319 (2001), http://www.sciencedirect.com/science/article/pii/S0167865501000769

11. Grice, H.: Meaning. Philosophical Review 66(1), 377–388 (1957), http://www.sciencedirect.com/science/article/pii/S0167865501000769

12. Jakobson, R.: Language in Literature, 2nd edn. Belknap Press Series. Harvard University Press (1987)

13. Kala, R., Vazirani, H., Shukla, A., Tiwari, R.: Offline handwriting recognition using genetic algorithm. International Journal of Computer Science Issues 7(1), 16–25 (2010)

14. Kimura, F., Shridhar, M.: Handwritten numerical recognition based on multiple algorithms. Pattern Recogn. 24(10), 969–983 (1991), http://dx.doi.org/10.1016/0031-32039190094-L

15. Kinect (2013), http://www.microsoft.com/en-us/kinectforwindows/

16. Shannon, C., Weaver, W.: The Mathematical Theory of Communication, Illini Books Edn., vol. 1. University of Illinois Press (1949)

17. Skeleton (2013),
http://microsoft.com/library/microsoft.kinect.jointtype.aspx

Toward an Integrated System for Surveillance and Behaviour Analysis of Groups and People

Edoardo Ardizzone, Alessandro Bruno, Roberto Gallea,
Marco La Cascia, and Giuseppe Mazzola

Dipartimento di Ingegneria Chimica, Gestionale, Informatica, Meccanica, Università degli
Studi di Palermo, Palermo, Italy
{edoardo.ardizzone,alessandro.bruno15,roberto.gallea,
marco.lacascia,giuseppe.mazzola}@unipa.it

Abstract. Security and INTelligence SYStem is an Italian research project
which aims to create an integrated system for the analysis of multi-modal data
sources (text, images, video, audio), to assist operators in homeland security
applications. Within this project the Scientific Research Unit of the University
of Palermo is responsible of the image and video analysis activity. The SRU of
Palermo developed a web service based architecture that provides image and
video analysis capabilities to the integrated analysis system. The developed architecture uses both state of the art techniques, adapted to cope with the particular problem at hand, and new algorithms to provide the following services: image cropping, image forgery detection, face and people detection, weapon detection and classification, and terrorist logo recognition. In the last phase of the
project we plan to include in our system new services, mainly oriented to the
video analysis, to study and understand the behaviour of individuals, either
alone or in a group.

Keywords: homeland security, weapon detection, weapon classification, image
analysis, video analysis, logo recognition, forgery detection, information fusion.

1 The SINTESYS Project

SINTESYS (Security and INTelligence SYSstem) [1] is an Italian research project,
funded by the PON R&C 2007-2013 program, which involves many scientific (Università del Salento, Università degli Studi di Palermo, Università degli Studi di Salerno,
ICAR-CNR, CeRICT) and industrial (Engineering Ingegneria Informatica, Expert System, Digital Video, System Management) partners. The goal of SINTESYS (Security
and INTelligence SYSstem) is to study, define and develop new technologies for the
realization of an innovative integrated system which can analyse, plan, investigate 'open'
multi-modal (text, images, video, audio, ...) data sources (OSINT - Open Source INTelligence) in an integrated, coherent and consistent way, in order to discover the presence
of links, relationships, connections which the disjointed evaluation of individual sources
would not be able to highlight, and thus to give an important contribution to the management of the case of interest in terms of Decision Support System. SINTESYS is

A. Petrosino, L. Maddalena, P. Pala (Eds.): ICIAP 2013 Workshops, LNCS 8158, pp. 474–481, 2013.

mainly, but not only, directed to analysts who work in institutional sectors, supporting them in the most advanced Intelligence processes for homeland security applications, through collection, processing, analysis and distribution of information. For this purpose, SINTESYS uses and combines techniques, technologies and innovative models for sound analysis, image recognition, movie recognition, social network analysis, text mining, human computer interaction, cognitive psychology, along with models and techniques for information fusion and artificial intelligence. SINTESYS is also establishing new models and innovative techniques to analyse the social dynamics within groups and communities, in order to provide hidden information which may be of importance for security issues. SINTESYS therefore proposes to create an integrated software system equipped with advanced tools for analyzing and correlating vast amounts of data from a variety of heterogeneous, multichannel and multimodal information sources. Using innovative techniques of feature extraction in a combined and integrated way on the same contents, enables synergy and "disambiguation" of data. This analysis, together with a study on correlation of the same data, leads to the emergence of situations of potential danger to public security, ranging from recognition and localization of socially dangerous groups of people or individuals, to the discovery of communicative dynamics which may suggest the need to monitor for prevention aims. With this goal the SINTESYS partners defined a taxonomy of interesting macro-events, which spans from People Detection, to Behavioural Recognition, to Terrorist Attacks, that the system should be able to detect, by analyzing and fusing micro-events, that are detected by each separate analysis module. Furthermore, the system is designed to be flexible to suit the various needs of intelligence analysts, who are able to navigate data using intelligent graphical user interfaces which adapts to different types of information sources and to the actual user needs, through a specific survey of the interaction habits and a psychological study on interaction patterns. The project is still in progress, and currently both state of the art technologies and new algorithms, with particular attention to open source environments, have been developed by the involved research units. We expect that the innovative character of the project results will lead to the growth of various markets and sectors related to the homeland security, individual behaviour understanding and social relationship analysis.

2   Image and Video Analysis

Within the SINTESYS project the Scientific Research Unit (SRU) of University of Palermo) is responsible for image and video analysis. For this purpose the SRU in the first year of the project, studied and developed algorithms for medium level feature extraction, for image data sources: a saliency based image cropping service, a state of the art face detection and people detection algorithms, two proposed methods for the detection and the classification of weapons, a service for the recognition of logo of terrorist groups, and an image forensics technique to verify the authenticity of a digital image. These algorithms are made available as web services and accessed by the integrated analysis system. In the next subsections we will describe the client-server architecture of the image and video analysis system, and the implemented services.

2.1   System Architecture

The selected architecture is based on the client–server model. The structure of the web services is distributed between client (service requester) and the server (service provider). The client and the server communicate over http interface.

The client-server communication is handled with a computer network. The request of the *client* is sent through http interface as it follows:

```
http://sintesys.dicgim.unipa.it/sintesys.php?service =
service_name&url=image_url&par=[par1,par2,…,parN];
```

The client request is made of the web server address (*http://sintesys.dicgim.unipa.it/*), the name of the php file that handles the executions of the services (*sintesys.php*), the name of the service (*service_name*), the URL of the input image (*image_url*) and a vector of parameters, if needed. After the execution of the web service by the server, the results are displayed via the http interface using a JSON object. A JSON Object is an unordered collection of name/value pairs. As an example:

```
{"name":"http://sintesys.dicgim.unipa.it/out/image_crop/c
at_shot_by_arrow-1_out.jpg","bbox":[133,114,918,865]}
```

The output JSON Object includes the URL of the processed image, if any, that is temporarily stored into the server and the other results of the invoked services (the bounding box in this case, for the image cropping service).

The platform of the SINTESYS project is distributed across multiple *servers*. Our SRU, which deals with image processing, installed the developed applications onto a web server that handles the processing of the data via Apache Web Server and the Matlab Application Server. Once the client request is sent via HTTP interface, the Apache server interprets the request of the service by analyzing the name of the service. More particularly, a PHP application handles the selection of the requested web service by extracting the name of the service, the input image and any parameters from HTTP interface, as described in the previous section. The PHP application also handles the execution of the service through the Microsoft Component Object Model (COM) protocol that allows the selection of the specific application, related to the requested service. In our project the services are implemented in Matlab code, but the source code can be written in any of the many programming languages that support COM. Upgrades to applications are simplified, as components can simply be swapped without the need to recompile the entire application. In addition, a component's location is transparent to the application, so components can be relocated to a separate process or even a remote system without having to modify the application. Matlab function returns a JSON Object, as described in the above section, which have different fields, with respect to the different web services.

2.2   Services

Within the SYNTESIS project we studied and developed several algorithms for medium level feature extraction and to support the analysis of an inspected image source.

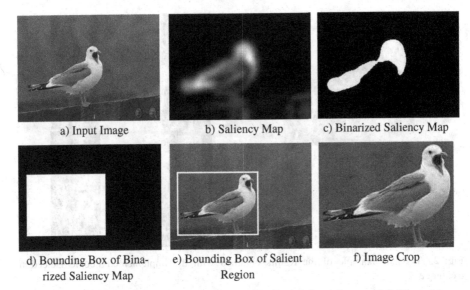

a) Input Image   b) Saliency Map   c) Binarized Saliency Map

d) Bounding Box of Bina-   e) Bounding Box of Salient   f) Image Crop
rized Saliency Map   Region

Fig. 1. The steps of the Image Cropping Method pipeline. a) Input Image, b) Saliency Map, c) Binarization, d-e) Bounding Box, e) Cropping.

2.2.1   Image Cropping

Image cropping is a technique that is used to resize an image by selecting its most relevant areas, discarding its useless or redundant parts. Our SRU developed a saliency based image cropping technique, which extracts salient information from the image to select the image crop. Our system can be subdivided into (see fig.1): Saliency Map Extraction, Saliency Map Binarization (Thresholding), Bounding Box Extraction, Photo Cropping. In our work we used the GBVS algorithm[2], which is one of the most popular state-of-the-art technique to extract the saliency map. The saliency map is then binarized using a threshold, which is experimentally set, and then the bounding box of all the pixels, which values are above the threshold, is selected and used to crop the photo (fig.1.f).

2.2.2   Face Detection

The Face Detection service is used to detected one of more faces into an input image. The implemented algorithm is based on the well-known Viola Jones descriptors [3], which are now adopted as a standard for the detection of faces in digital images.

2.2.3   People Detection

The People Detection service is based on the Dollar et al. algorithm [4]. It is designed to detect the position of people standing in the scene. The implemented technique use the Histogram of Gradients (HoG) which analyzes the distribution of the gradient of the image along different directions. Fig. 2 shows a visual example of the obtained results.

Fig. 2. A visual example of the results obtained with the implemented People Detection technique

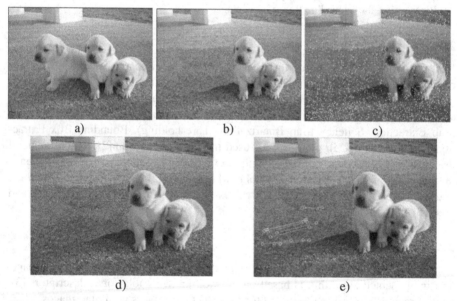

Fig. 3. Original image (a), Tampered image (b), superimposed SIFT keypoints (c), matching keypoints (d), after RANSAC (e)

2.2.4   Forgery Detection

The Forgery Detection service aims to verify the authenticity of a digital image, discovering if the image has been tampered by someone. The implemented algorithm is based on the work of Pan and Lyu [5], and it is based on the extraction of the interest points. Points are then matched, comparing their local features, to identify possible duplicated regions. Matches are filtered by using the RANSAC algorithm, to find groups of points that match according to an affine transformation (see fig. 3). This method proved to be robust to geometric transformations (rotation and scaling), but cannot be used whenever the copy-paste region is uniform. In that case, block-matching methods are preferable, but they are extremely slow, therefore we decided to use a point-based technique.

2.2.5   Weapon Detection

The Weapon Detection service is a new method that is designed to detect whether an input image is a weapon or not. The proposed algorithm initially segments the image (see fig.4), by thresholding the saliency map, as discussed for the Image Cropping service, and refines the segmentation by using active contours [6]. It then extracts features from the foreground of the scene: texture (Edge Histogram [7]), color (Color Histogram) and shape (Turning Angle [8] Histogram). These descriptors are used to train three separate SVM classifiers, and the image is classified as weapon by majority. Weapon images are taken from the Internet Movie Firearms Databases [9]. Negative examples are images of objects that "can be hand-held" (books, bags, umbrellas, etc.) and have been downloaded by the Google Image Search Engine. Experimental results shows that our weapon detector achieves above the 90% of accuracy.

2.2.6   Weapon Classify

The Weapon Classification service is able to classify an image of a weapon into one of the following categories: gun, revolver, rifle, machine gun, heavy machine gun (fig. 5). In this case there is not a "no weapon" class, as the service supposes that the input image represents a firearm. The service extracts the HoG descriptor from the image, and uses a trained multiclass SVM to classify it. Training images are taken from [9]. The classification accuracy is, also in this case, above the 90%.

2.2.7   Recognition of Terrorist Logos

The Terrorist Logo Recognition service, compares an input image with a dataset of images representing the logos of 13 of the most known terrorist groups in the world. We built a reference dataset by downloading from the Web 10 different instances of each logo of the 13 selected classes (some examples in fig.6). The implemented algorithm is a KNN classifier, which compares the SIFT interest points and descriptors of the input image to the descriptors extracted from a reference dataset images. The algorithm proved to be robust to scaling, translation and rotation, as the SIFT descriptors are robust to affine transformation. The average accuracy of the method is about 65%.

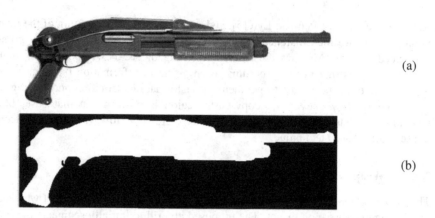

(a)

(b)

Fig. 4. Weapon Detection: input image (a), segmentation mask (b)

gun   revolver   machine gun

rifle   heavy machine gun

Fig. 5. Some visual examples of the weapon classes

Al-qaeda   Brigate Rosse   Tamil Tigers

Hezbollah   Mujahidin-e Khalq   Popular Front for the Libe-
                                                          ration of Palestine

Fig. 6. Some visual examples of the logo classes

Fig. 7. Some case studies. Photos downloaded from the Web

3   Conclusions and Future Works

Even though computer vision techniques are not yet able to resolve the complete image understanding problem, experiments on real data showed that they can play a significant role in particular cases and constrained scenarios (see fig.7). Moreover when they are used in an integrated system they can take advantage from the analysis of other sources of information, or they can give hints to the other analysis modules. Each module is designed to find micro-events that, fused with the other source information, could help experts in the detection of the macro-events of interest. The future works of the Palermo SRU will focus on the video analysis techniques. In fact, the spread of the broadband in the world is increasing the availability of video resources on the Web, therefore they represent a very important source of information. In particular we are working on algorithms about people and object tracking, action recognition, video saliency detection, video summarization and skimming, and video forgery detection. The integration of the these video analysis services into the system will give an essential contribution toward the understanding of the human activities in social context, and of the interaction of individuals with other people or objects.

References

1. http://sintesys.eng.it/en_GB/home
2. Harel, J., Koch, C., Perona, P.: Graph-based visual saliency. In: Advances in Neural Information Processing Systems 19, pp. 545–552. MIT Press (2007)
3. Viola, P., Jones, M.: Robust real-time face detection. International Journal of Computer Vision 5(2), 137–154 (2004)
4. Dollár, P., Belongie, S., Perona, P.: The Fastest Pedestrian Detector in the West. In: BMVC (2010)
5. Pan, X., Lyu, S.: Region duplication detection using image feature matching. IEEE Transactions on Information Forensics and Security, 857–867 (2010)
6. Kass, M., Witkin, A., Terzopoulos, D.: Snakes: Active contour models. Int. J. Comput. Vision 1, 321–331 (1987)
7. Won, C.S., Park, D.K.: Efficient Use of MPEG-7 Edge Histogram Descriptor. ETRI Journal 24, 23–30 (2002)
8. Niblack, W., Yin, J.: A pseudo-distance measure for 2D shapes based on turning angle. In: Proceedings of the Int. Conference on Image Processing, vol. 3, pp. 352–355 (1995)
9. http://www.imfdb.org/wiki/Main_Page

User-Oriented Social Analysis
across Social Media Sites

Ming Yan, Zhengyu Deng, Jitao Sang, and Changsheng Xu

National Lab of Pattern Recognition, Institute of Automation
CAS, Beijing 100190, China
China-Singapore Institute of Digital Media, Singapore, 139951, Singapore
{ming.yan,zydeng,jtsang,csxu}@nlpr.ia.ac.cn

Abstract. The vast amount of user-generated data in various and disparate social media sites contains rich and diverse information about what is happening around the world. Digging into such user-generated data distributed in different social media sites helps us better understand what people are interested in and how they feel about certain topics. In this paper, we investigate into users' behavior data in Twitter and YouTube to figure out whether people's attention on certain topics has some sort of temporal order between Twitter and YouTube on user level. We collected a real world dataset of 8,518 users with account associations between Twitter and YouTube as well as all their behavior data with timestamp since Jan. 2012. The results demonstrate that more users tend to get access to certain events earlier in Twitter than in YouTube and the ratio is somewhat topic-sensitive.

Keywords: temporal, cross-network, user-oriented, social behavior analysis.

1 Introduction

With the emergence and popularity of various and disparate social media sites, users are now frequently participating in multiple social media sites simultaneously. According to statistics, on average every user owns as many as 5.6 social media accounts while they visit about 3 different social media sites per day. Large amounts of information is generated, shared and exchanged by the users across various social media sites, which capture how people are spending their time and what they are interested in. This also makes user's information distributed in multiple social media sites, thus the aggregation and analysis of user-related information in multiple sites will inevitably give us a better understanding of users themselves.

Nowadays many social media aggregation tools such as about.me and FriendFeed make it convenient for users to provide and aggregate their separate accounts, which provides possibilities for the cross-network analysis on user level. We also find that more and more users are willing to provide their accounts in other platforms when registering into social network sites. For example, we

A. Petrosino, L. Maddalena, P. Pala (Eds.): ICIAP 2013 Workshops, LNCS 8158, pp. 482–490, 2013.

have observed from our Google+ dataset that a considerable proportion of users provide the external links to their other social sites such as YouTube, Flickr and Twitter at their Google+ homepages.

In recent years, cross-network social media analysis and application has attracted more and more academic attentions. The works mainly consist of multi-platform social network analysis [1][2], cross-network user identification [3][4] and cross-network collaboration [5,6,7,8], etc. [1][2] compared the social network topology structure and some corresponding SNA metrics of different social network sites and analyzed how information propagates through different network structures. [4] developed a new re-identification algorithm utilizing only the network topology to re-identify the anonymous Twitter graph from Flickr graph with relatively small error rate. [5][6] analyzed the characteristics of different social tagging sites and proposed some cross-network user modeling strategies. [8] explored ways in which event content identified on one social media site can be used to retrieve additional relevant event content on other social media sites so as to better understand the related events.

In this paper, our cross-network social analysis work focuses on investigating into the temporal order of user's access or reaction to certain topics shared across different social media sites: Twitter and YouTube. Take the event "US presidential election 2012" as an example, our motivation is to figure out if most users first post or reshare the tweets about "Obama vs Romney" or other topics related to this event in Twitter and then go to watch related videos in YouTube for more information or vice versa. Some researchers have already begun to explore and compare the speed of the emergence and spread of certain events among different text-based social sites [9][10]. [9] made some analysis on the identification of events using Twitter and Wikipedia and found that Wikipedia lags behind Twitter by about two hours. [10] found six main temporal shapes of attention of online content between Twitter and Webblogs. However, these existed cross-network temporal analysis works only focus on the global popularity of certain events. Our work made this temporal analysis on a user level, i.e., we try to find whether the temporal order exists for the majority of users. To the best of our knowledge, this is among the first work to make a temporal analysis of certain events in multiple platforms on a user level. Finally, we also find the temporal order is somewhat related to the category of the events. For example, a larger proportion of users first share their opinions about the newly-released electronic products in Twitter and then view the videos in YouTube which describe the new features of the products.

2   Data Collection

In this section, we first describe how we collect our cross-network user dataset. Then we introduce the way we extract some certain topics which are frequently talked about both in Twitter and YouTube and how we represent or track these topics on user level in detail.

2.1   Cross-network User Data Collection

In order to obtain a collection of users who have both accounts in Twitter and YouTube, we started from Google+ website where people provide many external links to their other social network homepages and collected about 100,000 users in total. Then we kept only the users who have both Twitter and YouTube accounts and removed those who have less than 10 videos in their upload list, which results in the final cross-network dataset with 8,518 users. The users' rich social behavior data from Jan. 2012 to Apr. 2013 were also downloaded from Twitter and YouTube respectively. In Twitter, we collected all the users' posted tweets with timestamp (including retweets). In YouTube, all the available information for a user such as uploading and favoriting a video were downloaded. As a result, we got more than 8 million tweets and 0.6 million video-related behaviors for our 8,518 user dataset. The following experiments are all based on this dataset.

2.2   Topic Extraction and Representation

To find some topics which are widely spread between Twitter and YouTube in our dataset, we combine the official statistics of the trending topics in 2012 with a simple sorting method by word frequency. In Twitter we use tweet words and hashtags to identify or represent a topic while in YouTube the video tags are utilized to identify a topic. We started from the top trending searches of 2012 revealed by Google [1] and collected all the trending topics with different locations and different categories it mentioned. Then we aggregated all the tags of the YouTube videos and all the tweet words as well as the hashtags involved in our dataset respectively. We further counted the word and tag frequency upon all the behavior data in Twitter and YouTube respectively and sorted the words and tags according to their frequency. Finally, we selected the trending topics with high frequency in our behavior dataset in both networks from all those collected through Google official data as our ultimate topics. As a result, we obtain 22 trending topics shown in Table 1. The following cross-network data analysis works in section 3 are all based on these 22 trending topics and we will only show the topic number in the subsequent experiment results for brevity.

Next, we will describe how we identify and represent the selected trending topics in Twitter and YouTube respectively since different social networks tend to use different terms to indicate the trending topics. For instance, people may use "obama election 2012" or "mitt romney election" to indicate the topic "US presidential election 2012" in YouTube while they may adopt the hashtags such as #USelection, #voteobama or #obama2012 to indicate the same topic in Twitter. To capture all the terms which can represent the trending topics in Twitter and YouTube respectively, we use the YouTube Search API to search for all the 22 trending topics in YouTube engine and aggregate the video tags of

---

[1] http://www.marketingcharts.com/wp/topics/entertainment/
google-reveals-2012s-top-trending-searches-25381/

Table 1. The final selected trending topic list

Topic	Topic	Topic
1. US presidential election 2012	9. Samsung Galaxy S III	17. google glasses
2. gangnam style	10. Michael Jackson	18. call me maybe
3. super bowl 2013	11. Christmas 2012	19. Spider Man
4. Olympic 2012	12. Google Nexus 4 release	20. Skyfall
5. Justin Bieber	13. Iphone 5 release	21. End of the World 2012
6. star wars film	14. Call of Duty: Black Ops II	22. Whitney Houston
7. The Dark Knight Rises	15. Doctor Who TV Series	
8. Minecraft Game	16. Prometheus	

the returned videos while in Twitter we search for the related tweets from a wider range of tweet dataset we downloaded since the Twitter Search API can only search the tweets currently posted. Then we adopt the same word frequency sorting method as in the previous Topic Extraction procedure and manually select the high frequency terms which can represent the topic as our indicator for the topic. In this way, we count how many of the 8,518 users have referred to the different selected topics via their user tag cloud in Twitter alone, YouTube alone and both in Twitter and YouTube respectively. The result is shown in Table 2. We can see that users are more active in Twitter and for all the topics the number of involved users are larger in Twitter than YouTube. Moreover, the topic overlap on user level between Twitter and YouTube is relatively small that only a small proportion of users pay attention to certain topics both in Twitter and YouTube.

Table 2. The user number who have referred to each of the selected trending topics (we only show 20 topics due to the space and T stands for Topic) in Twitter alone, YouTube alone and both in the two respectively.

	T1	T2	T3	T4	T5	T6	T7	T8	T9	T10
Twitter	2908	3850	1107	1376	1071	2385	2251	857	1164	519
YouTube	949	1181	239	310	405	1171	638	572	458	321
Both Two	521	602	82	115	78	350	219	221	192	62

	T11	T12	T13	T14	T15	T16	T17	T18	T19	T20
Twitter	4155	1434	2708	890	1114	791	1704	897	951	1254
YouTube	1270	361	497	174	586	231	658	508	264	249
Both Two	729	189	246	63	177	75	269	117	82	85

3   Cross-Network Data Analysis

In this section, we first present a global temporal dynamic analysis of the popularity of certain topics regarding all the users' behavior data in our dataset. Then we further investigate whether there are some temporal behavior patterns across different social media sites on user level and topic level respectively.

3.1   Global Attention of Certain Topics Starts Earlier in Twitter than in YouTube

To capture a full dynamic of some certain topics and verify the effectiveness of our method to represent and track certain topics, we select two popular topics in our trending topic list in Table 1, i.e. "US presidential election 2012" and "super bowl 2013", we then count how many users in our dataset begin to pay attention to these topics each day during an observation of two months. For the topic "US presidential election 2012", we observe from Oct.1 to Nov.30 in 2012 of which the final election day happened on Nov.6. Here we mainly present and illustrate our results on this topic for the sake of space limit. The temporal dynamic result of the users' attention on this topic is shown in Figure 1. We further track this topic with the real-world timeline in its wikipedia page [2] and the real events are labeled in the figure. We can find that the statistics from our dataset well capture the real events happened in "US presidential election 2012", since it can be seen from the Figure 1 that a peak of user attention occurs near each of the important events in the topic which in turn indirectly verify the effectiveness of our mechanism to represent and track the topics.

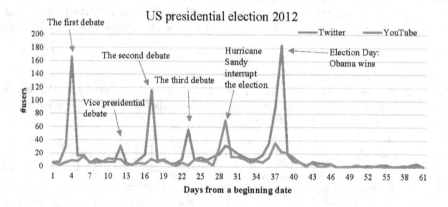

Fig. 1. The temporal dynamics of global user attention for the topic "US presidential election 2012"

Moreover, for a qualitative analysis of the temporal order of users' attention on this topic between Twitter and YouTube in a global view we can see from the figure that many users in Twitter begin to follow this topic since the first, second and third debate while users in YouTube mainly begin to follow this topic since the event "Hurricane Sandy interrupts the election" occurs. Finally, the attention in both networks achieves the peak when the final election day comes and Obama wins the election. Since Twitter network can identify more sub-topics and users

---

[2] http://en.wikipedia.org/wiki/United_States_presidential_election,
_2012_timeline

are more active and productive, users on average tend to get access to certain topics faster in Twitter than in YouTube. This is also reasonable by realizing the fact that users can speak almost whatever they like in Twitter just by typing some words while users in YouTube have to spend more efforts recording and uploading the videos before people can get to know this. The difference of the efforts it takes to create the content accounts for this gap to some extent. The similar characteristic also goes for the topic "super bowl 2013" and we omit it here in case of space limit.

Nevertheless, we've also observed an interesting phenomenon that most the emergence of the peak time of user attention lags behind the occurrence time of the real events by one day. For instance, the first, second and the third debate happened in Oct.3, Oct.16 and Oct.22 respectively according to Wikipedia statistics while our peak time for each of the three events all comes one day later than the actual occurrence time. It may be due to the fact that many users are not that active in social networks and they just begin to pay attention to this topic when they notice their friends or some real-time event reporters post some tweets about this topic. Besides, it takes some time that information spread widely to the general public in social media network .

3.2   Attention to Certain Topics is Earlier in Twitter on User Level

After the global temporal analysis of user behavior between Twitter and YouTube, we further investigate into the temporal patterns across different social media sites based on each single user. In other words, we try to figure out whether the majority of users are first involved in this topic in Twitter and then go to YouTube for more details or vice-versa when some topic emerges. Therefore, we first collect the users who have referred to the topics in our trending topic list both in Twitter and YouTube (the available number of the users can be found in Table 2). Then we analyze the users' behavior data to find when the users first referred to the topics in Twitter and YouTube respectively. We use the same method to identify the topic as in section 2.2 and if the topic indicator occurs in user's tweets or video tags, we consider that the user refer to the topic. We further get the date when users begin to pay attention to the topic for the first time and judge in which network the user pay attention to the selected topic earlier. We aggregate the votes from all the users who have referred to the topics both in Twitter and YouTube and calculate the ratio between the Twitter votes and YouTube votes. The result is shown in Table 3.

From Table 3, we can see that the number of user votes for "Twitter is earlier" is far larger than that for "YouTube is earlier" almost on all topics. In other words, a larger proportion of users tend to first focus on some trending topics in Twitter and then they will go to YouTube for more details on this topic. As a result, the local temporal analysis based on each single user also meets the global patterns demonstrated in section 3.1 indicating that information emerging and spreading in Twitter is faster than that in YouTube.

Table 3. The number of user votes for "Twitter is earlier" and "YouTube is earlier" and their ratio on the topics in our trending topic list

	T1	T2	T3	T4	T5	T6	T7	T8	T9	T10
#Twitter earlier votes	352	414	58	80	50	181	135	141	140	40
#YouTube earlier votes	169	188	24	35	28	169	84	80	52	22
The ratio	2.08	2.20	2.42	2.29	1.79	1.07	1.61	1.76	2.69	1.82

	T11	T12	T13	T14	T15	T16	T17	T18	T19	T20
#Twitter earlier votes	480	155	177	48	107	45	181	61	48	42
#YouTube earlier votes	249	34	69	15	70	30	88	56	34	43
The ratio	1.93	4.56	2.57	3.2	1.53	1.5	2.06	1.09	1.41	0.98

3.3   Reaction to Certain Topics is Somewhat Topic-sensitive

In section 3.2, we also find the user vote ratio is different for different topics and for the topic "Skyfall" even the number of YouTube earlier votes is a little larger than that of the Twitter earlier votes. So it naturally comes to our mind that whether the temporal order between Twitter and YouTube has something to do with the topic category. Therefore, we choose 5 categories which have obvious category labels, i.e. celebrity, technology, movie, game, sport. We further calculate the average user vote ratio in each category and the result is shown in Table 4. We can see that the ratio on technology category is relatively large while the ratio on movie category is small instead. It may be partly due to the fact that users are more likely to discuss and get to know full comments on electronic products before they search for the related videos, meanwhile a lot of users may share their opinions on the newly-released movies after they have completely viewed it in YouTube. Therefore, the user reaction to different topic categories also follows different temporal patterns and we should take topic category into consideration when analyzing the user behavior on certain topics.

Table 4. The user vote ratio between Twitter and YouTube on different categories

Category	Celebrity	Technology	Movie	Game	Sport
The ratio	1.87	3.27	1.31	2.48	2.35

4   Applications

The user-oriented temporal analysis across different social media sites can facilitate a variety of applications, including but not limited to:

1. **Cross-network User Collaboration.** Since we have found that for certain kinds of topics users are very likely to first talk about them in Twitter and then go to YouTube to better understand the evolution of the topics, we can further design some time-aware cross-network collaboration applications based on the temporal analysis. For example, we have been working towards the topic of the personalized real-time video recommendation from Twitter to YouTube. We first capture the temporal interests of certain users and

what topics they currently pay attention to in Twitter, then we can utilize the user interest learnt in Twitter to help recommend the relevant videos to the same user for his YouTube account as the user attention in YouTube lag behind that in Twitter.

2. **Trend-aware Prediction of Content Popularity.** As we can identify the trending topics and track the temporal dynamics of the topic popularity in Twitter precisely, we can well capture the trend of the corresponding topics in real world. In general, the topic trend in YouTube somewhat follows a similar pattern but with some delay than that in Twitter. Therefore, We can utilize the topic popularity trend obtained from Twitter to help predict the trend of the same topic in YouTube.

5   Conclusion

In this paper, we present a measurement study of users' temporal behavior between Twitter and YouTube. In particular, we explore the temporal patterns of users' attention to certain topics on user level. It is shown that most users' attention to certain topics is earlier in Twitter than YouTube and the situation is topic-sensitive. Further work may include a quantitative analysis on the users' temporal behavior patterns across different social media networks and some novel applications based on our social behavior analysis.

References

1. Ahn, Y.Y., Han, S., Kwak, H., Moon, S., Jeong, H.: Analysis of topological characteristics of huge online social networking services. In: Proceedings of the 16th International Conference on World Wide Web, pp. 835–844. ACM (2007)
2. Lerman, K., Ghosh, R.: Information contagion: An empirical study of the spread of news on digg and twitter social networks. In: Proceedings of 4th International Conference on Weblogs and Social Media, ICWSM (2010)
3. Carmagnola, F., Cena, F.: User identification for cross-system personalisation. Information Sciences, 16–32 (2009)
4. Narayanan, A., Shmatikov, V.: De-anonymizing social networks. In: 2009 30th IEEE Symposium on Security and Privacy, pp. 173–187. IEEE (2009)
5. Abel, F., Araújo, S., Gao, Q., Houben, G.-J.: Analyzing cross-system user modeling on the social web. In: Auer, S., Díaz, O., Papadopoulos, G.A. (eds.) ICWE 2011. LNCS, vol. 6757, pp. 28–43. Springer, Heidelberg (2011)
6. Abel, F., Gao, Q., Houben, G.-J., Tao, K.: Semantic enrichment of twitter posts for user profile construction on the social web. In: Antoniou, G., Grobelnik, M., Simperl, E., Parsia, B., Plexousakis, D., De Leenheer, P., Pan, J. (eds.) ESWC 2011, Part II. LNCS, vol. 6644, pp. 375–389. Springer, Heidelberg (2011)
7. Roy, S.D., Mei, T., Zeng, W., Li, S.: Socialtransfer: cross-domain transfer learning from social streams for media applications. In: ACM Multimedia, pp. 649–658 (2012)
8. Becker, H., Iter, D., Naaman, M., Gravano, L.: Identifying content for planned events across social media sites. In: Proceedings of the Fifth ACM International Conference on Web Search and Data Mining, pp. 533–542. ACM (2012)

9. Osborne, M., Petrovic, S., McCreadie, R., Macdonald, C., Ounis, I.: Bieber no more: First story detection using twitter and wikipedia. In: SIGIR 2012 Workshop on Time-Aware Information Access (2012)
10. Yang, J., Leskovec, J.: Patterns of temporal variation in online media. In: Proceedings of the Fourth ACM International Conference on Web Search and Data Mining, pp. 177–186. ACM (2011)

Towards the Parody Machine.
Qualitative Analysis and Cognitive Processes
in the Parody of a Politician

Isabella Poggi[1] and Francesca D'Errico[2]

[1] Dipartimento di Filosofia, Comunicazione e Spettacolo – Università Roma Tre
isabella.poggi@uniroma3.it
[2] Faculty of Psychology
Uninettuno International Telematic University (Utiu)- Rome
fderrico@uniroma3.it

Abstract. The paper presents a model of parody, viewed as a distorted imitation of a text, discourse, behavior or trait of a person performed in order to elicit laughter. Focusing on the parody of politicians as a way to discredit them for persuasive purposes, a qualitative analysis is presented of the parody of a Mayor of Rome by an Italian comedian. The role of allusion in parody, and its consequent dependency on culturally shared knowledge are highlighted, and the function of ridicule as a form of moralistic aggression is stressed. Finally a first flash of a procedure for the construction of a parody machine is provided, based on the cognitive process of parody in humans.

1   From Computational Humor to the Parody Machine?

Laughing at others is a formidable weapon against power; and a weapon of power. People make fun of others to abase them, to make them powerless and not to be afraid of them anymore. A way to do so is satire, and specifically to make a parody of someone: showing his flaws by making a caricature of his appearance or behavior.

The field of computational humor, has emerged in the last twenty years to build systems for the generation of humorous texts and images [1]. At the same time, multimodality and body signals have been so deeply studied as to lead to their simulation in Embodied Conversational Agents and Robots. Since humor is typically conveyed multimodally by the interaction of words and prosody with body movements, gestures, face, gaze, even suits or costumes, it should be possible now also to encompass multimodal bodily aspects within computational humor.

Parody is a such humorous behavior, in that it is often aimed at making people laugh about someone or something by funnily imitating it from semantic but also acoustic and visual points of view. So why not start thinking of a "parody machine"?

As for any case of simulation of a complex human activity, building a parody machine, one that given a person is able to extract her potentially ridicule flaws and to reproduce them in such a way as to make fun of them, might be motivated by at least two functions, a genuinely theoretical and an applicative one. The former is in the

A. Petrosino, L. Maddalena, P. Pala (Eds.): ICIAP 2013 Workshops, LNCS 8158, pp. 491–500, 2013.

loop of modeling a human process, simulating it, getting a feedback through evaluation, and re-formulating the model accordingly: simulation as a way to test a conceptual model; and a model capable to account for the production of parodies must necessarily model subtle but important devices of social interaction. On the application side, beside the traditional functions of computational humor [2, 3], a "parody machine" might provide an automatic tool for finding out and displaying the ridiculous aspects of a character or object: a machine able to single out the weak points of a behavior or person might anticipate possible future reactions of others and in some cases induce to change course of action. A such machine might be an "alter-ego" warning us when the way we appear or behave may trigger laughter; a sincere friend who, when understanding we become ridicule, imitates us and lets us clumsiness emerge. But to build a parody machine requires an adequate model of parody: such first step is the objective of our work.

This paper defines the notion of ridicule (Sect. 2) in terms of a socio-cognitive model of communication and social interaction, then it overviews previous definitions (n.3) and presents its own notion of parody (n.4). Through a qualitative analysis of the parody of a mayor of Rome by an Italian comedian (n.5), it highlights the cognitive processes occurring in a Parodist' mind, and finally (n.6) provides some first flashes of a computational model of parody, figuring out what capabilities an Artificial System should be endowed with to automatically generate parodies.

2   Ridicule: A Way to Discredit Others

Ridiculization is a communicative act conveying a negative evaluation of someone, aimed at a sort of "moralistic aggression" [4] toward him/her, to be used as a sanction against a-social behaviour, possibly even with a pedagogical function. According to [5], a negative evaluation is the belief that some object, event or person does not have (or does not provide someone with) the power to achieve some goal. We evaluate something negatively either when it lacks the power to achieve some goal (negative evaluation from lack of power) or when it has the power of thwarting some goal (negative evaluation from noxiousness). When A ridicules B, A conveys a negative evaluation of B for lack of power, but one that contrasts with some pretence of superiority exhibited by B. Such contrast between pretence of power and actual lack of power, whose outcome is though not threatening for A, can elicit laughter: the physiological expression of relief that follows the sudden disconfirmation of some expectation of danger, thus resulting in a sense of superiority. Ridiculization is then a communicative act through which a Sender S remarks, in front of some Audience A, a feature of a victim V evaluated as negative due to lack of power, contrasting with V's pretence of superiority, and seen as not threatening for S and A, so as to elicit relief and laughter. Ridiculization further implies S deliberately soliciting Audience A to laugh at V, with the goal of causing that:

  a.   S and A feel superior to V, because they feel above the inadequacy of the victim, and not threatened by it;

b. This common superiority strengthens the social bonds between S and A, through the shared positive emotion of laughing together, through feeling similar to each other as opposed to different from V, and a sense of alliance and complicity;

c. With image and possibly self-image attacked, the Victim feels emotions of shame, humiliation, abasement, s/he feels different, rejected, isolated from the group. All this may induce V to future different behaviour: which is the function of ridiculization as "moralistic aggression" [4]: aggression from the group aimed at changing a member's conduct.

In previous works, [6] analyzed verbal and multimodal cases of ridiculization in political debates, where political opponents try to make fun of each other, to lower each other's credibility before voters, thus performing a "discrediting move", i.e., spoiling the other's image before an audience, for persuasive purposes. In persuasion, Persuader P aims at convincing an Audience A not only by what he says (*logos*), but also by the emotions he induces (*pathos*) and by the reliable image he presents of himself (*ethos*). Further, as well as P needs to project a positive image of himself, to prevent the Audience from being persuaded by an opponent T, he may try to convey a negative image of him, i.e., cast discredit over T. In political persuasion, discredit is cast over opponents concerning three different features [8]: the politician's *benevolence* (caring the electors' goals, working on behalf of their interest, being trustworthy, honest, ethical), *competence* (expertise, skill, knowledge, planning and reasoning capacity), and *dominance* (capacity of winning in contests, of influencing others and imposing one's will). A politician may discredit the other on all three features through ridiculization, by signals in various modalities that call for the Audience's laughter: laughter or smile only or in combination with words; words only, withoutsmile or laughter; but also by irony and parody.

3   Related Work on Parody

What is parody? According to Holman and Harmon [8], parody is an imitation, intended to ridicule or criticize, that does not need a "pretense of ignorance" like in the socratic teacher, because familiarity with the original object is necessary: to be effective it has to "sound true" to the original [9].

A parody is not a simple imitation: first it has to be an "approximation" to an original source, since like in sarcasm "the subject is treated in a contradictory manner: elevated subjects are debased and "lowly" are elevated" [10].

The parodistic act presents a not so obvious nature from a linguistic and psychological point of view: Bachtin [11: 76] sees it as "an arena of conflict between two voices, they are detached but they are hostilely counterposed" and the second voice represents a "semantic authority". In his speculation on parody he specifies: "the audience knows for sure with whom it is expected to agree." The Parodist has a strong role of both communicating and informing the audience on a criticizable object or act. In fact Rossen-Knil and Henry [12] on the production side formally mention four pragmatic aspects of parody: (1) the intentional verbal representation of the object of parody, (2) the flaunting of the verbal representation, (3) the critical act, and (4) the comic act. On the comprehension side the parodistic act depends on the successful interaction between parodist and audience, since not only needs the latter recongnize the "authority" and the ethic or moralistic intention of the parodist, but it also needs to know vices and virtues of the character, if the parody is focused also on the body and verbal features (tic, stummer…) which are the innesco of the comic part.

A verbal parody involves a highly situated, intentional, and conventional speech act which re-presents the object of parody and flaunts that re-presentation in order to criticize that object in a humorous way [11].

4   A Socio-cognitive Model of Parody

In terms of our model, parody is a communicative act – a text or a verbal or multimodal communicative behaviour (discourse, song, film, fiction) – that performs a distorted imitation of another text or multimodal behaviour, with the aim of amusing and eliciting laughter. Not only a person, but also a text (a song, a novel, a drama) may be an object of parody.

In political satire, to make fun of the target T in front of the audience A, the Parodist P imitates the Target's traits and/or communicative or non-communicative behavior, performing a distorted imitation that enhances the Target's flaws. To do so, the Parodist must 1. single out the most characterizing features of Target T's physical traits or behaviors, and 2. imitate them while exaggerating them in such a way as to make them appear ridicule.

How can a feature exhibited by P evoke a similar (but less extreme, less exaggerated) feature of T? The key to parody is allusion. In Allusion, an Agent P wants an Addressee A to infer that P refers to X, though not by explicitly mentioning X but simply making reference to it in an indirect way. P does not mention X out of reasons of euphemism or other kind of protection, and yet wants A to understand both what P refers to and why P does not mention it explicitly.

In imitation, P produces the trait or behavior Y while asking A to recognize it as similar to trait or behavior X, so allusion in a sense is always present in any kind of imitation. But as I ask you to recognize Y as an imitation of X, I presuppose that you know X. Therefore imitation typically requires that the knowledge of X is shared by me and you: there must be a common culture, a shared frame of reference between the Imitator (the Parodist) and his Audience; so much so that both imitation and parody cannot be entirely understood across different cultures.

Due to its character of indirect, hence necessarily somewhat concealed type of communication, in both verbal and bodily allusion the referent cannot be mentioned in a clear and, so to speak, "central" way, but simply hinted at here and there during discourse or in the overall multimodal arrangement of the parodist. These hints, a sort of "key-words" that orient A to capture the allusion, concern the "allusion points": the contents in the background knowledge that are supposedly shared with A, and to which the Parodist wants to allude in his parody.

5   The Parody of a Politician. A Qualitative Analysis

To better illustrate our definitions of parody and allusion, we present a qualitative analysis of a real parody of a politician: the Italian comedian Max Pajella's parody of Gianni Alemanno, a former exponent of the Italian fascist party Alleanza Nazionale (National Alliance), mayor of Rome since 2008 to 2013, one often criticized for having been a fascist drubber in his youth and, during his role as a Mayor, for his familism, since he hired lots of relatives and friends in the town bus company. Max Pajella is a skilled imitator and parodist working in the left-wing satire show *"The show must go off"*, where he ridicule tics and behaviors of various right-wing politicians, appearing on the screen and talking to the show conductor, the comedian Serena Dandini, in the studio, while she comments on what he says and takes the role of his stooge. For his parody of Gianni Alemanno, Pajella picks up a recent episode in which the Mayor really made himself ridicule: the snow in Rome.

Below we describe the context and background of this event, with words in bold describing the "allusion points".

On February 3rd, 2012, a lot of snow came on Rome. Not so used to see snow, Rome is generally not well prepared to confront this challenge, but in this case, the disorganized management by Alemanno and his staff turned a meteorological event into a disaster. A **newsletter** from the national Civil Protection had warned him that **35 millimeters** of water were expected; actually, 1 millimeter of water equates 1 cm. snow, but Alemanno and his staff were not expert on this, so they expected 3,5 centimeters of snow instead of the 35 and more that came in fact. Probably due to this misunderstanding, no kind of prevention was undertaken: no **salt** to prevent streets from freezing, no **snow chains** for buses; buses stopped for hours with roman citizens inside, not to let them die for cold. Alemanno simply warned people to stay home, then he bought a stock of **shovels** and had them distributed to Roman citizens recommending to clean up their doors by themselves; he himself was videorecorded on TV while shoveling snow. Finally he often said he would **call the army** to cope with the emergency. When the emergency was over, Alemanno was accused of disorganization and inefficiency, and to justify himself he appeared in all possible TV news and talk shows imputing the disaster to the Civil Protection, who had not warned him how serious the situation was, and complaining that **he had been left alone** to confront the emergency.

Our hypothesis is that in a parody, each element of the parodist's imitation alludes to a relevant element of the story to cast ridicule on it; and analyzing a parody implies discovering the beliefs alluded to by each of the Parodist's words or visual behaviors, and the information, opinion, or evaluation they indirectly convey. In the following, we separately analyze Pajella's imitation of Alemanno's discourse and that of his multimodal behavior.

5.1   Allusions and Parody in Alemanno's Costume and Background

Pajella, acting Alemanno, shows on the screen with Coliseum in the background and **flocks of snow** gently falling down; he is dressed as a **Roman centurion**, his helmet on the ground, and holds a big **shovel** in his right hand and a **sheet of paper** in his left hand.

1. Coliseum with **flocks of snow** falling down alludes to snow in Rome: quite a "neutral" information, only aimed to set the stage of the parody.
2. Alemanno dressed as a **Roman centurion** alludes to the Roman tourist operators that welcome tourists around Coliseum dressed as centurions. This is not, though, a neutral information, but one loaded with somewhat negative evaluation: men playing centurions with tourists are generally connoted as underprivileged uneducated people from Roman slums, waiting for a tip after posing for a picture. This suit then conveys Alemanno a nuance of a lout, a buffoon.
3. The **shovel** in his hand alludes to (and ridicules) the shovels he distributed to Romans to help themselves, and to his showing himself shoveling, to project an image of a willing boy who, though left alone by civil protection, did everything he could to help. But one more inference can be drawn from this: Alemanno's impotence to manage emergency in Rome.
4. The sheet of paper in his left hand alludes to the **newsletter** from the Civil Protection about the centimeters of water expected: this points at Alemanno's ignorance in meteorology.

5.2   Allusions and Ridicule in Alemanno's Words

The same kind of analysis given in a discursive way on Pajella-Alemanno's costume and visual background is provided in a schematic way for his words in Table 1. In columns 1. and 2. we write the Parodist's words and their literal meaning, respectively; in col. 3 the belief each word or sentence alludes to, in 4 the indirect meaning conveyed by the allusion, and in 5 we finally classify the example in terms of the feature of the Target made fun of, whether Competence, Benevolence or Dominance. (Table 1)

Table 1. Pajella's words and their allusions

1.BELIEF MENTIONED	2.MEANING DIRECTLY CONVEYED	3.BELIEF ALLUDED TO	4.MEANING TO BE INFERRED	5.RIDICULED FEATURE
Io sono stato lasciato solo in questo Colosseo a spalare la neve io sono stato lasciato solo.	I have been left alone; in this Coliseum I have been left alone shoveling snow.	Alemanno often complained he had been left alone	Alemanno plays the victim to justify himself:	DOMINANCE
Io se continua così chiamo l'esercito. La Protezione Civile mi ha lasciato solo.	If things go on like this, I'll call the army. Civil Protection has left me alone	A. always threatened to call the army:	He threats but also plays the helpless	DOMINANCE
Dovevano dircelo che l'acqua ghiacciava a zero centigradi centimetri	They should have told us that water froze at zero centigrade centimeters	A.and his staff proved very ignorant about meteorological facts	A. is very ignorant	COMPETENCE

Table 1. (*Continued*)

Perché la Protezione civile aveva detto che sul Campidoglio sarebbero piovuti soltanto 35 millimetri di mmerda.	Because Civil Protection had said that only 35 millimeters **shit** would have fallen on Capitolium.	The snow was cause of a great loss of face for A.		DOMINANCE
a tutti coloro i quali, quei romani i quali sono rimasti dentro bloccati sugli autobus, i cinquantotti barrati, i sessanta notturni,	to all those who, those romans who remained blocked on the bus, barred fiftyeights, the night sixties,	*Cinquantotti* (the plural of a number) alludes to A.'s linguistic ignorance	He is ignorant also in Italian language	COMPETENCE
A: *vi sono vicino, è come se foste tutti quanti parenti miei.* D: *Come se fossero parenti suoi?? In realtà, molti lo sono... vabbè, lasciamo perdere*	A.:I am close to you, as if you all were relatives of mine. D: As if they were your relatives?? Actually, many are.... Ok, just let it go...	This alludes to A.'s familism in hiring all his relatives in the bus company.	He is dishonest because he is familistic in his administration	BENEVOLENCE
D: *Eh, non sarebbe il caso di tendere un po' più la mano alla Protezione Civile? Collaboriamo bene, mo?*	D: Well, shouldn't you lend a hand to Civil Protection more? Are we collaborating well, now?	People commented that the Mayor and the Civil Protection should have collaborated more	A. did not collaborate but only cast discredit on the Civil Protection	BENEVOLENCE
A: *Su questo le posso dire che ha ragione: è il momento di tendergli una mano ... e prenderli a ccatenate! Se solo si trovassero ste catene.... Però, 'n se trovano!*	A: About this I can tell you that you're right: it's time to lend them a hand.... And take them by chain hits! If only we might find these chains.... But you can't find them!	Alemanno as a fascist drubber in his youth, possibly using chains to hit political rivals Snowchains lacking in the emergency	A.was formerly a violent person A.was disorganized	BENEVOLENCE COMPETENCE

5.3   Allusion, Parody, and Culture

The annotation of Table 1 allows us to assess density and quality of the parody itself, measured, respectively, in terms of the number of ridiculing allusions, and of how much the Victim is made fun of concerning his immorality, incompetence, or impotence. But Table 1 shows as well how parody cannot exist without allusion, because it relies on the imitation of traits or behaviors of the Victim; the similarity between the trait exhibited or the behavior performed by the Parodist and the corresponding trait or behavior of the victim cannot be caught unless the Addressee is acquainted with the Victim's behaviors and traits. The Audience cannot understand who the Parodist is imitating and alluding to if it does not share the Parodist's culture, i.e. the same knowledge and values.

6   Toward the Parody Machine?

How could we build a Parody Machine? The cognitive process necessary for a Human to perform a parody – that we should simulate to make an Embodied Agent able to perform parodies – implies at least the following requirements:

1. having a goal of moralistic aggression toward a Victim, to be pursued through ridicule.
2. having "sense of humor", i.e., the capacity for grasping scenarios feasible to being the object of fun or laughter, while distinguishing them from those that cannot or should not.
3. singling out one or more traits or behaviors of the Victim that are worth being ridiculed.
4. having (and searching) one's Model of the Addressee: a representation of what knowledge about the Victim is shared, and whether it may be subject to negative evaluation by the Addressee too.
5. imitating the traits, body behavior, or verbal text or discourse singled out as potentially ridicule, by exaggerating them, and possibly accompanying them with signals of allusion to induce the Audience to search its memory for similar traits or behaviors in the Victim and attach a tag of ridicule to it.

In the same vein, an Artificial System capable of performing parodies should be endowed with:

a. a capacity for having goals of moralistic aggression;
b. "sense of humor", i.e., capacity for grasping traits and behaviors feasible to being made fun of;
c. a cultural database on the behaviors and traits of possible Victims of parody;
d. a User Model of the Audience, to set which cultural beliefs and values concerning the Victim are shared and which are not
e. a body signals detection module to capture the recurrent physical features that characterize the style of the Victim's body behavior
f. an Imitation module, i.e., the capacity to display the same traits or behaviors as the Victim imposing the same physical features to one's imitative body behavior
g. an exaggeration module, i.e., the capacity to imitate the Victim's features by exaggerating them, but up to a realistic threshold, not in such a way as to make them unrecognizable by an Audience.

A simplified scheme of the process leading from perception of ridicule features to their distorted imitation is represented in Fig. 1.

Future research should implement the various steps of this procedure to build a Parody Machine.

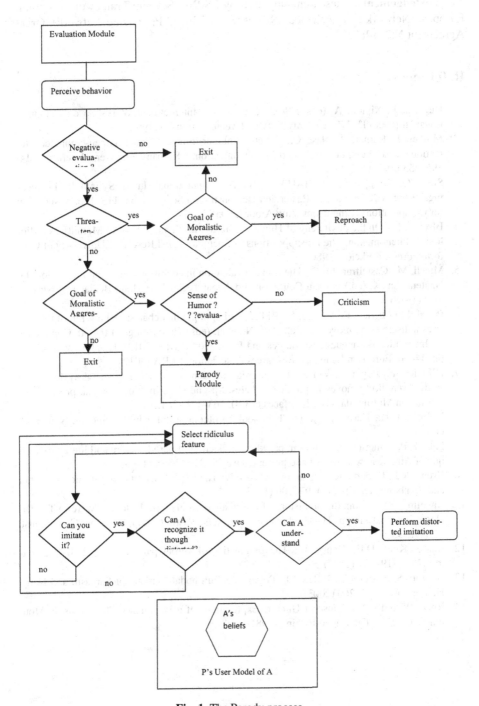

Fig. 1. The Parody process

Acknowledgements. Research supported by SSPNet Seventh Framework Program, European Network of Excellence SSPNet (Social Signal Processing Network), Grant Agreement N.231287.

References

1. Hulstijn, J., Nijholt, A. (eds.): Proceedings of the International Workshop on Computational Humour (TWLT 12). University of Twente, Enschede (1996)
2. Morkes, J., Kernal, H., Nass, C.: Effects of humor in task-oriented human-computer interaction and computer-mediated communication. Human-Computer Interaction 14, 395–453 (1999)
3. Stock, O., Strapparava, C.: HAHAcronym: A Computational Humor System. In: Proceedings of the ACL Interactive Poster and Demonstration Sessions, pp. 113–116. Association for Computational Linguistics, Ann Arbor (2005)
4. Bischof, N.: On the phylogeny of Human Morality. In: Stent, G.S. (ed.) Morality as a Biological Phenomenon. The Presuppositions of Sociobiological Research. University of California Press, Berkeley (1980)
5. Miceli, M., Castelfranchi, C.: The role of evaluation in cognition and social interaction. In: Dautenhahn, K. (ed.) Human Cognition and Agent Technology. John Benjamins, Amsterdam (1998)
6. Poggi, I., D'Errico, F., Vincze, L.: Ridiculization in public debates: making fun of the other as a discrediting move. In: Calzolari, N., et al. (eds.) Proceedings of the 8th Conference on International Language Resources and Evaluation (LREC 2012), Istanbul, May 21-27, pp. 44–50. European Language Resources Association, ELRA (2012)
7. D'Errico, F., Poggi, I., Vincze, L.: Discrediting signals. A model of social evaluation to study discrediting moves in political debates. Special issue in "Social signal processing". Journal on Multimodal User Interfaces 6(3-4), 163–178 (2012)
8. Holman, C.H., Harmor, W.: The handbook to literature, 5th edn. Macmillan, New York (1986)
9. Falk, R.P.: American literature in parody: a collection of parody, satire and literary burlesque of American writers past and present. Twayne, New York (1995)
10. Kreuz, R.J., Roberts, R.: On satire and parody: The importance of being ironic. Metaphor and Symbolic Activity 8(2), 97–109 (1993)
11. Bakhtin, M.M.: From the prehistory of novelistic discourse. In: Holquist, M. (ed.) The Dialogic Imagination, pp. 41–83. University of Texas, Austin (1981); Emerson, C., Holquist, M. (Trans.)
12. Rossen-Knill, D.F., Henry, R.: The pragmatics of verbal parody. Journal of Pragmatics 27(6), 719–752 (1997)
13. Attardo, S., Eisterhold, J., Hay, J., Poggi, I.: Multimodal Markers of Sarcasm and Irony. Humor 16(2), 243–260 (2003)
14. Ruch, W. (ed.): The Sense of Humor: Explorations of a Personality Characteristic. Mouton-de Gruyter, The Hague-Berlin (1998)

Natural Interactive System
for Hemispatial Neglect Rehabilitation

Gianpaolo D'Amico, Lea Landucci, and Daniele Pezzatini

MICC - Media Integration and Communication Center,
University of Florence, Italy
http://www.micc.unifi.it

Abstract. Experimentation of natural interaction principles and advanced interactive solutions for medical treatment of the neglect syndrome. Novel tools are provided for improving rehabilitation and evaluation of patients and overcome the conventional pen-and-paper approach. This project is the result of a multidisciplinary collaboration among Media Integration and Communication Center, the Faculty of Psychology of the University of Florence and Montedomini A.S.P., a public agency for disabled elders and healthcare services in Italy.

Keywords: User Interfaces, Information Interfaces and Presentation, Life and Medical Sciences.

1 Introduction

Hemispatial neglect (or neglect syndrome) is a neuropsychological condition in which, after a damage to one hemisphere of the brain, a deficit in attention to and awareness of one side of space is observed. It is defined by the inability of a person to process and perceive stimuli on one side of the body or environment that is not due to a lack of sensation.[1] For example a stroke affecting the right lobe of the brain can lead to neglect for the left side of the field of view, causing a patient to behave as if such side of sensory space does not exist. In such conditions the patient could be no more able to pass a door without hitting the jamb, or to eat the food on a dish without leaving the left half part completely untouched. Unfortunately, the only treatment consists of finding ways to bring the patient's attention toward the left, usually done incrementally, by going just a few degrees past midline, and progressing from there. Moreover the difficulty degree of such task increases with the age of the patient.

The Behavioural Inattention Test (BIT)[2] is a 15-item standardized test battery for assessing visual neglect, consisting of 6 of the most commonly used pen-and-paper tests (line crossing, letter cancellation, star cancellation, figure copying, line bisection, and free drawing) and 9 behavioral tasks (picture scanning, telephone dialing, menu reading, article reading, telling and setting the time, coin sorting, address and sentence copying, map navigation, and card sorting) (see fig.1). One component of the test battery is a simple test described by Albert [3] in which patients cross out lines on a sheet of paper (see fig. 1 - b);

A. Petrosino, L. Maddalena, P. Pala (Eds.): ICIAP 2013 Workshops, LNCS 8158, pp. 501–508, 2013.

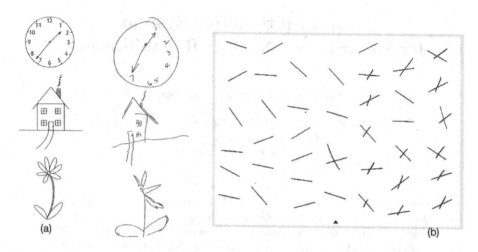

Fig. 1. Set of pen-and-paper tests from the BIT battery: (a) figure copying and (b) Albert's test

this is easy to administer and related closely to neglect diagnosed by the test battery as a whole [4]: that is the reason why we focused on Albert's test.

As reported by the medical staff we interviewed, the main issue in Albert's test is that particular negative results can be due to lack of stimulation, especially for elderly patients. That is why the idea of this work is to *translate* analog Albert's tests in digital tests able to stimulate the patient's attention.

For such delicate process we have exploited the help of the department of psychology at the University of Florence that suggested some real-world contexts able to put patients at ease and encourage them to actively participate in all the test and training phases.

2 Related Work

There is a wide variety of solutions for the study of the neglect syndrome still using paper based tools, as in [11], where drawing-based pencil-and-paper tests enable objectivity, repeatability and diagnostic capability in the scoring process of the disease. Anyway there is another part of research which experiments solutions for the development of neuropsychological assessment and rehabilitation tools via the adoption of computer-based advanced technologies.

A former approach is based on Virtual reality (VR), which is showed to be effective for dealing with cognitive and functional impairments due not only to traumatic brain injury, but also to neurological disorders and learning disabilities [6] [10]. VR-DiSTRO[5] is a solution which uses shutter stereoscopic glasses, a force feedback interface and a software, in order to provide an immersive experience and then estimate its accuracy and usability for patients affected by acute neglect syndrome. A similar approach is presented in [8], where a 3D-haptic virtual world is seen through stereo shutter-glasses, where hemispatial neglect patients interact by manipulating a haptic interface. A different approach is discussed in [7], where post-stroke neglect in the extrapersonal space was evaluated. Authors modeled a street crossing in VR, in which a battery of thirty-two patients with right-hemispheric stroke were asked to control a virtual avatar safe from a traffic accident. In [14] authors studied unilateral spatial neglect following stroke in recovered post-stroke patients with residual symptoms of unilateral spatial neglect. They compared the assessment and treatment results from standard paper and pencil tests with their VR solution. SeeMe is a system in which participants see themself in real time in a projected screen while they assess functional tasks touching virtual balls. A single screen-mounted camera and vision-based tracking system capture and convert the user's movements for processing on the big display.

Other computer-based approaches which differ from VR technology are presented in [12], where a game-based solution composed of a webcam, a computer and a video projector is used to guide the patient in exploring the space (included the neglected hemispace) with the goal to reach for targets with different levels of difficulty. In [13] a system to measure eye and head-neck movement is presented for the evaluation of the unilateral spatial neglect fields. Eye motion was estimated via a small CMOS camera attached to a head unit, while the head-neck movement was processed via a high-vision video camera attached to the front of the patient. In [9] authors proposed a computerized version of the cancellation test via the adoption of a touchscreen interface to large groups of control subjects and unilaterally brain-damaged patients (unilateral and non-unilateral spatial neglect).

3 The System

The proposed solution is represented by an interactive environment in which patients are asked to perform different tasks in order to estimate their neurocognitive condition (testing phase) and to support rehabilitation activities (training phase). Tasks, that have been defined under the supervision of a team of psychologists, consist of predefined exercises to address the following elements: memory, attention, perceptual disturbances, visualspatial disturbances and difficulties in executive functions. The main idea is to allow patients to interact with digital content through gestures in order to perform tasks similar to those that would occur in their daily life. On the other hand, we wanted to provide medical staff with an advanced tool to customize tasks configurations and to analyze data obtained from patients activity.

The system is composed by two main parts: a touch based interactive surface for patients and a desktop based application for medical staff. The interactive surface is visualized on a wide LCD screen (52") with multitouch capabilities provided by an infrared based overlay. The screen is mounted on a reclining and height-adjustable table, so that every patient could easily interact with every part of the screen. The chosen interface metaphor for the proposed use case is the action of cleaning a dirty table (see fig. 2). Patients are asked to move a real sponge on the interactive table in order to physically erase virtual dust or spots displayed on the screen.

Fig. 2. A patient performing the task of cleaning the interactive table from coffee spots

The testing phase consists of collecting information on the severity of the condition and progress of the patient, whilst the training phase encourages the exploration of the neglected hemifield through various procedures. The set of the spots (visual stimuli) displayed on the table can be configured according to four parameters: number, location, size and nature (e.g. coffee, oil, water; see fig.3).

Doctors and therapists can create different configurations of tasks using a desktop based GUI in order to tune difficulty according to patient conditions. As an example, a training task could be configured with a particular spatial distribution of stimuli on the basis of patients neglected hemifield. Therapists can also add audiovisual feedback to stimuli (e.g. blinking light, sounds etc.) that can be triggered during the training session helping patients to complete the task.

All the activities during the rehabilitation sessions are tracked and recorded in a database so that a personal history of each patient can be evaluated in order to estimate performances in terms of accuracy (number of erased spots), time spent in accomplishing the task and trajectory of movements. In this way, medical staff can work with a novel diagnostic tool which provides useful information, statistics, charts and high-level data for the evaluation of patients (see fig.4).

Both the desktop application and the interactive rehabilitation interface are developed using the AIR (Adobe Integrated Runtime) framework, allowing to bring ActionScript and Flex code into a native desktop installer. The multitouch

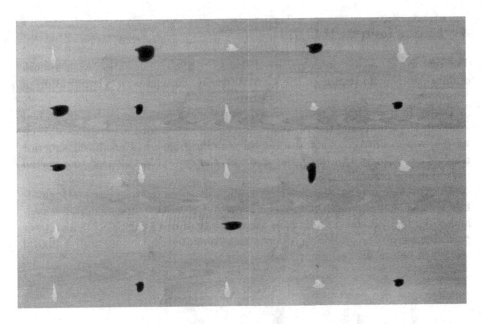

Fig. 3. Interactive table with water and coffee spots

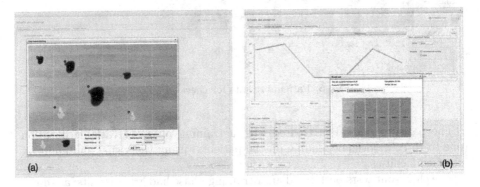

Fig. 4. (a) drag and drop GUI for training configuration and (b) statistical analysis tools

overlay sends data on tracked fingers and objects to the main application using the TUIO protocol [15].

4   Experimental Results

The real-world testing phase occurred thanks to the collaboration with Monte-domini A.S.P. who exploited the system for the experimental rehabilitation of approximately 30 patients in the last two years.

Taking into account a sample of ten representing patients, for whom we had available the traditional test of Albert as a check-in test for the experimentation, we discovered not only that the digital training phase has produced superior results than standard training, but also that the system has also led to a partial psycho-motor rehabilitation.

As expected, a table sprinkled with (digital) spots or dust has a strong affordance so that the instinct to clean is greater than that of concluding a pen-and-paper test: as shown in fig.5, in the majority of cases the patients had lower performance on the standard Albert's test compared to the interactive digital test, even before the training phase.

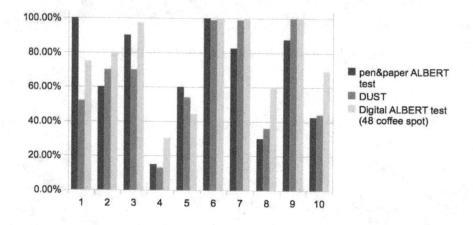

Fig. 5. Patients results for check-in test

The patients were then treated with a training phase of variable duration (one to three months depending on the patients) using the visual and auditory interface facilities.

The check-out tests performed after training phase had great results: as shown in fig.6, the patients improved the awareness of the left side of view (this was proved not only with the digital test but also with the traditional one).

The physical therapists who have followed them have also recorded an improvement in their physical condition. In fact, in order to reach the entire surface of the table, patients have unconsciously also worked on their body: the lower part has worked to support the whole body (training of body-balance) while the upper part had a benefit due to the stretching of arms performed in order to reach the upper and side areas of the table (such effect has obviously occurred also in patients forced to use the table on wheelchairs).

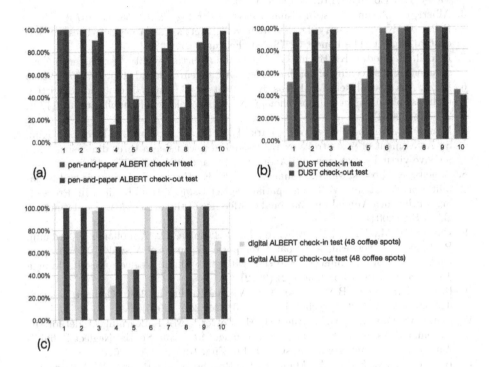

Fig. 6. Patients results for check-out test

Finally, medical staff has recognized added value in the efficacy of the performance analysis process due to the use of the computerised analysis tools provided by the system.

5   Conclusions and Future Work

The developed system allows effective analysis of the clinical status of patients affected by the neglect syndrome and a fine tool for the rehabilitation training. The idea is to use a real-world context in order to stimulate elder patients to perform tests and to improve their clinical condition through the training phase. First experimental results are very positive and encourage us to continue on this path. Future work includes the improvement of the evaluation on patients and the development of new natural interactive contexts for the rehabilitation also exploiting dynamic scenarios.

References

1. Unsworth, C.A.: Cognitive and Perceptual Dysfunction. In: Physical Rehabilitation, pp. 1149–1185 (2007)
2. Wilson, B.A., Cockburn, J., Halligan, P.W.: Behavioural Inattention Test. Thames Valley Test Company Ltd., Titchfield (1987)
3. Albert, M.: A simple test of visual neglect. Neurology 23(6), 58–64 (1973)
4. Fullerton, K.J., Mcsherry, D., Stout, R.W.: Albert's test: a neglected test of perceptual neglect. The Lancet 327(8478) (February 22, 1986)
5. Fordell, H., Bodin, K., Bucht, G., Malm, J.: A virtual reality test battery for assessment and screening of spatial neglect. Acta Neurol Scand. 123, 167–174 (2011)
6. Rizzo, A.A., Schultheis, M., Kerns, K.A., Mateer, C.: Analysis of assets for virtual reality applications in neuropsychology. Neuropsychological Rehabilitation 14(1/2), 207–239 (2004)
7. Kim, D.Y., Ku, J., Chang, W.H., Park, T.H., Lim, J.Y., Han, K., Kim, I.Y., Kim, S.: Assessment of post-stroke extrapersonal neglect using a three-dimensional immersive virtual street crossing. Acta Neurol Scand. 121, 171–177 (2010)
8. Baheux, K., Yoshikawa, M., Tanaka, A., Seki, K., Handa, Y.: Diagnosis and Rehabilitation of Patients with Hemispatial Neglect Using Virtual Reality. In: Proceedings of the 26th Annual International Conference of the IEEE EMB, San Francisco, CA, USA (2004)
9. Rabuffetti, M., Farina, E., Alberoni, M., Pellegatta, D., Appollonio, I., Affanni, P., Forni, M., Ferrarin, M.: Spatio-Temporal Features of Visual Exploration in Unilaterally Brain-Damaged Subjects with or without Neglect: Results from a Touchscreen Test. PLoS One 7(2) (2012)
10. Rose, F.D., Brooks, B.M., Rizzo, A.A.: Virtual Reality in Brain Damage Rehabilitation: Review. Cyberpsychol. Behav. 8(3), 241–262 (2005)
11. Liang, Y., Fairhurst, M.C., Guest, R.M., Potter, J.M.: A Learning Model for the Automated Assessment of Hand-Drawn Images for Visuo-Spatial Neglect Rehabilitation. IEEE Trans. Neural Syst. Rehabil. Eng. 18(5), 60–70 (2010)
12. Borghese, A.N., Sedda, A., Mainetti, R., Ronchetti, M., Pasotti, F., Bottini, G.: A reliable low-cost platform for neglect Virtual Rehabilitation. In: International Conference on Virtual Rehabilitation, Switzerland, June 27-29 (2011)
13. Sugihara, S., Miyasaka, T., Tanaka, T.: A study of assessment of unilateral spatial neglect using a system for motion analysis of eyes and a head-neck. In: IEEE/SICE International Symposium on System Integration, January 29, pp. 67–70 (2009)
14. Sugarman, H., Weisel-Eichler, A., Burstin, A., Brown, R.: Use of Novel Virtual Reality System for the Assessment and Treatment of Unilateral Spatial Neglect: A Feasibility Study. In: International Conference on Virtual Rehabilitation, Switzerland, June 27-29 (2011)
15. Kaltenbrunner, M., Bovermann, T., Bencina, R., Costanza, E.: TUIO - A Protocol for Table-Top Tangible User Interfaces. In: Proceedings of the 6th International Workshop on Gesture in Human-Computer Interaction and Simulation, Vannes, France (2005)

Customers' Activity Recognition in Intelligent Retail Environments

Emanuele Frontoni[1], Paolo Raspa[1], Adriano Mancini[1],
Primo Zingaretti[1], and Valerio Placidi[2]

[1] Dipartimento di Ingegneria dell'Informazione,
Università Politecnica delle Marche
Ancona, Italy
`{frontoni,raspa,mancini,zinga}@dii.univpm.it`
[2] Grottini Lab, Porto Recanati, Italy
`valerio.placidi@grottinilab.com`

Abstract. This paper aims to propose a novel idea of an embedded intelligent system where low cost embedded vision systems can analyze human behaviors to obtain interactivity and statistical data, mainly devoted to customer behavior analysis. In this project we addressed the need for new services into the shop, involving consumers more directly and instigating them to increase their satisfaction and, as a consequence, their purchases. To do this, technology is very important and allows making interactions between costumers and products and between customers and the environment of the shop a rich source of marketing analysis.

We construct a novel system that uses vertical RGBD sensor for people counting and shelf interaction analysis, where the depth information is used to remove the affect of the appearance variation and to evaluate customers' activities inside the store and in front of the shelf, with products. Also group interactions are monitored and analyzed with the main goal of having a better knowledge of the customers' activities, using real data in real time.

Even if preliminary, results are convincing and most of all the general architecture is affordable in this specific application, robust, easy to install and maintain and low cost.

Keywords: RGBD, depth images, activity recognition, interactions, retail environments, people counting, shelf interaction map.

1 Introduction

The concept of shop is changing during years and today it means many different things: shop became not only the place where customers go to buy a specific product, but also the place where customers go to spend part of their time; competition between different producers is made also in the shop structure, meaning of communication, graphics, position of products, shelf availability and many other aspects [21].

This project focuses on developing automated RGBD video analysis techniques for tracking customers in retail stores with the goal of recognizing various customer activities that may be relevant for marketing analysis with a particular focus on the interactions

A. Petrosino, L. Maddalena, P. Pala (Eds.): ICIAP 2013 Workshops, LNCS 8158, pp. 509–516, 2013.

between shoppers and products on shelves. The approach uses low-level segmentation and tracking methods, mapping the customers to the floor plan, identifying events such as picking up products in front of store shelves, group formations by customers, etc.

The aim of every retail environment is to attract customer attention: with technology and strategy, shop's owner has to attract customer attention on particular products, giving also the chance to interact physically with technology, making the experience absolutely complete and involving. The main goal of this new concept of retail environment is simple: make more business with respect to the old shop idea.

First of all, in some cases technology works as a virtual shop assistant, giving information to the customer directly; in this way shop's owners save money with staff.

Second, and more important, is the fact that technology let to provide many statistic data that, opportunely elaborated, can give much information about customers, customizing the shop to their needs and adapting product expositions to their behaviours. Data extracted in this way are objective, while often this kind of decision is made looking to subjective data.

Several aspects of these problems are currently solved using artificial intelligence and, in particular, vision. Visual analysis in dynamic scenes is currently one of the most active research topics in computer vision [1, 5, 9].

In general, the processing framework of visual surveillance in dynamic scenes includes the following stages: modelling of environments, detection of motion, classification of moving objects, tracking, understanding and description of behaviours, human identification, and fusion of data from multiple cameras [3, 6, 7].

As a result, more and more research has been conducted in this field involving a great quantity of different vision based approaches.

Automatic recognition of human actions and interactions, however, remains a very challenging problem. The key difficulty stems from the fact that the imaged appearance of a person performing a particular action can vary significantly due to many factors such as camera viewpoint, person's clothing, occlusions, variation of body pose, object appearance and the layout of the scene.

In addition, motion cues often used to disambiguate actions in video [9, 17, 20] are not available in vertical acquired RGBD images.

In this work, we seek to recognize common human actions, such as "picking up a product", "interacting with the shelf" or "moving in a group" in challenging realistic retail images. A number of previous works [2, 4, 8, 10] focus on exploiting body pose as a cue for action recognition. In particular, several methods address joint modeling of human poses, objects and relations among them [11-16].

Reliable estimation of body configurations for people in arbitrary poses, however, remains a very challenging research problem. Less structured representations, e.g. [18, 19] have recently emerged as a promising alternative demonstrating state-of-the-art results for action recognition in static images.

In this paper we will introduce the general framework of our system and we will discuss how vision and, in particular, people and object tracking, are involved in different tasks of the whole system. We will show successful applications for retail environment management and for products management, showing the visual tracking methodology and results of real scenarios with real time performances. Software analysis, tests and experiments developed are presented to show the feasibility of the proposed approach in large-scale applications, using only RGBD vision sensors.

The paper is more focused on the application of vision to retail environment and on the general application of visual tracking as a main information source; main novelties are in the original and wide application of the tracking system and activity analysis focused on shelf interactions. The other interesting point of the project is in the real experimental platform described in the result section and in the combination of vision based statistical approach with marketing analysis data.

The paper is organized as follows: Section 2 introduces the general concept of the system and describes the peculiarity of the particular methodology described in this paper. The experimental results are provided in Section 3. Conclusions are given in the last Section.

2   Metodology

2.1   Customers Counting and Single/Group Behaviors

The goal of the system is the use of vertical mounted RGBD camera (Fig.1a) to detect costumers activities and in particular their interactions with shelf and products. The first part of the activity recognition method is based on the water filling algorithm to identify people from a vertical depth image even when they are moving in group inside the store (e.g. a mam with child or a group of friends). This last aspect of group behaviors will be better investigated in future tests in real scenario and results on this side are not reported in this paper even if the methodology will be the same described here following.

The system needs to identify every   person moving in the scene (Fig. 1b) to track his activities and in particular to analyze the interaction of this certain person with the shelf. Section 2.2 will give more details on this second aspect.

Fig. 1. Example of a user interacting with the shelf (a) and the approach for people detection and activity analysis in our test environment. Test case (a) will be described in next section.

We take the depth image as a function f, where $f(x, y)$ stands for the depth information of pixel (x, y). Due to the noise of RGBD sensor, $f(x, y)$ can be non-derivable or even discontinuous. Finding people in depth image equals to finding local minimum regions in f. Mathematically, the problem can be defined as finding the region A and N that satisfy the following constraint:

$$E_A(f(x, y)) + \eta \leq E_{NA}(f(x, y)) \tag{1}$$

where $A \in N$, A is the local region and N is its neighborhood. $E(.)$ is an operation to pool the depth information in the region to a real value that reflects the total depth information in the region. η is a pre-defined threshold to ensure that depth in A should lower than N_A with a margin.

Note that A and N can be of arbitrary shape, and finding all the regions in image can be very time consuming. In [21] is possible to find detail about the water filling algorithm that can effectively find all the suitable regions as reported in the example of Fig.2.

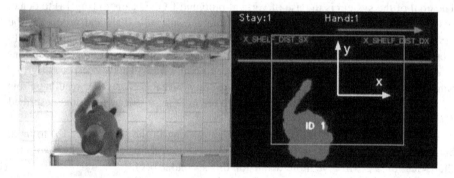

Fig. 2. Example of the water filling algorithm detecting customer with ID 1 together with the shelf line estimated by the depth sensor and the reference system. This second aspect will be better described in section 2.3

2.2   Costumer Interaction Aspects

The second methodological aspect of this work is the idea to have an estimation of the interaction with products on the shelf and a classification of the interaction type. In particular we define *positive* interaction when the product is picked up from the shelf and bought and *negative* one when the product is put back on the shelf after a pickup. This is very useful information when we try to identify customers' activities in front of shelves. This allows also the description of the activity also with an interaction map that will be discussed in the result section.

To solve the hand problem we designed a template matching method dealing with hand and products templates. A sample of two of these templates is reported in Fig. 3.

The template frame is identified when the hand is entering or exiting the shelf line identified by the depth sensor.

Fig. 3. Example of hand template and hand/product template, the first one entering the shelf line, the second exiting with product

In general template matching requires similarity measures between the features of a template and the query image. Image intensity patches are often compared by normalized cross-correlation whereas Hausdorff and chamfer measures are popular with edge-based features. A common approach is to have a number of prototype shape templates and search for them in the image. Templates used for hand with products and hands without were collected in real scenarios. Chamfer score and a closely related measure Hausdorff score have been used in many shape matching schemes. We use truncated chamfer score, which makes it more robust to outliers [10, 11].

3   Results

The system was installed in a real store using 5 sensors mounted in the ceiling of particular locations of the store (main entrance, high interest product categories, etc.).

The hardware was selected to respect the low cost aspect of the project and in particular the idea to use commercial components that are suitable for low maintenance and low cost requirements. The Raspberry processing unit was used to compute the RGBD video streaming at 10 frames/second using OpenCV and our software with drivers for the Asus Pro Live RGDB sensor.

The processing unit is devoted to all image-processing elaborations and only synthetic data are transmitted over the WiFi network of the store to a web server that collect numerical data in respect to privacy limitation.

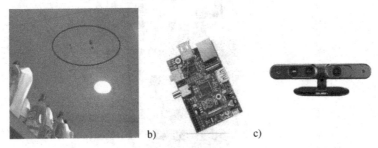

a)   b)   c)

Fig. 4. a: The system installed in the ceiling of a real store (5 of this unit was installed for test in particular areas of the store. **b:** the Raspberry used as processing unit (one for each RGBD camera with WiFi modules for synthetic data transmission) **c:** the Asus RGBD sensor.

The system on the web server collects several data suitable for customer activity analysis together with the interaction map of the shelf. Here following Tab. 1 presents a list of parameters that are grabbed from the real environments that was on line for 30 day. The table is related to a complete day analysis and is reported to give an idea of possible data comparisons that can be performed both between different categories (locations inside the store) and different periods.

Also change detection can be easily applied to this data to better understand what is the customers' reaction when a change is performed in the layout of the store, in the communication on the shelf or in the packaging or planogram of a certain category.

Table 1. List of parameters provided by the system for activity analysis in a day of test in a real scenario

Parameter	Value
1. Total number of people	465
2. Average attention time	36 sec
3. People passing by (no attention)	43%
4. Average group number	1,2
5. Number of shelf interactions	590
6. Interaction per person	2,1
7. Average X, Y (to evaluate attention)	134,20
8. Direction Left-Right	72%
9. Direction Right-Left	28%

Fig. 5 reports an example of the interaction map. This particular result, that is one of the novelties of this paper, is performed on the web application using data of hand interaction and their x, y, z labeled with the product/no-product features and with the id of the person that is performing the interaction. In particular the sequence of the interactions can be used to represent over the shelf image an intensity map that proves information about the interaction sequence: red areas are customers that picked up the products and put id back on the shelf; green areas represent positive interaction where customers bought the product.

Fig. 5. Example of a user interaction map. Red area represents negative interactions.

Also in this case change detection is the suggested way to perform comparisons between different planograms and packaging, or on-shelf communication.

Further results analysis are currently being developed mainly integrating data coming from 5 sensors. The system demonstrated to be affordable and robust and, until today, it collected data for 30 days with no evidence of particular errors. Even if preliminary and open to huge further investigations, results are convincing and also the discussion with marketing people involved in the project demonstrate a lot of interest for the application here described.

A subset of results (6 hours of store activities with 143 people passing by in a 1.33mt shelf) was compared with ground truth manually recorded by visual merchandising people, showing an accuracy in Table 1 data of 98,5% for parameters 1,2,8 and 9. Parameters 5 and 6 were compared with manual grabbed data with an accuracy of 97,2%.

4   Conclusion and Future Works

In this paper we presented a novel application of visual activity recognition, using a combination of techniques to better understand consumer behaviors also in the ability to interact with the environment and in particular with shelves and products; the proposed approach was tested in a real environment with interesting results in the field of retail marketing analysis.

The paper presented also an integrated architecture for mixing together different kind of vision based applications such as people and products tracking. Future work about this project is, first of all, the optimization of these systems in terms of stability, performances and robustness to environmental inconveniences, considering that in a shop there is no special worker able to reset or modify these systems in case of trouble.

The final step of this project is to provide the shop with a full automated user interaction model that can also give information about shelf refill, out of stock, crowded areas and walkability map. The goal is also to have a fast system to evaluate variations in the layout of the store, of the shelf and in on-shelf communication, to allow marketing people to work on the bases of real test with costumers in a real scenario.

Acknowledgements. Authors would like to thank all the staff of the company Grottini Lab S.r.l and Daniele Liciotti for their support and the provided test location.

References

[1]   Ascani, A., Frontoni, E., Mancini, A., Zingaretti, P.: Feature group matching for appearance-based localization. In: IEEE/RSJ, International Conference on Intelligent RObots and Systems, IROS 2008, Nice (2008)

[2]   Bourdev, L., Malik, J.: Poselets: Body part detectors trained using 3D human pose annotations. In: ICCV (2009)

[3]   Brox, T., Bourdev, L., Maji, S., Malik, J.: Object segmentation by alignment of poselet activations to image contours. In: CVPR (2011)

[4]   Csurka, G., Bray, C., Dance, C., Fan, L.: Visual categorization with bags of key-points. In: WS-SLCV, ECCV (2004)

[5]   Desai, C., Ramanan, D., Fowlkes, C.: Discriminative models for multi-class object layout. In: ICCV (2009)

[6]   Desai, C., Ramanan, D., Fowlkes, C.: Discriminative models for static human-object interactions. In: SMiCV, CVPR (2010)

[7]   Farhadi, A., Endres, I., Hoiem, D., Forsyth, D.: Describing objects by their attributes. In: CVPR (2009)

[8]   Felzenszwalb, P., Girshick, R., McAllester, D., Ramanan, D.: Object detection with discriminatively trained part based models. IEEE PAMI (2009)

[9]   Ferrari, V., Marin-Jimenez, M., Zisserman, A.: Pose search: retrieving people using their pose. In: CVPR (2009)

[10] Gupta, A., Kembhavi, A., Davis, L.: Observing human-object interactions: Using spatial and functional compatibility for recognition. IEEE PAMI 31(10), 1775–1789 (2009)

[11] Johnson, S., Everingham, M.: Learning effective human pose estimation from inaccurate annotation. In: CVPR (2011)

[12] Lampert, C., Nickisch, H., Harmeling, S.: Learning to detect unseen object classes by between-class attribute transfer. In: CVPR (2009)

[13] Laptev, I., Marszałek, M., Schmid, C., Rozenfeld, B.: Learning realistic human actions from movies. In: CVPR (2008)

[14] Lazebnik, S., Schmid, C., Ponce, J.: Beyond bags of features: spatial pyramid matching for recognizing natural scene categories. In: CVPR, pp. II: 2169–II: 2178 (2006)

[15] Li, L., Su, H., Xing, E., Fei-Fei, L.: Object bank: A high-level image representation for scene classification and semantic feature sparsification. In: NIPS (2010)

[16] Maji, S., Bourdev, L., Malik, J.: Action recognition from a distributed represen-tation of pose and appearance. In: CVPR (2011)

[17] Moeslund, T.B., Hilton, A., Kruger, V.: A survey of advances in vision-based human motion capture and analysis. CVIU 103(2-3), 90–126 (2006)

[18] Yao, B., Fei-Fei, L.: Grouplet: A structured image representation for recognizing human and object interactions. In: CVPR (2010)

[19] Yao, B., Fei-Fei, L.: Modeling mutual context of object and human pose in human-object interaction activities. In: CVPR (2010)

[20] Zhang, J., Marszalek, M., Lazebnik, S., Schmid, C.: Local features and kernels for classi-fication of texture and object categories: A comprehensive study. IJCV 73(2), 213–238 (2007)

[21] Mancini, A., Frontoni, E., Zingaretti, P., Placidi, V.: Smart vision system for shelf ana-lisys in intelligent retail environments. In: ASME/IEEE International Conference on Me-chatronic and Embedded Systems and Applications (MESA 2013), Portland, Oregon (2013)

Viewing the Viewers: A Novel Challenge for Automated Crowd Analysis

Davide Conigliaro[1,2], Francesco Setti[2], Chiara Bassetti[2],
Roberta Ferrario[2], and Marco Cristani[1,3]

[1] Università degli Studi di Verona, Strada Le Grazie 15, I-37134 Verona, Italy
[2] ISTC–CNR, via alla Cascata 56/C, I-38123 Povo (Trento), Italy
[3] Istituto Italiano di Tecnologia (IIT), via Morego 30, I-16163 Genova, Italy

Abstract. We focus on the automated analysis of *spectator crowd*, that is, people watching sport contests alive (in stadiums, amphitheaters etc.), or, more generally, people "watching the activities of an event [...] interested in watching something specific that they came to see" [2]. This scenario differs substantially from the typical crowd analysis setting (e.g. pedestrians): here the dynamics of humans is more constrained, due to the architectural environments in which they are situated; people are expected to stay in a fixed location most of the time, limiting their activities to applaud, support/heckle the players or discuss with the neighbors. In this paper, we start facing this challenge by following a social signal processing approach, which grounds computer vision techniques in social theories. More specifically, leveraging on social theories describing expressive bodily conduct, we will show how, by using computer vision techniques, it is possible to distinguish fan groups belonging to different teams by automatically detecting their liveliness in different moments of the match, even when they are merged in the stands. Moreover, we will show how, only by automatically detecting crowd's motions on the stands, it is possible to single out the most salient events of the match, like goals, fouls or shots on goal.

Keywords: spectator crowd, crowd analysis, spatio-temporal clustering.

1 Introduction

Emerged as a Video Surveillance niche, crowd analysis has become in the last 10 years a separate topic of Computer Vision, embracing heterogenous applicative fields like public crowd management, space design, virtual and intelligent environments [19]. Crowd analysis focuses on the modeling of large masses of people, where the single person cannot be finely characterized, due to the small visual resolution, the frequent total occlusions and the particular dynamics. Therefore, many of the standard Computer Vision technologies as person detection, multi-target tracking, action recognition, re-identification, cannot be considered in their classical form. As a consequence, crowd modeling has grown with its own set of peculiar techniques (as multiresolution histograms [20], spatiotemporal

A. Petrosino, L. Maddalena, P. Pala (Eds.): ICIAP 2013 Workshops, LNCS 8158, pp. 517–526, 2013.
© Springer-Verlag Berlin Heidelberg 2013

cuboids [12], appearance or motion descriptors [1], spatiotemporal volumes [14], dynamic textures [15]), calculating on top of them flow information. Such information is then employed to learn different dynamics like Lagrangian particle dynamics [16], and in general fluid-dynamic models. The most important applications of crowd analysis are abnormal behavior detection [15], detecting/tracking individuals in crowds [13], counting people in crowds [3], identifying different regions of motion and segmentation [18].

In this paper, we focus on a novel applicative field for crowd analysis, centered on the modeling of the so called *spectator crowd* [2] (or viewers' crowd, as we have called them in the title). The idea is to observe people while they are watching a public show, as in a sport arena, a movie theater, a classroom, a court, and recording and analyzing their activities. This scenario differs substantially from those analyzed by the typical crowd modeling techniques: due to *territoriality* principles, people are assumed to stay near a fixed location for most of the time, i.e., their seat [9,11], while what is mainly being monitored in the crowd analysis literature are moving people.

In addition, people here are assumed to have a strong relation with the event or contest they are watching, that becomes a kind of reference point, where the focus of attention [7] of the crowd is located, and around which the space is structured. In classical crowd modeling no such clear reference point is present.

These two key elements build a context where diverse techniques and applications can be developed, some of which are listed in the following:

Spectators Segmentation finding diverse groups of people among the spectators, for example the fans of the opposite teams in a sport match; attentive VS distracted students in a classroom; enthusiastic VS annoyed spectators at a theater play;

Excitement Calculation in a given time interval, quantizing the level of excitement of some part or of the entire crowd;

Event Segmentation segmenting diverse activities of the crowd (clapping hands, making a wave, heckling), and studying how these activities are related with the observed event (i.e. some people clap their hands when the favorite team scores a goal, or get excited when a foul is or is not signaled by the referee);

Augmented Video Summarization the spectator feedback, automatically recognized, may help in highlighting exciting or crucial events that should be included in a video summarization of the show;

Anomaly Detection given an expected crowd behavior, highlighting anomalous activities that may lead to dangerous situations, like fights, mass escapes, etc. in order to prevent them;

Comparative Analysis of Spectators various factors can be compared, like fans of different teams in the same sport [17], or fans of different sports [8], or the behavior of the same fans in different stadiums, where spectators are arranged differently etc.;

Interpretation of Crowd's Intentions discriminating whether a display of crowd excitement is determined by a rejoicing VS aggressive attitude, to foresee the subsequent crowd's behavior.

In the following, we will show how the first three aspects discussed above can be faced using Social Signal Processing methods [4], focusing on a sport scenario, where people watch hockey matches [1]. For the spectators segmentation and the excitement calculation issues, we use local flow information (position, flow intensity and direction), as input of a Gaussian clustering framework operating on the single frame. The spatial segmentations are then joined together along the temporal axis by a hierarchical clustering. The results are impressive, since it becomes possible to distinguish the different fan groups, even when they are merged; regions of activities indicating how much lively some supporters are can also be automatically found. In the event segmentation problem, we calculate global flow measures (intensity, entropy of the flow direction) at each frame, obtaining a 2D signal which is subsequently quantized by Mean Shift segmentation. This way, important events (goals, shots on goal) can be easily discovered.

Our framework has been evaluated on a dataset of 12 videos taken during the 2013 IIHF Ice Hockey U18 World Championship, for a total of 6 hours, showing qualitative and quantitative promising results.

In the rest of the paper we present our framework in Sec. 2, followed by preliminary results in Sec. 3; Sec. 4 draws some conclusions and future perspectives.

2   Our Framework

In the following, we will detail the methodologies adopted for solving the *spectators segmentation*, the *excitement calculation* and the *event segmentation* issues (see Sec. 1).

2.1   Spectators Segmentation and Excitement Calculation

As a first step, standard motion flow is computed on the image plane, extracting at each pixel direction and intensity. Then, assuming people as static [9, 11] and considering the size of people, flow information can be re-arranged into a grid of N squared patches $\{x\}$. On each patch x, at each time frame, we extract four measures: the first is the flow intensity $I(x)$, obtained by averaging over the flow intensity values of the patches' pixels; intuitively, this cue encodes how much movement characterizes a patch. The second cue is the flow direction entropy $E_{\mathrm{dir}}(x)$, , calculated over the related flow direction values (opportunely quantized). The entropy is defined as

$$E_{\mathrm{dir}}(x) = -\sum_{i=1}^{d} p(x_i) \log p(x_i) \tag{1}$$

where d is the total number of directions, and $p(x_i)$ is the probability to have the direction i in the patch. The entropy $E_{\mathrm{dir}}(x)$ describes the kind of movement in

---

[1] The last two aspects, in order to be studied seriously, imply the availability of a background behavioral model, which is not the case here; we thus leave such analyses to future studies. Finally, the augmented video summarization application implies multimedia aspects that cannot be dealt with here.

the patch: high entropy values mean random directions, while low values address homogeneous movement in the patch (a similar use of this entropic descriptor has been exploited in [5]). The last two measures are the x, y patch centroid coordinates. In other words, at each time step, each patch is described as a 4D point.

The segmentation occurs in two steps: first, a Gaussian clustering with automatic model selection [6] is applied on the values of all the patches in a given time frame. This way, an instantaneous grouping is inferred. This process is replicated for all the T frames.

At this point, a $N \times N$ similarity matrix is built, containing at entry i, j how many times patches i and j have been in the same cluster. Making the similarity matrix as a distance (computing the reciprocal) it is possible to perform single link hierarchical clustering, and to obtain the spectator segmentation, which partitions the scene in regions where the behavior of the crowd is similar (in terms of the measures quoted above).

For each region r, a *local* level of excitement is estimated by computing the value:

$$Exc(r) = \frac{I(r) \times E_{\text{dir}}(r)}{E_{\text{int}}(r)^2} \qquad (2)$$

over a short time interval (in the order of seconds); here, $E_{\text{int}}(r)$ is the entropy of the motion flow *intensities* at a given time step. The rationale of this measure is that we consider as an high excitement for a group of people an intense movement (high $I(r)$), with diverse directions (high $E_{\text{dir}}(r)$), computed in a coordinated fashion for all people belonging to that region (low E_{int}).

Finally, the average of $Exc(r)$ over all frames is considered as the excitement cue in a given interval for the region r.

2.2   Event Segmentation

The event segmentation task is meant to highlight events that globally trigger the excitement of the spectator crowd, against periods in which the level of excitement is generally low. To such aim, the intensity and the entropy of all the patches are collected at each frame and averaged, obtaining a single pair of values. Replicating this process for all frames gives a 2D signal which can be quantized in an unsupervised fashion by Mean Shift. In this case Mean Shift has been preferred to the Gaussian clustering, since pooling together the signal values of an entire sequence leads to highly irregular distributions, proper for a non parametric treatment.

After the quantization, looking at the mean values of each obtained cluster may serve to get insight on the kind of event being modeled. For example, clusters with high intensity and high entropy may be originated by an interesting event happened in the game.

3   Experiments

In order to test our framework, we built a novel repository which consists of videos taken during the 2013 IIHF Ice Hockey U18 World Championship, partially played in Asiago from the 7th to the 13th of April 2013. In particular, two entire matches were recorded (Italy VS Norway, Italy VS Slovenia), each by two cameras, mounted frontally at a distance of about 25 meters from the spectators' stand. Each camera was pointing at an half of the whole stand, the zoom being fixed. Therefore, for each match we have two sequences, further divided in 3 as the times of the hockey play. This resulted in 12 videos at 30 fps, with a resolution of 640x480 pixels for a total duration of about 6 hours. All videos were manually labeled by highlighting the main actions of the game, especially the fouls, shots and goals. Italy VS Norway ended 1-12, while Italy VS Slovenia 3-2.

The experiments have been partitioned in two groups. In the former, we focus on the spectators segmentation and the excitement calculation; in the latter we perform event segmentation (see Sec. 1). In all cases, a grid of rectangular patches of size 40×80 was built, with the patches overlapping for an half of their size, in both dimensions. Flow was computed on the entire scene each 10 frames, so we have 3 processed frames per second; after that, the flow direction was quantized in five values (up, down, left, right, none) where the fifth value corresponded to all those flow vectors whose intensity was inferior to a given threshold $I = 0.8$.

3.1   Spectators Segmentation and Excitement Calculation

The whole footage was analyzed by temporal windows of 3 minutes length, overlapped by 10 seconds. For each window, we computed first the frame-based Gaussian clustering and subsequently the temporal hierarchical clustering. This way, for each window we get interesting spectators segmentations, clearly explaining the occurred events; for longer windows, the segmentation tends to discriminate solely the presence of the crowd against the background. Some segmentation results are shown in Fig. 1 and Fig. 2.

In Fig. 1, the Norwegian stand is analyzed, in relation to a sequence of 3 minutes extracted from the first time of the Italy-Norway match. As shown in Figure 1b), we have 3 regions, one corresponding to the background (region 1), the other two (regions 2 and 3) focusing on the crowd. Looking at the dendrogram, one can see that the crowd regions are closer than the background, which is reasonable; the excitement level is shown as the color of the regions, highlighting region 3 (dark red) of highly excited people, continuously moving, clapping their hands, shaking flags and yelling; the other region, 2, shows people who are more quite, and in fact the zoomed image in the light red box of Figure 1d) shows a sitting spectator only shaking the flag. Of the focused images, the first one shows a spectator of the background region (blue): this person moves very little for the whole duration of the video and doesn't exult for the goal.

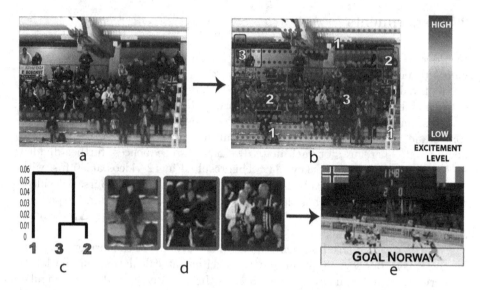

Fig. 1. Spectators segmentation and excitement calculation; a) an example frame of the sequence; b) spectator segmentation result, where the regions are colored considering their mean excitement level; c) dendrogram of the temporal clustering; d) zoomed images, highlighting the behavior of people of the different regions e) a frame of the match played in the considered interval.

In Fig. 2 we show the spectators segmentation and excitement calculation related to a sequence of 3 minutes extracted from the second time of the Italy-Norway match. In this case, we focus on a different stands area, where many Norwegian and some Italian supporters are blended. The sequence reports two goals, one for team. The segmentation gives surprising results, being able to distinguish 5 regions (4 plus the background). Regions 2 and 3 individuate Italian supporters, while regions 4 and 5 show Norwegian fans. The excitement calculation shows that Norwegian supporters are more energetic (at the end of the sequence the score was 5-1 for Norway) than the Italians. Excluding the background, the most quiet region is 2: probably, due to the mixing of the opposite teams, people prefer to be quiet not to offend fans of the other team.

3.2   Event Segmentation

For the event segmentation, we analyze the video for the entire duration of a game time to identify the salient moments for the audience. All the 12 videos are analyzed by considering a time window of 2 seconds with 1 second of overlapping. The bandwidth parameter of Mean Shift was obtained experimentally, and is kept the same for each match. Depending on the choice of bandwidth, different actions of the game can be detected, such as goals or shots on. For the Italy–Norway match a bandwidth value of 0.181 was fixed and 0.1464 for Italy–Slovenia.

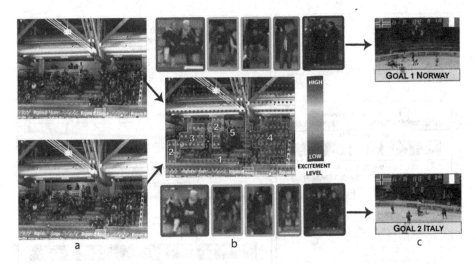

Fig. 2. Spectators segmentation and excitement calculation; a) two different frames of the sequence, the first extracted during the Norwegian goal, the second during the Italian goal. b) in the middle the spectator segmentation result, where the regions are colored considering their mean excitement level. Above and below zoomed images, highlighting the behavior of people in the different regions related with the goals of the different teams (Norwegians on top, Italians on bottom) c) the two goals.

The obtained results show that in the Italy–Norway match, the most salient events detected for the Norwegian spectators are 16, including 11 goals scored and 2 spectacular shots, the other 3 are false positives caused by people arriving or leaving from the stands at the start or end of the game time. For the Italian spectators, instead, only 3 salient events were detected, 1 goal of Italy, 1 goal of Norway and 1 is a false positive caused by spectators leaving at the end of the match.

On the other hand, in the Italy–Slovenia match spectators are mainly Italian and two different stands are filmed, but the results are mixed. The salient events detected are 9, including 3 Italian goals and 1 nice Italian shot. The other 5 events are false positives always related to people arriving or leaving.

An example of these results is shown in Figure 3. Plot A shows how the two different spectators crowds get excited by different events. Norwegian spectators went crazy at the goal of Norway, while Italians, quite as it was to be expected, when Italy scored a goal. To be noticed also the yellow box detected for the Italian spectators, in the moments immediately following the Norwegian goal, this is because Italians argue against Norwegian players.

Plot B, instead, shows the results calculated on Norwegian spectators over the whole the first time. We can see that the 4 goals are well detected as salient events by Mean Shift, but also another event wowed people, a great shot of a Norwegian player. The last yellow box in the strip shows the end of the first time, when the audience gets up and leaves the stand.

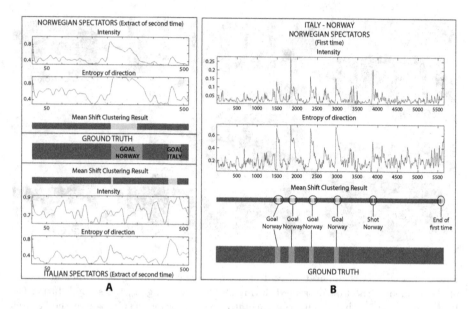

Fig. 3. Salient events detection. Plot A shows the results over the same video considered in Figure 2. Here, the extracted flow intensity and entropy of flow direction of both Norwegian and Italian spectators are shown. The small bars show the results of Mean Shift clustering (the yellow boxes represent detections of salient events). These bars are compared to the ground truth (the bigger bar in the middle) where goals are indicated (green bars). Plot B shows the same results over the first time of the Italy - Norway match, by filming Norwegian spectators.

4   Conclusions

The study of spectators crowd dynamics offers new perspectives in the crowd modeling field. In this paper we have performed a preliminary study, first of all reasoning on the possible applications that can be developed in such a scenario, and presenting effective implementations for some of them; in particular, we showed how spectators can be segmented on the basis of their behavior, how their excitement level can be inferred, and how the observed show can be segmented, by looking exclusively at the crowd activity. Much more can be done, by employing more sophisticated models: dynamic Bayesian networks may embed spatial and temporal reasoning in a unique model; gesture recognition, face detection and expression recognition may provide detailed cues to better understand the nature of the spectators activities, allowing the discrimination between supporting, heckling or just watching, absent in the present work. Further developments may be achieved by adopting different sensors, like microphones, infrared and pan-tilt-zoom cameras.

An important theme to be inquired is the establishment of the ground truth for such kinds of scenarios. In this paper we have adopted a sort of "expert based ground truth", in that we have compared our findings with what had been explained in sociological theories. Alternatively, a more complete approach of this kind (expert) would be based on an ethnographic study: in that case the ground truth would be built on the basis of participant observation carried out by several ethnographers (team ethnography), doing fieldwork on the stands of an arena, stadium, amphitheater, etc. This, moreover, could be complemented with ethnomethodologically oriented videoanalysis (see [10]). A completely different approach to ground truth would be to found it in a more "bottom-up" way, by asking directly to those belonging to the crowd, either exactly the crowd that was attending the recorded event, or, more generically, people that can report about an experience of participation to a public event as a viewer. Even in this case, there are various ways to implement such approach, ranging from structured questionnaires to in-depth interviews.

Notwithstanding all that have already been mentioned, of course privacy and ethical issues should also be taken more seriously into account in the nearest future developments of this study.

Acknowledgments. This work is part of the Oz ("Observing the attention") project, financed by the Winter Universiade Trentino 2013 Educational Programme.

D. Conigliaro, F. Setti, C. Bassetti and R. Ferrario are supported by the VisCoSo project grant, financed by the Autonomous Province of Trento through the "Team 2011" funding programme.

References

1. Andrade, E.L., Blunsden, S., Fisher, R.B.: Modelling crowd scenes for event detection. In: ICPR, pp. 175–178 (2006), http://dx.doi.org/10.1109/ICPR.2006.806
2. Berlonghi, A.: Undestanding and planning for different spectator crowds. Safety Science 18, 239–247 (1995)
3. Chan, A.B., Vasconcelos, N.: Bayesian poisson regression for crowd counting. In: ICCV, pp. 545–551 (2009)
4. Cristani, M., Murino, V., Vinciarelli, A.: Socially intelligent surveillance and monitoring: Analysing social dimensions of physical space. In: CVPRW, pp. 51–58 (2010)
5. Cristani, M., Pesarin, A., Vinciarelli, A., Crocco, M., Murino, V.: Look at who's talking: Voice activity detection by automated gesture analysis. In: AML Workshops, pp. 72–80 (2011)
6. Figueiredo, M., Jain, A.: Unsupervised learning of finite mixture models. PAMI 24(3), 381–396 (2002)
7. Goffman, E.: Behaviour in Public Places. Free Press of Glencloe. Notes on the Social Organization of Gatherings (1963)
8. Goldstein, J., Arms, R.: Effects of observing athletic contests on ostility. Sociometry 34(1), 83–90 (1971)
9. Guyot, G.W., Byrd, G.R., Caudle, R.: Classroom setting: An expression of situational territoriality in humans. Small Group Behavior 11, 120–128 (1980)
10. Heath, C., Hindmarsh, J., Luff, P.: Video in Qualitative Research. Analysing Social Interaction in Everyday Life. Sage, London (2010)

11. Kaya, N., Burgess, B.: Territoriality: Seat preferences in different types of classroom arrangements. Environment and Behavior 39(6), 859–876 (2007)
12. Kratz, L., Nishino, K.: Anomaly detection in extremely crowded scenes using spatio-temporal motion pattern models. In: CVPR, pp. 1446–1453 (2009)
13. Kratz, L., Nishino, K.: Tracking with local spatio-temporal motion patterns in extremely crowded scenes. In: CVPR, pp. 693–700 (2010)
14. Laptev, I.: On space-time interest points. Int. J. Comput. Vision 64(2-3), 107–123 (2005), http://dx.doi.org/10.1007/s11263-005-1838-7
15. Mahadevan, V., Li, W., Bhalodia, V., Vasconcelos, N.: Anomaly detection in crowded scenes. In: CVPR, pp. 1975–1981 (2010)
16. Raghavendra, R., Del Bue, A., Cristani, M., Murino, V.: Abnormal crowd behavior detection by social force optimization. In: HBU, pp. 134–145 (2011), http://dx.doi.org/10.1007/978-3-642-25446-8_15
17. Roadburg, A.: Factors precipitating fan violence: a comparison of professional soccer in britain and north america. The British Journal of Sociology 31(2), 265–276 (1980)
18. Sand, P., Teller, S.: Particle video: Long-range motion estimation using point trajectories. Int. J. Comput. Vision 80(1), 72–91 (2008), http://dx.doi.org/10.1007/s11263-008-0136-6
19. Zhan, B., Monekosso, D., Remagnino, P., Velastin, S., Xu, L.Q.: Crowd analysis: A survey. Machine Vision Applications 19(5-6), 345–357 (2008), http://dx.doi.org/10.1007/s00138-008-0132-4
20. Zhong, H., Shi, J., Visontai, M.: Detecting unusual activity in video. In: CVPR, pp. 819–826 (2004)

JAR-Aibo: A Multi-view Dataset for Evaluation of Model-Free Action Recognition Systems

Marco Körner and Joachim Denzler

Friedrich Schiller University of Jena
Computer Vision Group
Ernst-Abbe-Platz 3, 07743 Jena, Germany
{marco.koerner,joachim.denzler}@uni-jena.de
http://www.inf-cv.uni-jena.de

Abstract. We present a novel multi-view dataset for evaluating model-free action recognition systems. Superior to existing datasets, it covers 56 distinct action classes. Each of them was performed ten times by remotely controlled SONY ERS-7 AIBO robot dogs observed by six distributed and synchronized cameras at 17 fps and VGA resolution. In total, our dataset contains 576 sequences. Baseline results show its applicability for benchmarking model-free action recognition methods.

Keywords: action recognition, behaviour understanding, dataset.

1 Introduction and Recent Work

The automatic recognition of action and behaviour from video streams gained more and more scientific interest during the last decades, as pointed out by recent reviews[14,1,3]. In order to evaluate and compare algorithms for action recognition or behavior understanding, open-access datasets of high complexity are evidently needed. During the recent years of research on this topic, numerous of those datasets were published and used by the community. The vast majority is designed for single-view approaches, while datasets for multi-view scenarios are rare and only cover a small number of distinct action classes.

We present a multi-view dataset for evaluating model-free action recognition systems. To especially assess the performance of model-free approaches, 56 remotely triggered actions performed by SONY ERS-7 AIBO robot dogs were captured by six synchronized cameras resulting in 576 multi-view sequences.

1.1 Single-View Datasets

As the scientific efforts started to concentrate on recognition of actions and activities captured by single cameras, most of the early datasets show single persons performing basic actions captured from only one view in front of simple and static backgrounds. The most prominent are the Weizmann[7] and the KTH[16] dataset, where the latter shows varying clothing of the actors.

A. Petrosino, L. Maddalena, P. Pala (Eds.): ICIAP 2013 Workshops, LNCS 8158, pp. 527–535, 2013.

Table 1. Comparison of recent publicly available datasets for multi-view action recognition. The `JAR-Aibo` dataset mentioned in the last column will be presented in this paper.

	Dataset					
	`IXMAS`	`i3dPost`	`MuHAVi`	`VideoWeb`	`CASIA Action`	`JAR-Aibo`
Year	2006	2009	2010	2010	2007	2013
Application	Human Action Recognition	Human Movement Recognition, 3d Human Action Recognition	Human Action Recognition	Complex Human Activity Recognition	Human Behaviour Analysis	Action and Activity Recognition
Published in	[19]	[6]	[17]	[4]	[18]	—
Number of references[3]	59	10	11	11	18	—
Technicals						
Cameras	5	8	8	4,7,8	3	6
Format	390×291 px, png	1920×1080 px, png	720×576 px, jpg	640×480 px, mpeg1/jpg	320×240 px, avi	640×480 px, png
Frequency	23 fps	25 fps	25 fps	30 fps	25 fps	17 fps
Synchronized	(✓)	✓	✗	✗	(✓)	✓
Content						
Scenery	indoor	indoor	indoor	outdoor	outdoor	indoor
Number of actions	11	8	14	10	8	56
Interactions	none	none, Person-to-Person	none	none, Person-to-Person	none, Person-to-Person, Person-to-Object	none, Actor-to-Actors
Number of actors	13	11	17	2	24	1 (up to 4 in interactions subset)
Repetitions per action and actor	3	1	*several*	*several*	*several*	10
Ground truth data						
Action labels	✓	✓	✓	✓	✓	✓
Calibration	✓	✓	✓	✗	✗	✓
Silhouettes	✓	✗	✓	✗	✗	✗
Bounding boxes	✗	✗	✓	✗	✗	✓
3d models	✓	✓	✗	✗	✗	✗
Background images	✓	✓	✗	✗	✗	✓

As the recognition rates of many approaches obtained for these data got reasonably high, many other datasets were developed over time, *e.g.* CAVIAR[5], Hollywood 1/2[9,11], UCF Sports[15], UCF Youtube[10], *etc.* They concentrate on more realistic actions captured in uncontrolled environments showing changing lighting conditions, background, and activities.

Furthermore, datasets like BEHAVE[2], TV Human Interaction[13], *etc.* were designed to capture person-to-person interactions specifically.

1.2   Multi-view Datasets

After years of research, the interest today moves towards the detection and recognition of actions simultaneously captured by multiple cameras. Nevertheless, only a few datasets with specific limitations exist so far, as summarized and compared in Tab. 1.

The most commonly used is the IXMAS[19] dataset, which contains sequences of 11 types of actions performed three times by 13 actors in total. Images were recorded roughly synchronized at a resolution of 390×291 px at 23 fps and saved with lossless png compression. Background images, action labels, as well as body silhouettes and 3d models are delivered with the dataset. The i3DPost[6] dataset synchronously captured high-definition videos (1920×1080 px) at 25 fps in lossless png format from 8 points of view. A selection of 8 real-life actions and interactions was performed by 11 actors only once. The distributors provide background images, action labels, and 3d body models. The MuHAVi[17] dataset contains 8 views (720×576 px) with 14 actions performed several times by 17 actors. The images were recorded non-synchronously and stored in lossy jpeg format. Only action labels and body silhouettes are available with the data.

While these datasets mentioned so far were captured under controlled conditions and show a static and simple background, there are also some less commonly used outdoor datasets available, like VideoWeb[4] and CASIA action[18].

2   Multi-view Action Recognition Dataset

As can be seen, each of the already published datasets shows benefits and drawbacks, which makes them suitable or unsuitable for specific applications and problems. For this reason, we aim to fill a gap by providing a new dataset for evaluation of action recognition systems, especially for the case of appearance-based approaches without any higher-order model knowledge. The selection of actions recorded for our dataset includes well-distinguishable as well as rather similar actions. In this section we will introduce our setup and the provided data.

2.1   Camera Setup and Calibration

We created a setup of six interconnected and calibrated RGB SONY DFW-L500 FireWire cameras distributed around a rectangular region of size $2 \, \text{m} \times 3 \, \text{m}$ at a height of $90 - 100 \, \text{cm}$ as sketched in Fig. 1a. All cameras were oriented to

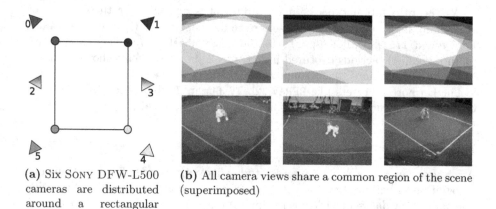

(a) Six Sony DFW-L500 cameras are distributed around a rectangular scene

(b) All camera views share a common region of the scene (superimposed)

Fig. 1. The setup of the dataset: (a) distribution of cameras, (b) example views with superimposed camera fields of view

    (a)   (b)   (c)   (d)

Fig. 2. Images were captured synchronously: (a),(c) and (b),(d) show succeeding frames of views 2 and 4 of the dataset, respectively

observe a common area of the scene, as displayed in Fig. 1b. Images were captured synchronously (*c.f.* Fig. 2) at VGA resolution (640 × 480 px) and a frame rate of approximatively 17 fps. We used the png image file format in order to avoid compression artifacts and loss of quality. Further camera parameters, *e.g.* the shutter speed, aperture size, and gain, were adapted once in the beginning of our recordings and kept further untouched. Fig. 4 visualizes the different lightning conditions per camera.

    Calibration of the intrinsic and extrinsic parameters of our camera system, was done using the OpenCV library and a "circular grid" calibration pattern and resulted in RMS errors of about 0.2 px (intrinsic) and 0.18 cm (extrinsic).

2.2   Individuals

We decided to use up to four Sony ERS-7 AIBO robot dogs (*c.f.* Fig. 3a) due to their ability to perform a variety of actions in different poses triggered remotely

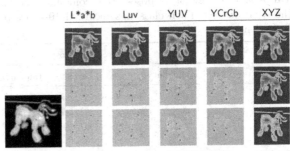

L*a*b   Luv   YUV   YCrCb   XYZ

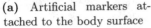

(a) Artificial markers attached to the body surface

(b) Image captured by a SONY DFW-L500 camera and the corresponding channels of different color spaces

Fig. 3. In order to assist model-based approaches, colored markers were attached to the Aibo body. These colors were chosen to be easily distinguishable in appropriate color spaces.

and in order to specifically benchmark model-free approaches. Comparable to human actors, their anatomy offers many degrees of freedom, which enables them to perform complex actions and to move smoothly. All robot dogs were wireless connected to a central computer, which was used to trigger certain actions. The body surface of the Aibo used in this dataset is bright, glossy and almost untextured. To allow comparisons between model-free and model-based approaches, we applied markers roughly at locations of anatomical joints. Marker colors where chosen to be easily detectable in various color spaces, as illustrated in Fig. 3b. The right half of the body was indicated by an additional blue marker.

2.3 Recorded Actions

While many of the existing datasets only cover a small number of different classes, our dataset was designed to show a high variety of activities. In total, 36 actions performed in up to 3 poses and additionally 6 pose transitions were recorded, which results in a total number of 56 different action classes. Each of them was performed 10 times at different locations and orientations within the scene. Our selection contains rather simple actions (*e.g.* bow, stretch) as well as complex activities (*e.g.* dance*, lookaround*). Some actions are easy to distinguish, while others only differ slightly in their type, speed, or order of execution (*e.g.* hello, greeting). Tab. 2 shows a summary of all recorded pose-action combinations and pose transitions included in our dataset. Additionally, we recorded 16 sequences of interactions between up to 4 dogs, some of them operating in a fully autonomous mode, others acting triggered by the operator.

A selection of actions included in the dataset is shown in Fig. 4.

Table 2. Overview of all pose-action combinations and pose transitions recorded for the Aibo dataset. Each class was recorded 10 times performed in different positions and orientations.   ✓– availlable, ✗– not availlable

Action	Pose			Action	Pose			Action	Pose		
	sit	stand	lie		sit	stand	lie		sit	stand	lie
sit	✗	✓	✓	knockdown	✗	✓	✗	dance2	✗	✓	✗
stand	✓	✗	✓	angry	✓	✓	✗	dance3	✗	✓	✗
lie	✓	✓	✗	disappointed	✓	✓	✗	dance4	✗	✓	✗
				stretch	✓	✗	✗	dance5	✗	✓	✗
greeting	✓	✓	✗	yawn	✓	✓	✗	liftleg	✗	✓	✗
hello	✓	✓	✗	scratch	✓	✓	✗	header	✗	✓	✗
welcomeback	✓	✓	✗	lookaround1	✓	✓	✗	kickright	✗	✓	✗
goodnight	✓	✓	✗	lookaround2	✓	✓	✗	scootleft	✓	✗	✗
bow	✓	✓	✗	snif	✗	✗	✓	scootright	✓	✗	✗
comehere	✓	✓	✗	struggle	✓	✓	✗	pickupbone	✓	✓	✗
yes	✓	✓	✗	bark2	✗	✓	✗	releasebone	✓	✓	✗
no	✓	✓	✗	dance1	✗	✓	✗	touchmyback	✓	✓	✗

2.4   Ground Truth Data

All sequences are distributed as frame-wise png images within an unique path such as $DATAHOME/<pose>_<action>/<sequence>/<camera>_<frame-id>. We additionally provide background images for each view and bounding boxes of foreground detections. For the interaction subset, a list of action labels sorted by their temporal occurrences is provided for each sequence.

3   Baseline Results

In order to show the applicability of our dataset, we present baseline results for model-free action recognition. For this reason, we used *Temporal Self-Similarity Maps (SSM)* as recently proposed by Körner *et al.*[8], where image sequences are represented by variations of frame-wise extracted low-level features. Within this framework, a SSM is a square-shaped matrix, which entries represent the pairwise similarity (or dissimilarity) of all frames. As can be seen in Fig. 5a, different atomic action primitives induce specific pattern structures in the corresponding SSM. Furthermore, these structures can be assumed to be stable under viewpoint changes. For a more detailed description of this method, we refer to [8].

In our experiment, we created SSMs by comparing truncated Fourier descriptors of the single frames. SIFT features were extracted from the diagonal lines of each SSM. After generating a global dictionary of features seen in the testing set, each SSM can be represented by a *Bag of Words* histogram. For training and testing we used disjoint partitions of all camera views. Classification was performed following a 10-fold cross validation scheme by using a *Gaussian Process* classifier and a histogram intersection kernel. Fig. 5b shows the performance of this approach applied to the JAR-Aibo dataset. When applied to the IXMAS[19]

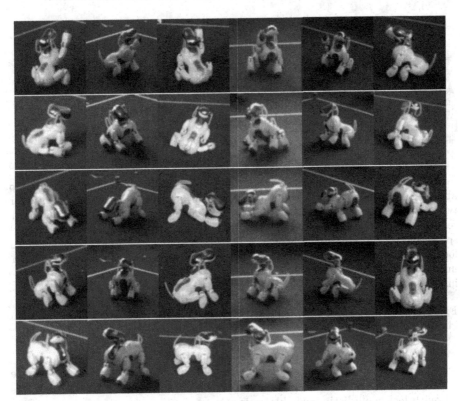

Fig. 4. Example images from the dataset. Each column represents one camera view, each row show one Aibo action exemplar.

dataset, the same method produced recognition rates of about 79%, which is competitive to other model-free methods. This shows that our dataset can be used to benchmark a wide range of appearance-based methods for action recognition.

4 Summary

We presented a new extensive dataset for automatic evaluation of appearance-based action recognition approaches. It contains a total number of 576 sequences showing 56 actions performed by remotely triggered SONY ERS-7 AIBO robot dogs observed by 6 synchronized cameras including 16 sequences showing interactions between several Aibos. This dataset shows some challenging properties, which have to be faced:

- Since the dataset was recorded in a windowed lab, the illumination conditions change from view to view as well as from sequence to sequence (*c.f.* Fig. 4).
- While numerous approaches for action recognition operate model-based, there are few standard techniques to extract the body pose of non-human actors [12]. Hence, this dataset is suitable to evaluate model-free approaches.

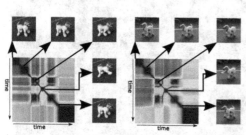 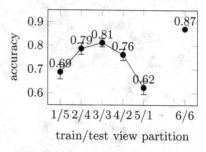

(a)   Two SSMs obtained for an stand_kickright action captured from two viewpoints. Cold and warm colors represent high and low self-similarities, respectively. Action primitives induce similar local patterns in the corresponding SSM even under changes of viewpoint, illumination, or image quality.

(b)   Results obtained on JAR-Aibo dataset: averaged recognition rates for different $n_{training}/n_{testing}$ view partitions. Errorbars show one standard deviation. Best results were obtained when using the same amount of cameras for training and testing.

Fig. 5. Multi-View Action Recognition by Temporal Self-Similarity Maps: (a) main idea of the SSM approach, (b) performance on JAR-Aibo dataset

– Due to the large number of action classes included in the dataset, the chance to confuse semantically related actions is higher compared to other datasets with less, well-distinguishable actions.

We also gave baseline results to show the applicability of our dataset for benchmarking a wide range of generic model-free action recognition approaches, as they are not limited to the case of recognizing actions performed by human actors.

We hope that this dataset is of use for the research community and can help to further improve the development of this pulsating and important field of research. The complete dataset can be downloaded from http://www.inf-cv.uni-jena.de/JAR-Aibo.

Acknowledgements. The authors would like to thank Anna Balbekova for technical assistance during acquisition of this dataset.

References

1. Aggarwal, J.K., Ryoo, M.S.: Human activity analysis: A review. ACM Computing Surveys 43(3), 16:1–16:43 (2011)
2. Blunsden, S., Fisher, B.R.: The behave video dataset: ground truthed video for multi-person behavior classification. Annals of the BMVA (4), 1–11 (2010)
3. Chaquet, J.M., Carmona, E.J., Fernández-Caballero, A.: A survey of video datasets for human action and activity recognition. Computer Vision and Image Understanding 117(6), 633–659 (2013)

4. Denina, G., Bhanu, B., Nguyen, H., Ding, C., Kamal, A., Ravishankar, C., Roy-Chowdhury, A., Ivers, A., Varda, B.: Videoweb dataset for multi-camera activities and non-verbal communication. In: Bhanu, B., Ravishankar, C.V., Roy-Chowdhury, A.K., Aghajan, H., Terzopoulos, D. (eds.) Distributed Video Sensor Networks, pp. 335–347 (2011)
5. Fisher, R.B.: The pets04 surveillance ground truth data set. In: Proceedings of the 6th IEEE International Workshop on Performance Evaluation of Tracking and Surveillance (PETS 2004), pp. 1–5 (2004)
6. Gkalelis, N., Kim, H., Hilton, A., Nikolaidis, N., Pitas, I.: The i3dpost multi-view and 3D human action/interaction database. In: Proceedings of the 2009 Conference for Visual Media Production, pp. 159–168 (2009)
7. Gorelick, L., Blank, M., Shechtman, E., Irani, M., Basri, R.: Actions as space-time shapes. IEEE Transactions on Pattern Analysis and Machine Intelligence (TPAMI) 29(12), 2247–2253 (2007)
8. Körner, M., Denzler, J.: Temporal self-similarity for appearance-based action recognition in multi-view setups ((to appear)). In: Wilson, R., Hancock, E., Bors, A., Smith, W. (eds.) CAIP 2013, Part I. LNCS, vol. 8047, pp. 163–171. Springer, Heidelberg (2013)
9. Laptev, I., Marszalek, M., Schmid, C., Rozenfeld, B.: Learning realistic human actions from movies. In: Proceedings of the 21st IEEE Conference on Computer Vision and Pattern Recognition (CVPR), pp. 1–8 (2008)
10. Liu, J., Luo, J., Shah, M.: Recognizing realistic actions from videos "in the wild". In: Proceedings of the 2nd IEEE Conference on Computer Vision and Pattern Recognition (CVPR), pp. 1996–2003 (2009)
11. Marszalek, M., Laptev, I., Schmid, C.: Actions in context. In: Proceedings of the 22nd IEEE Conference on Computer Vision and Pattern Recognition (CVPR), pp. 2929–2936 (2009)
12. Nierobisch, T., Hoffmann, F.: Appearance based pose estimation of aibo's. In: IEEE Conference on Mechatronics and Robotics, vol. 3, pp. 942–947 (2004)
13. Patron, A., Marszalek, M., Zisserman, A., Reid, I.: High five: Recognising human interactions in tv shows. In: Proceedings of the 21st British Machine Vision Conference (BMVA), pp. 50.1–50.11 (2010)
14. Poppe, R.: A survey on vision-based human action recognition. Image and Vision Computing 28(6), 976–990 (2010)
15. Rodriguez, M., Ahmed, J., Shah, M.: Action mach a spatio-temporal maximum average correlation height filter for action recognition. In: Proceedings of the 21st IEEE Conference on Computer Vision and Pattern Recognition (CVPR), pp. 1–8 (2008)
16. Schuldt, C., Laptev, I., Caputo, B.: Recognizing human actions: a local svm approach. In: Proceedings of the 17th International Conference on Pattern Recognition (ICPR), vol. 3, pp. 32–36 (2004)
17. Singh, S., Velastin, S., Ragheb, H.: Muhavi: A multicamera human action video dataset for the evaluation of action recognition methods. In: Proceedings of the 7th IEEE International Conference on Advanced Video and Signal-Based Surveillance (AVSS), pp. 48–55 (2010)
18. Wang, Y., Huang, K., Tan, T.: Human activity recognition based on r transform. In: Proceedings of the 20th IEEE Conference on Computer Vision and Pattern Recognition (CVPR), pp. 1–8 (2007)
19. Weinland, D., Boyer, E., Ronfard, R.: Action recognition from arbitrary views using 3d exemplars. In: Proceedings of the 11th IEEE International Conference on Computer Vision (ICCV), pp. 1–7 (2007)

Head Dynamic Analysis: A Multi-view Framework

Ashish Tawari and Moham M. Trivedi

University of California, San Diego, USA
{atawari,mtrivedi}@ucsd.edu

Abstract. Analysis of driver's head behavior is an integral part of driver monitoring system. In particular, head pose and dynamics are strong indicators of driver's focus of attention. In this paper, we present a distributed camera framework for head pose estimation with emphasis on the ability to operate reliably and continuously. To evaluate the proposed framework, we collected a novel head pose dataset of naturalistic on-road driving in urban streets and freeways. As oppose to utilizing all the data collected during the whole ride where for large portion of the time driver is front facing, we use data during particular maneuvers typically involving large head deviation from frontal pose. While this makes the dataset challenging, it provides an opportunity to evaluate algorithms during non-frontal glances which are of special interest to driver safety. We conduct a comparative study between proposed multi-view based approach and single-view based approach. Our analyses show promising results.

1 Introduction

Automatic analysis of driver behaviors is becoming an increasingly important aspect in the design of Driver Assistance System (DAS). With driver distraction and inattention being one of the prominent causes of automotive collision, we require new sensing approaches with ability to continuously infer driver's focus of attention. Eye gaze and movement are considered good measures to identify individual's focus of attention. Vision based systems provide non-contact and non-invasive solution, and are commonly used for gaze tracking. However, such systems are highly susceptible to illumination changes, particularly, in real-world driving scenario. Eye-gaze tracking methods using corneal reflection with infrared illumination have been primarily used in indoor [5] but are vulnerable to sunlight. While precise gaze direction provides useful information, coarse gaze direction, approximated by head pose and its dynamics, are often sufficient [6,3]. Head pose is a strong indicator of a driver's field-of-view and current focus of attention. It is intrinsically linked with visual gaze estimation, the ability to characterize the direction in which a person is looking. This paper presents an automatic head pose tracking system for uninterrupted driver monitoring using distributed cameras.

The two main contributions of this paper are the design of the hardware setup and annotation strategy for 'ground truth' data collection, and the development

A. Petrosino, L. Maddalena, P. Pala (Eds.): ICIAP 2013 Workshops, LNCS 8158, pp. 536–544, 2013.

of the multi-sensory framework for improved head pose estimation. Also, important for the driving application is the design of the experiments to evaluate the realistic requirement of the vision based system in driver assistance technology. Towards this end, we gather dataset which targets spatially large head turns (away from frontal pose) since those are the times interesting events, critical to driver safety, happens. We present comparisons between single- and multi-view systems using errors statistics in yaw, pitch and roll rotation as well as the failure-rate, percentage of the time system's output is not reliable.

2   Related Studies

In driving context, challenges lie in the design and development of a system which is robust and reliable, and can operate in a 'continuous' manner. For driver monitoring task, tracking driver's head has shown much more robust performance than that of tracking eyes. In the driving distraction studies, it is suggested that non-forward glances with detectable head deviation are more severe than that without head deviation. For either prolonged or large-eccentricity, because it is more comfortable, most drivers are likely to use a combination of head and eye movements to direct their gaze to the target. It is argued that although eye-gaze measures are better, head pose still provides good estimate of driver distraction [13]. Also, in meeting room scenario, which provides more free-viewing-like opportunity, it is shown that head orientation contributes over 68% to overall gaze direction while focus of attention estimation based on head orientation alone can get 88% accuracy [11].

While there exist number of studies for head-pose estimation and tracking, their performance in real-world driving lacks proper evaluation in it's ability to operate continuously. We encourage readers to study a comprehensive survey by Murphy-Chutorian and Trivedi [8] for a good overview of different techniques and approaches for head pose estimation. In our approach, we have used facial feature and their geometric configuration along with a generic 3D face model for head pose estimation. We present some relevant literature using shape feature and geometric configuration.

Methods based on shape features analyze the geometric configuration of facial features to estimate the head orientation. Many of these existing algorithms require certain number of specific features to be visible in the image plane of the camera and use geometric constraints such as face symmetry using lip corners and both eyes [4], anatomical structure of the eye and person specific parameters [1], parallel lines between eye corners and between lip corners [12]. To avoid errors associated with precise localization of detailed facial feature, Ohue et al. proposed simple facial features - the left and right borders, and the center of the face [9]. Along with these features, the authors used a cylindrical face model to find the driver's yaw direction. Meanwhile Lee et. al. [6] used similar shape feature with ellipsoidal face model to improve the yaw estimate when the head rotates significantly.

As oppose to hand design feature and their geometric configuration, our approach can work with any set of distinct features on the face since it utilizes the

3D face model. In recent years, there has been significant advancement in the area of facial feature detection and tracking [10,14]. Their usefulness and the performance for continuous head pose estimation in an unconstrained real world setup is still not clear. It's expected that the performance would degrade as head pose deviates from frontal pose which would be the case with any system with single frontal positioned camera. Towards this end, we propose a simple distributed camera solution and conduct comparative study with single and multi-camera setup. Finally, we collect a real world head-pose dataset of naturalistic driving. Although there exist many head-pose databases ranging from images to videos, our dataset is unique with multiple cameras and consists of events with large head turns. Details of the dataset preparation including hardware setup and annotation strategy are provided in the Section 4.

3   Proposed Multi-view Framework

Spatially large head pose deviation from the frontal pose targeted in this work requires improved operating range of the head pose tracking system. For this, we use distributed cameras where each camera independently computes head pose and their results are then combined to choose the best perspective.

3.1   Appearance Based Head Pose Estimation

Pose from Orthography and Scaling (POS) [2] is used to estimate head pose from the detected facial features. POS requires at least four facial features points in general positions in the image plane and their 3D correspondences. We used generic 3D mean face model which, even though not person specific, shows promising results. For facial feature detection and tracking, we used a variant of Constraint Local Model (CLM) [10] to suit our application.

CLM utilizes parametrized shape model to capture plausible deformation of landmark locations. Using ensemble of landmark detectors, it predicts the locations of the facial landmarks. In [10], the response map of these detectors is represented non-parametrically and the landmarks' locations are optimized via subspace constrained meanshifts while enforcing their joint motion via shape model. The fitting process on an image $I^{(m,n)}$ provides a row vector $P^{(m,n)}$ for each sequence m and frame n containing $l = 66$ detected landmark positions

$$P^{(m,n)} = [x_1, y_1; x_2, y_2; \cdots x_l, y_l]$$

CLM is generally used to fit faces of various orientations, positions and sizes in the image plane. However, when streaming images from a fixed camera looking at the driver's face while driving, there are constraints in orientation, position and size of the face that can be used to further improve facial feature tracking. For each perspective, we estimate the probable face location and face size. When the tracked features are not within the expected region or if the size of the face is beyond what is normal from that perspective, the tracked facial features are rejected. Similarly, if the head pose computed from these facial features is not realizable in a driving scenario, it is also rejected.

Procedure 1. Camera Selection

Input: *prevCam*
Output: *currCam, prevCam*
  Camera is numbered starting from 1 (left most) to N (right most)
  $i \leftarrow prevCam$
  if $i = 0$ **then**
    $i \leftarrow$ INIT()
  else
    if $yaw\_i \geq LEFT\_THR\_i$ **then**
      $i \leftarrow min(i - 1, 1)$
    else if $yaw\_i < RIGHT\_THR\_i$ **then**
      $i \leftarrow max(i + 1, N)$
    end if
  end if
  if Camera i is active **then**
    Comment: *A camera is active if it has measurements.*
    $currCam \leftarrow i$
  else
    $currCam \leftarrow$ INIT()
  end if
  $prevCam \leftarrow currCam$

---

  function INIT()
    For each camera calculate symmetry score S_i
    $S_k = 0 \ \forall k \in$ (Set of inactive camera)
    $i^* \leftarrow \arg\max_i(S_i)$
    if $S_{i^*} = 0$ **then**
      $i^* = 0$
    end if
    return i^*
  end function

3.2 Perspective Selection Procedure

The distributed camera setup tracks head independently in each stream and their decisions are pooled together to choose the 'best' perspective. Procedure 1 details the perspective selection criteria. During the tracking phase, the transition from one perspective to another is achieved using the thresholds in the yaw rotation angle. During initialization due to loss of track or at the very beginning, the camera is chosen based on symmetry of the face from the detected facial features. Higher symmetry-score ensures better frontal pose in the given perspective.

4 Data and Evaluation

4.1 Data Collection and Ground Truth Annotation Strategy

To evaluate our approach, we created head pose dataset consisting of multiple drivers with urban and freeway drives. The LISA-A experimental testbed, as

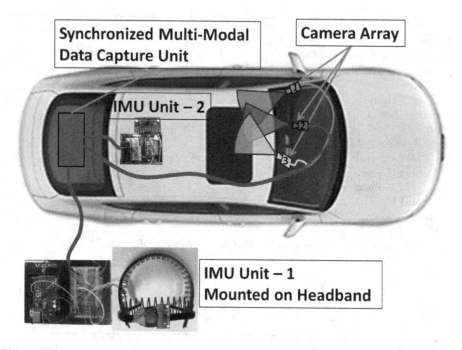

Fig. 1. LISA-A experimental testbed equipped with and capable of time synchronized capture of camera array and multiple Inertial Measurement Units (IMUs)

Fig. 2. An example of time-synchronized data capture from three distributed cameras

seen in Figure 1, was used to collect real-world test data. Three distributed webcameras mounted on A-pillar, on front windshield and near rear view mirror capture face data as shown in Figure 2. These cameras provide 640x360 pixel color video stream at 30fps. In addition, the vehicle is instrumented with Inertial Motion Units (IMUs) with sensors placed on the divers head and fixed at the back of the car to track respective motion. Sensor fusion of the IMUs' data provide

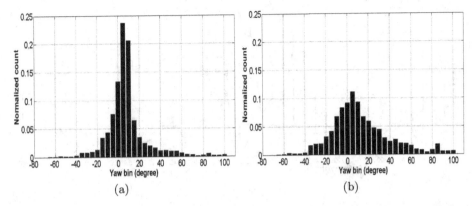

Fig. 3. Histogram of the yaw angle distribution (a) during a typical ride using all the data and (b) using select events in the dataset

Table 1. A list of events considered for evaluation, and their respective count and number of frames

Events	No. of events	Total no. of frames
Right turns	17	5062
Left turns	9	2936
Stop sign	32	7693
Right Lane change	9	1967
Left Lane Change	10	2050
Merge	5	1218
All	82	20926

precise ground truth head pose data for evaluation. Sensor fusion is required since the IMU attached to the drivers head is effected by the car movement, hence the compensation for the same is needed, which in turn, is captured by the IMU rigidly fixed to the car. The multiple IMUs involve calibrated accelerometer- and gyroscope-sensors. The IMU unit however, has some drift associated with the gyroscope, a commonly known phenomenon. This is overcome by resetting angle calculation in the beginning of each event where initial orientation is provided by hand annotation of the respective face image. Since on average each events lasts around 10 seconds the drift during this period is practically non existent.

The automobile was set up to collect data during naturalistic urban and freeway driving. Each of the two subjects drove the vehicle on similar routes through the University of California, San Diego campus in sunny weather condition causing varying lighting condition. The cameras were set to auto-gain and auto-exposure, but these adjustments have to compete with ever-shifting lighting conditions and dramatic lighting shift (e.g. sunlight diffracting around the driver) that at times saturated the camera image. All these situation are part of the evaluation, as they are typical phenomena that occur in natural driving. The placement of the cameras varies slightly for different drivers since at each

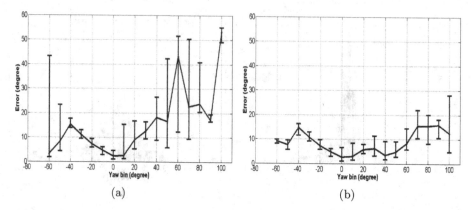

(a)   (b)

Fig. 4. Absolute yaw error vs yaw angle plot. Error bar shows first quartile, median and third quartile statistics. (a) Using single camera setup and (b) using multiple camera setup.

run cameras are secured again, in case they are loosened during the drive. The drives averaged 25 minutes in duration and we analyzed different maneuvers involving large head turns as detailed in the Table 1. During urban drive, the drivers passed through many stop signs and made multiple left/right turns, and while on the freeway, they made merge, multiple lane change etc. maneuvers. Note that it's a challenging data set not just because of the real-world drive but also because data consists of and is concentrated around events with large head movement. Fig 3 shows a typical histogram of yaw angle distribution during a test ride. It can be seen that while considering the entire ride, most of the time (Fig 3(a)) drivers look front. However, the spread of the yaw angle distribution is much more for the chosen events (Fig 3(b)).

4.2   Results

We compare the performance of multi-view approach using all the three cameras with that of single-view approach with front facing camera. We, first, show in Fig 4 the absolute yaw error statistics as a function of ground-truth yaw angle with respect to front camera. The figure shows first-, second- and third quartile of the errors associated with the respective yaw bins. It can be observed that the single camera system quickly loses track with high estimation error beyond 40^0 in either direction. The multi-camera system, on the other hand, is able to keep track over much wider span with better error statistics. For quantitative evaluation over the database, two metrics, mean absolute error (MAE) and failure rate (percentage of the time system's output is not reliable), are used. Head tracking is considered lost if the estimated head pose is not available or is more than 20^0 from the ground truth in either direction for the yaw rotation angle. Number of frames, where head tracking is lost, normalized with the total number of frames over all events gives the failure rate. As shown in Table 2, failure rate of the single-view system is over 20% and that of the multi-view approach is

Table 2. Comparative evaluation of the single- and multi-view framework

Methods	Mean Absolute Error			Failure rate
	Pitch	Yaw	Roll	
Multi-view	11.5°	7.3°	4.1°	10.9%
Single-view	11.1°	8.1°	4.8°	20.7%

~11%, a significant improvement. The MAE for pitch, yaw and roll for both approaches are comparable. This is expected since multi-camera system combines each camera independently and is bounded by the single camera accuracy.

5 Conclusion

Non-frontal glances with large head deviation are of special interest for driver safety. A Driver Assistance System (DAS) monitoring driver face/head is required to be robust and reliable in real-world conditions. Moreover, they need to perform uninterruptedly with high accuracy to be accepted and trusted by the driver. For the design and the development of such system, evaluation over real-world driving dataset is a must. There exist very few real-world naturalistic driving head pose databases. In one such database LISA-P, however, Martin et al. [7] showed using ground truth data that 95% of the time the driver's head pose was within 36° of forward facing in the yaw rotation angle. Therefore, there is a need for evaluating over databases more concentrated on large head movements during naturalistic on-road driving, in order to better evaluate any algorithm. Towards this end, we introduced a low cost hardware solution for ground truth data collection. Furthermore, the collected data is segmented into events with different maneuvers involving large head movement. Since a frontal single-view of the driver is insufficient for tracking head during large movements, we proposed a multi-view framework using distributed cameras. Our analysis using the collected dataset shows that the multi-view framework outperforms the single-view approach with failure rate below 11% while it's over 20% for the latter.

In future studies, we will pursue joint processing of distributed cameras for improved tracking performance. It would also be interesting to see how having more/less number of cameras than in current implementation affects the performance.

References

1. Chen, J., Ji, Q.: 3D gaze estimation with a single camera without ir illumination. In: 19th International Conference on Pattern Recognition, pp. 1–4 (December 2008)
2. Dementhon, D.F., Davis, L.S.: Model-based object pose in 25 lines of code. International Journal of Computer Vision 15, 123–141 (1995)
3. Doshi, A., Trivedi, M.M.: On the roles of eye gaze and head dynamics in predicting driver's intent to change lanes. IEEE Transactions on Intelligent Transportation Systems 10(3), 453–462 (2009)

4. Gee, A., Cipolla, R.: Determining the gaze of faces in images. Image and Vision Computing 12(10), 639–647 (1994)
5. Guestrin, E.D., Eizenman, M.: General theory of remote gaze estimation using the pupil center and corneal reflections. IEEE Trans. Biomed. Engineering 53(6), 1124–1133 (2006)
6. Lee, S.J., Jo, J., Jung, H.G., Park, K.R., Kim, J.: Real-time gaze estimator based on driver's head orientation for forward collision warning system. IEEE Transactions on Intelligent Transportation Systems 12(1), 254–267 (2011)
7. Martin, S., Tawari, A., Chutorian, E.M., Cheng, S.Y., Trivedi, M.M.: On the design and evaluation of robust head pose for visual user interfaces: Algorithms, databases, and comparisons. In: 4th ACM SIGCHI International Conference on Automotive User Interfaces and Interactive Vehicular Applications, AUTO-UI (2012)
8. Murphy-Chutorian, E., Trivedi, M.: Head pose estimation in computer vision: A survey. IEEE Transactions on Pattern Analysis and Machine Intelligence 31(4), 607–626 (2009)
9. Ohue, K., Yamada, Y., Uozumi, S., Tokoro, S., Hattori, A., Hayashi, T.: Development of a new pre-crash safety system. In: SAE 2006 World Congress & Exhibition. SAE Technical Paper 2006-01-1461 (April 3, 2006)
10. Saragih, J., Lucey, S., Cohn, J.: Face alignment through subspace constrained mean-shifts. In: Int. Conf. on Computer Vision, pp. 1034–1041 (2009)
11. Stiefelhagen, R., Zhu, J.: Head orientation and gaze direction in meetings. In: CHI 2002 Extended Abstracts on Human Factors in Computing Systems, CHI EA 2002, pp. 858–859. ACM, New York (2002), http://doi.acm.org/10.1145/506443.506634
12. Wang, J.G., Sung, E.: Em enhancement of 3D head pose estimated by point at infinity. Image and Vision Computing 25(12), 1864–1874 (2007), the age of human computer interaction
13. Zhang, H., Smith, M., Dufour, R.: A final report of safety vehicles using adaptive interface technology: Visual distraction (February 2008), http://www.volpe.dot.gov/coi/hfrsa/work/roadway/saveit/docs/visdistract.doc
14. Zhu, X., Ramanan, D.: Face detection, pose estimation, and landmark localization in the wild. In: 2012 IEEE Conference on Computer Vision and Pattern Recognition (CVPR), pp. 2879–2886. IEEE (2012)

Attention Control
during Distance Learning Sessions

Giuseppe Mastronardi, Vitoantonio Bevilacqua,
Roberto Fortunato Depasquale, and Massimiliano Dellisanti Fabiano Vilardi

Politecnico di Bari, Bari, Italy
{mastrona,bevilacqua,m.dellisantifabiano}@poliba.it,
{robertofortunato.depasquale}@gmail.com

Abstract. The distance learning (DL) is a teaching system that extends
the education beyond the physical barriers, providing access to remote
places and disabilities. The increasing need of procedures for DL certification is now involving biometric approach. An analysis of biometric
techniques is shown in order to ensure the users authentication, to verify
the individual's attention level and then to certificate the learning outcomes. That is necessary to implement a system to identify uniquely the
users and to track both path's carried (visited pages) and use's time, to
have a secure users identification and also validation of the environments
conditions in which they take place during possible tests of certification.
The appropriate biometric technique is appeared the Face Recognition
because it allows a real-time verification of the real presence, low implementation costs by use of webcam and reasonable degree of reliability.
To avoid the influence related to environmental conditions, it has been
realized a modular system that implements Detection and Recognition
operations. The implemented system is able to verify the presence of
learners beyond the screen during lessons or learning tests, to allow authentication and to verify the simultaneous presence of other individuals
in order to start an alarm if unregistered peoples are present during
learning or testing sessions. This system is also capable to recognize the
attention level of users through Request Random Windows (RRW). The
application opens casually a RRW in different screen position during the
DL and asks learner to click upon to close it within a few seconds. When
this window is closed, a new step of Face Recognitions is performed again
to validate the presence of the same user. Interesting results are obtained
in experimental cases employing these techniques on a individuals samples set.

Keywords: attention control, distance learning, biometric techniques.

1   Introduction

New communication technologies (synchronous and asynchronous) are pushing
to processes' development of learning and training. Today, it's possible to access training courses online through Internet connections and webcams. These

A. Petrosino, L. Maddalena, P. Pala (Eds.): ICIAP 2013 Workshops, LNCS 8158, pp. 545–549, 2013.
© Springer-Verlag Berlin Heidelberg 2013

technology supports are exploited interactive learning processes, facilitated by videos, quizzes and teleconferencing. In fact, the webcam can be used to recognize the DL's target users through biometric techniques. The scene analysis is crucial: a context, where more subjects are captured via a webcam (with low definition), highlights conditions less facilitating for face-detection. Using optimal environmental conditions of scenes (no more individuals, uniform and not white background) allows more precise face-detection [1] [3] and face-recognition [2] [3] (with a positive identification if a person's face belongs at a white-list). Then, to verify the continuous presence of the subject during communication and their attention level degree, there are required processes of face-recognition in both periodic and randomized way, depending to the confirm request upon windows appearing in random moments and in random screen positions.

2 Paper Preparation

In order to make the system more manageable and modular, the MVC pattern (Model-View-Controller) has been adopted. In this approach, the design of a web application is divided into three levels: the Presentation Layer (View) that implements modes and forms of data presentation to the user; the Application Logic Layer (Model), that interfaced the database with the procedures to extract and to process data (templates of faces and reaction times); the Control Layer (Controller) that implements the interactions between the other layers.

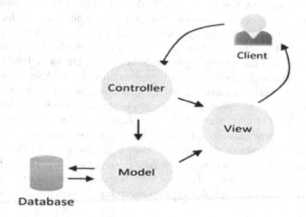

Fig. 1. MVC pattern (Model-View-Controller)

The recognition process must be based on an enrollment phase. This phase is characterized by: acquisition subject face; extraction subject features; saving obtained template; combining templates to respective individual data.

The proposed system is characterized by a step of pre-processing in which the image is processed by two subsystems connected in cascade: Haarcascade

Fig. 2. Enrollment phase with face-detection and face characterization processes

[2] [5] and than Principal Component Analysis (PCA) [6]. After the real-time acquisition of an image by webcam, the algorithm Haarcascade processes the one to detect the presence of the human face returning an image containing only one face. From the subsequent PCA application, a face image is obtained as face projection within the sub-space (face-space). This projection is saved in a database and then associated with the individual data. From the training-set (a training set consisting of all the known samples), containing the location in the subspace of all subjects, it will be possible to recognize the individual with the Eigenfaces method. The login phase involves the insertion of the username, the password and the verification of the associated individual face. After the recognition, the subject can access at the DL and attend the lesson. During the DL session, in random mode, checks are performed on the verification of the attention level. The application opens casually a Request Random Windows (RRW) in different screen position during the DL and asks learner to click upon to close it within a few seconds. The method used to calculate the attention degree is to record the reaction time. The reaction time is the time between appearance of the RRW and the mouse click on its to confirm the request.

When this window is closed, a new step of Face Recognitions is performed again to validate the presence of the same user. The training session (or test) is suspended if no face is present or it is not the same as starting. At the same way, the training session is suspended if the permissible response time exceeds the time threshold (time-out). Obviously, the user can pause the DL at any time.

3   Processing

The testing phase of the system has allowed to identify the ideal conditions of the PCA method, working on the number of components in order to improve the biometric classification. The considered images represent a small sample of

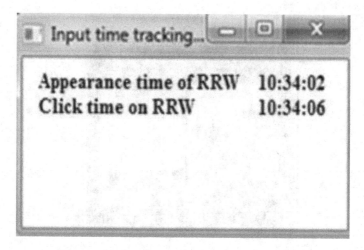

Fig. 3. Data on the reaction time of an experimental case

actual individuals. Each of them is asked for repeated exposure to the system for a period of sixty seconds in order to evaluate the recognition rate vs time of recognition tr (time of real recognition) and the exposure time te (time period of acquisition):

$$P_r = t_r/t_e \tag{1}$$

By way of example, the figure to right shows the rate of recognition in four individual experiment by varying the number of images (Eigenfaces). It's possible to show how the optimal value corresponds to 15 snapshots to get the best performance. Therefore, a greater number of Eigenfaces may be considered redundant.

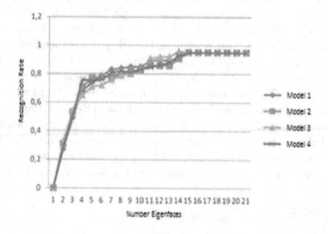

Fig. 4. Recognition Rate of 4 models included in a experimental case

4   Conclusions

Distance learning systems are in continuous evolutions and diffusion. In fact, the classic educational process is giving way to remote innovative systems to meet the expectations of users spread over a large geographical area, but also to satisfy the same education providers, who need to reduce the cost of location management and maintenance. The training online is growing everywhere and is therefore a reality that sees a growing involvement of biometrics for student identification. The biometric facial recognition, combined with response times to the requests for attention by RRW, allowed us to develop a valuable tool for secure authentication of individuals during the administration of a DL module. Therefore, this hybrid approach becomes strongly recommended in all those systems that require a minimum level of security to avoid misleading identity. The use of biometrics of face, less intrusive and more efficient, can be used in any structure with easy possibility to control lighting conditions and acquisition distance. The presented application is a prototype platform in continuous development. In this paper, an analysis was made of the state of art and technology related to the use of certain techniques biometrics, illustrating a possible application scenario that may also involve the subsequent possible process of testing sessions.

References

1. Sakai, T., Nagao, M., Fujibayashi, S.: Line Extraction and Pattern Detection in a photograph. Pattern Recognition 1(3), 233–248 (1969)
2. Kanade, D.: Computer Recognition of Human Faces. Birkauser, Basel and Stuttgart (1997)
3. Reifeld, T., Yeshurun, Y.: Robust Detection of Facial Features by Generalized Symmetry. In: Proceedings of 11th International Conference on Pattern Recognition (1992)
4. Bradski, G., Kaehler, A.: Learning: OpenCV. Computer Vision with the OpenCV Library. O'Reilly Media (2008)
5. Padilla, R., Costa Filho, C.F.F., Costa, M.G.F.: Evaluation of Haar Cascade Classifiers Designed for Face Detection. In: World Academy of Science, Engineering and Technology (2012)
6. Turk, M., Pentland, A.: Eigenfaces for Recognition. Journal of Cognitive Neuroscience 3(1), 71–86 (1991)

Statistical Person Verification Using Behavioral Patterns from Complex Human Motion

Felipe Gomez-Caballero, Takahiro Shinozaki,
Sadaoki Furui, and Koichi Shinoda

Tokyo Institute of Technology, Tokyo, Japan
`felipe@ks.cs.titech.ac.jp`

Abstract. We propose a person verification method based on behavioral patterns from complex human movements. Behavioral patterns are represented by anthropometric and kinematic features of human body motion acquired by a Kinect RGBD sensor. We focus on complex movements to demonstrate that independent and rhythmic movement of body parts carries a significant amount of behavioral information. We take a statistical approach by Gaussian mixture models to model the individual behavioral patterns. We demonstrate that subject-preferred movements are more robust against forgery attacks and variations over time than predetermined subject-independent movements. The obtained equal error rate was 15.7% when using subject-preferred movements and 27.3% when using a predefined sequence of movements.

Keywords: person verification, individuality, human movement, GMM.

1 Introduction

Automatic identity verification systems provide a secure means for access control to facilities or information. Traditionally, they have required the use of keys/cards or passwords. However, these identity tokens are easily lost or stolen. This can be solved by a biometrics approach, which identifies individuals based on their physiological or behavioral traits [9]. Physiological biometrics are stable since they rely on unique and permanent physical traits, such as fingerprint or iris [14]. However, they cannot be changed if the biometric data is counterfeited. In behavioral biometrics, identity is verified through action patterns which can be repeated in a unique manner, such as voice [5] and gait [1]. Behavioral biometrics are less stable since behavior may change due to the physical state of the individual. However, they are difficult to disguise or to imitate by others.

We focus on the individuality of *human motion* as an alternative cue when other behavioral biometrics can not be obtained or when their quality is low. Some previous studies for this application have used simple movements (e.g. arm raising) as the behavioral cue [17,16,7,8]. In this approach, it is easy for users to remember the movement and to repeat it in a stable manner. It is also easy for the identification systems to segment a person from the scene and track the movement. On the other hand, a psychology study has shown that such simple behavioral motions tend to be similar among different users [3], and thus, it may be difficult to be used for real authentication applications.

A. Petrosino, L. Maddalena, P. Pala (Eds.): ICIAP 2013 Workshops, LNCS 8158, pp. 550–558, 2013.
© Springer-Verlag Berlin Heidelberg 2013

Therefore, the use of more complex movements is promising to increase the accuracy of person verification using behavioral patterns. However, there have been two problems in this approach. First, it may be difficult for users to do the same gesture again and again, when it is complex. If the gestures from the same user vary, they cannot be used for authentication. Second, it becomes difficult for the system to segment and track such complex movement precisely. From these two reasons, such an approach has not yet been applied until now. As for the first problem, intra-subject motion variety, Chow et al. [2] reported in a motor control study that a person can repeat the same movement precisely even if it is complex, when he/she is familiar with the movement. For example, from a biomechanics perspective, volleyball players can perform spike jump movements in the same way repeatedly [20]. The use of such subject-dependent familiar motions may solve the first problem. Recently, 3D cameras such as Kinect sensors have been often used to capture human motions [15,4,10]. Without using any markers, they can segment and track complex human motions. The use of 3D cameras may solve our second problem.

This paper proposes person verification based on complex behavioral motions using Kinect sensors. We take a statistical approach using Gaussian mixtures models (GMM) to robustly model individual behavioral patterns. We evaluate our method using a dataset containing a variety of complex movements.

The remainder of the paper is organized as follows. Section 2 gives a brief overview of the proposed method. Section 3 describes the features and extraction process. Section 4 describes the statistical approach used to model the person's behavioral patterns. Section 5 describes the task and classifiers used in our system. In Section 6, experimental conditions are explained and results are presented. Finally, conclusion and future work are described in Section 7.

2 Proposed Method

Figure 1 shows an overview of the system implemented in our method, consisting of three major phases: feature extraction, model training and verification. In the feature extraction phase, the video input from a Kinect sensor is processed to extract features from skeletal joint points. In the model training phase, statistical models are created for each person using the extracted features. In the verification phase a sample video input is matched against the claimed person's model to produce a score. If the score is above a threshold the identity claim is accepted, otherwise rejected.

3 Feature Extraction

We implement an image processing front-end using the Kinect SDK to locate and track the skeletal joints shown on Figure 2(a). The input consists of video stream acquired from a Kinect sensor at 30 frames per second. For each frame, 3D position of the 20 joints found by the Kinect SDK is extracted. The positions are normalized by following the hierarchical skeleton structure which takes the

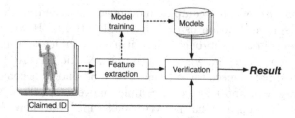

Fig. 1. Person identity verification system. (Dotted lines indicate process flow during training and solid lines indicate the flow during identity verification).

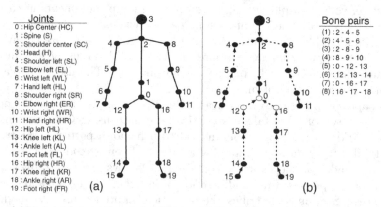

Fig. 2. (a)Skeletal joints found by Kinect SDK. (b)Hierarchical skeleton structure. Arrows indicate hierarchical dependence between joints. Dotted lines represent bones.

hip center joint as the origin. For each joint, velocity and acceleration values are calculated since these characteristics have been proved to be useful for recognition of self-generated actions [11]. In addition, the angle between each of eight bone pairs is calculated. A bone pair is defined by the two segments formed between three adjoining joints. Figure 2(b) illustrates the hierarchical skeleton dependence between joints and the bones considered during feature extraction.

The feature vectors created for the experiments in this paper include the 3D position, velocity and acceleration of 17 joints and the angle between eight bone pairs. By this setup, we create a 93 dimension feature vector that captures anthropometric and kinematic characteristics. The 'hip left' and 'hip right' joints are not included since these points exhibited limited motion in the captured samples. The joint 'hip center' is also not included since it is used for normalization.

4   Model Training

We take a statistical approach by Gaussian mixture models (GMM) [18] to robustly model the individual behavioral patterns. A GMM is a parametric probability density function represented as a weighted sum of M component Gaussian distributions given by the equation $p(\mathbf{x}|\lambda) = \sum_{i=1}^{M} w_i g(\mathbf{x}|\mu_i \Sigma_i)$, where $\mathbf{x}$ is a D-dimensional feature vector, w_i is the mixture weight, and $g(\mathbf{x}|\mu_i \Sigma_i)$ is the component Gaussian distribution with mean vector μ_i and covariance Σ_i. A GMM represents feature vectors by its mean components, as well as their average variations by the covariance matrix. Therefore it is possible to model the variations of features that characterize individual behavioral patterns.

To robustly estimate the GMM parameters with a limited amount of data, we use the maximum likelihood linear regression (MLLR) [13] method which is often used in speaker recognition. MLLR estimates a set of transformations that can be shared by several model components, hence reducing the required amount of adaptation data [12,6]. In MLLR, an affine transform $(\mathbf{A}, \mathbf{b})$ is applied to the Gaussian parameters (μ) of an initial model to create the parameters of a new person-dependent model $(\hat{\mu})$ by $\hat{\mu} = \mathbf{A}\mu + \mathbf{b}$, where $\mathbf{A}$ is an $n \times n$ transformation matrix (n is the dimensionality of the data) and $\mathbf{b}$ is a bias vector which maximizes the likelihood of the adaptation data. As an initial model, we use a universal background model (UBM) [19]. A UBM is a GMM trained by EM parameter estimation using the training data from all the subjects in the dataset. The UBM parameters are then adapted via MLLR to derive a person-dependent model by using the person's training data. The vector for each sample used to train the models has a dimensionality of $93 \times N$, where N is the number of frames in a given training sample and 93 corresponds to the feature vector size.

5   Identity Verification

In this task, an unknown person claims an identity and provides a sample to be compared with a model for the person whose identity is claimed. We implement a log-likelihood ratio (LLR) scheme [19] for the decision-making process. The LLR measures how much better the claimant's model scores for a test sample compared with a non-claimant model. As shown in equation 1, the LLR is obtained by the difference in scores resulting from testing a given sample (x) against the claimed person model (λ_{pm}) and the UBM (λ_{UBM}).

$$LLR = \log p(x|\lambda_{\text{pm}}) - \log p(x|\lambda_{\text{UBM}}) \qquad (1)$$

If the LLR is above a threshold the identity claim is accepted, otherwise rejected.

6   Experiments

6.1   Conditions

For evaluating the proposed method, we collected a dataset consisting of short videos depicting complex human movements recorded by a Kinect sensor over several sessions. A total of 16 subjects (4 females, 12 males) were recorded performing two different types of movements. We collected a 'predefined sequence

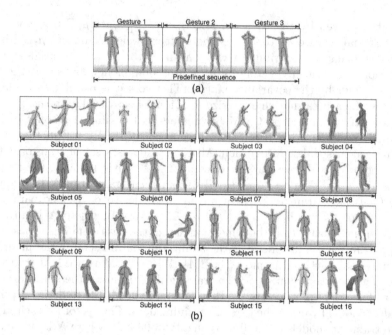

Fig. 3. (a) Example of the predefined sequence of movements. *Gesture 1*: Knock door, *Gesture 2*: Hand wave, *Gesture 3*: Open double sliding door. (b) Examples of subject-preferred movements, including: aerobics (subject 05, 06, 11), jumping (01, 03, 12), soccer kick (07, 13, 16), martial art (03), dance step (10), tennis swing (08), table tennis swing (14), badminton swing (09), batting (15) and pitch (04).

of movements' (FIXED) and a 'subject-preferred movement' (PREFERRED), in order to prove that movements familiar to the subject are more robust than other movements.

The FIXED movement consists of three consecutive gestures, knock door, hand wave and open double sliding door. Figure 3(a) shows its example. Each subject was instructed on how to perform the FIXED movement on the first recording. Figure 3(b) shows example frames of the PREFERRED movements. Subjects were asked in advance to select a preferred complex movement which they could easily repeat. Since the subjects are likely to select movements that are familiar for them, we expect that behavior patterns will be more stable. All subjects reported that they felt comfortable performing their preferred and familiar movement.

The dataset is organized in one training session and six testing sessions. Recording of the training and the first testing sessions were separated by a 28 days interval between them. The six testing sessions were recorded with an interval of seven days between them. The training session contains 20 samples per subject for each movement. Each testing session contains 10 samples per subject for each movement. Average length per sample for the FIXED and PREFERRED movement are 5.18 and 3.86 seconds respectively. Samples were recorded at 30fps.

For the verification test, 10 subjects were randomly chosen out of 16 as the target. In order to assess the robustness of PREFERRED movements against forgery attacks, we asked the 16 subjects to act as impostors and imitate the movement of the 10 target subjects. After watching a video showing the target subject executing his/her movement, subjects tried to imitate each movement five times. In the case of FIXED movements, we randomly select five samples from non-target subjects as impostor data since all subjects perform the same movement. Verification tests are conducted for each movement category using samples from the six testing sessions and the impostor samples collected in a single session. For each genuine target subject, we conduct 60 verification trials where each trial used a single sample from the subject. For the forgery attacks, we conduct 75 verification trials per target subject where each trial used a single sample from 15 impostors. Performance is measured by the equal error rate (EER) calculated a posteriori. The EER is the value where the false acceptance and false rejection rates are equal, hence an optimal threshold can be found. The subject models were created using 32 Gaussian mixture components.

6.2   Results

Table 1 shows the false rejection (FR) and false acceptance (FA) rates per target subject and EER using global optimal threshold of the systems when forgery attacks by impostors are introduced. It can be seen that performance of the system using PREFERRED movements is higher compared to using FIXED movements. This confirms that robustness against forgery attacks of PREFERRED movements is higher than FIXED movements.

The results also suggest that the choice of PREFERRED movement affects the performance of the system, since some movements are more robust against forgery than others. For example, subject-15 movement (batting) does not provide sufficient behavioral information due to its limited motion and little change in body pose, hence making it easy to be imitated by impostors. On the other hand, the movement selected by subject-08 (tennis swing) involves a characteristic rhythmic motion of both arms and legs that was difficult to mimic by impostors. This observation is consistent with the findings in [3], demonstrating that independent and rhythmic movement of body parts carries a significant amount of behavioral information. Although FIXED movement execution time is in average longer, it can be assumed that the amount of behavioral information encoded in PREFERRED movements is higher and more stable. The Detection Error Trade-off (DET) curves for both systems are shown in Figure 4.

7   Conclusions and Future Work

We have extended our previously proposed approach [8] for person verification based on behavioral patterns by using complex human motion. We focused on the behavioral patterns of subject-preferred and familiar movements. By using a Kinect sensor, accurate segmentation and tracking of the human body was

Table 1. False rejection (FR) and false acceptance (FA) rates per target subject and EER for systems using predefined sequence of movements (FIXED) and subject-preferred movement (PREFERRED)

	FIXED		PREFERRED	
Target	FR (%)	FA (%)	FR (%)	FA (%)
01	6.7	75.0	0.0	28.0
02	15.0	54.8	0.0	21.3
03	1.7	18.2	5.0	34.7
04	100	2.1	65.0	13.3
05	0.0	31.1	1.7	6.7
06	0.0	58.8	6.7	6.7
07	96.7	0.0	13.3	1.3
08	28.3	2.3	3.3	0.0
11	16.7	7.9	51.7	0.0
15	48.3	0.0	3.3	45.3
EER (%)	27.3		15.7	

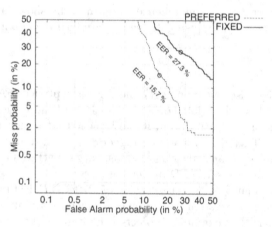

Fig. 4. DET curves for systems using FIXED and PREFERRED movements

feasible. We have shown that our system achieves higher performance by using subject-preferred movements (EER = 15.7%) compared to using predefined sequence of movements (EER = 27.3%) when forgery attacks by impostors are introduced. Results also suggest that the choice of subject-preferred movement directly affects the performance. We have also confirmed that our system is able to verify the identity of a person even when there is a time difference of 28 to 63 days between training and testing sessions. We consider the results are encouraging and further research is worthwhile to pursue. Moreover, the proposed method can serve as support to other biometric methods.

For the future work, we plan to increase the number of subjects in the dataset and include a wider variety of complex human movements. In order to further improve the performance, we would like to implement a Hidden Markov Model (HMM) based framework, taking advantage of the temporal information of complex movements. We also would like to improve the feature set to include richer information about each individual behavioral patterns.

References

1. Aqmar, M., Shinoda, K., Furui, S.: Robust Gait-Based Person Identification against Walking Speed Variations. IEICE on Information and Systems 95, 668–676 (2012)
2. Chow, J.Y., Davids, K.W., Button, C., Rein, R.: Dynamics of movement patterning in learning a discrete multiarticular action. Motor Control: The Int. Journal for the Multidisciplinary Study of Voluntary Movement 12(3), 219–240 (2008)
3. Daprati, E., Wriessnegger, S., Lacquaniti, F.: Kinematic cues and recognition of self-generated actions. Experimental Brain Research 177(1), 31–44 (2007)
4. Fernandez-Baena, A., et al.: Biomechanical validation of upper-body and lower-body joint movements of kinect motion capture data for rehabilitation treatments. In: Intelligent Networking and Collaborative Systems 2012, pp. 656–661 (2012)
5. Furui, S.: 40 Years of Progress in Automatic Speaker Recognition. In: Tistarelli, M., Nixon, M.S. (eds.) ICB 2009. LNCS, vol. 5558, pp. 1050–1059. Springer, Heidelberg (2009)
6. Gales, M.J.F., Woodland, P.C.: Mean and Variance Adaptation within the MLLR Framework. Computer Speech Language 10(4), 249–264 (1996)
7. Gomez-Caballero, F., Shinozaki, T., Furui, S.: User Identification Using Time-of-Flight Camera Image Streams. IPSJ Technical Report vol. 2, 615–616 (2010)
8. Gomez-Caballero, F., Shinozaki, T., Furui, S., Shinoda, K.: Person Authentication Using 3D Human Motion. In: Proc. of the 2011 Joint ACM Workshop on Human Gesture and Behavior Understanding, J-HGBU 2011, pp. 35–40. ACM (2011)
9. Jain, A., Ross, A., Prabhakar, S.: An Introduction to Biometric Recognition. IEEE Trans. on Circuits and Systems for Video Technology 14(1), 4–20 (2004)
10. Kato, K., et al.: Exploring analysis of football actions considering correlation of joints in the body. In: 2012 Int. Conference on Networked Sensing Systems (2012)
11. Knoblich, G., Prinz, W.: Recognition of Self-Generated Actions From Kinematic Displays of Drawing. Journal of Experimental Psychology: Human Perception and Performance 27(2) (2001)
12. Leggetter, C.J., Woodland, P.C.: Flexible Speaker Adaptation Using Maximum Likelihhod Linear Regression. In: Proc. ARPA Spoken Language Technology Workshop, vol. 9, pp. 110–115 (1995)
13. Leggetter, C.J., Woodland, P.C.: Maximum Likelihood Linear Regression for Speaker Adaptation of Continuous Density hidden Markov models. Computer Speech & Language 9(2), 171–185 (1995)
14. Lin, J.L., Hsu, H.L., Jong, T.L., Hsu, W.H.: Biometric Authentication. In: Pattern Recognition, Machine Intelligence and Biometrics, pp. 607–631. Springer (2011)
15. Munsell, B.C., Temlyakov, A., Qu, C., Wang, S.: Person identification using full-body motion and anthropometric biometrics from kinect videos. In: Fusiello, A., Murino, V., Cucchiara, R. (eds.) ECCV 2012 Ws/Demos, Part III. LNCS, vol. 7585, pp. 91–100. Springer, Heidelberg (2012)
16. Pratheepan, Y., Torr, P., Condell, J.V., Prasad, G.: Body Language Based Individual Identification in Video Using Gait and Actions. In: Elmoataz, A., Lezoray, O., Nouboud, F., Mammass, D. (eds.) ICISP 2008 2008. LNCS, vol. 5099, pp. 368–377. Springer, Heidelberg (2008)
17. Pratheepan, Y., et al.: Style of Action Based Individual Recognition in Video Sequences. In: Systems, Man and Cybernetics, pp. 1237–1242 (2008)

18. Reynolds, D.A.: Automatic Speaker Recognition using Gaussian Mixture Speaker Models. The Lincoln Laboratory Journal, 173–192 (1995)
19. Reynolds, D.A., Quatieri, T.F., Dunn, R.B.: Speaker Verification Using Adapted Gaussian Mixture Models. Digital Signal Processing 10(1-3), 19–41 (2000)
20. Tokuyama, M., et al.: Individuality and reproducibility in high-speed motion of volleyball spike jumps by phase-matching and averaging. Journal of Biomechanics 38(10), 2050–2057 (2005)

Author Index